**BU**

OF EUROPE

*This small volume is dedicated to the memory of*
*Dr Lionel G. Higgins and Mr Norman D. Riley,*
*and to all entomologists, amateur and professional, past and present,*
*who, collectively, are responsible for the vast, accumulated knowledge*
*of the western Palearctic butterfly fauna.*

# BUTTERFLIES

## OF EUROPE

TOM TOLMAN

With Illustrations by
RICHARD LEWINGTON

Princeton University Press
Princeton and Oxford

## Princeton Field Guides

Rooted in field experience and scientific study, Princeton's guides to animals and plants are the authority for professional scientists and amateur naturalists alike. **Princeton Field Guides** present this information in a compact format carefully designed for easy use in the field. The guides illustrate every species in color and provide detailed information on identification, distribution, and biology.

*Birds of Kenya and Northern Tanzania: Field Guide Edition*, by Dale A. Zimmerman, Donald A. Turner, and David J. Pearson
*Birds of India, Pakistan, Nepal, Bangladesh, Bhutan, Sri Lanka, and the Maldives*, by Richard Grimmet, Carol Inskipp, and Tim Inskipp
*Birds of Australia*, by Ken Simpson and Nicolas Day
*Birds of Europe*, by Killian Mullarney, Lars Svensson, Dan Zetterström, and Peter J. Grant
*Birds of Nepal*, by Richard Grimmet, Carol Inskipp, and Tim Inskipp
*Birds of the Seychelles*, by Adrian Skerrett and Ian Bullock
*Stars and Planets*, by Ian Ridpath and Wil Tirion
*Butterflies of Europe*, by Tom Tolman and Richard Lewington

Published in the United States, Canada, and the Philippine Islands by Princeton University Press, 41 William Street, Princeton, New Jersey 08540

Originally published in English by HarperCollins*Publishers* Ltd. under the title:

COLLINS FIELD GUIDE: BUTTERFLIES OF BRITAIN AND EUROPE

Library of Congress Control Number 2001088357

ISBN 0-691-09074-2

This book has been composed in Plantin

www.birds.princeton.edu

Printed and bound in Hong Kong by Printing Express Limited.

1  3  5  7  9  10  8  6  4  2

# Contents

# A Personal Tribute to the Memory of
# Lionel G. Higgins and Norman D. Riley

In the course of almost three decades, *A Field Guide to the Butterflies of Britain and Europe* by L. G. Higgins and N. D. Riley has become an almost indispensable travelling companion for many general naturalists and butterfly specialists alike. As a familiar prelude to many a reference to the European butterflies, the words '....according to Higgins and Riley.....' testify to the heavy reliance placed upon this standard work, as well as the high esteem in which these authors are universally held.

Norman Riley died in 1979, at about the time I began to take an active interest in the butterflies of continental Europe, and, although I never met with this gentleman, I was privileged to develop a close association with Lionel Higgins in the latter years of his life. This man, characterized by his mild, unassuming manner, incisive mind, great enthusiasm, gentle humour and generous nature, seemed never too busy to give attention to problems of butterfly identification for which I invariably sought his help. I was also impressed by his uncommon, although tacit regard for the need for circumspection in the pursuit of science: indeed, I do not believe we ever provided a complete solution to any problem. Our best efforts invariably raised more questions than answers, conclusions were, accordingly, always tentative, always calling for more data, more material and, of course, more work. The commendable caution of Lionel Higgins is well epitomized by the last example of our many co-operative efforts to resolve ambiguities in the characters of 'difficult' butterflies. Two days were spent preparing and comparing dissected components of insects. We each had our allotted tasks, and, as work progressed, silence prevailed except for essential exchanges, mostly to predetermine the availability of the one and only binocular microscope – the preferred instrument for insect dissection. During this period, the cramped conditions of Lionel's insect-storage room/laboratory/library were transformed into a state of near chaos, with every available work-surface strewn with books, journals, insect drawers, microscope slides, test-tube racks and a host of other paraphernalia. Only at the end of the second day, when all available avenues of investigation had been exhausted, did I ask the inevitable question 'Well, what do you think?' Lionel's furrowed brow provided the answer before he spoke 'Hmmm.... any chance of getting more material?'. Lionel Higgins will always stand out in my mind as one who needed no reminding that only fools rush in where wise men fear to tread.

After a brief illness, Lionel George Higgins died on October 9th 1985, at the age of 94. We spoke for the last time, by telephone, shortly before his death. The brief conversation – about butterflies, as usual – ended with Lionel making a joke, and the very last thing I recall were not words, but hearty laughter. A fitting, final farewell from a very fine, old gentleman and one whom I shall always feel honoured to have been able to call my friend.

# Preface

Since the first edition of *A Field Guide to the Butterflies of Britain and Europe* by L. G. Higgins and N. D. Riley in 1970, Europeans have witnessed many changes. Overall economic growth, reflected in greatly enhanced personal disposable income, increased leisure time, a vastly improved road network and, in most recent times, the very welcome removal of previously inhibiting travel restrictions in eastern Europe, have concerted in presenting the butterfly enthusiast with greater opportunities for travel within the subcontinent than perhaps might have been imagined or hoped for three decades ago. In direct consequence of one change, namely, the ever-growing interest in the butterflies of the Greek islands, those of the eastern Aegean region are covered by the Field Guide for the first time. These islands hold several species which are to be found nowhere else in the geo-political region of Europe. In the last decade or so, other additions to the list of Europe's butterfly fauna have brought the total, recognized and described in this work, to 440.

The previous field guide was intended largely for use in the field for the purpose of butterfly identification. The present volume, whilst, hopefully, fulfilling this same basic need, endeavours to encourage wider and deeper interest in the butterflies themselves. As most people, including most children know, a butterfly arises from a chrysalis, which, in turn, comes from a caterpillar. That these three states of development equate to one and the same entity, argues convincingly that no knowledge of the adult butterfly, however extensive, can be complete without that of its life-history. Moreover, the benefits bestowed by a wider understanding of the biology, ecology and behaviour of butterflies extends significantly beyond any theoretical consideration. In illustration of the practical benefit of wider knowledge, familiarity with habitat character, coupled with awareness of larval host-plants, is a general and often considerable advantage in locating adult butterflies, especially those of very restricted or uncertain distribution. Again, for purely practical purposes, knowledge of the early-stages of butterflies commends itself as a tool of potentially considerable convenience for searching out these insects even when they are not flying. As an activity far less susceptible to the vagaries of the weather, and one offering greater option in the use of time, searching for eggs or caterpillars can, through choice, be conducted in much more leisurely fashion. Of course, the concomitant advantage of almost inevitable, incidental discoveries of value to science is the greater source of gratification.

Within the constraints imposed by the size of this volume, every effort has been made to facilitate and encourage these potentially highly rewarding pursuits. A strong, personal commitment to the notion that no facet of butterfly science should suffer needless neglect, has provided more than sufficient stimulus for the task of extending the previous field guide. If this stimulates the reader to peer amongst leaves and flowers for butterfly eggs or caterpillars, or to pay closer attention to the activities of the adult insects, as well as the character of the habitat in which they reside, then the effort expended in preparing this work will have been justified.

# Acknowledgements

No work of the present kind is possible without the collective efforts of a great many people. As the content of scientific journals provide the indispensable basis of this volume, the author is deeply indebted to all who have taken the trouble to publish their observations. For their direct assistance, in providing information, helpful discussion and access to private butterfly collections, the writer also wishes to express his gratitude to the following – Dr Stanislav Abadjiev (Institute of Zoology, Bulgarian Academy of Sciences, Sofia - BU), Professor Zolta Balint (Magyar Természettudományi Múzeum Állattára, Budapest - H), Mr Dubi Benyamini (Santiago - Chile [Israel]), Mr Lubos Bieber (Lipuvka - Czech Republic), Dr Jean-Pierre Borie, (Compiègne - F), Mr Nils Brostrom (Hässelby - S), Dr John Brown (Department of Physiology, University of Cambridge - U.K.), Dr Clair Brunton (Department of Genetics, University of Cambridge - U.K.), Professor Jaroslaw Buszko (Institute of Biology, Copernicus University, Torun - PL), Mr Paola Casini (Firenze - I), Sir Cyril Clarke (West Kirby - U.K.), Mr John Coutsis (Athens - GR), Professor Sir John Dacie (Wimbledon - U.K.), Mr Charles Derry (Ironbridge - U.K.), Mr Jos Dils (Hoevenen - B), Mr Roland Essayan (Dijon - F), Mr David Hall (Litchfield - UK), Mr Hans Forslind (Kalmar - S), Mr Jürgen Fuchs (Feucht - D), Mr Nicos Ghavalas (Athens - GR), Mr Yves Gonseth (Neuchâtel - CH), Dr Jacques Hutsebaut (Brussels - B), Mr and Mrs David Howell (Broadstairs - U.K.), Mr Hans Henrickson (Stenstrup - DK), Dr David Jutzler (Effretikon - CH), Mr Ib Kreutzer (Arden - DK), Dr Torben Larsen (London - U.K.), Mr Ronnie Leestmans (Vilvoorde - B), Mr and Mrs Staf de Louker (Bouwel - B), Dr Marchi (Universitá degli studi di Cagliari, Sardinia - I), Mr Francisco Martinex (Valencia - E), Professor Steffen Oemig (Leverkusen - D), Mr Alain Olivier (Antwerp - B), Professor Dennis Owen (Oxford Brookes University - U.K.), Mr Jim Phelpstead (Southampton - U.K.), Mr Tony Pittaway (Moulsford - U.K.), Mr Dirk van der Poorten (Antwerp - B), Mr Willy de Prins (Antwerp - B), Mr Alex Riemis (Turnhout - B), Dr Patrick Roche (Sant Julià de Lòria - Andorra), Dr Klaus Schurian (Kelkeim-Fischbach - D), Professor C. B. Stace (Department of Botany, Leicester University - U.K.), Mr Per Tangen (Askim - N), Monsieur Michel Tarrier (Malaga - E[F]), Dr George Thomson (Lochmaben - U.K.), Mr Jerry Tremewan (Truro - U.K.), Mr Rainer Ulrich (Wiesbach - D), Mr Ken Wilmott (Leatherhead - UK), Mr and Mrs Joachim Wolf (Neu-Isenburg - D).

Staff of the Departments of Entomology of – Institut voor Taxonomische Zoologie, Amsterdam (Holland); Natural History Museum, London (U.K.); Oxford University Museum [Hope Department] (U.K.) for arranging access to butterfly collections and entomological libraries. Also, to Dr Stephen Simpson and Dr George McGavin of the Hope Department, and members of Vlaamse Vereniging Voor Entomologie, Antwerp for the loan of specimens used for illustration.

Dr Roberto Crnjar (Universitá degli studi di Cagliari, Sardinia - I) for checking and amending the text relating to the butterflies of Sardinia and Corsica: Mr Martin Gascoigne-Pees (Stonesfield - U.K.) and Dr Peter Russell (East Wittering - U.K.) for checking the main text, furnishing much useful comment and the loan of many specimens used for illustration: Dr N. Savenkov (Latvijas

Dabas Muzejs - Latvia) for detailed distributional and historical data on the butterflies of Latvia: Mr John Tennent (Fylingthorpe - U.K.) for very extensive and much needed information on the butterflies of Morocco, Algeria and Tunisia.

For their willing assistance in the identification of larval host-plants – Dr Brian Adams and Professor Frank Bisby (Department of Botanical Taxonomy, University of Southampton - U.K.); Professor K. Browicz (Pozan - PL); Mr Thomas Cope and Mr David Gardner (Royal Botanic Gardens, Kew - U.K.), Dr D. Champluria and Professor D. Fergusson (Rijksuniversitair Centrum Antwerpen (Antwerp - B); Mr Wolfram Hannig (Schladming - A); Dr Alfred Hansen (Botanical Museum, Copenhagen - DK); Dr Stephen Blackmore and Mr Nick Turland (Botany Department, Natural History Museum, London).

Dr P. H. Boting (Antwerp - B) for identifying many ant species, and to Dr Konrad Fiedler (Theodor-Boveri-Institut für Biowissenschaften [Biozentrum] der Universität Würzberg - D) for rendering a similar and extensive service, and for many helpful discussions on the Lycaenid butterflies: for assisting Dr Fiedler in the identification of some ant species from Greece, thanks are also due to Dr Donat Agosti (Zürich - CH).

Finally, it is with particular pleasure that I express my deep and heartfelt gratitude to my wife, Sally, for her dedicated and indispensable assistance in field work, especially in connection with the tedious and time-consuming tasks of locating and rearing the early-stages of butterflies: invaluable help in literature research is no less appreciated, as is her uncommon capacity to respond with patience and tolerance to the often immoderate restrictions imposed upon her life by her husband's entomological pursuits.

10

# Abbreviations

| | |
|---|---|
| Bco. | Barranco |
| CN | chromosome number |
| Dj. | Djebel (Mount/Mountain) |
| E | east |
| f. | form |
| fw | fore-wing |
| fwl | fore-wing length (from apex to point of attachment to thorax) |
| gc | ground-colour |
| hw | hind-wing |
| LHP(s) | larval host-plant(s) |
| m | metre |
| mm | millimetre |
| Mt./Mts. | Mountain/Mountains |
| Mte. | Mount/Mountain |
| N | north |
| NE | northeast |
| NW | northwest |
| pd | post-discal |
| Pl. | Planina (mountains) |
| Pso. | Passo |
| Pto. | Puerto |
| s | space (referring to the area of wing-membrane between the veins) |
| S | south |
| SE | southeast |
| SW | southwest |
| S. | Sierra |
| sp./spp. | species (singular)/species (plural) |
| ssp./sspp. | subspecies (singular)/subspecies (plural) |
| syn: | synonym |
| TL: | Type-locality |
| unf | fore-wing underside |
| unh | hind-wing underside |
| uns | fore-wing and hind-wing undersides |
| upf | fore-wing upperside |
| uph | hind-wing upperside |
| ups | fore-wing and hind-wing uppersides |
| v | vein |
| var. | variety |
| W | west |
| ♀ | male |
| ♂ | female |

# Introduction

Butterflies (Rhopalocera) and moths (Heterocera) together comprise the vast order of insects known as the Lepidoptera – a word of Greek origin meaning wings with scales (*lepis* = scale, *pteron* = wing). In most of Europe, butterflies may be distinguished from moths by one or more of the following characteristics:

1) Butterflies have clubbed antennae: those of moths are usually fine and filamentous and often markedly different between the sexes.

2) Unlike butterflies, moths possess a coupling device, linking fore-wing to the hind-wing during flight.

3) Butterflies roost with their wings tightly closed in the vertical plane above the body: moths usually roost and rest with the wings in roughly the horizontal plane with the fore-wing obscuring the hind-wing.

4) The flight of butterflies is confined mostly to sunny or at least bright conditions: most moths fly at night; those that fly in the daytime are easily recognized by their antennae and resting pose.

**The basic external anatomy of a butterfly**

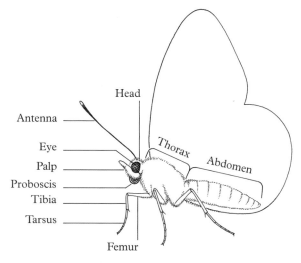

**Figure 1. Main external features.**

The head, which is capable of very limited movement, carries two large, compound eyes giving virtually all-round vision, but of low resolutional quality: the eyes are, however, very sensitive to movement in the field of vision. The frons – 'face' – is located between the eyes often bearing a hair-tuft. In place of jaws, the coiled and extendable proboscis, formed from two, co-acting tubes, finely tapered at their extremities, is an organ through which fluid nutrients are obtained by sucking. Located symmetrically about the proboscis, is a pair of jointed sensory organs known as the palpi. The clubbed antennae, important sensory organs, arise from the upper part of the head from between the eyes. Behind the head is the thorax, which carry the two pairs of wings and three pairs of legs: in some groups, the first pair of legs are degenerate and useless for walking, and may not be apparent without close inspection. All functional legs are jointed and comprise a femur, tibia and tarsus: the structure of the tarsus varies but usually terminates in a pair of claws. Olfactory sensors are present on the antennae, palpi, head, proboscis and legs. Compared to the head and thorax, the abdomen is soft and relatively much more flexible. It contains the organs of digestion and reproduction. The abdomen of a female, as it contains the eggs, is usually noticeably 'fatter' than that of the male. Male genitalia are often of critical value in the identification/separation of species. However, as the structural complexity of these essentially internal anatomical organs are not adequately describable without pictorial representation, reference to genitalia is limited to those instances where alternative, superficial diagnostic features are absent.

Androconia (singular, androconium) are specialized wing-scales (often referred to as scent-scales or androconial scales) possessing gland cells containing special chemicals known as pheromones which are released by male butterflies in courtship. Andronconia usually differ markedly in shape from ordinary scales and often have a terminal fibrous tuft. Androconia may be distributed and effectively hidden amongst ordinary wing-scales, or grouped in conspicuous patches: these sex-brands, as they are often called, are usually located on the upper surface of the fore-wing. In a few species, androconia are held in a kind of envelope formed by a fold in the fore-wing costal membrane.

An ordinary wing-scale is a very small, thin, chitinous platelet with a tiny peg at its base by which means it is attached to the wing-membrane. Wing-scales are usually pigmented, but bright 'metallic' colours of butterflies, such as the 'blues' and 'coppers', are due entirely to the diffraction of incidence light by the microscopic structure of the scale. The same phenomenon is responsible for the 'rainbow' colours created by a thin film of oil on water. The colours of these interference patterns, as they are called, are very sensitive to viewing angle, and explains why the purple flush of the Purple Emperor, for example, (see front book-cover) is not visible on both sets of wings at the same time. The subtle variations in the tone of the greenish or brassy iridescent sheen of many satyrid butterflies is similarly explained.

The wings are of prime importance in the identification of butterflies. To facilitate the description of wing-markings, the wing-surface is divided into specific areas as shown in figures 2 and 3.

The terminology and vein-notation is standard. Although demarcation of adjacent wing-areas is somewhat arbitrary, confusion over the described location of markings need never arise: for example, whether a row of spots is designated as 'post-discal' or 'submarginal' is immaterial if no other markings are present in this general region. All terms are explained in the glossary (page 293): abbreviations are given on page 10. The notation used for the veins and intervening spaces is self-explanatory, and designed to accommodate slight differences in venation between families without the need for altering the numbering system. Where, for example, one or more of the veins branching

**Figure 2. Wing venation.**

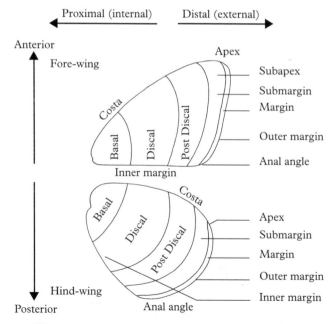

**Figure 3. Wing-area notation.**

from the fore-wing subcostal vein (v7, v8 or v9) are absent, the space above vein 6 is still called space 6. In the case of the Papilionidae, where v1a is absent on the hind-wing, v1b becomes v1 and the spaces below and above v1 becomes s1a and s1 respectively. One or more of the three discocellular veins on the hind-wing may be absent, in which case the cell is said to be open. The finer detail of venation in a dead butterfly can be seen more easily if the wings are moistened with a drop of petroleum spirit: this renders the wings briefly translucent without damage to the scales. (Organic solvents should only be used in well-ventilated areas, well away from naked flames: inhalation and contact with the skin should be avoided).

## The life-cycle of a butterfly

The egg (ovum), caterpillar (larva), chrysalis (pupa) and adult butterfly (imago) are the four distinct stages in the life-cycle. This remarkable process of transformations is known as metamorphosis.

　　Ova are usually laid on the plants upon which the larvae subsequently feed. Ova vary considerably in external appearance, and may be bottle-shaped, disc-shaped, spherical or dome-shaped according to the family to which they belong. The ovum stage lasts a few days, a few weeks or several months if hibernation (over-wintering) occurs in this stage. Larval development proceeds in stages (instars) corresponding to the need for skin-changes to accommodate growth. Most European species hibernate in the larval stage. Between families, a considerable variance in larval shape, colouring and markings, together with a wide range of adaptive behaviour, reflect a correspondingly wide range of survival strategies: similar adaptive variation is shown by pupae, the hibernation stage for many species.

## Butterfly identification

With the exception of the Danaidae, comprising the two, very distinctive species shown on Plate 96 a representative sample of each European butterfly family is illustrated on Plates A and B. A comparison of one or more of the characters of size, wing-shape and wing-markings of an unidentified specimen, with those of the sample, will show the group to which the specimen most probably belongs. By referring to the plate indicated by the number adjacent to the species bearing the closest resemblance to the unknown specimen, an immediate identification is sometimes possible, if not, reference to neighbouring plates, illustrating other species within the same family or genus, will usually prove more productive. Page numbers given for each species illustrated in the main plates, refer to the location of the species' description and other relevant information in the text, and, by this means, any tentative identification can be checked. All possible checks should be made, including a comparison with similar species and of the site of observation of the newly identified butterfly with its known geographical/altitudinal range. It is prudent, of course, to assume that not all is known about the distribution of European butterflies; it is, accordingly, always best to expect the unexpected. In particularly difficult cases, it may be helpful to list all possible candidates, and, after systematic elimination of the least likely, focus attention on the diagnostic features of those remaining.

# Arrangement of the Main Text

The following annotated description of subtitled elements of the main text, is intended to illustrate the essentially interactive nature of insect behaviour, ecology and biology, including that pertaining to early-stages, as well as demonstrating its relevance to the identification of butterflies and the investigation of their taxonomic relationships.

## Range

Unless otherwise qualified, range denotes the known, global limits of distribution.

## Species name, author and date: type-locality: synonymy

This brief, unsubtitled section, gives the Latin (scientific) name of the species, along with the author and date of its original description: the origin of the specimen (the type-specimen) pertaining to this description is the type-locality. The Latin name may be written as binomen or trinomen, e.g., *Pieris napi* (in abbreviation, *P. napi*) or *Pieris napi napi* (in abbreviation, *P. n. napi*): these names refer to exactly the same entity: the trinomen is required only to distinguish the nominate subspecies (strictly, nominotypical subspecies) from other subspecies; e.g., *Pieris napi napi* and *Pieris napi segonzaci*. Only the more recent or commonly encountered synonyms are given, and are restricted to species name.

Taxonomic classification is often the subject of much contention. However, such matters need not be a source of confusion or consternation if it is recognized that, in reality, a great deal of taxonomic classification equates to hypotheses yet to be tested by the rigorous application of investigative biological methods.

As no universally accepted arrangement of butterfly taxa appears to exist, the systematic order adopted by Higgins and Riley (1983), with a few minor adjustments, has been followed: this may prove convenient for readers familiar with the previous field guide. For the general purpose of this book, departures from the more recent and possibly more rigorous taxonomic evaluations is of little consequence. All butterfly taxa are indexed, and their location within the text should present no difficulty.

## Distribution

The geographical area covered is indicated on the map in figure 4 and includes the Canary Islands, Madeira, the Azores, and the Aegean Islands of Greece, but excludes Cyprus and eastern Mediterranean islands not under European political administration. The map provided with each species is intended as a rough, graphical summary of distribution. It will be appreciated that information is often incomplete, especially in some eastern regions. It should also be noted that, in general, a species will not be found at all sites within the designated area of distribution. The regions of temporary occupancy of migrants is indicated by a tint. The predictability of migration near the limits of migratory range, varies appreciably for species as does uncertainty regarding residency near the often ill-defined boundaries of permanent occupancy.

Altitudinal range is included with distribution. Apart from the advantage in locating butterfly habitats, knowledge of altitudinal range usually serves to account for otherwise anomalous disjunctions in the two-dimensional

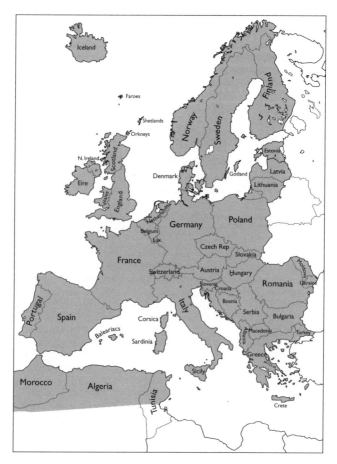

**Figure 4. Distribution map.**

distributional representation of many species: a cursory inspection of the maps will reveal recurring distributional patterns closely associated with higher mountain massifs, suggesting a restriction to colder conditions at higher altitude, a situation usually confirmed by the altitudinal range given in the text. Cold conditions also occur in higher latitudes, and some species found in central Europe only at high altitude, 'reappear' at or near sea-level in the arctic region. Whilst these examples furnish useful ecological information, other disjunctive patterns, equally evident in the maps, reveal, or at least suggest, a continuity of distribution in the distant past, subsequently disrupted by climatic change in more recent geological time: the study of these and related events in respect of other animals as well as plants – palaeobiogeography – often provides significant clues to the processes of evolution.

The quoted lower limit of altitudinal range, approximating to sea-level, has been refined, as far as available data allow, in an attempt to accommodate the significant and often rapid transition in habitat character, reflected in vegetation zones, which can occur between low-lying, inland coastal districts and the shore-line itself.

## Description

For several reasons, quantified estimates of butterfly size have been omitted; the best indication of approximate size is provided by the illustrations. No valid representation of size-variance is easily interpretable, nor indeed, easily obtainable: an estimate of the range of fore-wing length is apt to be misleading, as geographical variation is often appreciable and it is almost always possible to find individuals whose size falls beyond either limit of the range commonly quoted for most species.

With few exceptions, descriptions are restricted to important diagnostic features and characters not apparent in the illustrations. In cases where confusion between closely similar species may arise, comparative data are included with each description.

## Variation

The great many types and sources of variation, including that of larvae and pupae, are given in the text.

## Flight-time

For many geographically wide-ranging species, voltinism, the number of annual broods (generations), may vary appreciably according to general geographical location, altitude and regional climatic conditions. A species, single-brooded in colder, more northerly locations or at higher altitudes, may produce two or more broods in warmer regions at low altitudes. Some multiple-brooded (polyvoltine) species may be on the wing from early Spring until late Summer or Autumn in North Africa or coastal Mediterranean regions, or throughout the year in the Canary Islands. As a rule, a species occurring at low altitude in more southerly regions will emerge earlier. Emergence dates may also be influenced significantly by seasonal conditions and may even affect voltinism. A late Spring, combined with a cool Summer, can delay the emergence of some arctic species by more than a month: prolonged periods of drought may delay entirely the emergence of some desert-dwelling (eremic) butterflies for one or more seasons.

## Habitat

Whilst many widespread species are frequently found in commonly occurring habitats, others live in relative isolation in habitats of special character. The general character of habitat is described, along with any readily discernible features. Geology/soil-type is a factor of considerable, and sometimes definitive importance in respect to the character of vegetation, including, of course, larval host-plants. In company with other information, a knowledge of habitats is often very useful in locating butterflies, especially those having very specific requirements.

## Life-history

The limitation of space precludes detailed description of life-history. Larval host-plant (LHP) data have either been personally verified, or taken from sources deemed to be reliable. Uncertainties, in plant identity and use as LHPs, are indicated as appropriate: thus; (?) *Centaurea scabiosa* signifies confirmation of plant identity at species level, but only its suspected use as a LHP: *Centaurea* (?) *scabiosa* signifies a confirmed LHP whose identity has been determined with certainty at generic level, but only tentatively at species level: *Centaurea* sp. indicates confirmation of a LHP whose identity has been confirmed at generic, but not species level. Suspected, but unconfirmed errors in LHP records are indicated by the expressed need for confirmation. Where the reliability of a data source cannot be established with confidence, many, often very old records have been omitted without comment. Wherever possible, plant taxonomy/nomenclature follows that of *Flora Europaea*: beyond the geographical range covered by this work, other standard floras, e.g., *Flora of Turkey*, and original source publications have been consulted.

The distinction between the plants which butterfly larvae will accept as food in captivity and those selected in nature, is very important. The behaviour of any animal, including man, can be expected to change according to circumstance, most especially where survival is threatened. It should not be assumed that a species which accepts a particular plant as a food-source in captivity would thrive or survive, or, indeed, make any attempt to exploit the same plant in the wild. As the captive behaviour of larvae, as well as that of butterflies themselves, provides no dependable guide to natural behaviour, the sole, reliable criterion of a LHP is the plant upon which larvae are known to feed in nature. That not all butterflies lay their eggs on the plants upon which their larvae subsequently feed, argues strongly for caution in the interpretation of field observations.

For many reasons, a knowledge of LHPs is of great importance. Their distribution may reveal much of interest concerning that of the butterfly itself: in some cases, for example, the rarity and/or distributional pattern of a butterfly may correspond very closely with that of its LHP. Such information may be quite sufficient to locate a butterfly in its early stages, including that of hibernation: on this account, and as already indicated in the Preface, the field study of butterflies need not necessarily be confined to the period in which they normally fly.

For many reasons, it makes good sense to ensure that all necessary care is exercised in effecting the identification of LHPs. Given that mainland Europe hosts something of the order of 20,000 flowering plants, the scope for misidentification is considerable, and the responsibility for identifying LHPs is, in general, best delegated to the professional botanist.

## Behaviour

For our own species, success in life very much depends upon our behaviour. This is no less true of a butterfly. Of course, butterflies do not make choices, in the sense that we understand, but respond instinctively to specific stimuli as well as gradual seasonal or other changes in its environment. For this reason it is probably more useful, and certainly instructive, to regard a butterfly, not as a living creature, but as a small miniaturized, biological machine equipped with an array of sensors linked to a central processing unit (equivalent more to a computer than a brain) preprogrammed with all necessary inherited information required to ensure its survival. On this premise, we would at once dispose of any notion that a butterfly is capable of being 'frightened': instead, we would consider that it was programmed to react swiftly to any sudden movement in its immediate vicinity, simply to avoid being eaten by a bird: in reality, the butterfly is probably incapable of distinguishing a bird from a butterfly net or a windblown leaf. Through the process of natural selection, the genes carried by those insects failing to react appropriately to threat, would be quickly eliminated. By this means, the need for choice of action, which would imply intelligent behaviour, is also eliminated. In more complicated examples of behaviour, it would appear that programmes are often interactive. For example, in considering the factors controlling the emergence date of a spring butterfly which has hibernated as a pupa, it is clear that temperature is not the sole determinant: if it were, the insect might well emerge, prematurely, in winter and well out of synchronization with, say, the development of its LHP. In fact, it is virtually certain that butterflies have built-in clocks (just like modern computers) and are able to respond to the seasonal changes in day-length (photoperiod).

In view of the importance of camouflage as a survival strategy, it is not surprising that the behaviour of a butterfly is often highly correlated with its physical appearance and the character of its habitat. The presumed need for good underside camouflage of the Purple Hair-streak (*Quercusia quercus*) for example, required to evade the predatory attentions of birds whilst sitting on the leaves of oak trees – a common occupation – explains, so it would appear, the otherwise anomalous underside markings, namely, the silvery-greyish ground-colour which mimics, not the green pigment of the leaf itself, but the reflections of the shiny leaf-surface, and the white discal line which corresponds to the highlighted reflection from a leaf-vein. As may be confirmed by reference to the illustrations and main text, the underside ground-colours of the Brimstone (*Gonepteryx rhamni*), the Peacock (*Inachis io*) and the Comma (*Polygonia c-album*), three species which hibernate as adults, corresponds closely with the character of their respective hibernation quarters.

Refinement in the adaptive colouring of a species to suit the particular character of a particular habitat is also to be expected and in company with butterfly behaviour, often appears to explain local variation in wing-markings. In the genus *Pseudochazara*, for example, local variation in wing colouring and pattern, especially on the underside of the hind-wing, is observed frequently and is often presented as justification for subspecific separation. However, considering the unvarying preference of the genus for resting on or amongst rocks, superficial differences between populations, corresponding to refined adjustment to local geological conditions, are as readily attributable to the need for good camouflage. Roosting occurs in concealment amongst stones or in rock crevices. That such retreats are invariably cool, relative to ambient, sur- face conditions, precludes the predatory attention of lizards – always a serious threat to adult *Pseudochazara* species – but a roosted insect loses this security once it has crawled up towards the light, seeking the warmth of the morning sun, for then it becomes visible and, in its still torpid state, especially vulner- able: here, the importance of underside hind-wing camouflage is most obvious. The warming-up process always seems to be conducted in the same way, with the same meticulous care: thus, situated very close to or even in contact with a stone, the insect adjusts the plane of its tightly closed wings perpendicularly to the sun, thereby maximising exposure to its rays. Some vertical tilting is often necessary to gain precise adjustment, and it is noteworthy that subtle corrections corresponding to the movement of the sun are often observed during this normally lengthy procedure. It is apparent from these observations, that by exploiting the potential for heating both hind-wing surfaces simultaneously – the stone against which the butterfly stations itself will already have warmed – the period of greatest threat from predation is minimized. Here, it is interesting to reflect upon the interaction of elements within an ecosystem, for it appears that the behaviour and adaptation of a *Pseudochazara* species is intimately and competitively associated with the behaviour and adaptation of lizards.

A parallel example of adaptive colouring is apparent for the genus *Hipparchia*. However, it is often found that the range of variation in the underside hind-wing is greater than at first sight might be expected; possibly, because of equivalent variation in the character of the surfaces upon which the butterflies rest or roost: for example, the bark of a pine tree, a favoured resting site, usually displays a most complex array of colours, pattern and hard shadows created by texture.

An interesting survival strategy adopted by some species is that of migration. With seasonal regularity, such species – the 'nomads' of the butterfly world – disperse, sometimes in prodigious numbers, from areas of permanent residence, taking up accommodation in more or less any suitable site encountered along migratory routes. Colonies thus established, provide for further migration and colonization. In this way, the Painted Lady (*Vanessa cardui*), one of the better known migrants, extends its range progressively from early Spring onwards through Summer, from north Africa, throughout Europe, to well within the Arctic Circle: it is one of very few migrants to reach Iceland. The process of breeding and dispersion continues until the onset of cold weather, when all or nearly all colonists and offspring are presumed to perish in the winter months: however, the loss of such huge numbers of butterflies is of little or no consequence, as it is not the survival of individuals, but that of the species which determines its overall success. As a broad, unrefined hypotheses, the basis of migratory behaviour as a survival strategy is easily understood, for in the event of general climatic change, inevitable in geological time, some colonies, somewhere, are likely to be favourably placed for the purpose of establishing a new, permanent base from which future generations can migrate. Characteristically, migrants have, through necessity, adapted either to a wide variety of larval host-plants or at least one of common and widespread occurrence.

A few species, such as the Swallowtail (*Papilio machaon*) and the Nettle-tree Butterfly (*Libythea celtis*), appear to disperse with seasonal regularity, as indicated by their frequent occurrence in locations well-removed from potential breeding sites, that is, those containing larval host-plants. However, unlike typical migrants, dispersion is confined largely within the boundaries of permanent residence.

## Conservation

Nature conservation is the collective responsibility of all individuals, not just the relatively very few, active conservationists. Securing the very necessary wider commitment to the protection of the environment presents a problem of truly global dimensions for which no proportionately adequate solutions are currently available.

Enhancing the security of the natural world means damaging or destroying as little of it as possible. Given our present circumstances, responding to the challenge of meeting our responsibility to future generations will doubtless call for very profound and, quite possibly, very rapid changes to social, economic and, by implication, personal philosophies. It is all but a certainty that our survival depends upon divesting ourselves of the mythical belief in our own adaptability. Contrary to popular conviction, man is not the most adaptable of species: indeed, in direct consequence of his much celebrated superior intelligence, man distinguishes himself by being the only species not to have adapted to his environment. In contradistinction, the butterfly – a 'humble' creature of no intelligence – 'learned' to look after itself, with great proficiency, many millions of years before man first walked the Earth. It continues to live in harmony with the rest of nature. To ensure our own survival, we must learn to do the same.

Exploiting the popular appeal of creatures of great natural beauty, such as, but not exclusively butterflies, which arouse spontaneously our protective instincts, would appear to afford the best chance of securing the all-important protection of natural habitats. The late L. G. Higgins once remarked to the writer, that 'all butterflies must have a happy home', and, as a truism no less applicable to other animals and plants, the protection of a butterfly habitat serves, automatically, to protect all wildlife residing within the same domain. Assuming the efficacy of this aim and method, how is it best exploited? Wide-spread enlightenment – education – provides the general answer, but since children are the future custodians of our planet, it is perhaps their instruction which matters most. There are nothing but good reasons for encouraging children to take an interest in their planet. The wider and deeper the interest, the greater the desire to protect. The mind of a child is active, alert and inquisitive, but above all, it is impressionable, and, like a clean sheet of white paper, it may be the best place – it may be the only place – to write the messages required to reverse the fortunes of our species.

# Papilionidae Latreille 1802

The twelve European representatives of this family include some very large and colourful butterflies, of which the swallowtails are perhaps the best known. Sexual dimorphism is generally not well marked in wing-characters, but appreciable differences in abdominal size, shape, colour or colour-pattern enables sexual determination to be made with no difficulty. With the exception of that of the Scarce Swallowtail, larvae have bright 'warning' colours and are often conspicuous when feeding or resting. As an additional deterrent to predators, the larvae of some species possess an osmeterium, a soft, fleshy, orange-coloured, eversible, forked organ concealed within the first thoracic segment: when erected, this organ emits a powerful and offensive odour, which, coupled with the startling appearance of the osmeterium itself, is said to be an effective defence against predatory birds. Swallowtail (*Papilio*) pupae, as well as those of the festoons (*Zerynthia*), are cryptically coloured: pupae of other species are secreted amongst moss/leaf-litter, under stones or in loose soil.

## *Papilio machaon* Swallowtail                                    Plate 1

**Range.** NW Africa and Europe, through Middle East, Near East, Asia (30-70°N) to Japan. Represented in N America by several subspecies/forms.

*P. machaon* Linnaeus 1758 TL: Sweden (Verity 1947). syn: *sphyrus* Hübner 1823.
**Distribution.** Mediterranean coastal districts of NW Africa. Europe to N Fennoscandia and most Mediterranean islands. Absent from Atlantic Islands and British Isles, except for a very restricted area of SE England (Norfolk). Wide-ranging but usually encountered only in small numbers in any given site. 0-3000m: common occurrence at 1000-2000m above limit of available LHPs due to strong dispersive/migratory tendency.
**Description.** Second brood: ups black markings lightly dusted with pale yellow scales; black markings slightly reduced; blue markings better defined. Superficially indistinguishable from *P. saharae* (see *P. saharae*).
**Flight-period.** Univoltine, bivoltine or trivoltine according to latitude, altitude and seasonal conditions: February/October. Impression of flight-period in any given site may be confounded by occurrence of vagrant specimens.
**Habitat.** Diverse. In N Europe, mostly wet places: marshes; fens; river banks. In C Europe, dry or damp, grassy places. In Mediterranean region, general habitat character appears to be relatively unimportant, relating more to the fortuitous occurrence of LHPs and opportunism of vagrant, ovipositing females. At low/moderate altitudes, most egg-laying sites, which may contain very few LHP specimens, comprise hot, dry, sunny places, often areas of cultivation, roadsides, disturbed ground etc., and are often abundant in robust, nectar-rich plants such as thistles, which offer an efficient means of acquiring the energy needed to sustain a large insect (cf. *A. crataegi*; *P. brassicae*; *P. apollo*).
**Life-history.** LHPs: Apiaceae: *Foeniculum vulgare*; *Peucedanum palustre*; *P. cervaria*; *P. oreoselinum*; *P. officinale*; *Trinia glauca*; *Laserpitium halleri*; *L. latifolium*;

*Angelica sylvestris; A. archangelica; Carum carvi; Aegopodium podagraria; Anethum graveolens; Pimpinella saxifraga; Ammi visnaga; Ridolfia segetum; Silaum silaus; Daucus carota; Seseli varium; S. libanotis; Bupleurum fruticescens; B. falcatum; Petroselinum crispum; Crithmum maritimum; Ferula communis; Falcaria vulgaris; Meum athamanticum; Selinum carvifolia; Levisticum officinale; Heracleum sphondylium.* Rutaceae: *Dictamnus albus; Ruta graveolens; R. angustifolia; R. chalepensis; Haplophyllum balcanicum; H. tuberculatum; H. linifolium.* In S Europe, *F. vulgare* is perhaps the most commonly used LHP: in England, exclusively *P. palustre.* Ova laid on leaves. Larvae feed on leaves and/or flowers, depending on LHP. Larvae which lack the normal green colouring may be either substantially black or white with the usual orange segmental dots; such forms have been recorded from very hot localities in the Mediterranean region. Hibernates as a pupa. Pupates on robust stems or dead, woody plants. Pupa variable, light green or greyish-buff.
**Behaviour.** Males frequently 'hilltop'; several may remain flying together for some hours at mountain summit.

## *Papilio saharae* Desert Swallowtail					Not illustrated

**Range.** E Morocco, N and SE Algeria, C Tunisia, N Libya, N Egypt, W Saudi Arabia, W Yemen. Replaces *P. machaon* in N Africa south and east of Atlas Mts.

*P. saharae* Oberthür 1879 TL: Laghouat (Algeria).
**Distribution.** Morocco: Erfoud; Zagora; Tizi-n-Tinififft; Tizi-n-Bachkoum. Algeria: El Kantara; Laghouat; Biskra; Bou Saâda; Oued Mya; Oued Nsa; El Oulaya. Tunisia: Gafsa; Gabès; Djerba. 100-2000m. Overlaps with *P. machaon* in some areas, e.g. Tizi-n-Bachkoum.
**Description.** Indistinguishable from *P. machaon* on basis of wing-markings; genitalia differ but are too variable for reliable separation; antennal segments 30-31 (33-36 for *P. machaon*) – low-power magnification provides ready means of determination in the field; larvae morphologically distinct; divergent ecological needs and hybridization experiments provide evidence of separation at species level.
**Flight-period.** Univoltine. Generally mid April/late May; records span February/ October. Records for most summer months in Middle East suggest partial bivoltinism/polyvoltinism or delayed emergence due to exceptionally dry conditions. Pupal diapause may extend over two or more years, with seasonal population density varying accordingly: in consecutive seasons of exceptional dryness, the butterfly may fail to appear (cf. *E. falloui*).
**Habitat.** Rocky slopes or gullies with an abundance of LHP; arid, stony, flattish ground with sparse, low-growing vegetation; desert oases.
**Life-history.** LHPs principally *Deverra chloranthus:* also, *D. scopularia; Seseli varium:* elsewhere in range, *D. tortuosus; Ferula communis sinaica; Pycnocyla glauca.* Ovipositing and larval feeding behaviour similar to that of *P. machaon.* Larval markings (colour/pattern) differ considerably from those of *P. machaon:* also, in *P. saharae,* osmeterium is brown and twice the length of that of *P. machaon* which is orange. Hibernates as a pupa.
**Behaviour.** Males frequently 'hilltop': general behaviour very similar to that of *P. hospiton.*

**Note.** Apparently closely related to *P. hospiton*. Relationship between *P. saharae* and *P. machaon* appears to parallel that of *P. glaucus* Linnaeus and *P. canadensis* Rothschild and Jordan in N America.

## *Papilio hospiton* Corsican Swallowtail                                    Plate 1

**Range.** Corsica, Sardinia.

*P. hospiton* Géné 1839 TL: Tortoli, Sardinia.
**Distribution.** Corsica and Sardinia. Generally 500-1200m, but records range from sea-level to summits of highest mountains.
**Flight-period.** Univoltine. Generally mid May/late July in prolonged emergence: records span mid March/mid August.
**Habitat.** Open, grassy hillsides and valleys, often amongst bushes and rocks.
**Life-history.** LHPs: Corsica, *Ferula communis*; *Ruta corsica*; *Peucedanum paniculatum*: Sardinia, *F. communis*. Ova laid mostly near leaf-tips on plants in partial shade, or on lower, shaded leaves of plants growing in full sun. Larvae feed on leaves. Captive larvae readily accept *R. graveolans*. Captive larvae accept *Skimmia* (?)*japonia* cultivars (Rutaceae) – plant genus not indigenous in Europe. Hibernates as a pupa. Larvae often parasitized by a large, inky-blue hymenopteran (*Trogus violaceus*), which hibernates as a pupa within the pupal case of *P. hospiton*, or that of *P. machaon* subsequent to autumn emergence and parasitization of larvae of the latter species.
**Behaviour.** Males regularly 'hilltop' late morning and early afternoon. Females show no tendency to 'hilltop', but territorial range is extensive. Natural hybrids with *P. machaon* have been reported from Corsica and Sardinia.
**Conservation.** Protective European legislation for this species appears to be unwarranted: widely held to be under no threat from any cause.

## *Papilio alexanor* Southern Swallowtail                                    Plate 1

**Range.** SE France, NW and SE Italy, W Croatia, S Balkans, Greece, Turkey, Israel, Lebanon, N Iraq, Iran, Transcaucasus, Turkmenistan, Uzbekistan, S Kazakhstan, Afghanistan, Tajikistan, Kyrgyzstan, W Pakistan.

*P. alexanor* Esper 1799 TL: Nice and Provençe.
**Distribution.** SE France: Var; Alpes-Maritimes; Alpes-de-Haute-Provençe; Drôme; Hautes-Alpes; Isère; S Savoie. Extinct in Ardèche. Italy: Maritime Alps; Aspromonte; NE Sicily (Monti Peloritani). W Croatia: Istria; Dalmatia. Albania. Republic of Macedonia: Treska Valley; Titov Veles (Vardar River system). Greece: Mitzekeli Mts.; Parnassos massif (including Delphi; Arahova); Ghiona massif (including Amfissia); Mt. Hymettus; Mt. Parnis; northern coast of Peloponnesos; Panahaikion Mts.; Mt. Chelmos and environs (including Kalavrita; Zachlorou); Foli Mts.; Taygetos Mts.; Gythion; Corfu; Kefalonia; Lesbos; Samos. 0-1700m: generally below 1100m.
**Description.** Female larger; ups gc distinctly paler yellow.

**Variation.** On Lesbos and Samos, *eitschbergeri* Bollino and Sala: larger; ups gc paler; pd band narrower. (Typical form in W and C Turkey).

**Flight-period.** Univoltine. Mid April/mid July in prolonged emergence.

**Habitat and Behaviour.** Hot, dry, usually steep slopes on limestone or other consolidated calcareous substrates. In gliding or hovering fashion, both sexes exploit air currents associated with the topography of the terrain for their respective purposes – males in pursuit of females, females in search of egg-laying sites and both sexes open to any opportunity to take nectar. Frequently, habitats provide ideal conditions for *Centranthus ruber* (Red Valerian) – a much favoured nectar source.

**Life-history.** LHPs: France and Italy, *Opopanax chironium*; *Seseli montanum*; *Ptychotis saxifraga* [=*P. heterophylla*]; *Trinia glauca* [=*T. vulgaris*]: Greece, *Opopanax hispidus*; *Pimpinella saxifraga*; *Scaligeria cretica* [=*S. napiformis*]; *Ferula communis*; *Pastinaca sativa*. Captive larvae readily accept *Carum carvi*. Ova laid on floret-stem or calyx, or close to tips of filamentous leaves of plants so structured. Larvae feed on flowers or developing seeds. Hibernates as a pupa on robust stems of dead plants, sometimes at base of large rocks. In captivity, pupal diapause may extend over two seasonal cycles.

## *Iphiclides podalirius* Scarce Swallowtail                    Plate 2

**Range.** N Africa, S and C Europe, Turkey, Middle East, Near East, through temperate Asia to W China.

*I. podalirius* Linnaeus 1758 TL: Livorno, Tuscany (Verity 1947).
**Distribution.** Widespread, locally common. N Africa. 0-2700m: generally below 2400m. N France and Baltic coast to S Europe and most Mediterranean islands including Corsica but reportedly absent from Sardinia. 0-1500m.
**Description.** First brood: ups gc pale yellow; abdomen black. Second brood: ups gc whiter; black markings reduced; uph inner submarginal and pd bands narrow, greyish, often diffuse; unh twin black discal lines not filled with yellow-orange: female larger; abdomen greyish-white with dark grey dorsal line.

**Variation.** In NW Africa, Iberian Peninsula and S France (E Pyrenees), *feisthameli* Duponchel: first brood; ups gc greyish-white in male; with faint yellow flush in female; black markings heavier; uph inner black marginal border broad, solid. Second brood; ups gc white in male, female often with pale yellow flush; dark inner marginal and submarginal bands reduced, divided by pale line or narrow band.

**Flight-period.** Univoltine, bivoltine or trivoltine according to locality and altitude: March/early October.

**Habitat.** Diverse. Bushy places; woodland margins; open grassy places, rocky slopes or gullies, sometimes containing few and isolated LHP specimens; orchards of *Prunus* cultivars: often in very hot and dry situations.

**Life-history.** LHPs principally *Prunus*, including most cultivated species: *P. spinosa* (sloe/blackthorn); *P. amygdalus* (almond); *P. avium* (cherry); *P. domestica* (plum, damson, greengage); *P. persica* (peach); *P. armeniaca* (apricot); *P. mahaleb* (Mahaleb Cherry); *P. padus* (Bird Cherry): also, *Pyrus communis* (pear); *P.*

*amygdaliformis*; *P. longipes*; *Malus domestica*; *Crataegus monogyna*; *C. oxycantha*; *Sorbus aucuparia*. Ova laid on leaves. Larvae feed on leaves. In later instars, the green larva is shorter in proportion to its maximum diameter than any other European species and smoothly tapered towards its 'tail': in colour, texture and markings, well-camouflaged amongst leaves of principal LHP, *Prunus spinosa*. When crawling, the larva sways gently backwards and forwards: the reason for this curious behaviour is not clear – possibly it confuses predators: other well-camouflaged but very different animals, such as the chameleon and some Mantid species, move in a similar fashion. Pupates on thicker stems of LHP. Hibernates as a pupa. Pupa is green or buff, according to pupation site and season: pupae which hibernate – on plant stems devoid of leaves – are buff.

**Behaviour.** Adults are greatly attracted to nectar-rich shrubs and trees such as apple, cherry, lilac and buddleia. Air currents are often exploited in aiding flight. Males sometimes 'hilltop'.

**Note 1.** *I. p. feisthameli* considered specifically distinct by some authors: confirmatory experimental evidence (biochemical comparisons, hybridization experiments, etc.) appears to be lacking.

**Note 2.** Apparent absence from Sardinia is curious in view of widespread occurrence in coastal districts of S Corsica and the scope for fortuitous introduction in consequence of strong, prevailing north-westerly winds.

**Conservation.** Becoming increasingly scarce in C Europe, reputedly in consequence of changes in agricultural practices.

## *Zerynthia polyxena* Southern Festoon                    Plate 3

**Range.** Central S and SE Europe, NW Turkey, S Urals, NW Kazakhstan.

*Z. polyxena* Denis and Schiffermüller 1775 TL: Vienna.
syn: *hypsipyle* Schulze 1776: *hypermnestra* Scopoli 1763 (invalid homonym).

**Distribution.** Widespread but local. SE France: Hérault to Ardèche, Hautes-Alpes and Alpes-Maritimes. Italy. Sicily. S Switzerland: S Tessin: very local. SE Austria. SE Poland. Slovakia. Hungary. Balkans. Greece. European Turkey. Absent from Greek islands. 0-1700m – generally below 900m.

**Description.** Upf without red spots in s1b, s4-6, s9 or cell (cf. *Z. rumina*).

**Variation.** In S Europe, females with ochreous ups gc are common (f. *ochracea* Staudinger). In S France and Italy, f. *cassandra* Geyer: ups black markings more extensive; upf red spot usually absent in s9.

**Flight-period.** Univoltine. Late March/early July in prolonged emergence.

**Habitat.** Hot, dry grassy and bushy places; rocky slopes and gullies; cultivated areas, especially neglected terraces.

**Life-history.** LHPs *Aristolochia clematitis*; *A. rotunda*; *A. pallida*; *A. pistolochia*. Ova laid singly or in small batches on leaves, usually underside. Once established on a particular *Aristolochia* species, captive larvae may be reluctant to accept other, natural LHPs. Larvae often rest in full sun, usually on LHP leaves. Pupates on plant-stems, tree-bark or underside of stones. Hibernates as a pupa.

## *Zerynthia rumina* Spanish Festoon — Plate 3

**Range.** NW Africa, SW Europe.

*Z. rumina* Linnaeus 1758 TL: S Europe.
**Distribution.** Widespread, locally common. Morocco. Algeria. Tunisia. 0-2100m, generally below 1600m. Portugal. Spain. S France: Pyrénées-Orientales to Lozère and Provençe: sporadic and local. 0-1500m, generally below 1000m.
**Description.** Upf with red spots in s1b, s4-6, s7 and cell (cf. *Z. polyxena*).
**Variation.** F. *medesicaste* Hoffmannsegg: uph red spot some-
times present at cell-base – common in some localities in S France. F. *honnoratii* Boisduval (often spelt *honoratii* in error): ups and unh red markings greatly extended. In female, f. *canteneri* Staudinger: ups gc yellow-ochreous (a rare variant in male). In N Africa, f. *africana* Stichel: larger; all markings bolder, well developed; upf without red spot in s1b – replaced by black; uph with solid black pd band enclosing red spots: closely similar forms are common in S Spain.
**Flight-period.** Generally univoltine (late March/May) in prolonged emergence: records span February/July: a second brood (August/October) has been reported from N Africa and S Spain.
**Habitat.** Hot, dry rocky places amongst scrub, including coastal gullies; margins of dry riverbeds; cultivated areas; flowery meadows.
**Life-history.** LHPs: N Africa, *Aristolochia longa paucinervis*; *A. fontanesi*; *A. rotunda*; (?)*A. pallida*: Europe, *A. pistolochia*; *A. rotunda*; *A. longa*; *A. baetica*. Ova laid singly or in small batches on leaves: subsequent development similar to that for *Z. polyxena*.

## *Zerynthia cerisy* Eastern Festoon — Plate 2

**Range.** SE Europe, Turkey, Cyprus, Israel, Lebanon, Iraq, Iran.

*Z. cerisy* Godart 1824 TL: Ourlac [Province of Izmir].
**Distribution.** SE Serbia. S Romania. Albania. Republic of Macedonia. Bulgaria. European Turkey. N Greece: provinces of Kastoria, Drama and Evros: very sporadic and generally local: 75-1000m: Aegean Islands of Lesbos, Chios, Samos, Kos, Simi, Rhodes, Kastellorizo and Crete (0-1100m).
**Variation.** Uph submarginal red spots variable in size.
Female gc sometimes replaced by ochreous-yellow. On Samos: smaller; female ups gc appreciably darker yellow, red spots prominent. On Rhodes: both sexes: red spots replaced with orange in about 70% of specimens. On Crete, *cretica* Rebel: smaller; markings reduced; hw outer margin rounded: accorded specific status by some authors.
**Flight-period.** Univoltine. Mid March/late July in prolonged emergence: at highest altitude, emergence generally delayed by 3-4 weeks.
**Habitat.** Open, hot, sunny, dry, grassy places amongst thickets of mature bushes with dense undergrowth, or bordered by hedgerows with sparse deciduous trees: often in river valleys and cultivated areas.

**Life-history.** LHPs: N Greece and Bulgaria, *Aristolochia clematitis*: Samos, *A. bodamae*: Rhodes *A.* (?)*guichardii*; *A.* (?)*parvifolia*: Crete, *A. cretica*; *A.* (?)*sempervirens*. Ova laid singly or in small numbers on upperside of leaf: plants in close proximity to bushes or well-shaded by trees are favoured for oviposition. Captive larvae accept *A. rotunda*. Pupates at base of woody plants or rocks. Hibernates as a pupa.

## *Archon apollinus* False Apollo                    Plate 3

**Range.** Bulgaria, Greece, Turkey, Jordan, Israel, Lebanon, Syria, N Iraq, N Iran.

*A. apollinus* Herbst 1798 TL: Ourlac (Bay of Izmir).
**Distribution.** SW Bulgaria: reported in 1991 from Sandanski (Struma Valley). Greece: district of Thessalonika; Aegean Islands of Lesbos, Chios, Samos, Kos and Rhodes. European Turkey: Keban; Kuru Dag; Gelibolu Peninsula. 0-1100m. Records from Thrace (NE Greece and E Bulgaria) are somewhat confused by alterations in political boundaries and place names around the time of the Great War, but appear to relate solely to attempted introductions. In 1918 and 1919, larvae from European Turkey (Kuru Dag) were introduced by Iltschev to Badoma (presently known as Avas or Avandas), an area north of Alexandroupolis. Searches for the species in this area in 1914 and 1915 had proved negative: several, recent searches (1987-1993) have also been unsuccessful.
**Flight-period.** Univoltine. Mid March/mid April.
**Habitat.** Olive-groves; vineyards; rocky places amongst scrub or open woodland.
**Life-history.** LHPs: Lesbos and Samos, *Aristolochia bodamae*: Bulgaria, *A. clematitis*: Rhodes, *A.* (?)*guichardii*; *A.* (?)*parvifolia*. Ova bright green, laid on leaves. Larva black with red spots, feeding in small companies when young in loosely spun-up leaves. In later instars, larva feeds in a 'tent' fashioned from a leaf bound elaborately with silk – a curious practice, unique amongst European Papilionidae, for a larva with warning colours and an osmeterium to deter predators: however, the physical barrier would seem to offer some protection from dipterous and hymenopterous parasites. Captive larvae readily accept *A. clematitis* and *A. rotunda*. Pupates 1-2cm below ground-level in loose soil. Hibernates as a pupa.
**Conservation.** Use of herbicides in olive-groves and vineyards, the principal habitats, appears to have been responsible for extensive local extinction.

In the following three, rather distinctive species, fertilized females develop a large, chitinous structure – a sphragis – on the posterior segments of the abdomen to prevent further copulation.

## *Parnassius apollo* Apollo                    Plate 4

**Range.** Most larger mountainous regions of Europe to Tian Shan and W Siberia.

*P. apollo* Linnaeus 1758 TL: Sweden.
**Distribution.** Most larger mountain ranges from Spain to S Fennoscandia, Balkans and Greece, including NW Peloponnesos. Absent from British Isles

and Mediterranean islands except Sicily. Extinct in C
Germany, Denmark and Czech Republic. 500-2400m: generally above 1000m in S Europe.

**Description.** Male upf without red pd spot in s8; black pd
spot in s5 rarely with obscure red centre: equivalent markings in female variable but averagely slightly better developed – sometimes conspicuous. Antennal shaft pale grey,
narrowly ringed darker grey (cf. *P. phoebus*).

**Variation.** A large accumulation of formal descriptions has
resulted from attempts to account for marked, local/regional variation in size,
gc and development of markings. Many named forms differ only slightly, falling
within an overall range of variation which might be considered normal for other
species attracting less attention. An extensive, and therefore disproportionate
account of racial differences may serve only to mislead. Amongst the more
superficially distinctive forms are colour variants occurring at SW and SE
extremes of European range: in S Spain, *nevadensis* Oberthür (Sierra Nevada),
*filabricus* de Sagarra (S. de los Filabres) and *gadorensis* Rougeot and Capdeville
(S. de Gádor); all red markings replaced by yellow-orange: in S Greece (Mt.
Erimanthos, NW Peloponnesos), *atrides* van der Poorten and Dils: similarly
coloured. Other races of Spain (*hispanicus* Oberthür), Greece and S Balkans
(*rhodopensis* Markovic) have the more usual red markings.

**Flight-period.** Univoltine. Early May/September according to locality, altitude
and season.

**Habitat.** Breeding-grounds comprise rocky places with areas favouring the
establishment of LHP (*Sedum*) and the general exclusion of plant species
requiring a more substantial soil-base – a condition met partly by the relatively
high tolerance of LHP to desiccating conditions. Well-drained, often precipitous
rocky slopes; limestone pavements with narrow crevices or hollows, or other
flat, stony surfaces provide typical habitats where these occur in proximity to
deeper soils supporting robust nectar-rich plants such as knapweeds and
thistles.

**Life-history.** LHPs principally *Sedum album*: less often, *S. telephium*. Other
*Sedum* spp. and allied genera are often quoted in the literature – *S. roseum*; *S.
annuum*; *S. villosum*; *Sempervivum tectorum*; *Rhodiola rosea*. Ova laid on dead or
living woody plant stems, and the leaves of evergreen shrubs such as juniper or
lichens. Usually hibernates as a fully formed larva within ovum-case, less often
externally: may remain in diapause for two seasonal cycles: feeds in full sun on
leaves. Larva, velvety black, lateral spots yellow or brilliant orange-red according
to locality. Pupates in a flimsy cocoon under stones or moss.

**Note.** Declined rapidly in Germany, Norway, Sweden and parts of France
during the present century: climatic change appears primarily responsible.

## *Parnassius phoebus* Small Apollo                        Plate 5

**Range.** Central European Alps, C and Polar Urals, Altai, Tian Shan, S and C
Siberia, Yakutia, Magadan, Kamchatka, N America (Rocky Mts.).

*P. phoebus sacerdos* Stichel 1906 TL: Pontresina, Engadin.
syn: *delius Esper* 1800 (invalid homonym).

**Distribution.** Central European Alps of France (Alpes-Maritimes to Haute-

Savoie), Italy (Maritime Alps to E Alps), S Switzerland (Valais to Engadine) and S Austria (S Tirol to Styria and Carinthia). 1600-2800m: generally 1800-2200m.

**Description.** Male upf often with black-edged red pd spots in s5 and s8: equivalent markings better developed in female and usually contiguous with additional red spot in s6. Antennal shaft alternately ringed greyish-white and dark grey. (cf. *P. apollo*).

**Variation.** In Maritime Alps, f. *gazeli* Praviel: ups gc white; upf grey marginal border wider; black pd spot in s8 without red centre; uph black-ringed red ocelli smaller, without white pupils: variable and transitional to f. *sacerdos* in Hautes-Alpes. In E Switzerland, f. *cardinalis* Oberthür occurs frequently as a variant: ups dark markings more extensive; uph red ocelli joined by black bar. In Austrian Alps (Styria and Carinthia), f. *styriacus* Frühstorfer: resembles f. *gazeli*.

**Flight-period.** Univoltine. Late June/late August, according to altitude.

**Habitat.** Damp, sheltered gullies or hollows, often near the boggy margins of streams or similar sites suiting the needs of LHP.

**Life-history.** LHP *Saxifraga aizoides*. Ova laid on various substrates in vicinity of LHP, including moss, dead vegetation, stones and soil; less often on host-plant leaves. Hibernates as a fully formed larva within ovum-case or externally. Pupates in a flimsy cocoon, in leaf-mould beneath LHP or amongst moss. (In N America, *P. phoebus* larvae feed on *Sedum* and other Crassulaceae, whilst captive larvae reportedly reject *S. aizoides*: the acceptability, or otherwise, of *Sedum* to European larvae does not appear to have been investigated).

## *Parnassius mnemosyne* Clouded Apollo                    Plate 5

**Range.** Pyrenees, C and NE Europe, Turkey, Transcaucasus, Lebanon, Syria, Iraq, Iran, Afghanistan, C Urals, Siberia, Tian Shan.

*P. mnemosyne* Linnaeus 1758 TL: Finland.

**Distribution.** Sporadic and often local. Pyrenees and Massif Central through C Alps, Italy and N Sicily to S Poland, Balkans, Greece and European Turkey: rare and local in S Fennoscandia (except Denmark) and Baltic states. 75-2300m: generally 1000-1700m.

**Variation.** Many local variants have been described to account for development of ups dark suffusion. On Mt. Parnassos and mountains of Peloponnesos, *athene* Stichel: upf with 4-6 white pd spots in apical area: occurs as a variant in most S European populations, including Pyrenees, SE France, Apennines, Sicily and Republic of Macedonia: similar forms occur in Turkey, Middle East, Near East and C Asia.

**Flight-period.** Univoltine. Mid April/late August according to locality and altitude.

**Habitat.** Diverse. Light deciduous/coniferous/mixed woodland clearings, bushy places, open rocky and grassy slopes/gullies: in dry, damp or wet conditions in coastal and inland areas: less often, in hot, dry places near sea-level.

**Life-history.** LHPs *Corydalis solida*; *C. bulbosa* [=*C. cava*]; *C. intermedia* [=*C.*

*fabacea*]. In some sites where two host-plant species are present, e.g., *C. solida* and *C. bulbosa*, it appears that only one or other is used. Ova laid mostly on wilted leaves/stems of LHP; also, other dead plant stems, small stones or large rocks providing these are in close proximity to LHP. Hibernates as a fully formed larva within ovum-case or externally.

# Pieridae Duponchel 1835

Included in this large family, well-represented in Europe, are several of the more common and easily recognized butterflies, as well as some of the best known migrants, e.g., the Large White, Small White, Bath White and Clouded Yellow. Sexual dimorphism is generally well marked. The larvae of some species are cryptically coloured, whilst others are brightly marked with 'warning colours': larvae of the Large White and Small White, two very common pests on cabbages, exemplify the two extremes of these larval survival strategies.

## *Aporia crataegi* Black-veined White — Plate 6

**Range.** NW Africa, Europe, Turkey, Cyprus, Israel, Jordan, Lebanon, Syria, NE Iraq, N Iran, Transcaucasus, Asia (40-70°N), Japan.

*A. crataegi* Linnaeus 1758 TL: Sweden (Verity 1947).
**Distribution.** Widespread and common. Morocco. Algeria. Tunisia. Generally 500-2000m: occasional vagrants/(?)-migrants to 2600m. South of 64°N in Fennoscandia, throughout most of Europe including Sicily, Limnos, Lesbos, Chios, Samos, Ikaria and Rhodes. 0-2000m. Absent from C Norway, central W Sweden, Atlantic Islands, Balearic Islands, Corsica, Sardinia, Ionian Islands, Crete, Kykladian Archpeligo. Extinct in British Isles.
**Variation.** Rhodes (common and widespread), f. *fert* Turati and Fiori: uns veins with heavy black suffusion, expanding into triangular markings towards outer margins.
**Flight-period.** Univoltine. In N Europe, late May/early July: in S Europe, mid April/July according to altitude, locality and season.
**Habitat and Behaviour.** Diverse. Warm, sunny, bushy places; cultivated areas, especially orchards comprising species of LHP. Shows a marked preference for open ground containing an abundance of robust thistles upon which, during peak emergence, several butterflies may be found taking nectar on the same flower-head. Often found in areas devoid of LHPs, including high mountains. A dispersive/(?)migratory tendency would seem advantageous to a large species capable of very rapid population expansion: even at low population density, larvae may defoliate much of the available LHP: dispersion may be of further benefit in disrupting parallel population growth of larval parasites (commonly *Apanteles* spp.), which may infest over 90% of larvae.
**Life-history.** LHPs *Prunus spinosa* and most *Prunus* cultivars including *P. domestica* (plum); *P. avium* (wild cherry); *P. persica* (peach); *P. armeniaca* (apricot); *P. amygdalus* [=*P. dulcis*; *Amygdalus communis*; *A. dulcis*; *Pyrus communis*] (almond): also, *P. mahaleb*; *P. padus* (Bird Cherry); *Crataegus monogyna*; *C. pycnoloba*; *C. laciniata*; *Pyrus communis* (pear); *Malus domestica* [=*Pyrus malus*] (apple); *Sorbus aucuparia*; also, in Atlas Mts., *Euproctis chrysorrhoea*. Bright yellow ova laid in batches on underside of leaves. Small larvae feed in a silken web which also serves as a hibernaculum. In later instars, after hibernation, larvae feed singly or in small groups. Often pupates on grass stems.

## *Pieris brassicae* Large White                          Plate 6

**Range.** N Africa, Europe, Middle East and Asia to
Himalayas. Naturalized in Chile.

*P. brassicae* Linnaeus 1758 TL: Sweden (Verity 1947).
**Distribution.** Widespread and common. Throughout N
Africa and Europe to 66°N in Fennoscandia: at higher latitudes, appearance depends largely on migration. Recorded
from most Mediterranean islands. Infrequent reports from
Canary Islands most probably relate to accidental introduction or confusion with *P. cheiranthi* (below). 0-2600m: records
at highest altitudes more probably relate to migrants.

**Description and Variation.** First brood: unh dusted with dark scales; male
upf dark apical patch extending along outer margin to v3 or v2 (cf. *A rapae*).
Second brood: unh dark colouring reduced or absent; male upf apical patch
intensely black. On Madeira, f. *wollastoni* Butler (possibly extinct): ups markings with some of the character of *P. cheiranthi* (below). Wing-characters of
captively produced hybrids of *P. brassicae* and *P. cheiranthi* resemble f. *wollastoni*.
**Flight-period.** Polyvoltine. March/late October. Relative abundance of broods
seasonal/regional variations.
**Habitat.** Diverse. Most habitat-types containing LHPs and an adequate supply
of robust, nectar-rich plants, commonly thistles and knapweeds.
**Life-history.** LHPs: diverse genera and species of Brassicaceae: also *Capparis
spinosa* (Capparaceae); *Tropaeolum majus* (Tropaeolaceae). A frequent pest on
*T. majus* and *Brassica* cultivars. Ova laid in batches. Young larvae feed synchronously in close companies, dispersing in late instars. Larvae have conspicuous
'warning' colours and a chemical defence derived from sulphur-bearing com-
pounds (mustard oils) assimilated from LHP. Larvae often parasitized by
*Apanteles* spp. (Hymenoptera). Hibernates as a pupa.
**Behaviour.** A powerful migrant: vagrant specimens not uncommon on barren
ground at high altitudes.

## *Pieris cheiranthi* Canary Islands' Large White                  Plate 6

**Range.** Canary Islands.

*P. cheiranthi* Hubner 1808 TL: Canary Islands.
**Distribution.** La Palma: widespread, locally common. N Tenerife: apparently
restricted to northern coastal districts. 200-1400m. Presumed extinct on Gomera
– last recorded 1975. Records for Gran Canaria require confirmation: a record
for Lanzarote appears to have arisen from mis-identification.
**Variation.** On La Palma and (?)Gomera, f. *benchoavensis* Pinker: upf proximal
border of black apical patch more sharply defined, extending to v2: upf and
unf black discal markings averagely slightly reduced, showing tendency towards
disconnection: characters are said to associate with smaller specimens and are
suspected of being ecological in origin: closely similar forms occur sporadically
on Tenerife.
**Flight-period.** Polyvoltine. Recorded in all months in a succession of 7 or 8
slightly overlapping broods. No diapause stage reported.

**Habitat.** Wet, shaded gullies in laurel forests appear to comprise the primary (natural) habitat. Areas with equivalent microclimate outside of laurel zone, such as wet cliffs, provide alternative, secondary habitats.

**Life-history.** LHPs *Tropaeolum majus* (Tropaeolaceae); *Crambe strigosa* (Brassicaceae). *C. strigosa*, an endemic species confined to wet, rocky places in laurel forests, appears to be the only known, strictly natural LHP: *T. majus* (Nasturtium), an introduction from S America, is ecologically much more versatile. Ova laid on underside of leaves in batches of 5-50, batch-size roughly proportional to plant-size. Feeding behaviour and development similar to that of *P. brassicae*. Captive larvae accept many Brassicaceae species including *Brassica oleracea* (cabbage) which, if growing in appropriate microclimatic conditions (relatively cool/shady/damp) also appears to be acceptable in nature. Cabbage cultivars grown in more usual conditions, warm and dry, seem unattractive to the butterfly. In captive rearing, attempts to induce diapause by reduction of photo-period have been unsuccessful.

**Note.** Specific separation from *P. brassicae* supported by differences in:- biochemistry; early-stages (especially ovum: 13-14 longitudinal ribs in *P. cheiranthi*, 17-18 in *P. brassicae*); voltinism (*P. cheiranthi* has no diapause stage); ecological requirements; migratory behaviour (*P. cheiranthi* is essentially sedentary).

**Conservation.** Destruction of primary, natural habitat appears largely responsible for decline in many areas and possibly extinction on some islands.

Higgins and Riley (1983) cite adult morphology as a basis for generic separation of *Pieris* from the following, seven allied species. This proposal has been largely disregarded by other authors. However, as other taxonomically relevant differences are no less apparent (chromosome number, ovipositing behaviour and larval survival strategy – the latter reflected in morphology, behaviour and biochemistry), the proposal of Higgins and Riley is followed in the present treatment.

## *Artogeia rapae* Small White                                  Plate 7

**Range.** N Africa, Europe, Asia, Japan. Introduced to N America, Australia.

*A. rapae* Linnaeus 1758 TL: Sweden (Verity 1947).
**Distribution.** Azores. Madeira. Canary Islands (rare on Fuerteventura; a single record for Lanzarote). NW Africa. Throughout Europe, from Lappland to Mediterranean islands. Generally very common: less frequent in N Fennoscandia where occurrence may depend more on migration. 0-3000m: records at highest altitudes more probably relate to migrants.

**Description.** Upf apical patch extends along outer margin to v7 or v6 (cf. *A. mannii*).

**Flight-period.** Polyvoltine. Generally early March/November: recorded in all months in Canary Islands.

**Habitat and Life-history.** Diverse. Almost anywhere containing LHPs, principally Brassicaceae: also Capparaceae (*Capparis spinosa*); Tropaeolaceae; Resedaceae; Chenopodiaceae (*Atriplex* sp.). A common pest on cultivated

Brassicaceae. Ova laid singly on leaves. Larva green, densely clothed with very short, whitish hairs – cryptically coloured and similar to other European *Artogeia* (cf. *P. brassicae* and *P. cheiranthi*). Larvae often parasitized by *Apanteles* spp. (Hymenoptera). Hibernates as a pupa, often at 1-3m above ground-level on walls, fences, etc.

## *Artogeia mannii* Southern Small White                    Plate 7

**Range.** Morocco across S Europe to Turkey and Syria.

*A. mannii* Mayer 1851 TL: Split, Dalmatia.

**Distribution.** Morocco: Middle Atlas 2000m. Spain: very local: Provinces of Madrid and Málaga to Gerona and Huesca. SW and S France. S Switzerland: Valais; Tessin. Italy, eastwards to 51°N. Absent from Mediterranean islands except Sicily and Samos – possibly more widespread in E Aegean Islands. 0-2000m. Records for S Greece (Peloponnesos) require confirmation.

**Description.** Upf apex black, extending along outer margin to v4 or v3; distal margin of spot in s3 concave or linear (not round), often linked to outer margin by black scaling along v3 and v4 (usually only apparent in second brood); uph, distal margin of costal mark concave. (cf. *P. rapae*).

**Flight-period.** Generally polyvoltine, March/September: in Morocco, only one brood has been reported (July/August).

**Habitat.** Dry, usually hot, rocky places, often amongst sparse bushes or trees.

**Life-history.** LHPs *Iberis sempervirens*; *I. saxatilis*. Hibernates as a pupa.

## *Artogeia ergane* Mountain Small White                    Plate 7

**Range.** Spain, S France, N and C Italy, Balkans, Greece, Turkey, Middle East, Iran.

*A. ergane* Geyer 1828 TL: Ragusa (Hemming 1937).

**Distribution.** Spain: very local: Provinces of Palencia; Cuenca; Huesca; Lérida; Gerona. S France: Pyrenees to Provençe. Italy: extremely local in northern districts, commoner in C Apennines. Austria. Hungary. Balkans and Greece: widespread, often local. Absent from Mediterranean islands: records for Thassos and Crete require confirmation. 75-1850m: generally above 500m.

**Description.** Upf without black spot (cf. *P. rapae*). Second brood: ups markings greyish, somewhat diffuse.

**Flight-period.** Bivoltine/trivoltine according to locality: early April/late August.

**Habitat.** Hot, dry bushy and rocky places, on limestone or base rich-soils; also dry, grassy slopes and gullies at higher altitudes.

**Life-history.** LHP principally *Aethionema saxatile*: also, *A. orbiculatum*; *Isatis tinctoria*. Hibernates as a pupa.

**Behaviour.** Males often gather in large companies on damp soil.

## *Artogeia napi* Green-veined White                    Plate 8

**Range.** NW Africa, Europe, Middle East, Near East, Asia (40-70°N), N America.

*A. napi napi* Linnaeus 1758 TL: Sweden.
**Distribution.** Much of Europe, including Mediterranean islands of Corsica, Elba, Sicily, Corfu, Thassos and Lesbos. Generally widespread and common: more local in S Spain and S Greece. Absent from Atlantic islands, Shetland Islands and Sardinia. 0-2000m.
**Description.** First brood: ups veins lined greyish; unh yellow, veins suffused greenish: male upf apical black scaling on veins variable, sometimes vestigial; spot in s3 variable, sometimes absent: female ups and uns black markings better developed, with additional spot in s1b and s5 upf. Summer broods: ups grey scaling along veins reduced or absent, but usually with black scaling near outer margin; unh paler yellow, variable – sometimes almost white: female black markings well developed. Female upf with greyish line in s1b connecting outer margin to pd mark – the so-called *bryoniae*-streak – occurs occasionally in England, commonly in Scotland and is typical in N Scandinavia (cf. *A. bryoniae*). In S Italy and sporadically elsewhere in S Europe, f. *meridionalis* Heyne: first brood indistinguishable from nominate form: summer broods: generally larger; unh gc very pale yellow, geyish markings greatly reduced. A rare but recurrent aberration in most populations has white gc on all wing-surfaces replaced by bright yellow (f. *sulphurea* Schoyen): intermediate forms with yellowish-buff gc (f. *flavescens* Tutt) are more common, especially in northern range.
**Variation.** Considerable variation within European range is the subject of extensive research and debate. The species appears to be in an active state of evolution. The results of many experimental investigations are largely inconclusive and in some cases contradictory. The formal description of a great many local/regional ssp./forms presents a complicated and confused picture of biological relationships in which the contribution of ecological factors is very probably significant but difficult to isolate. The taxonomic status of the regional forms/sspp. described below is presently unclear.
**Flight-period.** Voltinism and emergence date dependent on locality, altitude and season: bivoltine (April/May and mid June/July) or trivoltine (April/early September) in N Europe, with a partial fourth brood in warmer areas (late September) in favourable seasons: in S Europe, three or more partially overlapping broods (March/October).
**Habitat and Behaviour.** Damp, grassy and flowery places with some shade; woodland margins; hedgerows; fertile meadows; wooded river valleys. In later broods, females may extend their local range to drier terrain in search of alternative LHPs: such habitats include dry, often rocky, flowery gullies; open bushy places; areas of neglected cultivation. In Mediterranean region, bushy margins of mountain streams/springs, or flood-plains of rivers comprise a common habitat-type in which *Nasturtium officinale* (watercress) is a common LHP.
**Life-history.** LHPs: Brassicaceae, including:- *Cardamine pratensis*; *C. amara*; *C. palustris*; *Nasturtium officinale*; *Lepidium heterophyllum*; *Lunaria rediviva*; *Hesperia matronalis*; *Arabis turrita*; *A. glabra*; *A. hirsuta*; *Sisymbrium officinale*;

*Alliaria petiolata; Sinapis arvensis; Alyssum spinosum; A. saxatile; Cheiranthus cheiri.*
Ova laid singly on underside of leaves, usually on smaller plants in partial shade.
Larva usually feeds on developing leaves: in the case of *L. rediviva* (Honesty),
oviposition/larval feeding appears to be restricted to young seed-capsules.
*Barbarea vulgaris*, a frequently quoted LHP, appears to be unacceptable to
captive larvae. Hibernates as a pupa.

*A. napi segonzaci* le Cerf 1923 TL: High Atlas.
**Distribution.** Morocco: High Atlas (Toubkal Massif; Tizi-n-Test; Dj. Ayachi).
1900-3800m.
**Description.** Large; unh pale yellow; veins broadly lined greyish: male upf
black spots in s3, s5 and s6 prominent: female ups veins lined grey.
**Flight-period.** Voltinism uncertain: records span May/early July.

*A. napi maura* Verity 1911 TL: Glacières de Blida, Algeria.
**Distribution.** Algeria: Glacières de Blida; Kabylie Mts. W Tunisia: Kroumerie.
900-1500m. Reported from Portugal.
**Description.** Resembles summer broods of nominate form closely.
**Flight-period.** Trivoltine. April/September.
**Life-history.** LHP *Ptilotrichum spinosum.*

*A. napi atlantis* Oberthür 1923 TL: Azrou, Morocco. Middle Atlas
**Distribution.** Morocco: Middle Atlas (Taghzeft Pass; Azrou; Dayet Achlef;
Timhadit; Col de Tambrata): very local and uncommon. 1500m.
**Description.** Large: unh veins almost without greyish suffusion: male upf
black spot in s3 prominent.
**Flight-period.** Voltinism uncertain: possibly bivoltine: recorded in May and
mid July.

*A. napi adalwinda* Frühstorfer 1909 TL: Finnmark.
**Distribution.** Fennoscandia north of 65°N. 0-500m.
**Description.** Male indistinguishable from *A. bryoniae* or spring brood of nominate form from N Britain: female ups resembles *A. bryoniae*; variable, gc white
to creamy-yellow, veins suffused greyish or greyish-brown, often extending to
whole wing surface; upf usually with narrow, greyish streak in s1b connecting
outer margin to pd mark (cf. *A. napi* and *A. bryoniae*). Local variation is marked
but a systematic difference between mountain and lowland populations south
of the Arctic circle is apparent in the gc of females which are more yellow
(*bicolorata* Petersen): although some ecological differences are associated with
these two forms, their taxonomic relationship is unclear.
**Flight-period.** Generally univoltine, mid June/mid July, partially bivoltine in
favourable seasons.
**Habitat.** Flowery mountain slopes/meadows; lowland grassland often near birch
woods: often associated with human habitation.

*A. napi flavescens* Wagner 1903 TL: Mödling [E Austria].
**Distribution.** Central E Europe: E Austria; E Slovakia; Carpathian Mts. 300-
1200m.
**Description and Variation.** Male resembles nominate form but variable; ups
and uns dark markings and greyish suffusion along veins sometimes greatly
reduced, unh gc sometimes white (f. *subtalba* Schima) – common or predominant in some localities: female extremely variable, ranging in overall character

from *A. napi* to *A. bryoniae* (below): such variability may be expressed in the progeny of a single female. No ecological separation of *flavescens* and nominate form is apparent, and cross-pairing experiments indicate a high degree of genetic compatibility.

## *Artogeia balcana* Balkan Green-veined White     Not illustrated

**Range.** Bosnia-Herzegovina, Republic of Macedonia, Bulgaria, N Greece.

*A. balcana* Lorkovic 1970 TL: Treska Valley [Republic of Macedonia].
syn: *canidiaformis* Drenowsky 1910 (nom. nud.)
**Distribution.** Bosnia-Herzegovina: Hrcavka; Zelenogora Pl. Republic of Macedonia: Treska Valley; Titov Veles; Katlanovo; Nikolic. Bulgaria: Osogovo Mts. (Kyustendil); Iskar Valley (Pancharevo Gorge); Struma Valley (Kresna Gorge). Greece: Phalakron massif: very local. 300-900m. Distributional relationship with *A. napi* unknown.

**Description.** Resembles *A. napi* closely: unh veins more poorly defined in summer broods. Sexual and reproductive isolation (pre-mating barrier and low fertility) from *A. napi* has been demonstrated in cross-pairing experiments (male *napi* x female *balcana* and female *napi* x male *balcana*).

**Flight-period.** Bivoltine or trivoltine according to locality and altitude: early April/October.

**Habitat.** Superficially indistinguishable from that of nominate form.

## *Artogeia bryoniae* Mountain Green-veined White     Plate 8

**Range.** C European Alps, Tatra Mts., Carpathian Mts., Turkey, Caucasus, Tian Shan, Altai.

*A. bryoniae* Hübner 1806 TL: Geneva.
**Distribution.** Jura Mts.; Central European High Alps; Julian Alps; Tatra Mts; Carpathian Mts. 800-2700m.
**Description.** Male resembles first brood *A. napi*: female ups variable; pale cream-yellow, suffused greyish/ greyish-brown; upf with narrow, greyish streak in s1b connecting outer margin to pd mark; uns veins well defined.

**Flight-period.** Generally univoltine. Mid June/early August: a partial second brood (August/September) has been recorded in warmer localities in S Switzerland.

**Habitat.** Damp alpine/subalpine meadows; flowery margins of streams.

**Life-history.** LHPs (Brassicaceae) include *Cardamine bellidifolia alpina*; *C. resedifolia*; *Biscutella laevigata*; *Thlaspi alpinum*; *T. montanum*. Ova laid singly on flowers or leaves.

**Note.** Hybrids with *A. napi* in areas of distributional overlap are reportedly infrequent: in captivity, cross-pairings result in progeny of poor viability. No significant biochemical difference between the two species has been discovered: greater differences have been found between different populations of *A. napi*.

## *Artogeia krueperi* Krueper's Small White — Plate 8

**Range.** S Balkans, Greece, Turkey, Syria, Oman, N Iraq, Iran, Baluchistan, Afghanistan, Turkmenistan, N Pakistan, NW India.

*A. krueperi* Staudinger 1860 TL: Arcana, Greece.
**Distribution.** Widespread but very local. Albania. Republic of Macedonia. Bulgaria. Greece, including Corfu, Samos, Chios and Kos. 75-1250m – generally above 600m.
**Variation.** In second and subsequent broods, unh markings progressively reduced, becoming paler and yellowish. Sporadic occurrence of typical first brood specimens in second generation suggests delayed emergence of hibernated pupae.
**Flight-period.** Polyvoltine. Late March/late August.
**Habitat and Behaviour.** Hot, dry, precipitous slopes of limestone or other calcareous rocks hosting a wide range of flowering plants, including LHP, in rock crevices or on small ledges. Patrolling males appear to exploit air currents, generated over areas of naked rock, in search of females: similar behaviour is shown by females in search of ovipositing sites and nectar.
**Life-history.** LHPs *Alyssum saxatile*; *A. montanum*. Ova laid singly on calyx. Larvae feed on flowers and developing seeds. Hibernates as a pupa.

## *Pontia edusa* Eastern Bath White — Not illustrated

**Range.** C, E and SE Europe, Turkey, N Iraq, N and NW Iran, C and E Asia (40-65°N).

*P. edusa* Fabricius 1777 TL: Kiel.
**Distribution.** NW France (Finistère and Ille-et-Vilaine): E France (E of Sâone Valley and Basses Alps), through S Switzerland (Valais), Italy (including Elba and Sicily), Germany (E of Rhine Valley and Bremen) to Gotland, Latvia, Balkans, Greece, European Turkey and most E Mediterranean islands. Recorded rarely as a migrant in S Ireland and S England. Occurrence in NE Europe largely dependent upon migration: with the exception of Gotland, no longer resident in Scandinavia. Distribution in N and E France and W Germany uncertain owing to possible confusion with *P. daplidice* and migratory behaviour of both species. 0-1500m, with migrants to at least 2300m.
**Description.** Morphologically inseparable from *P. daplidice* but biochemically distinct. Differences in male genitalia, although statistically significant, are too small to allow reliable separation. Specific distinction is supported by poor viability of progeny arising from hybridization: no pre-copulative barriers appear to separate the two species.
**Variation.** Second and subsequent broods, uns green markings less intense, tending to yellow. Size variable, sometimes very large; extremely small specimens appear to result from adverse effect of excessively hot/dry conditions on nutritional quality of LHP; similar observations apply to *P. daplidice* (below).
**Flight-period.** Polyvoltine. March/late October.

**Habitat.** Diverse – determined largely by presence of LHP. Open, hot, dry, sometimes barren, usually flattish, stony places: common on disturbed ground – roadsides, areas of cultivation, disused quarries and similar sites favouring colonization by LHPs.

**Life-history.** LHPs principally *Reseda alba*; *R. lutea*; *R. luteola*: in Scandinavia, *Descurainia sophia* [=*Sisymbrium sophia*]; *Teesdalia nudicaulis*; *Lepidium* sp. Ova laid mostly on underside of leaves. Larvae usually feed on flowers and developing seeds. Parasitization of larvae normally extensive and may exceed 99% (parasites often *Apanteles* spp., commonly *A. glomeratus* (Hymenoptera)). Hibernates as a pupa.

**Note.** Identification of British migrants are based on superficial characters only and must, therefore, be considered tentative.

## *Pontia daplidice* Bath White                    Plate 9

**Range.** Canary Islands, N Africa, SW Europe, SE Turkey, Middle East, W and S Iran to Afghanistan, Kazakhstan and Tahkistan.

*P. daplidice* Linnaeus 1758 TL: NW Africa (Wagener 1988).
**Distribution.** Canary Islands (La Palma; Gomera; Hierro; Gran Canaria; Fuerteventura; Tenerife: widespread and common (0-2400m); absent from Lanzarote except as a rare migrant – last recorded 1967. Madeira: as a very rare migrant. NW Africa 0-2700m. Portugal. Spain. Mallorca. France: west of Sâone Valley; Provençe. Corsica. Sardinia. Germany: west of Rhine Valley and Bremen. 0-2000m: migrants recorded at 2900m. Exact distribution and residential status uncertain in some regions (see *P. edusa*).

**Description and Variation.** See *P. edusa*.
**Flight-period.** Polyvoltine. Recorded in all months in Canary Islands. In Europe, March/October according to locality: generally more abundant in late summer/autumn brood.
**Habitat.** As for *P. edusa*.
**Life-history.** LHPs principally *Reseda luteola*; *R. alba*; *R. lutea*: several genera of Brassicaceae have been reported, including:- *Sisymbrium*; *Erysimum*; *Ptilotrichum*; *Arabis* [=*Turritis*]; *Moricandia*; *Alyssum*; *Sinapis*; *Iberis*; *Diplotaxis*; *Descurainia*; *Lepidium*; *Raphanus*; *Thlaspi*; *Fibigia* [=*Farsetia*]. Early-stage development as for *P. edusa*.
**Note.** Occurrence of migrants in Britain cannot be excluded (see *P. edusa*).

## *Pontia chloridice* Small Bath White                    Plate 9

**Range.** Republic of Macedonia, Bulgaria, NE Greece, Turkey, Iran, W and C Asia, N Pakistan, Siberia, Mongolia.

*P. chloridice* Hübner 1808 TL: not stated.
**Distribution.** Very local in widely scattered colonies. Republic of Macedonia: Vardar Valley (Titov Veles; Gradsko; Gevegelija). Bulgaria: Sliven; Belassita Mts.; Arda Valley. NE Greece: Evros. European Turkey. 25-500m. Reported rarely from S Finland: a single record (1932) exists for Latvia. A record from Thessalonika (N Greece) requires confirmation

(possibly a vagrant).
**Variation.** Second brood, ups black markings slightly reduced; uns green markings slightly paler, tending to yellow.
**Flight-period.** Bivoltine. Mid April/late May and June/July in prolonged emergence.
**Habitat.** Stony places; gravelly river-banks; dry river beds and associated sites containing rounded stones, often amongst low scrub.
**Life-history.** LHP *Cleome ornithopodioides*. Ova laid mostly on leaves. Larvae feed on leaves, flowers, and developing seeds. Pupates and hibernates on smooth, rounded stones. Pupa is remarkable in its striking resemblance to a bird-dropping. In captivity, pupa obtained from second brood enter diapause. (In Asia, *Cymatocarpus popovi*, *Sisymbrium polymorphum* [= *S. junceum*] and *Descurainia sophia* have been recorded as LHPs: the latter two species occur in SE Europe and may offer alternatives to the very rare and local *C. ornithopodioides*).
**Behaviour.** Population density subject to marked fluctuation. Dispersion accompanies rapid population growth, resulting in the sporadic occurrence of both sexes in seemingly unsuitable terrain – devoid of known LHPs.
**Conservation.** Grazing, water extraction for agriculture and, most particularly, gravel extraction threaten most habitats associated with river systems.
**Note.** Differences in larva and pupa indicates specific distinction from *P. beckerii* Edwards, a closely allied taxon in N America.

## *Pontia callidice* Peak White                                    Plate 9

**Range.** Pyrenees, C European Alps, Turkey, Middle East to Mongolia, China, N America.

*P. callidice* Hübner 1800 TL: Swiss Alps.
**Distribution.** Pyrenees. C European Alps: Alpes-Maritimes to Haute-Savoie; S Switzerland; N Italy, including Dolomites; Bavaria; Austria. 1500-3400m.
**Flight-period.** Univoltine. Early June/early August.
**Habitat.** Open, grassy and rocky alpine slopes.
**Life-history.** LHPs *Erysimum helveticum* [=*E. pumilum*]; *Reseda glauca*; *Cardamine bellidifolia*; *Hutchinsia alpina*. Hibernates as a pupa.

## *Euchloe crameri* Western Dappled White           Not illustrated

**Range.** NW Africa, Iberian Peninsula, S and SE France, NW Italy, E Libya, Egypt.

*E. crameri* Butler 1869 TL: S Spain.
**Distribution.** Widespread and common. NW Africa. 0-2700m. Iberian Peninsula. S and SE France. N Italy: Ligurian Alps to Bologna. 0-2000m. Limited distributional overlap with *E. simplonia* occurs in E Pyrenees and SE France.
**Description.** First brood, ups discoidal spot usually not projecting along costal vein (cf. *E. simplonia*); hw apex (v8) conspicuously angled (cf. *E. tagis*). Second brood larger; upf costa usually clear white – lacking dark striae; upf and unf discoidal spot often large, but variable;

unf apex and unh markings yellowish-green, often interspersed with small patches of yellow, especially on veins. Resembles *E. ausonia* closely: variation in wing-characters largely precludes reliable separation without reference to distributional data – itself inadequate in areas of possible overlap.

**Flight-period.** Bivoltine. Mid March/early June, with prolonged and overlapping broods. Very large specimens with paler yellow-green uns, which usually accompany the first brood, are possibly the progeny of the first brood of the previous season – partial univoltinism: an extended period for larval/pupal development under different conditions (temperature/humidity) may account for differences in size and markings.

**Habitat.** Open, hot, dry, flowery places: common on disturbed ground, especially in cultivated areas.

**Life-history.** LHPs include *Sinapis arvensis*; *Biscutella laevigata*; *Raphanus raphanistrum*; *Moricandia arvensis*; *Iberis sempervirens*; *I. pinnata*; *Isatis tinctoria.* Ova laid on flower-buds. Larva feeds on flowers and developing seeds. Hibernates as a pupa. May remain in diapause for two or more seasonal cycles.

## *Euchloe simplonia* Mountain Dappled White         Plate 10

**Range.** N Spain (Cantabrian Mts.), Pyrenees, Alps of France, SW Switzerland and NW Italy. (Closely allied taxa occur in NE Asia and N America).

*E. simplonia* Freyer 1829 TL: Croatia [?].
**Distribution.** N Spain: Cantabrian Mts; Pyrenees. SE France: Basses Alpes; Hautes Alpes. SW Switzerland: Valais (Pennine, Bernese and W Lepontine Alps; Rhône Valley). NW Italy: higher slopes of S Alps. 400-2400m, usually above 1500m.

**Description.** Upf black discoidal spot variable, usually narrow, curved, with short distal and proximal projections near costal vein (cf. *E. ausonia*; *E. crameri*). Hw apex (v8) conspicuously angled (cf. *E. tagis*).

**Flight-period.** Univoltine. April/August in prolonged emergence.

**Habitat.** Alpine/subalpine flowery meadows; grassy, rocky slopes.

**Life-history.** LHPs include *Biscutella laevigata*; *Iberis spathulata*; *Erucastrum nasturtiifolium.* Ova laid on flower-buds. Larva feeds on flowers and developing seed capsules. Hibernates as a pupa. May remain in diapause for two or more seasonal cycles.

## *Euchloe ausonia* Eastern Dappled White         Plate 10

**Range.** C and S Italy, Balkans, Greece, Turkey, Israel, Jordan, N Iraq, N Iran, Transcaucasus, Afghanistan, S Kazakhstan, Tibet. (Closely allied taxa occur in N America).

*E. ausonia* Hübner 1803 TL: Italy.
**Distribution.** Widespread and common. C and S Italy. Elba. Sicily. Balkans. Greece, including Crete, Limnos, Lesbos, Inousses, Chios, Forni, Samos, Ikaria, Kos, Rhodes and Kastellorizo. 0-1600m.

**Description.** Resembles *E. ausonia* very closely (See *E.*

*crameri* and *E. simplonia*).

**Flight-period.** Bivoltine. Early March/early July in prolonged, overlapping broods. Variation between broods as for *E. crameri*.

**Habitat.** As for *E. crameri*.

**Life-history.** LHPs *Sinapis arvensis; Isatis tinctoria; I. glauca; Aethionema saxatile; Iberis sempervirens; Biscutella mollis; B. laevigata; Bunias erucago; Alyssum saxatile.* Ova laid on flower-buds. Larva feeds on flowers and developing seed-capsules. Hibernates as a pupa. May remain in diapause for two or more seasonal cycles.

## *Euchloe insularis* Corsican Dappled White          Plate 10

**Range.** Corsica, Sardinia.

*E. insularis* Staudinger 1861 TL: Corsica.

**Distribution.** Corsica and Sardinia. 0-1300m. Common and widespread.

**Description.** Upf black discoidal spot narrow with fine proximal taper projecting along v12; unf black discoidal spot small; hw apex (v8) conspicuously angled (cf. *E. tagis*); unh white spots small (cf. *E. ausonia; E. simplonia*).

**Flight-period.** Bivoltine. Mid March/April and mid May/late June: second brood partial, generally of very low abundance.

**Habitat.** Flowery scrub, rocky slopes and gullies.

**Life-history.** LHPs include: *Iberis pennata* (Corsica); *Sinapis* sp.; *Hirschfeldia incana.*

## *Euchloe tagis* Portuguese Dappled White          Plate 10

**Range.** Morocco, Algeria, Portugal, Spain, S France, NW Italy.

*E. tagis* Hübner 1804 TL: Peidade, Portugal.
syn: *lusitanica* Oberthür 1909.

**Distribution.** Colonies very local, widely dispersed. Morocco: Middle Atlas (Ifrane; Immouzer-du-Kandar; Annoceur; 1600m); Rif Mts. (Chefchaoune; Dj. Tizuka; Dj. Lakraa; 1400-1600m). Algeria: Dj. Aurès; Batna; Dj. Kaïder; El Kantara; Guelt-Es-Stel; Dj. Senalba; Lambessa; 600-1200m. Portugal: Tagus Valley; Algarve. Gibraltar. Spain: Provinces of Cádiz; Málaga; Granada; Alicanti; Toledo; Madrid; Lérida; Burgos; Vitoria. S France: Hérault; Gard; Vaucluse; Bouches-du-Rhône; Var; Alpes-de-Haute-Provençe; Alpes-Maritimes; Lot; Lozère; Ardèche; Drôme; Ain. NW Italy: Maritime Alps; Apuane Alps (coastal foothills); Monti Calvi. 300-2400m: generally below 1000m in Europe.

**Description.** Hw apex smoothly curved (cf. *E. ausonia; E. simplonia; E. insularis; E. crameri*).

**Variation.** Marked regional variation, especially development of unh white markings, has given rise to many named forms/ssp. However, these taxa appear to conform to a well-defined, although slightly erratic cline. In Europe, unh white markings show progressive development from Portugal and SW Spain (*davidi* Torrez Mendez and Verdugo Paez, *granadensis* Ribbe and nominate form) through C and E Spain (*castellana* Verity) and S France and NW Italy (Maritime Alps) (*bellezina* Boisduval) to west-central Italy (Monti Calvi, Livorno) (*calvensis* Casini). From

SW Iberian Peninsula through Morocco (*reisseri* Back and Reissinger; *atlasica* Rungs), a general clinal reduction in unh white markings is apparent, culminating in NE Algeria (Aures Mts.) with *pechi* Staudinger in which the uns is uniform green except for small pale discoidal spot. Local and individual variation is significant, sometimes overlapping that of other regionally well-separated races; e.g., forms resembling *pechi* occur in Morocco and S Spain as occasional variants, whilst examples typical of French colonies occur in C Spain and *vice versa*.

**Flight-period.** Univoltine. N Africa, February/June: Europe, late March/May: according to locality, altitude and season.

**Habitat.** Hot, dry, rocky, slopes or gullies; rocky, flowery places, often amongst sparse scrub: usually on limestone.

**Life-history.** LHPs: N Africa, *Iberis grosmiqueli*; *I. linifolia*; *I. odorata*: *I.* (?)*ciliata* and *I.* (?)*taurica*: Europe, *I. pinnata*; *I. linifolia* (?)*welwitschii*; *I. saxatilis saxatilis*; *I. s. cinerea*; *I. sempervirens*; *I. ciliata*; *I. amara*; *I. umbellata*; (?)*Biscutella laevigata*. Larvae feed on flowers and young seed capsules. Hibernates as a pupa.

## *Euchloe falloui* Scarce Green-striped White — Plate 11

**Range.** Mauritania, eastwards to Sinai and Saudi Arabia.

*E. falloui* Allard 1867 TL: Biskra, Algeria.
**Distribution.** Morocco: Anti Atlas (Tafilalet; Tizi-n-Tinififft; Tafraoute); High Atlas; Middle Atlas. Algeria: (Biskra; Bou Saâda). Tunisia. 200-1800m.
**Description and Variation.** Upf black discal spot without white centre (cf. *E. belemia*). Unf apical and unh markings vary from yellowish, through greyish-yellow to greyish-green.
**Flight-period.** Generally bivoltine, February/June, emergence prolonged in both broods: whilst records for September/October have been attributed to a third brood, the possibility of delayed emergence of second brood, due to weather conditions, does not appear to have been excluded.

**Habitat.** Dry, stony ground; dry gullies; desert oases.

**Life-history.** LHP *Moricandia arvensis*: elsewhere in range, *M. sinaica*; *Diplotaxis acris*; *Schouwia thebaica*; *Zilla spinosa*; *Reseda muricata*. Ova laid on flowers/flower-buds. In Saudi Arabia, ovum/larval stage may occupy as little as 7 days: a survival (?)strategy to offset the risk of rapid dessication of LHP. Prolonged pupal diapause may occur in years of persistent drought.

**Behaviour.** Rarely strays far from LHP.

## *Euchloe belemia* Green-striped White — Plate 11

**Range.** Canary Islands, SW Europe, N Africa, N Chad, Middle East, Turkey, Iran, SW Pakistan.

*E. belemia belemia* Esper 1800 TL: Belem, Portugal.
**Distribution.** Generally widespread and common. Morocco Algeria. Tunisia. 0-1500m. Portugal: S. da Estrêla to Algarve. Spain: common in Andalusia; less frequent in Cuenca; Teruel; Madrid; Guadalajara; Valladolid; Burgos. 0-1350m.
**Description.** Upf black discal spot with white centre (cf. *E. falloui*). In first brood, upf apical patch and unh green stripes

dark, well defined: second brood larger; uns stripes paler green tending to yellowish, somewhat diffuse.

**Flight-period.** Bivoltine. February/mid April and late April/early June, in overlapping broods. Occasionally, single specimens have been observed in late summer/early autumn.

**Habitat.** Dry, flowery, often rocky places, amongst scrub or open woodland; neglected areas of cultivation; olive-groves; orchards.

**Life-history.** LHPs: Iberian Peninsula, *Diplotaxis siifolia*; *Biscutella laevigata*; *Sisymbrium*: NW Africa, *Diplotaxis tennuisiliqua*; *Biscutella didyma*. Larvae feed on developing seeds. Diapause stage: pupa.

*E. belemia hesperidum* Rothschild 1913 TL: Canary Islands.

**Distribution.** Fuerteventura 200-400m; Tenerife 1800-2300m; Gran Canaria 200-1000m. Reports from Gomera require confirmation.

**Description and Variation.** Similar to nominate form: smaller; upf black discal spot narrower; unh, margins of green stripes somewhat diffuse in both broods. On Tenerife, f. *eversi* Stamm: unf apical patch whitish.

**Flight-period.** Bivoltine. Gran Canaria and Fuerteventura, late December/early May: Tenerife, late March/early June. (Occasionally, single specimens have been observed well outside normal flight-times).

**Habitat.** Gran Canaria; dry, uncultivated places with *Sisymbrium*. Tenerife; sparse pinewood; semi-desert. Fuerteventura; damp meadows; neglected areas of cultivation containing *Sisymbrium*.

**Life-history.** LHPs: Tenerife, *Descurainia bourgeana*: Fuerteventura, *Carrichtera annua*; *Sisymbrium erysimoides*. Development as for nominate form.

## *Elphinstonia charlonia* Greenish Black-tip          Plate 11

**Range.** Canary Islands, Morocco, Algeria, Tunisia, Spain, N Chad, Egypt, Sudan, Saudi Arabia, Oman, Jordan, Israel, Lebanon, Syria, Iraq, Iran, Turkmenistan, Pakistan, NW India.

*E. charlonia* Donzal 1842 TL: Emsilah, Algeria.

**Distribution.** Canary Islands: Fuerteventura; Lanzarote; Graciosa. 0-400m. Morocco: S coastal region (Sidi R'bat); Middle Atlas; High Atlas (N'fiss Valley 1100m); Rif Mts. Algeria. Tunisia. 200-2000m. Spain: Granada (Baza 800m); Huesca (Fraga).

**Description and Variation.** Ups gc sulphur-yellow; apical patch dark brown with pale distal markings, proximal margin almost black, unmarked; unf costa and outer margin thinly lined red; discal spot solid black (cf. *E. penia*), appreciably variable in size; unh with a few obscure pale markings: hair-collar between head and thorax rose-pink (cf. *E. penia*). In Granada, S Spain, f. *bazae* Fabiano: all characters appear to be within range of variation of nominate form.

**Flight-period.** Bivoltine or polyvoltine according to locality: emergence in very arid regions appears to be governed by rainfall. Canary Islands, December/May: NW Africa, records span all months, more generally February/October: Spain, late February/late May (information limited).

**Habitat.** Hot, dry, rocky slopes; arid valleys; desert oases.

**Life-history.** LHPs: Canary Islands, *Reseda lancerotae* [= *R. crystallina*];

*Carrichtera annua*; reported use of *Kickxia sagittata* [=*K. heterophylla*] (Scrophul-
ariaceae), which captive larvae reject, has been discredited: Morocco, *Reseda
villosa*; *Succowia balaerica*; *Moricandia arvensis*; *Eryngium tenue*; *Eruca vesicaria*;
*Diplotaxis pendula*: Algeria, *Cleome arabica*; *Lonchophora capiomontana*: Tunisia,
*Diplotaxis acris*: Spain, *E. vesicaria*. Ova laid on underside of leaves. Larvae
feed on leaves and developing seeds. Hibernates as a pupa, which, on
Fuerteventura, reportedly has a more pointed head than non-hibernating pupae.
**Behaviour.** Recorded 'hilltopping' at 3000m in Atlas Mts.
**Note.** Range overlaps that of *E. penia* in S Syria and Jordan: limited sympatry
reported for S Syria.

## *Elphinstonia penia* Eastern Greenish Black-tip    Plate 11

**Range.** Republic of Macedonia, Bulgaria, Greece, Turkey,
Lebanon, Syria, N Iraq.

*E. penia* Freyer 1851 TL: not stated.
**Distribution.** Republic of Macedonia: Treska Gorge
(Skopje); Placenska Pl.; Pletvar Pass (Prelip); Vadar Valley
(Tetovo). SW Bulgaria: Pirin Mts. (850m). Greece: Mt.
Orvilos Mt.; W Phalakron massif; Mt. Pangeon; Lake
Vegoritis; Vermion Mts.; Askion Mts.; Vourinos Mts.; Mt. Olympus; Mt. Chelmos. European Turkey. 700-1750m.
**Description and Variation.** All black markings subject to appreciable
individual, inter-seasonal and intra-seasonal variation, with no clearly defined
systematic differences between broods. Upf black apical patch variable, sometimes solid black, more often broken with yellow marks; discal spot very variable
in size and shape; unf outer margin and costa sometimes lined rose-red; unf
with black discal spot showing through from ups – shadowy, not solid black (cf.
*E. charlonia*); unh gc greyish-green with variable pale obscure spots, more evident
along costa: hair-collar between head and thorax pale yellow, sometimes with
interspersed rose-pink dorsal hair (cf. *E. charlonia*). In addition to unf discal
spot, distinctive characters in male genitalia and larval/pupal morphology serve
to distinguish this species from *E. charlonia*. In Askion Mts. and Vourinos Mts.,
upf black discal mark generally larger, roughly rectilinear, atypically extending
across costal vein to wing-edge – a relatively constant and distinctive feature.
**Flight-period.** Voltinism uncertain: at least bivoltine in a prolonged emergence, early May/late July (in captivity, pupae obtained from second brood
usually enter diapause, emerging the following spring).
**Habitat.** Hot, dry, often precipitous limestone formations, where, evidently,
topography affords some protection of LHP from grazing animals.
**Life-history.** LHP *Matthiola tessela*. Ova laid on uns of leaves, less often on
seed-pods. Pupates at base of woody plant stems or rocks. Pupa may remain in
diapause for two seasonal cycles.
**Behaviour.** In hot, overcast conditions, both sexes often sit on warm rocks
with half-open wings. Seeks shelter under rock-ledges in hottest part of day.
Males show some tendency to 'hilltop'.

## *Anthocharis cardamines* Orange Tip                    Plate 12

**Range.** Europe, Middle East, eastwards through temperate
Asia to Japan.

*A. cardamines* Linnaeus 1758 TL: Sweden (Verity 1947).
**Distribution.** Common and widespread in most of Europe
to 69°N in Fennoscandia, including Ireland, Britain, Baltic
Islands, Corsica, Sardinia (above 500m), Sicily, Corfu,
Thassos, Lesbos, Chios, Samos, Tinos and Kastellorizo.
Absent from NW Africa, parts of SW Iberian Peninsula,
Balearic Islands, Malta, Crete and Rhodes. 0-2100m.

**Flight-period.** Univoltine. Late March/June according to locality and altitude.
**Habitat.** Diverse. Damp meadows; marshes; dry, lowland scrub; forest clearings; alpine grassland. On acidic or base-rich soils.
**Life-history.** LHPs include *Cardamines pratensis*; *Alliaria petiolata*; *Arabis
turrita*; *Lunaria annua*; *Biscutella mollis*; *Hesperis lacinata*. Hibernates as a pupa
on plant-stems.

## *Anthocharis belia* Moroccan Orange Tip                    Plate 12

**Range.** NW Africa, SW Europe.

*A. belia belia* Linnaeus 1767 TL: 'Barbaria' Algeria.
syn: *eupheno* Linnaeus 1767.
**Distribution.** Widespread, generally common. Morocco. Algeria. Tunisia. 0-2000m.

**Description and Variation.** Both sexes: unh greyish markings indistinct: female uph often flushed ochreous-yellow.
In S Morocco, *androgyne* Leech: both sexes, unh markings
reduced, sometimes restricted to indistinct wedge-shaped
marks on costa; female ups lightly flushed lemon yellow: distributional relationship with nominate form imperfectly known.
**Flight-period.** Univoltine. N Morocco, Algeria and Tunisia, April/May with
sporadic occurrence of fresh specimens in June/early July: S Morocco, late
February/April.
**Habitat.** Flowery places; woodland clearings.
**Life-history.** LHPs *Biscutella lyrata*; *B. didyma*; *B. raphanifolia*.

*A. belia euphenoides* Staudinger 1869 TL: Gibraltar.
**Distribution.** Widespread and common in Iberian Peninsula except NW
Portugal. France: Haute-Garonne, through S Massif Central to Provençe. S
Switzerland: very local, restricted to Tessin. Italy: very local: Cottian Alps; Ticino;
Abruzzi; Lazio. 0-1800m.
**Description and Variation.** Resembles nominate form: unh greyish mark-
ings more extensive, better developed. No significant variation noted in male
unh gc. Female upf orange apical patch with variable black suffusion.
**Flight-period.** Univoltine. Generally April/June according to locality: reported
from Gibraltar in early March.
**Habitat.** Dry, often hot, flowery places; margins of cultivated ground.
**Life-history.** LHPs *Biscutella laevigata*; *B. auriculata*; *B. ambigua*. Larva feeds
on developing seeds. Pupates and hibernates on dead plant-stems.

## *Anthocharis damone* Eastern Orange Tip                Plate 12

**Range.** Sicily, S Italy, Greece, Republic of Macedonia, Turkey, Israel, Lebanon, Syria, N Iraq, Iran.

*A. damone* Boisduval 1836 TL: Sicily.
**Distribution.** Italy: Sicily (Mt. Etna); Calabria; Aspromonte. Republic of Macedonia: Radika Valley; Treska Valley; Galicica Pl. Greece: Corfu (Mt. Panakrator); Mitzekeli Mts.; Parnassus and Ghiona massifs; Taygetos Mts. 350-1300m. European Turkey. Not reported from Albania. A record for Mt. Chelmos requires confirmation.
**Flight-period.** Univoltine. Early April/late May, according to season.
**Habitat.** Hot, rocky, south-facing, usually precipitous slopes on limestone.
**Life-history.** LHP *Isatis tinctoria*. Ova laid on flower buds. Larvae feed on flowers and developing seeds. Pupates on dried plant-stems.

## *Anthocharis gruneri* Gruner's Orange Tip              Plate 12

**Range.** Albania, Republic of Macedonia, Bulgaria, Greece, Turkey, Israel, Syria, N Iraq, Iran.

*A. gruneri* Herrich-Schäffer 1851 TL: 'Crete' [(?)Greece].
**Distribution.** Albania. Republic of Macedonia: Galicica Pl; Radika Valley; Vardar Valley and associated river systems. SW Bulgaria: Slavayanka Mts.; Belassitsa Mts. Greece: widespread but local: not reported from extreme NW Greece, E Thrace or Greek islands. 100-1800m.
**Flight-period.** Univoltine. Generally late March/May according to altitude: fresh males have been recorded in early July.
**Habitat.** Hot, dry, rocky calcareous slopes, often amongst scrub or small trees.
**Life-history.** LHPs *Aethionema saxatile*; *A. orbiculatum*. Larva feeds on leaves and developing seeds. Pupates on dried plant-stems. Pupa, light green or buff.

## *Zegris eupheme* Sooty Orange Tip                      Plate 11

**Range.** Morocco, S Spain, Turkey, Saudi Arabia, Iran, Caucasus, Ukraine, Volga, S Urals, Kazakhstan, Altai.

*Z. eupheme meridionalis* Lederer 1852 TL: Andalusia.
**Distribution.** Local, in widely separated colonies. Morocco: Middle Atlas (Anosseur, Ifrane, Forum-Kaharig, Azrou 1200-1800m); High Atlas (Oukaïmedan; Tizi-n'Ouguerd-Zegzaoune; Lake Tislit, 1200-2750m. Spain: Andalusia to Provinces of Salamanca; Burgos; Soria; Zaragosa; Huesca; Lérida; Alicante. 500-1400m.
**Variation.** Female ups orange apical patch sometimes reduced, rarely absent. In Morocco, f. *maroccana* Bernardi: superficially indistinguishable from f. *meridionalis*.
**Flight-period.** Univoltine. Late March/mid June according to locality.
**Habitat.** Dry, flowery often rocky places; most frequent in margins of cultivated land, neglected orchards and olive-groves.

**Life-history.** LHPs *Hirschfeldia incana* [=*Sinapis incana*]; *Isatis tinctoria*. Hibernates as a pupa.

## *Colotis evagore* Desert Orange Tip        Plate 11

**Range.** NW Africa, S Spain, SW Saudi Arabia, Ethiopia, Somalia.

*C. evagore nouna* Lucas 1849 TL: Oran, Algeria.
**Distribution.** Morocco: Middle Atlas; High Atlas. Algeria. Tunisia. Generally 800-2200m: recorded at 2500m in High Atlas. S Spain: mainly coastal areas below 100m: Provinces of Cádiz; Málaga; Granada; Almeria; Murcia. 0-400m.
**Variation.** Both sexes, ups black and grey markings follow a very complex, but systematic pattern of progressive develop ment through the broods: first brood, lightly marked, late summer broods heavily suffused black, with complementary greyish markings in nearly all wing-areas.
**Flight-period.** Polyvoltine. Spain, April/October: Morocco, generally February/November, but records span all months.
**Habitat.** Hot, dry gullies; steep, rocky slopes; stony margins of cultivated ground.
**Life-history.** LHPs: NW Africa, *Capparis spinosa*; *C. droserifolia*: Spain, *Capparis spinosa*. Ova laid on leaves, upon which larvae feed. Hibernates as a pupa.
**Behaviour.** In S Spain, population density increases progressively with each brood, apparently inducing territorial expansion and establishment of temporary colonies away from coastal regions in late summer/early autumn. In autumn, recorded from Middle Atlas and Rif Mts. in areas apparently devoid of LHPs.

## *Catopsilia florella* African Migrant        Plate 6

**Range.** All Africa south of the Sahara, Canary Islands, through Egypt to India and China.

*C. florella* Fabricus 1775 TL: Sierra Leone.
**Distribution.** First reported in Canary Islands from Tenerife in 1965: recorded subsequently from Gran Canaria (1966), Gomera, Fuerteventura and Lanzarote (1976), La Palma (1986) and Hierro (1995): residency now well established in coastal districts, rarely recorded above 500m. Occasional in S Morocco (possibly resident in Drââ Valley), S Algeria (Tamanrasset). Recorded from Malta in 1963.
**Description and Variation.** Male ups and uns gc white: female dimorphic: yellow gc sometimes replaced by white (f. *pyrene* Swainson): both forms common in Canary Islands.
**Flight-period.** Polyvoltine. Recorded in all months in a succession of perhaps 8 or 9 broods: no diapause stage.
**Habitat.** Flowery places: gardens, parks etc.
**Life-history.** LHPs: Canary Islands, *Cassia didymobotrya* (an ornamental plant introduced from Africa); possibly other introduced *Cassia* spp.: elsewhere in range, *C. odorata*; *C. occidentalis*; *C. petersiana*; *C. corymbosa*; *C. aschrek*. Ova laid singly on leaves, sometimes in large numbers, resulting in subsequent defoliation of LHP. Larval colouring depends on plant parts ingested: larvae feeding on leaves are green, those feeding on the yellow flowers are usually yellow – larval

coloration unrelated to female dimorphism. Larvae are heavily parasitized by dipterans (Braconidae; Tachididae).
**Behaviour.** Strongly migratory.

## *Colias phicomone* Mountain Clouded Yellow          Plate 13

**Range.** Europe (Cantabrian Mts., Pyrenees, Central Alps, Carpathians).

*C. phicomone* Esper 1780 TL: Styria.
**Distribution.** Spain: Cantabrian Mts. above 1800m; Pyrenees. France: Pyrenees. Alps of France; Italy; S, C and E Switzerland; Germany; Austria. Romania: N Carpathian Mts. 900-2500m.
**Variation.** At lower altitudes, ups greyish suffusion reduced; male gc brighter yellow.
**Flight-period.** Univoltine. Generally mid June/mid August, emerging late May at lowest altitudes: a partial second brood has been reported in warm localities in favourable seasons.
**Habitat.** Grassy slopes; alpine pasture.
**Life-history.** LHPs *Hippocrepis comosa*; *Trifolium repens*; *Lotus corniculatus*. Ova laid singly on upperside of leaves. Hibernates as a small larva.

## *Colias nastes* Pale Arctic Clouded Yellow          Plate 13

**Range.** Arctic Fennoscandia, Taimyr, Yamal Peninsula, Novaya Zemlya, Polar Urals, N America (including Rocky Mts.), Greenland.

*C. nastes werdandi* Zetterstedt 1840 TL: Torne-Lapland.
**Distribution.** Norway: just S of Arctic Circle to Arctic Sea. N Sweden. NW Finland. 100-1100m.
**Variation.** Male ups gc various delicate shades of whitish-yellow or green; marginal borders variable, light grey to black; upf proximal dark border of submarginal pale spots often reduced, sometimes absent. Males reflect UV light. Female uph dark markings sometimes limited to greyish dusting on veins at outer margin. Yellowish-orange variants (f. *christiernssoni* Lampa) are believed to result from hybridization with *C. hecla*.
**Flight-period.** Univoltine. Mid May/early July according to locality and season.
**Habitat.** Open grassy areas amongst scrub; gentle heathland slopes near marshes; dry grassy and rocky slopes in mountains.
**Life-history.** LHP *Vaccinium* spp. at lowest altitudes, *Astragalus alpinus* in mountains. Ova laid on leaves. Hibernates as a larva or pupa. Full larval development may require two seasonal cycles.

## *Colias palaeno* Moorland Clouded Yellow          Plate 13

**Range.** C, E and NE Europe, W and C Asia (50-70°N), Siberia, Sakhalin, Mongolia, NE China, Korea, Japan, N America.

*C. palaeno* Linnaeus 1761 TL: Uppsala.

**Distribution.** France: Jura; Vosges. Italy: very restricted in S Alps. Switzerland: Jura Mts.; C and S Alps. Germany to N Fennoscandia, Baltic states and N Balkans (Carpathian Mts.). 100-2500m. Extinct in Belgium.

**Variation.** Male ups gc ranges from white, faintly tinged with yellow, to pale sulphur-yellow: palest forms predominate in Lappland, yellowish forms in southern range (f. *europome* Esper); upf black discoidal spot variable; sometimes very small or absent, or replaced by thin oval ring, usually very faint in specimens from highest altitudes. In Central Alps, female ups sometimes pale lemon yellow (f. *illgneri* Rühl). At high altitudes, unh in both sexes more heavily dusted with dark scales (f. *europomene* Ochsenheimer).

**Flight-period.** Univoltine. Late June/early August in Lappland: mid June/July in S Scandinavia and C Alps: mid June/late August: emergence depending on altitude, locality and season.

**Habitat.** Acidic marshes and bogs with *Vaccinium* and other shrubs, usually near deciduous or coniferous woodland. At highest level in C Alps, habitats somewhat drier, more open and frequently associated with *Juniperous communis*.

**Life-history.** LHPs *Vaccinium uliginosum*; *V. myrtillus*. Ova laid on upperside of leaves. Larvae are said to feed at night, concealing themselves during the day. Hibernates as a larva.

**Conservation.** Habitat loss arising from land drainage has been responsible for widespread local extinction in many low-lying areas of C Europe.

## *Colias chrysotheme* Lesser Clouded Yellow                    Plate 14

**Range.** E Europe, C and E Asia (50-57°N), NE China.

*C. chrysotheme* Esper 1781 TL: Cremnitz, Hungary.

**Distribution.** Small, widely dispersed colonies. E Austria. Slovakia. Hungary. Romania. 300-1000m. Apparently extinct in Czech Republic. Records for Bulgaria appear to have arisen from misidentification.

**Description and Variation.** Male ups dark marginal borders crossed proximally by yellow veins; uph costa without androconial patch (cf. *C. crocea* and *C. myrmidone*): female fw pointed; upf costa dusky-green; uph lemon yellow submarginal spots well developed, extending to costa (cf. *C. crocea*): white female form is said to be very rare. First brood appreciably smaller than late summer brood.

**Flight-period.** Polyvoltine. Late April/late October in three or four broods according to season.

**Habitat.** Grassy, flowery bushy places.

**Life-history.** LHPs *Vicia hirsuta*; *Astragalus austriacus*. Captive larvae accept *A. glycyphyllos* readily.

## *Colias aurorina* Greek Clouded Yellow    Plate 15

**Range.** Greece, Turkey, Lebanon, Syria, N Iraq, NW Iran, Caucasus, Transcaucasus.

*C. aurorina heldreichii* Staudinger 1862 TL: Mt. Veluchi [=Mt. Timphristos].
syn: *libanotica* Lederer 1858
**Distribution.** Restricted to Greece: Pindos Mts. (Grammos massif; N Smolikas massif; Timfi Mts.; Mt. Vardhousia; Mt. Tymphristos; Mt. Iti; Mt. Ghiona; Mt. Kaliakouda; Mt. Parnassos). 550-2000m. Peloponnesos: Aroanian Mts. (Mt. Chelmos; mountains W of Vouvraitis Gorge; Panahaikon Mts.). 1100-1800m.
**Variation.** Female f. *fountanei* Aigner [=*alba* Rühl]: orange gc replaced by white: progressively commoner towards end of flight-period.
**Flight-period.** Univoltine. Mid May/mid July, emergence dependent upon altitude and locality: rarely, worn examples may occur in late August.
**Habitat.** Dry, usually open terrain, dominated by LHP: on limestone or base-rich soils.
**Life-history.** LHPs: Timfi Mts. and Smolikas massif, *Astracantha rumelica* [= *Astragalus creticus rumelicus*]: S Pindos Mts. and Aroanian Mts., *Astragalus parnassi cyllenus*. Ova laid on upperside of leaves. Hibernates as a small larva. Hibernated larvae feed quickly, completing their development within 14 days. In later instars, larva very distinctive: very dark olive-green with yellowish markings.

## *Colias myrmidone* Danube Clouded Yellow    Plate 15

**Range.** E Europe, Ukraine, Volga, C and S Urals, NW Kazakhstan.

*C. myrmidone* Esper 1781 TL: Turnau, Hungary.
**Distribution.** SE Germany. Austria. Czech Republic. Slovakia. Poland. S Lithuania. (?)Hungary. Romania. In SE Range, closely associated with Danube River system. Very local and sporadic. Recorded only once from Latvia (1949). Not confirmed for Bulgaria. 100-500m.
**Description and Variation** Male ups gc deep yellow; upf outer margin straight; black marginal borders unmarked by yellow veins but with tendency to faint yellow superscaling; uph costa, oval androconial patch conspicuous: female uph submarginal lemon yellow spots conspicuous: f. *alba* Staudinger, orange ground colour and yellow spots replaced by white, faintly tinged green. (cf. *C. crocea* and *C. chrysotheme*).
**Flight-period.** Bivoltine. Late May/mid June and mid July/mid September.
**Habitat.** Open bushy areas, dominated by LHP.
**Life-history.** LHPs *Cytisus ratisbonensis*; *C. capitatus*. Ova laid on upperside of leaves.
**Note.** Adverse climatic factors, coupled with poor viabilty of small, fragmented habitats appears to be responsible for recent, accelerated decline in Germany, Czech Republic and Hungary: possibly now extinct in the latter country.

## *Colias hecla* Northern Clouded Yellow                    Plate 14

**Range.** Arctic Fennoscandia, Kola and Yamal Peninsulas, Polar Urals, Polar Siberia, Arctic N America, Greenland.

*C. hecla sulitelma* Aurivillius 1890 TL: Mt. Sulitelma, Sweden.
**Distribution.** Norway: just south of Arctic Circle to Arctic Sea. Extreme north of Sweden and Finland. 50-900m – occurs near sea-level on Porsanger Peninsula.
**Description.** Male uph costa without androconial patch.
**Variation.** Male ups borders sometimes brownish with uniform whitish suffusion; ups gc occasionally with distinct pinkish-violet reflections – males reflect UV light. Female ups gc sometimes very pale yellowish-white. Believed to hybridize with *C. nastes* (see *C. nastes*).
**Flight-period.** Univoltine. Mid June/early August, emergence dependent on seasonal conditions.
**Habitat.** Open grassy slopes with low-growing shrubs.
**Life-history.** LHP *Astragalus alpinus*. Ova laid on LHP as well as other low-growing plants. Larvae feed on leaves, flowers and stems. Captive larvae readily accept *Medicago sativa*. Hibernates as a larva or pupa. Larvae require two seasonal cycles for full development.

## *Colias hyale* Pale Clouded Yellow                        Plate 16

**Range.** C Europe, NE Turkey, NW Asia, C Asia 43-63°N, NE China.

*C. hyale* Linnaeus 1758 TL: S England (Verity 1947).
**Distribution.** Spain: Granada (S. de Alfacar); Palencia; Guipuzeoa; Navarra; Catalonia (many records uncertain due to possible confusion with *C. alfacariensis*). Pyrenees to Denmark, Gotland (resident), Baltic states, S Finland and N Bulgaria. Migrants occur very rarely in Britain and S Norway, more frequently N Germany and S Sweden. 0-1800m. Absent from Italy, W and SW Balkans, Greece and Mediterranean islands.
**Description.** See *C. alfacariensis* (below).
**Variation.** Female white gc rarely replaced by yellow.
**Flight-period.** Bivoltine or trivoltine according to locality: early May/early October.
**Habitat.** Flowery, grassy places on base-rich soils; commonly associated with *Medicago sativa* (lucerne, alfalfa) under cultivation.
**Life-history.** LHPs, principally *Medicago sativa* (widely cultivated and naturalized): also, *M. lupulina*; *Lotus corniculatus*; *Trifolium pratense*; *Hippocrepis comosa*; *Securigera varia*; *Vicia cracca*. Hibernates as a small larva. Mature larva green with pale yellow subspiracular line (cf. *C. alfacariensis*).

## *Colias crocea* Clouded Yellow Plate 14

**Range.** N Africa, S and C Europe, Middle East, Turkey, Iran, Central W Asia C and S Urals.

*C. crocea* Geoffroy in Fourcroy 1785 TL: Paris.
syn: *edusa* Fabricus 1787.
**Distribution.** N Africa, Canary Islands, Azores, Madeira and Europe (including Mediterranean islands) to S Scandinavia and Baltic states. Appearance in Ireland, Britain, including Scotland, S Scandinavia and Baltic states depends exclusively on migration. Common and widespread in C and S Europe but probably not resident except in warmer regions of Mediterranean: resident in Rhône Valley and SW Iberian Peninsula (see Life-history). 0-3200m: more generally below 1600m: at highest altitudes observations more probably relate to migrants.
**Variation.** Male uph with oval androconial patch (cf. *C. erate*): ups orange gc sometimes replaced by pure yellow; rare in Greece, more frequent in Azores (5-10% of population). Female f. *helice* Hübner: gc replaced by pale creamy-white; outer marginal borders dark brown: comprises 5-10% of all populations.
**Flight-period.** Polyvoltine. March/November in warmer Mediterranean region: in Canary Islands, continuously brooded.
**Habitat.** Diverse. Found in most habitat-types; more common in warm/hot places with an abundance of flowers.
**Life-history.** LHPs: a wide range of genera and species of Fabaceae, including *Medicago sativa*; *M. lupulina*; *M. polymorpha*; *M. lappacea*; *M. hispida*; *M. sulcata*; *Trifolium pratense*; *Onobrychis viciifolia*; *Lotus*; *Coronilla*; *Melilotus*; *Hippocrepis*; *Astragalus*; *Astracanthus*; *Vicia*; *Chamaecytisus*; *Colutea*; *Erophaca*; *Acanthyllis*; *Anthyllis*. Ova laid on upperside of leaves, appears to be restricted to a single plant species at any given site. No diapause stage: most N and C European populations probably succumb to winter cold: in frost-free regions of S Europe, larvae continue to feed and develop slowly during winter.
**Note.** Hybridizes freely with *C. erate* in E and SE Europe.

## *Colias caucasica* Balkan Clouded Yellow Plate 15

**Range.** S Balkans, Greece.

*C. caucasica balcanica* Rebel 1903 TL: Bulgaria.
**Distribution.** Bosnia-Herzegovina: Jahorina Pl. (Trebevic); Ljubisnja Pl. SW Serbia (Montenegro): Mt. Durmitor; Sinjavina Pl. Republic of Macedonia: Sar Pl.; Bistra Pl.; Galicica Pl.; Mt. Pelister; Osogovske Pl. Bulgaria: Osogovo Mts.; Rila Mts.; Rhodopi Mts. Greece: Varnous Mts.; Voras Mts. 1200-2150m.
**Description and Variation.** Resembles *C. myrmidone*: larger; male ups gc deeper orange: female upf yellow spots in black marginal border variable in size and number, sometimes absent. Female f. *rebeli* Schawerda: orange gc replaced by white.
**Flight-period.** Univoltine. Mid June/mid August according to altitude.
**Habitat.** Open alpine grassland, rocky slopes or gullies dominated by LHP

(1700-2100m); bushy clearings in beech or pine forests at lower altitudes. In Greece, on acidic soil-base (granite).

**Life-history.** LHPs: Greece and Bosnia-Herzegovina, *Chamaecytisus hirsutus*; Bulgaria (Rila Mts.), *C. eriocarpus* [=*Cytisus absinthoides*]. Ova laid on upperside of leaves. Larvae feed on leaves. A second brood is easily produced in captive rearing: in Greece, in near natural conditions (normal photo-period) larval development is rapid, with 100% of pupae consistently producing imagines in August (cf. *C. myrmidone*). *Chamaecytisus hirsutus* is apparently repellent to grazing animals.

## *Colias alfacariensis* Berger's Clouded Yellow          Plate 16

**Range.** S and C Europe, Turkey. Eastern range uncertain due to possible confusion with *C. hyale*.

*C. alfacariensis* Ribbe 1905 TL: Sierra de Alfacar, Spain.
syn: *australis* Verity 1911
**Distribution.** Most of C and S Europe, including Balearic Islands, Corsica and Sicily, to 54°N in Poland. Absent from Britain, N Holland and N Germany except as a rare migrant: also absent from N Africa, S Greece, E Thrace, European Turkey and Sardinia. 0-2100m.

**Description.** Resembles *C. hyale* closely: distinction often difficult, especially in female. Genitalia very similar: chromosome numbers identical (CN=31). Readily separable in larval stage. For the male, the following wing-characters of *C. alfacariensis*, considered collectively, usually allow separation from *C. hyale*:-

1. Fw outer margin and apex relatively more rounded.
2. Ups gc slightly deeper tone – 'warmer' yellow.
3. Upf dark basal shading wedge-shaped, extending along inner margin. (In *C. hyale*, radially more uniform – fan-shaped).
4. Uph marginal black border often narrower and less extensive; submarginal markings absent or restricted to s6 and s7.
5. Uph discoidal spot usually larger and deeper orange.

**Variation.** Female white ups and uns gc rarely replaced by yellow.
**Flight-period.** Bivoltine or trivoltine. April/October according to locality.
**Habitat.** Rocky slopes, gullies, dry grassy places, often with open scrub: almost invariably on calcareous soils.
**Life-history.** LHPs *Hippocrepis comosa*; *Coronilla varia*; oviposition on upperside of leaves appears to be restricted to one or other of these plant species when both are present. In Slovakia, where *H. comosa* is not native, restricted to *S. varia*. Larva very distinctive: green with yellow dorsal/subspiracular lines and black segmental spots (cf. *C. hyale*). Hibernates as a small larva.

## *Colias erate* Eastern Pale Clouded Yellow          Plate 16

**Range.** SE Europe, NW Turkey, Central W Asia to E Kazakhstan, NW Siberia, Afghanistan, N Pakistan, N India, S Mongolia, China, Korea, Japan. Also Ethiopia and Somalia.

*C. erate* Esper 1804 TL: Sarepta, S Russia.
**Distribution.** SE Europe: distributional detail poorly known
owing to migration and establishment of colonies of indefinite
persistance. Resident in Slovakia, SE Poland, E Hungary,
Romania, Bulgaria, NE Greece and European Turkey. Since
about 1986, a progressive expansion in S Balkans has resulted in persistent colonies throughout Bulgaria (previously
known only from Black Sea coast, Danube Plain and Mt.
Sakar). Present situation in Republic of Macedonia unclear.
Colonies established in N Greece (Lake Doirani, Phalakron massive, Rhodopi
Mts. and Evros) in 1986/87 from extensive cross-border migration from generally low-lying areas of Republic of Macedonia and Bulgaria had largely expired
during 1988/89. Very small, isolated colonies persist in Evros (NE Greece), but
their existence before the influx of 1987 cannot be precluded. 0-1700m.
**Description and Variation.** Male fw pointed, outer margin linear; ups gc
pure lemon yellow; upf marginal borders uniformly black, but often with
yellow spots (f. *poliographus* Motschulsky) – the dominant form in some
colonies (see Note 1). Female ups gc and upf spots in marginal borders yellow
or white.
**Flight-period.** Polyvoltine. Mid March/October, voltinism and emergence
dependent on locality – in Slovakia and Bulgaria, 3 to 5 broods.
**Habitat.** Found in a wide variety of situations, mostly in regions containing an
abundance of LHP in cultivation.
**Life-history.** LHP: Europe, *Medicago sativa*: other genera/species of Fabaceae
have been reported from eastern range. Hibernates as a pupa.
**Note 1.** *C. erate* (?)f. *poliographus* accorded specific rank by some authors: distribution reportedly overlaps that of *C. erate* in Romania, NW Siberia and
Afghanistan, extending eastwards through N Pakistan, Kashmir, S Mongolia,
China and Korea to Japan.
**Note 2.** Hybridization with *C. crocea* well documented: in E Thrace (NE Greece),
specimens sharing characters of the two species – presumed to be hybrids – are
common (Plate 14).

## *Gonepteryx rhamni* Brimstone                   Plate 17

**Range.** NW Africa, Europe, Turkey to W Siberia, Kyrgyzstan
and Mongolia.

*G. rhamni* Linnaeus 1758 TL: Sweden (Verity 1947).
**Distribution.** Widespread and common. Mountainous
regions of NW Africa. 0-2800m. Europe, south of Scotland
and 64°N in Fennoscandia. Mediterranean islands of Corsica, Sardinia, Sicily, Corfu, Kefalonia, Zakynthos and
Kastellorizo. Absent from Atlantic Islands. 0-2500m.
**Description.** Male ups yellow gc uniform (cf. male *G.*
*farinosa*): female hw shape variable but dentation of inner margin better
developed than that of *G. cleopatra*. Distinction from female *G. farinosa* often
difficult: ups and uns white, faintly tinged greenish.
**Variation.** Throughout range, hw shape variable. In NW Africa and S Europe,

often very large (f. *meridionalis* Röber) but size locally and regionally variable. Gynandromorphism commonly reported.

**Flight-period.** Univoltine. In N and C Europe, June/July: in S Europe and NW Africa, May/October: hibernated specimens re-appear March/early May. Confirmation of partial bivoltinism reported for N Africa and S Europe requires detection of early stages in mid/late summer to eliminate possible confusion caused by disruption of diapause in summer/autumn: males, especially, are readily inclined to leave hibernation on warm days in late winter.

**Habitat.** Damp or dry bushy places especially associated with woodland; open grassy and rocky slopes with sparse bushes. Sympatric with *G. cleopatra* and *G. farinosa* in some areas of Greece.

**Life-history.** LHPs *Frangula alnus*; *Rhamnus catharticus*; *R. alaternus*; *R. alpinus* (?)*alpinus*; *R. a. fallax*; *R. myrtifolia*; *R. oleoides*. Ova laid singly on developing leaves or stems. Larva feeds on leaves. Pupates on LHP stems. Hibernates as an adult, often amongst the leaves of evergreen shrubs and trees.

## *Gonepteryx cleopatra* Cleopatra                                    Plate 17

**Range.** Canary Islands, Madeira, NW Africa, S Europe, Turkey, Middle East.

*G. cleopatra cleopatra* Linnaeus 1767 TL: Barbaria, Algeria.
**Distribution.** Widespread, generally common. Morocco. Algeria. Tunisia. 0-3000m. Portugal. Spain. Balearic Islands. S and C France: Pyrenees and Provençe to Vendée and Ain. Corsica. Peninsular Italy except C Apennines; sporadic in northern districts. Sardinia. Sicily. Dalmatian coast: sporadic. C and S Greece, Corfu, Kefalonia, Zakynthos, Lesbos, Chios, Samos, Ikaria, Rhodes, Karpathos, Crete, Skiathos, Skyros, Sifnos, Paros and Milos. European Turkey. Not reported from Albania and Republic of Macedonia. Records for S Switzerland, Bulgaria and N Greece appear to relate to vagrant specimens only. 0-1600m: generally below 1200m.

**Description.** Male ups gc yellow; upf with deep orange discal patch; unf discal area yellow, unh and unf costa pale yellowish-green or whitish: in f. *italica* Gerhard [=f. *massiliensis* Foulquier], uns dull yellow, except for slightly brighter upf discal area. Whilst these colour forms occur together in varying ratio in most regions, including NW Africa, f. *italica* becomes increasingly common in E Mediterranean, comprising 100% of specimens on some E Aegean islands. Female unf with delicate, pale orange streak above median vein; uph often with faint orange flush; hw angular projection at v3 very shallow (cf. female *G. rhamni* and *G. farinosa*).

**Variation.** Male upf orange flush variable in size and intensity. In SE Europe, female white gc (normal) sometimes replaced by pale yellow or bright sulphur-yellow (resembling male *G. rhamni*); these forms sometimes occur together, in locally or regionally widely varying ratios: in N and C Greece, white form preponderates: on Mt. Chelmos, mostly bright yellow: in Taygetos Mts., normal and intermediate forms common, the brightest yellow forms infrequent: on Rhodes (f. *fiorii* Turati and Fiori), universally bright yellow (a similar form has been reported from Tunisia): yellow variants appear to be rare on Karpathos and absent from Crete and some other E Aegean islands: an intermediate yellow form has been reported from Milos. On Mallorca, male upf orange flush averagely smaller and paler.

**Flight-period.** Univoltine. Mid May/August with hibernated specimens reappearing in early spring (late February/late April). Reportedly bivoltine in S Spain and N Africa, but possible, temporary suspension of diapause in late summer is a potential source of confusion.

**Habitat.** Open bushy, often rocky places: often associated with light woodland.

**Life-history.** LHPs *Rhamnus catharticus*; *R. alaternus*; *R. myrtifolia*; *R. oleoides*; *R. alpinus*; *R. sibthorpianus*; *R.* (?)*persicifolius* (Sardinia). Ova laid singly on developing leaves or stems. Larva feeds on leaves. Pupates on LHP stems. Hibernates as an adult.

*G. cleopatra maderensis* Felder 1862 TL: Madeira.

**Distribution.** Madeira:Terreirro da Luta; Ribeiro Frio; Encumeada Pass. 500-1500m.

**Description.** Male upf deep orange with very narrow, yellow marginal borders; fw and hw well marked with a reddish-brown marginal line, slightly expanded at veins: female ups pale greenish with faint yellow flush; unh and unf costal areas dull greenish; unf disc whitish.

**Flight-period.** Voltinism uncertain due to longevity of adults and perhaps sporadic, temporary suspension of diapause – if any. Recorded in all months but commoner April/September.

**Habitat.** Dense laurel forest containing other trees and shrubs including LHP. Butterfly appears to be confined to such areas – not as wide-ranging as Canary Island *Gonepteryx*.

**Life-history.** LHP *Rhamnus glandulosa*.

**Note.** Visible areas of female underside at rest (hw and fw costa) are non-reflective in UV-light, as are the leaves of laurel (*Laurus laurocerasus*) amongst which females normally roost, often rest and possibly hibernate: as insectiferous birds have good UV-colour vision, cryptic UV-coloration is an obvious functional advantage in habitat dominated by laurel. Canary Island *Gonepteryx* butterflies (below) have followed a different evolutionary path, resulting in strongly UV-reflective female undersides – an adaptive consequence, apparently, of less parochial behaviour in a more botanically diverse environment containing plants, e.g., bramble (*Rubus fruticosus*), whose leaves are also UV-reflective. Recent DNA studies have demonstrated a much closer affinity of *maderensis* to the nominate form than the *Gonepteryx* of the Canary Islands.

*G. cleopatra cleobule* Hübner 1825 TL: Tenerife.

**Distribution.** N Tenerife: Las Mercedes; Icod Alto; Anaga; Chinobre. 500-2000m.

**Description.** Fw outer margin almost linear; hw dentation very shallow; fw and hw with conspicuous, often striking, reddish-brown marginal line, slightly expanded at veins: male upf gc deep orange, extending almost to margins; uph yellow; unf greenish-yellow; unh greenish: female ups gc yellow, flushed orange; strongly UV-reflective.

**Flight-period.** Voltinism uncertain (see *maderensis*). Recorded in all months.

**Habitat and Behaviour.** Sunny clearings in laurel forests, but habitat of more diverse character than that of *maderensis*. Both sexes tend to fly at lower altitudes in winter and often feed on *Cedronella canariensis* blossom.

**Life-history.** LHPs *Rhamnus glandulosa; R. crenulata.* Larvae have been recorded in April, August and December. Early stages do not appear to differ from *palmae* or *eversi* (below). Captive larvae accept *R. catharticus.*

**Note.** Considered specifically distinct by many authors: recent, comparative DNA studies of this and related taxa have proved inconclusive.

*G. cleopatra palmae* Stamm 1963 TL: La Palma.

**Distribution.** La Palma: Santa Cruz; Quintero; Rio de las Nieves; Barranco del Agua; Bco. de la Galga; Bco. de Jieque; Los Sauces; Los Tilos. 300-1600m.

**Description.** Fw outer margin almost linear; hw dentation very shallow: male upf yellow with diffuse orange discal flush, variable; uph yellow; unh and unf costal area greenish-yellow: female ups very pale yellow – fw discal area almost white, hw and fw costal areas flushed pale yellow-orange; uns similar. Female ups non-reflective in UV-light.

**Flight-period.** Voltinism uncertain (see *maderensis*). Recorded in March/April, June/September and December.

**Habitat, Behaviour and Life-history.** As for *G. c. cleobule.*

*G. cleopatra eversi* Rehnelt 1974 TL: Gomera.

**Distribution.** Gomera: Las Rosas; Hermigua; La Palmita; Las Hayas; Mt. Garajonay; Laguna Grande; Roque de Agando; Montaña Quemada; Vallehermoso. 500-1400m.

**Description and Variation.** Resembles *cleobule*: upf orange discal flush slightly paler, variable: female resembles *palmae*: ups lemon yellow; upf often with strong orange discal flush. Female ups non-reflective in UV-light.

**Flight-period.** Voltinism uncertain (see *maderensis*). Recorded in March/May, July/September and December.

**Habitat, Behaviour and Life-history.** As for *G. c. cleobule.*

## *Gonepteryx farinosa* Powdered Brimstone                    Plate 16

**Range.** Albania, Republic of Macedonia, Bulgaria, Greece, Turkey, Israel, Lebanon, Syria, N Iraq, N and W Iran, Caucasus to Tajikistan.

*G. farinosa* Zeller 1847 TL: Macri (Fethiye), SW Turkey.

**Distribution.** Albania. Republic of Macedonia. Bulgaria: a single site in Struma Valley. Greece: E Thessaly; Sterea Ellas; Attika; Peloponnesos: very restricted in N districts (Kastoria; Kozani; Drama; Evros): recorded from Levkas, Kefalonia, Rhodes, Kastellorizo. European Turkey. 25-1450m.

**Description.** Male upf lemon yellow, with slightly roughened appearance; uph distinctly paler – constrast with fw apparent in flight: female ups white, sometimes faintly tinged bluish (cf. *G. rhamni*).

**Flight-period.** Univoltine. Mid June/July: hibernated specimens re-appear March/April.

**Habitat and Behaviour.** Hot, dry, bushy places, often on rocky slopes at higher altitudes; very hot, dry low coastal hills amongst sparse bushes of *Paliurus spina-christi*. In some localities, often roosts in bushes of *Phlomis fruticosa.*

**Life-history.** LHPs *Rhamnus alpinus fallax; R. sibthorpianus; R. lycioides graecus; Paliurus spina-christi.* Ova laid at leaf-nodes on stems.

## *Leptidea sinapis* Wood White                     Plate 18

**Range.** Europe, Turkey, Lebanon, Syria, Caucasus to W Siberia and Tian Shan.

*L. sinapis* Linnaeus 1758 TL: Sweden (Verity 1947).
**Distribution.** Widespread and common in most of Europe south of 66°N in Fennoscandia (very local north of Arctic Circle), including Mediterranean islands of Mallorca, Corsica, Sardinia, Elba, Sicily, Corfu, Levkas, Kefalonia, Zakynthos, Skyros, Thassos, Lesbos, Chios, Samos and Crete. Absent from Scotland, N England, Holland, N Germany and Denmark except Bornholm. 0-2300m: generally below 1900m.
**Description.** Antennal club black with extreme tip brown and small white ventral patch (cf. *L. duponcheli*). Second/third broods, dark markings reduced. Resembles *L. reali* closely.
**Flight-period.** Generally univoltine in N and C Fennoscandia, June/early August: bivoltine in most of C Europe May/June and July/August: trivoltine in parts of S Europe, late March/September according to locality and altitude.
**Habitat.** Diverse. Mature deciduous/coniferous/mixed forest clearings/margins; sparse woodland; bushy places; flowery meadows; coastal scrub; less often, grassy, rocky slopes/gullies above treeline: most habitat-types associate with a wide range of temperature, geology and ground-water conditions.
**Life-history.** LHPs *Lathyrus pratensis*; *L. grandiflorus*; *L. tuberosus*; *L. montanus*; *L. linifolius*; *L. vernus*; *L. niger*; *L. aphaca*; *Lotus uliginosus*; *L. corniculatus*. Ova laid on underside of leaves of partially shaded LHPs. Larvae feed on leaves. Pupates on robust plant-stems, usually in concealment amongst grasses. Hibernates as a pupa.

## *Leptidea reali* Réal's Wood White            Not illustrated

**Range.** Spain, France, S Belgium, N Switzerland, Austria, Slovenia, Croatia, SW Serbia, S Poland, SE Sweden, Ukraine.

*L. reali* Reissinger 1989 TL: La Montailla, E Pyrenees.
syn: *lorkovicii* Réal 1988 (invalid homonym)
**Distribution.** Spain: provinces of Cuenca (Uña); Teruel (Albarracin); Alava (Cantabrian Mts.); Lérida (Caldos de Bohit); Gerona. France: Ariège; Pyrénées-Orientales; Aude; Alpes-Maritimes; Alpes-de-Haute-Provençe; Hautes-Alpes; Ardèche; Isère; Jura; Moselle; Meuse. S Belgium: province of Luxembourg. N Switzerland: canton of Luzern (Herigswald; Sörenburg). Slovenia. Croatia. SW Serbia: Mt. Maglic. SE Poland. SE Sweden: Sönder-manland (including Island of Ingarö); Uppland. Tentative records for province of Alicante and Corsica require confirmation. 100-2000m. Geographical/altitudinal distribution uncertain due to probable confusion with *L. sinapis*: distribution possibly much less disjunctive than present records indicate.
**Description.** Resembles *L. sinapis* but density of black pigmentation in wing-markings averagely greater; in summer broods, female upf black, roundish apical patch usually well represented. Wing-characters variable, inadequate for reliable

determination, but, in either sex, readily separable from *L. sinapis* by substantial morphological and reproductively significant differences in genitalia: field observations and laboratory experiments indicate a significant pre-mating barrier between the two species: natural hybrids unknown.

**Flight-period.** Limited data indicate voltinism/flight-times similar to that of *L. sinapis*.

**Habitat.** Similar to that of *L. sinapis* with which it is usually to be found.

**Life-history.** LHP *Lathyrus pratensis*. Life-cycle/early-stages similar to that of *L. sinapis*: pupa slightly more yellowish, reddish lateral lines and wing-case markings less distinct.

## *Leptidea duponcheli* Eastern Wood White        Plate 18

**Range.** SE France, S Balkans, Turkey, Lebanon, N Iraq, N and W Iran, Transcaucasus.

*L. duponcheli* Staudinger 1871 TL: S France.
syn: *lathyri* Duponchel (invalid homonym)
**Distribution.** SE France: Var and Alpes-Maritimes to Drôme and Hautes-Savoie. NW Italy: Maritime Alps: very local. SW Serbia (Montenegro). Albania. Republic of Macedonia. Bulgaria: very local and sporadic. N and C Greece, including Zakynthos: local but widespread. 50-1150m.

**Description.** Fw pointed; uns of antennal club brown (white in *L. sinapis*); upf v1 with pronounced 'hump' below cell – curvature relatively slight in *L. sinapis*. First brood: colour and pattern of heavy uns markings distinctive, showing through to ups. Second brood: markings less intense. Separable from *L. sinapis* and *L. reali* in all broods and both sexes by wing-markings, antennal club and fw venation.

**Flight-period.** Bivoltine. Mid April/mid May and late June/July.

**Habitat.** Hot, sunny, bushy places; open woodland; rocky gullies. Habitats more restricted and averagely hotter/drier than those of the more ecologically diverse *L. sinapis* with which it usually occurs.

**Life-history.** LHPs *Lathyrus aphaca*; *L. pratense*; *Lotus uliginosus*. Ova laid on underside of leaves of LHP specimens usually well-shaded by undergrowth or large rocks. Larvae feed on leaves. Hibernates as a pupa.

## *Leptidea morsei* Fenton's Wood White        Plate 18

**Range.** Central E Europe to C and S Urals, SE Turkey, Altai, W Siberia to Japan.

*L. morsei major* Grund 1905 TL: Zagreb, Yugoslavia.
**Distribution.** S Poland. Slovakia. SE Austria. Hungary. N Croatia. Romania. Bulgaria. 250-1400m.
**Description.** Fw apex falcate – rounded in *L. sinapis* and *L. reali*. First brood, unh pattern and tone of greyish markings distinctive. Second brood, larger; markings greatly reduced. Antennal club resembles *L. sinapis*.

**Flight-period.** Bivoltine. Mid April/mid May and mid June/late July.

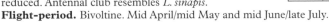

**Habitat.** Margins/clearings associated with mature, damp deciduous woodland. Habitat and LHP often shared with *Neptis sappho*.

**Life-history.** LHPs *Lathyrus verna*; *L. niger*: the latter appears to be the sole LHP in some habitats of N Croatia, despite presence of both plant species.

# Lycaenidae Linnaeus 1758

This very large family of generally small butterflies, represented in Europe by over one hundred species, include the blues, hairstreaks and coppers. For most species, sexual dimorphism is especially well marked, and the females of many 'blue' butterflies are brown. Close similarity between species sometimes renders identification difficult, but differences – often more easily seen than described – in ground-colour and the pattern of markings, particularly on the hind-wing underside, are generally clear. The greatest difficulties in determination are presented by the distinctive group known as the 'anomalous blues', so-called because the uppersides of both sexes are brown: sexual distinction is, however, clearly indicated by a sex-brand on the upper fore-wing of the male. The males of many species will often gather, sometimes in huge numbers and for pro-longed periods, on damp ground for the purpose of extracting sodium salts from the water. The larvae of the Lycaenidae are shaped much like a wood-louse, are usually well-camouflaged, and often show a high order of adaptation to larval host-plants. For most species, a 'honey' gland (dorsal nectary organ) on the 10th larval segment exudes a sugary fluid – a high-energy food – which is very attractive to ants. In exchange for this secretion, attending ants actively afford some protection against parasitic flies (diptera) and wasps (hymenop-tera). Whilst some associations (facultative), although mutually advantageous, are not essential, others (obligate) are quite necessary for the survival of some Lycaenid species such as the Large Blue, whose symbiotic relationship has evolved to the point of total dependence on (particular) ants species within whose nests the latter stages of larval, as well as pupal development occurs: the butterfly larvae feed exclusively on ant larvae, whilst receiving the full co-operation and protection of the adult ants. The association of many lycaenid larvae with ants (myrmecophily) is well-documented, but, as the rapid progress of research suggests, much detail remains to be discovered about these inter-esting relationships. Pupae are characteristically 'dumpy' – short in proportion to diameter. According to species, pupae may be secured by a girdle of fine silk to a leaf or stem, often of the larval host-plant, or, with no attachment, secreted in rolled-up leaves, secured by a few strands of silk, under basal leaves of the larval host-plant, or on the ground under stones, amongst leaf-litter, moss, etc.

## *Cigaritis zohra* Donzel's Silver-line　　　　　Plate 21

**Range.** Morocco, Algeria.

*C. zohra zohra* Donzel 1847 TL: Djebel Amour, Algeria.
**Distribution.** W and C Algeria: widespread but local: Sebdou; El Bayadh; Aflou; Djelfa; Saïda; Kralfalih. Records from Tunisia (Tozeur; Gafsa; Moulares) require confirma-tion.
**Description.** Male ups gc orange-brown; submarginal and marginal dark spots usually confluent; upf markings vari-able but usually well developed; unh gc brown. All markings subject to marked local variation.
**Flight-period.** Univoltine. Records span May/June.

*C. zohra monticola* Riley 1925 TL: Aghbalu Larbi, Taghzeff Pass, Morocco.
**Distribution.** Morocco: widespread but local: Middle and High Atlas (Annoceur; Ifrane; Tizi-n-Tretten; Boulmane; Col du Zad; Tizi-n-Taghzeft). 1600-2200m.
**Description.** Resembles nominate form: smaller; ups gc deeper orange: all markings subject to appreciable variation.
**Flight-period.** Univoltine. March/June according to season, generally late April/May.
**Habitat.** Grassy slopes.
**Life-history.** First and second instar larvae feed on *Coronilla minima*, thereafter, living in nests of *Crematogaster laestrygon* until adulthood.
**Behaviour.** Flies close to the ground: fond of resting on bare ground with wings closed.

## *Cigaritis siphax* Common Silver-line  Plate 21

**Range.** Algeria, Tunisia.

*C. siphax* Lucas 1849 TL: Constantine, Algeria.
**Distribution.** Algeria: Collo; Bône; Aflou; Khenchala; Timgad; Djurdjura massif. Tunisia: Aïn Draham; Cap Bon; Hammamet. 100-1000m.
**Variation.** Ups markings variable; black marginal spots sometimes absent; unh gc brown to purplish.
**Flight-period.** Voltinism uncertain, possibly trivoltine. Records span March/October.
**Habitat.** Dry hillsides with *Cistus*.

## *Cigaritis allardi* Allard's Silver-line  Plate 21

**Range.** Morocco, Algeria.

*C. allardi* Oberthür 1909 TL: Sebdou, Algeria.
**Distribution.** Morocco: W Middle Atlas (Abu Safra; Azrou; Immouzer; El Harcha; El Ksiba; 1200-1600m; W Anti-Atlas (Agadir; Tafraoute; Col du Kerdous; 800-1100m); High Atlas (Dj. Aourach; Tizi-n'Ouguerd-Zegzaoune 2000-2400m). Algeria: Sebdou; Masser Mines; Dj. Maktar; 1500-1800m.
**Variation.** Subject to variation in ups black markings and gc variable: the following taxa relate to small but systematic, regional differences: Middle Atlas Mts., *occidentalis* Le Cerf: High Atlas Mts. (Morocco and W Algeria), *meridionalis* Riley: Anti-Atlas Mts. *estherae* Brevignon.
**Flight-period.** Univoltine. March/June according to location and season.
**Habitat.** Hot, dry, rocky slopes, sometimes scrub-covered.
**Life-history.** LHPs *Genista quadriflora*; *Cistus salvifolius*; *Fumana thymifolia*; *Helianthemum hirtum ruficomum*. Larvae strongly myrmecophilous, attended by *Crematogaster auberti*; *C. antaris*; *C. scutellaris*.
**Behaviour.** Flight very rapid in hot conditions. Both sexes rest on low-growing shrubs and are easily disturbed.

## *Apharitis myrmecophilia* Desert Leopard         Not illustrated

**Range.** Tunisia, S and E Algeria, Libya, Egypt, Jordan, Cyprus, Saudi Arabia, Oman.

*A. myrmecophila* Dumont 1922 TL: Tozeur, Tunisia.
**Distribution.** E Algeria: Biskra. 100m. Extremely local, usually occurring in very small numbers. More widespread in S Algeria (Hoggar Mts.; Tassili n'Ajjer) and S Tunisia (Tozeur; Nefta).
**Description.** Ups gc bright orange; marginal borders thinly black; upf dark markings variable, prominent or absent; uph without submarginal and discal markings: both sexes, upf apex with distinctive creamy-white patch (*Cigaritis* spp. and *A. acamas*, a closely similar species from S Algeria, are without a white apical patch).
**Flight-period.** Voltinism uncertain: possibly bivoltine or polyvoltine: records span April/July.
**Habitat.** Very hot sandy places.
**Life-history.** LHP *Calligonum comosum* (Polygonaceae). Larvae strongly myrmecophilous, attended by *Crematogaster auberti*; (?) *Cataglyphis bicolor*. Larvae feed at night, residing in ants nests during the day. Pupates in ants nests.
**Behaviour.** Adults often rest on small stones in full sun in the hottest parts of habitat, or bushes to which they quickly return when disturbed.

## *Thecla betulae* Brown Hairstreak         Plate 19

**Range.** Europe through Asia to Korea.

*T. betulae* Linnaeus 1758 TL: Sweden (Verity 1943)
**Distribution.** Spain: S. de Gata; Cantabrian Mts.; Catalonia. E Pyrenees through most of Europe, including W Ireland and S England to S Fennoscandia, Balkans, N Greece (Voras Mts., Phalakron massif and N Pindos Mts.) and European Turkey. Absent from Portugal, S Italy and Mediterranean islands. 50-1500m.
**Flight-period.** Univoltine. Late July/early September.
**Habitat.** Deciduous woodland or mature scrub with open, sunny clearings containing an abundance of blackthorn (*Prunus spinosa*).
**Life-history.** LHP *Prunus spinosa*. Ova laid, often in pairs, mainly in forks at stem-junctions, usually on young plants. Hibernates as an ovum. Pupae attended by *Lasius niger*.

## *Quercusia quercus* Purple Hairstreak         Plate 19

**Range.** N Africa, Europe, Middle East, Turkey, Caucasus, Russia, S Urals, Kazakhstan.

*Q. quercus quercus* Linnaeus 1758 TL: England (Verity 1943).
**Distribution.** Common and widespread from Pyrenees, eastwards through most of Europe, including Britain, to S Fennoscandia, Greece, European Turkey and Mediterranean islands of Sicily, Corsica, Sardinia, Crete, Lesbos, Samos and Rhodes. 0-2000m. (Vagrant specimens have been found at 2300m).

**Flight-period.** Univoltine. Late June/early September.
**Habitat.** Diverse. Hot, dry oak scrub; damp or dry deciduous or mixed forests containing oak.
**Life-history.** LHPs *Quercus* spp., including *Q. robur*; *Q.
coccifera*; *Q. petraea*; *Q. ilex*; *Q. cerris*; *Q. pubescens*. Ova laid at
base of leaf buds. Hibernates as an ovum.
**Behaviour.** Adults show little interest in the nectar of plants,
carrion, excrement, and only rarely visit damp soil: nutrients
seem to be obtained largely from aphid secretion ('honey-
dew') on leaves of trees, especially LHP, to which adult activity is largely
confined.

*Q. quercus ibericus* Staudinger 1901 TL: S Spain and Morocco.
**Distribution.** Morocco: Middle Atlas; Rif Mts. Algeria: Middle Atlas. 1200-
2200m. Portugal. Spain. 900-2100m.
**Description.** Resembles nominate form except uns very pale silvery-grey,
markings reduced, including anal orange spot and ring.
**Flight-period.** Univoltine. June/mid September.
**Habitat.** Oak (*Quercus*) scrub; dry, oak woodland: often in very hot places.
**Life-history.** LHP *Quercus* spp., including *Q. coccifera*; *Q. ilex*.
**Note.** Intermediate forms, some closely approaching *ibericus*, occur north of
Pyrenees in Haute Garonne. Captive rearing in cool conditions produce
specimens indistinguishable from nominate form, indicating at least some
ecological control over distinctive characters.

## *Laeosopis roboris* Spanish Purple Hairstreak — Plate 19

**Range.** Portugal, Spain, S France.

*L. roboris* Esper 1793 TL: Stated in error as 'Frankfurt am
Main'
**Distribution.** Portugal except extreme south (Algarve).
Throughout Spain in scattered colonies. France: E Pyrenees
to Provençe. 100-1600m.
**Flight-period.** Univoltine. Late May/late July according to
locality and altitude.
**Habitat.** Open flowery bushy places with ash trees.
**Life-history.** LHP *Fraxinus excelsior*. Ova laid near dormant leaf-buds or main
trunk of host-tree, sometimes near ground-level. Larvae feed on flowers and
developing leaves. Hibernates as an ovum.
**Behaviour.** In early morning, both sexes often assemble in large numbers to
feed on tall umbellifers (Apiaceae), including fennel (*Foeniculum vulgare*). Flight
is confined mostly to higher branches of LHP in cooler conditions late afternoon/
early evening: adults rest on leaves of trees/shrubs during hottest periods.

## *Satyrium acaciae* Sloe Hairstreak — Plate 19

**Range.** Spain, S Europe, Turkey, S Russia.

*S. acaciae* Fabricus 1787 TL: S Russia.
**Distribution.** N Spain and Montes Universales, eastwards through France
(to 49°N), Germany and Poland (to 51°N), N Italy to Greece and European

Turkey. Absent from Portugal, S Italy and Mediterranean islands. 0-2000m.
**Description.** Male ups without sex-brand. Female abdomen with black anal hair-tuft.
**Flight-period.** Univoltine. June/July.
**Habitat.** Diverse. Dry scrub; open woodland; occasionally, damp forest clearings and open terrain above tree-line.
**Life-history.** LHP *Prunus spinosa*. Ova laid mostly at stem junctions. Immediately after ovipositing, the female uses the dark abdominal tuft to brush hair-like scales onto the whitish egg, rendering it less visible: as these scales are easily removed (hibernated ova are devoid of scales), the purpose of this practice is obscure. Hibernates as an ovum.
**Behaviour.** Both sexes attracted to flowers of *Achillea* and *Thymus*.

## *Satyrium ilicis* Ilex Hairstreak                     Plate 19

**Range.** Europe, S Fennoscandia, Israel, Lebanon, Turkey, W and S Urals, NW Asia.

*S. Ilicis* Esper 1779 TL: Erlangen, Germany.
**Distribution.** Portugal. N and E Spain: scattered colonies; Balearic Islands, eastwards to S Fennoscandia, Baltic states, Balkans, European Turkey and Greece, including Corfu, Thassos, Limnos, Lesbos, Samos, Ikaria, Chios, Kos, Simi, Poros and Tenos. 0-1600m. Absent from Britain, Corsica, Sardinia, Sicily and Crete.
**Description and Variation.** Male upf without sex-brand. Unh submarginal orange spots in s1b-s5 clearly defined, conspicuously edged black; white marginal line usually prominent (cf. *S. esculi*). In Portugal, Spain and S France, *cerri* Hübner: upf with variable orange discal patch, usually better developed in female.
**Flight-period.** Univoltine. Late May/early August according to altitude.
**Habitat.** Diverse. Hot, dry *Quercus coccifera* scrub; damp/dry heaths; forest clearings.
**Life-history.** LHP *Quercus* spp., including *Q. coccifera*; *Q. ilex*; *Q. robur*. Ova laid near dormant leaf-buds. Hibernates as an ovum. Larvae attended by *Camponotus aethiops*; *Crematogastor schmidti* or (?)*ionia*.
**Behaviour.** Attracted to flowers of *Thymus* and *Sambucus ebulus*.

## *Satyrium esculi* False Ilex Hairstreak                Plate 19

**Range.** N Africa, SW Europe.

*S. esculi* Hübner 1804 TL: Portugal.
**Distribution.** Morocco. Algeria. Tunisia. 900-2400m. Iberian peninsula except extreme N and NW; Balearic Islands (Ibiza and Mallorca). France: E Pyrenees to Alpes-Maritimes. 500-1300m.
**Description and Variation.** Male upf without sex-brand; ups gc light greyish-brown to dark brown; dull yellow-orange suffusion on fw disc and hw submargin extremely variable, often absent; unh reddish-orange submarginal spots in s1b-s5 clearly defined,

internally finely edged black; marginal white line vestigial (cf. *S. ilicis*): female ups and uns gc generally paler; ups pattern of orange suffusion similar, averagely better developed. In N Africa (*mauretanica* Staudinger), range of variation in wing-markings similar: in some localities, ups orange suffusion extensive and constant (f. *powelli* Oberthür): similar forms occur in Spain (*illicioides* Gerhard).
**Flight-period.** Univoltine. Late May/August according to locality.
**Habitat.** Hot, dry flowery scrub or sparse deciduous or mixed woodland.
**Life-history.** LHPs *Quercus coccifera*; *Q. ilex*. Larvae attended by *Camponotus cruetatus*.

## *Satyrium spini* Blue-spot Hairstreak      Plate 20

**Range.** S and C Europe to Turkey, Lebanon, Iraq and Iran.

*S. spini* Denis and Schiffermüller 1775 TL: Vienna.
**Distribution.** Most of Europe to about 54°N in Baltic states. Absent from N France, Belgium, Holland, Fennoscandia, Estonia, Latvia, S Italy and Mediterranean islands, except Mallorca, Corfu, Zakynthos, Kithira and Lesbos. 0-2000m.
**Description.** Male upf with sex-brand. Both sexes, unh with blue spot in anal angle.
**Variation.** In Iberian peninsula, female ups with variable orange suffusion, ranging from small, diffuse patch on fw disc and hw anal angle (f. *vandalusica* Lederer [=f. *lynceus* Hübner] to most of ups except marginal, costal and basal areas (f. *leonensis* Manley): female ups orange suffusion rare elsewhere in Europe.
**Flight-period.** Univoltine. Late May/late July according to locality.
**Habitat.** Hot, dry scrub; grassy, bushy places; woodland clearings; exposed mountain meadows with light scrub.
**Life-history.** LHPs Rhamnaceae, including *Rhamnus alaternus*, *R. lycioides*, *R. alpinus*: also, *Paliurus spina-christi* (Rhamnaceae) in Greece. Hibernates as an ovum.

## *Satyrium w-album* White-letter Hairstreak      Plate 20

**Range.** C and E Europe, Turkey, Urals, Kazakhstan, Japan.

*S. w-album* Knoch 1782 TL: Leipzig.
**Distribution.** From N Spain (Cantabrian Mts.), Italy (including Sicily) and Greece (in Peloponnesos, reported only from Mt. Chelmos) to S England and S Fennoscandia. Absent from European Turkey and Mediterranean islands except Sicily. 100-1300m.
**Description.** Male upf with small sex-brand above cell.
**Flight-period.** Univoltine. Generally mid June/late July: emergence may be delayed until August in S Scandinavia in unfavourable seasons.
**Habitat.** Mature woodland with open, sunny clearings.
**Life-history.** LHP *Ulmus*, principally *Ulmus glabra*. Ova laid at base of terminal leaf buds. Hibernates as an ovum. Newly-hatched larvae feed on developing flower-buds in early spring.
**Behaviour.** Both sexes attracted to bramble blossom.

## *Satyrium pruni* Black Hairstreak            Plate 20

**Range.** C and E Europe, S Siberia, Mongolia, Korea, Japan.

*S. pruni* Linnaeus 1758 TL Germany (Verity 1943).

**Distribution.** From E Pyrenees, N Italy (sporadic and very local) and N Greece (district of Drama: extremely local) to central S England, Denmark (restricted to Sjælland and Falster: very local), S Sweden (Skåne, Blekinge, Småland and Öland: very local), Lativa (widespread but scarce), (?) Estonia and S Finland. Absent from coastal Mediterranean districts and islands. 200-750m.

**Description and Variation.** Male upf with small sex-brand above cell. Ups submarginal orange markings variable, better developed in female.

**Flight-period.** Univoltine. Generally mid June/late July: mid May/early July in central E Europe.

**Habitat.** Mature blackthorn (*Prunus spinosa*) thickets in sheltered, sunny clearings or at margins of mature, deciduous woodland.

**Life-history.** LHP *Prunus spinosa*. Ova laid mostly at stem junctions on taller plants. Hibernates as a fully-formed larva within ovum-case. Newly-hatched larvae feed on flower-buds in early spring and developing leaf-buds towards maturity.

**Behaviour.** Adults take nectar from the blossom of shrubs, especially privet (*Lingustrum vulgare*) and bramble (*Rubus fruticosus*) rather than low herbage: often rest for prolonged periods in higher parts of LHP.

## *Satyrium ledereri* Orange-banded Hairstreak            Plate 20

**Range.** Greece (Samos), Turkey, Lebanon, Iran, Transcaucasus.

*S. ledereri* Boisduval 1848 TL: Caucasus.

**Distribution.** Greece: known only from Mt. Karvouni (1050-1145m) and Mt. Kerketefs (1000-1400m) on E Aegean island of Samos.

**Variation.** On Samos, *christianae* Olivier: wing-characters and male genitalia within range of variation of nominate form.

**Flight-period.** Univoltine. June.

**Habitat.** Above tree-line on exposed, dry, craggy limestone supporting sparse, low-growing vegetation.

**Life-history.** LHP *Atraphaxis billardieri* var. *billardieri* (Polygonaceae). Ova laid on woody stems of LHP. Hibernation stage uncertain: in early spring, torpid, second instar larvae have been found under bark and in crevices on stems of dormant LHP: in captivity, hibernates as a fully-formed larva within ovum-case (cf. *S. pruni*). Larvae feed on leaves. In captivity, larvae reject *Rumex acetosella*, *R. acetosa* and *Polygonum aviculare*.

**Note.** In North America, Polygonaceae shrubs are widely used by 'hairstreaks' of the genera *Callophrys* and *Strymon*.

## *Callophrys rubi* Green Hairstreak            Plate 20

**Range.** N Africa, Europe, Turkey, Russia, Siberia, Amur.

*C. rubi* Linnaeus 1758 TL: Sweden (Verity 1943).

**Distribution.** Widespread and common. Morocco. Algeria. Tunisia. 0-2500m. Throughout Europe, including arctic Fennoscandia, Baltic Islands and most

Mediterranean islands: reported from all Greek island-groups but apparently absent from Crete. Absent from Atlantic Islands (a record for Tenerife (1963) remains unconfirmed), Outer Hebrides, Orkney and Shetland Islands. 0-2300m: generally below 2000m.
**Description and Variation.** Frons green, eyes with very narrow white borders (cf. *C. avis*). Both sexes: ups smokey, greyish-brown; unh usually with white mark on costa, sometimes developed into a dotted white mediodiscal line, more rarely extending across unf: latter form relatively common in habitats shared with the similarly marked *C. avis*. In S Europe and NW Africa, f. *fervida* Staudinger: ups gc often more reddish-brown.

**Flight-period.** Univoltine. Generally March/June: single, fresh specimens are often recorded in July.

**Habitat.** Diverse. Woodland clearings; bushy places; scrubland; flowery meadows; heaths; marshes; sheltered rocky places or alpine grassland well above tree-line. Adapted to a remarkable range of climatic and other ecological conditions.

**Life-history.** LHPs include *Cytisus scoparius*; *C. nigricans*; *C. villosus*; *Genista tinctoria*; *G. angelica*; *G. pilosa*; *G. germanica*; *G. (?)corsica* (Corsica and Sardinia); *Chamaespartium sagittale*; *Chamaecytisus hirsutus*; *C. ciliatus*; *C. eriocarpus*; *Ulex europaeus*; *U. minor*; *Anthyllis vulneraria*; *Dorycnium hirsutum*; *D. suffruticosum* (Algeria); *Onobrychis viciifolia*; *Heliathemun nummularium*; flower-buds/fruits of *Arbutus*; *Vaccinium*; *Rhamnus*; *Frangula*; *Cornus*; *Rubus*. Larvae polymorphic, displaying a wide colour-range – pale greenish-blue, grass green or reddish. Pupa has an ability to make faint sounds by moving its abdominal segments – stridulation. Hibernates as a pupa under stones, leaves or moss at base of trees/ shrubs or amongst leaves on LHP.

## *Callophrys avis* Chapman's Green Hairstreak    Plate 20

**Range.** NW Africa, SW Europe.

*C. avis* Chapman 1909 TL: S France and Morocco.
**Distribution.** Morocco: Tangiers. Algeria: Algiers; Khenchela; Zehroun. Tunisia: Aïn Draham. 200-1700m. S Portugal. Spain: provinces of Cádiz, Málaga and Teruel. S France: Pyrénées-Orientalis to Alpes-Maritimes. 100-1000m: usually below 700m.
**Description and Variation.** Resembles *C. rubi*. Frons and eye borders rusty-red; ups reddish-brown; uns thin white line mediodiscal line on both wings (cf. *C. rubi*).

**Flight-period.** Univoltine. Late March/mid June according to locality and altitude.
**Habitat.** Dry scrub containing *Arbutus unedo* – usually in abundance.
**Life-history.** LHP principally *Arbutus unedo*: also, *Salvia verbenaca*; *Vibernum tinus* (NW Africa) and *Coriara myrtifolia* (NW Africa and Spain). Reported use of *Cytisus malacitanus catalaunicus* [=*Sarothamnus catalaunicus*] and *C. grandiflorus* [=*Sarothamnus grandiflorus*] requires confirmation. On *A. unedo*, ova laid on developing leaves adjacent to withered flowers or fruits on mature plants – young or newly coppiced plants are avoided. Hibernates as a pupa.

## *Tomares ballus* Provence Hairstreak          Plate 21

**Range.** Morocco, Algeria, Tunisia, Lybia, Egypt, Portugal, Spain, S France.

*T. ballus* Fabricus 1787 TL: Spain.

**Distribution.** Morocco: Anti-Atlas (Aït-Abdallah; Tafraoute). Algeria: El Kantara. Tunisia: Hammamet. 0–1700m. Portugal and Spain: scattered colonies: absent from northern provinces and W Pyrenees. France: E Pyrenees to Alpes-Maritimes. 300–1300m.

**Variation.** Male uns green or bluish-green disc sometimes greatly reduced; uph marginal orange spots in anal angle variable in number and size, sometimes absent: female ups orange areas sometimes replaced with dull yellow.

**Flight-period.** Univoltine. January/mid May according to locality and altitude.

**Habitat.** Open, dry, meadows and slopes with short grass-turf.

**Life-history.** LHPs principally *Medicago*: S Portugal, *Dorycnium hirsutum*; S Spain, *Medicago littoralis*; *M. truncatula*; *M. minima*; S France, *M. lupulina*: N Africa, *M. turbinata*; *Lotus hispidus*; *Anthyllis tetraphylla*. Ova laid singly in folds of developing leaves. Captive full-grown larvae, are extremely restless and many die without pupation, suggesting that, in nature, pupation occurs within an ant's nest. Larvae are cannibalistic. Larvae attended by *Plagiolepis pygmaea*. Hibernates as a pupa.

**Behaviour.** At higher altitudes, after severe overnight ground frost, very torpid adults have been observed laying with closed wings on rocks warmed by the early morning sun: after regaining the use of the legs, the insect raises itself from the prone position, adjusting the ventral surface of its wings perpendicular to the angle of the sun's rays: as warming progresses, further advantageous changes in wing-angle are made.

## *Tomares nogelii* Nogel's Hairstreak          Plate 21

**Range.** Romania, Turkey, Ukraine, Crimea, Syria, Lebanon, N Iran.

*T. nogelii dobrogensis* Caradja 1895 TL: Tulcea, Romania.

**Distribution.** Information limited. SE Romania: known only from the district of Dobrogea (Galati; Tulcea).

**Flight-period.** Univoltine. May/early July.

**Habitat.** Grassy scrub.

**Life-history.** LHP *Astragalus ponticus*.

## *Tomares mauretanicus* Moroccan Hairstreak          Plate 21

**Range.** NW Africa.

*T. mauretanicus* Lucas 1849 TL: Algeria.

**Distribution.** Widespread, often common. Morocco. Algeria. Tunisia. 0–2400m.

**Variation.** Subject to considerable local and individual variation: male uph orange markings in anal angle virtually absent or well represented (f. *undulatus*

Gerhard), sometimes projecting to pd area: female uns black markings well developed or greatly reduced.

**Flight-period.** Univoltine. January/April at sea-level, early March/June at higher altitudes.

**Habitat.** Grassy places; hot, dry stony slopes.

**Life-history.** LHPs *Astragalus epiglottis*; *A. pentaglottis*; *Hedysarum pallidum*; *Hippocrepis multisiliquosa*; *H. minor*. Ova laid on leaves in small batches – an unusual practice for Lycaenidae.

## *Lycaena helle* Violet Copper                                Plate 21

**Range.** C and N Europe, W Russia, C and S Siberia, Mongolia, Transbaikal, Amur.

*L. helle* Denis and Schiffermüller 1775 TL: Vienna.

**Distribution.** Locally very common in small, widely dispersed colonies. France: E Pyrenees (Ariège) to Jura Mts.; Doubs. NW Switzerland: Vaud; Valais; Fribourg; Berne; Luzern; Obwald. S Belgium: Ardennes. S Germany. Poland (very rare). Czech Republic. Slovakia. Fennoscandia, except S Norway and Denmark. Extinct in Latvia. 100-1800m.

**Variation.** In Fennoscandia, ups markings generally much reduced.

**Flight-period.** Univoltine. May/July, according latitude and altitude.

**Habitat.** Flowery, marshy meadows, usually associated with rivers or lakes; sphagnum bogs, often associated with *Vacinium* and open woodland.

**Life-history.** LHPs: C Europe, principally *Polygonum bistorta*: N and C Fennoscandia, *P. viviparum*: reputed use of *Rumex acetosella* and *R. acetosa* in S Scandinavia requires confirmation. Ova laid on underside of leaves. Small larvae feed on lower cuticle creating a characteristic pattern of translucent 'windows'. Hibernates as a pupa.

**Conservation.** Drainage and afforestation of habitats poses a serious threat in C and E Europe.

## *Lycaena phlaeas* Small Copper                                Plate 21

**Range.** Canary Islands, N and E Central Africa, Europe, temperate Asia, Japan, NE North America.

*L. phlaeas phlaeas* Linnaeus 1761 TL: Westermannia, Sweden.

**Distribution.** Widespread and common. Canary Islands (rare on Lanzarote: a record for Fuerteventura requires confirmation). NW Africa (0-2700m). South of Arctic Circle to all larger Mediterranean islands and island-groups. Absent from Outer Hebrides, Shetland and Orkney Islands. 0-2400m.

**Variation.** First brood: male ups brightly marked: subsequent broods: ups often suffused smokey greyish-brown, sometimes almost obscuring orange gc; hw 'tail' at v2 usually prominent, less marked in female (f. *elea* Fabricius). Uph sometimes with blue pd spots (f. *caeruleopunctata* Rühl). Extremely small specimens, common in late broods in very hot localities, appear to result from premature pupation induced by LHP desiccation.

**Flight-period.** Bivoltine in N Europe, May/early October: at least trivoltine in S Europe and N Africa, February/late October: polyvoltine in Canary Islands, throughout the year in a succession of overlapping broods.

**Habitat.** Diverse. Adapted to most habitat types.

**Life-history.** LHPs *Rumex* spp., including *R. acetosella*; *R. acetosa*; *R. hydrolapathum*; *R. scutatus*: also, in N Africa, *R. thyrsoideus*; *R. papilio*; *R. vesicarius*; *R. tingitanus*: Gran Canaria, LHP determined as *R. maderensis* or *R. vesicarius*. Less commonly, *Polygonum* spp., including *P. aviculare*, especially in very arid places where *Rumex* spp. are scarce or absent. Hibernates as a small larva.

*L. phlaeas polaris* Courvoisier 1911 TL: Norwegian Lappland.

**Distribution.** Arctic Fennoscandia (66-70°N): generally local. 0-400m.

**Description.** Ups resembles nominate form: unh gc dove-grey or greyish-buff, black spots prominent in contrast, pd series externally edged with whitish striae; submarginal red spots conspicuous.

**Flight-period.** Univoltine. Mid June/late July according to season and locality.

**Habitat.** Warm, sheltered, grassy, flowery places. 0-350m.

*L. phlaeas phlaeoides* Staudinger 1901 TL: Madeira.

**Distribution.** Madeira. 50-1800m.

**Description and Variation.** Ups resembles nominate form: unh colour and pattern distinctive: in late summer broods, ups darker; hw with 'tail' at v2.

**Flight-period.** Polyvoltine. March/October.

**Habitat.** As for nominate form.

**Life-history.** LHP unknown. Captive larvae accept *Rumex acetosella* and *R. acetosa*.

## *Lycaena dispar* Large Copper                              Plate 21

**Range.** Europe, N Turkey.

*L. dispar dispar* Haworth 1803 TL: Cambridgeshire, England.

**Distribution.** Restricted to Friesland, Holland. Became extinct in about 1848 in the fens of E England. Since 1927, a colony originating from Dutch race has been maintained at Woodwalton Fen, Huntingdonshire, England.

**Variation.** In Holland, *batava* Oberthür: resembles nominate form closely.

**Flight-period.** Univoltine. June/July.

**Habitat.** Fenland.

**Life-history.** LHP *Rumex hydrolapathum*. Ova laid mostly on upperside of leaves; small larvae feed by excavating lower cuticle. Hibernates as a small larvae. A second or third brood may be induced in captive rearing.

*L. dispar rutila* Werneburg 1864 TL: Berlin.

**Distribution.** Extremely local in widely dispersed colonies. France: Gironde; Doubs; Haute-Rhin; Bas-Rhin; Meuse; Ardennes; Nièvre; Côte d'Or; Haute-Marne; Aube. Doubtful in NW Switzerland. N Italy: W coastal Italy to Golfo di Gaeta. Germany. Latvia. S Finland. Poland to Balkans, N and C Greece. European Turkey. 0-1000m.

**Description and Variation.** Resembles nominate form: smaller; unh variable, but generally duller, tending to yellowish-grey; orange submarginal band paler. In Greece and Hungary, individuals of second brood sometimes approach or exceed size of *batava*.

**Flight-period.** Bivoltine in most localities: late May/June and August: univoltine in colder, northern districts: a third brood has been reported from some localities in S Europe.

**Habitat.** Boggy margins of lakes, rivers, ditches and canals.

**Life-history.** LHPs *Rumex hydrolapathum*; *R. crispus*; *R. aquaticus*. In second brood, oviposition and development as for nominate form. In Greece, larvae of the first brood have been known to enter diapause in June, remaining inactive until following spring.

**Conservation.** Changes in land use, particularly drainage of wetlands, pose a serious threat: in Greece, all known colonies appear to be at imminent risk on this account.

**Note.** Variation in voltinism and size tends to diffuse the taxonomic boundary separating *rutila* and *batava*. In general, variation in these two parameters provides an inadequate basis for subspecific differentiation, especially as voltinism and size are significantly correlated, effectively halving the number of allowable taxonomic discriminators: in present case, averagely greater size of *batava* may be attributed to the longer period available for larval growth and therefore causally related to voltinism. Such minor differences in wing-markings as are evident for the above forms, appear to fall within the variance of that which may be regarded as normal for most species.

## *Lycaena vigaureae* Scarce Copper                        Plate 22

**Range.** Europe, Turkey, C Asia, Mongolia.

*L. vigaureae vigaureae* Linnaeus 1758 TL: Sweden (Verity 1943).

**Distribution.** N Spain: N Cantabrian Mts.; Pyrenees. S France: Massif Central. From E Alps eastwards to Arctic Circle in Fennoscandia and NW and N central Greece. Absent from Britain, Belgium and Holland. 1000-2000m.

**Variation.** In N Europe, smaller. In Lappland, f. *oranulus* Freyer, male ups yellower; black marginal borders sometimes slightly wider: female ups suffused grey.

**Flight-period.** Univoltine. Mid July/mid September, according to altitude and locality.

**Habitat.** Flowery places, often dampish clearings or hillside bogs in woodland.

**Life-history.** LHPs Rumex spp., commonly *R. acetosa*. Hibernates as an ovum or small larva below crown of LHP. In habitats prone to flooding, hibernating larvae are often inundated for prolonged periods.

*L. vigaureae montanus* Meyer-Dür 1851 TL: Rhône Glacier.

**Distribution.** Alps of France, Switzerland, Italy, Germany, Austria. 1700-2000m.

**Description and Variation.** Male ups black marginal borders wider, some-

times with very small black discoidal spot: female ups dull golden-yellow with variable greyish suffusion, sometimes obscuring gc.
**Flight-period.** Univoltine. Late June/early September.
**Habitat.** Sheltered hollows and gullies on open flowery grassland.
**Life-history.** As for nominate form.

*L. virgaureae miegii* Vogel 1857 TL: Guardarrama, C Spain.
**Distribution.** N and C Spain: S. de Guardarrama; S. de Gredos; S. del Moncayo; Picos de Europa (Pto. de Pajares; Pto. de los Fierros). 600-1600m. No recent records from N Portugal.
**Description and Variation.** Upf with black cell-bar; black borders wider; 3-5 black pd spots in s2-6; uph with black cell-bar and sometimes 3 or 4 small, black pd spots.
**Flight-period.** Univoltine. July/August.
**Habitat and Life-history.** As for nominate form.

## *Lycaena ottomana* Grecian Copper                    Plate 22

**Range.** S Balkans, Greece, Turkey.

*L. ottomana* Lefèbvre 1830 TL: Greece.
**Distribution.** SW Serbia (Montenegro):Vipazar. Republic of Macedonia. Albania. Bulgaria. Greece, including Corfu and Evia. Absent from S Peloponnesos. A record for Thassos requires confirmation. Widespread but often very local. 50-1500m – generally below 1000m. Often occurs with *L. thersamon*.
**Variation.** Second brood: unh gc colour somewhat yellowish; hw 'tail' at v2 generally better developed but variable.
**Flight-period.** Bivoltine. Mid April/late May and July/early August.
**Habitat.** Dry, generally hot, grassy, flowery places, often amongst bushes or in light woodland.
**Life-history.** LHP *Rumex acetosella*. Ova laid on all plants parts. Larvae feed on leaves, less often on flowers. Captive larvae accept *Rumex hydrolapathum*, *R. acetosa* and *Polygonum aviculare*.
**Behaviour.** Males of summer brood are especially attracted to flowers of *Sambucus ebulus*. Females appear to retire to a different part of their habitat after pairing. This behaviour, coupled with relatively subdued female activity, may account for the commonly reported 'rarity' of females, even in colonies where males are abundant.

## *Lycaena tityrus* Sooty Copper                    Plate 22

**Range.** Europe, Turkey, Siberia, Urals, Kazakhstan, Altai Mts.

*L. tityrus tityrus* Poda 1761 TL: Graz, S Austria.
syn: *dorilis* Hufnagel 1766
**Distribution.** From N Spain (Cantabrian Mts. and Pyrenees) throughout Europe to about 58°N in Lithuania. Absent from Britain, Fennoscandia (except Fyen, Denmark) and Mediterranean islands except Sicily and Samos. 50-2500m.

**Variation.** First brood: male ups gc dark grey-brown; female ups orange submarginal bands and orange basal suffusion extensive: in later broods, male ups often with orange submarginal spots on hw, sometimes extending to fw; female ups brown, sometimes with orange discal suffusion; orange submarginal spots reduced.

**Flight-period.** Polyvoltine in hot, low-lying regions, mid April/October: bivoltine in cooler localities, late April/June and July/September.

**Habitat.** Diverse. Flowery grassy meadows; dry scrub; damp woodland clearings; sheltered alpine gullies.

**Life-history.** LHP *Rumex* spp., especially *R. acetosa*. Hibernates as a small larva at base of LHP.

*L. tityrus subalpinus* Speyer 1851 TL: Innsbruck, N Tyrol.

**Distribution.** Pyrenees (2100m). Alps of France, Switzerland, Italy, Germany, Austria. 1200-2500m.

**Description.** Ups dark brown in both sexes, unmarked except dark cell-bar and occasional submarginal orange markings, especially in female; uns gc yellowish-grey.

**Flight-period.** Bivoltine at lower altitudes, April/June and July/early September: univoltine above (?)1500m, late June/September.

**Habitat.** Sheltered grassy and flowery places.

**Life-history.** LHP *Rumex scutatus*.

*L. tityrus bleusei* Oberthür 1884 TL: Escorial and Madrid, Spain.

**Distribution.** Spain: S. de Guardarrama; S. de Guadalupe; S. de Gredos. 900-1100m.

**Description.** Male upf gc orange, spots large; female ups orange markings extensive.

**Flight-period.** Voltinism uncertain: probably as for nominate form.

**Habitat.** Grassy, flowery, bushy places.

## *Lycaena alciphron* Purple-shot Copper                    Plate 22

**Range.** Morocco, Europe, Turkey, Iran, S Siberia, S Urals, Mongolia, Altai.

*L. alciphron alciphron* Rottemburg 1775 TL: Berlin.

**Distribution.** S France. Germany. Czech Republic. Slovakia. Hungary. Lithuania. Latvia. (?)Estonia. 50-900m. Very sporadic and local.

**Flight-period.** Univoltine. Generally June/July: recorded in April from coastal districts of S France.

**Habitat.** Grassy, flowery places.

**Life-history.** LHP *Rumex acetosa*.

*L. alciphron melibaeus* Staudinger 1879 TL: Greece.

**Distribution.** Widespread and common. Balkans. N and C Greece, including Lesbos. European Turkey. 50-1750m.

**Description.** Male ups gc orange, suffused greyish with violet or pinkish tones:

female ups gc medium brown with variable, sometimes extensive orange
suffusion.
**Flight-period.** Univoltine. Mid June/July.
**Habitat.** Grassy flowery banks and meadows, sometimes in damp places;
sheltered gullies above tree-line.
**Life-history.** LHP *Rumex* spp. near polymorphic *R. acetosa*. Ova laid mostly
at stem-leaf junctions, less often on flowers. Hibernates as a small larva at base
of LHP.
**Behaviour.** Both sexes attracted to flowers of *Thymus*.

*L. alciphron gordius* Sulzer 1776 TL: Graubünden, Switzerland.
**Distribution.** N Portugal. Spain: widespread in mountains. Andorra. S and C
France: E Pyrenees; Massif Central; SW Alps. S Switzerland: Valais to
Graubünden. Italy: Maritime Alps to Dolomites and Calabria (Aspromonte);
generally absent from eastern coast. NE Sicily (Monti Nebrodi; Mt. Etna).
Generally 800-2000m: Sierra Nevada, 1100-2500m.
**Description.** Male ups violet suffusion reduced; uns brighter: female ups clear,
bright orange; black markings bold.
**Flight-period.** Univoltine. Late June/early August.
**Habitat.** Sheltered, flowery hollows and gullies.
**Life-history.** LHP *Rumex scutatus*.

*L. alciphron heracleana* Blachier 1908 TL: High Atlas, Morocco.
**Distribution.** Morocco: High Atlas; known only from Toubkal massif and Dj.
Siroua. 1700-2650m.
**Description.** Resembles *gordius*: large; male ups yellowish-orange without violet
or greyish suffusion. Female ups deeper yellow-orange, black markings more
prominent.
**Flight-period.** Univoltine. Mid June/July.
**Habitat.** Damp grassy places.
**Behaviour.** Males often 'hilltop', congregating on barren, stony ground –
recorded at 3000m.
**Life-history.** LHP *Rumex scutatus*; possibly also *R. acetosa*.

## *Lycaena thersamon* Lesser Fiery Copper      Plate 23

**Range.** Italy, E and SE Europe, Israel, Lebanon, Turkey,
Iraq, Iran, Afghanistan, Unkraine, S Urals, Altai.

*L. thersamon* Esper 1784 TL: Sarepta, S Russia.
**Distribution.** Widespread, generally very local. Central
peninsular Italy: E and SE Europe from about 50°N to N
Peloponnesos and E Aegean islands of Thassos, Kos and
Rhodes. 0-1600m. In Greece, distribution correlates closely
with that of *L. ottomana*.
**Variation.** Sometimes with filamentous 'tail' on hw at v2 (f.
*omphale* Klug): in Greece, 'tailed' individuals occur sporadically in first brood,
more commonly in subsequent broods.
**Flight-period.** Polyvoltine. Mid April/October according to locality and altitude.
**Habitat.** Dry grassy, flowery meadows or scrub clearings; sometimes very hot,
dry, rocky places.

**Life-history.** LHP *Polygonum aviculare*. Ova laid on leaves, stems and flowers. Larvae feed on leaves and flowers. Captive females refuse to oviposit on *Polygonum persicaria*, *P. hydropiper* or *Rumex acetosella*: captive larvae reject these, as well as *R. acetosa* and *Cytisus scoparius* (Fabaceae) and *Chamaecytisus hirsutus* (Fabaceae). The widely quoted use of *Rumex* and *Sarothamnus* [=*Cytisus*] appears to originate from mis-quotation of an early literature reference (Malicky 1969). On Cyprus, distribution of butterfly is said to correlate with that of '*Polygonum bellardi*' [=*P. patulum* or *P.* (?)*rurivagum*]

**Behaviour.** Both sexes greatly attracted to blossom of *Thymus* and *Sambucus ebulus*. Frequently, a colony may reveal its existence by the appearance of only one or two specimens.

## *Lycaena thetis* Fiery Copper                              Plate 23

**Range.** Greece, Turkey, Lebanon, Syria, Iraq, Iran.

*L. thetis* Klug 1834 TL: Syria.

**Distribution.** C and S Greece: Mt. Tymphristos; Mt. Ghiona; Mt. Kaliakouda; Mt. Iti; Mt. Chelmos; Taygetos Mts. 1500-2300m. A record for former S Yugoslavia appears to have arisen from confusion with *L. ottomana* or *L. thersamon*.

**Variation.** Hw 'tail' at v2 sometimes well developed (f. *caudata* Staudinger): although reputedly associated with a second brood, the species appears to be univoltine through-out its range. In Greece, *hephetstos* Dils and van der Poorten: wing-characters and male genitalia indistinguishable from nominate form.

**Flight-period.** Univoltine. Mid July/August.

**Habitat.** Open, dry, rocky sites on limestone supporting low-growing shrubs, including the spiny, cushion-forming LHP which shows a marked preference for consolidated rock formations in upper half of altitudinal range. Habitats may be as small as 2500m². All known habitats shared with *Turanana endymion*.

**Life-history.** LHP *Acantholimon androsaceum* (Plumbaginaceae). Oviposition not observed in Europe: in Turkey, females have been seen to eject ova into the centre of LHP. Hibernates as a small larva concealed amongst the densely packed stems and dead stem-leaves of LHP. Post-hibernated larvae feed on leaves and are evidently very closely adapted to LHP. Appears to be unique amongst the European Lycaeninae – 'coppers' – for its independence of the Polygonaceae – the 'dock' family. Although LHP is shared with *Turanana endymion* in the same habitats, competition between the two species appears to be negligible.

**Behaviour.** Both sexes strongly attracted to nectar of *Thymus*.

**Conservation.** Exploitation of many of the higher mountains of Greece for recreational and other purposes poses a direct threat to habitats.

## *Lycaena phoebus* Moroccan Copper                         Plate 23

**Range.** Morocco.

*L. phoebus* Blachier 1908 TL: High Atlas, Morocco.

**Distribution.** Very local but common. W Morocco: region of Marrakech (Asni; El-Kelaa-des-Srarhna; Nid de Cigogne; 400-2200m); High Atlas (Toubkal massif); Anti-Atlas (Tafraoute; Tizi-n-Taraktine; Ida-Ougnidf; Tizi-n-Taghatine;

1000-1800m). Records for Algeria and Tunisia have been discredited.

**Flight-period.** Voltinism uncertain, possibly regionally variable: district of Marrakech, late April/late September in at least two broods: in hot, dry, barren localities, March/May: at higher altitudes in High Atlas, late August/September.

**Habitat.** Grassy flowery places especially with *Thymus*; margins (drainage ditches) of cultivation; dry, barren places in Anti-Atlas.

**Life-history.** LHPs: High Atlas, possibly *Polygonum aviculare*: Anti-Atlas, *P. equisetiforme*. Reputed use of *Rumex* requires confirmation: field-observations indicate that, where opportunities exist, neither *R. papilio* nor *R. vesicarius*, are exploited by ovipositing females.

## *Lycaena hippothoe* Purple-edged Copper                    Plate 23

**Range.** Europe, C and S Siberia, S Urals, Altai.

*L. hippothoe hippothoe* Linnaeus 1761 TL: S Sweden.
**Distribution.** N Spain: Cantabrian Mts.; S. de la Demanda; S. Mancilla; S. Moncayo. From Pyrenees eastwards through much of Europe to about 62°N in Fennoscandia. Absent from Britain, NW France, coastal S France, N Holland, S Italy, S Balkans and Greece. 400-1800m.

**Description and Variation.** Male ups with striking purple flush: female upf orange discal area variable; uph orange submarginal markings prominent; unf orange discal flush variable. In central E Europe, *sumadiensis* Szabo: resembles nominate form closely: bivoltine.

**Flight-period.** Univoltine in W and N Europe (including NW Hungary), June/late July: bivoltine in central E Europe (including S and E Hungary), May and late July/August

**Habitat.** Marshy meadows, hillside bogs.

**Life-history.** LHPs *Polygonum bistorta*; *Rumex acetosa*. Hibernates as a small larva.

*L. hippothoe eurydame* Hoffmannsegg 1806 TL: Mts near Geneva.
syn: *eurybia* Ochsenheimer 1808.
**Distribution.** Alps of France, Switzerland, Italy, Austria: also, Apuane Alps and C Appennines. 1500-2500m. Altitudinal range overlaps that of nominate form but not on same mountains.

**Description.** Male ups without purple flush: female ups uniform brown, sometimes with vestigial orange submarginal markings; unf without orange flush.

**Flight-period.** Univoltine. July/mid September according to altitude.

**Habitat.** Damp alpine meadows.

**Life-history.** LHPs *Polygonum bistorta*; *Rumex acetosa*. Hibernates as a small larva.

*L. hippothoe stiberi* Gerhard 1853 TL: Lappland.
**Distribution.** Fennoscandia from about 62°N (Dovrefjeld) to North Cape.
**Description.** Male ups gc lighter golden-red; unf orange discoidal flush and unh orange band distinct: female upf discoidal area orange extending towards

outer margin. In both sexes, unh gc colour light greyish-buff; ups and unh submarginal bands well developed.
**Flight-period.** Univoltine. Late June/July.
**Habitat.** Grassy places, often near shoreline on Norwegian coast.
**Life-history.** LHP *Rumex acetosa*. Hibernates as an ovum.

## *Lycaena candens* Balkan Copper      Plate 23

**Range.** S Balkans, Greece, Turkey.

*L. candens* Herrich-Schäffer 1844 TL: Turkey.
**Distribution.** Locally common. Republic of Macedonia. S Serbia. Albania. Bulgaria. N and C Greece: Varnous Mts.; Voras Mts.; Rhodopi Mts.; Pindos Mts.; Mt. Olympos. 900-2000m.
**Description.** Resembles nominate form of *L. hippothoe* closely: larger; male genitalia distinctive.
**Flight-period.** Univoltine. Mid June/late July.
**Habitat.** Hillside bogs, in beech or pine woodland clearings, containing many distinctive plants, especially *Geum coccineum* and *Silene asterias*; less often exposed, dry, grassy places above tree-line.
**Life-history.** LHP *Rumex* sp. near polymorphic *R. acetosa*. Hibernating larvae are often inundated in early spring.

## *Lampides boeticus* Long-tailed Blue      Plate 24

**Range.** Worldwide temperate zones.

*L. boeticus* Linnaeus 1767 TL: Algeria.
**Distribution.** Canary Islands, NW Africa, Mediterranean islands and Europe to about 54°N (N Germany). Generally widespread and common in southern areas. Occasionally common in Channel Islands. Rare in S England and generally scarcer in northern range, where appearance probably depends solely on migration: residency uncertain in most regions, including S Europe (see below). 0-2700m.
**Flight-period.** Polyvoltine. Canary Islands, throughout year in several, overlapping broods. In N Africa and Europe, February/November according to locality.
**Habitat.** Diverse. Hot, dry, flowery places; cultivated ground.
**Life-history.** LHPs many genera of Fabaceae upon which larvae feed mainly on developing seeds: Canary Islands, *Cassia didymobotrya*; *Pisum sativum*; *Chamaecytisus palmensis*: N Africa and Europe, commonly *Colutea arborescens*: also in N Africa, *Helianthemum helianthemoides*. Sometimes a serious pest on cultivated *Pisum sativum* (Garden Pea) and *Phaseolus vulgaris* (Broad Bean). Whilst captively reared larvae appear willing to accept the seeds or flowers of an extraordinary range of Fabaceae, the natural exploitation of *Cercis siliquastrum* (Judas Tree) and *Robinia pseudacacia* (False Acacia), common Mediterranean species with large seed-capsules, does not appear to have been observed. Life-cycle in captivity 4-6 weeks, according to temperature. Apparent absent of a diapause stage suggests residency is possible only in warmer parts of the

Mediterranean where continuity of larval food source is maintained (cf. *D. chrysippus*). Larvae attended by *Lasius niger*, *Camponotus compressus*; *C. cruetatus*; *C. sylvaticus*; *C. foreli*; *Prenolepis clandestina*; *Plagiolepis* sp.; *Tapinoma melanocephalum*.

## *Cacyreus marshalli* Geranium Bronze          Plate 24

**Range.** S Africa: introduced to S Spain.

*C. marshalli* Butler 1898 TL: S Africa.
The immature stages of this South African species are believed to have been accidentally introduced to the Balearic Islands, Spain, through the importation of *Pelargonium* cultivars. First reported in 1990 on Mallorca, the species quickly became a pest throughout this island. It has since extended its range to other Balearic Islands as well as the Spanish mainland: two specimens were captured near Logrono in 1992, another in Granada city-centre in 1995. In 1991, a male specimen was captured in a Brussels garden containing *Pelargonium* and several colonies were noted in the vicinity of Rome in 1996. The widespread popularity of *Pelargonium* as ornamental plants would seem conducive to further dispersion. In South Africa, this continuously brooded insect also feeds on *Geranium* spp. and its establishment in the wild in the warmer parts of the Mediterranean region would seem possible. In captivity, life-cycle occupies about one month at 25°C. Whilst a preference is shown for flowers and flower-buds, larvae attack all aerial components of *Pelargonium*. Larva is pale green with red markings and long, stiffish white hairs: pupa; similarly coloured and ornamented.

## *Leptotes pirithous* Lang's Short-tailed Blue          Plate 24

**Range.** N Africa, S and C Europe, Turkey, Middle East, Saudi Arabia, C Asia, India.

*L. pirithous* Linnaeus 1767 TL: Algeria.
syn: *telicanus* Lang 1789.
**Distribution.** Widespread and common. N Africa. Mediterranean Europe, including islands. Iberian peninsula. SW France: Pyrenees. SW Balkans. Greece. Less common in C Europe to about 48°N as a migrant: residency in most regions unconfirmed (see below). 0-1200m. Not recorded from Atlantic islands.
**Flight-period.** Polyvoltine. February/October.
**Habitat.** Diverse. Hot, dry scrubland; cultivated areas, especially Lucerne fields (*Medicago sativa*).
**Life-history.** LHPs: many genera of Fabaceae: also, Lythraceae (*Lythrum salicaria*); Plumbaginaceae; Rosaceae; Ericaceae (*Calluna vulgaris*): in Greece, oviposition has been observed on *Sambucus ebulus* (Caprifoliaceae) and a *Jasminum* cultivar (Oleaceae) (captive larvae accept flower-buds of *J. nudiflorum*). Reported use of *Quercus suber* (Fagaceae) requires confirmation. Ovum stage usually 3 days, sometimes 6 days at same temperature. Life-cycle in captivity 4-8 weeks, depending on temperature. Larvae polymorphic: in Greece, larvae of various colours from pure white to dark green have been recorded on flowers of *Galega officinalis* (Fabaceae). Diapause stage – if any – unknown: attempts to

induce diapause in captivity have been unsuccessful. Resident status in N and E Mediterranean uncertain: occurrence in S Europe may depend on early season migration from N Africa.

## *Cyclyrius webbianus* Canary Blue                                    Plate 24

**Range.** Canary Islands.

*C. webbianus* Brullé 1839 TL: Canary Islands.

**Distribution.** Restricted to Canary Islands: Gomera; La Palma;Tenerife; Gran Canaria. Generally 200-2500m – recorded above this range near summit of Mt. Teide, Tenerife (3500m). A single record for Hierro requires confirmation.

**Flight-period.** Polyvoltine. Throughout year in a succession of several overlapping broods at lower altitudes: not recorded between early October and early May above 2000m on Tenerife (Cañadas Plateau).

**Habitat.** Rocky places amongst scrub at low altitudes; sometimes waste-ground close to human habitation; sheltered hollows with sparse vegetation on Mt. Teide, 2000-3000m.

**Life-history.** LHPs Fabaceae, including *Cytisus canariensis*; *Spartocytisus rubigenus*; *Lotus sessilifolius*; *L. hillebrandii*; *L.glaucus*; *Adenocarpus viscosus*; *Teline stenopetala*. Captive larvae readily accept leaves and flowers of *Lotus corniculatus*, *L. uliginosus* and *Onobrychis viciifolia* and the flowers of *Lathyrus pratensis*, *Ulex europaeus*, *Cytisus scoparius* and *C. sessilifolius*. Diapause stage/winter survival strategy at high altitude on Tenerife unknown.

**Behaviour.** Adults attracted to nectar of *Pterocephalus lasiospermum*; *Dittrichia viscosa*; *Micromeria* sp.

**Note.** Closest known relative, *C. mandersi* Druce 1907, endemic in Mauritius and believed to be extinct.

## *Tarucus theophrastus* Common Tiger Blue                           Plate 24

**Range.** N Africa, S Spain, Tropical Africa north of equator, SW Arabia.

*T. theophrastus* Fabricius 1793 TL: Morocco.

**Distribution.** Mainly coastal districts. Morocco: Anti-Atlas; High Atlas; Middle Atlas. Algeria. Tunisia. Generally 0-1400m – a single female recorded at 2600m near Oukaïmedan, High Atlas. S Spain: provinces of Cádiz; Almeria; Murcia. 25-250m. Reports from NW Sicily and Aspromonte require confirmation.

**Description.** Uns black pd line disrupted by veins on both wings (cf. *T. rosaceus* and *T. balkanicus*).

**Flight-period.** Polyvoltine. NW Africa, April/November (recorded in all months in southern deserts): Spain, mid April/September: first brood often very scarce.

**Habitat.** Hot, dry, open scrubland usually dominated by large bushes of LHP, often in cultivated areas.

**Life-history.** LHPs: Spain, *Ziziphus lotus*: NW Africa, *Ziziphus lotus*; *Z. jujuba* [=*Z. vulgaris*; *Z. sativa*] (cultivated in Mediterranean Europe, naturalized in some areas) and *Paliurus spina-christi* [=*Ziziphus spina-christi*]. (*Z. jujuba* and

*P.spina-christi* occur in S Spain: *Z. lotus* occurs in Sicily: *Z. jujuba* is naturalized in S Italy). Ova laid on stems, usually at the base of a thorn. Larvae feed in systematic fashion, excavating adjacent furrows in lower cuticle of leaves, resulting in a characteristic pattern of elongate, parallel, translucent 'windows' on unbroken upper cuticle. In Spain, larvae attended by *Crematogaster fuentei*. Hibernates as a pupa. In captivity, pupae from first brood may remain in diapause until following spring.

**Behaviour.** During most of the day, adults fly amongst branches or rest on leaves of LHP: in early evening, large numbers may sometimes gather at the tops of grass-stems near base of LHP.

## *Tarucus rosaceus* Mediterranean Blue                Plate 24

**Range.** N Africa, Egypt, Israel, Jordan, Saudi Arabia, Iraq, S Iran, NW India.

*T. rosaceus* Austaut 1885 TL: Algeria.
syn: *mediterraneae* Bethune-Baker 1917.
**Distribution.** Morocco. Algeria. Tunisia. 0-1400m.
**Description.** Unf black pd line unbroken except at v6. Examination of genitalia advisable to confirm identification, owing to variation in wing-characters and possible confusion with *T. theophrastus* and *T. balkanicus*.

**Flight-period.** Polyvoltine. March/September.
**Habitat.** Hot, dry ground. Habitats usually shared with *T. theophrastus*.
**Life-history.** LHP *Paliurus spina-christi*. In Saudi Arabia, *Ziziphus*. Larvae attended by *Plagiolepis pygmaea*; *Camponotus sicheli*; *Monomorium salomonis*.

## *Tarucus balkanicus* Little Tiger Blue                Plate 24

**Range.** NW Africa, Sudan, S Balkans, Greece, Turkey, Israel, Lebanon, Iran, Iraq, Saudi Arabia, Transcaucasus, C Asia.

*T. balkanicus* Freyer 1845 TL: 'Turkey'.
**Distribution.** Very sporadic and local. Morocco. Algeria. Tunisia. S Dalmatian coast. Albania. Republic of Macedonia. Bulgaria: Kresna; NE coast. N and C Greece; Corfu. A record for Samothraki requires confirmation. European Turkey. 50-850m.

**Description.** Resembles *T. rosaceus* and *T. theophrastus* but males usually separable by:- upf large, prominent black discal and pd spots; uns dark pd spots usually confluent: male genitalia distinct.
**Flight-period.** Polyvoltine. Mid April/October. First brood often very scarce, population density increases rapidly in summer.
**Habitat.** Hot, dry, open scrubland, often dominated by the distinctive bushes of LHP.
**Life-history.** LHP: Europe and N Africa, *Paliurus spina-christi*: also in N Africa, *Ziziphus lotus*. Ova laid on stems, usually at the base of a thorn. Larval feeding behaviour as for *T. theophrastus*. Larvae attended by ants. Hibernates as a pupa. In captivity, pupae from first brood may remain in diapause until following spring.

**Behaviour.** Both sexes warm themselves in the early morning by sitting on rocks, usually with wings closed. In Greece, a small, purple-flowered *Micromeria* species is a frequently used nectar-source.

## *Azanus ubaldus* Desert Babul Blue                                      Plate 24

**Range.** Gran Canaria, N and Tropical Africa, Egypt, Jordan, Israel, Saudi Arabia, S Asia.

*A. ubaldus* Stoll 1782 TL: Sri Lanka

**Distribution.** Canary Islands: Gran Canaria (recorded from Playa del Inglés (1982) and Maspalomas (1992)). S Morocco: 400-1000m. (Also reported from S Algeria (to at least 1500m) and S Tunisia).

**Description.** Resembles *A. jesous*: both sexes: smaller; unf without cell-spot – almost always present in *A. jesous*. Male ups pale blue; dark marginal borders dark very narrow; upf with well-defined slightly darker blue androconial patch – a useful diagnostic feature; androconial scales very narrow, length variable; uph marginal spots in s1c and s2 small, obscure; uns gc pale greyish-brown, with transverse whitish striae; unh with two conspicuous round spots on costa and two larger marginal spots in s1c and s2, basal spots smaller, variable, often indistinct: female ups brown, often with obscure, blue basal suffusion; uns whitish striae better developed, other markings as for male.

**Flight-period.** Voltinism uncertain: probably polyvoltine. Records for Gran Canaria relate to late January and late April: records for Morocco span March/ late summer: possibly continuously brooded in both regions – no diapause stage reported from elsewhere in range.

**Habitat.** Restricted to immediate vicinity of LHP – *Acacia* trees growing in very hot, dry places.

**Life-history.** LHPs: Gran Canaria, not recorded – probably *Acacia* sp.: Morocco, *Acacia raddiana; A. seyal.* Larvae attended by *Camponotus* sp.; *Prenolepis* sp.

**Behaviour.** Adults fly rapidly amongst branches of LHP, exploiting its flowers as a nectar-source. An entire colony may restrict itself to a single *Acacia* tree, despite the presence of others nearby. Both sexes take water from damp ground.

**Note.** In Saudi Arabia, apparently subject to very marked seasonal fluctuations in population density (cf. apparent sporadic occurrence on Gran Canaria).

## *Azanus jesous* African Babul Blue                                      Plate 24

**Range.** Africa, Egypt, Israel, Lebanon, Syria, Saudi Arabia, Yemen, Oman.

*A. jesous* Guérin 1849 TL: Abyssinia.

**Distribution.** S and W Morocco: widespread on plains north of Marrakech: more sporadic and local on southern slopes of High Atlas and Anti-Atlas. 200-(?)1000m, most frequent 400-800m: single specimens have been recorded at 1800m on Toubkal massif. (Known to occur at 2000m in Oman).

**Description.** Resembles *A. ubaldus*: both sexes: larger; unf black cell-spot distinct, very rarely absent – a useful diagnostic character. Male ups pale lilac-blue; brown marginal borders narrow, proximally diffuse; upf with dark spot at cell-end; androconial patch inconspicuous; androconial scales short, wide, coarsely striated; uph marginal spots in s1c and s2 small, obscure; uns gc greyish-brown, transverse whitish striae conspicuous; unf with small dark marginal spots in s2-6; unh spots as for *A. ubaldus* but larger, with an additional, large marginal spot in s6 and two indistinct spots in s4 and s5: female ups gc pale brown, sometimes with blue suffusion; upf dark discoidal spot often enclosed by pale suffusion, usually extending to inner margin; uns markings as for male.
**Flight-period.** At least trivoltine: February throughout summer in overlapping broods.
**Habitat.** As for *A. ubaldus*.
**Life-history.** LHP *Acacia gummifera*: elsewhere in range, commonly *Acacia* spp.; also, *Prosopis farcta* (Sinai Peninsula); *Medicago* sp.; *Entada* sp. In Yemen, large numbers of pupae recorded under stones at base of host-tree (*Acacia etbaica*).
**Behaviour.** As for *A. ubaldus*. (Shows some tendency towards migratory/dispersive behaviour in Saudi Arabia).

## *Zizeeria knysna* African Grass Blue                    Plate 24

**Range.** Canary Islands, N Africa, S Portugal, S Spain, Egypt, Israel, Lebanon, Syria, Iraq, E Saudi Arabia, Turkey, Cyprus, S Asia, Australia.

*Z. knysna knysna* Trimen 1862 TL: South Africa.
syn: *lysimon* Hübner 1805 (invalid homonym)
**Distribution.** Canary Islands: local in coastal districts: La Palma; Tenerife; Gran Canaria: very few records for Gomera; Hierro; Lanzarote: a record for Fuerteventura requires confirmation. 0-100m. Morocco. W Algeria. 0-1500m. S Portugal. Spain: mainly coastal valleys in Provinces of Cádiz; Málaga; Granada; Almeria: also recorded in river valleys on northern slopes of Sierra Nevada and elsewhere in similar inland sites. Recorded from districts of Madrid, Santandar and Benidorm. Apparently extinct in Rio Guadalaviar (S. de Albarracin, Teruel). 25-800m.
**Variation.** Male ups, width of black marginal borders variable: female ups gc brown, sometimes with blue scaling at wing-bases extending into discal area: both sexes, uns markings variable.
**Flight-period.** Polyvoltine. Canary Islands: throughout the year in a succession of overlapping broods: NW Africa and Spain, February/October.
**Habitat.** Damp places in hot, coastal gullies; damp, sunny clearings in densely wooded river valleys; desert oases.
**Life-history.** LHPs: Gran Canaria, *Amaranthus* sp. (Amaranthaceae): NW Africa, *Medicago sativa*; *M. tribuloides*; *Acanthyllis* sp.; *Melilotus messanensis* (Fabaceae); *Polygonum equisetiforme* (Polygonaceae); *Armeria delicatula* (Plumbaginaceae); *Tribulus terrestris* (Zygophyllaceae): S Spain, *Medicago minima*; *M. lupulina*; *M. sativa* (Fabaceae). Elsewhere in range, use of Oxalidaceae,

Malvaceae and Euphorbiaceae has been reported. Captive larvae (Canary Islands) readily accept leaves and flowers of *Lotus corniculatus*, *L. uliginosus*, *Trifolium pratense*, *T. repens*, *Coronilla varia* and flowers of *Ulex europaeus*, *Cytisus scoparius* and *C. sessilifolius*. Captive larvae (Malta) are said to reject *Oxalis* and *Medicago* spp. but accept *Polygonum aviculare*. For some LHPs, larval coloration depends upon particular plant parts ingested. Ants attending larvae: *Tapinoma melanocephalum*; *Pheidole* sp. Ova parasitized by Chalcididae. On Gran Canaria, larvae parasitized by *Cotesia cupreus* (Braconidae).

*Z. knysna karsandra* Moore 1865 TL: India.
**Distribution.** Widespread in E Algeria and Tunisia. 0-1500m. Malta. Sicily. Reports from Rhodes and Crete unconfirmed. Distributional relationship with nominate form in E Algeria unclear.
**Description and Variation.** Resembles nominate form closely: distinguished by small difference in male genitalia: both sexes, uns markings extremely variable: female ups blue suffusion variable.
**Flight-period.** Polyvoltine. Late February/October.
**Habitat.** As for nominate form.
**Life-history.** LHPs: NW Africa, *Melilotus indica*; *Medicago sativa*.

## *Everes argiades* Short-tailed Blue                    Plate 25

**Range.** N Spain, C, S and E Europe, Asia, Japan.

*E. argiades* Pallas 1771 TL: Samara, S Russia (April).
**Distribution.** N Spain (Cantabrian Mts.; S. de la Demanda; Pyrenees) through France, C Germany (very local in Bavaria), Switzerland (sporadic) N and western C Italy, NE Sicily to Gotland, Lithuania, Latvia, Balkans, European Turkey (Gelibolu) and N Greece (very local). A rare migrant in Britain, more frequent in Belgium, Holland, N Germany, S Sweden (resident only on Gotland), Estonia and S Finland. 0-1000m.
**Description.** Male ups violet-blue in first brood, less violet and darker in second brood; uph sometimes with small, black antemarginal spots in s1b-s4; unh orange spots in s1c and s2; hw 'tail' at v2 variable: female ups greyish-brown, often with blue discal and basal suffusion on fw and posterior submargin and disc of hw.
**Flight-period.** Bivoltine. Late April/mid June and July/August.
**Habitat.** Flowery bushy places, grassy banks, woodland clearings.
**Life-history.** LHPs *Lotus corniculatus*; *L. uliginosus*; *Coronilla varia*; *Medicago sativa*; *M. lupulina*; *Trifolium pratense*; *Astragalus glycyphyllos*. Larvae cannibalistic.

## *Everes decoloratus* Eastern Short-tailed Blue          Plate 25

**Range.** SE Europe, (?) Turkey.

*E. decoloratus* Staudinger 1886 TL: Vienna, Hungary, Bulgaria.
syn: *sebrus* Hübner 1824 (name rejected by ICZN Op. 970)
**Distribution.** S Austria. Hungary. Slovenia. Romania. Republic of Macedonia. Albania. Bulgaria. N Greece: very local: known only from Phalakron massif and foothills of Rhodopi Mts. 250-1000m.

**Description.** Male ups dusky-blue, scales are easily lost, giving somewhat dull appearance even in fairly fresh specimens; black outer marginal borders narrow, indenting along veins; upf with small black discoidal spot (cf. *E. alcetas* and *E. argiades*): female ups dark chocolate brown.

**Flight-period.** Trivoltine. May/June, July/August and September.

**Habitat.** Flowery, bushy places; sunny clearings in light deciduous woodland.

**Life-history.** LHPs *Medicago lupulina*; *M. sativa*. Ova laid on flowers upon which larvae feed. Hibernates as a full-grown larva.

## *Everes alcetas* Provençal Short-tailed Blue                Plate 25

**Range.** Spain, S Europe, Balkans, Turkey, S Siberia, Urals, Altai.

*E. alcetas* Hoffmannsegg 1804 TL: Austria.

**Distribution.** Generally sporadic and local. Spain: Pyrenees. S France. N and C Italy. S Austria. S Poland. (?)Slovakia. Hungary. Slovenia. Bosnia-Herzegovina. (?)Albania. Romania. Bulgaria. N Greece. 50-1200m.

**Description and Variation.** Male ups with very narrow black borders; hw 'tail' at v2 often vestigial; upf without black discoidal spot (cf. *E decoloratus*): female ups dark greyish-brown. In N Greece, unh orange mark in anal angle often reduced or absent.

**Flight-period.** Trivoltine. Late May/June, July/August and late September.

**Habitat.** Clearings in light deciduous woodland. In N Greece, all known habitats are associated with rivers, ditches or springs – favourable to the establishment of the LHP, *Galega officinalis*.

**Life-history.** LHPs *Coronilla varia*; *Galega officinalis*. Ova laid on leaves. Larva feeds on leaves and flowers. Larvae attended by *Formica* (?)*cinerea* group.

## *Cupido minimus* Little Blue                Plate 25

**Range.** N and C Spain, through Europe, Asia and Mongolia to Amur.

*C. minimus minimus* Fuessly 1775 TL: Switzerland.
syn: *alsus* Denis and Schiffermüller 1775.

**Distribution.** Widespread and common. From Spain (Cantabrian Mts.; Montes Universales; Catalonia; Pyrenees) to Ireland, Britain, S and W Norway to 69°N, S and E Sweden, S Finland, Baltic states, Balkans and Greece, including Corfu and Kos. 50-2800m.

**Variation.** Male ups pale blue scaling subject to variation, sometimes absent.

**Flight-period.** Univoltine (April/July) or bivoltine (April/June and late July/September) according to altitude and locality: in very hot conditions, desiccation of LHP may delay or even preclude a second brood.

**Habitat.** Diverse. Open grassy places; dry, rocky slopes and gullies; forest clearings. Restricted to calcareous soils.

**Life-history.** LHP *Anthyllis vulneraria*. Ova laid on flowers, usually at base of calyx. Whitish larva feeds on developing seed through hole at base of calyx. Aligned with the similarly coloured calyx-tube, the larva is well-camouflaged when feeding, resting or during skin-changes (cf. *C. carswelli* and *C. lorquinii*). Hibernates as a full-grown larva. In captivity, pupation appears to be induced by contact with fresh, spring leaves of LHP. Larva may remain in diapause for 15 months. Larvae attended by *Lasius alienus*; *L. niger*, *Formica fusca*; *F. rufibarbis*; *Plagiolepis vindobonensis*; *Myrmica rubra*. Pupates in loose soil at base of LHP.

*C. minimus trinacriae* Verity 1919 TL: Palermo, Sicily.
**Distribution.** Sicily. 100-1500m.
**Description.** Resembles nominate form: smaller; ups gc black; lacking blue scales. A similar form (*noguerae* Haig-Thomas) occurs in Montes Universales, E Spain.
**Flight-period.** Univoltine. April/May. Absence of second brood is possibly due to loss of aerial components of LHP through desiccation in summer months (cf. *C. minimus*).
**Habitat.** Dry limestone rocks.
**Life-history.** LHP *Anthyllis vulneraria*.

## *Cupido carswelli* Carswell's Little Blue                 Plate 25

**Range.** S Spain.

*C. carswelli* Stempffer 1927 TL: Sierra de Espuña, Spain.
**Distribution.** Restricted to mountains of S and SE Spain. S. de Tejeda; S. de Cazorla; S. de la Sagra; S. Segura; S. de Alcaraz; S. de Espuña. 1000-1800m. (*C. lorquinii* occurs in S. de Tejeda below 850m.).
**Description.** Resembles *C. minimus*, except male ups have a small patch of purple scales at the base which may extend along some veins of the hw. Regarded by some authors as a form/ssp. of *C. minimus*.
**Flight-period.** Univoltine. Late April/early June. As in the case of *C. minimus*, desiccation of LHP in early/mid summer may inhibit larval development, precluding a second brood in late summer.
**Habitat.** Limestone rocks or dry grassland, often amongst open scrub.
**Life-history.** LHP *Anthyllis vulneraria*. Oviposition and larval development parallels that of *C. minimus*: however, LHP is a colour variant in which upper part of calyx tube is sparsely mottled with the same dark reddish hue of the flowers. Similar mottling occurs on the posterior segments of the adult larva, apparently, for the purpose of mimicking the calyx tube, along which, like the larva of *C. minimus*, it aligns itself when feeding or resting. The yellow-flowered form of *A. vulneraria*, which has a pure white calyx, is apparently absent in the range of *C. carswelli*.

## *Cupido osiris* Osiris Blue                                Plate 25

**Range.** Spain, S Europe, Turkey, C Asia.

*C. osiris* Meigen 1829 TL: not stated
syn: *sebrus* auct. Name rejected by ICZN OP. 970.

**Distribution.** N, S and E Spain. S France. W Switzerland. NW coastal and central peninsular Italy. (?)Slovakia. Austria. Hungary. Balkans. Greece, including Limnos. European Turkey. 500-1800m.

**Description.** Male ups violet-blue with sharply defined very narrow black marginal borders: female ups dark brown; upf with occasional blue basal flush.

**Flight-period.** Univoltine (late May/July) or bivoltine (late April/late June and late July/early September) according to locality and altitude: second brood sometimes partial or may fail to appear in exceptionally dry conditions – LHP desiccation (cf. *C. minimus*).

**Habitat.** Open grassy, flowery places.

**Life-history.** LHP*s Onobrychis* spp., including *O. viciifolia*; *O. montana*; *O. arenaria*. Ova laid on flowers upon which larvae feed. Hibernates as a larva. Larvae of first brood may enter and remain in diapause until following spring. Larvae attended by *Lasius alienus*.

## *Cupido lorquinii* Lorquin's Blue                    Plate 25

**Range.** Morocco, Algeria, S Portugal, S Spain.

*C. lorquinii* Herrich-Schäffer 1851 TL: Spain.

**Distribution.** Morocco. Algeria. 1400-2700m. S Portugal: Serra de Monchique. S Spain: provinces of Cádiz and Málaga (Sierras of Tejeda, Almijara, Mijas, Blanca, Ronda, Bermeja, Crestellina and Grazalema); Granada (Sierra Nevada; S. de Alfacar); Jaen (S. de Jabalcuz). 100-2000m. (*C. carswelli* occurs above 1000m in S. de Tejeda).

**Description.** Male ups violet-blue with broad black marginal borders: female ups dark greyish brown, occasionally with a few, blue, basal scales.

**Flight-period.** Univoltine. Generally mid April/mid June, sometimes emerging mid February in Anti-Atlas.

**Habitat.** Similar to that of *C. carswelli*.

**Life-history.** LHP *Anthyllis vulneraria*. Ovipositing behaviour, larval development and adaptation to LHP, similar to that of *C. carswelli*. Larvae attended by *Plagiolepis pygmaea*; *Tapinoma nigerrimum*. Hibernates as a pupa.

## *Celastrina argiolus* Holly Blue                    Plate 25

**Range.** N Africa, Europe, Turkey to C Asia (40-67°N), Japan, N America.

*C. argiolus* Linnaeus 1758 TL: England (Verity 1943).

**Distribution.** Widespread and common in NW Africa (0-2600m) and most of Europe (0-1900m). Sporadic in Ireland and N Scandinavia: generally absent from Scotland, where records appear to relate to dispersal from N England or accidental introduction: widespread on Mediterranean islands.

**Variation.** Female seasonally dimorphic: second brood, upf black borders wider, blue basal flush, darker violet-blue; uph black costal margin wider.

**Flight-period.** Bivoltine. NW Africa, March/May and mid June/August (occasional fresh specimens September/October may represent a third brood or delayed emergence): Europe, early April/June and July/August.

**Habitat.** Diverse. Dry or damp bushy places, usually associated with woodland clearings/margins.

**Life-history.** LHPs comprise a wide range of plant families:- *Rubus fruticosus*; *R. idaeus*; *R. discolore*; *Filipendula ulmaria*; *Discolores* sp.; *Pyracantha coccinea* (Rosaceae): *Ulex europaeus*; *Genisa tinctoria*; *Spartium junceum*; *Dorycnium pentaphyllum* (?)*germanicum*; *Astragalus glycyphyllos*; *Medicago sativa*; *Melilotus alba*; *M. officinalis*; *Galega officinalis*; *Colutea arborescens*; *Robinia pseudacacia* (Fabaceae): *Euonymus europaeus* (Celastraceae): (?)*Clematis vitalba* (Ranunculaceae); *Rhamnus cartharticus*; *Frangula alnus* [=*Rhamnus frangula*] (Rhamnaceae): *Humulus lupulus* (Cannabaceae): *Calluna vulgaris*; *Erica arborea*; *Arbutus unedo* (Ericaceae): *Escallonia macrantha* (Escalloniaceae): *Lingustrum vulgare*; *Syringa vulgaris* (Oleaceae): *Ilex aquifolium* (Aquifoliaceae): *Cornus sanguinea* (Cornaceae): *Hedera helix* (Araliaceae): *Lythrum salicaria* (Lytheraceae); (?)*Alnus glutinosa* (Betulaceae). Ova laid on calyx or stem of flower-buds or developing seeds: larvae feed on these components, less often on young, succulent leaves. In some woodland habitats, LHPs comprise *I. aquifolium* (Holly) and *H. helix* (Ivy) in first and second broods respectively. Larvae attended by *Lasius niger*; *L. alienus*; *L. fuliginosus*; *Camponotus japonicus*; *C. nearcticus*; *Formica subsericea*; *F. truncorum*; *Myrmica* sp. Hibernates as a pupa. Cyclical variation in inter-seasonal abundance has been attributed to larval parasitism.

## *Glaucopsyche alexis* Green-underside Blue                Plate 27

**Range.** Algeria, Tunisia, Europe, C Asia, Amur.

*G. alexis* Poda 1761 TL: Graz, Austria.
syn: *cyllarus* Rottembur 1775.

**Distribution.** Algeria: scarce and local: Saida; Aflou; Batna; Khenchela; Coverdo; Col de Ben-Chiacao; Lambessa. Tunisia: Hammamet. 500-1300m. Widespread and common in much of Europe, including S Fennoscandia, Corsica, Sicily and many Greek islands including Corfu. Absent from Atlantic Islands; Portugal; W Spain; Britain; N Belgium, Holland, N Germany; Denmark; Baltic states; Balearic Islands; Sardinia; Crete. 25-1500m.

**Description and Variation.** Male ups dark borders sometimes wide and suffuse; uns light grey, without marginal markings; unf pd spots may be greatly reduced: female ups blue basal suffusion variable. In some populations, in both sexes, unh greenish-blue flush may extend almost to margin e.g., Dijon, S France. In Scandinavia, unh black pd spots greatly reduced. In N Africa, *melanoposmater* Verity, male uns pd spots and blue basal flush reduced; female ups usually with blue basal suffusion: similar forms occur in Europe.

**Flight-period.** Univoltine. April/early July. Whilst the typical form occurs in N Greece in April, males with wide, ups dark borders have been reported in the same localities in early July: a similar form, emerging early June, occurs in Taygetos Mts. (1400-1600m) .

**Habitat.** Diverse. Flowery banks, open scrub, damp meadows, woodland clearings.
**Life-history.** LHPs: several genera of Fabaceae including, *Astragalus onobrychis*; *A. glycyphyllos*; *Galega officinalis*; *Vicia* spp.; *Coronilla varia*; *Calicotome villosa*; *Spartium junceum*; *Medicago* spp.; *Melilotus alba*; *Onobrychis* spp.; *Cytisus* spp.; *Colutea arborescens*. Ova laid on flowers upon which larvae feed. Larvae are usually greenish or dusky-pink, with brownish variegations, but sometimes pure, bright yellow if reared on the similarly coloured flowers of *Spartium junceum*: all larvae tend towards a whitish colour prior to pupation. Larvae attended by *Lasius alienus*; *Formica pratensis*; *F. selysi*; *F. fusca*; *F. cinerea*; *F. nemoralis*; *F. subrufa*; *Camponotus aethiops*; *C. maxiliensis*; *Myrmica scabrinodis*; *Crematogaster auberti*; *Tapinoma erraticum*. Hibernates as a pupa. In captivity, pupa may remain in diapause for two winters.

## *Glaucopsyche melanops* Black-eyed Blue   Plate 27

**Range.** N Africa and SW Europe.

*G. melanops melanops* Boisduval 1828 TL: Aix-en-Provence.
**Distribution.** SE France: Haute Garonne and Pyrénées-Orientales to Ardèche and Basses Alpes. Italy: W Ligurian Alps. 100-800m
**Description.** Uns pale greyish-brown with faint marginal markings (cf. *G. alexis*): female ups blue suffusion variable, may be absent or extend to outer margin.
**Flight-period.** Univoltine. Mid April/May.
**Habitat.** Scrub or open woodland, often containing *Erica arborea* and *Spartium junceum*.
**Life-history.** LHPs: *Dorycnium decumbens*; *D. suffruticosum*; *Genista* sp.; *Lotus hispidus*; *Anthyllis cytisoides*. Ova laid on flowers upon which larvae feed. Larvae attended by *Camponotus foreli*; *C. cruentatus*; *C. micans*; *C. sylvaticus*. Hibernates as a pupa. In captivity, pupa may remain in diapause for two seasonal cycles.

*G. melanops algirica* Heyne 1895 TL: Nemours.
**Distribution.** Morocco. Algeria: Algiers; Lambessa. Tunisia. 600-2600m. N Portugal. Spain. 600-1100m.
**Description and Variation.** Male ups marginal borders 2-3mm wide; uns marginal markings bolder; unh with faint grey marginal and antemarginal spots: female ups basal blue suffusion reduced or absent. Transitional to nominate form in Catalonia. In High Atlas (up to 2600m), *alluaudi* Oberthür: male ups tinged violet; dark, marginal borders usually wider; female ups blue suffusion reduced, often vestigial or absent.
**Flight-period.** Univoltine. February/June. Report of a second brood in Tunisia (September/October) requires confirmation.
**Habitat.** Dry scrub containing a tall Broom (?*Cytisus*).
**Life-history.** LHPs: *Ononis atlantica*; *Adenocarpus anagyrifolius*; *Hedysarum flexuosum*.

## *Turanana endymion* Odd-spot Blue                Plate 27

**Range.** Greece, Turkey, Turkestan.

*T. endymion taygetica* Rebel 1902 TL: Mt. Taygetos, Greece.
syn: *panagaea* Herrich-Schäffer 1851 (invalid homonym)
**Distribution.** S Greece: Mt. Chelmos; Mt. Taygetos. 1500-2300m.
**Description and Variation.** Male ups dull blue; black marginal borders 2mm
wide; upf cell-end marked by fine black, often crescent-shaped mark; uns gc
greyish; unf black pd spots large – that in s3 conspicuously displaced distad;
unh with dull yellow-buff submarginal spot in s2 (usually vague, sometimes
absent in majority of specimens – (?)seasonally variable): female ups brown;
uns gc greyish-brown. Mt. Chelmos: male uns gc distinctly browner; unh submarginal spot in s2 orange, usually conspicuous, but sometimes absent even in
female. Male genitalia of Mt. Chelmos and Mt. Taygetos populations structurally identical, but different from that of nominate form (TL: Amasya, Turkey).
**Flight-period.** Univoltine. Late May/mid July in prolonged emergence.
**Habitat.** Exposed, dry limestone rocks, supporting low-growing, mostly
cushion-forming shrubs. Colonies are generally very small, sometimes limited
to a few hundred square metres. All known habitats shared with *Lycaena thetis*.
**Life-history.** LHP *Acantholimon androsaceum* (Plumbaginaceae). Ova laid
on calyx of flowers, within which the newly-hatched larva feeds. Hibernates as a
pupa. Apparently highly adapted to LHP, which it shares with *Lycaena thetis* in
the same habitats; however, competition between the two species appears to be
negligible. Association with ants does appear to have been observed in Europe.
**Behaviour.** Males sometimes stray considerably from LHP in search of water
and have been noted on damp patches at 1150m. In warm windless conditions,
adults sometimes assemble in large numbers on bushes of *Cratageus pycnoloba*
to bask in late afternoon sun. Attracted to the flowers of *Thymus*.
**Conservation.** On Mt. Chelmos, human activity poses a serious threat to this
species as well as *Lycaena thetis*.

## *Maculinea alcon* Alcon Blue                    Plate 26

**Range.** N Spain, C and E Europe, Denmark, S Sweden,
Turkey, Caucasus, Siberia, C and S Urals, Kazakhstan,
Mongolia, Altai.

*M. alcon* Denis and Schiffermüller 1775 TL: Vienna.
**Distribution.** Very local, sporadic in most regions. N Spain:
Province of Santander (Herrera 50m). France. NE Belgium.
Germany. SW Sweden and W Denmark. N Italy. Switzer-
land, Austria through (?)Slovakia and Hungary to Poland
and Lithuania. Distribution uncertain in some regions owing
to possible confusion with *M. rebeli* (below). 0-1000m.
**Description.** Male ups gc dull dusty-blue.
**Flight-period.** Univoltine. Mid June/mid August according to locality and
season: peak emergence normally late July.
**Habitat.** Marsh meadows, usually associated with flood-plains of rivers or lakes.
**Life-history.** LHPs *Gentiana pneumonanthe*; *G. asclepiadea*; (?)*G. cruciata*. Ova
laid singly but often in large numbers, mainly on flower-buds. Small larvae

feed and live within the calyces of flowers until late summer, thereafter in symbiotic relationship with *Myrmica ruginodis*, *M. rubra*, or *M. scabrinodis* ants.
Further larval development, hibernation and pupation occurs within nest of
adoptive ant species.

**Conservation.** As for all wetland species, land-drainage at sites well-removed
from habitats may be no less consequential than direct interference, which, if
coincident with periods of prolonged drought, poses a serious threat to ecologically sensitive species – adverse climatic events are probable rather than
possible, and most marshland insects are already disadvantaged by the small
size of most of their habitats.

**Note.** That the reputedly distinctive features of ecology and altitudinal range
of *M. alcon* and *M. rebeli* (below) are not infrequently at variance with wing-
morphology, has given rise to uncertainties in identification and distribution.
Intermediate forms of the two taxa, reported as *M. rebeli*, occur at low altitude
in the environs of Paris. In S Scandinavia, (?)*M. alcon* occurs at low altitudes
and utilizes *Gentiana pneumonanthe* as a LHP, but wing-characters are reported
to correspond to those of *M. rebeli*. The only two, known colonies of *M. alcon* in
Belgium occur approximately at sea-level in damp/wet habitats and both utilize
*G. pneumonanthe*: reports of *M. rebeli* in Belgium appear to be unsubstantiated.
The ground-water level of some habitats of *M. rebeli* in N Italy and N Greece is
more typical of those of *M. alcon*. A taxon resembling *M. alcon* but utilizing
*Gentiana cruciata* as a LHP in habitat approximating to that of *M. rebeli* has
been reported from Croatia. In Bakony Mts. (W Hungary), altitudinal separation of *M. alcon* and *M. rebeli* may be as little as 200m. Possibly, *M. alcon* and *M.
rebeli* are conspecific, with adaptive wing-morphology corresponding to marked
ecological diversity. Within the genus, *M. arion* displays a wide range of altitudinal
variation in wing-morphology: additional, lesser variation, apparently of ecological origin but unrelated to altitude, is also apparent.

## *Maculinea rebeli* Mountain Alcon Blue                     Plate 26

**Range.** N Spain, SC, E and SE Europe.

*M. rebeli* Hirschke 1904 TL: Austria.

**Distribution.** Very sporadic and very local. N Spain: Picos
de Europa; S. de la Demanda; provinces of Soria; Santander;
Huesca (Ordessa); Gerona; (?)Teurel. France: E Pyrenees;
Massif Central; Basses and Hautes Alps. Italy: C Apennines;
Dolomites; Apuane Alps; C Apennines. Switzerland. S Ger-
many, Czech Republic, Slovakia and S Poland to S Balkans
and N Greece (Pindos Mts.; Mt. Phalakron; Rhodope Mts.;
Mt. Cholomon). 600-2250m.

**Description and Variation.** Resembles *M. alcon* closely: male ups gc brighter
blue, lacking violet overtones. In Bakony Mts. (W Hungary), *xerophila* Berger:
resembles nominate form: both sexes larger; female ups gc very dark grey.

**Flight-period.** Univoltine. Mid June/July.

**Habitat.** Typically, damp or wet meadows, also in drier situations. In N Greece,
occurs in boggy woodland clearings in Rhodope Mts. (1500m), but in dry,
grassy, gullies above tree-line on Mt. Phalakron (1450-1850m).

**Life-history.** LHP principally *Gentiana cruciata*: also, *G. germanica*; *G.*

*asclepiadea*. Oviposition and life-cycle similar to *M. alcon*: adoptive ant species *Myrmica scabrinodis*, *M. sabuleti*, *M. schenki* or *M. sulcinodis*.

**Conservation.** Many colonies are vulnerable in consequence of small habitat-size: damage to LHPs from grazing, trampling and, in populated areas, flower-picking, poses a significant threat.

## *Maculinea arion* Large Blue                                   Plate 26

**Range.** Europe, Turkey, Russia, W Siberia, S Urals, N Kazakhstan, Mongolia, China, Japan.

*M. arion* Linnaeus 1758 TL: Nuremberg, Germany (Fruh-storfer).

**Distribution.** N and C Spain, Italy, N and C Greece and European Turkey to S Sweden, Lithuania, Latvia (rare and local), (?)Estonia and S Finland. Absent from Portugal, N Belgium, N Holland, N Germany and Mediterranean islands except Corsica. 50-2000m. Indigenous British population extinct.

**Variation.** Coastal regions of SE France, NW Italy and Corsica, f. *ligurica* Wagner ups black markings well developed – similar and transitional forms occur in most lowland populations. Above 1500m in C Alps, Balkans and Greece, *obscura* Christ: ups pd areas greyish; black pd markings largely obscured; basal flush dull blue with violet overtone: a closely related, but well-characterised form occurs at 1000-1400m in SE Switzerland and Greece: ups brighter blue flush extending to submargin; black marginal borders and pd markings clearly defined: transitional forms are common in Greece. Progressive ups darkening with increasing altitude would appear to be a clinal adaptation, possibly relating to a compensatory need to absorb solar energy more rapidly in prevailing cooler conditions.

**Flight-period.** Univoltine. Late May/July according to altitude and locality.

**Habitat.** Dry, grassy, bushy places; woodland clearings.

**Life-history.** LHPs *Thymus* spp., including *T. serpyllum* and *T. praecox*. Ova laid on flowers. Life-cycle similar to that for *M. alcon*: larvae/pupae attended by *Myrmica sabuleti* or *M. scabrinodis*.

## *Maculinea telejus* Scarce Large Blue                         Plate 26

**Range.** Pyrenees, C Europe, Caucasus, C and S Urals, Siberia, Kazakhstan, Mongolia, N China, Korea, Japan.

*M. telejus* Bergsträsser 1779 TL: Hanau, W Germany. syn: *euphemus* Hübner 1800.

**Distribution.** Very scarce and local. France: Gers; Gironde; Dordogne; Charante; Isère; Savoie; Haut-Rhin. N Switzerland: very local. N Italy: Piedmont; Trieste. C and S Germany. Austria. Hungary. Slovakia. S Poland. SW Latvia: a single known colony. Extinct in Belgium. Reports from Spain (Valle d'Aran) require confirmation. 700-1600m. Often occurs with *M. nausithous*.

**Flight-period.** Univoltine. Mid June/mid August.

**Habitat.** Marsh meadows, containing an abundance of LHP.

**Life-history.** LHP *Sanguisorba officinalis*. Ova laid on flowers. Life-cycle similar to that for *M. alcon*: Larvae/pupae attended by *Myrmica sabuleti, M. rubra, M. scabrinodis* or *M. vandeli*.

## *Maculinea nausithous* Dusky Large Blue                Plate 26

**Range.** N Spain, E France, C Europe to 52°N, Turkey, Caucasus, C and S Urals, Altai.

*M. nausithous* Bergsträsser 1779 TL: Hanau, W Germany.
syn: *arcas* Rottemburg 1775 (invalid homonym).
**Distribution.** Very scarce and local. N Spain: Picos de Europa; Soria; S. de la Demanda. E France: Savoie; Isère; Ain; Côte-d'Or; Haut-Rhin; Vosges. N Switzerland. C and S Germany. Austria (absent from Tirol). Czech Republic. Slovakia. Hungary. 700-1600m. Often occurs with *M. telejus*.
**Flight-period.** Univoltine. Mid June/mid August according to locality.
**Habitat.** Marsh meadows, containing an abundance of LHP – habitat as for *M. telejus*, but with some preference for drier margins.
**Life-history.** LHP *Sanguisorba officinalis*. Ova laid on flowers. Life-cycle similar to that for *M. alcon*: Larvae/pupae attended by *Myrmica rubra* or *M. scabrinodis*.

## *Iolana iolas* Iolas Blue                Plate 26

**Range.** Morocco, Algeria, C Spain, SC and SE Europe, Turkey, Iran.

*I. iolas* Ochsenheimer 1816 TL: Hungary.
**Distribution.** Widespread, usually very local. Morocco: very local: High Atlas (Tizi-n-Test): possibly now extinct in Col de Jerada, E Morocco. Algeria: Medea; Berrouaghia; Blida; Aflou; El Bayadh; Djelfa; Batna. 800-1600m. S and E Spain: Sierra Nevada; Montes Universales; Catalonia. S France: E Pyrenees to Provençe and Savoie. Switzerland: restricted to Rhône Valley. N and C Italy. Austria and Hungary to Balkans and Greece. 100-1700m.
**Variation.** In NW Africa, uns marginal markings indistinct in both sexes; male ups more violet-blue; female ups bluish suffusion extensive (*debilitata* Schultz): similar forms occur in Spain. Taxon *debilitata* accorded specific rank by some authors, with or without further differentiation in recognition of local forms: Montes Universales, *thomasi* Hemming; Catalonia, *farriolsi* de Sagarra.
**Flight-period.** Univoltine, May/early July: single or very small numbers of fresh specimens have been recorded in August/September, indicating a partial second brood or possibly delayed emergence due to exceptional weather conditions: state of development of LHP is an important consideration in respect to either possibility – an absence of seed-capsules would necessitate a profound departure from normal, larval feeding regime (see below).
**Habitat.** Dry, bushy places, usually on calcareous soils.
**Life-history.** LHPs principally *Colutea arborescens*: NE Greece, *C. cilicica*. Ova laid on seed-capsules or inside calyx. Larvae feed exclusively on seeds, sometimes in company with larvae of other lycaenids (*L. boeticus*; *P. argus*; *C. argiolus*;

*G. alexis; L. pirithous*). Larvae strongly myrmecophilous: attended by *Tapinoma erraticum*. Pupates under stones. Hibernates as a pupa. In captivity, diapause may extend over two seasonal cycles.
**Behaviour.** Single males have been recorded several kilometres from areas containing known LHP.

## *Pseudophilotes baton* Baton Blue                     Plate 27

**Range.** N Portugal, N Spain, France, S and C Europe.
*P. baton* Bergsträsser 1779 TL: Hanau, Germany.
**Distribution.** N Portugal. N Spain. France to 49°N. Corsica. Switzerland. Italy. Sicily. S Germany. W Czech Republic. Poland. W Austria. 200-2000m.
**Flight-period.** Generally bivoltine, April/June and late July/early September: univoltine in some localities at higher altitudes, June/July.
**Habitat.** Dry grassy and flowery places; sheltered slopes; rocky gullies.
**Life-history.** LHPs *Thymus serpyllum*; *T. vulgaris*; *T. nitens*; *T. praecox* (?)*polytrichus*; *Satureja montana*; *S. hortensis*; *Lavendula staechas*; *L. angustifolia*; *L. latifolia*; *Mentha suaveolens*; *M. longifolia*; *M. rotunda*; *Calamintha nepeta*. Ova laid on flowers, sometimes on leaf stems. Larvae feed on flowers and developing seeds. Like other European members of this genus, captively reared larvae appear to require direct sunlight and high temperatures for healthy development. Larvae attended by *Lasius alienus*; *Myrmica scabrinodis*. Hibernates as a pupa.

## *Pseudophilotes panoptes* Panoptes Blue             Plate 27

**Range.** Portugal, Spain.
*P. panoptes* Hübner 1813 TL: Spain.
syn: *P. baton panoptes* auct.
**Distribution.** Portugal and Spain south of Cantabrian Mts. and Pyrenees: widespread and common. 600-1900m.
**Description.** Resembles *P. baton*. Male unh pale orange or yellow submarginal spots vestigial or absent.
**Flight-period.** Bivoltine. Late March/June and July/August.
**Habitat.** As for *P. baton*.
**Life-history.** LHP *Thymus mastichina*; *T. villosus*; *Saturja montana*.
**Note.** Justification for separation from *P. baton* at species level unclear.

## *Pseudophilotes vicrama*                              Plate 27

**Range.** E Europe, Balkans, Greece, Turkey, C Asia, Tian Shan, China.
*P. vicrama schiffermuelleri* Hemming 1929 TL: Dom Altenberg, Austria.
**Distribution.** S Finland. Baltic states. Poland. SE Germany. Czech Republic. Slovakia. Austria. NE Italy: Trentino-Alto Adige (western limit). Hungary. Balkans and Greece, including Corfu, Kithira, Crete, Skyros, Andros, Paros, Sifnos, Limnos, Lesbos, Chios, Ikaria, Samos, Karpathos, Rhodes and Kos. European Turkey. 0-1900m.

**Variation.** Resembles *P. baton*. Appreciably larger, especially female: unh orange submarginal spots well developed in s1b-5. Readily separable from *P. baton* by distinctive character of valve in male genitalia (individually and regionally variable).
**Flight-period.** Bivoltine. April/early June and July/August according to altitude and location.
**Habitat.** Dry scrubland; grassy banks; rocky gullies; woodland clearings.
**Life-history.** LHPs *Thymus longicaulis chaubardii*; *T.*

*glabresens*; *T.* (?)*comptus*; *T.ocheus*; *T.striatus* or *atticus*; *Saturja montana*; *S.thymbra*. Oviposition, early development and hibernation as for *P. baton*. Larvae strongly myrmecophilous: attending ant species not determined: captive larvae appear reluctant to pupate, possibly due to absence of ants.

## *Pseudophilotes abencerragus* False Baton Blue          Plate 27

**Range.** Morocco, Algeria, Tunisia, Portugal, Spain, Egypt, Israel, Jordan, W Arabia.

*P. abencerragus* Pierret 1837 TL: Province of Oran, Algeria.
**Distribution.** Widespread but local. Morocco. Algeria. Tunisia. 100-2500m. S Portugal: S. da Estrêla, Alemtejo, Algarve. C and S Spain: Provinces of Madrid (Arganda; Camporeal; Loeches; Aranjuez); Extremadura (Alcácer do Sal); Cuenca (S. de Cuenca); Jaen (S. de Jabalcuz; S. de la Pandera); Málaga (Antequera; Rhonda; Foljambe). 100-1500m.
**Variation.** In N Africa, uns paler than Iberian populations, sometimes yellowish-grey.
**Flight-period.** Univoltine in Iberian peninsula, April/May (early April at 100m in Algarve). Bivoltine in High Atlas, late March/early June and August/September (occasionally, fresh specimens have been recorded in July).
**Habitat.** Dry flowery places usually associated with light scrub.
**Life-history.** LHPs: NW Africa, *Thymus hirtus*; *T.fontanesii*; *Salvia taraxicifolia*; *Medicago* (?)*turbinata*: Spain, *Cleonia lusitanica*. Ova laid on underside of leaves of *C. lusitanica* but larvae live entirely within flower-heads, refusing to eat leaves in captivity. Larval colouring differs appreciably from that of *P. baton*, *P. panoptes* and *P. vicrama*.

## *Pseudophilotes barbagiae* Sardinian Blue          Plate 27

**Range.** Sardinia.

*P. barbagiae* de Prins and van der Poorten 1982 TL: Sardinia.
**Distribution.** Sardinia: Monti del Gennargentu (Fonni; Lanusei; Desulo). 800-1500m. Reports from Monte Limbara require confirmation.
**Description.** Male ups darkish, somewhat greyish-brown; intensity of blue basal flush diminishing progressively towards pd area; black discoidal spot small or vestigial; uns gc darker than for *P. baton*; unh submarginal orange markings

poorly developed, usually vestigial: female similar; ups uniform dark brown.
Separable from closely allied taxa by distinctive characters in male genitalia.
**Flight-period.** Univoltine. May/June.
**Habitat.** Dry rocky, scrub clearings and slopes.
**Life-history.** LHP *Thymus* (?)*herba-barona*.

## *Pseudophilotes bavius* Bavius Blue                   Plate 27

**Range.** Morocco, Algeria, SE Europe, Turkey, Caucasus,
Crimea, S Urals.

*P. bavius bavius* Eversmann 1832 TL: S Urals.
**Distribution.** Widely separated colonies. Romania: districts
of Cluj and Bistrita Nasaud (Transylvania). Republic of
Macedonia: Skopje (Treska Valley); Gradsko. NW Greece:
Askion Mts. 700-1200m. S Greece: Mt. Chelmos and
environs (Kalavrita, Zachlorou), southwards to Sparta.
Turkey in Europe. 600-1100m.
**Variation.** In Romania, *hungaricus* Doiszeghy 1913 [TL: Vita, Bistrita Nasaud]:
male ups silvery-blue. In Republic of Macedonia, *macedonicus* Schultze: male
ups dull, somewhat greyish-blue; uph usual submarginal spots absent except
for small, pale orange mark in anal angle. In Peloponnesos, *casimiri* Hemming:
male ups bright blue; uph orange submarginal spots well developed. In Askion
Mts., resembles *casimiri* but variable – in same colony, some individuals closely
correspond to *macedonicus*.
**Flight-period.** Univoltine. Mid May/June.
**Habitat.** Dry, sheltered rocky slopes, gullies or small clearings amongst scrub
on calcareous soils.
**Life-history.** LHPs *Salvia* spp.: Romania, *S. nutans*; NW Greece, *S. officinalis*;
S Greece, *S. verbenaca*. In S Greece, ova laid on tips of developing flower-
stems, upperside of young basal leaves and at base of stem-leaves. Larvae feed
on flowers, less often on leaves and stems. Most larvae are green but a pinkish
form appears to correspond to those feeding exclusively on flowers. Captive
larvae readily accept *Salvia argentea*, *S. aethiopis*, *S. sclarea*, *S. nemorosa* and *S.
verticillata*. In Romania, larvae are susceptible to heavy parasitization (>95%)
by *Apanteles lycaenae* (Diptera). Hibernates as a pupa: in nature, a single example
has been recorded under basal leaf of *S. sclarea*. Larvae of *hungaricus* attended
by ants (sp. not determined).
**Conservation.** In S Greece, most known habitats appear to be threatened
grazing – sheep and goats are very partial to the flower-stems of *S. verbenaca*.

*P. bavius fatma* Oberthür 1890 TL: Lambessa, Algeria.
**Distribution.** Very local. Morocco: Middle Atlas (Anosseur; Ifrane; Azrou;
Immouzer). Algeria: Aures Mts. (Lambessa; Col de Telmet). 1500-1800m.
**Description.** Male uph prominent submarginal orange spots extends to s7.
Female ups blue flush generally more extensive.
**Flight-period.** Univoltine. Late April/early June.
**Habitat.** Dry scrub; flowery meadows; clearings in light woodland.
**Life-history.** LHP *Salvia argentea*.
**Behaviour.** Adults often rest on basal leaves of LHP.

## *Scolitantides orion* Chequered Blue                     Plate 27

**Range.** Spain, S France, N Italy, E and SE Europe, S
Fennoscandia, Turkey, C Asia, Japan.

*S. orion orion* Pallas 1771 TL: E Russia.
**Distribution.** Very local in coastal areas. S Norway, S
Sweden and S Finland. Absent from Baltic states. 0-300m.
**Description.** Male ups extensive bright silvery- or violet-
blue, somewhat disrupted by black veins; upf black marginal
spots with proximal whitish/silvery-greyish band, somewhat
broken and striated; uph black marginal spots faintly ringed
pale blue or white: female ups gc very dark greyish-brown, blue flush vestigial,
variable but rarely absent.
**Flight-period.** Univoltine. Mid May/June.
**Habitat.** Rocky slopes/rock ledges largely devoid of vegetation except LHP.
**Life-history.** LHP *Sedum album*. Hibernates as a pupa.

*S. orion lariana* Frühstorfer 1910 TL: Lake Como.
**Distribution.** Very local and sporadic. Spain: S. de Espuna; Montes Universales;
Alicante to Catalonia; Huesca. S France: Gironde; Lot-et-Garonne; Massif
Central; E Pyrenees to Basses Alps; Corsica. N Italy and S Switzerland to S
Poland, Hungary, Balkans and N Greece: Mt. Orvilos; Phalakron massif;
Rhodopi massif; Askion Mts.; Mt. Olympus. European Turkey. 200-1100m.
**Description.** Male ups darker blue markings less extensive, rarely extending
beyond discoidal spot: female ups very dark greyish-brown, almost black, usually
without blue basal flush.
**Variation.** Subject to marked local and regional variation. In Republic of Mac-
edonia (Treska Valley) and NW Greece (Askion Mts.): resembles nominate form
closely.
**Flight-period.** Generally univoltine (late May/June), bivoltine in some areas
of Switzerland (April/May and July /August).
**Habitat.** Dry, often very hot, stony slopes/soil-banks/gullies, often amongst
scrub; sometimes grassy, rocky clearings in light deciduous woodland: usually
on calcareous substrates.
**Life-history.** LHPs *Sedum album*; *S. telephium*; *S. hispanicum*; *S. maximum*.
Ova laid at base of leaves, upon which larvae feed. Captive larvae accept many
*Sedum* species. Larvae attended by *Camponotus vagus*; *C. aethiops*; *Tapinoma
erraticum*. Hibernates as a pupa under stones or sometimes in small hollows in
loose sandy soil near base of LHP.

## *Chilades trochylus* Grass Jewel                          Plate 27

**Range.** Greece, Turkey, Egypt, Middle East, Iran, Afghanistan, C Africa.

*C. trochylus* Freyer 1844 TL: Turkey.
**Distribution.** Very local and sporadic. Greece: Lake Vegoritis; Olympus massif;
Mt. Hymettus; Pastra Mts; Mt. Parnassos; Delphi; N Peloponnesos (Xilocastro);
Evia; Samos; Chios; Rhodes; Crete. 25-900m.
**Variation.** Ups discoidal spots sometimes faintly ringed white.
**Flight-period.** Polyvoltine. Late March/late October.
**Habitat.** Hot, dry, stony places; sometimes on disturbed soils in areas of

cultivation. Some habitats are extremely small – 200m².

**Life-history.** LHP on Mt. Parnassos massif, *Andrachne telephioides* (Euphorbiaceae): natural use of *Heliotropium hirsutissimum* (Boraginaceae) in Europe not confirmed, although both plant species are exploited in Israel and Sinai peninsula. Captive larvae feed readily on flowers and leaves of *Heliotropium hirsutissimum*. Hibernates as a pupa. On Mt. Parnassos, larvae attended by *Acantholepis* near *caucasica*: outside of Europe, *Pheidole quadrispinosa*; *Prenolepis* sp.; *Iridomyrmex* sp.

## *Maurus vogelii* Vogel's Blue                    Plate 28

**Range.** Morocco.

*M. vogelii vogelii* Oberthür 1920 TL: Tizi-n-Taghzeft, Morocco.

**Distribution.** Very local. Morocco: Taghzeft Pass; district of Timhadit and Itzer. 1900-2200m.

**Flight-period.** Univoltine. Mid August/mid September.

**Habitat.** Dry, stony places with very sparse vegetation.

**Life-history.** LHP *Erodium petraeum crispum* [=*Erodium cheilanthifolium*].

*M. vogelii insperatus* Tennent 1994 TL: Tizi-n-Test, High Atlas, Morocco.

**Distribution.** Morocco: High Atlas (Tizi-n-Test). 2400-2880m.

**Description.** Resembles nominate form closely. Male uns gc browner, tinged yellow; submarginal orange markings paler, with proximal whitish markings vestigial or absent; white rings enclosing discal and pd spots slightly reduced.

**Flight-period.** Probably univoltine: data very limited: late May/June.

**Habitat.** Steep, stony slopes.

**Life-history.** LHP *Erodium petraeum crispum* [=*Erodium cheilanthifolium*]. Larvae feed at night, resting at base of LHP during the day. Larvae attended by ants.

## *Plebejus martini* Martin's Blue                    Plate 28

**Range.** E Morocco, N Algeria.

*P. martini martini* Allard 1867 TL: Algeria.

**Distribution.** Algeria: Batna; Lambessa; Khenchela; Oran; Algiers; Kabylie; Tlemcen Mts. 1400-1900m.

**Flight-period.** Univoltine. Mid May/early July according to locality.

**Habitat.** Dry, stony, flowery places with some scrub, e.g., *Quercus ilex*; *Chamaerops humilis*; *Thymus*.

**Life-history.** LHPs *Astragalus massiliensis*; *Acanthyllis numidia*. Larvae attended by *Crematogaster* sp.

*P. martini ungemachi* Rothschild 1926 TL: Aselda (High Atlas), Aghbalu Larbi, Taghzeft Pass (Middle Atlas) (Morocco).

**Distribution.** Morocco: widespread but local: High Atlas (Tizi-n-Talremt;

Imilchil; Reraya Valley); Middle Atlas (Boulemane; Sefrou; Tizi-bou-Zabel). 1400-2200m.
**Description.** Resembles nominate form closely. Uns white rings, enclosing black discal and pd spots, better defined; female ups submarginal orange spots usually larger but variable; uns gc greyer.
**Flight-period.** Univoltine. Mid May/June.
**Habitat.** Stony, flowery places.
**Life-history.** LHP *Astragalus incanus incurvus.*

*P. martini regularis* Tennent 1995 TL: Dj. Lakraa, Morocco.
**Distribution.** Morocco: W Rif Mts. (Dj. Lakraa). 1900-2100m.
**Description.** Resembles nominate form: male ups slightly darker blue; upf and uph lacking black cell-spots.
**Flight-period.** Univoltine. Late June/July.
**Habitat.** Open, stony slopes.
**Life-history.** LHP *Astragalus armatus.*

## *Plebejus allardi* Allard's Blue                    Plate 28

**Range.** Morocco, Algeria, Tunisia, W Libya, Israel.

*P. allardi* Oberthür 1874 TL: Sebdou, W Algeria.
**Distribution.** Widely scattered and local. Morocco: Anti-Atlas. 1300-1500m. Algeria: Sebdou (Tlemcen Mts.) 900m. Tunisia: Isle of Jerba 10-25m; Zriba 480m.
**Description.** Resembles *P. martini.* Ups black veins more prominent near outer margin; uns gc darker, greyish-brown; uns markings better developed.
**Flight-period.** Univoltine. Mid April/mid May according to altitude.
**Habitat.** Hot, dry, rocky slopes or sandy ground with sparse, low-growing vegetation.
**Life-history.** LHP *Astragalus caprinus.* Ova laid on underside of developing leaves.
**Behaviour.** Both sexes fond of resting on LHP.

## *Plebejus pylaon* Zephyr Blue                    Plate 28

**Range.** Spain, Switzerland, Italy, Balkans, Greece, Turkey, Middle East, N Iran, SW Russia.

*P. pylaon sephirus* Frivaldsky 1835 TL: Slivno, Bulgaria.
**Distribution.** Generally sporadic, often locally common. Hungary. Serbia. (?)Albania. Republic of Macedonia. Romania. Bulgaria: Pirin Mts. NW and C Greece: Varnous Mts.; Vernon Mts; Askion Mts.; Mt. Parnis; Pindos Mts. S Greece: Mt. Chelmos; Mt. Menalon. European Turkey. Records for Taygetos Mts. require confirmation. 500-2050m.
**Description and Variation.** Male ups violet-blue; unh antemarginal black spots without silvery-bluish/greenish scales. In Republic of Macedonia and Greece, f. *brethertoni* Brown: resembles nominate ssp. closely (probably synonomous): size variable, usually large; male uph sometimes with reddish spots in

anal angle: female ups submarginal orange spots variable in colour, size and number, sometimes confluent, rarely with obscure, proximal, ray-like projections on fw.

**Flight-period.** Univoltine. Mid May/July according to locality and altitude.

**Habitat.** Usually open dry, grassy, sometimes sandy places containing an abundance of LHP: exceptionally, damp woodland clearings: on calcareous soils.

**Life-history.** LHPs: Hungary, *Astragalus exscapus*; *A. dasyanthus*: Greece, *A. exscapus* (Smolikas massif: extremely local); *A. parnassi cyllenus* (S Pindos Mts., Mt. Chelmos); *A. angustifolius* (Askion Mts.; Mt. Menelon); *Astracantha rumelica* [=*Astragalus creticus rumelicus*] (Sarantaporus Valley, Pindos Mts.). Ova laid on leaves, upon which larvae feed. Hibernates as a small larva. Pupates at base of LHP, often at entrances to galleries of ant's nest. Larvae attended by *Bothriomyrmex gallicus*; *Tapinoma simrothi*; *Lasius niger*; *Lasius* near *alienus*; *Camponotus* (?)*aethiops*; *C.* (?)*laconicus*; *Tetramorium* near *caespitum*; *Formica pratensis*.

**Behaviour.** Males often assemble in large numbers on damp ground.

*P. pylaon trappi* Verity 1927 TL: Simplon.
syn: *lycidas* Trapp 1863 (invalid homonym)

**Distribution.** (?)SE France: Savoie (Val d'Isère). S Switzerland: Bernese Alps (Gemmi Pass); Pennine Alps (Simplonpass; Saastal; Zermatt). N Italy: Piedmont (Val di Cogne; Val d'Ossola); Venosta Alps (Schlandrounertal; Val Passiria). 1000-2000m.

**Description and Variation.** Male ups darker violet-blue; black marginal borders slightly wider: female ups dark brown; often with blue basal suffusion; uph dark orange spots in anal angle vestigial or absent, often replaced by black dots. In Piedmont, f. *augustini* Mentzer: slightly smaller. In S Tirol, f. *delattini* Junge: slightly larger.

**Flight-period.** Univoltine. Late June/early August according to season and altitude.

**Habitat.** Sheltered grassy places; small, pinewood clearings.

**Life-history.** LHP *Astragalus exscapus*. Early-stage development as for *L. p. sephirus*. Larvae attended by *Formica lugubris*; *F. lemani*.

*P. pylaon hespericus* Rambur 1839 TL: Sierra de Alfacar, Andalusia.

**Distribution.** Spain: Teruel (S. de Albarracin 1000-1500m); Madrid (Loeches; Camporeal; Arganda; 700-800m); Toledo (La Mata 700-800m); Granada (Sierra Nevada; S. de Alfacar; 1150-1300m). Most colonies extremely local.

**Description and Variation.** Male ups bright turquoise blue; uph black antemarginal spots sometimes faintly ringed pinkish-violet; uph, ochreous mark sometimes present in s1a: female ups medium brown; uph with 2-4 submarginal orange spots in anal angle, variable, sometimes absent. In provinces of Madrid and Toledo: averagely slightly larger; male ups slightly brighter.

**Flight-period.** Univoltine. Mid May/June.

**Habitat.** Dry, rocky gullies, often amongst scrub; dry grassy places in woodland clearings. LHPs usually extremely local.

**Life-history.** LHPs: S. de Albarracin, *Astragalus turolensis* [=*A. aragonensis*]; *A. sempervirens muticus*: Madrid and Toledo, *A. alopecuroides* [=*A. narbonensis*]: Granada, *A. clusii* [=*A. tumidus*]. Oviposition and development as for *sephirus*.

104                           BUTTERFLIES OF EUROPE

Larvae/pupae attended by *Formica cinerea*; *F. subrufa*; *Plagiolepis pygmaea*; *P. schmitzi*; *Camponotus* near *aethiops*; *C. cruentatus*; *C. foreli*; *C. sylvaticus*; *Crematogaster auberti*. Pupates near base of LHP, often at entrances to galleries of ant's nest.

**Conservation.** Most colonies appear to be vulnerable, particularly those in close proximity to areas of intensive cultivation: at least two colonies have been eradicated in Sierra Nevada in last two decades by urban expansion.

## *Plebejus argus* Silver-studded Blue                    Plate 28

**Range.** Europe, Turkey, temperate Asia, N China, Japan.

*P. argus argus* Linnaeus 1758 TL: S Sweden (Verity 1943). syn: *aegon* Denis and Schiffermüller 1775.
**Distribution.** Widespread, locally common. From N and E Spain to 69°N in Fennoscandia, Balkans, Greece (including Corfu and Thassos) and European Turkey. 0-1500m. A record for Kykladian island of Tenos requires confirmation. Absent from Ireland and Scotland.
**Description.** Male fore-tibia with spine (cf. *Plebejus idas*).
**Variation.** Numerous ssp./forms have been described to account for minor variation in size; development of markings; ups and uns gc, especially female ups blue suffusion. Generally, uns gc correlates with character of habitat: darker forms occur on dark, acidic soils (heaths, bogs etc.), paler forms on limestone. In S Greece, males with reddish marginal spots in s1-3 uph occur rarely. On Mt. Erimanthos (NW Peloponnesos) above 1500m: large; male ups black borders exceptionally narrow – uph black submarginal spots largely obscured by gc; uns gc whitish, markings well developed: female ups brown: in E Spain, *montesiai* de Sagarra: male ups and uns closely similar: female ups extensively suffused bright blue.
**Flight-period.** Bivoltine. May/June and July/August.
**Habitat.** Diverse. Most habitat types in altitudinal range: in very damp to very dry conditions.
**Life-history.** LHPs: Fabaceae, spp. of the genera:- *Lotus*; *Ulex*; *Cytisus*; *Genista*; *Colutea*; *Astragalus*; *Ononis*; *Medicago*; *Hippocrepis*; *Coronilla*; *Galega*: Cistaceae, *Helianthemum*: Ericaceae, *Calluna vulgaris*; (?)*Erica* sp. In northern Europe, hibernates as a fully-formed larva within ovum-case: in one example in Greece, a second instar larva was found hibernating within its exuvium attached to the underside of a stone. Larvae strongly myrmecophilous. Ova laid on plants in close proximity to ant's nests. Larvae attended by *Lasius niger*; *L. alienus*; (?)*Formica cinerea*. Adult larvae pupate in ants' nest into which they are ushered by attending ants. Without ants, captive adult larvae become very 'agitated' and usually die (cf. *Tomares ballus*).

*P. argus caernensis* Thompson 1941 TL: Great Ormes Head, N Wales.
**Distribution.** N Wales: coastal areas: Great Ormes peninsula. 10-100m.
**Description and Variation.** Small. Male ups, bright blue; uns white with pale blue, basal suffusion: female upf and uph usually suffused blue to submargin; ups orange submarginal spots usually well developed, especially hw. A similar but larger race, *cretaceae* Tutt, appears to be close to extinction on

the chalk-grassland of SE England: a related form, occurring on coastal limestone of central S England (Dorset), appears less vulnerable.
**Flight-period.** Univoltine. Mid June/late August. Emerges 2-4 weeks earlier
than other British populations.
**Habitat.** Dry, sheltered, grassy places on limestone.
**Life-history.** LHP *Helianthemum nummularium*. Development as for nominate
form.

*P. argus aegidion* Meisner 1818 TL: Grimsel Pass, Switzerland.
**Distribution.** Central Alps. 1500-2000m.
**Description and Variation.** Resembles nominate form. Male ups black
marginal borders 2-3mm wide; uns greyish: female ups orange submarginal
spots reduced, confined to hw. Transitional to nominate form below 1500m.
**Flight-period.** Univoltine. Early July/August.
**Habitat.** Alpine grassland.

*P. argus hypochionus* Rambur 1858 TL: Andalucia.
**Distribution.** N Portugal. S and C Spain. Not reported from Gibraltar. 600-
2400m.
**Description and Variation.** Larger; male ups brighter blue; uns chalky-white:
female ups orange submarginal spots well developed, usually in complete series
on fw and hw. Transitional forms and geographical/altitudinal overlap with other
races, presents a complex and poorly understood distributional pattern in Iberian
Peninsula.
**Flight-period.** Univoltine. Early June/late July.
**Habitat.** Flowery, grassy places; rocky gullies.

*P. argus corsicus* Bellier 1862 TL: Corsica.
**Distribution.** Corsica. 500-1000m. Very local. (A tentative record from the
island of St. Maria (within political boundary of Sardinia, 15km SE of Corsica)
merits investigation – possibly arises from confusion with *P. idas*).
**Description and Variation.** Resembles nominate form: male uns gc yellowish
or brownish grey; markings ill-defined; unh submarginal spots yellowish or
pale orange: female ups usually with blue suffusion, especially hw. On St. Maria,
smaller; male ups and uns gc and uns markings said to be identical to that of
nominate form: female ups blue suffusion extensive.
**Flight-period.** Univoltine. July.
**Habitat.** Grassy, woodland clearings.
**Life-history.** LHP yellow-flowered (?)*Genista* sp.

## *Plebejus loewii* Loew's Blue                                   Plate 29

**Range.** Greece (E Aegean Islands), Turkey, Iraq, Iran, Afghanistan, Pakistan.

*P. loewii* Zeller 1847 TL: Turkey.
**Distribution.** Aegean Islands: Kos; Patmos; Kalimnos; Tilos; Rhodes. 0-800m.
**Flight-period.** Voltinism uncertain: only one brood (late May/late June)
observed on Rhodes. Reportedly univoltine in Turkey.
**Habitat.** Dry rocky places.
**Life-history.** LHP unknown in Europe and Turkey. (Saudi Arabia, *Astragalus
spinosus*; *A. sieberi*).

## *Plebejus idas* Idas Blue                                   Plate 28

**Range.** Europe, Turkey, Middle East, Asia, N America.

*P. idas* Linnaeus 1761 TL: Sweden
**Distribution.** Spain: local in Sierra Nevada; Montes Universales; Soria; Burgos; Cantabrian Mts.; Pyrenees; Catalonia. France, eastwards throughout most of Europe. 200-2100m. Absent from Britain; S Greece; Mediterranean islands.
**Description and Variation.** Male fore-tibia lacking spine (cf. *P. argus*). Range/character of variation broadly similar to that of *P. argus*: many forms/ssp. have been described to account for local/regional variation. Above 1800m in central Alps, *haefelfingeri* Beuret: small; male ups bluer; uns, greyish-buff. Below 1000m in Alps and Pyrenees, *opulentus* Verity: large; uns well marked. At 1000-1500m in Alps and Pyrenees, *alpinus* Berce: transitional to *opulentus*. In N Scandinavia, *lapponicus* Gerhard: resembles *haefelfingeri*: small; uns discal and pd spots small; female ups gc brown, often suffused blue; uph orange spots vestigial. Above 1800m in Sierra Nevada, S Spain, *nevadensis* Oberthür: resembles *magnagraeca* (below) but averagely smaller.
**Flight-period.** Univoltine (late June/August) or bivoltine (late May/June and July/August) according to altitude and locality.
**Habitat.** Bushy places; grassy woodland clearings; heaths, in dry or damp situations; sheltered grassy banks and hollows at highest levels.
**Life-history.** LHPs *Cytisus scoparius*; *Genista pilosa*; *Lotus corniculatus*; *Melilotus alba*; *Anthyllus vulneraria*; *Calluna vulgaris*. Hibernates as an ovum. Larvae are strongly myrmecophilous and pupate within an ant's nest. Larvae/pupae attended by *Lasius niger*; *Formica* cinerea; *F. selysi*; *F. exsecta*; *F. lemani*; *F. pressilabris*; *F. lugubris*; *F. cunicularia*; *F. lefrancoisi*; *F.* (?)*fusca*.

*P. idas calliopis* Boisduval 1832 TL: Grenoble.
**Distribution.** France: Basses Alpes; Haut Alpes. 500-1000m.
**Description.** Male uns discal and pd spots reduced: female ups dark brown, often with blue basal suffusion.
**Flight-period.** Univoltine. July/early August.
**Habitat.** Habitats dominated by bushes of LHP.
**Life-history.** LHP *Hippophae rhamnoides* (Elaeagnaceae). Adult activity confined largely to proximity of LHP. Larvae attended by *Formica* spp. patrolling LHP.

*P. idas magnagraeca* Verity 1936 TL: Mt. Olympus, Greece.
**Distribution.** Republic of Macedonia. Bulgaria. N and C Greece. Widespread but local. 500-1800m.
**Description.** Large: male ups black borders 2-3mm wide; ups gc generally darker blue, sometimes with purplish tint; black veins usually prominent: female ups brown; uph submarginal orange spots usually well developed, sometimes extending to fw in a complete series: both sexes, uns markings bold.
**Variation.** Somewhat variable in all characters. Above about 1500m on Mt. Pangeon, Mt. Timphristos and Mt. Parnassos: smaller; male ups paler blue; black borders narrower; veins less conspicuous – resembles *nevadensis* Oberthür.

**Flight-period.** Univoltine. June/July.
**Habitat.** Grassy, flowery clearings in scrub or light woodland: above 1500m, dry gravelly slopes on acidic soils or dry grassy banks on limestone.
**Life-history.** LHPs: Vernon Mts., *Genista depressa*; Rhodopi Mts., *Cytisus villosus*. Pupates amongst leaf-litter or on leaves of LHP. Larvae/pupae attended by *Formica pratensis*.

*P. idas bellieri* Oberthür 1910 TL: Bastelica, Corsica.
**Distribution.** Corsica. Sardinia. 0-1400m.
**Description and Variation.** Male ups black marginal borders, 1-2mm (Corsica) or 2-3mm (Sardinia); uns gc yellowish or brownish-grey, markings very prominent in both sexes: female ups darkish brown with extensive blue basal flush, especially hw.
**Flight-period.** Univoltine. Late June/July.
**Habitat.** Scrub and woodland clearings.

## *Plebejus argyrognomon* Reverdin's Blue — Plate 28

**Range.** France, C, E and SE Europe, Turkey.

*P. argyrognomon* Bergsträsser 1779 TL: Hanau, Germany.
syn: *ismenias* Meigen 1829 (invalid homonym); *aegus* Chapman 1917
**Distribution.** France: Dordogne; Charante; Vienne; Isère and Haute Savoie to Paris and Aisne. NW Switzerland. Italy. Germany to S Norway (including Oslofiord island of Borøya), S Sweden, E Latvia (very local), Balkans and N Greece (very local). Records for Mt. Parnassos require confirmation. 200-1500m.
**Description.** Resembles *P. idas*: individual wing-characters not diagnostic but overall appearance usually sufficient for identification. Male genitalia distinctive.
**Variation.** In Scandinavia, *norvegica* Nordstrom: female ups bright, shiny blue. In Balkans and Greece: often large; female ups invariably brown. In France, Germany and Austria, female ups blue suffusion variable within and between populations but usually limited to wing-bases. Geographical variation in degree and incidence of female ups blue suffusion suggests a clinal change, possibly associated with climatic conditions (cf. *P. amanda*).
**Flight-period.** Generally bivoltine, mid May/June and late June/July: univoltine in Scandinavia, late June/late August according to season.
**Habitat.** Grassy, flowery, bushy, dry or damp places.
**Life-history.** LHPs *Coronilla varia*, *Astragalus glycyphyllos*. In Scandinavia, *A. glycyphyllos* is the sole LHP, also apparently in Greece – despite presence of *S. varia* in all known habitats. Ova laid on either surface of leaves. Hibernates as an ovum or small larva. In Greece, hibernated larvae feed on developing leaves below base of LHP. Larvae attended by *Lasius niger*; *L. alienus*; *Myrmica scabrinodis*; *M. sabuleti*; *Camponotus vagus*.

## *Vacciniina optilete* Cranberry Blue                    Plate 27

**Range.** Central Alps, NE Europe, Republic of Macedonia, Japan, N America.

*V. optilete* Knoch 1781 TL: Braunschweig, Germany.

**Distribution.** Central Alps of SE France (Hautes-Alpes; Haute-Savoie), N Italy, Switzerland and W Austria (Gross Glockner). 1500-2800m. S and C Germany to Czech Republic, Slovakia, Poland, Baltic states and Fennoscandia. 100-1400m. Republic of Macedonia: Sar Pl.; Vraca Pl.; Pelister massif. Above 2000m.

**Flight-period.** Univoltine. Late June/August according to latitude and altitude.

**Habitat.** Heaths; moors; raised bogs; dry or damp forest clearings on acidic soils.

**Life-history.** LHPs: Central Alps, *Vaccinium uliginosum*: Fennoscandia, *V. uliginosum*; *V. myrtillus*; *V. oxycoccus*; *Erica tetralix*. Ova laid on various plant parts including stems. Larvae feed on leaves and flowers. Hibernates as a small larva, sometimes on dead, fallen leaves of LHP.

## *Kretania psylorita* Cretan Argus                    Plate 29

**Range.** Crete.

*K. psylorita* Freyer 1845 TL: Mt. Ida, Crete.

**Distribution.** Restricted to Crete: Psyloritis Mts. (Mt. Ida); Dikti Mts. 1300-2000m. Locally abundant.

**Flight-period.** Univoltine. June/July.

**Habitat.** Rocky ground, dominated by LHP.

**Life-history.** LHP *Astragalus* or *Astracantha*; not reliably determined at sp. level (cf. *K. eurypilus*).

**Behaviour.** Flight very low, maintaining close proximity to LHP, seemingly to minimize danger of windswept terrain.

**Conservation.** Habitats reportedly threatened by increasing human activity.

## *Kretania eurypilus* Eastern Brown Argus                    Plate 29

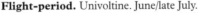

**Range.** Greece, Turkey, Middle East, Iran, S Russia.

*K. eurypilus eurypilus* Freyer 1851 TL: Amasya, Turkey.

**Distribution.** Greece: Samos (Mt. Kerketefs 1000-1450m). Two records (1901 and 1968) of female specimens from Mt. Chelmos are generally presumed to have arisen from confusion with closely similar female *Plebejus pylaon*.

**Variation.** Female ups submarginal orange-red spots variable in number and size, sometimes large and in complete series on fw and hw, sometimes entirely absent.

**Flight-period.** Univoltine. June/late July.

**Habitat.** Open rocky limestone slopes/gullies/hollows, with sparse low-growing vegetation: above tree-line.

*K. eurypilus pelopides* van der Poorten 1984 TL: 'S Peloponesos' [Taygetos Mts.].

**Distribution.** S Greece: Taygetos Mts. 1400-2200m.

**Description.** Resembles nominate form. Male ups gc greyer, lighter brown; submarginal orange spots paler; uph sometimes with slight greyish suffusion, broken by veins; uns gc greyer, brighter; submarginal and pd spots interposed with whitish band, broken by veins: female similar; fw outer margin more rounded; ups orange submarginal spots better developed; uph greyish suffusion apparent in about 50% of specimens.

**Flight-period.** Univoltine. Early June/late July in prolonged emergence.

**Habitat.** Sheltered gullies/hollows on limestone or metamorphic rocks, generally above tree-line.

**Life-history.** LHP *Astracantha rumelica* [=*Astragalus creticus rumelicus*]. (In Lebanon, *Astracantha gummifera*). Ova laid on upperside of leaves. Hibernates as a small larva. Hibernated larva generally feeds in a concealed position by boring laterally into stem, just below new season's growth, and then axially downwards into stem: newly developed leaves are left intact, concealing posterior segments of larva. Larvae attended by *Camponotus kiesenwetteri*; *C. universitatus*. A high proportion of larvae are parasitized.

## *Eumedonia eumedon* Geranium Argus          Plate 29

**Range.** Europe, Turkey, Urals, Mongolia, Tian Shan, Altai.

*E. eumedon* Esper 1780 TL: Erlangen, W Germany.
syn: *chiron* Rottemburg 1775 (invalid homonym).

**Distribution.** Spain: S. de Maria; S. de Tejeda; Cantabrian Mts.; S. de la Demanda; S. de Cuenca; Pyrenees. France: Pyrenees; Massif Central; Provençe to Jura. Italy: very sporadic. N Sicily. Commoner in NE range: Switzerland to N Fennoscandia (including Öland and Gotland) and Romania. Sporadic and local in W Croatia, Republic of Macedonia, Bulgaria and N and C Greece. Absent from NW Europe, Denmark and N Norway. In C and S Europe, 750-2400m: in Fennoscandia, 0-1300m: generally below 900m.

**Variation.** At lower altitudes and in S Europe: generally larger; uns markings better developed. In N Fennoscandia and at higher altitudes in C Alps: small; uns greyish; uns markings reduced; male unf pd spots often very small, sometimes absent. In Balkans and Greece: generally much larger; uns gc light golden-brown, all markings bold, especially orange submarginal spots. Throughout range, uph submarginal spots variable in both sexes, better developed in female. On Mt. Parnassos, unh white stripe usually absent.

**Flight-period.** Univoltine. Mid May/mid August according to altitude, latitude and locality.

**Habitat.** Warm, sheltered, flowery, woodland or scrub clearings; sheltered alpine meadows. In dry or damp situations on calcareous or acidic soils.

**Life-history.** LHPs *Geranium sanguineum*; *G. sylvaticum*; *G. tuberosum*; *G. palustre*; *G. pratense*; *G. cinereum*. Ova laid at base of stamens. Before hibernation, larvae feed almost exclusively on developing fruits. Hibernates as a small larva. Hibernated larvae feed on developing leaves. Larvae attended *by Lasius alienus*; *Myrmica* sp.; *Tapinoma* sp. In captive rearing, a second brood is easily induced.

**Behaviour.** Adult activity confined largely to vicinity of LHP.

## *Aricia agestis* Brown Argus                                    Plate 29

**Range.** N Africa, S and C Europe, Turkey, Middle East, Iran, Tian Shan, Siberia, Amur.

*A. agestis agestis* Denis and Schiffermüller 1775 TL: Vienna, Austria.

syn: *astrache* Bergsträsse 1779; *medon* Hufnagel 1776 (invalid homonym)

**Distribution.** Widespread and common. N Spain, eastwards through S Britain to Denmark (including Fyen, Sjælland, Lolland, Falster and Bornholm) and S Sweden. Lithuania: rare and very local. Recorded from most Mediterranean islands. Absent from Balearic Islands (replaced by *A. a. cramera* (below)), Ireland, Scotland, W Denmark, Latvia and Estonia. 0-1700m.

**Description and Variation.** First brood uns gc grey; second brood sandy to rusty-brown. In S Europe, including Mediterranean islands, *calida* Bellier: ups and uns submarginal orange spots well developed.

**Flight-period.** Generally bivoltine in N and C Europe, May/June and July/September: possibly univoltine in Lithuania, June/July: trivoltine at lower altitudes in S Europe, April/October.

**Habitat.** Dry or damp, grassy, flowery places in diverse range of climatic conditions: on calcareous soils.

**Life-history.** LHPs, *Helianthemum nummularium*; *Erodium cicutarium*; *E. ciconium*; *Geranium tuberosum*; *G. asphodeloides*; *G. sanguineum*. Ova laid on upperside of leaves upon which larvae feed. Hibernates as a small larva. Larvae attended by *Lasius niger*; *L. alienus*; *L. flavus*; *Myrmica sabuleti*.

**Note.** Sympatric with *A. artaxerxes allous* in Lithuania.

*A. agestis cramera* Eschscholtz 1821 TL: Canary Islands.

syn: *canariensis* Blachier 1889.

**Distribution.** Canary Islands: Gomera; Hierro; La Palma; Tenerife; Gran Canaria. 300-1600m. Morocco. Algeria. Tunisia. 0-2500m. Portugal. Spain, south of the Cantabrian Mts. and Pyrenees. Balearic Islands: Ibiza; Mallorca; Menorca. 0-1900m.

**Description and Variation.** Resembles nominate form. Ups submarginal orange spots strongly developed, often forming a continuous band disrupted by veins. Uns gc variation as for nominate form. Male genitalia distinctive: accorded specific status by some authors.

**Flight-period.** Polyvoltine in Canary Islands, recorded in all months, broods partially overlapping: bivoltine or trivoltine in NW Africa and S Europe (April/October), according to altitude.

**Habitat.** Dry, usually rocky, flowery places on calcareous soils.

**Life-history.** LHPs: Tenerife, *Tuberaria guttata*; *Helianthemum nummularium*: Spain and NW Africa, *Helianthemum*; *Erodium*; *Geranium*. Ova laid mainly on upper surface of leaves. Larvae feed on leaves. Larvae are polymorphic: attended by *Lasius* sp.; *Myrmica* sp. Captive larvae accept many species of *Erodium* and *Geranium*.

# *Aricia artaxerxes* Mountain Argus                     Plate 29

**Range.** N Africa, Europe Turkey, eastwards to Altai Mts.

*A. artaxerxes artaxerxes* Fabricius 1793 TL: Scotland.
**Distribution.** Scotland. N England. 0-350m.
**Description and Variation.** In Scotland, upf discoidal spot
invariably white: in N England, this distinctive feature
comprises only about 5-10% of specimens – more usually
black, sometimes faintly ringed white (*salmacis* Stephens);
in Scotland, unh ocelli often reduced to black points, rarely
absent, better developed in *salmacis*, transitional in some
colonies in S Scotland. In all populations, ups orange submarginal spots variable,
often reduced to obscure markings in s1 and s2 uph, rarely absent.
**Flight-period.** Univoltine. Mid June/late July according to locality and season.
**Habitat.** Mostly, sunny south-facing slopes with short grass; usually on limestone but always on calcareous soils. Many habitats occur on coastal cliffs.
**Life-history.** LHP principally *Helianthemum nummularium*; use of *Erodium*
and *Geranium* are suspected alternatives in some localities. On *Helianthemum*,
ova laid on ups surface of leaves, upon which small larvae feed on the lower
cuticle. Hibernates as a small larva amongst leaf litter at base of LHP. Larvae
attended by *Lasius* sp.

*A. artaxerxes allous* Geyer 1837 TL: Alps of Provence.
syn: *inhonora* Jachontov 1909.
**Distribution.** Pyrenees. Alps of central Europe. Sicily (above 2000m). S Germany. S Poland. Czech Republic. Slovakia. Hungary. Baltic countries (very local
and rare). Fennoscandia to 70°N. Republic of Macedonia: Sar Pl. Bulgaria.
Greece. Absent from Tatra and Carpathian Mts. 1400-2200m in S Europe,
progressively lower altitudes north of C Alps, sea-level in S Fennoscandia.
**Description and Variation.** Generally small; ups dark brown; fw apex pointed,
especially in male; ups orange submarginal spots usually confined to hw, often
reduced to obscure patch in anal angle; fringes poorly chequered. Female
markings generally better developed. Development of markings appears to be
clinal, with smaller, darker and poorly marked forms predominating in colder
conditions – higher altitudes and latitudes. The affinity of *A. a. artaxerxes* and *A.
a. allous* is indicated by characters of the former (ups white discoidal spot; uns
reduced ocelli) arising, sporadically, in populations of the latter: such forms
occur in Sweden: forms resembling *salmacis* have been recorded in NW Greece.
**Flight-period.** Univoltine. Early June/Mid August; emergence dependent on
locality.
**Habitat.** Sheltered, flowery slopes, generally with short grass; on calcareous
soils, including base-rich sand dunes in Scandinavia.
**Life-history.** LHPs *Helianthemum nummularium*; *Geranium sanguineum*; *G.
sylvaticum*; *G. asphodeloides*; *G. cinereum subcaulescens*; *Erodium cicutarium*. In
NW Greece, oviposition has been observed on *Potentilla recta*. Ova usually laid
on ups surface of leaves, upon which larvae feed. In some localities, oviposition
on *H. nummularium* is confined largely to plant specimens growing in heavy
shade of other plants, such as *Verbascum*. Hibernates as a small larva amongst
leaf-litter or moss at base of LHP. Larvae attended by *Lasius* sp.

**Note.** Sympatric with *A. agestis* in Lithuania.

*A. artaxerxes montensis* Verity 1928 TL: Andalusia.
syn: *montana* Heyne 1895 (invalid homonym); *nevadensis* Oberthür 1910 (invalid homonym).
**Distribution.** Morocco: Anti-Atlas (scarce); High Atlas; Middle Atlas; 900-2800m. Spain. S France: Massif Central; Vosges; Jura; Basses Alpes. Italy. Sicily. Balkans. S Greece. 1000-2200m.
**Description and Variation.** Generally large; fw pointed; uns gc creamy-grey to light, creamy-brown; orange spots well developed. Forms with upf white markings do not appear to have been reported. In some regions, small specimens may be difficult to distinguish from *A. a. allous*. Balkan and Greek populations, sometimes referred to as *macedonicus* Verity, appear to fall within the range of variation of *A. a. allous*.
**Flight-period.** Univoltine. Late June/September according to altitude and locality.
**Habitat.** Warm, flowery, grassy or rocky places on calcareous soils.
**Life-history.** LHPs *Helianthemum*; *Erodium*.
**Note.** Distributional relationship (geographical/altitudinal) of *A. a. montensis* and *A. a. allous* is not well understood. Generally, *A. a. montensis* frequents warmer and drier terrain at lower altitudes in Mediterranean region: often sympatric and synchronous with *A. agestis*. In N and C Greece, and on Mt. Erimanthos (NW Peloponnesos), populations closely resembling *A. a. allous* occur at 1500m and above: in Taygetos Mts. (S Peloponnesos), *A. a. montensis* occurs from 1000m to at least 1600m. *A. a. montensis* is accorded specific rank by some authors.

## *Aricia morronensis* Spanish Argus                    Plate 29

**Range.** Spain, France (E Pyrenees).

*A. morronensis morronensis* Ribbe 1910 TL: Mt. Morron, S. de Espuña, Murcia.
syn: *idas* Rambur 1840 (invalid homonym); *ramburi* Verity 1929.
**Distribution.** Very sporadic and very local. Spain: S. de Maria; S. de Cazorla; S. de Segura; S. de Espuña; S. de Gredos; S. de Guadarrama; Picos de Europa; S. de Prieta; S. de Andia; Pyrenees (Ordesa). France: E Pyrenees (Col du Tourmalet). 900-2200m.
**Variation.** Size and development of markings variable between populations. Ups black discoidal spot sometimes faintly ringed white; upf apex with some white scaling.
**Flight-period.** Voltinism unconfirmed for all populations: univoltine above 1800m, July/August.
**Habitat.** Sparsely vegetated, sometimes dry, rocky ground.
**Life-history.** LHPs *Erodium cicutarium*; *E. ciconium*; *E. malacoides*. Ova laid on leaves upon which larvae feed. Hibernates as a small larva. Larvae attended by *Lasius niger*; *Crematogaster auberti*; *Tapinoma erraticum*; *T. nigerrimum*.

*A. morronensis ramburi* Verity 1913 TL: Sierra Nevada, Granada.
**Distribution.** Spain: Sierra Nevada, Granada. 2050-3000m.

**Description.** Small; ups gc medium brown; submarginal orange spots absent; upf discoidal spot, small, black; uns gc café-au-laît; unh pale yellow-orange submarginal spots inconspicuous, sometimes absent.

**Flight-period.** Univoltine. Late June/July.

**Habitat.** Exposed, extensively rocky, usually flattish terrain with sparse, low-growing vegetation locally dominated by LHP: on dark-coloured slates (carboniferous schists). Colonies widely dispersed: usually very small.

**Life-history.** LHP *Erodium petraeum crispum* [=*Erodium cheilanthifolium*]. Larvae feed on leaves. Hibernates as a small larva: attended by *Tapinoma* sp.

**Behaviour.** Flight very fast and low. In very hot or windy conditions, shelter usually sought amongst or under small, broken slates: roosts in similar positions. Rapid heating of dark, slaty rock by early morning sun is exploited by both sexes; after basking with fully opened wings, full activity is achieved within 15-20 minutes, even with air (shade) temperature of 9-12°C.

*A. morronensis hesselbarthi* Manley 1970 TL: Abejar, Soria.

**Distribution.** Spain: known only from environs of Abejar, Province of Soria. 950-1100m.

**Description.** Both sexes: large; ups dark brown; uph with orange submarginal spots in anal angle; uns gc darker than nominate form; uns markings well developed.

**Flight-period.** Bivoltine. Late May/June and July/August.

**Habitat.** Flowery meadows.

**Life-history.** LHP *Erodium cicutarium cicutarium* [=*Erodium primulaceum*]. Larvae feed on leaves. Hibernates as a small larva: attended by ants.

**Conservation.** Possibly threatened with extinction from local development and exploitation of habitat for agricultural purposes: a significant proportion of known habitat has been destroyed in recent years.

## *Ultraaricia anteros* Blue Argus                                    Plate 30

**Range.** Balkans, Greece, Turkey, Iran.

*U. anteros* Freyer 1838 TL: Constantinople.

**Distribution.** Croatia: Velebit Mts. SW Serbia: Sinjajevica Pl.; Komovi Pl. Republic of Macedonia: Sar Pl.; Jakupica; Galicica Pl. Albania. S Romania. Bulgaria: Rila Mts.; Rhodope Mts. Greece: widespread, locally common: Vernon Mts.; Varnous Mts.; Voras Mts.; Mt. Orvilos; Rhodope Mts; Phalakron massif; Mt. Pangeon; Mt. Olympus; Grammos massif; Epano Arena; Pindos Mts.; Mt. Chelmos. Records from E Thrace and Taygetos Mts. require confirmation. European Turkey. 550-2000m.

**Description and Variation.** Male upf with small, black discoidal spot; unf basal spot absent in about 30% of individuals. Male ups gc variation appears to relate to density or disposition of blue scales: some specimens are shiny, bright blue, others appearing dull and relatively non-reflective even in fresh condition. First brood, unh gc greyish or buff; subsequent broods, unh gc rich, ochreous-tan, especially female.

**Flight-period.** Voltinism dependent on altitude: possibly univoltine (late June/July) at 2000m: bivoltine or trivoltine (early May/September) at lower altitudes.

**Habitat.** Generally open grassy, flowery places; sometimes bushy places or clearings in light woodland: usually on limestone.

**Life-history.** LHPs *Geranium asphodeloides* or *G. sanguineum* at lower altitudes; *G. macrorrhizum* or *G. cinereum subcaulescens* above 1600m. Ova laid on under-side of basal leaves (cf. *A. artaxerxes*), upon which larvae feed (cf. *E. eumedon*). A third generation is produced consistently from captive rearing of ova obtained from second brood.

## *Pseudaricia nicias* Silvery Argus          Plate 30

**Range.** Pyrenees, Alps of C Europe, Fennoscandia, Russia, W and S Siberia.

*P. nicias nicias* Meigen 1830 TL: Rhetian Alps (Verity 1943). syn: *donzelii* Boisduval 1832.

**Distribution.** Spain: Pyrenees; Pto. de la Bonaigua; Valle de Arán. Andorra. France: Pyrenees; Basses Alps. NW Italy. S and E Switzerland (Valais; Engadine). 1000-2300m.

**Flight-period.** Univoltine. Early July/early September according to altitude.

**Habitat.** Warm, sheltered, often damp places with an abundance of flowers and long grasses: typically, luxuriant meadows/hayfields bordered by wood-land.

**Life-history.** LHPs *Geranium sylvaticum*; *G. pratense*. Ova laid on flowers. Small larvae feed on flowers and developing seeds before hibernation, developing leaves and flower-buds after hibernation. Larvae attended by ants.

*P. nicias scandica* Wahlgren 1930 TL: Sweden.

**Distribution.** Eastern central Sweden from 60°N to 66°N. S Finland except W coast. 0-300m.

**Description.** Male ups brighter pale blue, sometimes with greenish tinge; marginal borders greyer, narrower, well defined.

**Flight-period.** Univoltine. Early July/Mid August.

**Habitat.** Grassy slopes, flowery meadows or large forest clearings with a SW aspect; bushy, low-lying coastal districts, including beaches.

**Life-history.** LHP *Geranium pratense.*

## *Albulina orbitulus* Alpine Blue          Plate 30

**Range.** C European Alps, Norway, S Urals.

*A. orbitulus* de Prunner 1798 TL: Piedmont, N Italy. syn: *pheretes* Hübner 1805.

**Distribution.** Central European Alps of France, Italy, S and E Switzerland and Austria. 1000-2700m. Mountains of Norway and Sweden from 61°N to 64°N. 800-1200m.

**Variation.** Female ups blue basal suffusion variable, some-times extensive, especially on hw.

**Flight-period.** Univoltine. July/August in Alps; June/July in Scandinavia.

**Habitat.** At lower altitudes: flowery, often damp places: at higher altitudes:

exposed, sometimes steep but well-consolidated flowery slopes with short grass; habitats are often small 'islands' amongst screes or extensive rocky outcrops. **Life-history.** LHP *Astragalus alpinus*. Hibernates as a small larva.

## *Agriades glandon* Glandon Blue                                    Plate 30

**Range.** S Spain (Sierra Nevada), Pyrenees, Alps of C Europe, N Fennoscandia, Arctic Asia, Siberia, Arctic Urals, Arctic N America.

*A. glandon glandon* de Prunner 1798 TL: W Alps.
syn: *orbitulus* Esper 1800 (invalid homonym).
**Distribution.** France: Pyrenees; Basses Alpes. Alps of S and E Switzerland, Italy, Germany and Austria. 1800-2700m.
**Variation.** Male ups silvery-blue often diffuse towards margin; upf and uph discoidal spots sometimes small, rarely absent; uns black pupils in white spots sometimes reduced to minute points, occasionally, white spots absent except on costa (*albocellatus* Osthelder); unh orange spots variable, rarely absent: both sexes, ups discoidal spots sometimes ringed white, especially in female.
**Flight-period.** Univoltine. Early July/Late August.
**Habitat.** Rocky ground with short grass, often sparsely vegetated rocky outcrops. Colonies often extremely small, sometimes apparently quite isolated. Often sympatric with *A. orbitulus* at higher altitudes.
**Life-history.** LHP *Vitaliana primuliflora* [=*Androsace vitaliana*] or *Androsace obtusifolia* on acidic substrates; *A. chamaejasme* on acidic or calcareous substrates. Ova laid on various plant parts, including dead leaves. Larvae feed on flowers, developing seeds and leaves. Hibernates as a small larva. Larvae not attended by ants.
**Behaviour.** Males may wander a considerable distant from breeding ground to drink from damp patches. Flight is fast and low. Uses the cover of small stones to shelter from strong winds.

*A. glandon zullichi* Hemming 1933 TL: Sierra Nevada.
syn: *nevadensis* Zullich 1928 (invalid homonym).
**Distribution.** S Spain: confined to Sierra Nevada, Granada. 2500-3000m.
**Description.** Resembles nominate form: male ups silvery pale blue suffusion variable, sometimes extending to outer margin.
**Flight-period.** Univoltine. Late June/August.
**Habitat.** Shallow depressions or small gullies on otherwise exposed, wind-swept and barren greyish-brown soils supporting sparse, low-growing, vegetation dominated by LHP. Colonies mostly widely dispersed and usually extremely small.
**Life-history and Behaviour.** LHP *Vitaliana primuliflora* [=*Androsace vitaliana*]. Development as for nominate form. Even in close proximity to fallen snow and at low air temperatures (diurnal range, +5°C to -10°C), hibernated larvae begin feeding in early spring – activity resulting, apparently, from rapid solar heating of LHP and surrounding soil/rocks. Pupal colouring slightly variable, generally darker than that of nominate from.

*A. glandon aquilo* Boisduval 1832 TL: North Cape.
**Distribution.** Norway: 66°N to North Cape: Nordland; Troms; Finnmark.

Sweden: Lycksele Lappmark; Torne Lappmark (Björkliden; Jieprenjokk). NW Finland: Kilpisjärvi. 50-900m.

**Description.** Resembles nominate form: smaller; male ups pale silvery or greyish-blue; marginal borders narrow; unh white marginal spots confluent, generally lacking ocelli: female upf pale submarginal spots elongate, sometimes with an incomplete series of similar pd markings.

**Flight-period.** Univoltine. Late June/early August, according to season.

**Habitat.** Short, grass turf associated with slate or shale rocks, especially eroded ledges with south-eastern exposure: also relating barren, rocky places, including consolidated areas of steep, screes where vegetation can establish itself.

**Life-history.** LHP *Saxifraga aizoides*; *S. oppositifolia*. Ova laid on underside of leaves. On *S. aizoides*, small larvae feed on flower-buds, but principally on leaves by excavating soft tissue between cuticles. Reputed use of *Astragalus alpinus* requires confirmation: butterfly is known to occur in habitats devoid of this plant, which is also rejected by captive larvae. Hibernates as a small larva.

**Behaviour.** Flies very fast and low, often resting on or between stones. Large numbers may sometimes congregate on flat rocks.

## *Agriades pyrenaicus* Gavarnie Blue — Plate 30

**Range.** N Spain (Picos de Europa and Pyrenees), France (Pyrenees), Balkans, Greece, Turkey, Transcaucasus.

*A. pyrenaicus pyrenaicus* Boisduval 1840 TL: Pyrenees.

**Distribution.** Spain: Gerona (La Molina). France. Hautes-Pyrénées: Gavarnie, Cauterets, Col du Tourmalet. 1800-2200m.

**Variation.** Male ups submarginal white markings subject to slight individual variation, sometimes transitional to *A. p. asturiensis* (below).

**Flight-period.** Univoltine. June/July.

**Habitat.** At lower altitudes, short turf on well consolidated ground: at higher level, south-facing, barren outcrops of limestone rocks or craggy cliff-faces supporting often very isolated LHP specimens on small ledges or in crevices.

**Life-history.** LHP *Androsace villosa*. Hibernated larvae feed on developing leaves and flowers. Larvae not attended by ants.

*A. pyrenaicus asturiensis* Oberthür 1910 TL: Picos de Europa.

**Distribution.** N Spain: Picos de Europa. 1550-2100. Locally common in widely scattered colonies.

**Description.** Resembles nominate form. Male ups brighter, more silvery-blue; submarginal obscure white markings extending to fw in a continuous narrow band broken by veins: female ups slightly paler brown, with obscure whitish striae submarginal white markings disrupted, often obscure; dark discoidal spots usually ringed white.

**Flight-period.** Univoltine. Mid June/early August.

**Habitat and Life-history.** As for nominate form.

*A. pyrenaicus dardanus* Freyer 1844 TL: Turkey [(?) Balkans].

**Distribution.** Bosnia-Herzegovina: Vran Pl.; Cvrsnica. SW Serbia (Monte-

negro): Mt. Durmitor. Republic of Macedonia: Sar Pl.; Jakupica Pl. Bulgaria: Mt. Alibotus. N Greece: Mt. Orvilos (the southernmost extension of Alibotus massif). 1500-2300m.
**Description.** Similar to nominate form. Smaller.
**Flight-period.** Univoltine. June/July.
**Habitat.** Exposed, expansive, grassy slopes on dry calcareous soils.
**Life-history.** LHP *Androsace villosa*. Hibernated larvae feed on developing leaves and flowers.

## *Cyaniris semiargus* Mazarine Blue                    Plate 30

**Range.** Morocco, Europe, Turkey, Middle East, C Asia, N China, Korea.

*C. semiargus semiargus* Rottemburgh 1775 TL: Saxony, Germany.
syn: *acis* Denis and Schiffermüller 1775.
**Distribution.** Morocco: Anti-Atlas; High Atlas 2300-2700m; Middle Atlas 1600m. N Portugal. N and E Spain: Cantabrian Mts.; Pyrenees. S and C Spain: S. de Alfacar; Sierra Nevada; S. de Segura; S. de Espuña; Montes Universales; S. de Guadarrama; S. de la Demanda; province of Soria (Abejar). Pyrenees to N Fennoscandia (rare and local north of Arctic Circle), N Greece and European Turkey. Absent from Peloponnesos and Mediterranean islands except Sicily. Extinct in Britain. 0-2200m.
**Variation.** In Morocco, and occasionally in S Spain, female ups basal areas extensively blue. In NW Greece, female unh often with brown or dark grey spot in anal angle, sometimes replaced by orange. In C Greece, Mt. Timphristos and Mt. Parnassos, nominate form replaced by *parnassia* Staudinger: small; male ups brighter blue; black marginal borders narrower, better defined; unh rarely with orange spot in anal angle: female uph occasionally with one or two orange spots in anal angle, unh orange spotting in anal angle more frequent. A similar form has been reported from Mt. Parnis and Athens basin.
**Flight-period.** Generally univoltine (NW Africa and Europe), early May/early August according to altitude and locality: reportedly bivoltine or trivoltine in Switzerland, May/October.
**Habitat.** Grassy, flowery, often damp places; meadows; hayfields; scrub or woodland clearings.
**Life-history.** LHP *Trifolium pratense*. Confirmation of natural use of other, frequently quoted Fabaceae appears to be lacking: however, in C Greece, opportunistic use of *T. physodes*, growing amongst an abundance of *T. pratense* has been recorded. Ova laid on flowers, upon which larvae feed prior to hibernation. Hibernated larvae feed on developing leaves. Striking similarity of colour/colour-pattern of larva and various plants parts upon which it feeds, rests and hibernates, suggests a close adaptation to *T. pratense*. Larvae attended by *Lasius* sp.

*C. semiargus helena* Staudinger 1862 TL: Mt. Taygetos, S Greece.
**Distribution.** Greece. Restricted to the Peloponnesos: Mt. Panakhaikon; Mt. Chelmos; Mt. Menalon; Mt. Oligirtos; Mt. Taygetos. 650-1800m.
**Variation.** Submarginal orange markings variable, especially in female. In

respect to development of female ups blue suffusion and orange markings, gradation of *C. semiargus* forms in Europe (especially Greece), Turkey and Middle East, is suggestive of a cline: within this range, male genitalia appear to be sensibly constant, chromosome numbers identical.

**Flight-period.** Univoltine. Late April/late June according to altitude.

**Habitat.** Grassy, flowery, often damp places, usually amongst open scrub and scattered trees: LHP usually abundant.

**Life-history.** LHP *Trifolium physodes*. Ova laid amongst flowers. Before hibernation in third instar, larvae feed entirely within the swollen calyces of the developing flowers. Larvae hibernate on underside of stones near LHP and/or ant's nests. Hibernated larvae feed on developing leaves. Usually pupates at the entrance to ant galleries in close proximity to LHPs. Larvae/pupae attended by *Camponotus vagus*; *C. aethiops*. Captive larvae accept many *Trifolium* species: in nature, where density of larvae may be very high, opportunistic use of isolated plants of *T. purpureum*, growing in a carpet of *T. physodes*, has been observed.

**Behaviour.** In calm, warm conditions, adults often assemble in large numbers on grass stems to bask in late afternoon sun.

## *Agrodiaetus iphigenia* Chelmos Blue                    Plate 31

**Range.** S Greece, Turkey, Transcaucasus.

*A. iphigenia nonacriensis* Brown 1977 TL: Mt. Chelmos, Greece.

**Distribution.** Scarce and local. Confined to Mt. Chelmos and environs. 1100-1750m.

**Description.** Female may be readily distinguished from other sympatric *Agrodiaetus* by its dark chocolate brown ups; distinctive white fringes; greyish uns gc; small diffuse, orange-brown submarginal spots in s1a-4: other markings in normal pattern.

**Flight-period.** Univoltine. Mid June/end July, according to season and altitude.

**Habitat.** Mostly dry, open treeless ground, usually with low scrub; always on a calcareous substrate, but not exclusively limestone. Some colonies occur in small clearings amongst tall scrub, or, more rarely, woodland.

**Life-history.** LHP *Onobrychis alba*. Hibernates as small larvae on underside of stones. Larvae attended by *Lasius alienus*.

**Behaviour.** Males occasionally wander considerable distances to visit damp ground. Females rarely leave the confines of their breeding ground. Both sexes bask with partially open wings early morning and late afternoon. Males (?)invariably feed with closed wings.

**Conservation.** Intensive grazing of habitat appears to pose a significant threat. It is evident that much of the LHP owes its survival to the protective, browse-deterring, spiny plants, such as *Astragalus parnassi*, amongst which it is mostly to be found.

## *Agrodiaetus damon* Damon Blue                    Plate 31

**Range.** Spain, S, C and E Europe, Turkey, S and C Urals, Mongolia, Altai.

*A. damon* Denis and Schiffermüeller 1775 TL: Vienna.

LYCAENIDAE

119

**Distribution.** Sporadic, locally common. N and E Spain:
provinces of Cuenca; Teruel; Palencia; Santander; Burgos;
Huesca; Lérida; Gerona; Barcelona. France: C Pyrenees;
Cevennes; Haute-Savoie; Jura Mts. N and central peninsular
Italy. Switzerland. S Germany. Czech Republic. Slovakia.
Hungary. S Poland. Estonia. SE Latvia (a single known
colony). S Croatia. Bosnia-Herzegovina. SW Serbia. Repub-
lic of Macedonia. NW Greece (Grammos massif to Mt.
Timphristos). 1000-2100m.

**Variation.** In Estonia and (?)Latvia, *ultramarina* Schawerda: large; male ups
deeper blue; wing veins prominent. In Montes Universales (Teruel, Spain),
*noguerae* de Sagarra: resembles nominate form closely.

**Flight-period.** Univoltine. Mid July/August.

**Habitat.** At lower altitudes, dry scrub or open woodland: at highest altitudes,
sheltered gullies/hollows on open grassy slopes.

**Life-history.** LHPs *Onobrychis* spp., including *O. montana*; *O. alba*. Hibernated
larvae feed in characteristic and systematic manner on upper cuticle of leaflets
by removing soft tissue between veins. Larvae attended by *Lasius niger*, *L. alienus*; *Formica pratensis*. Hibernates as an ovum or first instar larva in C Europe;
as second instar larva on Mt. Tymphristos, Greece (2000m).

## *Agrodiaetus dolus* Furry Blue

Plate 31

**Range.** SW Europe, Italy.

*A. dolus dolus* Hübner 1823 TL: Maritime Alps (Verity 1943).

**Distribution.** Spain: provinces of Santander; Navarra;
Burgos; Alava; Longono; Huesca; Lérida; Gerona; Barce-
lona. S France: Bouches-du-Rhône; Vacluse; Drôme; Var;
Alpes-de-Haute-Provence; Alpes-Maritimes. NW Italy:
Maritime Alps: very local. 600-1500m.

**Description and Variation.** Male upf brown basal androconial patch with slightly roughened appearance. Unh
white stripe absent or vestigial in both sexes. In Catalonia, *fulgens* de Sagarra:
resembles nominate form closely: slightly larger; male uns gc somewhat greyer:
female ups darker brown. Chromosome number, 123-125: cf. *A. ainsea*, CN=108.

**Flight-period.** Univoltine. Mid July/August.

**Habitat.** Flowery, grassy places amongst scrub; untended margins of cultivated ground.

**Life-history.** LHP *Onobrychis viciifolia*. Ova laid on flowers. Hibernates as a
small larva.

*A. dolus vittatus* Oberthür 1892 TL: Lozère, France.

**Distribution.** S France: Aveyron; Hérault; Gard; Lozère. 500-1000m.

**Description.** Male ups gc whitish or pale bluish grey, basal area with bluish
suffusion; brownish veins well defined: female ups appreciably darker brown
than nominate form.

**Flight-period, Habitat and Life-history.** As for nominate form.

*A. dolus virgilius* Oberthür 1910 TL: Sulmona, Abruzzi.

**Distribution.** Peninsular Italy: from Emilia-Romagna (Bologna) to Calabria

(Monte Pollino) in widely dispersed colonies. 600-1100m.
**Description.** Male ups gc white, narrow marginal border, internally somewhat diffused, especially along veins; upf with pale blue basal suffusion, brown
androconial patch rough: female ups darker brown than nominate form.
**Flight-period, Habitat and Life-history.** As for nominate form.

## *Agrodiaetus ainsae* Forster's Furry Blue          Plate 31

**Range.** N Spain.

*A. ainsae* Forster 1961 TL: Ainsa, N Spain.
**Distribution.** N Spain: Burgos (Villasur; Pto. de Paramo
de Masa; Villanueva de Argaño; Peñahorada; Monasterio de
Rodilla; Sotopalacios; Briviesca; Monasterio de Fresdelva);
Alava (S. de Urbasa); Huesca (Ainsa; S. de la Peña; Jaca).
Locally common. 950-1200m.
**Variation.** Populations in the province of Burgos (*pseudo-
virgilius* de Lesse) differ slightly, in wing markings and size,
from nominate form in Huesca: chromosome numbers identical (CN=108)
(cf. *A. dolus*).
**Flight-period.** Univoltine. July/August.
**Habitat.** Dry, grassy, bushy places; clearings in light deciduous or pine woodland.
**Life-history.** LHP *Onobrychis* (?)*viciifolia*.

## *Agrodiaetus escheri* Escher's Blue          Plate 31

**Range.** Morocco, Europe.

*A. escheri escheri* Hübner 1823 TL: Var, S France (Verity 1943)
syn: *agestor* Godart 1824.
**Distribution.** Spain: Sierra Nevada to Cantabrian Mts. and
Pyrenees: Sporadic, locally common. France (Massif Central;
Bouche du Rhône; Basses Alps). Switzerland (Rhône Valley;
Simplon; Graubunden). N Italy (Ortler Alps; Dolomites).
Records for N Portugal require confirmation. 500-2000m.
**Description.** Male ups black borders very narrow; uph
marginal border vaguely undulate: female ups submarginal orange spots variable,
ranging from 2 or 3 diffuse spots in anal angle hw, to a continuous band hw
and fw: both sexes, unf without cell-spot; all markings bold (cf. *Polyommatus
icarus*).
**Flight-period.** Univoltine. Late May/August according to locality and altitude.
**Habitat.** Flowery, rocky places.
**Life-history.** LHPs: principally, *Astragalus monspessulanus*; also, *A. sempervirens*;
*A. exscapus*; *A. incanus*. Ova laid on underside of leaves. Hibernates as a small
larva. Hibernated larvae feed below plant-crown on developing leaves. Larvae
attended by *Myrmica specioides*; *Formica cinerea*.

*A. escheri splendens* Stefanelli 1904 TL: Florence.
**Distribution.** N Italy: Liguria; Tuscany; Emilia-Romagna to Campania: very
sporadic. 300-1000m.
**Description and Variation.** Generally smaller; male ups paler blue; black
borders slightly wider; uns gc tending to white; uns markings slightly reduced:

female ups submarginal spots well developed. Individual specimens closely resembling or transitional to nominate form reputedly not uncommon.
**Flight-period.** Univoltine. Early June/July.
**Habitat.** Flowery rocky places, usually amongst low scrub.

*A. escheri dalmaticus* Speyer 1882 TL: Dalmatia.
syn: *olympena* Verity 1936.
**Distribution.** SW Croatia. S Bosnia-Herzegovina. SW Serbia. Republic of Macedonia. Bulgaria. Albania. Greece. Reports from Taygetos Mts. require confirmation. 500-1500m.
**Description.** Male ups silvery-blue sometimes with greenish reflections; marginal black borders 1-2mm (cf. nominate form): female ups resembles nominate form: uns markings prominent in both sexes.
**Flight-period.** Univoltine. Mid May/late June.
**Habitat.** Dry, flowery, often rocky places amongst sparse vegetation; damp woodland clearings above 1000m.
**Life-history.** LHPs principally *Astragalus monspessulanus*; also *A. spuneri*. Ova laid on underside of leaves. Hibernates as a larva. Hibernated larvae feed on developing leaves below plant-crown. Larvae attended by *Plagiolepis* sp.

*A. escheri ahmar* Le Cerf 1932 TL: Djebel Ahmar, Morocco.
**Distribution.** Morocco: Anti-Atlas (Dj. Ahmar; no recent reports from Tizin-Tiskine); Middle Atlas (Dj. Bou-Iblane). 1750-2000m. Very local – rarely reported.
**Description.** Resembles nominate form. Smaller; male ups dull blue; female ups submarginal spots yellow. Uns markings less prominent in both sexes.
**Flight-period.** Univoltine. June.
**Habitat.** Flowery slopes.

## *Agrodiaetus amanda* Amanda's Blue					Plate 32

**Range.** N Africa, Spain, Europe, Turkey, W Asia Iran.

*A. amanda amanda* Schneider 1792 TL: S Sweden.
syn: *icarius* Esper (after 1792)
**Distribution.** Spain (Sierra Nevada; Montes Universales; S. de la Demanda; Cantabrain Mts.; Pyrenees) through S France, Italy, C Switzerland and E Germany to S Fennoscandia, Balkans, Greece and European Turkey. Largely absent from coastal districts of Italy: absent from Mediterranean islands except NE Sicily and Lesbos. 100-2000m.

**Variation.** Male ups fuscous borders variable in width. In Scandinavia, female ups often suffused blue (*isias* Frühstorfer).
**Flight-period.** Univoltine. Late May/July according to locality.
**Habitat.** Warm grassy, often damp places containing an abundance of LHP, usually associated with bushes or light woodland; sheltered gullies above tree-line.
**Life-history.** LHPs *Vicia* spp., including *V. c. cracca*; *V. c. stenofolia*; *V. villosa*; *V. onobrychioides*; *V. terasperma*; *V. incana*; *V. sibthorpii*; *V. cassubica*. Ova laid on both surfaces of leaves. Hibernates as a small larva amongst leaf-litter at base of

LHP. Hibernated larvae feed on developing leaves. In NW Greece, larvae attended by *Tapinoma simrothi*; *Lasius alienus*: elsewhere, *L. niger, Myrmica specioides, Formica cinerea*.

*A. amanda abdelaziz* Blachier 1908 TL: Atlas Mts., Morocco.

**Distribution.** Morocco: High Atlas (Oukaïmeden; Dj. Ahmar). Middle Atlas (Azrou). Rif Mts. (Dj. Lakraa; Ketama). Algeria: Djurdjura Mts. 1300-2600m.

**Description.** Male ups paler silvery-blue; uns markings reduced; unh orange spots in anal angle vestigial or absent: female ups brown, sometimes with a few, blue basal scales; yellowish-orange submarginal spots well developed, sometimes forming continuous band on hw and fw; upf sometimes with faint orange, somewhat striated suffusion.

**Variation.** Female ups sometimes extensively suffused blue (*cyanea* Aigner): proportion of brown to blue females seasonally variable, suggesting influence of climatic factors (temperature/humidity) on form: possibly, cooler and/or damper conditions in larval/pupal development favour the blue form (cf. *isias* in Scandinavia).

**Flight-period.** Univoltine. Late May/mid July.

**Habitat.** Flowery, grassy places, especially alpine meadows.

**Life-history.** LHPs *Vicia ononbychioides; V. atlantica*.

## *Agrodiaetus thersites* Chapman's Blue                    Plate 31

**Range.** Morocco, S Europe, Turkey, Middle East, Iran, Caucasus, S Urals, Tian Shan.

*A. thersites* Cantener 1834 TL: Vosges, NE France.

**Distribution.** Morocco: Middle Atlas 1500-2000m. S Portugal. Spain. France (Pyrenees), north-eastwards to 51°N in Germany. E and SE Europe. Absent from Mediterranean islands except Sicily, Samos, Kos and Rhodes. European Turkey. 0-1500m.

**Description and Variation.** Male upf androconial patch conspicuous at oblique angles. Spring brood: both sexes, unh gc grey: female ups blue suffusion often extending to outer margins. Summer brood: both sexes unh sandy-brown; female ups brown; unf yellowish-grey. Both sexes, unf without cell-spot (cf. *Polyommatus icarus*).

**Habitat.** Warm dry, rocky, bushy places; grassy clearings in scrubland; meadows; areas of neglected cultivation.

**Flight-period.** Bivoltine. April/June and June/August: emergence of summer brood possibly depending on weather conditions (see below).

**Life-history.** LHPs *Onobrychis caput-galli; O. viciifolia; O. peduncularis* (Morocco). Ova laid on leaves. Larva feeds on leaf cuticles, leaving major veins intact. In drier habitats where *O. caput-galli*, an annual, is the only *Onobrychis* sp. available, aestivation as an ovum or undeveloped larva is possibly required pending germination of LHP seeds arising from spring flowering. In Greece, females of first brood (April) have been observed to oviposit freely on *O. caput-galli*, whilst, in the same habitat, ova of the second brood (June) are laid on dried grass stems, in total absence of LHPs – except the distinctive seeds of *O. caput-galli*. In absence of alternative LHPs, observed variance in flight-time of summer brood may relate to absence of rain required for seed germination. Hibernates as small larva. Larvae attended by *Lasius alienus*; *Myrmica scabrinodis*; *Tapinoma erraticum*.

## *Agrodiaetus admetus* Anomalous Blue               Plate 32

**Range.** Central E and SE Europe, Turkey.

*A. admetus* Esper 1785 TL: Hungary.
**Distribution.** Hungary. Croatia. W Bosnia-Herzegovina. SW Serbia. W Republic of Macedonia. Albania. Bulgaria. Greece. European Turkey. Sporadic, locally common. 50-1500m.
**Description.** Male unh white stripe poorly developed; female uns marginal and submarginal markings prominent, white chevron along v4 often reduced or absent.
**Flight-period.** Univoltine. Mid June/July.
**Habitat.** Hot dry, grassy, flowery scrubland.
**Life-history.** LHPs *Onobrychis viciifolia*; *O. caput-galli*. Oviposition observed on flowers of both plant species, by same female in same habitat. Larvae attended by *Camponotus gestroi*; *Crematogaster sordidula*; *C. sordidula* var. *mayri*. Hibernates under stones as a small larva.

## *Agrodiaetus fabressei* Oberthür's Anomalous Blue         Plate 32

**Range.** Spain.

*A. fabressei* Oberthür 1910 TL: Albarracin, C Spain.
**Distribution.** N and E Spain: provinces of Teruel (S. de Albarracin), Cuenca (Serrania de Cuenca), Soria (Abejar) and Burgos (Peñahorada; Sotopalacios). 900-1500m.
**Description.** Male unh without white stripe along v4: female unh small white chevron sometimes present on v4. Both sexes: uns marginal and submarginal markings vestigial or absent.
**Flight-period.** Univoltine. Late June/August.
**Habitat.** Rocky gullies with scrub; dry grassy slopes.
**Life-history.** LHP *Onobrychis viciifolia*; Ova laid on flowers. Hibernates as a small larva. Larvae attended by ants.

## *Agrodiaetus agenjoi* Agenjo's Anomalous Blue            Plate 32

**Range.** NE Spain.

*A. agenjoi* Forster 1965 TL: Spain (Catalonia).
**Distribution.** NE Spain: provinces of Gerona, Barcelona and Lérida. 700-1500.
**Description.** Resembles *A. fabressei* closely. Male ups dark brown; unh without white stripe along v4.
**Flight-period.** Univoltine. July/August.
**Habitat.** As for *A. fabressei*.
**Note.** Taxonomic status uncertain: perhaps better regarded a local variant of *A. fabressei*.

## *Agrodiaetus humedasae* Piedmont Anomalous Blue    Plate 32

**Range.** N Italy.

*A. humedasae* Toso and Balleto 1979 TL: Cogne, N Italy.
**Distribution.** NW Italy: known only from Valle d'Aosta (Cogne Valley). 800-950m.
**Description.** Male uns gc pale creamy-brown, somewhat darker than *A. violetae* (below); unh without white stripe.
**Flight-period.** Univoltine. Mid July/August.
**Habitat.** Flowery slopes amongst scrub and small trees.
**Life-history.** LHP *Onobrychis viciifolia*. Ova laid on flowers, upon which larvae feed. Hibernates as a small larva. Hibernated larvae attended by ants.
**Conservation.** Known habitat very restricted and in close proximity to human habitation and areas of cultivation.

## *Agrodiaetus violetae* Andalusian Anomalous Blue    Plate 33

**Range.** S Spain.

*A. violetae* Gomez Bustillo and Borrego 1979 TL: Sierra de Almijara, Andalusia.
**Distribution.** S Spain: Málaga (S. de Tejeda); Granada (S. de Almijara; S. de La Losa); Jaen (S. de Segura; S. de Cazorla); Albacete (S. de Alcaraz). 1200-1750m.
**Description.** Resembles *A. ripartii* closely. Male uns gc pale creamy-brown (less grey than *A. ripartii*); unh white stripe prominent.
**Flight-period.** Univoltine. Late June/early August.
**Habitat.** Grassy, flowery places.
**Life-history.** LHPs *Onobrychis viciifolia*; *O. peduncularis*. Ova laid on flowers, upon which larvae feed. Hibernates as a small larva. Hibernated larvae attended by *Camponotus piceus*.
**Note.** Taxonomic status uncertain: possibly conspecific with *A. ripartii*.

## *Agrodiaetus aroaniensis* Grecian Anomalous Blue    Plate 32

**Range.** Greece.

*A. aroaniensis* Brown 1976 TL: Mt. Chelmos, Greece.
**Distribution.** Greece: Phalakron massif; Vernon Mts.; Smolikas massif; Mt. Timphristos; Parnassos massif; Panakhaikon Mts.; Chelmos massif; Menalon Mts; Taygetos Mts. Widespread but generally very local. 800-1550m.
**Description.** Uns gc distinctive, uniform yellowish-grey; unh lacking white stripe on v4.
**Flight-period.** Univoltine. July/early August.
**Habitat.** Dry bushy or rocky places; sometimes in light woodland.
**Life-history.** LHP *Onobrychis arenaria*. Ova laid on flowers upon which larvae feed. Larvae attended by *Camponotus gestroi*; *Crematogaster sordidula* var. *mayri*. Hibernates as a small larva.

## *Agrodiaetus ripartii* Ripart's Anomalous Blue    Plate 33

**Range.** Spain, S and SE Europe, Poland, Turkey, S Ural, S Siberia, Tian Shan, Altai.

*A. ripartii* Freyer 1830 TL: Spain.

**Distribution.** N and E Spain: Cuenca; Teruel (Montes Universales); Segovia; Logrono; Burgos (Peñahorada; Sotopalacios); Huesca (S. de la Peña; Jaca; Ainsa; Toila). France: Var; Alpes-Maritimes; Vacluse; Alpes-de-Haute-Provençe; Ardèche; Drôme; Hautes-Alpes. NW Italy: Maritimes Alps: very local. S Poland. Republic of Macedonia. Bulgaria. Albania. Greece. European Turkey. 50-1800m.

**Description.** Unh white stripe along v4 prominent.

**Variation.** In Greece, *pelopi* Brown: unh white stripe often narrower, less conspicuous.

**Flight-period.** Univoltine. Late June/early August.

**Habitat.** Dry bushy places, often grassy; sometimes in light woodland.

**Life-history.** LHPs *Onobrychis viciifolia*; *O. arenaria*; *O. saxatilis*; *O. alba*; *O. montana*. Ova laid on flowers upon which larvae feed. In Greece, larvae attended by *Crematogaster sordidula*; *C. sordidula* var. *mayri*; *Camponotus gestroi*; *Lasius alienus*. Hibernates as a small larva.

## *Agrodiaetus nephohiptamenos* Higgins' Anomalous Blue   Plate 33

**Range.** N Greece, Bulgaria.

*A. nephohiptamenos* Brown and Coutsis 1978 TL: NE Greece.

**Distribution.** N Greece: Mt. Pangeon; Mt. Phalakron; Mt. Orvilos. Bulgaria: Mt. Alibotush (the northerly extension of Mt. Orvilos in Greece). 1500-2000m.

**Description.** Male hw fringes conspicuously white.

**Flight-period.** Univoltine. Mid July/late August: emergence time very dependent upon local weather conditions.

**Habitat.** Open grassy, flowery slopes above tree-line on limestone.

**Life-history.** LHP *Onobrychis montana scardica* – a distinctive ssp. confined to Balkan peninsula. This plant has not been noted below the lower altitude limit of the butterfly: biotopes do not appear to contain other *Onobrychis* species. Hibernates as a small larva. Hibernated larvae feed on leaves at base of LHP. Larvae attended by ants.

**Behaviour.** Whilst *A. nephohiptamenos* is essentially an allopatric member of its group, males have been recorded drinking on damp ground in company with *A. admetus*, *A. pelopi* and *A. aroaniensis* at lower limit of altitudinal range.

## *Agrodiaetus galloi* Gallo's Anomalous Blue    Plate 33

**Range.** S Italy.

*A. galloi* Bolleto and Toso 1979 TL: Monte Pollino, Reggio Calabria.

**Distribution.** S Italy: Reggio Calabria; Mt. Pollino, Piano de Ruggio, Serra del Prete, Vallone di Malvento, Campo Tenese, Orsomarso Mts. (Piano di

Campolungo). 1100-2200m, most abundant at 1750-1900m.
**Description.** Male ups gc chestnut brown with olive tones;
fringes brown; upf sex-brand conspicuous; uns gc sandy-
brown; antemarginal markings vestigial, obscure; fringes
cream-white; unh white stripe on v4 conspicuous: female
ups gc slightly browner, tinged reddish; fw less pointed; uns
black spots conspicuously ringed white; ups and uns fringes
creamy-white.

**Flight-period.** Univoltine. July/August.
**Habitat.** Grassy slopes; beechwood clearings; screes at highest altitudes.

## *Neolysandra coelestina* Pontic Blue         Plate 34

**Range.** S Greece, Turkey, S Urals.

*N. coelestina hera* Eckweiler and Schurian 1980 TL: Mt.
Chelmos, S Greece.
**Distribution.** S Greece: Aroánian Mts. (Chelmos massif)
and mountains to NW of Kalavrita. 700-1800m.
**Variation.** Male unh sometimes with pale orange spots in
s1-3: female ups rarely with blue basal suffusion.
**Flight-period.** Univoltine. Late May/mid June. At upper

limit of altitudinal range, fresh specimens occur sporadically
early/mid July .
**Habitat.** Woodland clearings at lower altitudes; open grassy gullies; sheltered
hollows above the tree-line; screes: on calcareous substrates.
**Life-history.** LHP *Vicia cracca stenophylla* [= *Vicia dalmatica*]: other *Vicia* sp.,
present in some habitats, do not appear to be exploited. Ova laid on stems and
stipules. Captive larvae accept many *Vicia* sp., but neither flowers nor leaves of
*Anthyllis vulneraria*. In S England, larvae hibernated in second instar from late
August to mid March. Habitat and LHP often shared with *A. amanda*.

## *Plebicula dorylas* Turquoise Blue         Plate 34

**Range.** S and C Europe, Turkey, Transcaucasus.

*P. dorylas* Denis and Schiffermüler 1775 TL: Vienna.
syn: *argester* Bergsträsser 1779; *hylas* Esper 1793 (invalid
homonym)
**Distribution.** N and C Spain (Montes Universales, S. de
la Demanda, Cantabrian Mts., Pyrenees). NW Pyrenees to
S Sweden (including Öland and Gotland) and Lithuania
(very rare and local). E Europe, Balkans and Greece.
Probably extinct in Latvia. Records from Sicily require
confirmation. Records for Corfu, Tenos and Syra probably arise from
nomenclatural confusion. 75-2300m.
**Description and Variation.** In C Spain, males ups gc and wing shape varies
appreciably: female ups sometimes with blue basal flush; wing bases always
with a few blue scales (cf. female *P. nivescens*).
**Flight-period.** Bivoltine at lower altitudes, May/June and late July/August;
univoltine at high altitude, late June/August.

**Habitat.** Grassy, flowery places, usually amongst scrub at lower altitudes; sheltered hollows on open grassy slopes on high mountains: on calcareous soils.
**Life-history.** LHP *Anthyllis vulneraria*. Ova laid on leaves, upon which larvae feed. Hibernates as a small larva beneath the crown of LHP: post-hibernated larvae feed below crown of plant exclusively on the leaves. Larvae attended by *Lasius alienus*; *Myrmica scabrinodis*; *Formica cinerea*.
**Note.** Although *C. minimus* shares *Anthyllis vulneraria* with *P. dorylas* in most habitats in S Europe, competitive feeding is avoided by the exploitation of different plant components – *C. minimus* feeds exclusively on seeds (captive larvae accept leaves if offered no alternative).

## *Plebicula golgus* Nevada Blue                Plate 34

**Range.** S Spain.

*P. golgus golgus* Hübner 1813 TL: Sierra Nevada, S Spain.
**Distribution.** S Spain: confined to Sierra Nevada. 2400-3000m. Locally abundant.
**Flight-period.** Univoltine. Late June/Late July.
**Habitat.** Exposed slopes, with low-growing, often with very sparse vegetation on greyish/brownish substrate, often strewn with dark, slaty rock – carboniferous schists.
**Life-history.** LHP *Anthyllis vulneraria arundana*. Ova laid singly on either leaf-surface near midrib. Larvae hibernate beneath crown of LHP. Larvae attended by *Tapinoma nigerrimum*.
**Note.** At peak emergence, both sexes observed in roughly equal abundance (cf. *P. dorylas*; *P. nivescens*; *P. atlantica*).

*P. golgus sagratrox* Aistleitner 1984 TL: Sierra de la Sagra, S Spain.
**Distribution.** S Spain: S. de la Sagra (Province of Granada). 1900-2350m. Locally abundant.
**Description.** Both sexes readily distinguishable from nominate form by overall brighter appearance. Male ups paler blue; uns gc white: female ups paler brown; ups often with orange submarginal spots, better developed on uph; uph often with blue scales at wing-base and along veins; uns gc paler, tending to white. Male genitalia as for nominate form (See Note 1).
**Flight-period.** Univoltine. Late June/late July.
**Habitat.** Steep, dry slopes with sparse, low-growing vegetation on limestone.
**Life-history.** LHP *Anthyllis vulneraria arundana*. Ova laid singly on either leaf-surface near midrib. Limited observations indicate that larvae feed exclusively on leaves in nature: captive larvae readily accept leaves and flowers of several varieties/subspecies of *A. vulneraria* other (undetermined) *Anthyllis* spp. Hibernates as a small larva beneath crown of LHP. Larvae attended by *Lasius niger.*
**Note 1.** Taxon erected at species level on basis of geographical isolation and phenotypic distinction from *P. g. golgus*: however, specific separation remains unsubstantiated. That geographical/ecological isolation of a species does not guarantee evolutionary divergence is exemplified by the taxonomic inseparability of respective LHPs. The principal superficial difference in the two taxa (colour tone) may be attributed to widely differing geological character (slate

grey-brown in the case of nominate form, white limestone in the case of *sagratrox*) of the terrain in which each form needs to survive and to which, therefore, each may be expected to adapt. Equivalent adaptation to geological substrate coloration is apparent for many European butterflies.

**Note 2.** As for nominate form, both sexes observed in roughly equal abundance at peak emergence (cf. *P. dorylas*; *P. nivescens*; *P. atlantica*).

## *Plebicula nivescens* Mother-of-pearl Blue          Plate 34

**Range.** Spain.

*P. nivescens* Keferstein 1851 TL: Sierra de Alfacar, Granada. **Distribution.** SW Spain to S Cantabrian Mts. and S Pyrenees. Widespread, generally very local. 1000-1900m. **Flight-period.** Univoltine. Late May/early August in prolonged emergence. **Habitat.** Hot, dry, limestone rocks, usually amongst scrub. **Life-history.** LHP *Anthyllis vulneraria*. Ova laid on either leaf-surface near midrib; a small leaf on a small plant is most often selected. Small larvae hibernate beneath crown of LHP. Larvae attended by *Tapinoma nigerrimum*.

**Note.** Females generally not commonly observed (cf. *P. dorylas*; *P. golgus*; *P. atlantica*).

## *Plebicula atlantica* Atlas Blue          Plate 34

**Range.** Morocco, Algeria.

*P. atlantica* Elwes 1905 TL: High Atlas, Morocco. **Distribution.** Widespread, generally very local. Morocco: High Atlas (1700-2700m); Middle Atlas (Tizi-n-Taghzeft; Col du Zad; Dj. bou Iblane; 1300-2100m); W Rif Mts. (Dj. Lakraa; Dj. Tissouka; Ketama; 1300-2100m). Algeria (Aures Mts.; Djurdjura Mts.; 1700-2500m). **Variation.** Male uph black submarginal spots sometimes with proximal pinkish-orange scales (*rosea* Tennent). In all populations, female ups submarginal orange markings sometimes forming a wide band with proximal ray-like projections extending to fw cell. In Middle Atlas and W Rif Mts., *weissi* Dujardin: generally smaller; female upf submarginal orange spots reduced, with those in s6-8 sometimes absent. In Algeria, *barraguei* Dujardin: male ups white marginal markings better developed; uns orange spots and unh discal and pd markings reduced or absent; female uph blue basal scaling usually well developed. **Flight-period.** Bivoltine. Late May/July and August/September. **Habitat.** Flowery places; dry, stony slopes with scrub. **Life-history.** LHP *Anthyllis vulneraria*: reputed use of *Vicia tenuifolia* requires confirmation. Ova laid singly near midrib on upperside of leaf.

**Note 1.** Females generally very uncommon (cf. *P. dorylas*; *P. nivescens*).

## *Meleageria daphnis* Meleager's Blue                Plate 34

**Range.** S Europe, Turkey, Lebanon, Syria, Iran, Trans-caucasus, S Urals.

*M. daphnis* Denis and Schiffermüller 1775 TL: Vienna. syn: *meleager* Esper 1779.

**Distribution.** Spain: very local and uncommon: province of Madrid; Burgos; Cuenca and Teruel (Montes Universales); Logrono (S. de la Demanda); foothills of Pyrenees (Huesca to Gerona). S France: Pyrénées-Orientales to Massif Central, Savoie and Alpes-Maritimes. Switzerland: Valais (Rhône Valley); NE Engadine. Italy. Sicily. S Germany (Tauberland; Baulandes) through S Poland to Balkans, European Turkey and Greece (widespread, locally common), including SE Aegean island of Simi. 200-1700m.

**Variation.** Female f. *steeveni* Treitschkes: ups gc greyish-brown; markings outlined with whitish or greyish suffusion, sometimes extending along veins: (?) exclusive form in Spain: intermediate forms occur in N and C Greece: in S Greece, f. *steeveni* (often with ups white scaling reduced) predominant.

**Flight-period.** Univoltine. Mid June/August according to locality.

**Habitat.** Grassy or bushy places, usually on limestone/base-rich substrates.

**Life-history.** LHP *Coronilla varia*. Ova laid on leaves upon which larvae feed. In hot, dry situations, plants heavily shaded by rocks or bushes are usually preferred for oviposition. Hibernates as an ovum or small larva: attended by *Lasius alienus*; *Formica pratensis*; *Tapinoma erraticum*.

## *Lysandra coridon* Chalk-hill Blue                Plate 35

**Range.** Europe, Ukraine, S Urals.

From Spain to Bulgaria, chromosome numbers (CN=87-92) appear to be roughly clinal, with higher counts predominating in E Europe. It should perhaps be mentioned that a narrow range of variance in chromosome number is not indicative of speciation: experiment demonstrates that cross-pairing of individuals from populations having slightly different chromosome number occurs easily and produces viable offspring: the process of fertilization (fusion of gamete cells – ovum and sperm) involves pairing of chromosomal elements, with functional exclusion of supernumerate components. Although it would appear that some genetic information is necessarily lost in this process, chromosomal pairing during fertilization is probably not – if at all – entirely random, suggesting that such loss as occurs, is selective and of little or no material consequence – indeed, a possibility implied by the viability of progeny. For many species, including our own, it is known that many genes carried on chromosomes are essentially redundant, persisting only as a legacy of evolutionary history.

Spanish races of *L. coridon* present a complex distributional and taxonomic problem. Theoretically, the problem may, at least in part, relate to the sympatric occurrence of the allied taxon, *L. albicans*, itself subject to considerable local/regional variation. That the two species share the same LHP in many habitats and, in the larval stage, may even compete for the same species of attending ant, represents, in effect, mutual ecological pressure which, so it may be surmised, has induced adaptive responses from both species. In some habitats, further complication may arise from the presence of *L. hispania*. Such influences, if applicable, are almost exclusive to Spain where the greatest range of phenotypic variation in *L. coridon* is to be found. In the limiting case, adaptation may lead to speciation and, indeed, some Spanish *Lysandra* taxa described here below species level are accorded specific rank by some authors. However, whilst many taxonomically relevant questions remain unanswered, the following provisional assignments are considered appropriate pending acquisition of definitive biological data.

*L. coridon coridon* Poda 1761 TL: Graz, Austria.
**Distribution.** From N Spain (Pyrenees: very local on southern slopes: 1200-2000m), eastwards through most of Europe, including S England, to Lithuania, Balkans and Greece. Absent from Fennoscandia, S Peloponnesos and Mediterranean islands. A record for European Turkey requires confirmation. 100-2000m.
**Variation.** Male ups gc locally/regionally variable. In Julian Alps: male ups distinctly bluer than nominate form, and without yellowish reflections. In Greece, *graeca* Rühl: male ups duller, greyish-blue with yellowish reflections: a similar form occurs in Apennines. Uns gc colour and development of markings also varies geographically, with paler and less well-marked forms predominant in Mediterranean regions. Female ups with various degrees of blue suffusion are very rare in most populations but frequent in others: in f. *syngrapha* Keferstein, ups heavy blue suffusion extends to submargin: a dominant form in some localities in SW France.
**Flight-period.** Univoltine. Late June/early October according to altitude and locality. Univoltine in most of Slovakia (late June/early August), consistently bivoltine (May/June and August/September) in one small area – details lacking.
**Habitat.** Dry, bushy, flowery places, usually associated with short grass: restricted to calcareous soils.
**Life-history.** LHP *Hippocrepis comosa*. Ova laid on leaves of LHP and other substrates, including dead grass-stems and stones. In N and C Europe, hibernates as an ovum: in Greece, as a second instar larva on underside of a stone covering an entrance to an ant's gallery. Larvae attended by *Lasius niger*; *L. alienus*; *L. flavus*; *L. (?) fuliginosus*; *Plagiolepis vindobonensis*; *Formica rufa*; *Myrmica scabrinodis*; *M. sabuleti*; *M. schencki*; *Tetramorium caespitum*.
**Note 1.** Males which appear to be hybrids of *L. coridon* and *L. bellargus* (f. *polonus* Zeller), appear regularly and not uncommonly on Mt. Chelmos, Peloponnesos: rare elsewhere in Europe.

*L. coridon caelestissima* Verity 1921 TL: C Spain, Albarracin.
**Distribution.** E Spain: provinces of Teruel and Cuenca (Montes Universales). Locally abundant. 1050-1800m.
**Description and Variation.** Male ups gleaming sky-blue: female ups usually brown, very rarely silvery sky-blue (f. *deliciosa* de Sagarra – cf. *L. c. coridon* f. *syngrapha*): both sexes, variation in ups and uns markings, including that relating to common aberrations, parallels that of nominate form.
**Flight-period.** Univoltine. July/August.
**Habitat.** Sheltered slopes/gullies/hollows in pinewood clearings on short grassy turf: restricted to limestone/calcareous substrates of Montes Universales.

(Reported occurrence on exclusively non-calcareous substrates is untenable: upper strata of Montes Universales consists almost exclusively of limestone; at lowest altitudinal range, soils of non-calcareous rocks are base-rich in consequence of ground-water alkalinity – run-off from higher levels).

**Life-history.** LHP *Hippocrepis comosa*. Ova laid on leaves. In captivity, hibernates as an ovum or unfed larva.

**Note.** Males with very pale blue ups, f. *caerulescens* Tutt, are presumed to be hybrids of *L. c. caelestissima* and *L. albicans arragonensis*. Overlap in altitudinal range of these taxa is apparently quite limited; *L. a. arragonensis* appears to be very local and sporadic above 1400m.

*L. coridon asturiensis* de Sagarra 1924 TL: Puerto de Pajares (Cantabrian Mts.)
**Distribution.** N Spain: provinces of Oviedo; Leon; Palencia; Santander; Burgos; Logrono; Alava; Guipúzcoa; Vitoria; Huesca. Locally abundant. 600-1950m.

**Description and Variation.** Male ups gc shiny, silvery-blue, lacking yellowish reflections – blue shade locally/regionally variable: size, regionally variable: female indistinguishable from nominate form or pale silvery-blue (f. *syngraphoides* de Sagarra – cf. *L. c. coridon* f. *syngrapha*); proportion of blue females regionally variable:- Pto. de Pajares (Oviedo), 50%; Picos de Europa (Leon and Santander), 0%: Huesca 80-95%. In Huesca (S. de la Peña and environs of Jaca), f. *manleyi* de Lesse: resembles nominate ssp. closely: both sexes slightly larger: male ups gc slightly paler blue; upf dark marginal border wide: female f. *syngraphoides* closely similar to that of nominate ssp. Near Peñahorada (Burgos), f. *burgalesa* Agenjo: males averagely very small; upf dark marginal border wide: female, normal size; ups gc brown in (?)all specimens.

**Flight-period.** Univoltine. July/August.

**Habitat.** As for nominate form: restricted to calcareous soils. (Reported presumed occurrence on acidic, 'red' soils is probably erroneous: in consequence of a high iron content, limestone soils are often red: LHP not (?) known on acidic soils).

**Life-history.** LHP *Hippocrepis comosa*. Ova laid on leaves. In captivity, hibernates as an ovum or unfed larva.

**Note.** Males with pale blue ups, reported from Burgos, are presumed to be hybrids of *L. c. asturiensis* and *L. albicans arragonensis*.

*L. coridon gennargenti* Leigheb 1987 TL: Barbagia Seulo [Sardinia]
**Distribution.** Sardinia. Very local and uncommon. 800-1300m.
**Description.** Male ups gc shiny, pale blue, without yellowish reflections (cf. nominate form): female ups light blue (cf. *L. c. coridon* f. *syngrapha*, *L. c. asturiensis* f. *syngraphoides* and *L. c. caelestissima* f. *deliciosa*): both sexes, uns as for nominate form.

**Flight-period.** Univoltine. July/August.

**Habitat.** As for nominate form: restricted to calcareous soils.

**Note.** Recent DNA studies indicate significant genetic departure from nominate form.

*L. coridon nufrellensis* Schurian 1977 TL: Mufrella Hauptkamm [Corsica]
**Distribution.** Corsica: apparently known only from type-locality. 1900-2200m.
**Description.** Resembles nominate form.

**Flight-period.** Available data very limited: presumed to be univoltine: type-series acquired 23-27th July 1975.

**Note.** Disparity in spelling of taxon and toponym is a *lapsus calami*.

## *Lysandra philippi* Macedonian Chalk-hill Blue        Plate 35

**Range.** N Greece.

*L. philippi* Brown and Coutsis 1978 TL: mountains of NE Greece.

**Distribution.** N Greece: Mt. Pangeon; Mt. Phalakron. 600-1900m.

**Description and Variation.** Resembles *L. coridon* closely: differentiated by much lower chromosome number (CN=20-26, *L. coridon*, CN=84-92). Male ups pale silvery-blue, lacking yellowish reflections: female resembles *L. coridon*. On Mt. Pangeon, female ups with extensive blue suffusion in about 50% of specimens: equivalent forms not reported from Mt. Phalakron. Male ups gc very rarely pale, sky-blue, intermediate between *L. philippi* and *L. bellargus* suggesting possible hybridization.

**Flight-period.** Univoltine. Early July/August.

**Habitat.** Dry, open scrub at lower altitude; grassy slopes at higher levels: always on limestone.

**Life-history.** LHP *Hippocrepis comosa*. Ova laid on leaves. Hibernates as a second instar larva on underside of a stone covering an entrance to an ant's gallery. Larvae attended by ants.

## *Lysandra hispana* Provençe Chalk-hill Blue        Plate 35

**Range.** E Spain, SE France, N Italy.

*L. hispana* Herrich-Schäffer 1852 TL: Spain
syn: *rezneciki* Bartel 1905

**Distribution.** Spain: Jaén; Granada; Albacete; Murcia; Alicante; Valencia; Castellon; Tarragona; Barcelona; Gerona; Lérida; Huesca; Navarra. France: Pyrénées-Orientales; Aude; Hérault; Ardèche; Drôme; Basses Alpes; Var; Alpes-Maritimes. Italy: Liguria; N Tuscany. 400-1000m.

**Description.** Male ups somewhat dull, bluish-grey with silvery-yellowish reflections; unh somewhat darker and greyer than *L. coridon*, with which it flies in most localities in the second brood. Female indistinguishable from *L. coridon*.

**Flight-period.** Bivoltine. Mid April/late May and August/early October.

**Habitat.** Dry flowery, usually grassy places, often amongst scrub: on calcareous soils.

**Life-history.** LHP *Hippocrepis comosa*; (?)*Anthyllis gerardi*. Ova laid on leaves. Larvae attended by *Plagiolepis pygmaea*; *Crematogaster sordidula*.

**Note.** Hybridizes with *L. bellargus*.

## *Lysandra albicans* Spanish Chalk-hill Blue                     Plate 35

**Range.** Morocco, Spain.

*L. albicans* Herrich-Schäffer 1851 TL: Spain.

**Distribution.** Morocco: Middle Atlas (Boulemane; Dj. bou Iblane; 900-1700m); W Rif Mts. (Dj. Bouhalla; Dj. Lakraa; 1300-1800m). Spain, except Cantabrian Mts., western provinces, Catalonia and eastern coastal districts. 500-1500m.

**Variation.** Several races have been described to account for local/regional variation. Individual variation in some colonies is often appreciable. In Middle Atlas Mts., *berber* Le Cerf: small; male ups pale greyish-blue, marginal borders well defined. In W Rif Mts., *dujardini* Barragué: resembles *berber* closely: both sexes, markings reduced; male unf discal and basal spots often absent. In S Spain: large; male ups generally very pale, almost white. In E and N Spain, *arragonensis* Gerhard: both very variable in all wing-characters: male ups gc silvery blue-grey; upf border variable in width and colour – very pale grey to black: forms transitional to nominate form occur between Sierra Nevada and Montes Universales. In provinces of Madrid and Toledo, *bolivari* Romei: male ups gc almost white; submarginal markings usually well defined. In Spain, variation appears to be roughly clinal, with larger, paler forms with reduced uns markings predominating in the south. Taxa *arragonensis* and *bolivari* accorded specific rank by some authors: chromosome number of *arragonensis* (Estepar, province of Burgos) and nominate form 82.

**Flight-period.** Univoltine. Mid June/August according to locality.

**Habitat.** Dry rocky places, often with sparse vegetation.

**Life-history.** LHP *Hippocrepis comosa*; (?)*H. multisilquosa*. Ova laid on upper-side of leaves. Larvae attended by ants.

## *Lysandra bellargus* Adonis Blue                     Plate 36

**Range.** Europe, Turkey, Iraq, Iran, Caucasus, Transcaucasus.

*L. bellargus* Rottemburg 1775 TL: W Germany.
syn: *adonis* Denis and Schiffermüller 1775.

**Distribution.** Most of Europe from Mediterranean coast, European Turkey to S England and Lithuania. Absent from N Belgium, Holland, N Germany, S peninsular Italy, S Peloponnesos and Mediterranean islands except Mallorca. Extinct in Latvia. 100-2000m. A solitary record for NW Africa (Dj. Lakraa, Rif Mts.), merits investigation.

**Variation.** Male ups gc somewhat variable, sometimes with greenish reflections; upf rarely with a few black submarginal spots; uph very rarely with orange spots in anal angle: females ups blue suffusion, sometimes extending to outer margins (*ceronus* Esper) – frequent in some localities in C Spain; uph sub-marginal orange spots variable, sometimes in a complete series on hw and fw. In both sexes, larger and more boldly marked forms are commoner in S Europe.

**Flight-period.** Bivoltine. Mid May/June and late July/mid September. Reputedly univoltine on Mt. Chelmos and elsewhere S Greece.

**Habitat.** Generally dry grassy places, often amongst scrub: on calcareous soils.

**Life-history.** LHPs *Hippocrepis comosa*; *Coronilla varia*: in Greece, both LHPs are exploited, but not, apparently, in the same habitat. Ova laid on leaves. Hibernates as a small larva. Larvae attended by *Lasius alienus*; *L. niger*; *Plagiolepis pygmaea*; *Myrmica sabuleti*; *M. scabrinodis*; *Tapincma erraticum*. Often pupates under a stone or amongst leaf-litter/moss at an entrance to an ant's nest.

**Note.** Known to hybridize with *L. coridon* (*polonus* Zeller): such specimens have intermediate but variable chromosome numbers: cf. *L. c. coridon*. Hybridizes with *L. hispana*. Pale blue male *Lysandra* specimens occur in circumstances suggesting hybridization of *L. bellargus* and *L. philippi*. Hybrids with *L. albicans* appear to be unknown.

## *Lysandra punctifera* Spotted Adonis Blue          Plate 36

**Range.** Morocco, Algeria, Tunisia.

*L. punctifera* Oberthür 1876 TL: Lambessa, Algeria.
**Distribution.** Widespread, locally common. Morocco. Algeria. Tunisia. 700-2800m.
**Description and Variation.** Male uph black submarginal spots prominent, sometimes with proximal reddish marks (*rubromaculata* Oberthür); uns markings well developed; white fringes boldly chequered: female ups blue suffusion shows a marked altitudinal cline, with bluest forms predominating at higher altitudes (cf. blue female forms of other lycaenids occurring in generally cooler/damper habitats at higher latitudes).
**Flight-period.** Bivoltine. Generally May/June and late August/September: emergence much dependent on altitude and locality; recorded in March in Anti-Atlas Mts. and late October in Tunisia.
**Habitat.** Flowery places; grassy hollows; dry slopes.
**Life-history.** LHPs *Hippocrepis scabra*; (?)*Onobrychis* sp. Larvae attended by *Monomorium salomonis*; *Crematogaster scutellaris*.
**Note.** In S Spain, male *L. bellargus* specimens sometimes resembles *L. punctifera* very closely: chromosome number of *L. bellargus* (CN=45) differs significantly from that of *L. punctifera* (CN=24): male genitalia distinctive. The close integral proportionality in chromosome numbers suggests the theoretical possibility of polyploidy (cf. *G. pumilio*): the results of cross-pairing experiments would seem especially worthwhile.

## *Polyommatus icarus* Common Blue          Plate 36

**Range.** Canary Islands, temperate N Africa, Turkey, Middle East, temperate Asia.

*P. icarus* Rottemburg 1775 TL: Saxony, Germany.
**Distribution.** Canary Islands: very local: Fuerteventura; Lanzarote; Tenerife (Punta Hidalgo – recently confirmed). Records for La Palma and Gran Canaria require confirmation. Widespread and very common in NW Africa (0-2700m) and Europe, including all major and most smaller Mediterranean islands. Absent from Madeira and Azores. 0-2900m.

**Description.** Male upf without androconial patch (cf. male *A. thersites*): male and female unf with black cell-spot – rarely absent (cf. male and female *A. thersites*): female ups gc brown often with blue basal and discal shading.

**Variation.** In both sexes, appreciable local, regional, inter-seasonal and intra-seasonal variation in size and wing-markings appears largely attributable to the extraordinary ecological adaptability of this, the most widespread of the European Lycaenids. In N and W Ireland and NW Scotland, *mariscolore* Kane: univoltine: large; male fw more pointed; ups gc brighter blue; uns gc pale, markings conspicuous: female ups bright blue suffusion extending to all wing-margins. (Larvae of Scottish populations, captively reared in S England retain univoltine character, but produce females devoid of ups blue scaling, indicating ecological control of blue suffusion, the extent of which, more generally, appears to correlate positively with cooler and/or damper conditions during larval/pupal development). Some populations of S Norway above 500m, resemble *mariscolore* closely: in N Fennoscandia, generally more typical of nominate form. In N Spain (provinces of Oviedo and Burgos), f. *boalensis* Verhulst and Verhulst: size regionally/seasonally variable; male ups slightly darker blue, black marginal borders slightly wider: female ups gc brown: both sexes, uns gc darker, all markings conspicuously bolder – in overall appearance, quite distinctive: in Burgos, *boalensis* occurs on acidic bogs in close proximity (within 200m) to nominate form flying synchronously on a calcareous substrate – a combination of circumstances indicative of ecological adaptation. In adaptive response to unusually acidic conditions, alteration of wing-characters, especially gc, is not uncommon for some species; in the present example, the sympatric and synchronous *C. glycerion iphioides*, *C. euphrosyne* and *C. selene* are abnormally dark on all wing-surfaces. In Sardinia and Corsica, f. *sardoa* Wagner: female upf submarginal orange spots well developed, often confluent, sometimes with ray-like projections towards cell, or with faint orange suffusion in discal and pd areas. In S Europe and NW Africa, f. *celina* Austaut: male ups black marginal borders slightly wider; uph with black marginal dots (variable in number and size), sometimes extending to fw: a recurrent form in some localities.

**Flight-period.** Voltinism dependent on locality and altitude. Univoltine (June/July) in colder climates – at higher latitudes (N Ireland, Scotland and Lappland) and altitudes (Sierra Nevada above 2700m): bivoltine/trivoltine (May/early October) in S Britain and C Europe: at least trivoltine at sea-level S Europe (late March/early November). In Canary Islands, recorded in all months, less commonly in summer – possibly aestivating in ovum or larval stage in hottest periods.

**Habitat.** Very diverse. Occurs in almost all habitat-types.

**Life-history.** LHPs: many genera/species of Fabaceae, including: *Galega*; *Ononis*; *Lotus*; *Medicago*; *Trifolium*; *Melilotus*; *Genista*; *Astragalus*; *Astracantha*; *Onobrychis*; *Anthyllis*; *Coronilla* in most of Europe, commonly *Lotus corniculatus* and *Medicago lupulina*: Lanzarote and Fuerteventura, *Lotus lancerottensis*. Larvae attended by *Lasius alienus*; *L. flavus*; *L. niger*; *Formica subrufa*; *F.* (?)*cinerea*; *Plagiolepis pygmaea*; *Myrmica sabuleti*; *M. lobicornis* var. *alpestris*.

**Note.** *Polyommatus abdon* Aistleitner and Aistleitner 1994, described from mountains of SE Spain, appears to be conspecific with *Polyommatus icarus*: minor differences reported in male ups gc and genitalia appear to fall within the range of variation of the latter taxon.

## *Polyommatus andronicus* Phalakron Blue          Not illustrated

**Range.** N Greece.

*P. andronicus* Coutsis and Chavalas 1995 TL: Mt. Phalakron
(N Greece)

**Distribution.** N Greece. Mt. Orvilos; Menikion Mts.;
Phalakron Mts. 1000-1800m.

**Description.** Resembles *P. icarus* closely: both sexes larger;
male ups gc slightly darker and shinier: female ups largely
devoid of blue basal scales: compared to *P. icarus*, male genitalia disproportionately larger, elements of female genitalia
similarly distinctive. Cross-pairing experiments with *P. icarus* would be of value
in the further investigation of this taxon.

**Flight-period.** Univoltine. Late June/early July. Flies with second brood *P. icarus*.

**Habitat.** Sheltered grassy or rocky slopes.

## *Polyommatus eroides* False Eros Blue          Plate 36

**Range.** E and SE Europe, Turkey, Urals, N Kazakhstan, W
Siberia.

*P. eroides* Frivaldsky 1835 TL: Balkans.

**Distribution.** Slovakia. Poland. (?)Albania. Republic of
Macedonia. Bulgaria: Pirin Mts. Greece: Grammos Mts.;
Epano Arena; Varnous Mts.; Vernon Mts.; Voras Mts.;
Rhodope Mts.; Mt. Pieria. 950-2100m.

**Description.** Male ups black marginal borders 1-2mm wide;
uns gc uniform dove grey: both sexes, uns markings well
developed: female ups gc uniform medium brown, sometimes with very faint
greyish tint, lacking blue basal suffusion.

**Flight-period.** Univoltine. Mid June/late July according to altitude.

**Habitat.** Open flowery banks or slopes with short grass, often amongst rocks
above treeline: (?)always on acidic substrates, especially granite: parts of habitat are often damp or wet, but LHP appears to favour well-drained, dry, often
gravelly banks/slopes with short vegetation.

**Life-history.** LHP *Genista depressa*. Ova laid on leaves. Small larvae feed on
leaves: hibernated larvae feed on flowers. Larvae attended by *Tapinoma* sp.

**Behaviour.** Males often gather in large numbers on damp ground.

## *Polyommatus eros* Eros Blue          Plate 36

**Range.** Spain (Pyrenees), France, European Alps, Italy
(Apennines), Balkans, Turkey, NW and C Asia.

*P. eros* Ochsenheimer 1808 TL: Alps of Tyrol and Switzerland.

**Distribution.** Spain: Pyrenees; Pto. de Bielsa; Pto. de Viella;
Pto. de La Bonaigua; La Molina. France: C and E Pyrenees;
Massif Central (Cantal); Central European Alps of France,
Italy, S Switzerland and W Austria (Gross Glockner). Italy:
C Apennines. Bosnia-Herzegovina: Prenj Pl.; Jahorina Pl. SW

Serbia: Mt. Durmitor. Republic of Macedonia: Placenska Pl.; Baba Pl. (Mt. Pelister). Bulgaria: Rila Mts. 1200-2700m, generally above 1800m.
**Flight-period.** Univoltine. July/September according to altitude.
**Habitat.** Grassy, flowery slopes on limestone, usually with short turf.
**Life-history.** LHPs *Oxytropis halleri*; *O. campestris*. Ova laid on leaves upon which larvae feed. Hibernates as a small larva. Larvae attended by *Formica lemani*; *Myrmica gallienii*.
**Behaviour.** Males often gather in large numbers on damp ground.

## *Polyommatus menelaos* Taygetos Blue                     Plate 36

*P. menelaos* Brown, 1976 TL: Langhanda Pass, Taygetos Mts.
**Distribution.** Greece: known only from Taygetos Mts. 1250-2000m.
**Description.** Resembles *P. eros*. Both sexes, larger, uns gc paler, tending to white.
**Flight-period.** Univoltine. Early June/late July according to season.
**Life-history.** LHP *Astragalus taygeteus* – endemic to Taygetos Mts. Ova laid on leaves, upon which small larvae feed. Hibernated larvae feed on flower-buds. Larvae attended by *Camponotus aethiops*.
**Habitat.** Sheltered gullies and hollows, generally above the treeline, on limestone or metamorphic rocks. Often occurs with *K. eurypilus*.
**Behaviour.** In hot conditions, males gather in large numbers on damp ground.

# Riodinidae Grote 1895

Closely related to the Lycaenidae. A large family whose distribution centres on tropical America. A few genera occur in the eastern Palearctic region, as well as tropical Asia and Africa. Represented in Europe by a single species.

## *Hamearis lucina* Duke of Burgundy Fritillary     Plate 37

**Range.** From N and C Spain eastwards throughout S and C Europe, European Turkey, Urals.

*H. lucina* Linnaeus 1758 TL: England (Verity 1943).

**Distribution.** N and C Spain, eastwards through most of Europe (including S England: very local) to SE Sweden and Latvia (a single known colony). N and C Greece: very local: not reported east of Rhodope Mts. or south of Mt. Timphristos. Absent from N Germany, Denmark, Finland, S Italy and Mediterranean islands except N Sicily. 50-1600m.

**Variation.** S Europe, usually larger. Second brood: ups dark markings more extensive, sometimes obscuring orange uph gc.

**Flight-period.** Univoltine (May/June) or bivoltine (April/June and July/September) according to altitude, latitude and local conditions – univoltine in hot Mediterranean localities where LHP may become desiccated in summer.

**Habitat.** Grassy, flowery clearings in woodland or scrub.

**Life-history.** LHPs *Primula vulgaris*; *P. veris*; *P. elatior*. Ova usually laid singly or in pairs, less often 3-6, on underside of leaves. Larvae feed on leaves. Hibernates as a pupa.

# Libytheidae Boisduval 1833

Related to the Nymphalidae. Represented in the Palearctic region by three species of which one occurs in Europe. The conspicuous palpi are over three times the length of the head.

## *Libythea celtis* Nettle-tree Butterfly　　　　　　　　　　Plate 37

**Range.** Algeria, Tunisia, S Europe, Turkey, C and NW Asia, N India, Siberia, China, Taiwan, Japan.

*L. celtis* Laicharting 1782 TL: Bolzano, S Tirol.
**Distribution.** N Algeria and NW Tunisia: local and un-common. Portugal and Spain: very sporadic and generally rare, more frequent in Pyrenees. Andorra: locally common. S France (Pyrénées-Orientales to Ardèche and Alpes-Maritimes) through Italy, SE Switzerland (extremely local) to S Slovakia (very occasional – residency in doubt), Hungary, Balkans, Greece (widespread, locally common) and European Turkey: generally sporadic and very local in northern range: reported from Corsica, Elba, Sardinia, Sicily, Lipari Islands, Malta, Crete and Lesbos. 400-1500m.
**Description.** Male unh greyish: female unh light brown, with buff or pinkish tints in fresh specimens.
**Flight-period.** Univoltine. June/August: reappearing after hibernation, late March/late April.
**Habitat.** Mostly open, bushy areas with scattered, generally small, deciduous trees.
**Life-history.** LHP *Celtis australis.* Ova laid close to leaf-buds. Larvae feed on leaves. When disturbed, larvae descend 2-3m from LHP on silken threads. Adults sometimes enter hibernation as early as August. In SE European, where *C. australis* appears to be uncommon, the possible alternative use of other *Celtis* species is suggested by the reported utilization of *C. caucasica* in NW Asia. Captive larvae accept *Ulmus* (?)*minor* and *Ulmus glabra* reluctantly.
**Behaviour.** Disperses over a wide area in mid or late summer, vagrant specimens having been recorded as high as 2300m. Dispersion appears to be confined largely within established residential range: in terms of survival strategy, behaviour therefore differs fundamentally from that of migrant species (cf. *C. cardui*). Freshly emerged adults often congregate in large numbers to drink on damp ground.

# Danaidae Boisduval 1933

This large family of large butterflies is confined mostly to tropical zones. Two of the eight species recorded in the Palearctic region occur, somewhat sporadically in Europe. Both are well-known migrants whose brightly coloured, conspicuous larvae feed on plants from which toxic substances are assimilated, rendering larva, pupa and adult butterfly generally unpalatable to birds: in fact, the harmful chemicals are concentrated in the wings and abdomen, and, in North America, some birds species have exploited this disparity by feeding only on the thoracic segments: for one bird species, known to be immune to the poison, adult *Danaus plexippus* butterflies provides the main part of its diet.

## *Danaus plexippus* Milkweed or Monarch      Plate 96

**Range.** Azores, Canary Islands, S Portugal, S Spain, Mauritius, India, Papua New Guinea and other E Indian islands, Australia, New Zealand, Hawaii, S Peru to Canada.

*D. plexippus* Linnaeus 1758 TL: Pennsylvania.

**Distribution.** Resident in coastal districts of Canary Islands (except Lanzarote) and S Spain (province of Málaga): resident below 100m: occasional as vagrants/migrants to 400m. Occasional as migrants in Azores, Lanzarote, S and W Portugal, Gibraltar, more rarely, Ireland, SW England and S France.

**Description.** Male uph with black sex-brand on v2: female similar but lacking sex-brand.

**Flight-period.** Polyvoltine in Canary Islands: continuously brooded: recorded in all months. (Hibernates as an adult in Mexico and SW U.S.A.).

**Habitat.** Hot, dry places: in Canary Islands, coastal areas, including parks and gardens: in S Spain, coastal gullies, almost invariably in close proximity to cultivated areas.

**Life-history.** LHPs: Mediterranean region, *Asclepias curassavica*: Canary Islands, *A. curassavica* and *Gomphocarpus fruticosus* – neither of which are native species; other Asclepiadaceae, including native *Periploca laevigata*, endemic *Ceropegia* spp. and non-native *Calotropis procera* are apparently not exploited. In Canary Islands, larvae recorded in all months.

**Behaviour.** This well-known, C and N American migrant is known to have greatly extended its range since the middle of 19th century, colonizing New Zealand in 1840, Australia in 1870 and Canary Islands in 1880: first noted as a resident of Spain in 1980: reported from S France, Corsica and Mauritius in 1983.

**Conservation.** In S Spain, the use of herbicides/insecticides, weed-burning and rubbish-disposal threatens extinction of resident colonies, most of which are small and isolated.

## *Danaus chrysippus* Plain Tiger      Plate 96

**Range.** Canary Islands, Africa, sporadic in coastal Mediterranean regions, central E Turkey, Saudi Arabia, tropical Asia, Australia.

*D. chrysippus* Linnaeus 1758 TL: S China.

**Distribution.** Canary Islands: resident on La Palma; Gomera; Fuerteventura (very local); 0-600m: probably no longer resident on Tenerife and Gran Canaria, but recorded as an occasional migrant. N Africa: resident and locally common in W Morocco (Sous Valley), N Algeria (Gharddia and Touggourt) and Tunisia (Douz; Sfax; Gabes; Sousse): more widely observed as single, migrant specimens. Recorded from mainly coastal districts of S Spain (Málaga and Almeria), S France, Corsica, Sardinia, Sicily, W Italy, Montenegro, Albania, Corfu, W and S Greece and Crete: temporary/(?)permanent breeding populations appear to have become established in some localities.

**Description.** Male ups gc variable, light orange-brown to chestnut brown; upf apex dark brown, enclosing transverse white spots, sometimes coalescing into a band broken by veins; uph with black sex-brand on v2: female similar but lacking sex-brand.

**Variation.** Polymorphism marked: f. *alcippus* Cramer, uph tawny-brown gc replaced by white: f. *alcippoides* Moore, white area less extensive, transitional to nominate form: incidence of both forms regionally and seasonally variable.

**Flight-period.** Polyvoltine. Canary Islands: continuously brooded: recorded in all months: N Africa, March/November: N and E Mediterranean region, May/October.

**Habitat.** Bushy, rocky places; hot, coastal gullies, usually in close proximity to cultivated areas; gardens.

**Life-history.** LHPs: Canary Islands: *Asclepias curassavica*; *Gomphocarpus fruticosus*; *Caralluma burchardii* (Fuerteventura); possibly also *Ceropegia hians* and *Calotropis procera* on La Palma and Gran Canaria respectively: Morocco and S Europe, *A. curassavica atropurpurea*; *C. procera*: Algeria and Tunisia, *Pergularia tomentosa*; *Cynanchum acutum*: S Europe, *A. curassavica*. Reported use of *Calystegia sepium* (Convolvulaceae) requires confirmation. Larvae recorded in all months in Canary Islands. Life-cycle in tropical Africa approximately one month. For a species having no diapause stage, winter residence in the often very cold eastern Mediterranean region seems unlikely; the impression of persistence in particular habitats more probably due to recurring early spring migration and subsequent establishment of temporary colonies which survive until onset of cold weather (cf. *C. cardui*; *C. crocea*; *L. boeticus*).

**Behaviour.** A powerful and wide-ranging migrant. In northern Corfu, in late September 1989, large numbers were observed, apparently migrating southwards. (In N America, migrates northwards from over-wintering quarters in spring and summer, returning in autumn).

**Conservation.** As in the case of *D. plexippus*, human activity poses a significant threat to resident colonies in S Spain.

142

# Nymphalidae Swainson 1827

This large family, well represented in Europe, contains many well-known, common and widespread species. A few, colourful and conspicuous species such as the Peacock, Small Tortoiseshell, Painted Lady and Red Admiral are often to be found in gardens and parks, even in large cities: this group comprises the so-called 'vanessids'. A few are migrants, capable of extending their range throughout most of the subcontinent during summer months. The largest group, the fritillaries, are to be found throughout the region. Some species occur well within the Arctic circle, whilst a few inhabit the equally inhospitable semi-deserts of N Africa. Larvae are often conspicuously coloured and spectacularly adorned with spiny protruberances: these 'warning colours' and unappetising structural features serve to discourage the predatory attention of birds. Small larvae of the genera *Melitaea*, *Mellicta*, *Hypodryas* and *Eurodryas* feed and hibernate gregariously in silk-webs, dispersing in later instars after hibernation to feed singly or in small companies: pupae are suspended on plant-stems, often of robust grasses, the underside of leaves or sometimes on stones.

## *Charaxes jasius* Two-tailed Pasha                           Plate 37

**Range.** Mainly coastal Mediterranean region. Represented by two subspecies in Ethiopia and equatorial Africa.

*C. jasius* Linnaeus 1767 TL: Barbaria (Algeria).
**Distribution.** Locally common in coastal districts of Morocco, Algeria, Tunisia, W Portugal and elsewhere in Mediterranean region, including Balearic Islands, Corsica, Sardinia, Sicily, Corfu, Crete, Samos, Ikaria, Chios and Rhodes: also, in isolated inland regions of Spain (Huelva and Málaga to Salamanca and Madrid) and France (Provençe to Ayeron, Lozère and Ardèche). Absent from N Adriatic coast (central peninsular Italy to Istria). Generally 0-1200m but recorded sporadically to 2400m in High Atlas.
**Flight-period.** Bivoltine. May/June and mid August/mid October.
**Habitat.** Hot, dry, often dense, mixed scrub containing an abundance of LHP: often on hillsides.
**Life-history.** LHP principally *Arbutus unedo*: the structure, colour-pattern and behaviour of the larva suggests a high-level of adaptation to *A. unedo*. In Gibraltar, oviposition has been reported on *Osyris quadripartita* (restricted to S Iberian peninsula and Balearic Islands). Ova/larvae have been recorded on *Nicotiana glauca* on Samos and *Citrus nobilis* and *C. sinensis* in N Africa. Captive rearing of larvae on *Rhamnus* sp. merits confirmation. Hibernates as a larva.
**Behaviour.** Exhibits marked territorial and 'hilltopping' behaviour. Both sexes greatly attracted to fermenting fruit; ethanol appears to be the key attractant – wine and other alcoholic beverages are potent baits.

## *Apatura iris* Purple Emperor                           Plate 37

**Range.** Europe, NW Kazakhstan, S Urals, Amur, NE China, Korea.
*A. iris* Linnaeus 1758 TL: Germany and England.

**Distribution.** N Portugal: Minho. N Spain: scattered colo-
nies: S. de Guadarrama; S. de la Demanda; Cantabrian Mts;
Pyrenees, Valle de Aran. Eastwards from Pyrenees through
S England, N Italy to Denmark (including Fyen, Sjælland,
Lolland, Falster and Bornholm), S Sweden (Skåne: first noted
1985), Baltic states, Balkans and NW Greece Varnous Mts.;
Vernon Mts.; Pindos Mts. (Grammos massif to district of
Trikala). 50-1500m.
**Description and Variation.** Upf dark spot in s2 obscured
by gc; uph inner edge of white discal band linear (cf. *A. ilia*). Rarely, ups white
markings greatly reduced or absent (f. *iole* Denis and Schiffermüller).

**Flight-period.** Univoltine. Mid June/mid August.

**Habitat.** Mature, deciduous woodland, with small clearings or tracks bordered
by LHP.

**Life-history.** LHPs, *Salix caprea*; *S. cinerea*; *S. alba*; *S.* (?)*atrocinerea*. Ova laid
on upperside of leaves in the shaded, interior parts of the tree, most frequently
1-2m above ground-level. Larva feeds near leaf-tip, producing a characteristic
symmetrical pattern, leaving main rib and tissue at leaf-tip intact. Hibernates
as a small larva in a stem-fork on LHP.

**Behaviour.** Males strongly attracted to carnivore excrement, human perspiration, hot road-tar and fumes of petroleum spirit. Both sexes often rest on
leaves of trees (commonly oak) several metres above the ground.

**Note.** *A. iris* and *A. ilia* often share same habitat and sometimes the same LHP
(*Salix alba*).

## *Apatura ilia* Lesser Purple Emperor                          Plate 38

**Range.** C and S Europe, Caucasus, S Urals, NW Kazakhstan, NE China.

*A. ilia* Denis and Schiffermüller 1775 TL: Vienna.
**Distribution.** N Portugal: Minho. N Spain: Cantabrian
Mts.; provinces of Huesca and Catalonia. From Pyrenees
eastwards to Latvia, Balkans and NW Greece. Absent from
Britain, Holland, N Germany, Poland, Fennoscandia and S
Italy. 300-1300m.
**Description and Variation.** Upf dark spot in s2 well defined,
ringed orange; uph inner edge of pale discal band non-linear (cf. *A. iris*); pd
spots rounded, sometimes confluent, conspicuous against orange background
(cf. *A. metis*). Both sexes polymorphic: f. *clytie* Denis and Schiffermüller: ups
yellow to orange-brown; ups white markings, except apical spots, replaced by
yellow: characters and incidence regionally variable. In Catalonia, f. *barcina*
Verity: ups and uns all white markings well developed; discal band wide; pale
submarginal markings usually present; uns gc colour paler: polymorphism rare:
a similar form occurs in W Peninsular Italy.

**Flight-period.** Univoltine (late May/July) or bivoltine (June and August/
September).

**Habitat.** Deciduous woodland clearings, tracks etc., bordered by LHP; wooded
river valleys, especially river banks where LHPs, often *Salix alba*, occur in
abundance.

**Life-history.** LHPs *Populus tremulae*; *P.alba*; *P.nigra*; *Salix alba*: also, NE Spain, *S.* (?)*atrocinerea catalaunica*. Ova laid on upperside of leaves. Hibernates as a small larva.
**Behaviour.** As for *A. iris*.

## *Apatura metis* Freyer's Purple Emperor                    Plate 38

**Range.** E and SE Europe, European Turkey, SW Russia, Kazakhstan, W Siberia, Amur, NE China, Korea, Japan.

*A. metis* Freyer 1829 TL: Pecs (Fünfkirchen), Hungary.
**Distribution.** Associated largely with river systems in:- Austria (Danube), Hungary (Danube; Drava), Slovenia (Sava), N Serbia (Danube), Bulgaria (widespread but local in river valleys), N Greece (Thiamis; Voidomátis; Strimonas; Nestos; Evros; Lake Doirani) and European Turkey (Evros Valley; Balli; Inecik). Not reported from Republic of Macedonia. 0-650m.
**Description and Variation.** Resembles *A. ilia*: generally smaller; ups brighter; upf orange pd band expanded at apex; uph dark pd spots obscured by dark background; uph outer edge of pale discal band well marked by discontinuity at v4 – component of band in s4, large, sharply angular (diamond-shaped). Polymorphism unknown. (Cf. *A. ilia*).
**Flight-period.** Bivoltine. Late May/June and mid July/August.
**Habitat.** Wooded river margins containing mature specimens of LHP.
**Life-history.** LHP *Salix alba*. Ova laid on upperside of leaves. Hibernation as for *A. ilia*.
**Behaviour.** In very hot conditions, adults may rest for several hours on leaves in higher branches of LHP. Males are attracted to carnivore excrement and often take water from riverside sand-bars: both sexes sometimes assemble on LHP to take sap issuing from wounded bark.
**Note.** In N Greece, *A. metis* and *A. ilia* are sympatric in the region of Lake Doirani: sympatry not known in the interconnected Sarantàporos and Voidomátis river systems, where both species occur with no obvious ecological separation.

## *Thaleropis ionia*                    Not illustrated

**Range.** (?)Greece (Kastellorizo), Turkey, NE Iraq, NW Iran, Caucasus.

*T. ionia* Eversmann 1851 TL: Amasya
The sole European record relates to a male, noted by Mr J. G. Coutsis, in the Goulandris Museum, Athens: the site of capture is given as Kastellorizo, a small island 120km east of Rhodes. Known on nearby Turkish mainland. In overall appearance, bears a slight superficial resemblance to *A. metis*, but readily separable by upf and unf white spots in s3-s5, in addition to several other distinctive wing-characters. LHP in Armenia, *Salix* sp.

## *Limenitis populi* Poplar Admiral                Plate 39

**Range.** C and E Europe, C and S Urals, W and S Siberia, Mongolia, NE China, Japan.

*L. populi* Linnaeus 1758 TL: Sweden (Verity 1950).

**Distribution.** N and E France (very local in Brittany; local in Drôme and Vacluse (Rhône Valley)), Switzerland, N Italy, eastwards to 66°N in Fennoscandia (including Gotland), Republic of Macedonia, Bulgaria and N Greece (Rhodopi Mts.). Absent from SW France, Britain, N Holland, N Germany and W Norway. Extinct in Denmark. 200-1500m.

**Variation.** Male ups gc somewhat variable, dark brown to dark slate-grey with bluish overtone; white discal markings sometimes reduced or absent (f. *tremulae* Esper), common in some populations.

**Flight-period.** Univoltine. Late May/late July: emergence seasonally variable in some localities. Flight-time short, usually 8-12 days.

**Habitat.** Mixed deciduous woodland, with clearings, roads etc. bordered by LHP.

**Life-history.** LHP *Populus tremula*. Ova laid on upperside of leaves. Larva feeds in a similar fashion to *A. iris* except that tissue at leaf-tip is also consumed. For hibernation, the small larva forms a hibernaculum from a partly consumed leaf, bound to its adjacent stem with silk. Pupates on upperside of LHP leaf.

**Behaviour.** Males attracted to carnivore excrement, human perspiration, hot road-tar, petroleum spirit and damp wood-ash.

## *Limenitis reducta* Southern White Admiral            Plate 39

**Range.** S and C Europe, Turkey, Middle East, W Iran, Caucasus.

*L. reducta* Staudinger 1901 TL: Hankynda.
syn: *camilla* Denis and Schiffermüller 1775 auct.: *anonyma* Lewis 1872 auct.: *rivularis* Stichel 1908 auct.

**Distribution.** N Portugal. N and EC Spain. NW and SW France (Brittany and Normandy: very local) eastwards through S Germany, Slovakia, Balkans, Greece and European Turkey, including Mediterranean islands of Corsica, Sardinia, Elba, Sicily, Corfu, Lefkas, Kefalonia, Zakynthos, Kithira, Kea, Thassos, Limnos, Lesbos, Chios, Ikaria, Samos, Kos, Nissiros and Rhodes. 0-1650m. Absent from Balearic Islands and Crete.

**Flight-period.** Univoltine in northern range (mid June/early August); bivoltine in Mediterranean region (mid May/June and mid July/August).

**Habitat.** Dry, rocky or grassy places amongst scrub; sheltered, dry or damp woodland clearings.

**Life-history.** LHPs *Lonicera periclymenum*; *L. etrusca*; *L. implexa*; *L. xylosteum*; *L. alpigena*; *L. nummulariifolia*; *L. caprifolium*. Ova laid singly on upperside of leaves, upon which larve feed. Larval colouring variable: bright green and reddish in C Europe, dull green and greyish-violet in Mediterranean region. Hibernates as a small larva within a hibernaculum formed from a leaf secured to LHP stem with silk.

## *Limenitis camilla* White Admiral　　　Plate 39

**Range.** C Europe, Turkey, Urals, NW Kazakhstan, Amur, NE China, Korea, Japan.

*L. camilla* Linnaeus 1763 TL: Germany
syn: *sibilla* Linnaeus 1767

**Distribution.** N Spain: Cantabrian Mts.; Pyrenees. Eastwards from Pyrenees through S England, E Denmark (including Fyen, Sjælland, Lolland, Falster and Bornholm) to Baltic states, Balkans, N Greece (Rhodopi Mts.: extremely local) and European Turkey. Sporadic in SE France, absent from S and E peninsular Italy and Mediterranean islands. 0-1500m. No recent records from S Sweden (Skåne).

**Flight-period.** Univoltine. Mid June/mid August.

**Habitat.** Sunny clearings in large deciduous woodlands, often in damp, humid situations; conifer plantations and pine forests with deciduous wooded margins.

**Life-history.** LHPs *Lonicera periclymenum*; *L. caprifolium*; *L. xylosteum*; *Symphoricarpus racemosa*. Ova laid singly on upper surface of leaves of shaded plants. Larva feeds from leaf-tip towards the stem, leaving mid-rib intact, along which it rests. Hibernates as a small larva within a hibernaculum formed from a leaf secured to LHP stem with silk.

**Behaviour.** Adults greatly attracted to bramble blossom.

## *Hypolimnas misippus* False Plain Tiger　　　Not illustrated

**Range.** Egypt, Lebanon, central S Turkey, Saudi Arabia, Tropical Africa and Asia, C America, Australia.

*H. misippus* Linnaeus 1764 TL: America.

**Distribution.** This powerful migrant was first reported from the Canary Islands (Tenerife) in 1895. Since 1987, appears to have become resident on Gomera, although the persistence of some colonies is in doubt. Vagrant specimens have been noted in the Azores. Absent from N Africa.

**Description.** Large; fw length 30mm; male ups very dark brown or black; large, white, round discal spots, fw and hw, and upf apex white oval spot with brilliant violet reflections at distal borders; uns gc brownish with ups pattern of white spots repeated. Sexual dimorphism striking: except for absence of hw black discal spots, the female is a close mimic of both white and orange forms of female *Danaus chrysippus*.

**Flight-period.** Polyvoltine. All confirmed records relate to October/February, suggesting that colonies may be temporary and due only to recurring late-season migration from Tropical Africa.

**Habitat.** The few extant records relate to gardens in coastal regions.

**Life-history.** LHP on Gomera unknown: elsewhere in range, species of:- *Portulaca*; *Talinum*; *Ficus*; *Ipomoea*; *Amaranthus*; *Hibiscus*; *Sedum*: species of at least the latter four genera occur on Gomera. Larvae are gregarious.

## *Neptis sappho* Common Glider                          Plate 39

**Range.** SE Europe, C and SE Asia, N China, Taiwan, Korea, Japan.

*N. sappho* Pallas 1771 TL: Volga, S Russia.
syn: *aceris* Esper 1783; *hylas* auct.
**Distribution.** NE Italy (Gorizia). Slovenia. Slovakia. Hungary. NE Croatia. N Serbia. Romania. Republic of Macedonia (Treska Valley, Skopje district). Bulgaria. N Greece (Rhodopi Mts. and southern foothills). Very local in many regions. Extinct in Austria. 200-1550m.
**Flight-period.** Bivoltine. Mid May/late June and July/August.
**Habitat.** Damp deciduous woodland, usually associated with river valleys: in Hungary, predominantly associated with (?)'Acacia' trees.
**Life-history.** LHPs *Lathyrus vernus*; *L. niger*. Hibernates as a small larva. Pupa mimics a dead leaf attached to stem of LHP. One locality in N Greece, in which *L. vernus* and *L. niger* appear to be absent, is dominated by *Robinia pseudacacia*, reportedly a LHP in Japan: cf. habitat character in Hungary.
**Behaviour.** Characteristic gliding flight is confined mostly to dappled shade of woodland canopy, where both sexes also rest or bask with outspread wings.
**Note.** Often associated with *L. morsei* in northern range.

## *Neptis rivularis* Hungarian Glider                    Plate 39

**Range.** S European Alps, E Europe, Turkey, Caucasus, C Asia, S Siberia, Mongolia, N China, Taiwan, Korea, Japan.

*N. rivularis* Scopoli 1763 TL: Graz, Austria.
syn: *lucilla* Schiffermüller 1775.
**Distribution.** SE Switzerland. N Italy. Slovenia. E Austria. Slovakia. Hungary. S Poland. W Croatia (Dalmatian coast) through C Serbia, Bosnia-Herzegovina to E Romania: very sporadic and local in S Balkans; Republic of Macedonia (Galicica Pl.; Treska Valley), SW Bulgaria and N Greece (Rhodopi Mts.: very local). 500-1600m.
**Flight-period.** Univoltine. Late May/early August.
**Habitat.** Open deciduous, more rarely, coniferous woodland.
**Life-history.** LHPs *Spiraea chamaedryfolia*; *S. salicifolia*; *Aruncus dioecus*; *Filipendula ulmaria*. Ova laid on leaf-edge, mostly at tip coincident with medial vein; about 25% are deposited a short distance from this point. Young larva feeds from below leaf-tip towards stem, leaving mid-rib intact: rests and sometimes hibernates in a tube formed from terminal leaf-remnant. Captive larvae accept *S. bumalda*. Pupa mimics a dead leaf attached to stem of LHP.

## *Nymphalis antiopa* Camberwell Beauty                  Plate 40

**Range.** Europe, Turkey, throughout temperate Asia and most of N America.

*N. antiopa* Linnaeus 1758 TL: Sweden (Verity 1950).
**Distribution.** Occasional in N Portugal. N Spain (S. de Guadarrama; S. de la Demanda; Cantabrian Mts.; Pyrenees) eastwards through most of Europe to

N Fennoscandia, S Greece and European Turkey.
Demarcation of residency and migration uncertain in some
northern areas, perhaps seasonally variable. Progressively less
frequent towards NW Europe; a rare migrant in Britain. Reported from Mallorca ((?)migrant): not recorded from other
Mediterranean islands. Generally 0-2000m: occasional as
migrants/vagrants in barren terrain above 2600m.
**Flight-period.** Univoltine. S Europe, mid June/July; Scandinavia, August/September. Hibernated specimens appear
March/June according to locality.

**Habitat.** Diverse. Sunny woodland glades; river valleys; dry rocky gullies; sand
dunes; parks; suburban gardens. Hibernated butterflies are usually found in
sites with an abundance of LHP: fresh specimens may appear almost anywhere
in summer.

**Life-history.** LHPs *Salix alba*; *S. cinerea*; *S. atrocinerea*; *S. caprea*; *S. aurita*; *S.
viminalis*; *Populus tremula*; *P. nigra*; *P. alba*. Ova laid in large batches around
circumference of a stem in upper part of LHP. Larvae feed gregariously in a
silken web in early instars – singly towards maturity. Pupation sites include
bushes and trees, but not usually the plant upon which larvae have fed. Hibernates as an adult in cool dark places, e.g., hollow trees, wood-stacks, road-
drains.

**Behaviour.** A powerful migrant, dispersing from its breeding grounds soon
after emergence. Usually encountered in very small numbers or singly. Attracted
to fermenting fruit, the sap of wounded trees and nectar-rich plants: hibernated specimens are fond of *Salix* blossom. Recorded taking nectar from *Urtica
dioica* in largely barren terrain at 2300m and moisture from snow at 2200m.

## *Nymphalis polychloros* Large Tortoiseshell          Plate 41

**Range.** N Africa, S and C Europe, Turkey, S Russia, C and
S Urals, Kazakhstan, Himalayas.

*N. polychloros* Linnaeus 1758 TL: Sweden (Verity 1950).
**Distribution.** Morocco. Algeria. Tunisia. 200-2600m. From
Iberian peninsula through most of Europe, including S
England (very rare and local, extinct in many areas) to Baltic
states, SE Sweden (including Bornholm and Öland) to Bal-
kans, Greece and European Turkey. Occasional in Denmark,
S Norway and S Finland as a migrant. Reported from Sicily,
Corsica, Sardinia, Elba, Corfu, Crete, Lesbos, Ikaria, Samos, Kos and Rhodes.
0-1700m. Not reported from Balearic Islands.

**Description.** Ups gc rusty-orange; inner margin well defined; legs and palpi
dark brown, nearly black (cf. *N. xanthomelas*).

**Variation.** In N Africa, *erythromelas* Austaut: ups gc brighter: transitional to
nominate form in S Spain.

**Flight-period.** Univoltine. Late June/August. Hibernated specimens appear
March/April.

**Habitat.** Diverse. Mature deciduous woodland with warm, sunny clearings;
light, open woodland, often in hot, dry areas in Mediterranean region.

**Life-history.** LHPs *Ulmus procera*; *U. glabra*; *U. campestris*; *U. americana*; *Salix* *caprea*; *S. alba*; *S. pedicellata*; *S. viminalis*; *Prunus avium*; *P. domestica*; *P. padus*; *Pyrus communis*; *Malus domestica*; *Populus tremula*; *P. nigra*; *P. alba*; *Sorbus tormilis*; *Crataegus monogyna*. Ova laid in a single batch around circumference of a stem, usually sited in upper part of LHP. Larvae feed gregariously in a silken web in early instars, singly towards maturity. Pupates frequently on branches of LHP. Hibernates as an adult in cool dark places, e.g., hollow trees, wood-stacks, road-drains.

**Behaviour.** Migrant. Appears to disperse quickly following its emergence. Fond of basking in late afternoon sun.

**Note.** Has become increasingly uncommon in NW Europe in recent decades.

## *Nymphalis xanthomelas* Yellow-legged Tortoiseshell    Plate 41

**Range.** E Europe, Turkey, C Asia, China, Korea, Japan.

*N. xanthomelas* Esper 1781 TL: Germany, Austria.

**Distribution.** Probably resident in E Slovakia, SE Poland, E Hungary and Romania: possibly resident in W Republic of Macedonia and NW Greece (very local and rare): occurrence in S Fennoscandia, Baltic states and most of S Balkans possibly dependent on migration, with perhaps establishment of temporary colonies. In Bulgaria, common and widespread in the 1920's, now possibly extinct as a resident species: becoming increasingly uncommon in other parts of European range. 0-2000m.

**Description.** Resembles *N. polychloros*: ups gc reddish-orange, brighter; inner edge of dark submarginal borders suffused – indistinct; legs and palpi light brown or buff.

**Flight-period.** Univoltine. July/September. Hibernated specimens appear in May.

**Habitat.** Damp deciduous woodland, especially in river valleys.

**Life-history.** LHPs *Salix* spp.; *Populus* spp. Oviposition, development and hibernation as for *N. polychloros*.

**Behaviour.** Migrant.

## *Nymphalis vau-album* False Comma                    Plate 41

**Range.** E Europe, Turkey, C Asia, NE China, Korea, Japan, S Canada and northern U.S.A.

*N. vau-album* Denis and Schiffermüller 1775 TL: Vienna. syn: *l-album* Esper 1781.

**Distribution.** Reported from S Finland, Baltic states, Poland, Czech Republic, Slovakia, E Austria, Hungary, Romania, W Balkans (last reported 1972 in Bosnia-Herzegovina) and Bulgaria (a single record, 1942). Distinction between permanent populations, migration and temporary colonies established through migration difficult to establish: occurrence in W, N and S limits of European range most probably relate to migration. Becoming increasingly uncommon in European range. 0-(?)1500m.

**Description.** White markings near upf apex and uph costa prominent (cf. *N. polychloros* and *N. xanthomelas*).

**Flight-period.** Univoltine. June/July. Hibernated specimens appear in March/April.
**Habitat.** Clearings in deciduous woods.
**Life-history.** LHPs *Salix* spp.; *Populus* spp.; *Ulmus* spp. Small larvae live in silken webs.
**Behaviour.** Migrant.

## *Inachis io* Peacock Butterfly                                    Plate 41

**Range.** Europe, Turkey, throughout temperate Asia to Japan.

*I. io* Linnaeus 1758 TL: Sweden (Verity 1950)
**Distribution.** Widespread and common in most of Europe south of 64°N to northern half of Iberian peninsula, Sierra Nevada, N central Greece, European Turkey and Mediterranean islands of Sicily, Corsica, Sardinia (above 400m), Corfu, Samos and Simi. Reported only once from NW Africa (Algiers, 1961). Records for N Scotland appear to relate to migration. 0-2500m.
**Flight-period.** Univoltine. Normally June/August but enter diapause between late July and early October according to weather conditions. Hibernated specimens appear March/May.
**Habitat.** Open, sunny places in woodland; wooded river-banks; damp meadows; fallow fields or disturbed ground; sheltered rocky gullies with bushes/small trees at upper limit of altitudinal range. LHP usually in great abundance.
**Life-history.** LHPs: mainland Europe, *Urtica dioica*: Samos (where *U. dioica* is not indigenous) *Parietaria officinalis*. Larvae feed in companies until almost full-grown. At low altitude (150m) in NW Greece, mature larvae have been recorded in late August. Hibernates as an adult in cool, dark places: hollow trees, dense vegetation, wood-stacks, outhouses, rock-crevices, stone walls etc.
**Behaviour.** Hibernated adults feed on *Salix* blossom in spring. Common on the blossom of *Buddleia davidii* in summer.

## *Vanessa atalanta* Red Admiral                                    Plate 40

**Range.** Azores, Canary Islands, N Africa, Europe, Turkey, Iran. N America to Guatemala. Haiti and New Zealand.

*V. atalanta* Linnaeus 1758 TL: Sweden (Verity 1950).
**Distribution.** Azores. Canary Islands. Morocco. Algeria. Tunisia. Throughout Europe, including all larger and many smaller Mediterranean islands, as a resident or migrant: in northernmost range, Ireland, Britain and most of Fenno-scandia, appearance probably depends largely on migration. 0-2500m.
**Flight-period.** Univoltine. June/October: hibernated specimens usually appear in March/April; has been recorded on warm days in winter months near Mediterranean coast.
**Habitat.** Diverse. Occurs in many habitats other than those containing its LHPs.
**Life-history.** LHPs: Canary Islands, *Urtica urens*; rarely *Parietaria* sp.: NW Africa, *Urtica membranacea, U. pilulifera; U. urens; Parietaria officinalis*: Europe,

*U. dioica*; (?) *U. urens*; *P. officinalis*; *P. diffusa*; *P. debilis*. Ova laid usually near tip of leaves of plants growing in open sunny positions. Larvae feed singly in rolled-up leaves. Larvae are polymorphic. Pupates on LHP stems. Hibernates as an adult, sometimes successfully in Britain.

**Behaviour.** Migrant. Often basks on walls, rock faces etc. Greatly attracted to nectar-rich plants, e.g., *Rubus fruticosus*, *Eupatorium cannabinum*, *Hedera helix*, *Sedum spectabilis* and *Buddleia davidii*.

## *Vanessa indica* Indian Red Admiral                                          Plate 40

**Range.** Canary Islands, Madeira, India, China, Japan, Korea.

*V. indica vulcania* Godart 1819 TL: Canary Islands (Kirby 1904)
syn: *callirhoe* Millière 1867; *occidentalis* Felder 1862.

**Distribution.** Madeira; occasional on nearby island of Porto Santo. Canary Islands: Gran Canaria; Tenerife; Gomera; La Palma; Hierro. Occasional (?) migrant on Fuerteventura. Not recorded from Lanzarote – suitable habitat appears to be absent. Absent from Azores, N Africa and European mainland. 0-1500m.

**Flight-period.** Polyvoltine. Occurs throughout the year, apparently without diapause.

**Habitat and Behaviour.** Laurel forests where LHP grows as an undershrub. Often found outside of natural habitat, in gardens, parks etc., where it visits nectar-rich plants. On Tenerife often found on laurel blossom.

**Life-history.** LHPs *Urtica morifolia*; *Parietaria* sp. On *U. morifolia*, ova laid singly, more rarely in pairs, on terminal leaves of shaded plants (cf. *V. atalanta*). Larva feeds within a rolled-up leaf in which it also pupates.

**Note.** Type locality of *V. indica calliroe* Hubner 1808 is given as 'China' – presumably in error. No populations are known between Atlantic islands and India.

## *Vanessa cardui* Painted Lady                                                Plate 42

**Range.** Cosmopolitan, except S America.

*C. cardui* Linnaeus 1758 TL: Europe, Africa.

**Distribution.** Most of the region as a migrant, progressing northwards from N Africa in early spring, extending its range to within the Arctic Circle during summer months. Permanent resident of N Africa, Canary Islands, Madeira and some warmer Mediterranean areas: possibly semi-permanent in other, southerly localities in a succession of favourable seasons. Relatively rare in Ireland and Scotland. Reported occasionally from Iceland, which has no indigenous butterflies. Generally 0-3000m: migrants often occur at high altitudes.

**Flight-period.** Polyvoltine. Has no diapause stage; flies in all months in areas of permanent residence. In northern Europe, migrants usually appear May/June: breeding and further dispersal persists until onset of cold weather.

**Habitat.** Virtually any site containing LHPs, most commonly areas containing an abundance of Thistles.

**Life-history.** Worldwide, LHPs comprise an extraordinary range of plant families of which Cucurbitaceae; Asteraceae; Fabaceae; Vitaceae; Malvaceae;

Brassicaceae; Boraginaceae have been recorded for N Africa and/or Europe: *Cirsium, Carduus* (thistles), *Echium* and *Malva* (especially *M. sylvestris*) appear to be most commonly used. Larvae have been recorded on cultivated *Glycine max* (Soya Beans) in Germany. Ova laid singly, usually on upperside of leaves upon which larvae feed. Ovum stage may be as short as 3 days in S Europe: life-cycle 5-8 weeks according to conditions. Larvae are polymorphic. On Fuerteventura (LHP commonly *Malva parviflora*), larvae often parasitized by *Cotesia vanessae* (Braconidae).

**Behaviour.** Thistles serve a dual purpose as rich nectar-sources and LHPs. A common summer visitor to *Buddleia davidii* bushes in gardens and parks.

## *Vanessa virginiensis* American Painted Lady          Plate 42

**Range.** Madeira, Canary Islands, S Canada, N America to Venezuela, Guatemala: occasional in Hawaii.

*V. virginiensis* Drury 1773 TL: New York.
syn: *huntera* Fabricius 1775.
**Distribution.** Canary islands: Tenerife; apparently extinct on Gomera and La Palma. Occasional migrant in W and S Portugal (especially Algarve), Azores, more rarely in Spain (including Huesca), very rarely in SW Ireland, W Wales and S England. Not reported from N Africa or (?)Madeira. 0-1500m.
**Flight-period.** Polyvoltine. Recorded in all months on Tenerife except February and November.
**Habitat.** Flowery places.
**Life-history.** LHP on Tenerife unknown: in N America, several genera of Asteraceae; Fabaceae; Malvaceae; Boraginaceae; Urticaceae; Balsaminaceae; Scrophulariaceae. Suspected of entering diapause in winter months as an adult: diapause may be disrupted temporarily during warm periods.

## *Aglais urticae* Small Tortoiseshell          Plate 41

**Range.** Europe, eastwards to Pacific coast.

*A. urticae urticae* Linnaeus 1758 TL: Sweden (Verity 1950).
**Distribution.** Common throughout Europe. Absent from Atlantic Islands, NW Africa and Mediterranean Islands except Sicily (replaced by *A. u. ichnusa* on Corsica and Sardinia). 0-3000m.
**Variation.** At high altitude: generally larger; ups gc brighter. In Lappland, generally smaller; ups gc slightly darker.
**Flight-period.** Univoltine in colder regions in N Europe and at high altitudes in S Europe, late May/August according to season and locality: bivoltine or trivoltine in warm localities, May/October. Hibernated specimens appear March/April.
**Habitat and Life-history.** Diverse. Occurs in almost all sites containing LHP *Urtica dioica*. Especially common in areas of human habitation and heavily grazed pasture where soil enrichment favours establishment of LHP. Natural use of *U. urens* as a LHP requires confirmation. Ova laid in large batches on underside of leaf. Small larvae feed on leaves in companies in silken webs, singly or in small groups as development proceeds. Hibernates as an adult,

often in human dwellings, out-houses, etc. In common with many other 'vanessids', a high proportion of larvae are lost to dipterous parasites.

**Behaviour.** Commonly observed at mountain summits – 'hilltopping'. Fond of basking on walls, paths etc. Hibernated specimens are fond of *Salix* blossom: attracted to *Buddleia davidii*, *Sedum spectabilis* and *Aster novi-belgii* in summer. Hibernation sometimes disrupted on warm days in late winter.

*A. urticae ichnusa* Hübner 1824. TL: not stated.
**Distribution.** Corsica. Sardinia. 700-2500m.
**Description.** Ups brighter; upf black spots in s2 and s3 absent or vestigial.
**Flight-period.** Bivoltine. May/October, reappearing March/April after hibernation.
**Habitat.** As for nominate form but restricted to mountainous areas.
**Life-history.** LHP (?)*Urtica dioica*. Captively reared *ichnusa* is said to produce imagines identical to or resembling nominate form.
**Behaviour.** Often 'hilltops'.

## *Polygonum c-album* Comma Butterfly · Plate 42

**Range.** N Africa, Europe, Turkey, C Asia, N China, Korea, Japan.

*P. c-album* Linnaeus 1758 TL: Sweden
**Distribution.** Morocco. Algeria. Tunisia. 500-2700m. Most of Europe, including England, Wales, Fennoscandia to 68°N and European Turkey. Absent from SW Iberian peninsula, Ireland and Mediterranean islands except Sicily, Corsica, Sardinia and Corfu. Occasional in N Holland, N Germany and Denmark. Apparently extinct in Scotland. 0-2000m.

**Description.** Unh cell-end with white 'comma', variable. In summer broods – those which do not enter winter diapause – uns gc yellowish-brown with bright, variegated pattern (f. *hutchinsoni* Robson). Specimens destined for hibernation in late summer or autumn, uns dark brown with obscure, dark greenish marbling; this cryptic pattern, appropriate for hibernating adults, appears to arise from photo-period influence on larval/pupal development.

**Flight-period.** Bivoltine in most of Europe, late May/June and July/August, reappearing March/April after hibernation: usually univoltine in Scandinavia, June/August: trivoltine in warmest areas of S Balkans and Greece, May/October.

**Habitat.** Woodland clearings, often in damp places.

**Life-history.** LHPs: NW Africa, *Ribes grossularia*; *R. uva-crispa*: Europe, *Urtica dioica*; *Salix caprea*; *S. alba*; *Humulus lupulus*; *R. uva-crispa*; *R. nigrum*; *R. rubrum*; *Corylus avellana*; *Ulmus glabra*; *U. minor*; *U. procera*; *U. laevis*. Captive larvae accept *Parietaria officinalis*. Ova laid singly on upperside of leaves. Hibernates as an adult amongst dense vegetation, tree roots, overhanging banks, road-drains, out-houses, etc.

**Behaviour.** Hibernation sometimes disrupted briefly on warm days in late winter. Adults often feed on *Salix* blossom in early spring.

**Note.** Declined rapidly in Britain about the turn of the century, but has recovered much of its former range since 1920/1930: now common and widespread in S England and Wales (cf. *L. camilla*). Short/medium term residency in areas close to limit of range possibly relate to erratic or periodic increases in adjacent, permanent populations accompanied by dispersion.

## *Polygonum egea* Southern Comma                Plate 42

**Range.** SE France, Italy, S Balkans, Greece, Turkey, Middle East, Iran to N India.

*P. egea* Cramer 1775 TL: Istanbul and Izmir.

**Distribution.** SE France. Corsica. NW coastal and peninsular Italy. Sicily. Dalmatian coast. Albania. Republic of Macedonia. Bulgaria. Greece, including Corfu, Crete and many other Aegean Islands. European Turkey. Absent from Sardinia and Rhodes. 0-1700m: uncommon above 1100m.

**Description.** First brood: ups yellowish-brown with dark brown markings, variable in size and number; uns yellowish with complex pattern of variegation; unh with small, white 'y'-shaped mark at cell-end. Summer brood(s): ups and uns usually slightly darker.

**Flight-period.** Bivoltine or trivoltine. May/October. Hibernated specimens reappear late March.

**Habitat.** Hot, dry, steep rocky places: often common in villages where old walls provide a foot-hold for LHP.

**Life-history.** LHP *Parietaria officinalis*. Captive larvae reluctantly accept *Urtica dioica* but reject *Salix caprea* and *Ulmus glabra*. Hibernates as an adult.

**Behaviour.** Fond of basking on rock faces, walls, hot paths, etc.

## *Araschnia levana* Map Butterfly                Plate 40

**Range.** N Spain, C and E Europe, Caucasus, C Asia to NE China, Korea and Japan.

*A. levana* Linnaeus 1758 TL: Germany.

**Distribution.** N Spain (E Pyrenees: very local) eastwards through N and C France, Switzerland to E Denmark (including Fyen, Sjælland, Lolland and Falster), S Sweden (SW Skåne – first recorded in 1992); Baltic states, Bulgaria and N Greece (Nestos and Evros river systems). Absent from S France, Italy, Dalmatian coast, (?)Albania and Republic of Macedonia. 0-1400m. Reports for Portugal require confirmation.

**Description and Variation.** Seasonal dimorphism well marked. First brood (f. *levana*): ups gc dusky-orange with black markings. Second brood (f. *prorsa* Linnaeus): ups gc dark brown; creamy-yellow or white discal band disrupted at v4 upf. Intermediate forms (f. *porima* Ochsenheimer) are not uncommon.

**Flight-period.** Generally bivoltine. May/June and July /August: sometimes a partial third brood in favourable localities/seasons.

**Habitat.** Deciduous woodland clearings or bushy margins.

**Life-history.** LHPs *Urtica dioica*; *U. urens*. Ova laid in chains suspended from underside of leaf – closely resembles character of flowers/flower-buds. Small larvae live in companies, dispersing towards maturity. Hibernates as a pupa.

## *Argynnis pandora* Cardinal Plate 43

**Range.** Canary Islands, N Africa, S Europe, Turkey, Middle East, Iraq, Iran, S Russia, Kazakhstan, Afghanistan, N Pakistan, N India.

*A. pandora* Denis and Schiffermüller 1775 TL: Vienna. syn: *maja* Cramer 1776.

**Distribution.** Canary Islands: La Palma; Gomera; Hierro; Tenerife. 500-1500m. Morocco. Algeria. Tunisia. 200-2600m. Portugal. Spain. Balearic Islands. W and S France. Corsica. Sporadic in N Italy, widespread in S Italy. Sardinia. Elba. Sicily. S Switzerland, Austria. Czech Republic. Slovakia. Hungary. Balkans. Greece, including Corfu, Crete, Thassos, Limnos and Samos. European Turkey. 50-1650m.

**Variation.** Aberrant form *maruxa* Agenjo, uns normal greenish gc replaced by pinkish-buff: reputedly recurrent in some localities of C Spain.

**Flight-period.** Univoltine in much of Europe, generally mid May/early July: bivoltine in NW Africa, May/June and August/late September: possibly bivoltine in parts of S Europe (univoltine in Sardinia, mid June/late August): in Canary Islands, late May/mid September with no apparent discontinuity.

**Habitat and Behaviour.** Open clearings, bordered by bushes, in deciduous or open pine woodland. Habitats invariably contain, or are in proximity to an abundance of robust, nectar-rich plants, *Carduus, Cirsium, Centaureae* etc., upon which both sexes are avid feeders.

**Life-history.** LHPs *Viola* spp., including *V. cheiranthifolia* (Tenerife). Ova laid on dead vegetation, less often on LHP in shade of dense undergrowth. Hibernates as a small larva.

## *Argynnis paphia* Silver-washed Fritillary Plate 43

**Range.** Algeria, Europe, Turkey, temperate Asia to Yakutia.

*A. paphia* Linnaeus 1758 TL: Sweden.

**Distribution.** Algeria (Blida; Djurdjura massif; Lambessa; Batna; Dj. Aures; Collo; S'Gag; 800-1600m). Generally widespread and common from N Portugal, N and E Spain (including S. de Cazorla and S. de Segura: sporadic) through Ireland and S Britain to S Fennoscandia (including Fyen, Sjælland, Lolland, Falster, Bornholm and Gotland), Greece and European Turkey: recorded from Sicily, Corsica, Sardinia, Elba, Crete, Lesbos, Samos, Ikaria and Andros. 0-1500m.

**Variation.** Unh gc and 'silver-wash' subject to appreciable variation, especially in Mediterranean region. In Algeria, *dives* Oberthür: ups black markings well developed; unh 'silver-wash' generally obsolete, replaced by yellowish-green. In Corsica and Sardinia, f. *immaculata* Bellier: unh 'silver-wash' replaced by extensive silvery-golden suffusion: forms transitional to nominate form not uncommon in Mediterranean region. In Spain, Italy and occasionally in S Greece, *anargyria* Staudinger: uns gc yellowish; 'silver-wash' replaced by pale, diffuse discal band. In NW Africa and S Europe, unh silver-white markings sometimes well developed, prominent (*argyrea* Oberthür). Female dimorphic: f. *valezina* Esper: ups suffused greyish-green or greenish-brown; usual black markings replaced by dark brown: recurrent form in most European populations, but unknown in N Africa and Sardinia.

**Flight-period.** Univoltine. Late May/September according to locality.

**Habitat.** Sunny, woodland clearings with bushy margins, usually containing bramble or other nectar-rich plants.

**Life-history.** LHPs: *Viola* spp.: Algeria, *V.* (?)*mumbyana*: Europe, *V. reichenbachiana*; *V. canina*; *V. odorata*; *V. riviniana*. Ova laid in crevices in tree-bark, where newly-hatched larvae hibernate: deciduous trees, less often conifers, sited near an abundance of well-shaded LHP, are usually selected.

## *Argynnis laodice* Pallas's Fritillary — Plate 44

**Range.** Central E Europe, C and S Urals, S and W Siberia, NW Kazakhstan, Amur, Japan.

*A. laodice* Pallas 1771 TL: S Russia.

**Distribution.** Latvia. Lithuania. E Poland. Slovakia. E Hungary. Romania. An occasional migrant in Estonia, SE Sweden (including Gotland) and S Finland.

**Variation.** Ups dark markings and black suffusion variable.

**Flight-period.** Univoltine. July/August.

**Habitat.** Damp, flowery meadows in open woodland at low altitudes.

**Life-history.** LHP *Viola palustris*.

**Behaviour.** Both sexes attracted to bramble blossom.

## *Argynnis aglaja* Dark Green Fritillary — Plate 44

**Range.** Morocco, Europe, Turkey, Asia, China, Japan.

*A. aglaja* Linnaeus 1758 TL: Sweden (Verity 1950).
syn: *charlotta* Haworth 1802.

**Distribution.** Morocco: Middle Atlas (Ain Leuth; Azrou; Ifrane; 1500-1800m); Rif Mts. (Bab-Berred; Dj. Lakraa; Ketama; 1200-1500m). Widespread and common in most of Europe, including Britain, Ireland, Orkney Islands and European Turkey: absent from Mediterranean islands except Sicily. 0-2200m.

**Variation.** In Middle Atlas, *lyauteyi* Oberthür: large; male ups gc dusky orange-buff; black markings well developed; unf with pale pinkish-orange basal flush; unh green suffusion brighter, more extensive: female ups pale yellowish-buff, with greyish-green suffusion. In Rif Mts., *excelsior* Rothschild: resembles *lyauteyi*: ups gc brighter; unf basal flush deeper pink. In colder climates, e.g., Scotland, ups black markings are often heavy.

**Flight-period.** Univoltine. June/August, according to locality and altitude.

**Habitat.** Open grassy, flowery slopes; clearings in light woodland; damp meadows; heaths; moorlands. Most frequent on calcareous soils.

**Life-history.** LHPs *Viola hirta*; *V. tricolor*; *V. palustris*. Ova laid on both surfaces of leaves. At rest, small larvae often secrete themselves in the smaller, furled leaves of LHP. Hibernates as an unfed larva amongst leaf-litter or in bark-crevices at base of small shrubs or trees. Pupates on robust plant-stems near ground-level.

# *Argynnis adippe* High Brown Fritillary    Plate 45

**Range.** NW Africa, Europe, Turkey, temperate Asia.

*A. adippe adippe* Denis and Schiffermüller 1775 TL: Vienna.
syn: *cydippe* Linnaeus 1761
**Distribution.** Most of Europe, including England and Wales, to 66°N in Fennoscandia (including Fyen, Sjælland, Lolland, Falster, Bornholm, Öland and Gotland), Greece and European Turkey. Absent from Mediterranean islands except Sicily. 0-2100m.
**Description.** Male upf sex-brands on v2 and v3 conspicuous; uph with hair-fringe along v7.
**Variation.** F. *cleodoxa* Ochsenheimer: unh gc buff or yellowish, without green basal suffusion; all markings reduced; silver spots obsolete except as pupils of pd reddish-brown spots: very rare in N Europe, progressively more frequent through central S Europe to Balkans, preponderating south of central Alps and replacing nominate form in Greece: nominate form occurs only rarely in S Balkans and has once been reported from N Greece. F. *cleodoxa* is common in Pyrenees, occurring with nominate form and the intermediate f. *cleodippe* Staudinger: these three forms become rapidly less common south of Pyrenees where they are replaced by f. *chlorodippe* Herrich-Schäffer: unh suffused olive-green; silver spots fully developed; series of reddish pd spots complete.
**Flight-period.** Univoltine. Late May/August according to locality and altitude.
**Habitat.** Generally dry, grassy bushy places; clearings in light woodland.
**Life-history.** LHPs *Viola* spp., including *V. canina*; *V. odorata*; *V. hirta*. Ova laid on leaves. Hibernates as a fully formed larva within ovum-case. Pupates on robust plant-stems near ground-level.
**Note.** In decline in Britain.

*A. adippe auresiana* Früstorfer 1908 TL: Djebel Aures, Algeria.
**Distribution.** Morocco: Anti-Atlas (Tizi-n-Melloul); High Atlas (Tizi-n-Talrhemt; Tizi-n-Test; Oukaïmeden; Dj. Aourach; 1750-2800m); Middle Atlas (Ifrane; Tizi-Tarhzeft; Azrou; 1300-1700m); Rif Mts. (Bab-Berred; Dj. Lakraa; Ketama; Taghsut; 1000-1800m). Algeria: Dj. Aures; Kabylie; 1300-1700m.
**Description and Variation.** Resembles *chlorodippe* closely: unh green suffusion darker; basal silver spots often smaller or absent. Male ups sex-brand vestigial; uph hair-fringe on v7 sparse. In High Atlas, f. *astrifera* Higgins: smaller; paler; black markings reduced. In Rif Mts., f. *hassani* Weiss: resembles *auresiana* closely: slightly larger; ups gc brighter; black markings heavier; unh green suffusion more extensive. All forms of *auresiana* appear to lack unh rounded, black-pupilled yellow/silver spot near cell-base – characteristic of *A. niobe*.
**Flight-period.** Univoltine. June/early August according to locality.
**Habitat.** Open, dry, bushy places; grassy, flowery slopes; rocky slopes with sparse vegetation; open woodland.
**Note.** Regarded as specifically distinct by some authors, and as a ssp. of *A. niobe* by others. In the absence definitive biological data, present provisional taxonomic assignment, based on close superficial similarity to *A. adippe* populations of S Spain, seems appropriate.

## *Argynnis niobe* Niobe Fritillary                    Plate 45

**Range.** Europe, Turkey, Middle East, Iran, C Asia, Mongolia, Amur.

*A. niobe* Linnaeus 1758 TL: Sweden (Verty 1950).

**Distribution.** Most of Europe to 62°N in Fennoscandia (including Sjælland, Falster, Bornholm, Öland and Gotland) and European Turkey. Absent from NW Africa, SW coastal district of Iberian peninsula, central N Italy, most coastal areas of peninsular Italy, Ireland, Britain and Mediterranean islands except N Sicily. 0-2400m.

**Description and Variation.** Male ups resembles *A. adippe*: upf sex-brand on v2 and v3 narrow – often greatly reduced or absent in C and S Spain; unh usually with small, roughly circular, yellow or silver spot, often with black pupil or thin black ring, near cell-base – a useful distinguishing character (cf. *A. adippe* and *A. aglaja*). F. *eris* Meigen: unh silver spots absent, but usual positions outlined black; gc variable, pale greenish-yellow to yellowish-buff: a wide variety of transitional forms are not uncommon in Fennoscandia and some localities of C Europe. F. *eris* appears to be present in all C European populations, in widely varying ratios to nominate form, replacing the latter entirely in Iberian peninsula, S Balkans and Greece (reports of nominate form from Sierra Nevada and Portugal require confirmation). In some localities of Massif Central and in C Apenines, nominate form preponderates. In (?)much of Spain, f. *altonevadensis* Reisser: a variant of f. *eris*: both sexes smaller, ups gc paler: female ups and uns black markings reduced.

**Flight-period.** Univoltine. Late May/August according to locality and altitude.

**Habitat.** Open grassy places often amongst scrub; rocky gullies with sparse vegetation; woodland clearings.

**Life-history.** LHPs *Viola* (?)*canina*; *V. odorata*; *V. hirta*; *V. palustris*. Ova laid on dead vegetation near LHP. Hibernates as a fully-formed larva within its ovum-case. Large larvae often rest in full sun on pieces of fallen tree-bark or dead wood.

## *Argynnis elisa* Corsican Fritillary                  Plate 46

**Range.** Corsica, Sardinia.

*A. elisa* Godart 1823 TL: Corsica and Sardinia.
**Distribution.** Corsica. Sardinia. 800-1500m.
**Flight-period.** Univoltine. Late June/mid August.
**Habitat.** Dry, open heaths; bushy places; light woodland.
**Life-history.** LHP *Viola corsica*. Hibernates as a fully formed larva within ovum-case.

## *Issoria lathonia* Queen of Spain Fritillary          Plate 46

**Range.** Madeira, Canary Islands, N Africa, Europe, Turkey, Middle East, W and C Asia to N India, Mongolia.

*I. lathonia* Linnaeus 1758 TL: Sweden (Verity 1950).

**Distribution.** Madeira and Canary Islands (Gran Canaria; Tenerife; Gomera; La Palma) as migrants only. Morocco. Algeria. Tunisia. Most of Europe to 63°N in Fennoscandia as a resident, and 66°N as a migrant in W Finland. Resident on Corsica, Sardinia and Sicily: not reported from eastern Mediterranean islands. Rare as a migrant in S England. 0-2700m: vagrants/migrants occur at higher altitudes. Commoner in summer months as populations expand and disperse. In S Europe in late summer, relatively greater  abundance at higher altitudes is possibly due to superior condition of LHPs which are less likely to have become desiccated.

**Flight-period.** Trivoltine. March/October.

**Habitat.** Diverse. Almost all habitat-types.

**Life-history.** LHPs: *Viola* spp. belonging principally to the distinctive, but taxonomically unseparated group recognizable as 'pansies' – *Viola tricolor; V. arvensis; V. aetolica; V. lutea; V. biflora; V. calcarata; V. corsica; V. odorata.* Reliable data regarding widespread, natural use of 'violets' appear to be lacking – species of this group are occasionally rejected by captive larva. Ova laid singly on leaves of LHP, where growing in dry conditions amongst sparse vegetation: in damp conditions, ova are often deposited on low, soft herbage other than LHP. In captivity, newly-hatched larvae from early broods, as well as small wild larvae, often wander – apparently aimlessly – amongst the leaves of 'pansies' and/or 'violets' for several days before dying without attempting to feed. In nature, small or large larvae often rest in exposed positions on stones, fallen wood-bark and a variety of plants. Pupates near ground-level, suspended from plant-stems or underside of leaves. Pupal colouring variable: shiny, uniform greyish-green or brownish with white dorsal patch, in either case, resembling a bird-dropping. Reputedly hibernates as an ovum, small larva, pupa or adult.

**Behaviour.** A well-known migrant. In late afternoon sun, adults often bask on hot paths, walls, etc.

## *Brenthis hecate* Twin-spot Fritillary                                    Plate 46

**Range.** S Europe, Turkey, Iran, C Asia, Altai.

*B. hecate* Denis and Schiffermüller 1775 TL: Vienna.

**Distribution.** Spain: scattered colonies: Sierra Nevada; S. de Segura; Montes Universales; S. de la Demanda; Cantabrian Mts.; Soria; Huesca; Catalonia. S France: very local in Provençe; Basses Alpes. N Italy. Commoner in E Europe: Czech Republic and Slovakia to Balkans, N and C Greece and European Turkey. 25-1500m.

**Description and Variation.** Ups pd spots of uniform size (cf. *B. daphne*). In E Europe, unh markings darker.

**Flight-period.** Univoltine. Generally late May/late July: Bulgaria and NE Greece, late April/early May in favourable seasons.

**Habitat.** Flowery, grassy meadows, usually sheltered by bushes or light woodland.

**Life-history.** LHP principally *Filipendula ulmaria.*

## *Brenthis daphne* Marbled Fritillary                   Plate 46

**Range.** S Europe, NE Turkey, Iraq, Iran, S Urals, NW Kazakhstan, S Siberia, Mongolia, China, Japan.

*B. daphne* Denis and Schiffermüller 1775 TL: Vienna

**Distribution.** Spain: S. de Guadarrama; Montes Universales; Cantabrian Mts.; Pyrenees; Catalonia. Local in S and C France. Italy. Switzerland and S Germany to S Poland, Balkans, N and C Greece and European Turkey. Absent from Mediterranean islands except N Sicily and Samos. 75-1750m.

**Description.** Ups pd spots irregular in size (cf. *B. hecate* and *B. daphne*): both sexes, unh base of s4 (adjacent to cell-end) yellow, partly shaded or striated orange-brown (cf. *B. ino*).

**Flight-period.** Univoltine. Late May/early August.

**Habitat.** Bushy, flowery places, often in woodland clearings.

**Life-history.** LHPs *Rubus fruticosus*; *R. idaeus*. Ova laid on upperside of leaves. Larvae often rest on upperside of leaves of LHP. Hibernates as an ovum or small larva.

## *Brenthis ino* Lesser Marbled Fritillary                   Plate 46

**Range.** Europe, Turkey, throughout temperate Asia, Polar Urals, Yakutia, Japan.

*B. ino* Rottemburg 1775 TL: Halle, Germany.

**Distribution.** Spain: Cantabrian Mts.; Province of Burgos; S. de la Demanda; Pyrenees. From E Pyrenees to 66°N in Fennoscandia and Balkans. In Italy, restricted to foothills of S Alps and Calabria. Absent from Portugal, Britain, N France, N Belgium, N Holland, Greece, European Turkey and Mediterranean islands. 0-2000m.

**Description and Variation.** Both sexes: unh base of s4 (adjacent to cell-end) wholly yellow – apparent as a discrete, rectilinear spot separating cell and dark pd area (cf. *B. daphne*): ups black markings and dark suffusion very variable.

**Flight-period.** Univoltine. In C and S Europe, early June/late July: in Scandinavia, late June/mid August according to season, altitude and latitude.

**Habitat.** Damp flowery places, sheltered by bushes or light woodland, usually near rivers or marshes; also hillside bogs.

**Life-history.** LHP principally *Filipendula ulmaria*: also, *F. petalata*; *Rubus chamaemorus*; *R. idaeus*; *Aruncus dioecus*; *Sanguisorba officinalis*. Reported use of *S. minor* (?)*minor* and *S. minor muricata* in Spain requires confirmation. On *F. ulmaria*, ova laid singly or in pairs mostly amongst flower-buds which they closely resemble. Small larvae feed on flowers and leaves. Hibernates as an ovum or small larva.

# Colour Plates

Plates A & B contain a representative sample of each European butterfly family, with the exception of the distinctive members of the family Danaidae shown on Plate 96. In each case the reader is refered to the exact Plate that each species is found on, or the Plates on which all European members of that family can be found.

# Plate A

## PAPILIONIDAE Plates 1-5

*Papilio machaon*
(plate 1)

♂

*Zerynthia polyxena*
(plate 3)

♀

*Parnassius apollo*
(plate 4)

♂

## PIERIDAE Plates 6-18

*Artogeia napi*
(plate 8)

♀

*Anthocharis
cardamines*
(plate 12)

♂

*Euchloe ausonia*
(plate 10)

♀

*Colias crocea*
(plate 14)

♂

*Gonepteryx rhamni*
(plate 17)

♂

# LIBYTHEIDAE

# RIODINIDA

♂

*Libythea celtis*
(plate 37)

♂

*Hamearis lucina*
(plate 37)

## LYCAENIDAE Plate 19-36

♀

♂

♂

*atyrium ilicis*
(plate 19)

*Quercusia quercus*
(plate 19)

*Thecla betulae*
(plate 19)

*Callophrys rubi*
(plate 20)

♂

♀

*Lycaena phlaeas*
(plate 21)

*Aricia agestis*
(plate 29)

♂

♀

*Polyommatus icarus*
(plate 36)

♀

*Lysandra coridon*
(plate 17)

e B

HESPERIIDAE Plates 97-104

♂

*Pyrgus malvae*
(plate 97)

♂

*Thymelicus sylvestris*
(plate 103)

NYMPHALIDAE Plates 37-54

♂

*Apatura iris*
(plate 37)

♂

*Limenitis camilla*
(plate 39)

♀

*Polygonum c-album*
(plate 42)

♂

*Vanessa atalanta*
(plate 40)

♂

*Mellicta athalia*
(plate 52)

♀

*Euphydryas aurinia*
(plate 54)

# SATYRIDAE Plates 55-95

*Melanargia galathea*
(plate 55)

*Hipparchia semele*
(plate 61)

*Satyrus ferula*
(plate 70)

*Erebia aethiops*
(plate 76)

*Erebia epiphron*
(plate 75)

*Erebia tyndarus*
(plate 80)

*Maniola jurtina*
(plate 87)

*Lasiommata megera*
(plate 87)

*enonympha pamphilus*
(plate 90)

*Coenonympha hero*
(plate 92)

*Pararge aegeria*
(plate 93)

# Plate 1  Papilionidae

♀

*Papilio alexanor*

*Papilio machaon*

*Papilio hospiton*

*Papilio alexanor*

# Plate 2  Papilionidae

Z. c. cerisy (Samos)        Z. c. cretica

*Zerynthia cerisy*

*Iphiclides podalirius*

♂

*I. p. feisthameli*

♂

♂

♀

*Zerynthia cerisy*

# Plate 3  Papilionidae

*Archon apollinus*

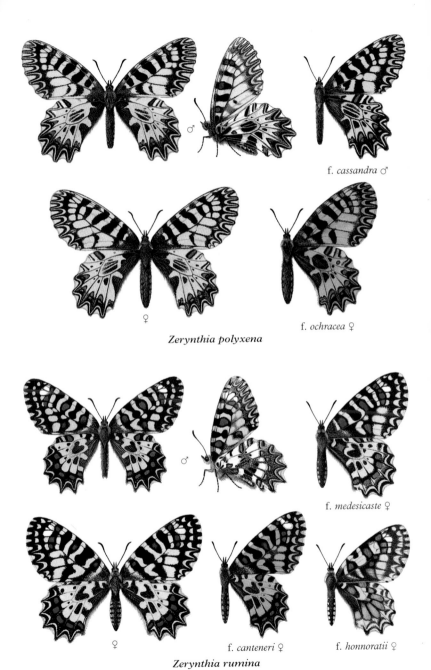

f. *cassandra* ♂

♀

f. *ochracea* ♀

*Zerynthia polyxena*

♂

f. *medesicaste* ♀

♀

f. *canteneri* ♀

f. *honnoratii* ♀

*Zerynthia rumina*

# Plate 4  Papilionidae

*Parnassius apollo*  Apollo p. 29

♂      ♀

*P. a. rhodopensis*

*P. a. nevadensis* ♀      *P. a. atrides* ♂

*Parnassius apollo*

♂

*P. a. apollo*

♀

*P. a. apollo*

**Parnassius apollo**

# Plate 5  Papilionidae

*P. m. athene* ♀

*P. m. mnemosyne* ♂

**Parnassius mnemosyne**

♂

♀

f. *cardinalis* ♀

*Parnassius phoebus*

♂

*Parnassius mnemosyne*

# Plate 6  Pieridae

♂

♀

*Catopsilia florella*

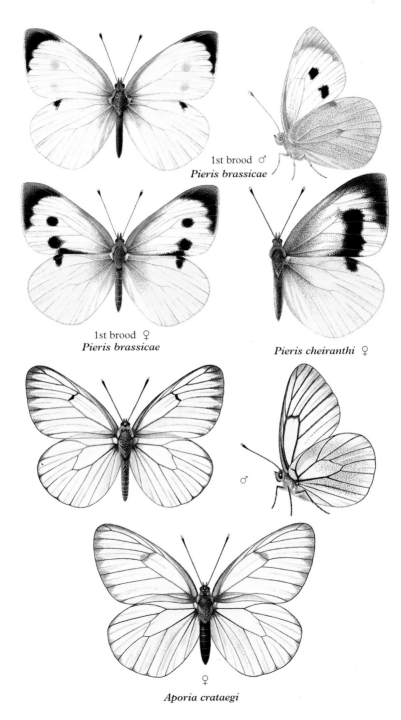

1st brood ♂
*Pieris brassicae*

1st brood ♀
*Pieris brassicae*

*Pieris cheiranthi* ♀

♂

♀

*Aporia crataegi*

# Plate 7   Pieridae

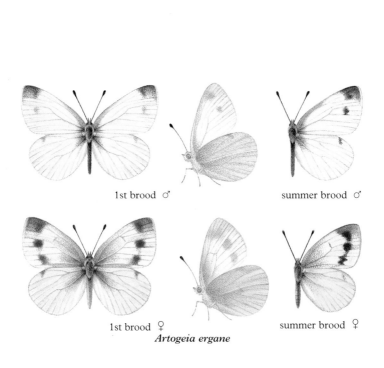

1st brood ♂                                    summer brood ♂

1st brood ♀                                    summer brood ♀
*Artogeia ergane*

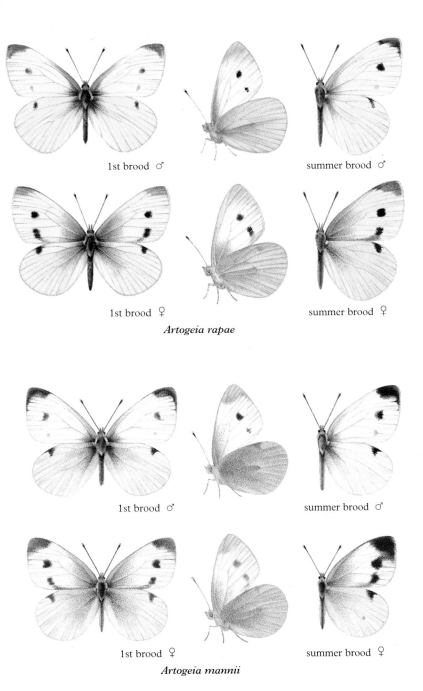

1st brood ♂                    summer brood ♂

1st brood ♀                    summer brood ♀

*Artogeia rapae*

1st brood ♂                    summer brood ♂

1st brood ♀                    summer brood ♀

*Artogeia mannii*

# Plate 8  Pieridae

*Artogeia bryoniae*

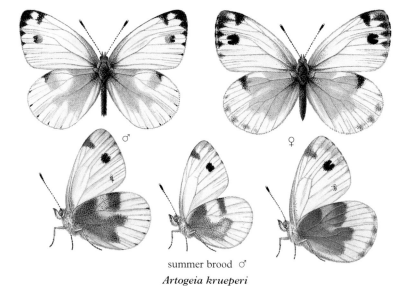

summer brood ♂

*Artogeia krueperi*

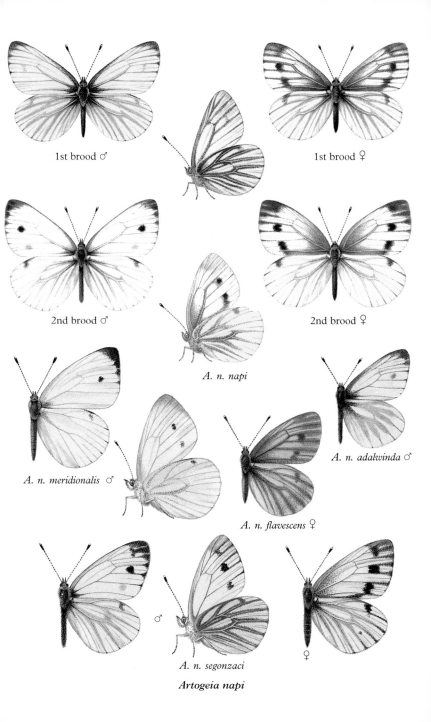

1st brood ♂

1st brood ♀

2nd brood ♂

2nd brood ♀

*A. n. napi*

*A. n. meridionalis* ♂

*A. n. flavescens* ♀

*A. n. adalwinda* ♂

♂

*A. n. segonzaci*

♀

*Artogeia napi*

# Plate 9    Pieridae

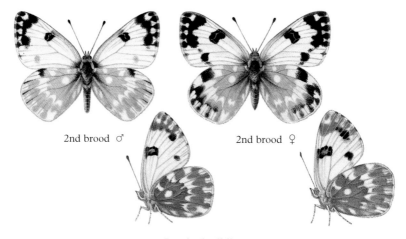

2nd brood ♂                              2nd brood ♀

*Pontia daplidice*

*Pontia callidice*

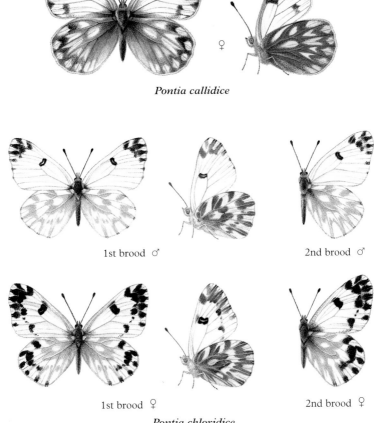

1st brood ♂

2nd brood ♂

1st brood ♀

2nd brood ♀

*Pontia chloridice*

# Plate 10 Pieridae

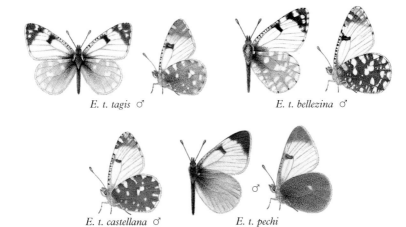

*E. t. tagis* ♂            *E. t. bellezina* ♂

*E. t. castellana* ♂      *E. t. pechi* ♂

*Euchloe tagis*

♂  ♀

*Euchloe simplonia*

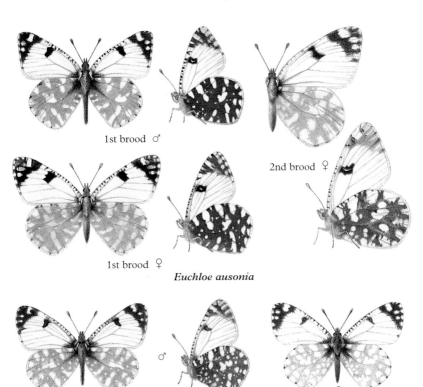

1st brood ♂

2nd brood ♀

1st brood ♀

*Euchloe ausonia*

♂  ♀

*Euchloe insularis*

# Plate 11 Pieridae

*Elphinstonia penia*

*Elphinstonia charlonia*

*Colotis evagore*

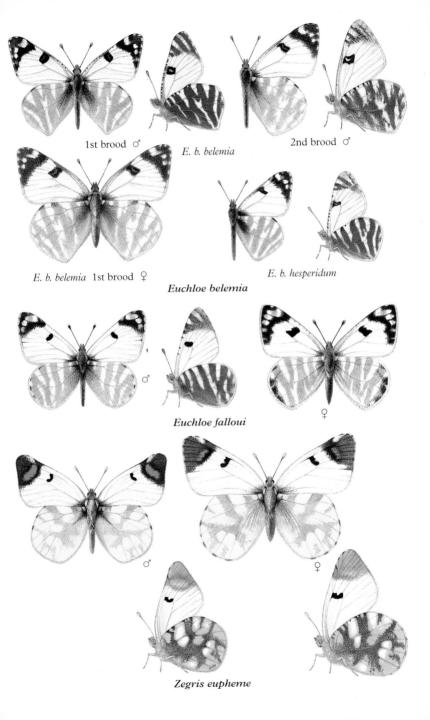

1st brood ♂

*E. b. belemia*

2nd brood ♂

*E. b. belemia* 1st brood ♀

*E. b. hesperidum*

**Euchloe belemia**

♂

**Euchloe falloui**

♀

♂

♀

**Zegris eupheme**

# Plate 12 Pieridae

*Anthocharis cardamines*

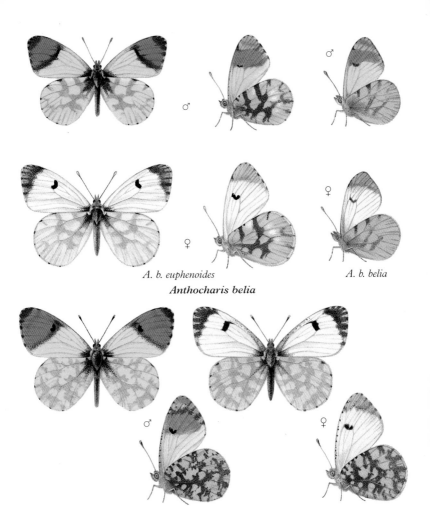

*A. b. euphenoides*                *A. b. belia*

**Anthocharis belia**

**Anthocharis damone**

**Anthocharis gruneri**

# Plate 13  Pieridae

*Colias nastes werdandi*

*Colias phicomone*

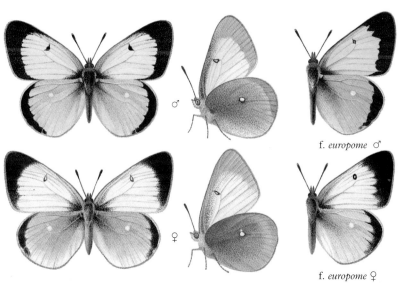

f. *europome* ♂

f. *europome* ♀

*Colias palaeno*

# Plate 14  Pieridae

*Colias hecla sulitelma*

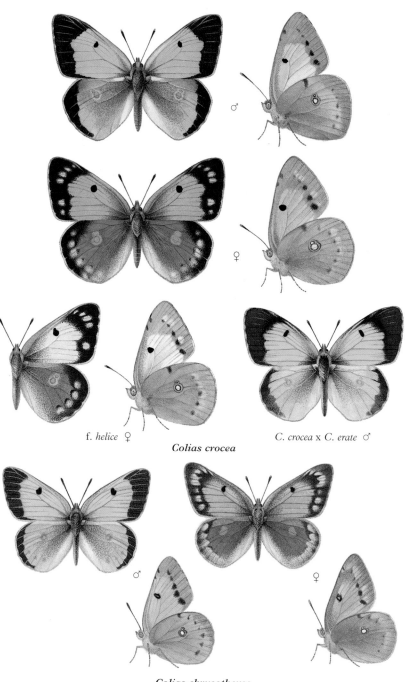

f. *helice* ♀

**Colias crocea**

*C. crocea* x *C. erate* ♂

**Colias chrysotheme**

# Plate 15  Pieridae

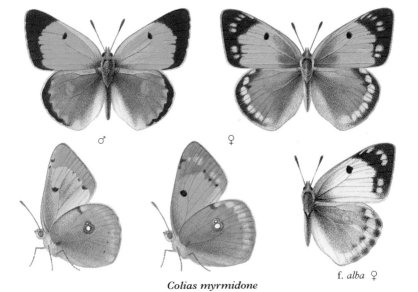

♂                    ♀

f. *alba* ♀

*Colias myrmidone*

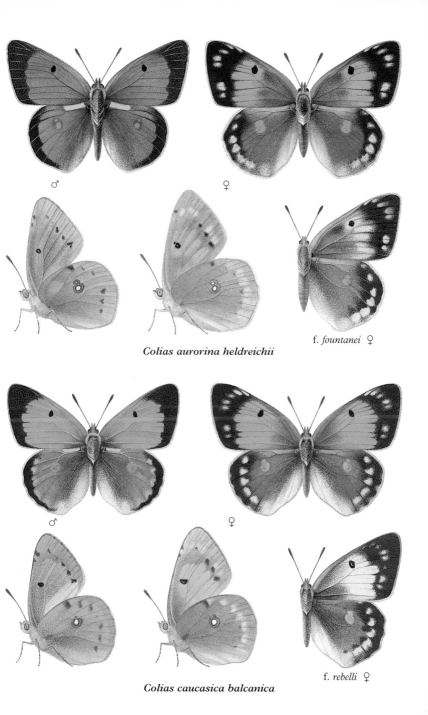

♂ ♀

f. *fountanei* ♀

*Colias aurorina heldreichii*

♂ ♀

f. *rebelli* ♀

*Colias caucasica balcanica*

# Plate 16  Pieridae

*Gonepteryx farinosa*

♂ ♀

*Colias hyale*

♂ ♀

*Colias alfacariensis*

♂ ♀

*Colias erate*       white ♀ form

# Plate 17  Pieridae

♂

♀

*Gonepteryx rhamni*

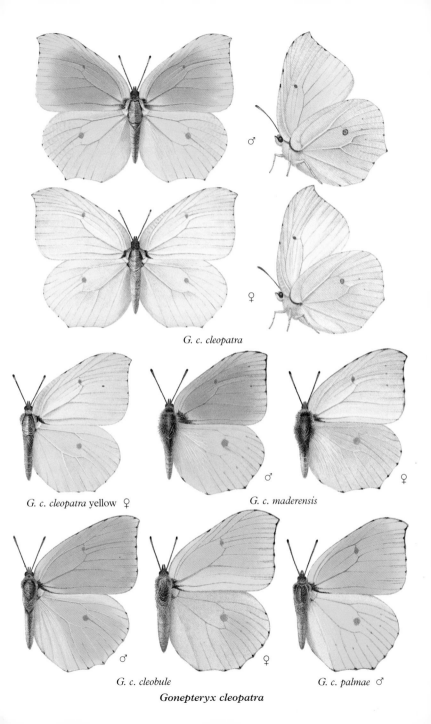

*G. c. cleopatra* ♂

*G. c. cleopatra* ♀

*G. c. cleopatra* yellow ♀

*G. c. maderensis* ♂

*G. c. maderensis* ♀

*G. c. cleobule* ♂

*G. c. cleobule* ♀

*G. c. palmae* ♂

**Gonepteryx cleopatra**

# Plate 18  Pieridae

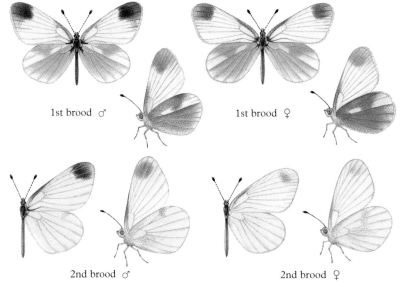

1st brood ♂            1st brood ♀

2nd brood ♂            2nd brood ♀

*Leptidea duponcheli*

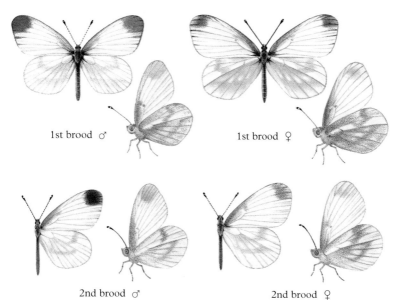

1st brood ♂

1st brood ♀

2nd brood ♂

2nd brood ♀

*Leptidea sinapis*

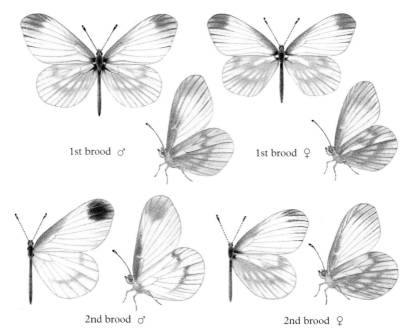

1st brood ♂

1st brood ♀

2nd brood ♂

2nd brood ♀

*Leptidea morsei*

# Plate 19 Lycaenidae

♂  ♀  f. *cerri* ♀

*Satyrium ilicis*

♂  ♀  f. *illicioides* ♀

*Satyrium esculi*

*Quercusia quercus*

*Q. c. ibericus* ♀

*Laeosopis roboris*

*Thecla betulae*

*Satyrium acaciae*

# Plate 20  Lycaenidae

*Satyrium ledereri*

*Satyrium spini*

*Satyrium w-album*

*Satyrium pruni*

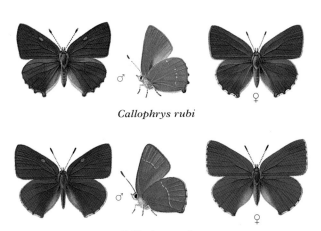

*Callophrys rubi*

*Callophrys avis*

# Plate 21 Lycaenidae

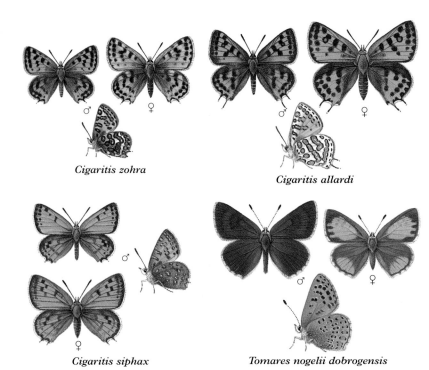

*Cigaritis zohra*

*Cigaritis allardi*

*Cigaritis siphax*

*Tomares nogelii dobrogensis*

*Tomares ballus*

*Tomares mauretanicus*

f. *undulatus* ♂

*Lycaena helle*

3rd brood ♀   *L. p. polaris* ♀   *L. p. phlaeoides* ♂

*Lycaena phlaeas*

*Lycaena dispar*

*L. d. rutila* ♂

# Plate 22  Lycaenidae

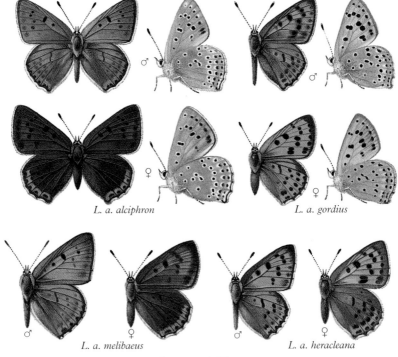

*L. a. alciphron*        *L. a. gordius*

*L. a. melibaeus*        *L. a. heracleana*

**Lycaena alciphron**

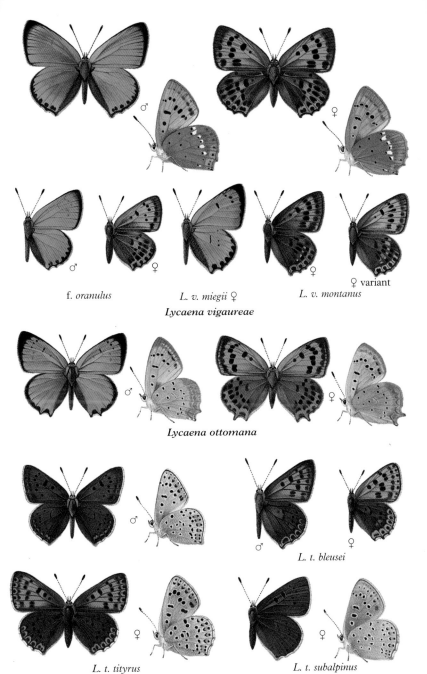

f. *oranulus*

*L. v. miegii* ♀

*L. v. montanus*

♀ variant

**Lycaena vigaureae**

**Lycaena ottomana**

*L. t. bleusei*

*L. t. tityrus*

*L. t. subalpinus*

**Lycaena tityrus**

# Plate 23  Lycaenidae

*Lycaena candens*

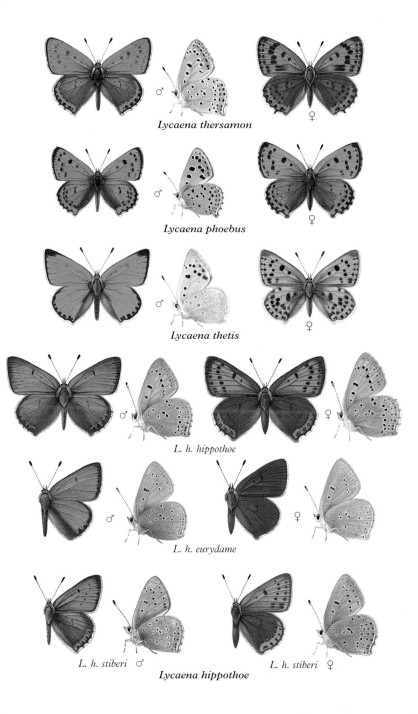

*Lycaena thersamon*

♂ ♀

*Lycaena phoebus*

♂ ♀

*Lycaena thetis*

♂ ♀

*L. h. hippothoe*

♂ ♀

*L. h. eurydame*

♂ ♀

*L. h. stiberi* ♂          *L. h. stiberi* ♀

*Lycaena hippothoe*

# Plate 24  Lycaenidae

*Lampides boeticus*                    *Leptotes pirithous*

*Cacyreus marshalli*

*Cyclyrius webbianus*

*Tarucus theophrastus*

*Tarucus rosaceus*

*Tarucus balkanicus*

*Azanus jesous*

*Azanus ubaldus*

*Zizeeria knysna*

colour variants

# Plate 25 Lycaenidae

1st brood ♀

2nd brood ♀

*Celastrina argiolus*

*Everes argiades*

*Everes decoloratus*

*Everes alcetas*

*Cupido minimus*

*Cupido carswelli*

*Cupido osiris*

*Cupido lorquinii*

# Plate 26  Lycaenidae

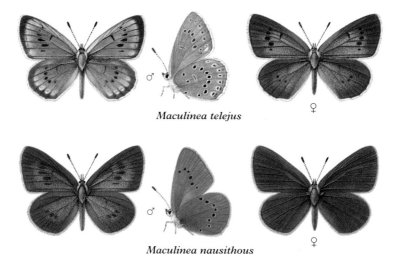

*Maculinea telejus*

♂  ♀

*Maculinea nausithous*

♂  ♀

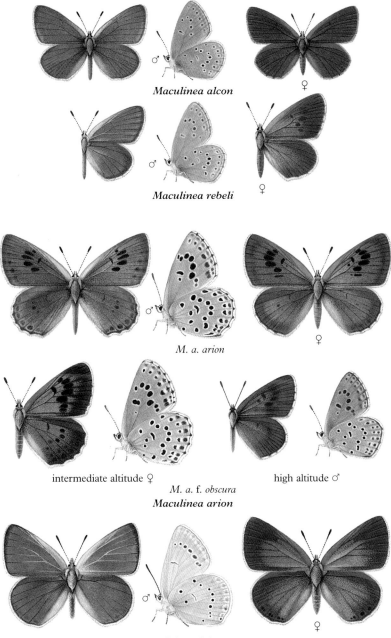

*Maculinea alcon* ♂ ♀

*Maculinea rebeli* ♂ ♀

M. a. arion ♂ ♀

intermediate altitude ♀     M. a. f. *obscura*     high altitude ♂

**Maculinea arion**

*Iolana iolas* ♂ ♀

# Plate 27  Lycaenidae

*Vacciniina optilete*

*Glaucopsyche alexis*

*Turanana endymion taygetica*

*Glaucopsyche melanops*

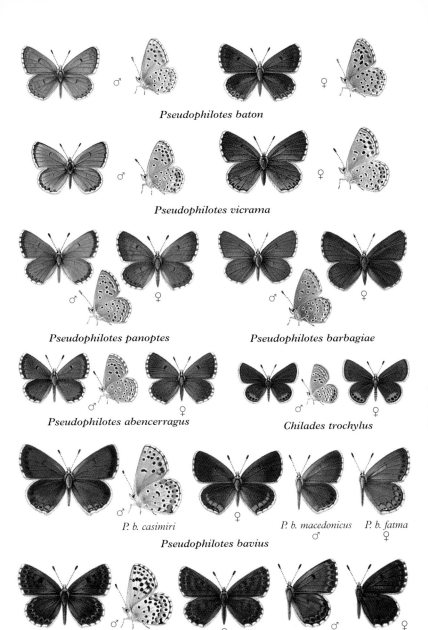

*Pseudophilotes baton*

*Pseudophilotes vicrama*

*Pseudophilotes panoptes*

*Pseudophilotes barbagiae*

*Pseudophilotes abencerragus*

*Chilades trochylus*

P. b. casimiri

P. b. macedonicus
♂

P. b. fatma
♀

*Pseudophilotes bavius*

S. o. lariana

colour variants

*Scolitantides orion*

# Plate 28 Lycaenidae

*P. a. argus*

*P. a. aegidon* ♂

*P. a. hypochionus*

*P. a. corsicus*

**Plebejus argus**

*P. i. idas*

*P. i. lapponicus* ♂

*P. i. calliopsis* ♀

*P. i. bellieri*

*P. i. magnagraeca*

*P. i. haefelfingeri* ♂

**Plebejus idas**

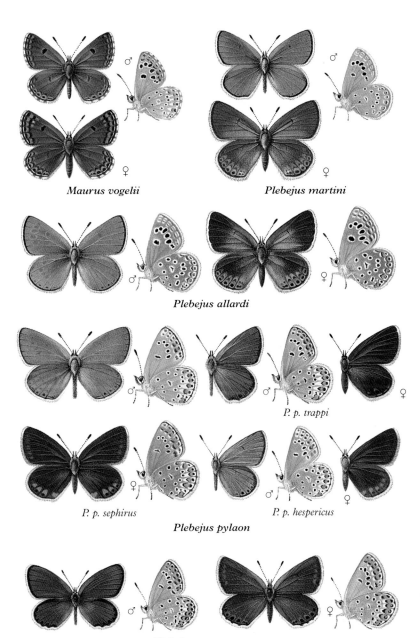

*Maurus vogelii* ♂ ♀

*Plebejus martini* ♂ ♀

*Plebejus allardi* ♂ ♀

*P. p. trappi* ♂ ♀

*P. p. sephirus* ♀

*P. p. hespericus* ♂ ♀

*Plebejus pylaon*

*Plebejus argyrognomon* ♂ ♀

# Plate 29  Lycaenidae

*Plebejus loewii*

*Kretania eurypilus pelopides*

*Kretania psylorita*

A. m. ramburi                        A. m. hesselbarthi
*Aricia morronensis*

*Eumedonia eumedon*

Greece ♂

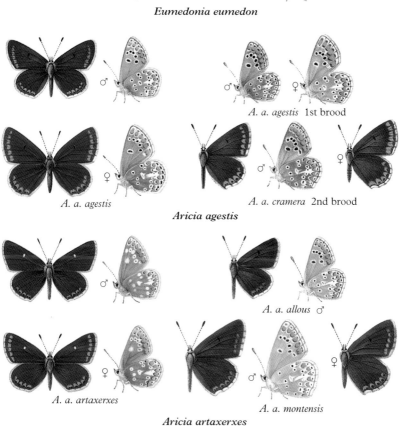

A. a. agestis 1st brood

A. a. agestis

A. a. cramera 2nd brood

*Aricia agestis*

A. a. allous ♂

A. a. artaxerxes

A. a. montensis

*Aricia artaxerxes*

*Aricia morronensis* (France)

# Plate 30  Lycaenidae

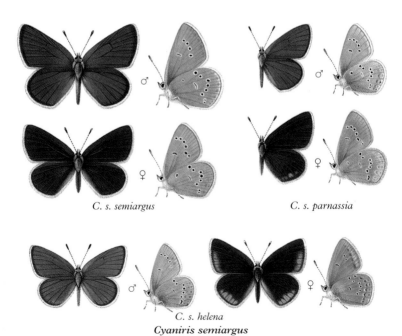

C. s. semiargus

C. s. parnassia

C. s. helena

Cyaniris semiargus

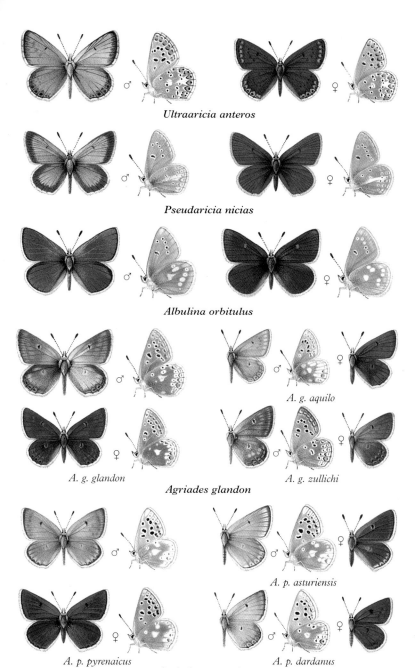

♂ ♀
*Ultraaricia anteros*

♂ ♀
*Pseudaricia nicias*

♂ ♀
*Albulina orbitulus*

♂ ♀
*A. g. aquilo*

♀ ♂ ♀
*A. g. glandon*  *A. g. zullichi*
*Agriades glandon*

♂ ♀
*A. p. asturiensis*

♀ ♂ ♀
*A. p. pyrenaicus*  *A. p. dardanus*
*Agriades pyrenaicus*

# Plate 31  Lycaenidae

*Agrodiaetus iphigenia*                *Agrodiaetus damon*

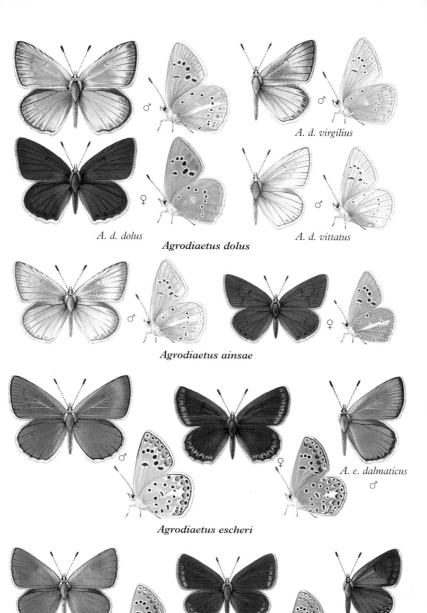

A. d. virgilius

A. d. dolus ♀

A. d. vittatus

**Agrodiaetus dolus**

**Agrodiaetus ainsae**

A. e. dalmaticus ♂

**Agrodiaetus escheri**

2nd brood ♂

2nd brood ♀

1st brood ♀

**Agrodiaetus thersites**

# Plate 32  Lycaenidae

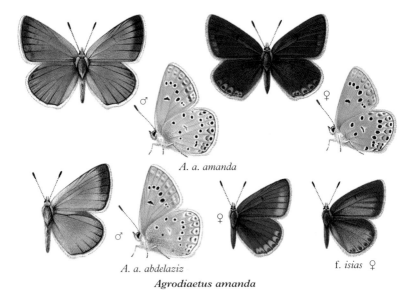

*A. a. amanda*

*A. a. abdelaziz*

f. *isias* ♀

*Agrodiaetus amanda*

*Agrodiaetus admetus*

*Agrodiaetus fabressei*

*Agrodiaetus agenjoi*

*Agrodiaetus humedasae*

*Agrodiaetus aroaniensis*

# Plate 33  Lycaenidae

*A. r. ripartii*

*A. r. pelopi*
**Agrodiaetus ripartii**

**Agrodiaetus violetae**

**Agrodiaetus nephohiptamenos**

**Agrodiaetus galloi**

# Plate 34  Lycaenidae

*Meleageria daphnis*

f. *steeveni* ♀

*Neolysandra coelestina*

*Plebicula dorylas*

*P. g. golgus*

*P. g. sagratrox*
**Plebicula golgus**

*Plebicula nivescens*

*Plebicula atlantica*

# Plate 35  Lycaenidae

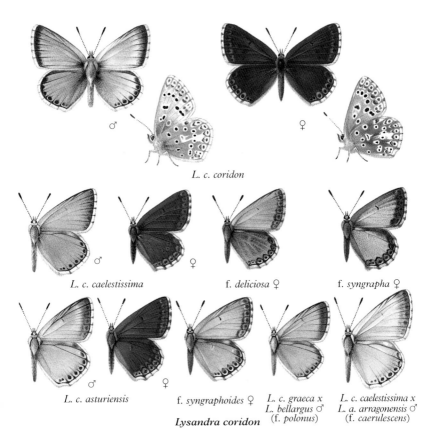

♂      ♀

*L. c. coridon*

*L. c. caelestissima* ♂ ♀      f. *deliciosa* ♀      f. *syngrapha* ♀

*L. c. asturiensis* ♂ ♀      f. *syngraphoides* ♀

*L. c. graeca* x *L. bellargus* ♂ (f. *polonus*)

*L. c. caelestissima* x *L. a. arragonensis* ♂ (f. *caerulescens*)

*Lysandra coridon*

blue ♀

*Lysandra philippi*

*Lysandra hispana*

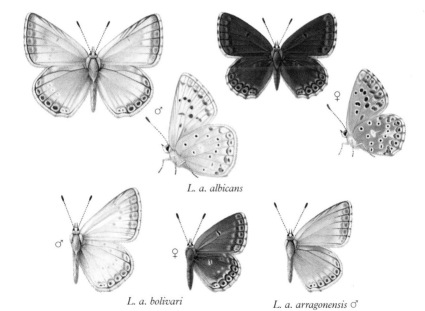

L. a. albicans

L. a. bolivari

L. a. arragonensis ♂

*Lysandra albicans*

# Plate 36  Lycaenidae

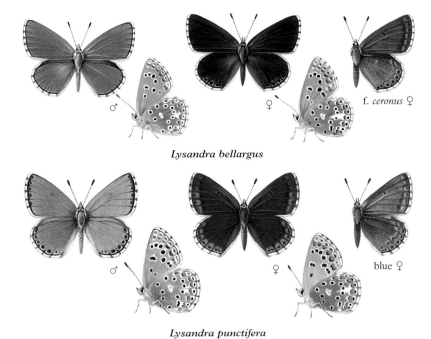

♂                    ♀                    f. *ceronus* ♀

*Lysandra bellargus*

♂                    ♀                    blue ♀

*Lysandra punctifera*

*P. i. icarus*

f. *boalensis* ♂          f. *celina* ♂          blue ♀          f. *sardoa* ♀

**Polyommatus icarus**

**Polyommatus eroides**

**Polyommatus eros**

**Polyommatus menelaos**

# Plate 37 Libytheidae, Riodinidae and Nymphalidae

*Hamearis lucina*

*Libythea celtis*

*Charaxes jasius*

♂

♂

♀

*Apatura iris*

# Plate 38  Nymphalidae

*Apatura metis*

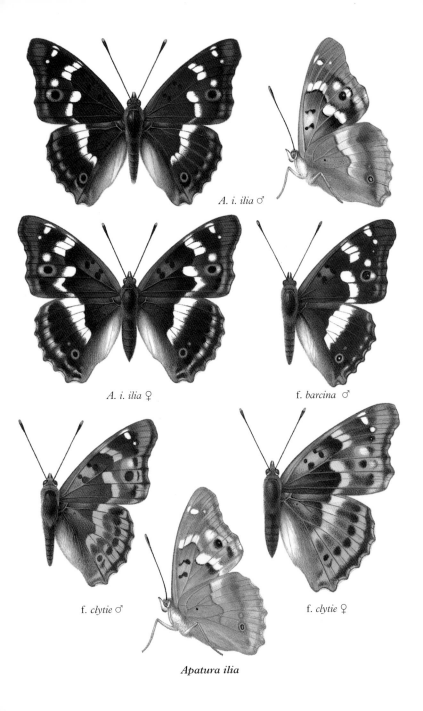

*A. i. ilia* ♂

*A. i. ilia* ♀

f. *barcina* ♂

f. *clytie* ♂

f. *clytie* ♀

**Apatura ilia**

# Plate 39 Nymphalidae

♂

*Limenitis camilla*

♂

♂

*Neptis sappho*

*Neptis rivularis*

*Limenitis populi*

*Limenitis reducta*

# Plate 40  Nymphalidae

♂

♀

1st brood

♂

♀

2nd brood

*Araschnia levana*

♂

*Nymphalis antiopa*

♂

*Vanessa atalanta*

♀

*Vanessa indica*

# Plate 41  Nymphalidae

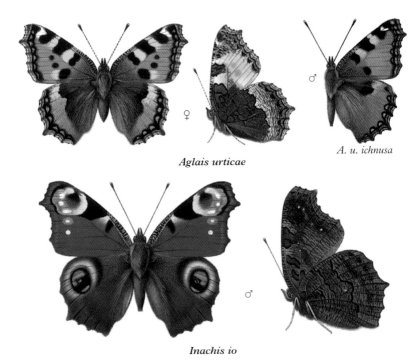

♀

*A. u. ichnusa*

*Aglais urticae*

♂

*Inachis io*

*Nymphalis polychloros*

*Nymphalis xanthomelas*

*Nymphalis vau-album*

# Plate 42 Nymphalidae

*Vanessa cardui*                                 *Vanessa virginiensis*

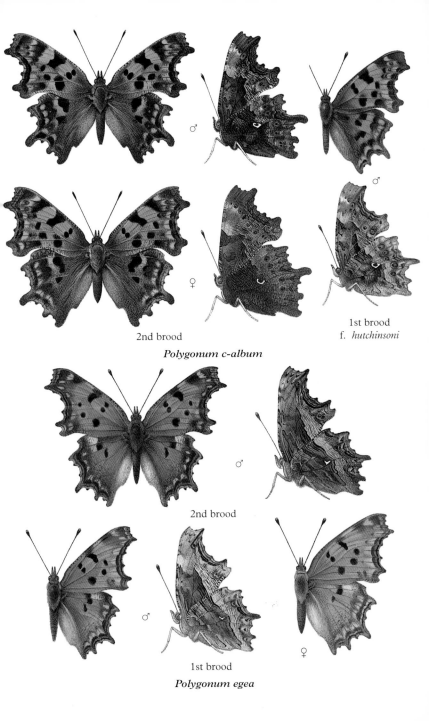

♂

♂

♀

1st brood
f. *hutchinsoni*

2nd brood

*Polygonum c-album*

♂

2nd brood

♂

♀

1st brood

*Polygonum egea*

# Plate 43  Nymphalidae

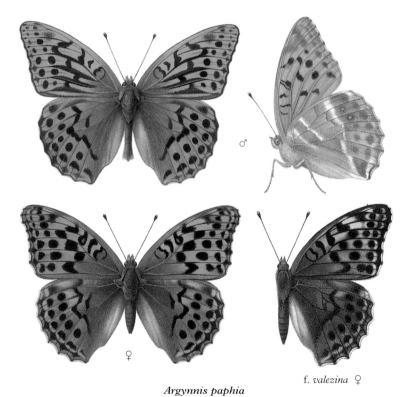

♂

♀

f. *valezina* ♀

*Argynnis paphia*

*Argynnis pandora*

♂

♀

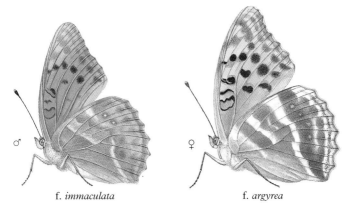

f. *immaculata*          f. *argyrea*

*Argynnis paphia*

# Plate 44 Nymphalidae

♂

♀

*Argynnis laodice*

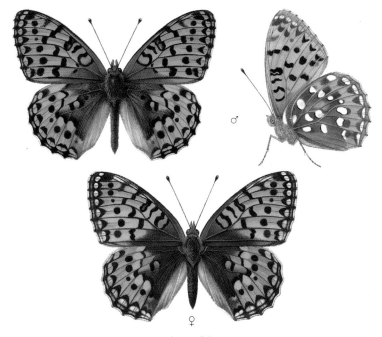

♂

♀

*A. a. aglaja*

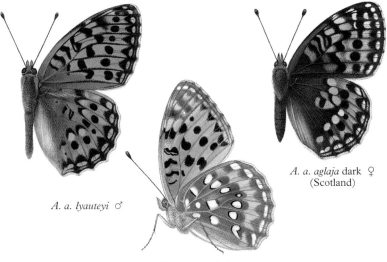

*A. a. lyauteyi* ♂

*A. a. aglaja* dark ♀
(Scotland)

**Argynnis aglaja**

# Plate 45  Nymphalidae

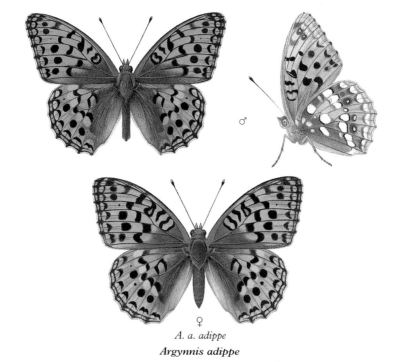

♂

♀

*A. a. adippe*

**Argynnis adippe**

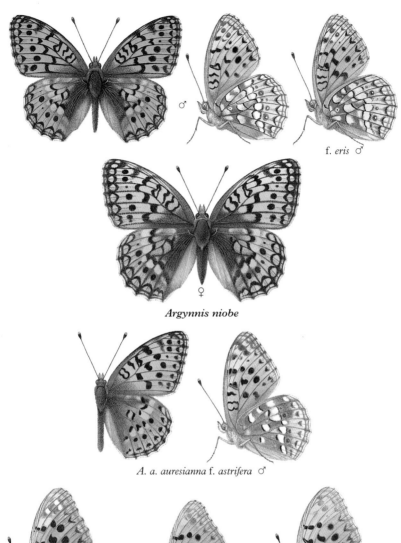

♂

f. *eris* ♂

♀

*Argynnis niobe*

*A. a. auresianna* f. *astrifera* ♂

f. *chlorodippe* ♂

f. *cleodippe* ♂
*A. a. adippe*
*Argynnis adippe*

f. *cleodoxa* ♂

# Plate 46 Nymphalidae

*Brenthis daphne*

*Brenthis ino*

♂    ♀

*Argynnis elisa*

♂    ♀

*Issoria lathonia*

♂    ♀

*Brenthis hecate*

# Plate 47 Nymphalidae

*P. e. eunomia*          *P. e. ossiana*

*Proclossiana eunomia*

*Boloria graeca*

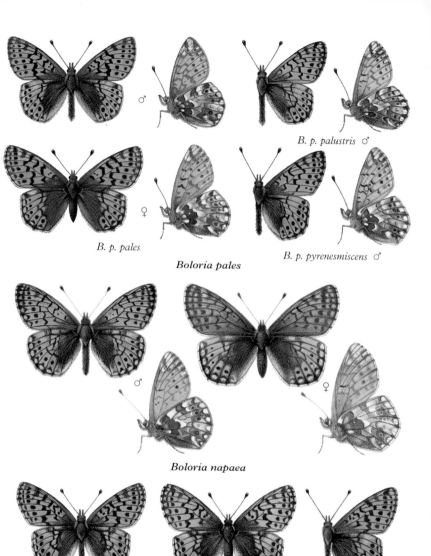

♂

*B. p. palustris* ♂

♀

*B. p. pales*

*Boloria pales*

*B. p. pyrenesmiscens* ♂

♂

♀

*Boloria napaea*

♂

♀

f. *alethea*

*Boloria aquilonaris*

# Plate 48 Nymphalidae

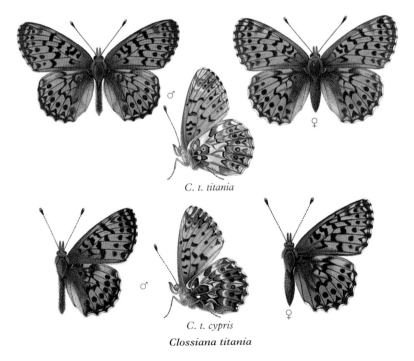

C. t. titania

C. t. cypris

*Clossiana titania*

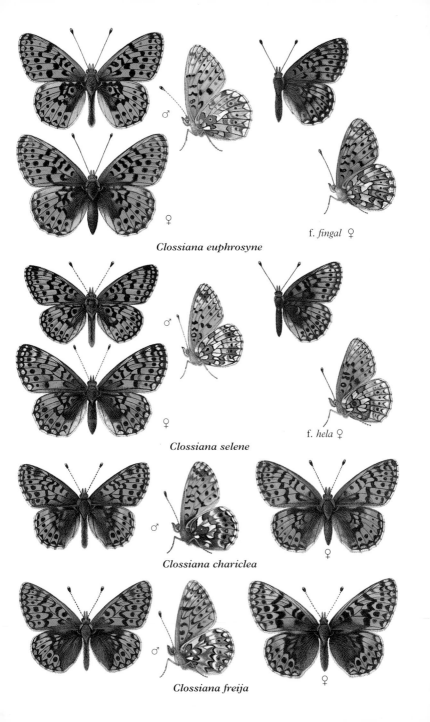

♂

♀

f. *fingal* ♀

*Clossiana euphrosyne*

♂

♀

f. *hela* ♀

*Clossiana selene*

♂

♀

*Clossiana chariclea*

♂

♀

*Clossiana freija*

# Plate 49  Nymphalidae

*Clossiana frigga*

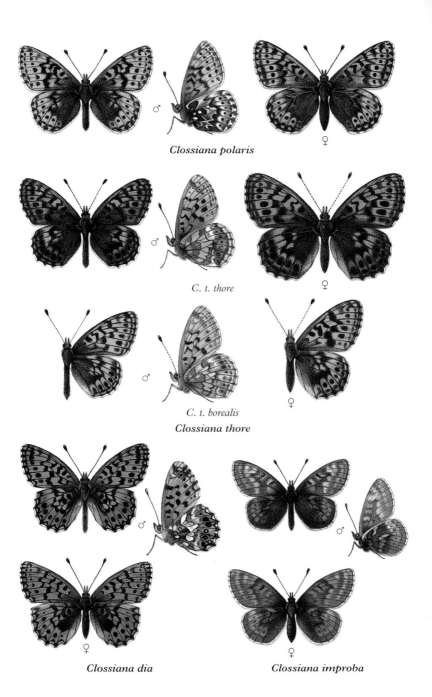

*Clossiana polaris*

♂ ♀

*C. t. thore*

♂ ♀

*C. t. borealis*

*Clossiana thore*

♂ ♀

*Clossiana dia*

♂ ♀

*Clossiana improba*

# Plate 50  Nymphalidae

*Melitaea cinxia*

*Melitaea arduinna*

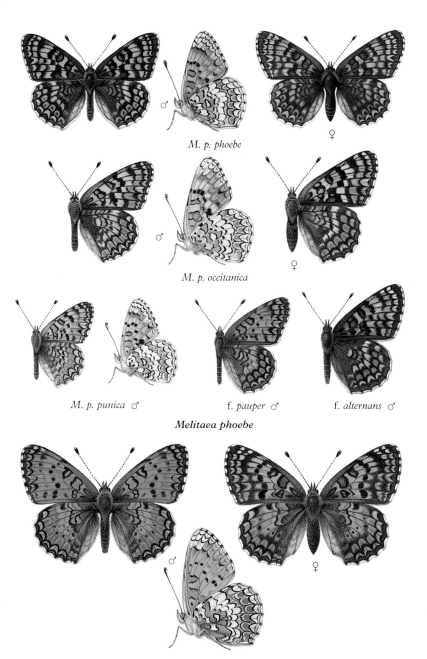

*M. p. phoebe*

*M. p. occitanica*

*M. p. punica* ♂          f. *pauper* ♂          f. *alternans* ♂

**Melitaea phoebe**

**Melitaea aetherie**

# Plate 51 Nymphalidae

♂   ♀

*Melitaea deserticola*

*M. t. trivia*        *M. t. ignasti*

*Melitaea trivia*

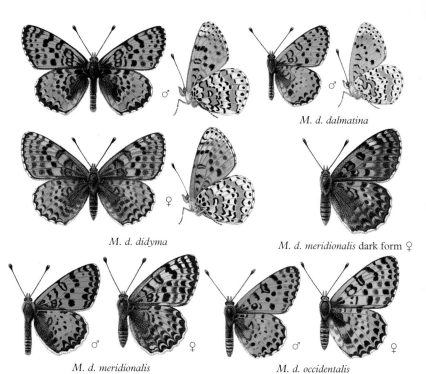

M. d. dalmatina

M. d. didyma

M. d. meridionalis dark form ♀

M. d. meridionalis

M. d. occidentalis

**Melitaea didyma**

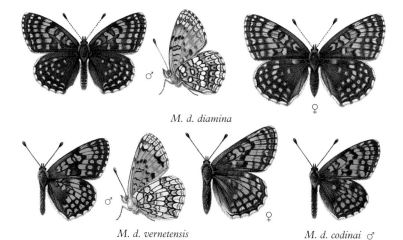

M. d. diamina

M. d. vernetensis

M. d. codinai ♂

**Melitaea diamina**

# Plate 52  Nymphalidae

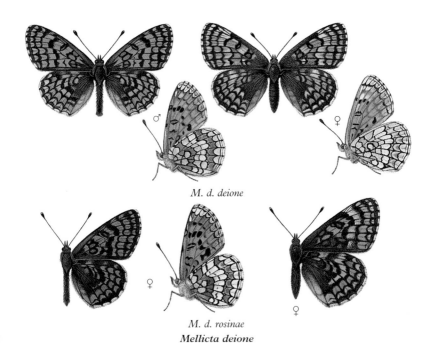

M. d. deione

M. d. rosinae

Mellicta deione

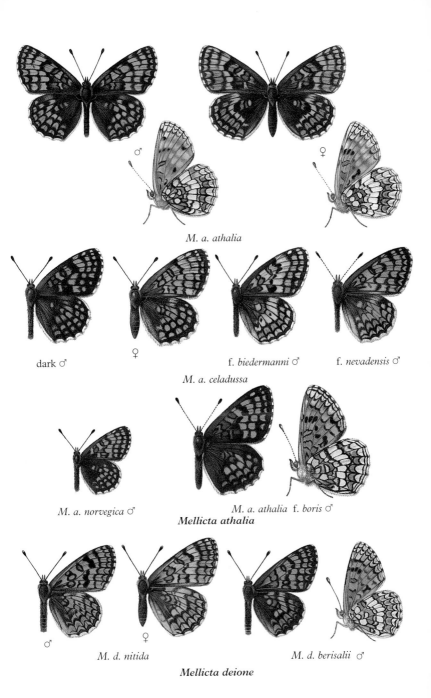

♂ ♀

*M. a. athalia*

dark ♂      ♀      f. *biedermanni* ♂      f. *nevadensis* ♂

*M. a. celadussa*

*M. a. norvegica* ♂      *M. a. athalia* f. *boris* ♂

**Mellicta athalia**

♂      ♀

*M. d. nitida*      *M. d. berisalii* ♂

**Mellicta deione**

# Plate 53 Nymphalidae

*Hypodryas maturna*

*Hypodryas intermedia*

*Mellicta asteria*

♂

♀

dark ♀

*Mellicta varia*

♂

♀

dark ♀

*Mellicta parthenoides*

♂

♀

*Mellicta aurelia*

♂

♀

*Mellicta britomartis*

# Plate 54 Nymphalidae

*Hypodryas cynthia*

*Hypodryas iduna*

E. a. bulgarica

E. a. debilis

E. a. beckeri

**Euphydryas aurinia**

**Euphydryas desfontainii**

# Plate 55  Satyridae

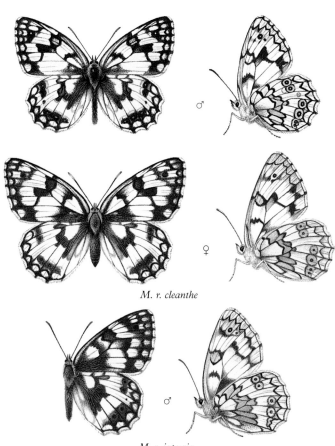

♂

♀

*M. r. cleanthe*

♂

*M. r. japygia*

*Melanargia russiae*

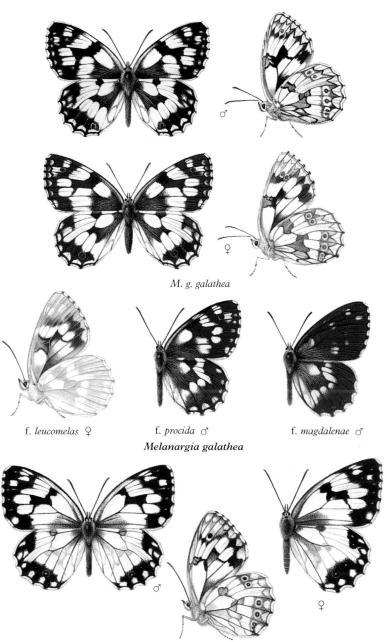

*M. g. galathea*

f. *leucomelas* ♀      f. *procida* ♂      f. *magdalenae* ♂

**Melanargia galathea**

**Melanargia lachesis**

# Plate 56  Satyridae

♂

f. *herta* ♂

*Melanargia larissa*

♂

♀

*M. o. occitanica*

*M. o. pelagia* ♂          *M. o. pherusa* ♂

**Melanargia occitanica**

♀

**Melanargia larissa**

# Plate 57  Satyridae

*Melanargia ines*

*Melanargia arge*

# Plate 58  Satyridae

♀

*Hipparchia alcyone*

*Hipparchia fagi*

*Hipparchia alcyone*

# Plate 59  Satyridae

*Hipparchia ellena*

*Hipparchia syriaca*

*Hipparchia ellena*

# Plate 60  Satyridae

*Hipparchia neomiris*

*Hipparchia volgensis delattini*

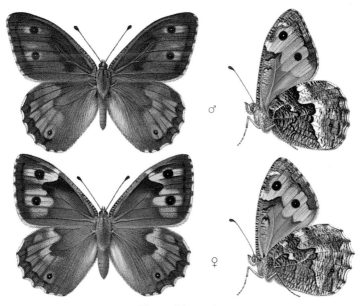

*Hipparchia cretica*

# Plate 61  Satyridae

*Hipparchia semele*

*Hipparchia pellucida*

*Hipparchia mersina*

# Plate 62  Satyridae

*Hipparchia caldeirense*

*Hipparchia azorina*

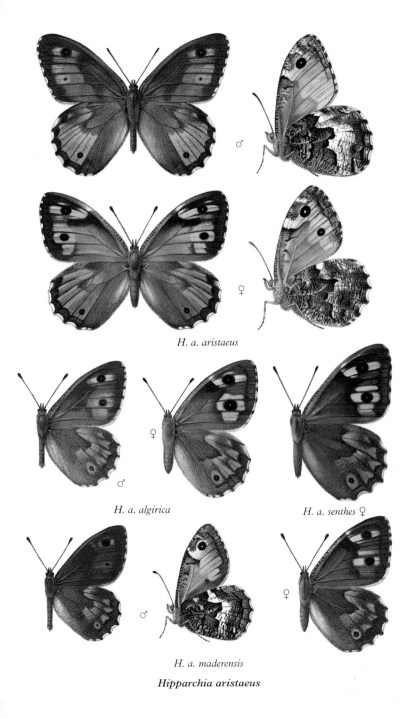

*H. a. aristaeus*

*H. a. algirica*

*H. a. senthes* ♀

*H. a. maderensis*

**Hipparchia aristaeus**

# Plate 63  Satyridae

*Neohipparchia fatua*

*N. s. statilinus* ♂          *N. s. sylvicola* ♂          *N. s. statilinus* ♀

**Neohipparchia statilinus**

♂          ♀

**Neohipparchia hansii**

# Plate 64  Satyridae

*Neohipparchia powelli*

*Pseudotergumia fidia*

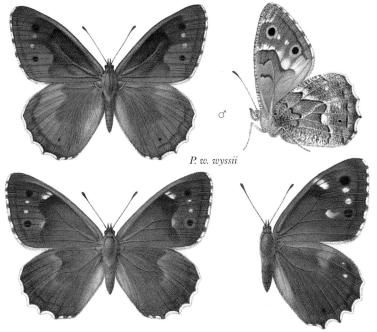

*P. w. wyssii* ♀  *P. w. bacchus* ♀

*Pseudotergumia wyssii*

# Plate 65  Satyridae

*Chazara prieuri*

♂

♀

*Chazara briseis*

♀

f. *uhagonis* ♀

*Chazara prieuri*

# Plate 66  Satyridae

♂     ♀

*Pseudochazara atlantis*

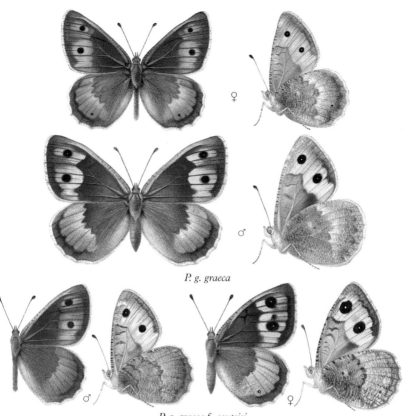

*P. g. graeca*

*P. g. graeca* f. *coutsisi*

**Pseudochazara graeca**

**Pseudochazara hippolyte**

# Plate 67  Satyridae

*P. m. amymone*

*Pseudochazara mamurra*

♂ ♀

*Pseudochazara geyeri*

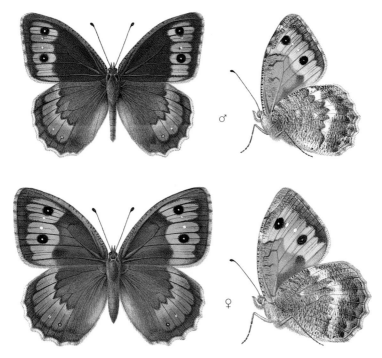

♂

♀

*Pseudochazara orestes*

# Plate 68  Satyridae

P. a. anthelea ♀

P. a. almathea

*Pseudochazara anthelea*

♂

♀

*Pseudochazara cingovskii*

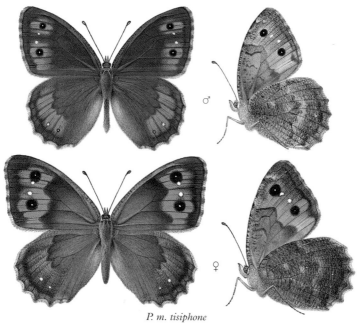

♂

♀

*P. m. tisiphone*

**Pseudochazara mniszechii**

# Plate 69  Satyridae

*Oensis bore*

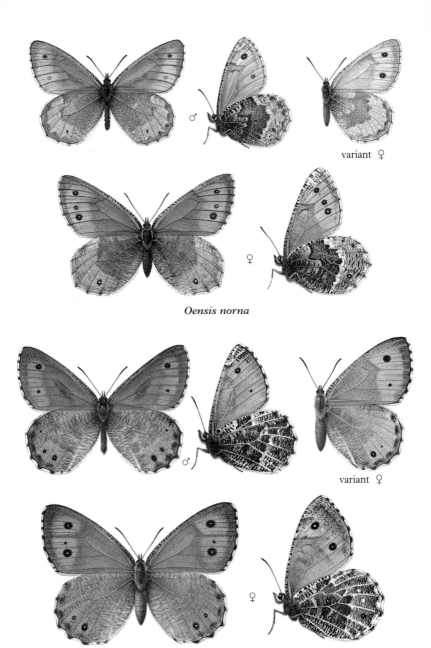

♂

variant ♀

♀

*Oensis norna*

♂

variant ♀

♀

*Oensis glacialis*

# Plate 70  Satyridae

♂    ♀

*Oensis jutta*

*Satyrus actaea*

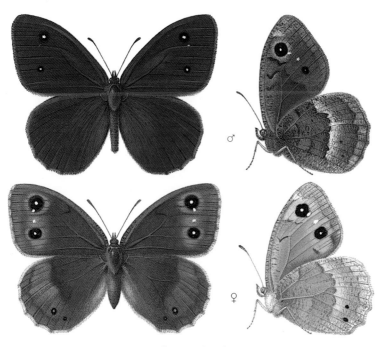

*Satyrus ferula*

# Plate 71  Satyridae

*Minois dryas*

*Berberia abdelkader*

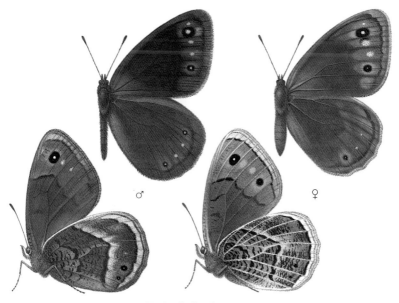

*Berberia lambessanus*

# Plate 72  Satyridae

♂                                                        ♀

*A. a. arethusa*
**Arethusana arethusa**

♂

*Kanetisa circe*

♀

*A. a. boabdil* ♂

*A. a. dentata* ♀

dark ♂

*Arethusana arethusa*

# Plate 73  Satyridae

*Erebia ligea*

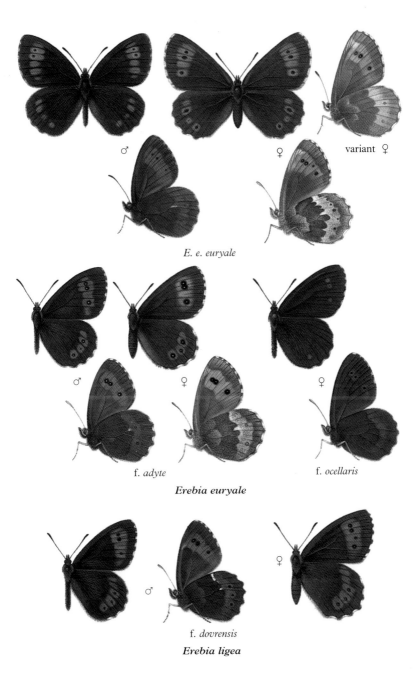

♂       ♀       variant ♀

*E. e. euryale*

♂       ♀       ♀

f. *adyte*       f. *ocellaris*

**Erebia euryale**

♂       ♀

f. *dovrensis*

**Erebia ligea**

# Plate 74  Satyridae

♂                    *Erebia claudina*                    ♀

♂                    *Erebia flavofasciata*              ♀

*Erebia eriphyle*

*f. tristis* ♂

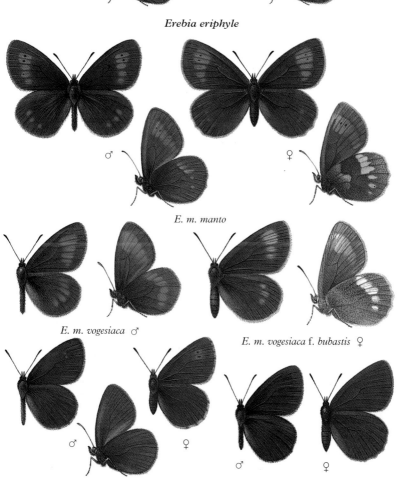

*E. m. manto*

*E. m. vogesiaca* ♂

*E. m. vogesiaca* f. *bubastis* ♀

*E. m. manto* f. *pyrrhula*

*E. m. constans*

*Erebia manto*

# Plate 75 Satyridae

♂         ♀

*Erebia christi*

♂         ♀

*Erebia orientalis*

*E. e. silesiana*

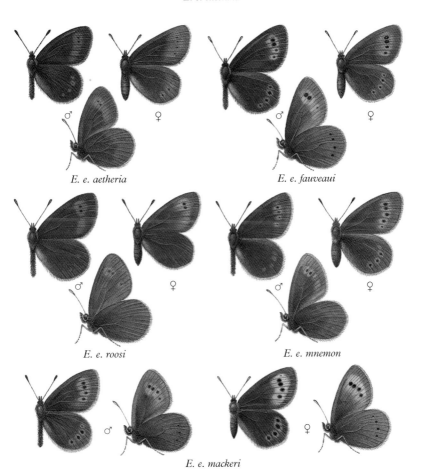

*E. e. aetheria*

*E. e. fauveaui*

*E. e. roosi*

*E. e. mnemon*

*E. e. mackeri*

**Erebia epiphron**

# Plate 76  Satyridae

♂                    ♀

variant ♀

*Erebia aethiops*

f. *phartina* ♂

f. *eupompa*

E. p. pharte

**Erebia pharte**

**Erebia melampus**

E. s. sudetica

E. s. liorana

**Erebia sudetica**

# Plate 77  Satyridae

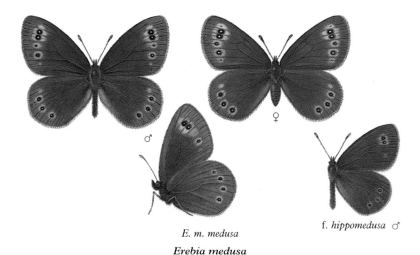

♂

♀

*E. m. medusa*

f. *hippomedusa*  ♂

**Erebia medusa**

*Erebia embla*

*Erebia disa*

*Erebia polaris*

# Plate 78 Satyridae

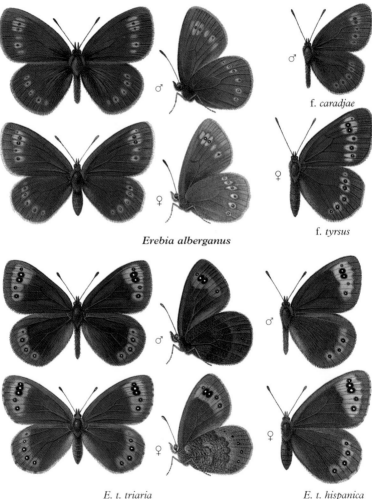

f. *caradjae*

f. *tyrsus*

*Erebia alberganus*

E. t. triaria

E. t. hispanica

*Erebia triaria*

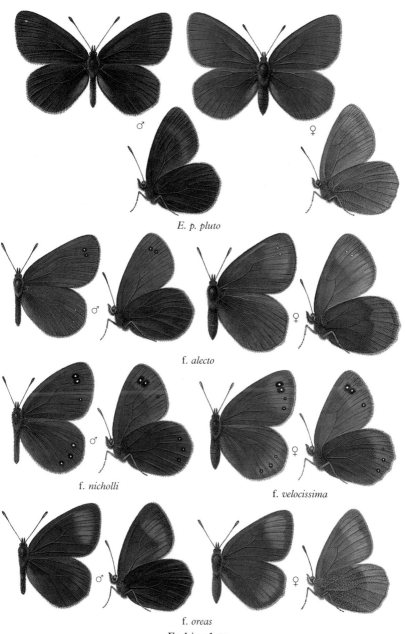

♂

♀

*E. p. pluto*

♂ ♀

f. *alecto*

♂ ♀

f. *nicholli*

f. *velocissima*

♂ ♀

f. *oreas*

**Erebia pluto**

# Plate 79 Satyridae

*Erebia aethiopella*

*Erebia rhodopensis*

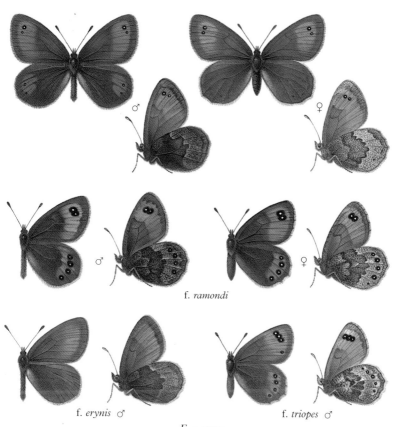

f. *ramondi*

f. *erynis* ♂          f. *triopes* ♂

E. g. gorge

**Erebia gorge**

**Erebia mnestra**

# Plate 80  Satyridae

♂     ♀     f. *arvernensis* ♀

*Erebia cassioides*

*Erebia gorgone*

*Erebia epistygne*

*Erebia tyndarus*

# Plate 81  Satyridae

♂

♀

♂

♀

*E. o. benacensis*

*Erebia ottomana*

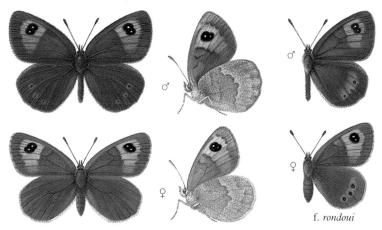

♂

♀

♂ ♀

f. *rondoui*

*Erebia hispania*

♂ ♀

*Erebia nivalis*

♂ ♀

*Erebia calcaria*

# Plate 82  Satyridae

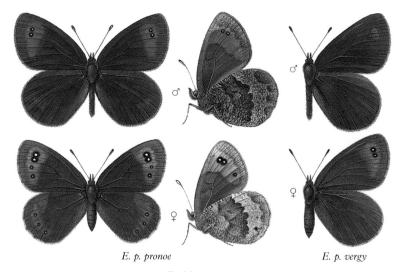

E. p. pronoe                                    E. p. vergy

*Erebia pronoe*

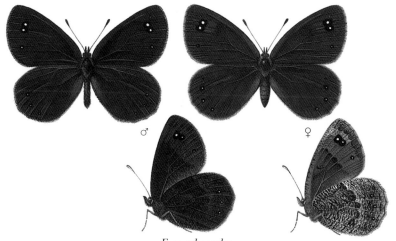

♂          ♀

*E. m. schanerdae*

**Erebia melas**

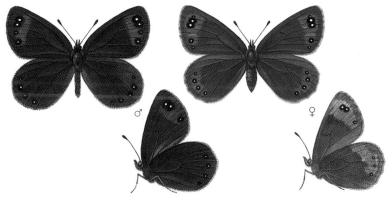

♂          ♀

*E. l. lefebvrei*

♂          ♀

*E. l. astur*

**Erebia lefebvrei**

# Plate 83  Satyridae

♂        ♀

*Erebia stirius*

*Erebia scipio*

♂

♀

*E. s. styx*

*E. s. trigilites*

♂

♀

*E. s. trentae*

**Erebia styx**

# Plate 84  Satyridae

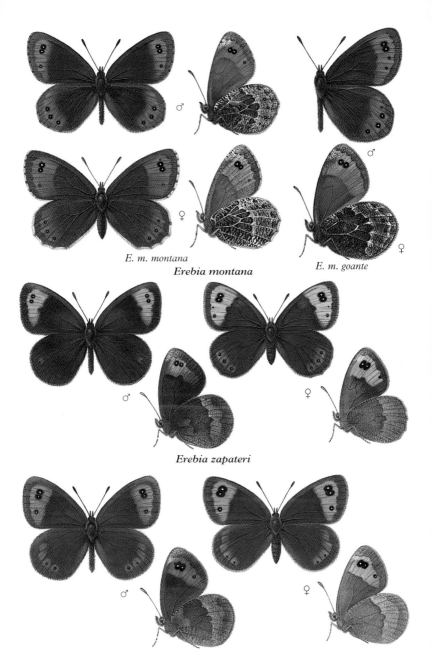

*E. m. montana*

**Erebia montana**

*E. m. goante*

**Erebia zapateri**

**Erebia neoridas**

# Plate 85  Satyridae

*Erebia palarica*

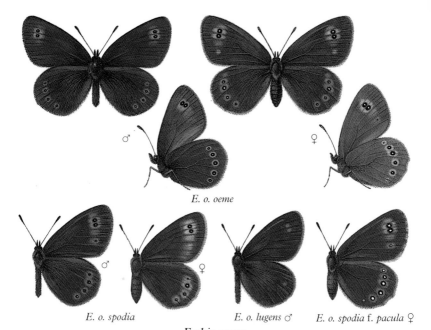

♂

♀

*E. o. oeme*

*E. o. spodia*    ♂    ♀       *E. o. lugens* ♂    *E. o. spodia* f. *pacula* ♀

**Erebia oeme**

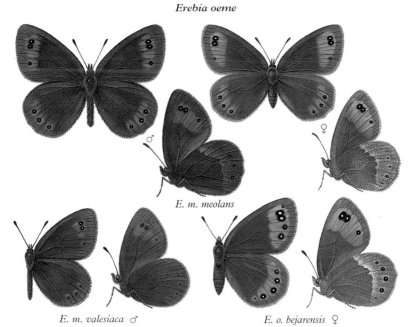

♂

♀

*E. m. meolans*

*E. m. valesiaca* ♂             *E. o. bejarensis* ♀

**Erebia meolans**

# Plate 86  Satyridae

♂                              ♀

*Maniola nurag*

♂          ♀

*Erebia pandrose*

♂          ♀

*Erebia stheynno*

♂          ♀

*Proterebia afra dalmata*

# Plate 87  Satyridae

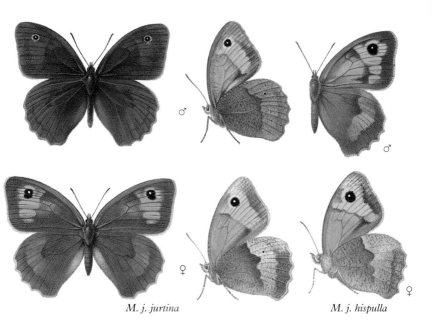

*M. j. jurtina* ♂ ♀ *M. j. hispulla*

**Maniola jurtina**

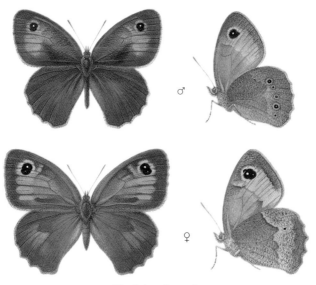

**Maniola telmessia**

# Plate 88 Satyridae

*Aphantopus hyperantus*

*Hyponephele maroccana*

*Hyponephele lycaon*

*H. l. rhamnusia* ♂

*H. l. lupina*

*Hyponephele lupina*

# Plate 89  Satyridae

*Pyronia janiroides*

*P. t. decolorata* ♀

**Pyronia tithonus**

variant ♂
(Greece)

**Pyronia cecilia**

**Pyronia bathsheba**

# Plate 90  Satyridae

♀

♂                                    ♀

f. *lyllus*

♂

*Coenonympha pamphilus*

♂                    ♂                    ♂

♀                    ♀                    ♀

*Coenonympha thyrsis*    *Coenonympha corinna*    *Coenonympha elbana*

*C. t. tullia*

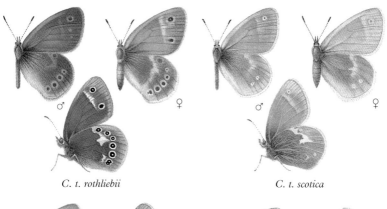

*C. t. rothliebii*                    *C. t. scotica*

*C. t. tiphon*

**Coenonympha tullia**

**Coenonympha rhodopensis**

# Plate 91  Satyridae

*Coenonympha gardetta*

*Coenonympha darwiniana*

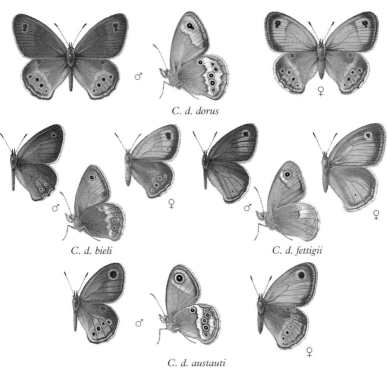

*C. d. dorus* ♂ ♀

*C. d. bieli* ♂ ♀

*C. d. fettigii* ♂ ♀

*C. d. austauti* ♂ ♀

**Coenonympha dorus**

**Coenonympha vaucheri** ♂ ♀

**Coenonympha arcania** ♂ ♀

# Plate 92  Satyridae

*Coenonympha oedippus*

*Coenonympha hero*

*Coenonympha arcanioides*

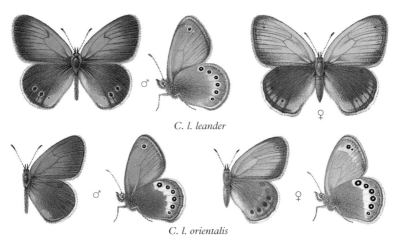

*C. l. leander*

*C. l. orientalis*

**Coenonympha leander**

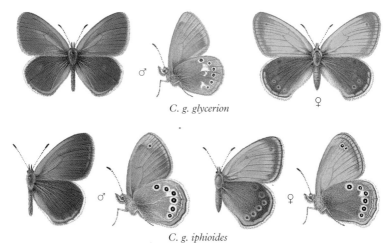

*C. g. glycerion*

*C. g. iphioides*

**Coenonympha glycerion**

# Plate 93  Satyridae

*Pararge xiphia*

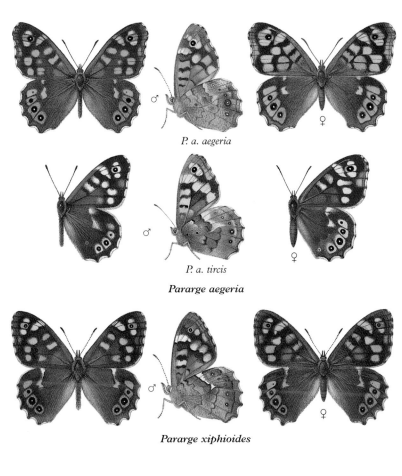

♂

*P. a. aegeria*

♀

♂

*P. a. tircis*

♀

**Pararge aegeria**

♂

♀

**Pararge xiphioides**

♀

♀

**Pararge xiphia**

# Plate 94  Satyridae

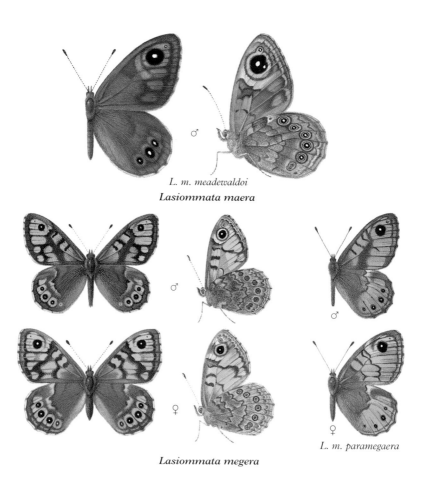

♂

*L. m. meadewaldoi*

**Lasiommata maera**

♂

♂

♀

♀

*L. m. paramegaera*

**Lasiommata megera**

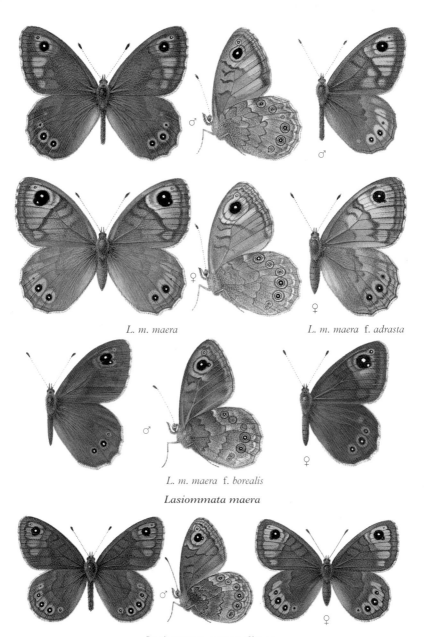

*L. m. maera*

*L. m. maera* f. *adrasta*

*L. m. maera* f. *borealis*

**Lasiommata maera**

*Lasiommata petropolitana*

# Plate 95  Satyridae

*Ypthima asterope*

*Lopinga achine*

*Kirinia roxelana*

*Kirinia climene*

# Plate 96  Danaidae

♂

*Danaus chrysippus*

♀

*Danaus plexippus*

♂

*Danaus plexippus*

# Plate 97 Hesperiidae

*Pyrgus warrensis*

♂ ♀

*Pyrgus malvae*

♂ ♀

*P. a. alveus*

♂ ♀ ♂ ♀

*P. a. centralhispaniae* *P. a. scandinavicus*

*Pyrgus alveus*

♂ ♀

*Pyrgus armoricanus*

♂ ♀

*Pyrgus foulquieri*

# Plate 98  Hesperiidae

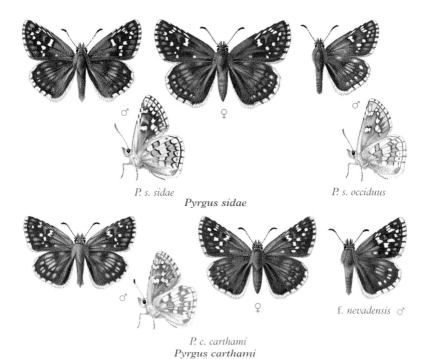

♂         ♀         ♂

*P. s. sidae*          *P. s. occiduus*

**Pyrgus sidae**

♂         ♀         f. *nevadensis* ♂

*P. c. carthami*

**Pyrgus carthami**

*Pyrgus serratulae*

f. *major* ♀

P. c. carlinae

P. c. cirsii

*Pyrgus carlinae*

*Pyrgus onopordi*

P. c. cinarae

P. c. clorinda ♂

*Pyrgus cinarae*

# Plate 99  Hesperiidae

*Spialia doris*

*Spialia phlomidis*

*Pyrgus andromedae*

*Pyrgus cacaliae*

*Pyrgus centaureae*

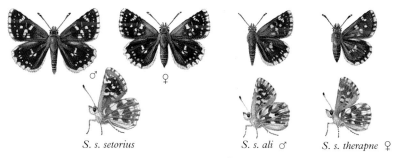

S. s. setorius          S. s. ali ♂          S. s. therapne ♀

*Spialia sertorius*

1st brood

*Spialia orbifer*

# Plate 100  Hesperiidae

*Muschampia tessellum*

*Muschampia cribrellum*

*Muschampia proto*

*Muschampia mohammed*

*Muschampia leuzeae*

# Plate 101  Hesperiidae

*Carcharodus alceae*

*C. l. lavatherae*     *C. l. tauricus*

*Carcharodus lavatherae*

*Carcharodus boeticus*

*Carcharodus stauderi*

# Plate 102  Hesperiidae

*Heteropterus morpheus*     ♀

*Carcharodus flocciferus*

*Carcharodus orientalis*

♀                    f. *baynesi* ♀

*Erynnis tages*

♂                                        ♀

*Erynnis marloyi*

# Plate 103  Hesperiidae

*Carterocephalus palaemon*

*Carterocephalus silvicolus*

*T. a. christi* ♂

*Thymelicus acteon*

*Thymelicus hamza*

*Thymelicus lineola*

f. *syriacus* ♂

*Thymelicus sylvestris*

*Thymelicus hyrax*

# Plate 104  Hesperiidae

f. *cantena*  ♂

*Hesperia comma*

*Gegenes nostrodamus*

*Gegenes pumilio*

*Borbo borbonica*

*Pelopidas thrax*

*Ochlodes venatus*

## *Boloria pales* Shepherd's Fritillary                    Plate 47

**Range.** Alpine and subalpine levels in S Europe.

*B. pales pales* Denis and Schiffermüller 1775 TL: Vienna.
**Distribution.** Eastern Alps of Bavaria and N and E Tirol.
Dolomites. Julian Alps. Tatra Mts. Carpathian Mts. 2200-
2700m.
**Description.** Upf black discal markings bold, macular (cf.
*B. napaea*); unf markings obscure – 'ghosted'; unh basal and
pd areas reddish. F. *tatrensis* Crosson du Cormier (Tatra Mts.)
and f. *carpathomeridionalis* Crosson and Popescu-Gorj (S
Carpathian Mts.) superficially indistinguishable from nominate form.
**Flight-period.** Univoltine. Late June/early September.
**Habitat and Life-history.** Flowery alpine meadows. LHP *Viola calcarata*.

*B. pales palustris* Frühstorfer 1909 TL: Zermatt, Switzerland.
**Distribution.** Alpes-Maritimes, through S Alps to SW Tirol. Local in C
Appenines. Bosnia-Herzegovina: Prenj Pl. SW Serbia: Mt. Durmitor. Albania.
Republic of Macedonia; Sar Pl.; Mt. Pelister. Bulgaria: Rila Mts.; Pirin Mts.
Generally 1500-2800m, occasionally at 1200m.
**Description.** Smaller; ups paler; upf discal markings thinner; unh reddish
coloration more extensive. F. *contempta* Rebel and Zerny (SW Serbia and
Republic of Macedonia) and f. *rilaensis* Varga (Rila Mts.) superficially indistin-
guishable from *B. p. palustris*.
**Flight-period.** Univoltine. Mid July/mid August.
**Habitat.** Flowery alpine/subalpine meadows.
**Life-history.** As for nominate form.

*B. pales pyrenesmiscens* Verity 1932 TL: Gèdre, Haute-Pyrénées.
**Distribution.** Cantabrian Mts; Pyrenees. 1500-2100m.
**Description.** Both sexes: larger; ups gc slightly paler; uph black basal suffusion
reduced, not encroaching cell: female ups sometimes suffused greyish-violet.
**Flight-period.** Univoltine. Late June/August.
**Habitat and Life-history.** As for nominate form.

## *Boloria napaea* Mountain Fritillary                    Plate 47

**Range.** E Pyrenees, Central Alps, Fennoscandia, S Siberia,
Altai, Amur, Alaska, Wyoming.

*B. napaea* Hoffmannsegg 1804 TL: Alps of Tirol.
**Distribution.** Spain and France: very local: E Pyrenees
(Gerona; Puy de Puymorens; Val d'Eyne; Cambre d'Aze; Pic
du Carlit). Andorra. Alps of France, S Switzerland, Italy and
Austria. 1500-2500m. Norway and W Sweden from 60°N
to North Cape. 0-1100m. A report for Cantabrian Mts. (Pto.
de San Glorio 1600m) requires confirmation.
**Description.** Resembles *B. pales*. Male ups paler; upf black discal markings
thin – not macular; unh paler: female ups suffused grey, often with strong violet
reflections and greenish basal overtones, most noticeable in fresh specimens.

**Flight-period.** Univoltine. Late June/August.

**Habitat.** In S Europe, flowery alpine/subalpine meadows: habitat-character similar Scandinavia, but at lower altitudes – sometimes on shoreline in N Norway.

**Life-history.** LHPs *Viola* spp. including *Viola biflora*; *Polygonum viviparum*. Ova laid on leaves of LHP or other nearby soft herbage. Hibernates as a small larva. At higher altitudes and latitudes, larval development occupies two seasonal cycles.

## *Boloria aquilonaris* Cranberry Fritillary                     Plate 47

**Range.** C Europe, Fennoscandia, Arctic Russia, S Urals, W Siberia, Altai.

*B. aquilonaris* Stichel 1908 TL: Gellivare, Sweden.
syn: *arsilache* Knoch 1781 (invalid homonym)

**Distribution.** Small, widely scattered colonies in S Belgium (Ardennes), France (Massif Central; Orne; Eure; Seine-Maritime; Nièvre; Jura; Doubs; Haute-Saône; Haute-Rhin; Vosges) and Switzerland (Jura Mts.; Prealps; Engadine). Progressively less sporadic from Bavaria and Austria, through Czech Republic, Slovakia, Poland to Baltic states. Widespread, locally common in Fennoscandia, including Sjælland. 100-2000m.

**Description and Variation.** Male ups bright fiery-red; ups and unf black basal and discal spots well developed; upf spots in s1b v-shaped, arranged horizontally thus > < or, less often, joined at apices or connected by a short streak (cf. *B. napaea*). In S Fennoscandia and C Europe, usually larger (f. *alethea* Hemming).

**Flight-period.** Univoltine. Mid June/August.

**Habitat.** Raised peat bogs or wet heaths, often sheltered by light woodland and usually in close proximity to permanent water.

**Life-history.** LHP *Vaccinium oxycoccos* [= *Oxycoccus quadripetalus*; *O. palustris*]. Ova laid on stems and leaves. Hibernates as a small larva. Development may occupy two seasonal cycles in northernmost range.

**Behaviour.** Despite their exceptional brilliance, males have a remarkable ability to 'vanish' in flight.

**Conservation.** As with all other wetland species, habitats are especially vulnerable to drainage in adjacent areas.

## *Boloria graeca* Balkan Fritillary                     Plate 47

**Range.** SW Alps, Balkans, Greece.

*B. graeca* Staudinger 1870 TL: Mt. Veluchi [Timphristos], Greece.

**Distribution.** SW Alps of France and Italy. Bosnia-Hercegovina: Prenj Pl. SW Serbia: Mt. Durmitor. Republic of Macedonia: Mt. Pelister; Placenska Pl.; Galicica Pl.; Sar Pl.; Kozuf Pl. Bulgaria: Rila Mts.; Pirin Mts.; Rhodopi Mts.; Slavayanka Mts. Greece: Varnous Mts.; Vernon Mts.; Voras Mts.; Mt. Orvilos; Pindos Mts. (Epano Arena and Grammos massifs to Mt. Ghiona). 1450-2600m.

**Variation.** In Bosnia-Herzegovina and Rila Mts., f. *balcanica* Rebel: slightly smaller, otherwise closely similar to nominate form – no ecological barriers are apparent between Greek and Balkan populations where these share the same mountain massives at political boundaries. In SW Alps, f. *tendensis* Higgins: unh ocellated pd spots generally better developed.

**Flight-period.** Univoltine. Mid June/early August.

**Habitat.** Open grassland, often containing *Juniperus communis nana*. On calcareous or acidic soils.

**Life-history.** LHP *Viola* sp.; *V.* (?)*tricolor macedonica*. Ova laid on leaves of LHP, as well as other plants, e.g., *Teucrium chamaedrys* and *Juniperus communis nana*. Hibernates as a small larva.

## *Proclossiana eunomia* Bog Fritillary                     Plate 47

**Range.** Europe, Russia, Mongolia, NE China, Sakhalin, N America.

*P. eunomia eunomia* Esper 1799 TL: Prussia.
syn: *aphrape* Hübner 1799/80.

**Distribution.** Very sporadic and local in W Europe. N Spain: E Cantabrian Mts. Andorra. France: Pyrénées-Orientales; Vosges; Ardennes. S Belgium: Ardennes. N Italy: ValVenosta. S Germany. Austria. Czech Republic. Slovakia. Poland. 300-1500m. Bulgaria: Stara Pl. 1600-1900m. Absent from Ireland, Britain, Holland, Denmark and Hungary.

**Description.** Both sexes: unh series of dark brown or black pd rings with pale yellow or white centres; basal, discal and pd spots yellow.

**Flight-period.** Univoltine. Late May/early July.

**Habitat.** Marsh meadows by rivers or lakes; raised peat bogs.

**Life-history.** LHP *Polygonum bistorta*. Ova laid on underside of leaves, singly or in small clusters. Hibernates as a small larva.

**Conservation.** Most habitats are extremely small and correspondingly vulnerable; many have been destroyed by drainage and afforestation: commercial forestry activity continues to pose a threat in S Belgium.

*P. eunomia ossiana* Herbst 1800 TL: Not stated.

**Distribution.** Norway, Sweden and Finland: widespread and common. Baltic states: sporadic but locally common. 50-900m. Absent from Denmark.

**Description and Variation.** Resembles nominate form, sometimes very closely. Both sexes: generally smaller; ups and uns markings well defined; unh basal, discal and pd spots white or silver; ups often with dark suffusion, especially in female. Slight regional variation in size, ups gc and markings, often obscured by significant individual variation.

**Flight-period.** Mid June/mid July: emergence date subject to seasonal conditions.

**Habitat and Life-history.** LHPs *Polygonum viviparum*; *Viola palustris*. Hibernates as a larva. Larval development may occupy two seasonal cycles.

## *Clossiana euphrosyne* Pearl-bordered Fritillary          Plate 48

**Range.** Europe, Turkey, Russia, N Kazakhstan.

*C. euphrosyne* Linnaeus 1758 TL: Sweden (Verity 1950).
**Distribution.** Widespread, locally common. N Spain, east-
wards through most of Europe, including Britain and central
W Ireland, to North Cape and S Greece (Mt. Chelmos and
Taygetos Mts.). Absent from W and C Denmark, E Italy and
Mediterranean islands except N Sicily. 0-1900m. Records
for N Portugal require confirmation.
**Description.** Unh cell-base reddish; chevrons enclosing
marginal silver spots proximally blunt, often obscure (cf. *C. selene*).

**Variation.** In Fennoscandia: generally smaller; ups markings with variable dark
suffusion, sometimes obscuring gc, especially in female: relationship of named
forms, e.g. f. *fingal* Herbst, f. *lapponica* Esper, f. *septentrionalis* Nordström, largely
obscured by individual and local variation.

**Flight-period.** Univoltine in N Europe and at high altitudes in S Europe, late
May/July: elsewhere, a partial second brood may occur, April/June and July/
September.

**Habitat.** Deciduous or coniferous woodland clearings.

**Life-history.** LHPs *Viola* spp., including *V. reichenbachiana*; *V. canina*; *V. palustris*;
*V. odorata*; *V. riviniana*; *V. (?) rhodopeia*; *V. hirta*. Ova laid on low herbage as well as
LHP. Hibernates as a half-grown larva.

## *Clossiana titania* Titania's Fritillary          Plate 48

**Range.** Central Alps of Europe, Poland, S Finland, Latvia,
Balkans, Urals, Siberia, Transbaikal, Mongolia, Amur,
Sakhalin, N Korea, N America, Canada.

*C. titania titania* Esper 1793 TL: 'Sardinia' [Piedmont].
**Distribution.** France: Massif Central; Hautes-Alps; Isère.
Italy: Cottian Alps. 300-1800m.
**Description.** Male ups brownish-orange; black markings
fine: unh marbled yellow and brown with greenish or violet
tints: female ups and uns paler.

**Flight-period.** Univoltine. Mid June/late August.

**Habitat.** Flowery meadows in woodland clearings.

**Life-history.** LHP *Polygonum bistorta*. Hibernates as a fully-formed larva within
ovum case. Pupates on plant-stems near ground-level.

*C. titania cypris* Meigen 1828 TL: Bavaria and Switzerland.
syn: *amathusia* Esper 1784 (invalid homonym)
**Distribution.** Alps of E Italy, S and C Switzerland (also Jura Mts.), Bavaria
and Austria. Poland. (?)Hungary. Latvia. Estonia. S Finland. (?)NW Croatia.
Bosnia-Herzegovina: Vranica Pl.; Jahorina Pl.; Zelengora Pl. SW Serbia: Mt.
Durmitor; Sinjajevina Pl. (?)Albania. Romania: Transsylvania. 800-1600m.
**Description.** Male ups reddish; all black markings heavy: unh darker, with
complex marbling – brown, purple, maroon, pale violet and yellow: female ups
gc paler.
**Flight-period, Habitat and Life-history.** As for nominate form.

## *Clossiana selene* Small Pearl-bordered Fritillary    Plate 48

**Range.** Europe, Russia, Mongolia, Sakhalin, Korea, N America.

*C. selene* Denis and Schiffermüller 1775 TL: Vienna.

**Distribution.** N Portugal. Spain: S. de Guadarrama; S. de la Demanda; Cantabrian Mts.; Pyrenees. France, eastwards through most of N and C Europe (including Britain), Baltic Islands to North Cape, N Balkans and SW Bulgaria. Sporadic in S France. Absent from Ireland, Ligurian Alps and peninsular Italy. 0-2200m.

**Description.** Unh cell-base yellow; chevrons enclosing marginal silver spots, well developed, sharply angled at proximal apex; size of dark pd spots irregular – large in s2, largest in s5 (cf. *C. euphrosyne*).

**Variation.** In Fennoscandia, f. *hela* Staudinger: generally smaller with variable dark ups suffusion. Inter-seasonal variation has been attributed to the influence of temperature on larval/pupal development.

**Flight-period.** Univoltine at higher latitudes and altitudes, mid May/early July: bivoltine in warmer regions, early May/late June and mid July/early September: second brood appears to be partial in some parts of C Europe.

**Habitat.** Forest clearings, often in damp places; meadows in wooded river valleys; moorland; marshy areas near lakes.

**Life-history.** LHPs *Viola canina*; *V. palustris*; *V. riviniana*; *V. hirta*. Ova laid on low herbage as well as LHP. Hibernates as a half-grown larva or sometimes as a pupa in Scandinavia.

## *Clossiana chariclea* Arctic Fritillary    Plate 48

**Range.** Arctic Fennoscandia, Arctic Siberia, Greenland, Labrador, Arctic America.

*C. chariclea* Schneider 1794 TL: Lapland.

**Distribution.** N Fennoscandia north of 68°. Sweden, mountains north and south of Lake Torneträsk (Pallentjåkka; Nissuntjårro; Snurijåkkåtan; Pessivare; Vilgesgierdu). Norway: mountains north of Swedish border to Gargia and Porsanger. Mountains of NW Finland (Saana; Malla; Kilpisjärvi; Enontekiö). 100-1400m.

**Flight-period.** Univoltine. Usually emerges late June/early July, flying for about two weeks: emergence may be delayed until early August in adverse seasonal conditions.

**Habitat.** Open, windswept, dry, rocky tundra with small grassy hollows, patches of dwarf Birch (*Betula nana*) and other low shrubs.

**Life-history.** LHP not reported: ova are sometimes laid on dead vegetation – twigs and grasses.

**Behaviour.** Even in overcast conditions, often rests with outspread wings in shelter of stones or shrubs.

**Note.** In N America, treated as a ssp. of *C. titania* by some authors.

## *Clossiana freija* Frejya's Fritillary          Plate 48

**Range.** Scandinavia, Baltic countries, Arctic and S Siberia, Transbaikal, Mongolia, Yakutia, Khamchatka, Japan, N America including scattered colonies in Rocky Mts. to 35°N.

*C. freija* Thunberg 1791 TL: Sweden.

**Distribution.** Norway, Sweden and Finland: widespread, generally common. NE Latvia: very rare and local – last recorded in 1980. (?)Estonia. Absent from Denmark, coastal areas of Norway, Sweden south of 59°N and Lithuania. 200-1000m.

**Description.** Unh with distinctive 'zig-zag' discal line in s1b-s3.

**Flight-period.** Univoltine. Generally late May/late June: fresh specimens may appear in late July/early August in retarded seasons.

**Habitat.** Dry grassy/rocky slopes/hollows with scattered, low-growing shrubs; marshes/peat bogs with *Vaccinium uliginosum* and *Rubus chamaemorus*, often sheltered by trees.

**Life-history.** LHPs *Vaccinium uliginosum*; *Rubus chamaemorus*; *Arctstaphylos alpina*; *A. uva-ursi*; *Empetrum nigrum*: (In Japan, *Rhododendron aureum* – *R. lapponicum* is widespread in Lappland). Ova laid on leaves.

## *Clossiana dia* Weaver's Fritillary          Plate 49

**Range.** Europe, Turkey, Caucasus, Transcaucasus, Russia, N Kazakhstan, Mongolia.

*C. dia* Linnaeus 1767 TL: Austria.

**Distribution.** Spain: Cantabrian Mts.; provinces of Burgos, Soria, Huesca, Gerona and Barcelona. From Pyrenees, eastwards through much of C and E Europe to Baltic states, Balkans, European Turkey and Greece: Varnous Mts.; Phalakron massif; Mt. Olympus; Pindos Mts. (Grammos massif to Mt. Timphristos). Absent from SW France, N Germany, S Italy, Britain, Fennoscandia and Mediterranean islands except N Sicily. 500-1550m.

**Description.** Resembles *C. titania cypris*. Smaller; ups gc paler; hw more sharply angled at v8; unh variegated yellow, brown, purple and violet, variable, sometimes very pale; discal and marginal spots silvery-white.

**Flight-period.** Bivoltine or trivoltine, late April/early September.

**Habitat.** Dry or damp, bushy, grassy and flowery clearings in light woodland or mature forests.

**Life-history.** LHPs *Viola* spp., including, *V. odorata*; *V. hirta*; *V. canina*; *V. reichenbachiana*; *V. tricolor*. Ova laid on leaves of well-shaded LHPs. Hibernates as a half-grown larva.

## *Clossiana polaris* Polar Fritillary          Plate 49

**Range.** Circumpolar: Arctic regions of Europe north of 68°N, Asia, Greenland, N America.

*C. polaris* Boisduval 1828 TL: North Cape.

**Distribution.** Generally very local and uncommon. Sweden: Torne Lappmark; mountains north of Lake Torneträsk. 1000-1400m. Norway: E Troms; Finnmark; Gargia (Grönnasen); Porsanger; Varanger. 100-1400m. Finland: Pallastunturi; Kilpisjärvi (Mt. Saana); Karigasniemi (Mt. Ailigas). 600-1000m.
**Flight-period.** Univoltine. Late May/early August; normally appears early July but emergence much dependent on seasonal conditions.
**Habitat.** Open tundra. Females particularly, tend to associate closely with small, dry, south or west-facing rock-ledges or gentle slopes, characterised by an abundance of *Dryas octopetala*, *Cassiope tetragona* and *Astragalus alpinus* and the absence of low shrubs; the base of such slopes are damp and carpeted by *Betula nana* (dwarf Birch), usually with some inclusion of *Salix* spp. and *Vaccinium uliginosum*.
**Life-history.** LHP(s) unconfirmed in Europe: in N America, *Dryas integrifolia*; *D. octopetala*; *Vaccinium uliginosum*. In N America, hibernates as a newly-hatched or large (third or fourth instar) larva.
**Behaviour.** Similar to that of *C. chariclea*.

## *Clossiana thore* Thor's Fritillary                    Plate 49

**Range.** Central European Alps, NE Europe, Russia, Sakhalin, Mongolia, NE China, N Korea, Japan.

*C. thore* Hübner 1803 TL: Alps of Tyrol
**Distribution.** Sporadic and local. Alps of Switzerland, (local north of Rhône Valley; Engadine), Bavaria and Austria. Italy: Dolomites; Carinthian Mts. 800-1800m. Norway, W Sweden (62°-70°N) and NW Finland. 300-1000m.
**Description and Variation.** Ups black markings heavy; uph margin wide, obscuring large submarginal spots; unh dark with pale discal and marginal spots. In N Scandinavia, *borealis* Staudinger: ups gc slightly paler; ups black markings much reduced; unh paler, pale discal and marginal spots obscure: individuals with ups dark markings closely resembling nominate form recur in most Lappland colonies. In S Fennoscandia, *carelia* Valle: transitional to nominate form.
**Flight-period.** Univoltine. C Alps Mid June/early August: Lappland, late June/early August according to locality and season. Records of a (?)partial second brood in Austria require confirmation.
**Habitat and Behaviour.** In central Alps, shaded clearings in deciduous or coniferous woodland. In Lappland, damp wooded margins of rivers or small mountain streams, characterised by *Geranium sylvaticum*, *Trollius europaeus* and an abundance of *Viola biflora*: both sexes frequent areas of dappled sunlight, often basking on leaves of *G. sylvaticum*.
**Life-history.** LHPs *Viola* spp., including *V. biflora*. In central Alps, possibly also in Lappland, larval development occupies two seasonal cycles, giving rise to relatively greater abundance in alternate years.

## *Clossiana frigga* Frigga's Fritillary          Plate 49

**Range.** Fennoscandia, Baltic states, N Asia, Mongolia, Amur, Kamchatka, N America, including isolated colonies in Rocky Mts. to Colorado.

*C. frigga* Thunberg 1791 TL: Lappland.

**Distribution.** Norway and Sweden (60-71°N): generally local and uncommon, more widespread in the far north; absent from coastal districts of Norway south of 66°N. Widespread in Finland. Baltic states: very rare and local (last recorded in Latvia in 1987). 100-450m.

**Variation.** Ups gc and black markings variable; basal, discal and pd spots sometimes confluent; veins often with dark suffusion; unh basal and discal gc pale reddish-brown to maroon with pinkish or violet overtones.

**Flight-period.** Univoltine. Late June/late July according to season.

**Habitat.** Marshes, peat bogs and wet heaths in vicinity of birch and willow scrub, usually bordering permanent water.

**Life-history.** LHP *Rubus chamaemorus*. Ova laid singly on leaves. Hibernates as a larva. Newly-hatched captive larvae sometimes refuse *R. chamaemorus* but accept *Polygonum viviparum*, and, in later instars, *Rubus fruticosus*.

## *Clossiana improba* Dusky-winged Fritillary          Plate 49

**Range.** N Fennoscandia, Novaya Zemlya, Arctic Urals, Yamal and Gydan Peninsulas, Arctic Siberia, Chukot Peninsula, Arctic America.

*C. improba improbula* Brykner 1920 TL: Lappland.

**Distribution.** Fennoscandia north of 68°N. From Mt. Nuolja and mountains north of Lake Torneträsk (Torne Lappmark, Sweden) to Rosta Ankerlia, Norway. NW Finland: Kilpisjärvi. 600-1050m. Local population density subject to very marked seasonal variation – can occur in great abundance.

**Flight-period.** Univoltine. Late June/early August according season.

**Habitat.** Open, flat, grassy terrain or gentle slopes with SE aspect providing shelter from prevailing NW winds.

**Life-history.** LHP(s) unknown: oviposition on *Polygonum viviparum* reported, but natural use as LHP apparently not confirmed. In N America, adults associate closely with *Salix* spp. of which *S. arctica* and *S. reticulata* are confirmed LHPs: oviposition, but not larval feeding, has also been observed (rarely) on *P. viviparum*: early-stages occupy two seasonal cycles. In Lappland, *S. reticulata* and other arctic *Salix* spp. occur within distribution of butterfly.

**Behaviour.** Flies fast and very close to the ground when disturbed. Well-camouflaged when settled with outspread wings on similarly coloured patches of bare ground. Both sexes are especially fond of the nectar of *Silene acaulis*: males sometimes take moisture from damp peaty soil.

## *Melitaea cinxia* Glanville Fritillary          Plate 50

**Range.** Morocco, W. Algeria, Europe, Turkey, Lebanon, Russia, N Kazakhstan, Mongolia.

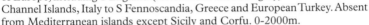

*M. cinxia* Linnaeus 1758 TL: Sweden.

**Distribution.** Morocco: W High Atlas (Toubkal massif 2000-2600m); Middle Atlas (Azrou; Ifrane; Col du Zad; Tizin-Tretten; 1500-2000m). W Algeria. N Portugal. Spain: S. de Guadarrama; Montes Universales; Cantabrian Mts. to Pyrenees and Catalonia. Extending eastwards through most of Europe, including S England (restricted to Isle of Wight), Channel Islands, Italy to S Fennoscandia, Greece and European Turkey. Absent from Mediterranean islands except Sicily and Corfu. 0-2000m.

**Variation.** In S Europe, female ups gc uniform sandy-buff with variable dark or greyish suffusion. In High Atlas, *atlantis* le Cerf: ups gc paler; black markings heavy but lacking dark suffusion.

**Flight-period.** Generally univoltine: NW Africa, late April/June; N, C and W Europe, early May/mid July; SE Europe, late April/early August in prolonged emergence: bivoltine in some regions of NE Spain, France, Switzerland and Italy, May/June and August/September.

**Habitat.** Diverse. Grassy, flowery places: open hillsides; scrub/woodland clearings; areas/margins of cultivation.

**Life-history.** LHPs: Middle Atlas, *Centaurea pullata*; *Scorzonera pygmaea*: Europe, *Plantago lanceolata*; *P. subulata*; *P. bellardii deflexa*; *P. argentea*; *P. cynops*; *P. major*; *P. media*; *Centaureae* (?)*graeca*; *Centaureae* sp.; *Veronica teucrium*. Ova laid in large batches on underside of leaf. Small larvae feed and hibernate in a silken web, dispersing in late instars. Pupates near ground on grass or other plant-stems.

## *Melitaea arduinna* Freyer's Fritillary          Plate 50

**Range.** SE Balkans, Greece, Turkey, Israel, Iraq, Iran, N Afghanistan, Caucasus, Volga, S Urals, (?)Uzbekistan, E Kazakhstan, Kyrgyzstan, Altai.

*M. arduinna rhodopensis* Freyer 1836 TL: 'European Turkey' [Bulgaria].

**Distribution.** Republic of Macedonia: Mt. Pelister; Prilep; Vardar Valley. Bulgaria: Ludogorie; Sboryanovo; Burgas; Kula; Vrushka Tchuka. Romania: Tultscha. Greece: Varnous Mts.; Vernon Mts.; N and C Pindos Mts. Very local, often common. 500-1500m.

**Variation.** Female ups often with dark suffusion.

**Flight-period.** Univoltine. Late May/early August: peak emergence, usually late June.

**Habitat.** Grassy, flowery banks in sheltered, bushy woodland clearings.

**Life-history.** LHP *Centaurea* (?)*graeca*. Ova laid in large batches on underside of leaf. Small larvae feed on leaves and stem cuticle (stem leaves are small and sparse) in silken web where they also hibernate: after hibernation, larger larvae disperse. Small larvae ((?)second instar) are unusual for having a

decidedly greenish appearance. Mature larvae superficially very similar to Spanish *M. phoebe*. Pupates on robust plant stems near ground-level. Captive larvae
accept many *Centaurea* spp., but reject *Plantago lanceolata* and *P. bellardii deflexa*
(cf. *M. cinxia*).

## *Melitaea phoebe* Knapweed Fritillary                    Plate 50

**Range.** N Africa, Europe, Turkey, Middle East, C Asia,
Mongolia, N China.

*M. phoebe* Denis and Schiffermüller 1775 TL: Austria.
**Distribution.** Morocco. Algeria. 900-2700m. Portugal and
Spain, through C and S France, Italy, C Germany to SE
Latvia, Balkans, European Turkey and Greece. Common and
widespread in much of S and C Europe: often sporadic in
northern range: not reported recently from Lithuania or
Estonia. Absent from Britain, northern C Europe, Fennoscandia, N and C Switzerland, much of Bavaria and Mediterranean islands
except Sicily, Chios and Lesbos. 0-1900m.
**Variation.** Geographical, seasonal and altitudinal variation marked, especially
in Spain. Nominate form occurs in most regions from Pyrenees eastwards,
north of C Alps to Balkans and Greece. South of Alps, also in Bavaria, f. *alternans*
Seitz: ups contrasting areas of pale and darker orange-fulvous gc well delineated by heavy black markings. In Iberian Peninsula, *occitanica* Staudinger:
resembles *alternans*: ups colour contrast similar, black markings generally less
intense, characters better developed in summer brood. Late summer broods in
S Europe, often small; ups pale, black markings reduced; unh gc pale (f. *pauper*
Verity): reduced size possibly due to retarded larval development arising from
desiccation of LHPs. In hot/dry localities in NW Africa, *punica* Oberthür: small;
ups yellowish with some variegation on hw; upf black discal markings well
developed; uns gc white: a larger, well-marked form (f. *gaisericus* Hemming)
occurs in Morocco (Middle and High Atlas) and is said resemble that of S
Europe.
**Flight-period.** Largely bivoltine, Mid April/mid June and late June/early
September. Voltinism uncertain at higher altitudes: emergence prolonged.
**Habitat.** Diverse. Dry, open flowery and grassy places, often amongst scrub
or light woodland.
**Life-history.** LHPs *Centaurea* spp., including *C. jacea*; *C. montana*; *C. graeca*;
*C. scabiosa*; *C. nigrescens*; *C. alba*; *C. columbaria*: NW Africa, also, possibly *Leuzea
acaule* [=*Rhaponticum acaule*]: natural use of *Plantago* spp. requires confirmation. Ova laid in batches on underside of leaf. Small larvae live in a silken web
before and after hibernation, feeding on leaves. Larvae tend to disperse in final
instar. Pupates near ground on plant stems or at base of stones. Colouring of
mature larvae regionally variable in S Europe: in Spain, resembles that of *M.
arduinna*: dorsum black with inconspicuous white marks (variable); sides rusty-
orange, spiny tubercles whitish/pale grey: in central S Europe and Greece; gc
black with conspicuous white speckling; spiny tubercles pale orange.
**Note.** F. *punica* considered specifically distinct by some authors: a single male
specimen has been reported recently from Bulgaria.

## *Melitaea aetherie* Aetherie Fritillary — Plate 50

**Range.** NW Africa, S Portugal, S Spain, Sicily.

*M. aetherie* Hübner 1826 TL: Spain

**Distribution.** Very sporadic and local. Morocco: Middle Atlas (Azrou; Taghzeft Pass; Aghbala Larbi; Meknes; Ifrane; Oulmes; Dj. bou Iblane; 1300-1800m); High Atlas (Oukaïmeden; Asif-n-Ait-Iren; Toubkal massif; 2000-2800m). Algeria: Kabylie; Aures Mts.; Oran; Teniet-el-Had; Tlemcen; Col du Ben-Chicao; Algiers; Ain-Draham; Sebou; Lambessa; Bainen; Khenchela; 1200-1800m. Tunisia: Kroumerie; Tunis. S Portugal: Algarve; 25-250m. S Spain: provinces of (?)Huelva; Cádiz; Málaga; Jaen; 50-800m. NW Sicily: Petralia; La Madonie; Ficuzza; Lupo; 800-1100m.

**Variation.** In NW Africa, *algirica* Rühl: resembles nominate form: unf black discal spots well developed: female ups gc pale orange usually with upf and uph posterior area suffused greyish. In Sicily, *perlinii* Turati: very similar: smaller; female ups suffusion slightly accentuated (cf. *M. didyma meridionalis*).

**Flight-period.** Univoltine in Iberian Peninsula (mid April/May) and NW Africa (May/July, according to altitude): reportedly bivoltine in Sicily, May/June and September.

**Habitat.** Hot, dry, grassy, flowery places: scrub clearings; marginal/neglected areas of cultivation.

**Life-history.** LHPs: Spain, *Centaurea calcitrapa*; *C. carratracensis*; *Cynara cardunculus*: suspected use of *Centrophyllum coeruleum* (?)unconfirmed. Ova laid in batches on underside of leaf. Hibernates as a small larva. Captive larvae accept leaves of *Cynara scolymus* (Globe Artichoke).

**Conservation.** In Iberian peninsula, close proximity to cultivated areas or human habitation poses a serious threat to residual habitats: coastal development in S Portugal (Algarve) is directly responsible for extinction of many colonies.

## *Melitaea didyma* Spotted Fritillary — Plate 51

**Range.** NW Africa, S and E Europe, Turkey, Middle East, N Iran, Afganistan, N Pakistan, Kazakhstan, Russia, Mongolia, W China.

*M. didyma* Esper 1779 TL: Bavaria.

**Distribution.** Widespread and common. Morocco: Anti-Atlas; High Atlas; Middle Atlas. Algeria. Tunisia. 0-2700m. Most of S and C Europe to S Belgium, Harz Mts., Lithuania and SE Latvia (locally common): Mediterranean islands of Sicily, Elba, Corfu, Levkas, Evia, Thassos, Limnos, Lesbos, Chios and Samos. 0-2300m. Absent from Britain, Holland, N Germany, N Poland, Estonia and Fennoscandia.

**Description and Variation.** Several forms have been described in recognition of considerable individual, local and geographical variation. From NW France, N of Alps to central E Europe (0-750m), nominate form: male ups fulvous-red; black markings variable; unh orange basal band usually continuous; black marginal spots rounded (cf. *M. trivia*): female ups gc paler, usually with some greyish suffusion. From N Spain, through southern of Alps to SE Europe (500-1700m), *meridionalis* Staudinger: male ups fiery orange-red; pd spots vestigial: female ups gc paler; upf and uph posterior area with variable greyish suffusion, less pronounced at lowest altitudes. In N Africa, S Iberian peninsula, Mediterranean region, Balkans and Greece (800-2300m), *occidentalis* Staudinger: ups gc pale fulvous or buff; black markings reduced; pd spots usually absent; unh basal orange band disrupted: female ups grey suffusion usually absent. A consideration of geographical, altitudinal, intra-seasonal, inter-seasonal variation, and the results of captive rearing under varied conditions, suggests diversity of form is at least partly attributable to ecological factors, the most influential of which are possibly those of temperature and/or humidity on larval/pupal development. Generally, extent of female ups dark suffusion appears to follow an altitudinal cline, with darkest females occurring at higher altitudes, that is, at lower average ambient temperature. First brood in S Greece, above 900m, corresponds to *meridionalis*, whereas second brood (larval/pupal development at relatively higher temperature) fits description of *occidentalis*: at sea-level in Greece, *occidentalis* occurs in spring and summer broods. Small, pale and lightly marked forms, e.g., *dalmatina* Staudinger, occur in late summer broods throughout Mediterranean region, especially at low altitude: reduced size is possibly the consequence of poor nutritional quality of desiccated LHPs.

**Flight-period.** Bivoltine or trivoltine. NW Africa, March/October: Europe, Mid April/September.

**Habitat.** Diverse. Dry flowery places; woodland or scrub clearings; meadows; dry rocky gullies; neglected and marginal areas of cultivation.

**Life-history.** LHPs include *Linaria vulgaris*; *L. peloponnesiaca*; *L. alpina*; *Antirrhinum brevifolium*; *Misopates orontium* [=*Antirrhinum orontium*]; *Plantago subulata*; *P. amplexicaulis*; *P. bellardi deflexa*; *P. lanceolata*; *P. major*; *Veronica teucrium*; *V. chamaedrys*; *Digitalis grandiflora*; *D. pupurea*; *Stachys recta*; *Valeriana officinalis*; *V. montana*; *V. persica*; *Verbascum thapsus*. Ova laid in batches. Hibernates gregariously as small larvae, often in the shelter provided by leaves or bracts of dead flower-heads of LHP. Large larvae roost singly at the tops of grass stems. Dry grass stems and stones are favoured pupation sites.

**Note.** Parallel between female *M. didyma meridionalis* and *M. aetherie algirica* is striking: ups pattern of greyish suffusion similar: both species occur at higher altitudes, suggesting equivalent or similar factors ((?)temperature/humidity) of ecological control of phenotypes.

## *Melitaea deserticola* Desert Fritillary Plate 51

**Range.** Morocco, Algeria, Tunisia, Libya, Egypt, Jordan, Israel, Lebanon, Syria, Saudi Arabia, Yemen.

*M. deserticola* Oberthür 1876 TL: Algeria.

**Distribution.** Morocco: Anti-Atlas: Tafraoute. High Atlas (Ourika; Amizmiz; Dades and Todra gorges); Middle Atlas. Algeria: Biskra; Mecheria; Laghout; Aflou. Tunisia: Tamerzad. 400-1800m.

**Description.** Resembles *M. didyma* closely: separable on basis of following characters: unh black chequering restricted to distal half (extending to wing margin in *didyma* – especially noticeable near veins): ventral surface of terminal one-third of antennal shaft orange, dorsal surface black (both surfaces black in *didyma*): antennal club entirely black (club-tip ringed orange in *didyma*): ventral surface of abdomen sandy-yellow/orange (white in *didyma*).

**Flight-period.** Voltinism uncertain in all regions: generally bivoltine, February/April and June: in some localities, apparently univoltine, April/May. (In eastern range, voltinism (one to four broods) appears to vary according to seasonal conditions: time of appearance of later broods vary, possibly due to aestivation. **Habitat.** Hot, dry gullies; sandy places; rocky slopes.

**Life-history.** LHPs: principally *Linaria aegyptiaca*: natural use of *Plantago media* and *Anarrhinum fruticosum* requires confirmation. Larva black, almost unicolorous. Circumstantial evidence suggests larvae aestivate in unfavourably hot conditions – (?)desiccation of LHP.

## *Melitaea trivia* Lesser Spotted Fritillary — Plate 51

**Range.** S Europe, Turkey, Middle East, Iran, Afghanistan, S Russia, Kazakhstan, N Pakistan, N India.

*M. trivia trivia* Denis and Schiffermüller 1775 TL: Vienna.
syn: *fascelis* Esper 1784
**Distribution.** N Italy (Turin; Lake Garda; Bolzano); S Apennines (Mte. Pollino): very sporadic and local. Slovenia to Slovakia, Balkans, Greece and European Turkey. Absent from Mediterranean islands except Thassos, Lesbos, Chios, Samos, Ikaria and Kos. Widespread and common in SE range. 0-1700m.

**Description and Variation.** Unh marginal spots somewhat triangular, usually not round; discocellular vein present in hw (cf. *M. didyma*). Second brood: often small; ups gc paler, black markings reduced. In Italy, transitional to *ignasiti* de Sagarra (below).

**Flight-period.** Bivoltine. Mid April/early May and June/August.

**Habitat.** Usually hot, dry, flowery places, often amongst scrub; neglected cultivated ground.

**Life-history.** LHPs *Verbascum thapsus*; *V. densiflorum*; *V. longifolium*; *V. speciosum*; *V. delpicum*. Small larvae feed and hibernate in a silken web. Large larvae tend to live in loose companies, resting on upperside of LHP leaves. Captive larvae accept *Buddleia davidii*. Often pupates on grass stems, sometimes at base of stones.

*M. trivia ignasiti* de Sagarra 1926 TL: Portugal.
**Distribution.** N and C Portugal: Provinces of Beira Baixa; Beira Alta; Beira Litoral; Trás-os-Montes. Spain: Cantabrian Mts.; S. de Guadarrama; S. de la Demanda; Huesca; Catalonia; Montes Universales; S. de Gádor. (?)500-1200m. Very local, generally uncommon. Detailed distribution uncertain owing to possible confusion with *M. didyma*.

**Description and Variation.** Ups gc uniform pale yellow-orange; black markings clearly defined. In S. de Gádor, f. *augustini* Augustin: similar.

**Flight-period and Habitat.** As for nominate form.

**Life-history.** LHP *Verbascum thapsus*. Development as for nominate form.

## *Melitaea diamina* False Heath Fritillary          Plate 51

**Range.** N Spain, C, E and SE Europe, NE Turkey, S and NW Russia, S Siberia, Transbaikal, Amur, Mongolia, NE China, Korea, Japan.

*M. diamina* Lang 1789 TL: Augsburg.
syn: *dictynna* Esper 1779 (invalid homonym)
**Distribution.** N Spain: Cantabrian Mts.; Pyrenees; Cata-
lonia. SW, central W and E France. N Italy to S Belgium, S
Holland, through Poland to Republic of Macedonia
(Jablanica Pl.; Galicica Pl.) and Bulgaria (Rila Mts.; Rhodopi
Mts; Musala massif). S Norway, Sweden (including Öland) and Finland to
62°N. Denmark: restricted to Sjælland: formerly very rare – no recent records.
Latvia: sporadic, locally common. Absent from Britain, N and C France, S
coastal areas of France, N Germany, N Poland, Lithuania, Estonia, peninsular
Italy, Greece and European Turkey. 100-2000m.
**Description and Variation.** Male ups gc orange-fulvous on disc, pale yellow
or white near outer margins; black markings extensive, obscuring much of gc,
especially near outer margins; uns gc very pale; marginal yellowish band bordered by fine black lines: female ups gc paler. In N Italy, generally at lower
altitudes, *wheeleri* Chapman: ups dark suffusion absent, markings clearly defined;
upf with dumb-bell shaped discal mark in s1b. In N Spain (E Pyrenees and
Cantabrian Mts.), *vernetensis* Rondou: resembles *wheeleri*: unh coloration more
uniform, averagely paler. In Catalonia, *codinai* de Sagarra: resembles *vernetensis*;
slightly larger; ups black markings further reduced; upf dumb-bell shaped mark
prominent in s1b. These and related variants, occur regularly in most populations
in S Alps: development of ups dark suffusion follows an altitudinal cline, with
darkest forms preponderating at higher level.
**Flight-period.** Univoltine at higher latitude and altitude, May/July; bivoltine
at low level in S Alps and Spain, May/July and August/September.
**Habitat.** Damp, grassy, flowery places, sometimes associated with woodland.
**Life-history.** LHPs *Valeriana officinalis*; *V. officinalis* (?) *collina* [= *V. wallrothii*]; *V.
dioica*; *V.* (?) *repens*; *V.* (?) *pratensis*. Natural use of *Plantago lanceolata*; *Filipendula
ulmaria*; *Melampyrum nemorosum*; *M. pratense*; *Veronica chamaedrys*; *Polygonum
bistorta* requires confirmation. Captive larvae accept *Centranthus ruber* and reject
*Plantago lanceolata*. Ova laid in batches on leaves. Small larvae feed and hibernate in silken web, dispersing shortly after hibernation. Pupates on plants near
ground. In one captive rearing experiment, a proportion of larvae from Monte
Baldo required two seasonal cycles for full development.

## *Mellicta athalia* Heath Fritillary          Plate 52

**Range.** Europe, Turkey, throughout temperate Asia to Japan.

*M. athalia athalia* Rottemburg 1775 TL: Paris.
syn: *neglecta* Pfau 1945.
**Distribution.** Common and widespread. Most of N and E Europe, including
S England (very local) and European Turkey from a line connecting NW
Pyrenees, N Alps and W Slovenia: SW of this region, replaced by *M. athalia
celadussa* (below). Absent from Mediterranean islands and S Greece. 0-2200m.

**Description.** Unf marginal pale spots in s2 and s3 usually with conspicuous black internal borders, sometimes including s1b and s4, more rarely reduced to a black mark or thick line bordering s2: this character, and overall appearance, usually allows separation from other members of the genus. Male genitalia distinct.

**Variation.** Many forms/ssp. have been described, reflecting appreciable local and regional variation: most are perhaps better regarded as ecological variants or segments of geographical or altitudinal clines. In Bulgaria (Stara Pl.), f. *boris* Früstorfer: ups dark marginal borders heavy: reportedly does not represent the average Bulgarian population which corresponds more closely to nominate form.

**Flight-period.** Generally univoltine in a prolonged emergence (mid May/mid August): a partial second brood (mid to late August/September) has been reported in favourable localities/seasons.

**Habitat.** Diverse. Dry or damp, grassy, flowery places, often amongst bushes or in woodland clearings.

**Life-history.** LHPs include *Plantago lanceolata*; *P. alpina*; *Veronica chamaedryas*; *V. montana*; *V. officinalis*; *Melampyrum pratense*; *M. sylvaticum*; *Digitalis purpurea*; *D. ferruginea*; *D. lutea*; *Linaria vulgaris*. Ova laid in batches on underside of leaf. Larvae feed and hibernate in silken webs. Larger larvae disperse after hibernation, feeding singly or in small groups, sometimes switching to alternative LHPs. Pupates on plant stems or leaves near ground.

*M. athalia norvegica* Aurivillius 1888 TL: Dovrefjeld, Norway.
**Distribution.** Fennoscandia: 62-70°N. 0-800m.
**Description and Variation.** Small; ups markings regular, well defined; unf pale marginal spots in s2 and s3 absent, replaced by gc, but dark proximal border retained. In C Sweden and Finland, f. *lachares* Frühstorfer: ups black markings finer, creating wider fulvous discal and pd bands: transitional forms occur in low-lying districts of S Sweden.
**Flight-period.** Univoltine. June/July according to season.
**Habitat.** Grassy, flowery places with bushes and small trees (400-800m). In S Fennoscandia, flowery woodland clearings, usually on dry, sandy heaths (0-300m).
**Life-history.** LHPs *Plantago* sp., *Veronica* sp., *Melampyrum* sp. Development as for nominate form.

*M. athalia celadussa* Frühstorfer 1910 TL: Maritime Alps.
syn: *pseudathalia* Reverdin 1921.
**Distribution.** N Portugal. N Spain and Sierra Nevada. S France. S Switzerland. Italy and Sicily – complementing distribution of nominate form. 0-2600m.
**Description and Variation.** Resembles nominate form. Male genitalia distinct: male ups markings generally finer; female ups dark suffusion uncommon. Interface with nominate form wide, extending to over 150km in parts, populated by intermediate forms. In Portugal and NW Spain, f. *biedermanni* Querci: large; ups submarginal and pd black lines fine, discal line thicker: transitional forms occur in central W Spain. In Sierra Nevada (S Spain), f. *nevadensis* Verity: univoltine: ups golden-yellow; black markings fine. In S Europe, late broods usually small with ups black markings reduced (f. *tenuicola* Verity).

**Flight-period.** Univoltine at higher altitudes, June/July; bivoltine below subalpine level, May/June and late July/August.
**Habitat and Life-history.** As for nominate form.

## *Mellicta deione* Provençal Fritillary                    Plate 52

**Range.** N Morocco, W Algeria, SW Europe.

*M. deione deione* Geyer 1832 TL: Aix-en-Provence.
**Distribution.** Widespread in Spain except central W and NW districts. S France: C and E Pyrenees to Massif Central and Hautes-Alps. N Italy: very sporadic: Maritime Alps; Cottian Alps; Val d'Aosta to Dolomites. 200-1600m.
**Description and Variation.** Male ups gc uniform yellow-orange; black markings fine; ups black discal mark in s1b heavy, usually dumb-bell, bell or club-shaped; unf dark proximal shading of marginal spots in s1b-s4 vestigial or absent (cf. nominate form); uns gc pale; unh submarginal and discal bands bright, uniform yellow-orange; submarginal band with distinctive rounded orange spots in each space: female ups gc paler, usually with distinctly paler shade in fw pd area. Nominate form is prevalent in S France and C Spain. In S and SE Spain (?)1000-1600m (*magna* Seitz) and E Pyrenees 1500m ((?)*praestantior* Verity; (?)*mirabilis* Rutimeyer): first brood: larger; ups brighter. In Cantabrian Mts. 1500m, S. de la Demanda and Montseny Mts., (*signata* de Sagarra) and C Pyrenees (*rondoui* Oberthür), (?)1000-1600m: smaller; ups darker. In N Italy (200-1500m), *vesubiana* Verity, *tessinorum* Frühstorfer and *phaisana* Frühstorfer: larger; ups black markings heavier – transitional to *berisalii* (below). In all regions, expected altitudinal clines, that is, with larger, brighter forms at low level, replaced progressively by smaller, darker races at higher altitudes, are generally not apparent.
**Flight-period.** Bivoltine. Mid May/June and mid August/early September.
**Habitat.** Open, flowery meadows; grassy, flowery woodland margins; bushy places.
**Life-history.** LHPs *Linaria vulgaris*; *L. alpina*; (?)*Antirrhinum sempervirens*; *A. hispanicum*; *Chaenorhinum minus* [=*Linaria minor*]; (?)*Digitalis lutea*; (?)*Cymbalaria muralis*. Ova laid in batches on underside of leaves. Larvae feed and hibernate gregariously.

*M. deione berisalii* Rühl 1891 TL: 'Simplon' [in error].
**Distribution.** Switzerland: apparently restricted to Rhône Valley (Saillon; Martigny; Folly; Varen). 300-1200m.
**Description and Variation.** Male ups dark fulvous; black markings heavy, marginal borders wide: female ups gc more uniform.
**Flight-period.** Univoltine. Mid May/mid July.
**Habitat.** Dry, bushy places, often near cultivated areas.
**Life-history.** LHPs *Linaria vulgaris*; *L. alpina*; *Chaenorhinum minus* [=*Linaria minor*]; (?)*Antirrhinum latifolium*; (?)*Digitalis lutea*. Development as for nominate form. Captive larvae accept *Antirrhinum majus* and *Linaria purpurea*.

*M. deione rosinae* Rebel 1910/1911 TL: Cintra [S Portugal].
syn: *philomena* Frühstorfer 1917

**Distribution.** S Portugal: widespread but local: Minho to Algarve (S. de Monchique; Serra do Caldeirão). 100-400m.
**Description.** Male ups gc dark fulvous; black markings heavy; unf pale marginal spots with proximal dark line in s2 and s3 – not as thick as in *M. athalia*; unf discal spot in s1b heavy, irregular in shape: female ups dark suffusion more intense and extensive; uns orange-red markings prominent.
**Flight-period.** Bivoltine. Early April/May and July.
**Habitat.** Dry, flowery, bushy places.
**Life-history.** LHPs *Linaria vulgaris*; *L.* (?)*micrantha*. Development as for nominate form. Captive larvae accept *Antirrhinum majus*.

*M. deione nitida* Oberthür 1909 TL: Tlemcen, Sebdou (Algeria).
**Distribution.** N Morocco: W Rif Mts. (Dj. Lakraa; Dj. Kelaa; Izlan). W Algeria: Sebou; Tlemcen. 900-1800m.
**Description and Variation.** In both sexes, fw outer margin strongly convex in most specimens; ups paler, yellowish-orange; ups black markings fine, marginal lines very narrow, sometimes paired; unh discal markings reduced; unh pale discal band usually unmarked: female similar. Male genitalia conform to nominate form. In W Rif Mts.: in July, smaller, with female ups gc more uniform (lacking usual contrastive colour bands) than specimens from same locality in late April/May.
**Flight-period.** Voltinism uncertain: possibly bivoltine (cf. seasonal variation) in Rif Mts. (mid April/early August) and univoltine in Algeria (May/June).
**Habitat.** Dry, flowery valleys; open grassy slopes; *Quercus* scrub.

## *Mellicta varia* Grisons Fritillary                    Plate 53

**Range.** European Alps, Apennines.

*M. varia* Meyer-Dür 1851 TL: Graubünden Alps.
**Distribution.** France: Alpes-Maritimes, through Drôme to Haute-Savoie (not W of Rhône Valley). 1500-2500m. Switzerland: Valais (Alpes Valaisannes; Bernese Alps); Grisons (mountains bordering Engadine Valley). Austria: Tirol. Italy: Maritime Alps; S Alps including Ortler; 2000-2650m; C Apennines (Monte Livata; Monte Sibillini; Gran Sasso; Abruzzi; 1200-2600m).

**Description and Variation.** Upf pd line often thin and broken; discal mark in s1b variable, often dumb-bell, sigma or club-shaped, repeated on unf with conspicuous adjoining black basal bar: female ups usually with extensive greyish suffusion. Development of ups black markings, and dark suffusion in female, subject to marked individual/local variation. In Ligurian Alps 1800m, *piana* Higgins: larger.
**Flight-period.** Univoltine. Late June/late August according to altitude
**Habitat.** Sheltered flowery slopes and hollows with short grass.
**Life-history.** LHPs *Plantago alpina*; *Gentiana verna*; *G. acaulis*. Ova laid in batches on leaves. Larvae hibernate in groups, dispersing after hibernation.

## *Mellicta parthenoides* Meadow Fritillary          Plate 53

**Range.** SW Europe.

*M. parthenoides* Keferstein 1851 TL: Soucy, France.
syn: *parthenie* Godart 1819 (invalid homonym).
**Distribution.** Widespread in Iberian Peninsula. France,
except NE. Very local in S Germany, Switzerland (Jura;
Schaffhausen), NW Italy (Ligurian and Cottian Alps). 400-
2400m.
**Description and Variation.** Male ups bright fulvous-
orange, hw discal field usually clear of black markings; upf
marginal and submarginal black lines of uniform thickness; pd line fine, often
disrupted in s4; black discal markings heavy; upf discal mark in s1b variable in
thickness but distinctly oblique (cf. *M. varia*). Regionally and locally very
variable: in Spain, ups markings generally better defined, contrasting sharply
with clear, bright gc.
**Flight-period.** Univoltine at higher altitudes, early June/July; bivoltine at lower
levels, May/June and August/September.
**Habitat.** Open, flowery, grassy places bordering woodland.
**Life-history.** LHPs *Plantago lanceolata*; *P. alpina*; *P. media*. Ova laid in batches
on underside of leaves. Larvae feed and hibernate in companies, dispersing in
later instars.

## *Mellicta aurelia* Nickerl's Fritillary          Plate 53

**Range.** C and E Europe, Turkey, Transcaucasus, S Urals, N
Kazakhstan, W Siberia, Tian Shan.

*M. aurelia* Nickerl 1850 TL: Erlangen, Germany.
syn: *parthenie* Borkhausen 1788 (invalid homonym).
**Distribution.** W France to Latvia, Balkans and N Greece
(Vernon Mts.; Rodopi Mts.: very local). Absent from Britain,
NW and SW France, N Belgium, Holland, Fennoscandia, C
and S Italy and Republic of Macedonia. Reports from S
Sweden unconfirmed. 100-1500m.
**Description and Variation.** Male ups black markings often suffused greyish;
upf marginal pd line complete (cf. *M. parthenoides*); spacing of marginal, submarginal, pd and discal lines roughly even, creating a uniform macular gc pattern
(cf. *M. parthenoides*); unh double marginal lines infilled yellow, slightly darker
than adjacent spots: female ups gc generally somewhat paler. Darker forms
often occur on damp peaty soils.
**Flight-period.** Univoltine. Early June/late July, in prolonged emergence in
some southern localities.
**Habitat.** Open, grassy and flowery places, with sparse bushes or small trees;
damp peat mosses; heaths.
**Life-history.** LHP *Plantago lanceolata*. Ova laid in batches on underside leaves.
Larvae feed and hibernate in companies, dispersing in later instars.

## *Mellicta britomartis* Assmann's Fritillary      Plate 53

**Range.** C Europe, C Asia, Transbaical, Mongolia, NE China, Korea.

*M. britomartis* Assmann 1847 TL: Breslau, Germany.

**Distribution.** Central E Germany to NE Poland and SE Sweden. N Italy: very local: Val d'Aosta; Val di Susa; Turin; Lake Maggiore; Lake Guarda; Friuli-Venezia. Slovenia. Hungary. N Serbia. Romania. Bulgaria: very local: Stara Pl. (Sliven); Burgas. Reported presence in NE Switzerland relates to one male and two female specimens taken on separate occasions from same, general locality. 300-900m.

**Description and Variation.** Male ups resembles *M. aurelia*. Larger; male ups gc darker, black markings heavier, lacking dusky suffusion; unh submarginal spots often with chocolate brown proximal border; double marginal lines infilled dusky-orange or brown – distinctly darker tone than adjacent yellow spots (cf. *M. aurelia*). In some cases, examination of male genitalia may be necessary to effect separation from *M. aurelia*: larval and pupal stages readily separable.

**Flight-period.** Univoltine in most localities, late May/early August: reportedly bivoltine in NW Italy (Ticino Valley), May/June and late July/early August.

**Habitat.** Warm, sheltered grassy and bushy places at woodland margins.

**Life-history.** LHPs *Plantago lanceolata*; *Veronica teucrium*; *Rhianthus minor*. Ova laid in batches on underside of leaves. Larvae feed and hibernate in a silken web.

## *Mellicta asteria* Little Fritillary      Plate 53

**Range.** Central European E Alps.

*M. asteria* Freyer 1828 TL: Chur, Switzerland.

**Distribution.** Very local. E Switzerland: Grisons, high mountains bordering Engadine Valley. Italy: C and E Alps, including Ortler. Austria: Tirol to Gross Glockner; Gurktaler Alps. 2000-2700m.

**Description.** Small; ups often heavily suffused greyish in both sexes.

**Flight-period.** Univoltine. Early July/late August.

**Habitat.** Confined to alpine tundra: open valleys and slopes with short grass.

**Life-history.** LHP *Plantago alpina*. Ova laid in clumps on underside of leaves. Larval development occupies two seasonal cycles.

## *Hypodryas maturna* Scarce Fritillary      Plate 53

**Range.** C and E Europe, Caucasus, Urals, E Kazakhstan, S and W Siberia, Transbaikal, Mongolia.

*H. maturna* Linnaeus 1758 TL: Not stated.

**Distribution.** Generally very local: colonies widely dispersed. France: Oise; Seine-et-Marne; Yonne; Nièvre; Allier; Saône-et-Loire; Côte-d'Or; Haute-Marne; Haute-Saône. Germany. Czech Republic. Slovakia. Poland. SE Sweden:

Uppland; Dalarne; Västmanland. Baltic states. S Finland.
Austria. Hungary. Romania. Slovenia. Croatia. Serbia.
Bosnia-Herzegovina. Albania. W Republic of Macedonia: Sar
Pl.; Radika Valley. Bulgaria: Ludogorie Hills. 200-1000m.
**Flight-period.** Univoltine. Late May/early July according
to locality and season.
**Habitat.** Small, bushy clearings containing young Ash or
Aspen trees in mixed deciduous woodland, often in lime-
stone valleys, sometimes in damp situations.
**Life-history.** LHPs (before hibernation) *Fraxinus excelsior*;
*Populus tremula*; (?)*Salix caprea*. Ova laid usually in a single large batch on
underside of leaf of a small specimen (<6m) of LHP. Larvae feed and hiber-
nate gregariously in a silken web which, in autumn, falls to the ground along
with dead leaves. After hibernation, larvae disperse and feed singly on *F. excelsior*,
*P. tremula*, *Plantago lanceolata*, *Veronica chamaedrys*, *Lonicera periclymenum* or
*Succisa pratensis*. In captivity, a proportion of larvae require two seasonal cycles
to achieve maturity (cf. *H. intermedia*).
**Behaviour.** Adults rest and roost in trees and seem to prefer the nectar of
shrubs, e.g., *Lingustrum vulgare* and *Viburnum lantana*, to that of low-growing
plants.
**Conservation.** Decline in many regions (N France; Bavaria; S Sweden) has
been attributed to forestry management, land drainage and habitat destruction
for agricultural purposes.

## *Hypodryas intermedia* Asian Fritillary                    Plate 53

**Range.** C European Alps, S and C Urals, S and W Siberia,
Transbaikal, Mongolia, Amur, NE China, Sakhalin, Korea.

*H. intermedia wolfensbergeri* Frey 1880 TL: Maloja Pass,
Engadine.
**Distribution.** France: Haute-Savoie; Savoie; Izère; Hautes-
Alpes. Switzerland: Valais (S of Rhône Valley) to Engadine.
Italy: N Cottian Alps; Ortler Alps; Dolomites; Karinthian
Mts. Slovenia: Julian Alps (Triglav Massif). 1500-2400m –
more often 1700-2000m.
**Description.** Unh pale discal band with medial thin black line, often broken
(cf. *H. cynthia*).
**Flight-period.** Univoltine. Late June/early August.
**Habitat.** Small clearings in light coniferous woodland, often associated with
small streams and low-growing shrubs, e.g., *Juniperous communis nana*, *Rhodo-
dendron ferrugineum* and *Alnus viridis*.
**Life-history.** LHP *Lonicera caerulea*. Ova laid in batches on underside of leaves.
Hibernates as a larva, the full larval development of which occupies two sea-
sonal cycles.
**Note.** Sympatric with *H. maturna* in some parts of E Palearctic range (Kentei
Mts.).

## *Hypodryas cynthia* Cynthia's Fritillary                Plate 54

**Range.** European Alps, Bulgaria.

*H. cynthia* Denis and Schiffermüller 1775 TL: Vienna.
**Distribution.** France: Alpes-Maritimes to Haute-Savoie.
Switzerland: Valais to St. Gallen and Engadine. Italy: W
Ligurian Alps, S Alps, Ortler Alps to Dolomites. Austria: W
Tirol to Niedere Tauern. 900-3000m. Bulgaria: Pirin Mts.
2200-2700m; Rila Mts. 2000-2800m. Records for Bavarian
Alps require confirmation.
**Description and Variation.** Male ups white discal and
basal markings definitive: female resembles female *H. intermedia*, but lacking
unh black line in pale discal band and with black points in each space of uph
and unh red pd band. Above 1800m, west of Hohe Tauern, *alpicola* Galvagni:
smaller; ups black suffusion more extensive, almost obscuring pale submarginal
band; red markings reduced, sometimes absent on fw. In E Austria, sporadic
occurrence of transitional forms at high and intermediate altitudes (east of
Brenner), and larger, brighter forms than nominate form at lowest altitudes,
suggests ecological modification with the combined characters of geographical
and altitudinal clines. In Bulgaria, *leonardi* Frühstorfer (Rila Mts.) and *drenowskii*
Röber (Pirin Mts.): large; brightly marked.
**Flight-period.** Univoltine. Late June/early August.
**Habitat.** Open, grassy slopes dominated by low shrubs, which often include
*Juniperous communis nana* (Central Alps) or *J. sibirica* (Bulgaria).
**Life-history.** LHPs *Plantago alpina*; *Viola calcarata*. Ova laid in batches on
underside of leaves. Hibernates as a larva, the full larval development of which
occupies two seasonal cycles.

## *Hypodryas iduna* Lappland Fritillary                Plate 54

**Range.** N Fennoscandia, E Turkey, Kola Peninsula, Caucasus, Polar and Subpolar Urals, NE and S Siberia, Yakutskaya,
Mongolia, Altai.

*H. iduna* Dalman 1816 TL: Sweden.
**Distribution.** N Fennoscandia from Arctic Circle to Arctic
Sea. In Finland, restricted to a few sites close to Norwegian
border. Sporadic and very local in some regions. 300-700m.
**Flight-period.** Univoltine. Late June/mid July: date of emergence dependent on local/regional weather conditions.
**Habitat.** Damp heathland with sparse scrub, often in close proximity to marshes
with small open areas of standing water; hillside bogs; drier rocky terrain at
highest altitudes.
**Life-history.** LHPs *Veronica alpina*; *V. fructicans*; *Plantago*; *Vaccinium*. Ova laid
in small batches on leaf. Larvae feed and hibernate gregariously in small groups
in a silken web.
**Behaviour.** In rapid flight close to the ground, males appear surprisingly grey
and bear a striking resemblance to a large *Pyrgus* sp. Adults often bask or seek
shelter from strong winds amongst dwarf Birch (*Betula nana*).
**Note.** Although predominantly an arctic species, occurs in lower latitudes where

equivalent ecological conditions are provided, evidently, by the compensating influence of high altitude; e.g., Mt. Ararat, 40°N, 4000m (*H. i. inexpectata* Sheljuzhko) and in the Altai Mts., 50°N, 1800-2700m (*H. i. sajana* Higgins) where further compensation derives from the more general, cooler conditions of a subarctic zone.

## *Euphydryas aurinia* Marsh Fritillary        Plate 54

**Range.** Morocco, Algeria, Europe, Turkey, temperate Asia, Korea.

*E. aurinia aurinia* Rottemburg 1775 TL: Paris.
**Distribution.** From Pyrenees, through most of Europe, including Britain, to 62°N in Fennoscandia, including Öland and Gotland. 0-2200m. Absent from C and S Greece, Mediterranean islands and peninsular Italy, except Monti Aurunci and Monti del Matese. 0-1950m.
**Variation.** Ups gc and black markings subject to considerable individual, local and regional variation. Divergence within a colony and between isolated colonies, even within a small area of distribution, is often appreciable. To a lesser extent, significant inter-seasonal differences are also apparent, indicating an ecological origin for at least some of the observed variation. Whilst a large number of subspecies have been described to accommodate regional differences, difficulties of taxonomic classification are compounded by the widespread occurrence of transitional forms, interspersed with distinctive, local ecological variants. In the absence of a biological basis for distinction, the greater proportion of descriptions at subspecies level lack justification, thereby creating, in some instances, a false impression of genetically distinct and geographically restricted populations. Subspecific assignments to S Balkan and N Greek races (*balcanica* Schawerda and *bulgarica* Frühstorfer), for example, is confounded by the sporadic occurrence, in the same region, of mountain populations indistinguishable from those of NW and C Europe. Similarly, *kricheldorffi* Collier (Asturia Mts., N Spain), shares much of the character of *scotica* Robson (W Scotland) and *iberica* Oberthür (Ireland): these forms, characterised by extensive ups dark suffusion and orange pd bands/cellular spots contrasting with yellowish discal markings, appear to be ecological modifications arising from damp and/or cold conditions: in warmer/drier conditions of central S and SE Europe, tendency towards bicoloured forms with dark markings is largely reversed. Distinctive forms/sspp. occupying substantial geographical areas are described below.
**Flight-period.** Univoltine. Mid April/Mid July, according to altitude.
**Habitat.** Diverse. Damp or dry flowery, grassy places; deciduous or coniferous woodland margins or clearings on calcareous or acidic soils; damp, open heathland; sheltered places on exposed mountain slopes.
**Life-history.** LHPs include, *Succisa pratensis* (N and C Europe); *Scabiosa columbaria*; *S.* (?)*ochroleuca* (NW Greece); *Lonicera periclymenum*; *L. implexa*; *Gentiana lutea* (Switzerland); (?)*Digitalis* sp. (Slovenia). Reported use of *Plantago* spp. in Slovakia requires confirmation. Ova laid in batches on underside of leaves. Larvae feed and hibernate in a silken web.

*E. aurinia provincialis* Boisduval 1828 TL: Provence, France.
**Distribution.** SE France: Bouches-du-Rhône; Var; Alpes-Maritimes; Alpes-de-Haute-Provençe; Hautes-Alpes; Isère. N Italy. 300-1000m – exceptionally to 2250m.
**Description and Variation.** Ups gc almost unicolorous pale orange, pd bands slightly darker; black markings fine; uns very pale sandy-orange. F. *comacina* Turati; smaller and paler, very local near Lake Como and Lake Lugano at 900m. West of Rhône Valley to Catalonia, transitional to *beckeri* Herrich-Schäffer (below). At higher altitudes in Piedmont, transitional to nominate form. In Croatia, *rotunda* Röber: resembles *provincialis*: averagely larger: transitional to nominate form in parts of Bosnia-Herzegovina and W Serbia.
**Flight-period.** Univoltine. May/June.
**Habitat.** Dry, flowery clearings in light woodland or scrub.
**Life-history.** LHPs *Succisa pratensis*; *Scabiosa columbaria*; *Cephalaria leucantha*; *Knautia arvensis*.

*E. aurinia beckeri* Herrich-Schäffer 1851 TL: Cádiz.
**Distribution.** Morocco: very local: Middle Atlas; Rif Mts; 300-1800m. C Algeria: very local: Blida; Col de Ben-Chicao; Berrouaghi; 1000-1200m. Portugal. Spain: Pyrenees and Cantabrian Mts. to Andalusia. 10-1700m.
**Variation.** At lowest altitudes in Algarve (10-100m), very large; gc tone averagely darker on both surfaces; ups black markings heavier; unh pale rings enclosing black points in marginal band reduced or absent. Transitional to nominate form in foothills of Cantabrian Mts. and Pyrenees. In C Algeria, *barraguei* Betz: upf and uph mediodiscal bands and upf pd band yellow – contrasting with orange gc; uns gc paler, unh orange pd paler.
**Flight-period.** Univoltine. NW Africa April/June according to locality: S Portugal (Algarve, 10-100m), early April/late May: Spain, late May/late June.
**Habitat.** Hot, dry, flowery places, often amongst rocks and open scrub: in NW Africa, flowery, grassy slopes, often on damp or marshy ground; clearings in dense or light woodland.
**Life-history.** LHPs: Spain, *Lonicera periclymenum*; *L. implexa*; *L. etrusca*; *Scabiosa columbaria*; *S. atropurpurea*; (?)*Knautia arvensis*: Morocco, *L. implexa*; (?)*L. biflora*; (?)*L. etrusca*; (?)*L. periclymenum*.

*E. aurinia debilis* Oberthür 1909 TL: E Pyrenees.
syn: *merope* de Prunner (invalid homonym)
**Distribution.** Andorra. France: Ariège; Pyrénées-Orientales; Alpes-de-Haute-Provençe to Haute-Savoie. Switzerland. Germany: Allgäuer Alps. Austria: Tirol; Carnic Alps. 1500-2600m: rarely below 1800m.
**Variation.** At high altitudes in Central Alps, *glaciegenita* Verity: male ups pale dusky-yellow, heavily suffused grey, variable; reddish-orange submarginal and cellular markings reduced. Clinal variation in wing-markings is apparent, with brighter forms occurring at lower altitudes in S and W Alps: expected accompanying clinal variation in size is, however, reversed with larger forms occurring in N and E Alps – possibly explained by a two year life-cycle at highest altitudes, thus providing more time for larval development.
**Flight-period.** Univoltine. Late June/late August according to altitude.
**Habitat.** Open grassy slopes; damp alpine meadows: on calcareous or non-calcareous soils.

**Behaviour.** Flight fast and low.
**Life-history.** LHPs *Gentiana verna*; *G. acaulis*; *G. clusii*; *G. alpina*; *Primula viscosa*. Ova laid in clusters on underside of leaves. Larvae feed on flowers. Hibernates as a small larva.

## *Euphydryas desfontainii* Spanish Fritillary        Plate 54

**Range.** Morocco, Algeria, Iberian peninsula.

*E. desfontainii desfontainii* Godart 1819 TL: Algeria.
**Distribution.** Morocco: Middle Atlas (Azrou; Annoceur; Tizi-n-Tretten; Ifrane; Mrassine; Douar de Garde; Mischliffen; Timhadit; Zehroun Massif; 500-2100m); High Atlas (Dades Valley; Tilmi; Djebel Siroua; Col du Kerdous; 2800m); Rif Mts. (Chechaouen); Algeria: (Sebdou; Daya; El Hacaiba; Tlemcen Mts.; 1500-1800m).
**Description and Variation.** Fw outer margin curvature slightly irregular near v6; unf discal area pale rose-red; black markings prominent (cf. *E. aurinia*). F. *gibrati* Oberthür, ups gc brighter, appears to fall with range of variation of nominate form.
**Flight-period.** Univoltine. Mid April/early June
**Habitat.** Dry, rocky or grassy gullies/slopes, often amongst scrub; grassy/flowery meadows.
**Life-history.** LHP *Knautia arvensis*. Larvae feed and hibernate in silken webs, which have been found on plants other than the LHP. Larvae are said to aestivate in summer heat, becoming active with the onset of autumn rain.

*E. desfontainii baetica* Rambur 1858 TL: Andalusia.
**Distribution.** S Portugal: Algarve. Spain: Province of Burgos, W Pyrenees and Catalonia through Madrid to Andalusia. France: Pyrénées-Orientales (Sournia: very local). Absent from Cantabrian Mts. Sporadic and generally very local. 50-1800m.
**Description and Variation.** Unf discal area yellow but variable – individuals indistinguishable from nominate form occur in Teruel and Andalusia. In provinces of Teruel, Alicante and Huesca, uns markings often better defined (*zapateri* Higgins). In S Portugal (Algarve 100-200m): very large, especially female; ups pale spots in marginal band vestigial; female ups gc pattern less contrastive.
**Flight-period.** Univoltine. Mid April/early June according to altitude.
**Habitat.** Hot, dry, grassy scrubland; rocky gullies; dry stream beds; neglected areas of cultivation.
**Life-history.** LHPs *Dipsacus fullonum*; *D. comosus*; *Cephalaria leucantha*; *Scabiosa* sp; *Knautia* sp.; (?) *Centaurea* spp. Ova laid in batches on underside of leaves. Captive larvae accept *Succisa pratensis*.

# Satyridae Boisduval 1833

A very extensive family of small, medium and large butterflies comprising about one-third of European species. Most are some shade of brown, usually with distinctive ocelli on the underside of the hind-wing and one or more prominent ocelli in the apical region of the upper and underside fore-wing: as observation shows, these ocelli – so-called 'eye-spots' – tend to divert the point of attack of a predatory bird or lizard from the more vital parts of the insect. An atypical group are the 'marbled whites', so-called because of their white ground-colour and intricate pattern of black markings. The genus Erebia comprise a large and distinctive group of mostly small or medium-sized insects, easily recognizable by their very dark brown, sometimes almost jet black ground-colour: these are mostly inhabitants of mountains, with some species occurring at altitudes as high as 3000m. Of the many endemic European Erebia species, more than a dozen are confined to the Central Alps. Amongst several other endemic species, having equally or even more restricted distributions, some are found only on the Atlantic islands. As far as is known, larva of all European Satyrid butterflies feed on grasses (Poaceae), mostly during the hours of darkness (this information is not repeated in the following account of species). Grasses are low in proteins and larval development is greatly protracted, often requiring several months. Most species hibernate as immature larvae (where confirmed for individual species, this information has been omitted from the general account). Although larval shape varies appreciably according to the relative proportions of component structures, the larvae of most species are quite distinctive and characterized by a smooth taper originating in the thorax or abdomen and terminating in twin 'tails' in the last abdominal segment. Larvae are generally quite sensitive to any form of disturbance and, if touched, will usually drop immediately from their feeding station and burrow into the base of the larval host-plant; the same reaction is sometimes induced by bright, artificial light. Pupae are suspended from plant-stems or secreted within or below the compact base of the larval host-plant, or amongst moss or in small hollows under stones.

## *Melanargia galathea* Marbled White                Plate 55

**Range.** NW Africa, Europe, Turkey, Transcaucasus.

*M. galathea galathea* Linnaeus 1758 TL: Germany (Verity 1953).
**Distribution.** N Spain (Cantabrian Mts. to W and C Pyrenees), eastwards through most of Europe, including S England and Sicily, to Lithuania, C Greece and European Turkey. 0-1750m. Absent from N Holland, N Germany and Peloponnesos. Last reported from Latvia in 1950. Generally widespread and common, but absent from substantial areas within main region of distribution. Largely replaced by *M. lachesis* (below) in Pyrénées-Orientales; Aude; Hérault; Gard: intermediate forms, believed to be hybrids, are frequent in areas of contact.
**Description.** Upf cell without medial transverse black bar (cf. *M. russiae*); upf basal and distal areas of cell black; unf distal one-third of cell grey, separated

from white area by irregular transverse black line; cell-base with limited dark suffusion. (Cf. *M. lachesis*).
**Variation.** Ups black suffusion variable: in C and S Italy, S Balkans and Greece, dark forms predonderate (f. *procida* Herbst): in NE Italy (f. *magdalenae* Reichl), black markings further extended, totally obscuring white gc in extreme examples. Ups and uns gc sometimes yellow, commonly associated with f. *procida*, in which ups female costa is often conspicuously buff. F. *leucomelas* Esper: unh uniformly white, unmarked – a recurrent form, commoner in the south. F. *galene* Ochsenheimer: unh pd ocelli absent.
**Flight-period.** Univoltine. Generally June/July, exceptionally late May/early September.
**Habitat.** Diverse. Grassy, flowery, bushy places.
**Behaviour.** Adults are especially fond of the nectar of *Centaurea*, *Scabiosa*, *Cirsium* and *Carduus* spp.
**Life-history.** LHPs include *Brachypodium pinnatum*; *B. sylvaticum*; *Bromus erectus*; *Poa trivialis*; *Phleum pratense*; *Agrostis capillaris*; *Dactylis glomerata*; *Molinia caerulea*; *Avena pubsecens*; *Festuca rubra*. Ova are ejected amongst grasses during flight. Mature larvae are polymorphic.

*M. galathea lucasi* Rambur 1858 TL: Bougie, Algeria.
**Distribution.** Morocco. Algeria. Tunisia. 800-2600m. Common and widespread.
**Description.** Ups black marginal markings averagely more extensive; distal part of cell greyish, closed by transverse black bar near cell-end: female unh pd ocelli with blue pupils.
**Variation.** Development of ups black marginal markings appear to follow an east-west cline, with darkest forms (f. *fumata* Mokhles) prevalent in Morocco. Variants equivalent to f. *leucomelas* Esper not reported.
**Flight-period.** Univoltine. Mid May/July at lower altitudes; June/early September at highest altitude.
**Habitat.** As for nominate form.

## *Melanargia lachesis* Iberian Marbled White               Plate 55

**Range.** Portugal, Spain, S France.

*M. lachesis* Hübner 1790 TL: Languedoc [S France].
**Distribution.** Portugal and Spain: widespread and common. France: Pyrénées-Orientales; Aude; Hérault; Gard (not reported east of Rhône Valley). 0-1600m.
**Description.** Upf cell white except for black suffusion at distal extremity (cf. *M. g.* galathea), lacking medial transverse black bar (cf. *M. russiae*).
**Variation.** Ups dark suffusion variable in extent and colour (brownish to black); uns gc whitish or yellowish. F. *cataleuca* Staudinger: unh uniformly white – equivalent to *M. galathea* f. *leucomelas* Esper.
**Flight-period.** Univoltine. Early June/early August.
**Habitat.** Dry, grassy, bushy, flowery places.

## *Melanargia russiae* Esper's Marbled White          Plate 55

**Range.** SW and SE Europe, Italy, E Turkey, Transcaucasus, S Russia to W Siberia, E Kazakhstan.

*M. russiae russiae* Esper 1783 TL: S Russia
**Distribution.** Occurred formerly in Hungary, now presumed extinct in Europe: extant in Caucasus, S Urals Mts., Tien Shan and Altai Mts.
**Description.** Ups marginal and subapical markings clearly defined, associated dark suffusion minimal.

*M. russiae cleanthe* Boisduval 1833 TL: Basses Alpes.
**Distribution.** N Portugal: Serra da Estrêla. N, C and E Spain. S France: E Pyrenees; S Massif Central; Vaucluse; Alpes-de-Haute-Provençe; Drôme; Hautes-Alpes. 600-1650m.
**Description.** Upf cell with medial transverse irregular black bar, often diffuse or partly obscured by greyish or fuscous cellular suffusion (cf. *M. galathea*; *M. lachesis*; *M. larissa*).
**Variation.** Ups dark suffusion variable in extent and colour – dark brownish to black. Lightly marked specimens resembling nominate form are not uncommon. A female form equivalent to *M. galathea* f. *leucomelas* has been recorded from Burgos, N Spain.
**Flight-period.** Univoltine. Late June/mid August.
**Habitat.** Dry, grassy places, often in bushy clearings in sparse pinewood.

*M. russiae japygia* Cyrillo 1787 TL: S Italy.
**Distribution.** Italy: Apennines (Florence to Avellino); Apulia; Calabria; N Sicily (Madonie; Monte Nebrodi; Monti Peloritani). 1000-1450m. Albania: Jablanica Pl. W Republic of Macedonia: Bistra Pl.; Jablanica Pl.; Placenska Pl.; Mt. Pelister. NW Greece: Vernon Mts.; Varnous Mts.; Voras Mts.; Timfi Mts.; Mitsikeli Mts. 1300-2100m.
**Description and Variation.** Ups dark suffusion more extensive, especially in Italy, but variable. In Italy and Greece, lightly marked forms, closely resembling nominate form, occur commonly, preponderant in some colonies.
**Flight-period.** Univoltine. Late June/mid August.
**Habitat.** Dry, rocky limestone slopes and open gullies dominated by grasses: less often, dry, gravelly slopes with short grasses on non-calcareous substrates.
**Life-history.** LHPs *Stipa pennata*; *Aegilops geniculata*; *Brachypodium pinnatum*; *B. sylvaticum*. In Greece, mature larvae are usually entirely green, but a small proportion have green bodies and light brown heads.

## *Melanargia larissa* Balkan Marbled White          Plate 56

**Range.** SE Europe, Turkey, Transcaucasus, N Iran.

*M. larissa* Geyer 1828 TL: Cres (Cherso Is.), Croatia (Hemming 1937).
**Distribution.** Croatia: Dalmatian coastal region. S Serbia. Albania. Republic of Macedonia. S Bulgaria: Pirin Mts.; Rhodopi Mts. Greece, including Corfu, Levkas, Limnos, Lesbos and Siros. European Turkey. 0-2150m – most often below 1500m.
**Description and Variation.** Upf, distal one-third of cell closed by dark line

(cf. *M. russiae*), basal area of cell largely suffused fuscous-grey; ups basal areas extensively suffused fuscous-grey, often obscuring uph cell completely (cf. *M. russiae*). In some localities, especially S Dalmatia, ups marginal and pd dark suffusion greatly reduced (*herta* Geyer): intermediate forms not uncommon. Female forms with unh light buff or whitish occur in Greece (cf. *M. galathea* f. *leucomelas*). On Limnos and Lesbos, *lesbina* Wagener: ups dark suffusion extensive, partly or largely obscuring white marginal chevrons.

**Flight-period.** Univoltine. Late May/early August according to locality.
**Habitat.** Warm, dry, grassy, flowery, places; often amongst bushes and rocks in open woodland.

## *Melanargia occitancia* Western Marbled White          Plate 56

**Range.** NW Africa, SW Europe.

*M. occitanica occitanica* Esper 1793 TL: Toulouse.
syn: *psyche* Hubner 1800; *syllius* Herbst.
**Distribution.** N and C Portugal. Spain: widespread but local: absent from NW, NC and extreme SW. France: E Pyrenees to Ardèche and Provençe. Italy: Maritime Alps: very local. 0-1500m. A record for Corsica requires confirmation.

**Description.** Unh veins brownish – overall pattern very distinctive; curved longitudinal brownish line in s1b linked at both ends to v1b.
**Flight-period.** Univoltine. Late April/late June, according to locality.
**Habitat.** Hot, dry, grassy, rocky places.
**Life-history.** LHPs *Brachypodium pinnatum*; *Dactylis glomerata*; *Lygeum spartum*. In captivity, newly-hatched larvae have been observed to enter and remain in diapause for 15 months.

*M. occitanica pelagia* Oberthür 1911 TL: Sebdou, Algeria.
**Distribution.** Morocco: Middle Atlas; High Atlas. W Algeria. Widespread but local. 500-2000m. Not recorded from E Algeria or Tunisia.
**Description and Variation.** Upf base of s3 always white – transverse black cellular bar clearly separated from discal markings (cf. nominate form). Moroccan populations resemble nominate form closely, those of Algeria show closer affinity to those of Sicily (cf. *M. o. pherusa* (below)).
**Flight-period.** Univoltine. Mid May/June.
**Habitat.** As for nominate form.

*M. occitanica pherusa* Boisduval 1833 TL: Sicily.
**Distribution.** NW Sicily: very local: mountains south of Palermo. 600-1000m.
**Description and Variation.** Ups black markings reduced, especially uph discal area; upf, base of s3 always white; uph and unh ocelli, smaller, sometimes absent (f. *plesaura* Bellier); unh veins brown, finer.
**Flight-period and Habitat.** As for nominate form.
**Note.** Clinal variation in wing-markings from Iberian Peninsula through N Africa to Sicily is clearly evident. The disjunctive distributional relationship with the closely similar, but allopatric *M. arge* (below) is striking: it would appear

that *M. arge* is the evolutionary culmination of a once uninterrupted cline of *M. occitanica* extending to southern Italian mainland: a small, but constant difference is apparent in valve of male genitalia; chromosome numbers unknown.

## *Melanargia arge* Italian Marbled White                Plate 57

**Range.** Peninsular Italy.

*M. arge* Sulzer 1776 TL: Kingdom of Sicily [included Appenines in 1776].

**Distribution.** NE Sicily (Monte Nebrodi; Monti Peloritani): W and C Italian mainland: Monti di Tolfa; Monti della Laga to S Calabria. Absent from E Italy, except Gargano and Salentina Peninsulas. 350-1500m.

**Description and Variation.** Resembles *M. occitanica pherusa*. Ups and uns black markings reduced; upf posterior extremity of cell-bar tapered to a fine line, not quite reaching median vein; black oval/circular mark at cell-end often enclosing bluish scales; base of s3 usually with some dark suffusion; unh veins black; dark longitudinal curved line in s1b linked at both ends to v1b (cf. *M. ines*). In E Italy, f. *couzzana* Stauder: unh markings reduced: intermediate forms (f. *turati* Rostagno) occur in SW Italy (Aspromonte).

**Flight-period.** Univoltine. early May/mid June.

**Habitat.** Dry, rocky and grassy places.

## *Melanargia ines* Spanish Marbled White                Plate 57

**Range.** Morocco, Algeria, Tunisia, Portugal, Spain, N Libya.

*M. ines* Hoffmannsegg 1804 TL: Spain.

**Distribution.** Morocco. Algeria. Tunisia. 300-2600m. Portugal. Spain: south of Cantabrian Mts. and Pyrenees. Widespread, locally common. 50-1500m.

**Variation.** Fairly constant in Europe. At high altitudes in Morocco, ups black markings often heavier (f. *jehandezi* Oberthür).

**Flight-period.** Univoltine. Late March/late June according to locality.

**Habitat.** Dry, grassy and rocky places: habitats often shared with *M. occitanica*.

**Behaviour.** Males recorded 'hilltopping' at 2788m in High Atlas.

**Life-history.** LHP: in S Spain, *Brachypodium pinnatum*. In dry conditions in captivity, newly-hatched larvae enter diapause without feeding.

## *Hipparchia fagi* Woodland Grayling                Plate 58

**Range.** N Spain, S and C Europe, N Caucasus, Volga, S Urals, W Kazakhstan.

*H. fagi* Scopoli 1763 TL: Krain, Yugoslavia.
syn: *hermione* Linnaeus 1764

**Distribution.** N Spain (Aragon; Catalonia), through C, S and E France (sporadic in central regions, commonest in SE), C Germany (sporadic and local in Bavaria), S Poland, Italy to Balkans and S Greece. Absent from N France,

Belgium, (?)S Holland, N Germany, European Turkey and
Mediterranean islands except Sicily and Levkas. Records for
Portugal, Corfu and Lithuania require confirmation. 50-
1800m, usually below 1000m.
**Description.** Resembles *H. alcyone* and *H. syriaca* very
closely: reliable separation probably impossible without
reference to male/female genitalia.
**Flight-period.** Univoltine. Early June/mid September
according to locality.
**Habitat.** Bushy, grassy, woodland clearings; margins of pine forests.
**Life-history.** LHPs *Bromus erectus*; *Festuca rubra*; *Brachypodium pinnatum*.
**Behaviour.** Often rests, sometimes in assembly, in shade on tree-trunks or
interior of bushes.

## *Hipparchia alcyone* Rock Grayling                    Plate 58

**Range.** Morocco, SW, C and E Europe, S Norway, Ukraine.

*H. alcyone alcyone* Denis and Schiffermüller 1775 TL: Vi-
enna, Austria.
syn: *aelia* Hoffmannsegg 1804.
**Distribution.** Spain. France: mainly in E and W Pyrenees;
S Massif Central; Basses Alpes; Yonne; Saône-et-Loire; Jura.
Italy: Liguria; C Apennines; Aspromonte. Switzerland (Jura;
Valais; Tessin) to Austria, Hungary, Poland, S Norway
(Telemarken; Augder) and SE Latvia. Local and generally
scarce in northern range. 0-1600m: most often above 500m. Distribution
uncertain in many regions owing to confusion with *H. fagi.*
**Description and Variation.** See *H. fagi.* Ups and uns gc, coloration of ups pd
band (white to yellowish) and development of markings subject to marked
variation.
**Flight-period.** Univoltine. Late June/mid August.
**Habitat.** Bushy, grassy, rocky woodland clearings/margins; in Norway,
extensive, glacial rock-formations, with sparse, low-growing vegetation and
scattered pine trees.
**Life-history.** LHPs *Brachypodium pinnatum*; *B. sylvaticum*; *Festuca ovina*.

*H. alcyone caroli* Rothschild 1933 (June) TL: Morocco.
syn: *natasha* Hemming 1933 (December).
**Distribution.** Morocco: Middle Atlas (Azrou; Ifrane; Mischliffen; Aïn Leuh;
Taghzeft; Zad; Aïn Kola; Rae El-Ma; Tizi-n-Treken; Timhadit; Daiet-Achlef;
Dj. Hebri); Rif Mts. (Chefchaoune; Dj. Lakraa; Ketama). 1000-2000m.
**Description.** Differs from nominate form by small differences in genitalia;
character of Julian organ regionally variable.
**Flight-period.** Univoltine. Late June/early October.
**Habitat.** Steep, rocky slopes; open woodland.

## *Hipparchia syriaca* Eastern Rock Grayling    Plate 59

**Range.** SE Europe, Turkey, Transcaucasus, Lebanon, Syria, Iran.

*H. syriaca* Staudinger 1871 TL: Syria, Cyprus.
**Distribution.** Croatia: Dalmatian coast. SW Serbia (Montenegro). Albania. Republic of Macedonia. Bulgaria. Greece, including Corfu, Kefalonia, Thassos, Lesbos, Chios, Samos and Rhodes. 0-1300m.
**Description and Variation.** See *H. fagi*. Male ups pale pd band variable, often partly obscured by dark suffusion: on Rhodes, *ghigii* Turati: ups pd band largely obscured by dark suffusion.

**Flight-period.** Univoltine. Generally June/August, records span early May/mid September suggesting possibility of aestivation.

**Habitat.** Hot, dry, bushy places in woodland, most often open pinewoods; hot, dry oak forests in Bulgaria; hot, dry, deciduous or pine woodland in NE Greece; very small clearings in dense pine forests reported for some colonies on Rhodes.

**Behaviour.** Males rest on stones, more often on tree trunks; several may assemble on a single tree.

## *Hipparchia ellena* Algerian Grayling    Plate 59

**Range.** Algeria, Tunisia.

*H. ellena* Oberthür 1894 TL: Bône, Algeria.
**Distribution.** E Algeria: Bône; Lambessa; Yakouren; Bou Youseff; Blida; Batna; W Tunisia: Aïn Draham; Kroumirie. 1500-1800m. Locally common.
**Description.** Ups white pd band well defined – devoid of dark suffusion (cf. *H. alcyone caroli*).
**Flight-period.** Univoltine. July/September.
**Habitat.** Oak forests (*Quercus mirbecki*).

**Life-history.** LHP *Brachypodium ramosum*. Hibernation stage unconfirmed.

## *Hipparchia neomiris* Corsican Grayling    Plate 60

**Range.** Corsica, Sardinia, Elba.

*H. neomiris* Godart 1824 TL: Corsica.
**Distribution.** Corsica: Soccia; Cap Corse; La Face; Haut Asco; Tattone; Col de Sorba; Vizzavona. 300-2000m. Sardinia: Monti di Alà; Monti del Gennargentu; Fonni; Lanusei; Seulo. 300-1800m. Capraia. Elba: Mte. Peronne; Mte. Maolo; Mte. Capanne. 300-1200m.
**Flight-period.** Univoltine. Mid June/August.
**Habitat.** Open, rocky slopes with low-growing vegetation and scrub, usually associated with pinewoods.

## *Hipparchia volgensis* Delattin's Grayling          Plate 60

**Range.** Albania, Republic of Macedonia, Bulgaria, Greece.
*H. volgensis delattini* Kudrna 1975 TL: Pristina [Republic of
Macedonia].
**Distribution.** Albania. Republic of Macedonia: Vadar Valley
and associated river systems. Bulgaria: mainly in southern
region. Greece: NW Macedonia; W Thessaly; N Peloponnesos (Aroanian Mts.); Zakynthos. 700-1450m.
**Description and Variation.** Inseparable from *H. semele*
without reference to male genitalia. Fertilized females possess
a rudimentary sphragis (cf. *H. semele*, *H. christenseni* and *H. cretica*). On Mt.
Chelmos (Aroanian Mts.) *muelleri* Kudrna: ups slightly darker; male genitalia
differ slightly, but very variable – distinction possible only by quantified (statistical) evaluation.
**Flight-period.** Univoltine. Early June/August.
**Habitat.** Hot, dry, rocky gullies; screes; dry scrub; open pine woodland.

## *Hipparchia semele* Grayling          Plate 61

**Range.** Europe to 63°N in Fennoscandia: distribution uncertain E of Europe.

*H. semele semele* Linnaeus 1758 TL: Sweden (Verity 1953).
**Distribution.** Generally widespread and common. Most
of Europe, from Portugal to S Fennoscandia (including Fyen,
Sjælland, Lolland, Falster, Borholm, Öland, Gotland and
Aland), S Serbia, S Romania and Bulgaria. In Britain, Scandinavia and Baltic states, shows marked preference for coastal
margins. Absent from Albania, Republic of Macedonia, much
of S Bulgaria and Mediterranean islands except N and E Sicily (1000-1800m).
Records for N Greece require confirmation. 0-2000m. Distribution in E and
SE Europe uncertain due to confusion with related taxa.
**Variation.** Variation in size, gc and development of markings (especially unh)
appears largely attributable to ecological adaptation. Darker forms tend to occur
on peat-based soils, paler forms on limestone. Many forms have been described
to account for local/regional character. In C and S Europe, f. *cadmus* Frühstorfer:
larger: male ups yellow-orange pd band greatly reduced, often restricted to s2
and s5, enclosing ocelli; uph yellow-orange pd area and unh white pd band
usually well developed: female upf pd better developed. In Sicily, *wilkinsoni*
Kudrna: resembles nominate form closely: male genitalia structurally similar
but disproportionately larger.
**Flight-period.** Univoltine. June/September according to locality.
**Habitat.** Diverse. Heathland; grassy, bushy places; open woodland; sand dunes;
coastal cliffs; dry rocky slopes/gullies: on calcareous and non-calcareous soils.
**Life-history.** LHPs *Festuca ovina*; *Koeleria pyramidata*; *Agrostis curtisii* [=*A.
setacea*]; *Phleum phleoides*; *Ammophlia arenaria*; x *Ammocalamagrostis baltica*
[=*Ammophlia arenaria* x *Calamgrostis epigejos* (=*Ammophlia arundinacea*)];
*Deschampsia cespitosa*; *Vulpia myuros*; *Aira praecox*; *Elymus repens* [=*Agropyron
repens*]; *Bromus erectus*; *Briza media*; *Sesleria albicans*; *Lolium prenne*. In some

habitats, ova are laid exclusively on dead vegetation. Distribution of the hybrid, x *A. baltica* ('marram' grass – an inhabitant of coastal margins) shows some correlation with that of the butterfly in its northern range.

*H. semele leighebi* Kudrna 1976 TL: Isola di Vulcano [Lipari Islands].
**Distribution.** Italy: Lipari [=Eolian] Islands (Volcano; Panarea). 0-500m. Widespread and very common.
**Description.** Ups orange markings well developed, bright; male genitalia probably indistinguishable from nominate form but androconial scales 30% longer. Resembles *H. aristaeus blachieri* very closely: male genitalia distinct: reputedly, fw/hw size-ratio of *H. a. blachieri* comparatively greater.
**Flight-period.** Univoltine. Mid May/early August.
**Habitat.** Diverse. Rocky slopes; gullies; scrub; open pinewoods; gardens.

## *Hipparchia cretica* Cretan Grayling                   Plate 60

**Range.** Crete (Greece).

*H. cretica* Rebel 1916 TL: Crete.
**Distribution.** Crete: widespread and common. 100-1500m.
**Description.** Resembles *H. semele* very closely: male genitalia larger; androconia differ slightly. Fertilized females possess a prominent sphragis (cf. *H. semele*, *H. christenseni* and *H. volgensis*).
**Flight-period.** Univoltine. Mid May/mid August.
**Habitat.** Dry, rocky slopes with bushes and sparse trees: olive groves.
**Life-history.** Hibernation stage unconfirmed.
**Behaviour.** Rests on shaded side of tree-trunks in very hot conditions.

## *Hipparchia christenseni*                   Not illustrated

**Range.** Karpathos (Greece).

*H. christenseni* Kudrna 1977 TL: Mt. Lastros, Karpathos.
**Distribution.** Karpathos; Mt. Lastros; Kali Limnos. Very local. 300-750m.
**Description.** Resembles *H. semele* and *H. cretica* very closely: separable on basis of male genitalia and androconia. Fertilized females possess a rudimentary sphragis (cf. *H. semele*, *H. volgensis*, *H. cretica*, *H. mersina* and *H. pellucida* – taxonomic relationship to these species presently unclear).
**Flight-period.** Univoltine. Early June/late June.
**Habitat.** Dry, bushy, stony places; pinewood clearings.
**Life-history.** Hibernation stage unconfirmed.
**Behaviour.** Adults often rest on the trunks of pine trees; in treeless, bushy terrain, males often settle on stones.

## *Hipparchia aristaeus* Southern Grayling                   Plate 62

**Range.** Madeira, NW Africa, Mediterranean Islands, S Balkans, Greece, Turkey.

*H. aristaeus aristaeus* Bonelli 1826 TL: Monti Gennargentu, Sardinia.
syn: *sardoa* Spuler 1902.
**Distribution.** France: Corsica (Evisa; Col du Lavezo; Vizzavona; Corte; Ajaccio).

Italy: widespread on islands: Sardinia; Capraia; Elba; Giglio; Ponza. 500-1800m.
**Description.** Large; ups orange markings bright, well developed.
**Flight-period.** Univoltine. June/late August.
**Habitat.** Dry, rocky places with sparse scrub.

*H. aristaeus senthes* Frühstorfer 1908 TL: Taygetos Mts. [S Greece].
**Distribution.** Albania. Republic of Macedonia. S Bulgaria. Greece, including Levkas, Thassos, several islands of Cycladian Archipeligo and E Aegean chain: not reported from Crete, Karpathos or Rhodes. European Turkey. 50-1600m.
**Description.** Ups orange/yellowish areas reduced, suffused greyish-brown. Resembles *H. s. semele* and *H. volgensis delattini*: male genitalia distinctive.
**Flight-period.** Univoltine. Late May/mid August according to locality.
**Habitat.** Dry, rocky and bushy places; bushy, woodland clearings.

*H. aristaeus algirica* Oberthür 1876 TL: Daya, Lambessa, Collo [Algeria].
**Distribution.** Morocco. Algeria. Tunisia. Widespread and common. 1200-2400m.
**Description.** Resembles *H. a. senthes* and *H. s. semele*.
**Flight-period.** Voltinism uncertain: records span late April/October: reportedly univoltine at high altitudes (June/July); elsewhere, the possibility of prolonged emergence, aestivation and wide, regional and/or seasonal variation in emergence date may create false impression of bivoltinism.
**Habitat.** Dry, rocky slopes with sparse vegetation; grassy, flowery places.
**Life-history.** LHP *Lygaeum spartum.*

*H. aristaeus blachieri* Früstorfer 1908 TL: Italy, Sicily.
syn: *siciliana* Oberthür 1915.
**Distribution.** Sicily: Puerta Antena; Messina; Palermo; Madonie; Mt. Elbei; Taormina; Isnello; Palazzolo Acreide; Ficuzza; Cefalu. 700-1900m.
**Description.** Ups pd orange-fulvous areas extensive. Superficially inseparable from *H. semele leighebi* but male genitalia distinct.
**Flight-period.** Univoltine. Mid June/August.
**Habitat.** Dry, rocky slopes with sparse vegetation.

*H. aristaeus maderensis* Bethune-Baker 1891 TL: Madeira.
**Distribution.** Madeira: Aira de Serrado; Poiso; Pico Arieiro. Local and uncommon. 800-1800m.
**Description.** Male ups markings largely obscured by dark brown suffusion; unh white discal band prominent: female ups markings better developed.
**Flight-period.** Univoltine. Late July/mid September.
**Habitat.** South-facing, steep rocky slopes in sparse deciduous or coniferous woodland.
**Life-history.** LHPs *Holcus* sp.; *Agrostis* sp.

## *Hipparchia azorina* Azores Grayling                    Plate 62

**Range.** Azores.

*H. azorina* Strecker 1899 TL: Azores
**Distribution.** Azores: Pico 600-2000m; Sao Jorge 480-720m; Faial 700-above 1000m; Terceira 1000m.

**Description and Variation.** Male ups sex-brand conspicuous. Three forms/ sspp., corresponding to their islands of origin, have been described:- *picoensis* Le Cerf (Pico); *ohshimai* Esaki (Faial); *jorgense* Oehmig (Sao Jorge); *barbarensis* (Terceira): differentiated by systematic differences in imago size, wing-coloration, androconia, male genitalia and early-stage morphology.
**Flight-period.** Univoltine. June/October.
**Habitat.** Sheltered grassy slopes.
**Life-history and Behaviour.** LHP: Pico and Faial, *Festuca jubata*: Sao Jorge and Terceira, (?)*F. jubata*: circumstantial evidence indicates monophagacity. Ova laid exclusively on LHP. Hibernation stage unconfirmed. Sex of mature larvae of *ohshimai* ((?)*picoensis*; (?)*jorgense*; (?)*barbarensis*) is readily determined by the width of the head. Adults take nectar from *Rubus ulmifolius*, *R. hochstetteranum*, *Pontentilla erecta* and *P. anglica*. Despite the paucity of flowering plants on the Azores, *Vaccinium cylindraceum*, *Thymus caespititius* and *Daboecia azorica*, where available, do not appear to be exploited as nectar sources by *Hipparchia azorina*, *H. caldeirense* (below) or *H. miguelensis* (below).

## *Hipparchia caldeirense* Oehmig's Grayling　　　Plate 62

**Range.** Azores.

*H. caldeirense* Oehmig 1981 TL: Caldeira Seca, Flores.
**Distribution.** Azores: Flores (Caldeira Seca; Pico dos Sete Pes). Above 700m.
**Description.** Male upf without androconial scales (cf. *H. azorina* and *H. miguelensis*).
**Flight-period.** Univoltine. June/late September.
**Habitat.** Grassy sheltered valleys on the slopes of the Caldeira Seca and Pico dos Sete Pes.
**Life-history and Behaviour.** LHP *Festuca jubata*: circumstantial evidence indicates monophagacity. Hibernation stage unconfirmed. Captive larvae reject *F. ovina* but accept *F. scoparia*. For both sexes, nectar sources as for *H. azorina*.

## *Hipparchia miguelensis* Le Cerf's Grayling　　　Not illustrated

**Range.** Azores.

*H. miguelensis* Le Cerf 1935 TL: Sao Miguel.
**Distribution.** Azores: Sao Miguel. 600-1000m.
**Description.** Male ups sex-brand conspicuous. Specific distinction from other *Hipparchia* species of the Azores based on adult and early-stage morphology.
**Flight-period.** Univoltine. Late June/late September.
**Habitat.** Sheltered, grassy hollows and small valleys.
**Life-history and Behaviour.** LHP *Festuca jubata*: circumstantial evidence indicates monophagacity. Hibernation stage unconfirmed. For both sexes, nectar sources as for *H. azorina*, in addition to *Calluna vulgaris*.

## *Hipparchia mersina*　　　Plate 61

**Range.** Greece (E Aegean Islands), Turkey.

*H. mersina* Staudinger 1871 TL: Mersin, SW Turkey.
**Distribution.** Greece: Lesbos 150-600m; Samos 300-1150m.

**Description.** Androconia scales long and slender. Fertilized females possess a rudimentary sphragis (cf. *H. pellucida* and *H. christenseni*).
**Flight-period.** Univoltine. Mid May/mid July.
**Habitat.** Dry, grassy clearings amongst rocks, sparse bushes and trees.
**Life-history.** On Samos, very small larvae, together with full-grown examples have been recorded in April.

## *Hipparchia pellucida*                              Plate 61

**Range.** Greece (E Aegean Islands), Turkey, Cyprus, N Iraq, N Iran, Crimea, Transcaucasus.

*H. pellucida* Stauder 1924 TL: Terter [Azerbaijan].
**Distribution.** Greece: Lesbos; Ikaria. 400-700m.
**Description.** Fertilized females possess a prominent sphragis (cf. *H. mersina* and *H. christenseni*).
**Flight-period.** Univoltine. Late May/July (data limited).
**Habitat.** Dry, grassy, rocky slopes or screes with scattered bushes; dry, gently sloping, stony ground with sparse, low-growing vegetation and scattered pine trees.

## *Neohipparchia statilinus* Tree Grayling            Plate 63

**Range.** NW Africa, S and C Europe, Turkey.

*N. statilinus* Hufnagel 1766 TL: District of Berlin.
**Distribution.** Morocco. Algeria. Tunisia. 900-2500m. S Europe (including European Turkey, Sicily, Elba, Corfu and Thassos) to NW France, Poland and Lithuania (first recorded 1971): common and widespread in Portugal, Spain, SE France, C and S Italy, S Balkans and Greece: very local and sporadic in SW and C France, Czech Republic, Slovakia and Hungary: possibly extinct in Germany. Absent from Britain, NE France, Belgium, Holland, N Switzerland, Bavaria, NW Austria, Carpathian Mts. and Fennoscandia. 0-1400m.
**Description and Variation.** Unh submarginal line variable, often obscure (cf. *N. fatua*). Many forms have been described in recognition of marked regional and local variation, especially unh gc – dark greyish-brown, through medium grey, devoid of brownish tones, to light greyish-brown or pale grey; variation in submarginal, discal, mediobasal lines and irroration varies independently of gc. In N Africa, *sylvicola* Austaut: unh dark greyish-brown; antemarginal band darker brown: similar forms occur in S Spain.
**Flight-period.** Univoltine. Late June/October with peak emergence generally late July/early August in most southern localities.
**Habitat.** Hot, dry, rocky areas, often amongst scrub or in open pinewoods, less often, deciduous or mixed woodland.
**Life-history.** LHPs include *Bromus erectus*; *B. sterilis*; *Bothriochola ischaemum*; *Stipa pennata*; *Lygaeum spartum*.

## *Neohipparchia fatua* Freyer's Grayling    Plate 63

**Range.** S Balkans, Greece, Turkey, Transcaucasus, Israel, Jordon, Lebanon, Syria.

*N. fatua* Freyer 1844 TL: Gediz, Province of Kütahya, W Turkey (Kudrna 1977).

syn: *allionii* Hübner 1824 (invalid homonym)

**Distribution.** Sporadic, locally common. S Croatia. S Bosnia-Herzegovina. SW Serbia. Republic of Macedonia. Albania. S Bulgaria. Greece, including Lefkas, Kithera, Thassos, Paros and most E Aegean islands. European Turkey. Not reported from Corfu or Crete. 0-600m.

**Description.** Resembles *N. statilinus*: larger; male ups very dark; unh dark mediobasal, discal and submarginal lines well defined (cf. *N. statilinus*).

**Flight-period.** Univoltine. Late May/early October according to locality.

**Habitat.** Hot, dry, stony gullies and rocky slopes, often with bushes in sparse, usually coniferous woodland; olive groves; orchards.

**Life-history.** Hibernated larvae recorded feeding only on well-shaded plants of a tall, robust, clump-forming grass.

**Behaviour.** Often rests in shade on tree-trunks.

## *Neohipparchia hansii* Austaut's Grayling    Plate 63

**Range.** Morocco, Algeria, Tunisia, NW Libya.

*N. hansii* Austaut 1879 TL: Daya, Algeria.

**Distribution.** Morocco: Anti-Atlas; Middle Atlas (Tizi-Tanout-ou-Fillali; Azrou; Aïn Leuh; Tirhboula; Foum Khereg); High Atlas (Dj. Ayachi; Tizi-n-Talhremt; Tizi-n-Test). Algeria: El Mizab; Sebdou; Blida. Tunisia: Tunis; Korbous; Cap Bon. 1000-2100m.

**Description and Variation.** Resembles *N. statilinus* closely: upf sex-brand smaller. In both sexes, all wing-characters subject to marked variation: male genitalia and androconia allow reliable separation from *N. statilinus* with which it sometimes occurs.

**Flight-period.** Univoltine. Late August/November.

**Habitat.** Rocky, slopes with sparse vegetation.

**Life-history.** Hibernation stage unconfirmed.

## *Neohipparchia powelli* Powell's Grayling    Plate 64

**Range.** Algeria.

*N. powelli* Oberthür 1910 TL: Djebel Amour, Algeria.

**Distribution.** C and E Algeria: scarce and local: Aflou; Guelt-es-Stel; Dj. Senalba; Dj. Amour; El Bayadh. 1100-1200m.

**Description.** Resembles *N. hansii*. In both sexes, fw apical angle distinctly sharper; male ups darker; ocelli obscure, faintly ringed yellow; upf sex-brand poorly defined; unf pd area brown, ocelli ringed yellow; unh whitish discal band narrow, diffuse on outer margin; veins greyish. Wing-characters constant in known range.

**Flight-period.** Univoltine. August/October.

**Habitat.** Hot, dry, rocky places with sparse vegetation.

**Life-history.** LHP *Lygaeum spartum*. Hibernation stage unconfirmed.

**Note.** Taxonomic and distributional relationship with *N. hansii* not clearly understood: male genitalia and androconia closely similar.

## *Pseudotergumia fidia* Striped Grayling                    Plate 64

**Range.** NW Africa, SW Europe.

*P. fidia* Linnaeus 1767 TL: 'Barbarie' Algeria.

**Distribution.** Widespread but local. Morocco: Middle Atlas; High Atlas. Algeria. Tunisia. 1000-2200m. Iberian Peninsula, except W Pyrenees and N Spain. Mallorca. France: E Pyrenees to Ardèche and Provence. NW Italy: Maritime Alps: very local. 0-1400m.

**Variation.** In NW Africa, unh veins conspicuously paler (f. *albovenosa* Austaut).

**Flight-period.** Univoltine. Europe, late June/late August according to locality: NW Africa, July/October.

**Habitat.** Hot, rocky slopes with scrub; dry soil-banks with bushes and sparse, low-growing vegetation; rocky places in light woodland.

**Life-history.** LHPs include *Cynodon dactylon*; *Dactylus glomerata*; *Brachypodium* sp.; *Poa annua*; *P. pratensis*; *Milium multiflorum*; *Oryzopsis* sp.

## *Pseudotergumia wyssii* Canary Grayling                    Plate 64

**Range.** Canary Islands.

Distinction between following forms based on small morphological differences in wing-markings, male genitalia and, in some cases, size/structure of ova. Hibernation stage unconfirmed.

*P. wyssii wyssii* Christ 1889 TL: Tenerife, Canary Isles.

**Distribution.** Tenerife: widespread but local in central mountains. 1400-2000m.

**Flight-period.** Univoltine. Early June/early September according to altitude.

**Habitat.** Rocky gullies in pine forests.

*P. wyssii bacchus* Higgins 1967 TL: Hierro, Canary Isles.

**Distribution.** Hierro: confined to Frontera; Sabinosa. 300-1500m.

**Flight-period.** Univoltine. Mid July/late August.

**Habitat.** Very steep, grassy cliffs and associated vineyards at cliff-base.

*P. wyssii gomera* Higgins 1967 TL: Gomera, Canary Isles.

**Distribution.** N and W Gomera: known largely from coastal districts: Barranco de Argaga; Barranco de Arure; Vallehermoso; Hermigua; Agulo; 200-300m: recently recorded inland at higher (unspecified) altitude.

**Flight-period.** Univoltine. Late May/early September.

**Habitat.** Rocky gullies and slopes; steep grassy/bushy cliffs; vineyards; scrub margins of laurel forest.

*P. wyssii tilosi* Manil 1984 TL: Los Tilos, La Palma.

**Distribution.** NE La Palma: Barranco del Agua; Los Tilos; Santa Cruz;

Barranco de la Rio de las Nieves; La Cumbrecita. 400-1300m.
**Flight-period.** Univoltine. Late July/early September.
**Habitat.** Rocky gullies in laurel or pine forests.

*P. wyssii tamadabae* Owen and Smith 1992 TL: Pinar de Tamadaba, Gran Canaria.
**Distribution.** Gran Canaria: Pinar de Tamadaba; Morgan; Pozo Nieves; Tiraiana; Maspalomas; Roque Nublo; Barranco de los Palmitos. 400-2000m
**Description.** Distinguished from other forms by unf apical ocellus with white pupil in 50% of males, 100% in females.
**Flight-period.** Univoltine. Early April/early September according to altitude.
**Habitat.** Rocky gullies in pine forests.

## *Chazara briseis* The Hermit                         Plate 65

**Range.** NW Africa, Spain, C Europe to 50°N, Turkey, Iran, Afghanistan to NW China.

*C. briseis* Linnaeus 1764 TL: Germany.
**Distribution.** Widespread. Morocco. Algeria. Tunisia. 0-2500m. From Spain (except extreme N and W), C Italy, S Greece and European Turkey to S Poland. 0-2000m. Absent from Portugal, NW and N France, Belgium, Holland, N Germany, S Italy and Mediterranean islands except Sicily. In France, range has contracted considerably in recent decades, now largely confined to SE: also extinct in parts of Germany. Sporadic in Switzerland and N Italy.
**Variation.** In S Europe, female ups white markings sometimes replaced by yellowish-buff or creamy-brown (f. *pirata* Esper – not known in N Africa). In SE Europe, female unh sometimes suffused pink.
**Flight-period.** Univoltine. Late May/October according to locality and altitude.
**Habitat.** Dry, often hot, stony places amongst scrub; dry, bushy grassland.
**Life-history.** LHPs include *Bromus erectus*; *Festuca ovina*.

## *Chazara prieuri* Southern Hermit                    Plate 65

**Range.** Spain, Morocco, Algeria.

*C. prieuri* Pierret 1837 TL: Bougi [Bejaïa], Algeria.
**Distribution.** Local and often very scarce. Morocco: Middle Atlas (Col du Zad); High Atlas (Tizi-n-Talrhemt; Aït Oumghar; Dj. Ayachi). Algeria: Sebdou; Télagh; Beni-Ounit; Sidi-bel-Abbes; Dj. Senalba; Dj. Metlili; El Bayadh; Aflou; Djelfa. 1200-2000m. Spain: provinces of Granada (S. de Baza; S. de La Sagra); Murcia (S. de Espuña); Teruel (Montes Universales); Madrid; Huesca; Zaragoza; Alicante. Mallorca. 900-1450m.
**Description and Variation.** Male upf with conspicuous buff patch in cell: in both sexes, unh veins conspicuously pale (cf. *C. briseis*). In Spain, female ups white markings replaced by fulvous in about 50% of specimens (f. *uhagonis* Oberthür): not reported from N Africa.
**Flight-period.** Univoltine. NW Africa, June/July: Spain, Mid July/mid August.

**Habitat.** Hot, dry, rocky gullies with scrub; dry, grassy, stony slopes in open coniferous woodland.
**Life-history.** LHP *Lygeum spartum*: in captivity, larvae accept *Festuca ovina*; *Poa annua*.

## *Pseudochazara atlantis* Moroccan Grayling　　　Plate 66

**Range.** Morocco.

*P. atlantis* Austaut 1905 TL: High Atlas Mts., Morocco.
syn: *maroccana* Meade-Waldo 1906
**Distribution.** Morocco: Anti-Atlas (Tizi-n-Melloul; Tizi-n-Tieta); High Atlas (Tizi-n-Talrhemt; Imilchit; Oukaï-meden); Middle Atlas (Col du Tagzheft; Col du Zad; Tizi-Tarhzeft); W Rif (Bab Taza; Dj. Lakraa). 1600-3000m.
**Description and Variation.** Upf rounded white spots in s3 and s4, sometimes vestigial, occurs in about 50% of specimens from the High Atlas. Fringes not chequered or only weakly so. Androconial scales variable between individuals in the same colony; scale-base rounded or shouldered. Development of markings and gc locally variable: f. *benderi* Weiss and f. *colini* Wyatt, relating to minor differences in size and gc, fall within range of variation of nominate form.
**Flight-period.** Univoltine. Mid June/early August according to altitude.
**Habitat.** Barren, rocky slopes.
**Life-history.** Hibernation stage unconfirmed.

## *Pseudochazara graeca* Grecian Grayling　　　Plate 66

**Range.** Greece, Republic of Macedonia.

*P. graeca* Staudinger 1870 TL: Mt. Parnassos and Mt. Chelmos, Greece.
syn: *Satyrus mamurra* var. *graeca* Staudinger 1870
**Distribution.** Republic of Macedonia: Pelister massif. NW and C Greece: Mt. Olympus; Mt. D'rfis (1000-1745m). Pindos Mts. (Smolikas massif to Mt. Parnassos) 1200-2200m. S Greece: Mt. Chelmos; Mt. Panakhaïkón; Mt. Ménalon; Mt. Taygetos. 1000-2200m. Not recorded from Varnous Mts. (NW Greece) – the southern extension of Pelister massif.
**Description.** Upf white pd spots in s3 and s4 sometimes poorly represented. Androconial scale-base, rounded.
**Variation.** Small but systematic local variation in size and coloration, especially unh, appears to be due to ecological adaptation to the geological character of habitat. Amongst several variants, described formally as ssp., *coutsisi* Brown [=*zagoriensis* Aussem] is the most distinctive: ups suffused smokey, greyish-brown; upf ocelli often lacking white pupils; uns darker: known only from N Smolikas massif, Timfi Mts. and Katara Pass 1200-1600m.
**Flight-period.** Univoltine. Mid July/late August.
**Habitat.** Mostly open, grassy places amongst limestone rocks above treeline: f. *coutsisi* occurs on dry, grassy slopes amongst scrub and light, mostly pine woodland; on Smolikas massif, on friable, greyish, metamorphic rocks.

**Life-history.** On Mt. Timphristos, larvae feed on a pleasantly perfumed grass.
**Note.** *P. graeca* appears to be closely related to *P. aurantiaca* Staudinger 1871
from N Iran (Elburz Mts.): minor differences in wing-markings are possibly
attributable to ecological adaptation, but androconial scales of *P. aurantiaca* are
wider at the base and almost double the length. In the absence of a full understanding of taxonomic significance of androconial morphology (cf. *P. atlantis*),
the relationship of *P. graeca* and *P. aurantiaca* remains unclear.

## *Pseudochazara hippolyte* Nevada Grayling          Plate 66

**Range.** S Spain, eastwards with marked distributional dis-
junction to S Urals, Kazakhstan, Kyrgyzstan, S Siberia,
Mongolia.

*P. hippolyte williamsi* Romei 1927 TL: Sierra Nevada, S Spain
**Distribution.** S Spain: Sierra Nevada 2000-2700m; S. de
los Filabres 1850-2020m; S. de Gádor 2000-2200m; S. de
Maria 1400-2040m; S. de Guillimona 1500-2000m. Records
for S. de Espuña require confirmation.
**Description and Variation.** Fringes chequered. Upf with-
out submarginal white spots in s3 and s4. Androconial scale-base shouldered.
Two forms have been described to account for minor, local variation: S. de
Maria, *aislada* Eitschberger and Steiniger: larger; paler; S. de Gádor, *augustini*
Weiss: slightly smaller; uns gc slightly brown.
**Flight-period.** Univoltine. Late June/late July.
**Habitat.** Dry, grassy slopes, with patches of bare, stony soil: on greyish or
greyish-brown non-calcareous rocks.
**Life-history.** LHP *Festuca ovina*. Larvae, captively reared in S England, (cf.
photo-period) hibernate in second instar.
**Note.** Type locality of *P. hippolyte hippolyte* Esper 1784 lies in the Ural Mts. of
S Russia, about 5000km from Spain: no intermediate populations are known.
Nominate form replaced by *mercurius* Staudinger 1887 in SE limit of Palearc-
tic range (Alexander Mts., Kyrgyzstan).

## *Pseudochazara geyeri* Grey Asian Grayling          Plate 67

**Range.** Albania, Republic of Macedonia, Greece, Turkey.

*P. geyeri occidentalis* Rebel and Zerny 1931 TL: Albania.
**Distribution.** Albania: mountains near Lake Ohrid. SW
Republic of Macedonia: Galicica Pl.; Pelister massif. 1500-
1700m. NW Greece: Mt. Malimadi; Triklarion Mts. 1450-1650m.
**Description.** Fringes chequered. Upf without submarginal
white pd spots in s3 and s4. Androconial scale-base bulbous.
**Flight-period.** Univoltine. Mid July/late August according
to season.
**Habitat.** Dry, rocky and grassy limestone slopes above treeline.
**Life-history.** Ova stage 10 days, hatching synchronously. Captive larvae accept
*Festuca ovina*. Hibernation stage unconfirmed.
**Behaviour.** Both sexes fond of sitting on stones or bare soil: attracted to nectar
of purplish *Centaureae* sp.

## *Pseudochazara mamurra* Brown's Grayling Plate 67

**Range.** NW Greece, Turkey.

*P. mamurra amymone* Brown 1976 TL: District of Ioannina, NW Greece.

**Distribution.** Reported only once from one area N of Ioannina, NW Greece.

**Description.** Male upf and unf with small white spots in s3 and s4. Androconial scale-base bulbous, shouldered; similar to nominate form. Female known but not formally described (illustrated).

**Flight-period and Habitat.** The few specimens reported from Greece so far were captured 5-10th July 1975, on rocky ground at 650m just N of Ioannina.

**Life-history.** Early-stages unknown.

**Note.** In Turkey, *P. mamurra* is markedly variable; also, characteristically local and uncommon, a feature shared, evidently, with *amymone*: more usually, *Pseudochazara* spp. are abundant, if often local.

## *Pseudochazara orestes* Dils' Grayling Plate 67

**Range.** Greece, Bulgaria.

*P. orestes* de Prins and van der Poorten 1981 TL: Drama, N Greece.

**Distribution.** N Greece: Phalakron massif 800-1650m; Menikion Mts. 800-1000m; Mt. Orvilos 1000-1800m. Bulgaria: Pirin Mts. 900m.

**Description.** Upf and unf white spots in s3 and s4 usually prominent. Fringes chequered. Androconial scale-base shouldered.

**Flight-period.** Univoltine. Mid June/late July.

**Habitat.** Hot, dry, mostly south-facing limestone cliffs/steep rocky slopes; gentler slopes containing large areas of flat, naked rock amongst small, shrubby deciduous trees, principally *Carpinus*, *Quercus*, *Fraxinus* and *Ulmus*.

**Life-history.** Ova laid in shade, on dead leaves of tufted-grasses lodged in crevices or under rock ledges. In captivity, life-cycle from ovum is completed without diapause in extended photo-period of S England. Captive larvae accept a variety of grasses, including *Agrostis stolonifera*.

**Behaviour.** Both sexes retire to the shade and relative cool of rock crevices and ledges in exceptionally hot conditions. Occasional population 'explosions' are accompanied by dispersion to lower altitudes – recorded at 250m in 1987.

## *Pseudochazara mniszechii* Dark Grayling Plate 68

**Range.** NW Greece, Turkey, N Iran, Armenia.

*P. mniszechii tisiphone* Brown 1980 TL: NW Greece.

**Distribution.** NW Greece: S Vernon Mts. 850-1100m; environs of Grammos Mt. 1000-1500m; N Smolikas massif 1000-1450m. Local, usually very common.

**Description.** Upf and unf elongate white pd spots in s3 and s4 prominent. Fringes chequered. Androconial scale-base shouldered.

**Flight-period.** Univoltine. Mid July/late August.

**Habitat.** Dry, slopes comprising a greyish, friable, metamorphic rock supporting sparse, low-growing vegetation amongst light scrub and open woodland. All known habitats contain same species of a robust, purple-flowered thistle (?)*Carduus* sp. which appears to be an important nectar source for both sexes.

**Life-history.** In captivity, life-cycle from ovum is completed without diapause in extended photo-period of S England. Captive larvae accept *Festuca ovina*: pupates 1-2cm below soil-level. Hibernation stage unconfirmed.

**Behaviour.** At peak emergence, fresh males and females occur in approximately equal numbers. Both sexes show a marked preference for sitting on bare patches of soil, rather than stones. Roosts in well-concealed spaces, usually deep between large stones.

## *Pseudochazara cingovskii* Macedonian Grayling     Plate 68

**Range.** Republic of Macedonia.

*P.cingovskii* Gross 1973 TL: Prilep [Republic of Macedonia]. syn: *Satyrus (Pseudochazara) sintenisi cingovskii* Gross 1973

**Distribution.** Republic of Macedonia: known only from Pletvar massif, near Prilep, south of Skopje. 1000-1200m.

**Description.** Upf and unf elongate white pd spots in s3 and s4 prominent. Fringes chequered. Androconial scale-base shouldered.

**Flight-period.** Univoltine. Late July/early August.

**Habitat.** Dry, white limestone rocks with sparse vegetation.

**Life-history.** Hibernation stage unconfirmed.

**Note.** Considerable confusion has persisted for many years in respect to taxonomy, nomenclature, morphology and distribution of *P. cingovskii* and *P. mniszechii tisiphone*: these taxa are superficially, at least, quite distinct and are not known to share the same habitats, nor indeed, the same countries.

## *Pseudochazara anthelea* White-banded Grayling     Plate 68

**Range.** Albania, Republic of Macedonia, Bulgaria, Greece, Turkey, N Iraq.

*P. anthelea anthelea* Hübner 1825 TL: Turkey.

**Distribution.** Greece: in Europe, known only from E Aegean islands: Lesbos; Samos; Kos; Kalimos; Chios; Rhodes. 550-1500m.

**Description and Variation.** Male ups sex-brand prominent and distinctive; androconial scales small, rounded at base; fringes strongly chequered. Sexual dimorphism very marked; female ups yellowish-brown. On Rhodes (Mt. Ataviros 500m), *atavirensis* Coutsis: female ups transitional to *amalthea* Frivaldsky (below).

**Flight-period.** Univoltine. Late May/early July.

**Habitat.** Dry, stony slopes and gullies, usually on limestone: at lower altitudes,

often amongst sparse bushes and/or light pine or deciduous woodland.
**Behaviour.** Males are very territorial, often taking up advantageous positions on rocks.

*P. anthelea amalthea* Frivaldsky 1845 TL: Crete.
**Distribution.** Albania. Republic of Macedonia: widespread. SW Bulgaria: very local: Struma Valley. NW, C and S Greece: local but widespread; local on Crete. 500-1800m.
**Description and Variation.** Male closely resembles nominate form: female ups yellowish-brown areas replaced by white – form unknown in Asia. On Smolikas massif, female upf often with white pd spots in s3 and s4.
**Flight-period, Habitat and Behaviour.** As for nominate form.
**Life-history.** Ova are appreciably smaller than those of other European *Pseudochazara* spp.
**Note.** Morphologically closely related to Asiatic *P. telephassa* Hübner 1827.

## *Oeneis norna* Norse Grayling                    Plate 69

**Range.** Fennoscandia, Kola and Yamal Peninsulas, Urals, Siberia, Baikal, Japan.

*O. norna* Thunberg 1791 TL: Lappland.
**Distribution.** Norway: 62-70°N. W Sweden: Jämtland to Torne-Lappmark. NW Finland. Local, but widespread. 250-800m.
**Variation.** Extremely variable in respect to all wing-characters including size and shape. Small and lightly marked specimens sometimes resemble *O. bore*, but ups are never quite as grey.
**Flight-period.** Univoltine. Mid June/mid July according to season.
**Habitat.** Heathy margins of bogs, often associated with open birch scrub; boggy and rocky slopes with scrub; damp grassy and mossy clearings in forests. Sympatric and synchronous with *O. jutta* in some habitats of C Sweden.
**Life-history.** LHPs *Phleum pratense*; *Poa alpina*; *Carex* sp.; *Nardus* sp. Larval development requires two seasonal cycles: in captivity, newly-hatched larvae often die without attempting to feed.

## *Oeneis bore* Arctic Grayling                    Plate 69

**Range.** N Fennoscandia, Kola Peninsula, Polar Urals, Polar Siberia, N America.

*O. bore* Schneider 1792 TL: Lappland.
**Distribution.** Very local. N Fennoscandia from 67°N to Arctic Sea. 100-1000m.
**Description.** Ups gc with distinct greyish tone – lacking 'warmer', brownish tone of *O. norna*: upf and unf with small, round, very pale pd dot in s5, sometimes very obscure but usually present – absent in *O. norna*.
**Flight-period.** Univoltine. Mid June/late July according to season.
**Habitat.** Damp grassy/boggy places, characteristically dominated by small, slightly elevated areas of almost barren rock, which appear to be meeting places for males and females – (?) 'hilltopping'.

**Life-history.** LHP *Festuca ovina*. Larval development requires two seasonal cycles: in captivity, hibernates as an ovum in first winter.
**Behaviour.** Both sexes sometimes rest on rocks for prolonged periods, even in bright sunshine: displays remarkable tenacity in clinging to exposed rock faces in strong winds.

## *Oeneis glacialis* Alpine Grayling Plate 69

**Range.** C European Alps.

*O. glacialis* Moll 1783 TL: Zillertal, Austria.
**Distribution.** Alps of France (Alpes-Maritimes to Haute-Savoie), Switzerland (Valais to Engadine), Italy (including Dolomites), Bavaria, Austria (including Carnic Alps). 1400-2900m.
**Description and Variation.** Unh veins white (cf. *O. norna*). Ups ocellation and male ups orange pd areas subject to marked variation.
**Flight-period.** Univoltine. Early June/mid August according to altitude.
**Habitat.** Dry, grassy places amongst rocks or scree.
**Life-history.** LHP *Festuca ovina*. Larval development requires two seasonal cycles.

## *Oeneis jutta* Baltic Grayling Plate 70

**Range.** Fennoscandia, Kola Peninsula, Urals, Siberia, N Mongolia, Amur, Yakutia, Madagan, N America.

*O. jutta* Hübner 1806 TL: Lappland.
**Distribution.** Norway: 61-65°N except SW region. Sweden: locally common: 58-68°N. Finland. Baltic states: very local. NE Poland.
**Flight-period.** Univoltine. Early June/mid July according to latitude and season.
**Habitat.** Marshes dominated by grasses, especially *Carex* spp.; usually near open areas of water, invariably with scattered pine trees and often bordered by pine woodland.
**Life-history.** Hibernation stage unconfirmed.
**Behaviour.** Often rests on trunks of pine trees.

## *Satyrus actaea* Black Satyr Plate 70

**Range.** SW Europe.

*S. actaea* Esper 1780 TL: S France.
**Distribution.** N Portugal: Serra da Estrêla. Spain: wide-spread, locally common. S France: E Pyrenees to Provençe, northwards to Savoie and Puy-de-Dôme. NW Italy: Maritime Alps; Cottian Alps. 100-2000m.
**Description.** Male upf with androconial patch in s1-3; unf brown (cf. *S. ferula*).
**Variation.** Very marked in respect to all wing-markings, gc

and size. Ups gc usually very dark brown or black, sometimes paler brown, especially in female: unh often very pale, but pale pd and discal bands remain conspicuous: female upf often with small white pd spots in s3 and s4.

**Flight-period.** Univoltine. Early June/late August according to locality and altitude.

**Habitat.** Dry, grassy, often rocky slopes; amongst rocks and scrub with scattered trees at lower altitudes.

**Note.** Absent from Turkey, Middle East and W Asia: records from this region have been shown to relate to *S. ferula* (below).

## *Satyrus ferula* Great Sooty Satyr                    Plate 70

**Range.** Morocco, S Europe, Turkey, Middle East, Iran, Transcaucasus, Ukraine, S Urals, Kazakhstan, SW Siberia, W China.

*S. ferula ferula* Fabricus 1793 TL: Italy.
syn: *bryce* Hübner 1800; *cordula* Fabricus 1793.
**Distribution.** Spain: province of Lérida (Val d'Aran; Rio Esera; Rio Noguera; 500-1400m). France: Pyrenees to Dordogne in small, widely dispersed colonies; more frequent in Massif Central, eastwards to Provençe and Basses Alps (largely absent from Bouches-du Rhône and Var). Italy: foothills of C Alps; C Apennines; Calabria. S Switzerland (Valais; Tessin), eastwards to Balkans and Greece. 400-1800m.
**Description.** Male upf without androconial patch (cf. *S. actaea*); upf gc orange or orange-fulvous.
**Variation.** Both sexes: ups and uns gc (very pale to very dark) and ocelli subject to considerable variation: female unh brightly marbled white/grey in some limestone localities.
**Flight-period.** Univoltine. Mid June/early August.
**Habitat.** Open, grassy and rocky slopes at higher altitudes; grassy, often bushy woodland clearings at lower altitudes.
**Life-history.** LHP (Greece and Switzerland) *Festuca ovina*. A high proportion of larvae (up to 90%) have been found to be parasitized in some colonies. In cool, wet or overcast conditions, larvae recorded feeding in daylight hours.

*S. ferula atlantea* Verity 1927 (September) TL: Meknes, Morocco.
syn: *meknesensis* Strand 1927 (October).
**Distribution.** W Morocco: widespread but local. 1500-3000m. Reports from Rif Mts. require confirmation.
**Description.** Male upf without androconial patch, otherwise resembles *S. actaea*.
**Flight-period.** Univoltine. Late June/mid September in prolonged emergence.
**Habitat.** Dry, grassy places or rocky slopes with sparse vegetation.

## *Minois dryas* Dryad                    Plate 71

**Range.** N Spain, C Europe, Turkey, W and C temperate Asia, Mongolia, Japan.

*M. dryas* Scopoli 1763 TL: Carniola.
syn: *phaedra* Linnaeus 1764.

**Distribution.** N Spain: very local: Cantabrian Mts.; Pyrenees. France (sporadic, commoner in E and SE), through N Italy, Switzerland, S Germany to N Poland, Balkans, N Greece (Rhodopi Mts.: very local) and European Turkey. 100-1600m.

**Variation.** Female upf ocelli markedly variable in size.

**Flight-period.** Univoltine. Late June/early September according to locality.

**Habitat.** Grassy, bushy margins of mixed deciduous woodlands: often in damp places.

## *Berberia abdelkader* Giant Grayling                     Plate 71

**Range.** Morocco, Algeria, Tunisia, NW Libya.

*B. abdelkader* Pierrett 1837 TL: Oran [Constantine] Province, Algeria.

**Distribution.** Morocco: High Atlas; Middle Atlas. N Algeria: Aures Mts. W Tunisia. 200-2300m.

**Description.** Male ups gc medium to dark brown; upf subapical ocellus (s5), large, blue-pupilled; pd ocellus in s2, often small, sometimes vestigial, rarely absent; small, bluish pd spots in s3 and s4, sometimes also in s6; creamy-white, yellowish or creamy pale brown apical scaling extremely variable, sometimes extending to enclose ocellus in s2; unh brown mediobasal and discal lines prominent, angled at v4: female similar: markings better developed: upf outer margin often golden-brown; unh gc paler; whitish veins prominent.

**Variation.** E Algeria (Bou-Saada to Dj. Metlili and Aures massif) to W Tunisia (700-1100m), *nelvai* Seitz [syn: *marteni* Chneour]: upf apex creamy-white, usually enclosing subapical ocellus, sometimes extending to pd ocellus (when present) in s2; uph pd ocelli in s2 and s5, when present, usually enclosed by pale or golden scales, sometimes extending to outer margin; uns resembles nominate form; unf subapical ocellus enclosed by whitish scales, sometimes extending to costa and outer margin to s2. In a restricted area of Middle Atlas, Morocco (1900-2300m), *taghzefti* Wyatt: characters intermediate of those of nominate form and *nelvai* Seitz. W Algeria (1200m), *saharae* Slaby: about 60% of males transitional to, or indistinguishable from *taghzefti*, the remainder resembling nominate form. Taxa *alfae* Slaby and *arvorum* Slaby appear to be synonymous with nominate form. The possibility that some, if not all, of the above variants are examples of ecological adaptation or polymorphism has not been precluded: subspecificity of some taxa is, in any case, precluded by sympatry.

**Flight-period.** Univoltine. June/early November according to altitude and locality.

**Habitat.** Open rocky slopes and sandy places containing extensive stands of LHP.

**Life-history.** LHP *Stipa tenacissima*: also, possibly *S. parviflora*. Hibernation stage unconfirmed.

**Behaviour.** Both sexes take nectar from *Colchicum autumnale*.

## *Berberia lambessanus*                           Plate 71

**Range.** Morocco, Algeria, Tunisia, (?)Libya.

*B. lambessanus* Staudinger 1901 TL: Lambessa, Algeria.
**Distribution.** Morocco: High Atlas; Middle Atlas; Rif Mts.
N Algeria: Aures Mts. NE Tunisia: Cap Bon. 50-3160m.
**Description.** Male ups gc very dark, tending to black; whitish apical suffusion entirely lacking; blue pd spots between
ocelli (ups and unf) usually wedge-shaped and larger than
those of *B. abdelkader*; uns gc very dark compared to *B.
abdelkader*; veins not lined white: female very variable: sometimes resembling male: more generally, markings better developed with upf
apical and marginal areas to s2 pale brown; unh veins conspicuously pale.
**Variation.** Constant in known range: *romeii* Rothschild (W Rif Mts., Morocco)
and *alexander* Chneour (Cap Bon, Tunisia) reportedly synonymous with nominate form.
**Flight-period.** Univoltine. April/November according to altitude and locality.
**Habitat.** Sometimes similar to that of *B. abdelkader*, but generally with more
varied vegetation including light woodland.
**Life-history.** LHP *Ampelodesmos tenax*: also, possibly *Stipa parviflora*. Ova laid
mainly on dead leaves near base of LHP. A high proportion of ova have been found
to be parasitized by a (?)hymenopteran which hibernates within ovum case.
**Note.** *B. abdelkader* and *B. lambessanus* reportedly fly together at Lac Tislit,
High Atlas Mts., Morocco, 2150-2250m.

## *Kanetisa circe* Great Banded Grayling                Plate 72

**Range.** C and S Europe, Turkey, Iran to Himalayas.

*K. circe* Fabricus 1775 TL: Europe (Germany, Verity 1953).
syn: *proserpina* Denis and Schiffermüller 1775.
**Distribution.** Widespread and common. From Mediterranean,
including Corsica, Sardinia, Sicily, Thassos, Lesbos and Euro-
pean Turkey, through most of C Europe to S Poland. 0-1650m.
**Flight-period.** Univoltine. Early June/mid September.
**Habitat.** Dry, grassy, bushy places; cultivated ground.
**Life-history.** LHPs include *Festuca ovina*; *Bromus erectus*.
Ova are ejected into low-growing vegetation during flight.

## *Arethusana arethusa* False Grayling                  Plate 72

**Range.** Morocco, S Europe, Turkey to Tian Shan.

*A. arethusa arethusa* Denis and Schiffermüller 1775 TL: Vienna.
**Distribution.** From N Portugal, N and C Spain, France
(Charante-Maritimes to Eure, Somme, Meurthe-et-Moselle
and Haut-Rhin) to (?)NW Switzerland and S Germany (very
local and rare), NE Italy, E Austria, Slovakia, Balkans, Greece
and European Turkey. 0-2000m. Very sporadic in parts of C
Europe and NW Balkans.

**Description and Variation.** Most wing-markings subject to marked local/ individual variation. Ups orange pd markings often macular and obscure; unh gc brownish, cryptically irrorated; diffuse pale discal band variable.

**Flight-period.** Univoltine. Mid July/mid September according to locality. Grassy, bushy places; woodland borders; rocky gullies: on calcareous and non-calcareous soils.

*A. arethusa dentata* Staudinger 1871 TL: W France.

**Distribution.** W Morocco: High Atlas (Toubkal massif 2400-2700m: very local). Spain: Catalonia; (?)Granada. France: Pyrénées-Orientales to Ardèche and Provençe. NW Italy (Maritime Alps: very local). 0-1000m.

**Description and Variation.** Ups orange pd bands well developed, but disrupted by veins; unf pd area with proximal brown line; unh paler, conspicuously irrorated; discal area bordered by diffuse whitish band; veins pale greyish or buff. In Morocco, *aksouali* Wyatt: resembles *dentata* closely: unh gc tending to yellowish-brown. In all regions, wing-markings subject to marked variation: closely similar forms have been recorded in Hungary and Greece.

**Flight-period and Habitat.** As for nominate form.

*A. arethusa boabdil* Rambur 1842 TL: Andalusia.

**Distribution.** S Spain: Andalusia (Sierra Nevada; S. de Alfarcar; S. de Almijara; S. de Los Filabres). 700-1700m.

**Description.** Ups orange pd bands greatly reduced, often obscured by gc in male; unf pd area and apical ocellus with irregular proximal brown line; unh white discal band and white veins conspicuous.

**Flight-period.** Univoltine. Late June/August.

**Habitat.** Hot, dry, grassy places amongst scrub and limestone rocks.

**Note.** Uncertainty in distributional relationship of above forms appears to relate to confusion arising from marked individual and local variation.

## *Erebia ligea* Arran Brown                                    Plate 73

**Range.** E Europe to Urals, Siberia, Altai, Transbaikal, Amur, Kamchatka, Japan.

*E. ligea* Linnaeus 1758 TL: Sweden (Verity 1953).

**Distribution.** France (Massif Central; Alpes-Maritimes to Vosges Mts.), through S Alps and Apennines to Czech Republic, S Poland, Balkans and N Greece (Varnous Mts.; Vernon Mts.; Rhodope Mts.). Fennoscandia, including Öland. Baltic states. Absent from C Switzerland, parts of Dalmatian coast, Denmark and S Lithuania. 0-1800m.

**Description.** Male upf with sex-brand (cf. *E. euryale*).

**Variation.** Ups reddish pd bands vary in colour and width; ocelli variable in size and number, sometimes small, lacking white pupils. In N Fennoscandia, f. *dovrensis* Strand: smaller; ups pd bands reduced; ocelli smaller, usually blind; unh white pd band reduced, usually restricted to s5 and s6: transitional to nominate form in S Scandinavia.

**Flight-period.** Univoltine. Mid July/late August.

**Habitat and Behaviour.** Sheltered, grassy, flowery, woodland/forest clearings, usually damp and humid, sometimes containing an abundance of bracken upon which adults often bask, even in warm, overcast conditions.

**Life-history.** LHPs include *Carex sylvatica*; *C. strigosa*. Hibernates as an ovum or larvae. Larval development occupies two seasonal cycles in N Fennoscandia. Wing-characters of captively reared specimens of f. *dovrensis* reputedly approach those of nominate form.

## *Erebia euryale* Large Ringlet                    Plate 73

**Range.** Mountains of Europe from N Spain to Balkans, Urals, Kanin Peninsula.

*E. euryale* Esper 1805 TL: Riesengebirge.

**Distribution.** Widespread, locally common. Cantabrian Mts.; W and E Pyrenees; Massif Central; Jura Mts.; C European Alps; Bohemian Mts.; High Tatra Mts.; Carpathian Mts.; Ligurean Alps; C Apennines; Julian Alps; Dinaric Pl. to mountains of Albania, Republic of Macedonia, Bulgaria and N Greece (Varnous Mts.; Mt. Phalakron; Rhodope Mts.). 750-2500m, more generally 1200-2000m.

**Description.** Male upf without sex-brand (cf. *E. ligea*). Male ups reddish pd bands or spots enclosing blind, usually elongate ocelli; uns ocelli usually white-pupilled; unh proximal edge of pd band sometimes with obscure, white tooth-like mark in s4, occasionally extending to costa as a narrow, obscure whitish band: female upf and unf ocelli sometimes with small white pupils; unh whitish or yellowish pd band broad, conspicuous.

**Variation.** Very marked local and regional differences has given rise to many named forms, variants of which are common and often transitional to each other or to the nominate form. From Haute-Savoie, through W and C Switzerland to N Austrian Alps, Bohemian Mts., Tatra Mts. and NW Carpathian Mts., f. *isarica* Heyne: male ups elongate ocelli blind; unh pd band variable, usually obscure: female uns markings similar to nominate form. In S Switzerland, f. *adyte* Hübner: ocelli usually white-pupilled: male unh darker; whitish, proximal pd markings similar to nominate form, generally less obscure but variable – tooth-like mark in s4 usually present: female unh pale pd band lightly irrorated with white scales, proximal border more regular, white markings in s4 to costa better developed. In SE Austria and Dolomites, f. *ocellaris* Staudinger: male ups markings reduced to small, red-ringed, blind ocelli, sometimes absent: female ups markings generally better developed, but occasionally entirely absent: both sexes, unh markings similar to nominate form.

**Flight-period.** Univoltine. Late July/August.

**Habitat.** Grassy, flowery places in pinewood clearings; grassy slopes above treeline.

**Life-history.** LHPs include *Sesleria varia*; *Festuca ovina*; *F. rubra*; *F. alpina*; *Poa nemoralis*; *Carex flacca*; *C. ferruginea*; *Calamagrostis varia*.

## *Erebia eriphyle* Eriphyle Ringlet                    Plate 74

**Range.** C European Alps.

*E. eriphyle* Freyer 1839 TL: Grimsel Pass, Switzerland.

**Distribution.** Switzerland: Bernese Alps, Lepontine Alps to Alpstein and Engadine. Germany: Allgäuer Alps (Nebelhorn). Austria: Lechtaler Alps; Ötztaler Alps; Stubaier Alps; Hohe Tauern (Gross Glockner); Niedere Tauern;

Sau Alp; Kor Alps. Italy: Ortler Alps; Dolomites. Widespread but very local. 1200-2250m.

**Description.** Uph reddish spot in s4 constant, those in s2, s3 and s5 variable; unf often with reddish suffusion projecting from proximal border of paler pd band to wing-base; unh reddish-orange spots in s2-5 variable, lacking black pupils, spot in s4 larger, always present. (cf. *E. manto f. pyrrhula* and *E. melampus*).
**Variation.** In E Alps, f. *tristis* Herrich-Schäffer: brighter, all markings better developed. Transitional to nominate form in E Switzerland and NW Tirol.
**Flight-period.** Univoltine. Late June/mid August according to locality and altitude.
**Habitat.** Damp, sheltered, herb-rich, alpine meadows, often associated with pinewoods; open areas amongst scrub in rocky gullies.
**Life-history.** LHPs *Anthoxanthum odoratum*; *Deschampsia caespitosa*. Larval development occupies two seasonal cycles: in captivity, a proportion of larvae reportedly remain within ovum-case during first winter.

## *Erebia manto* Yellow-spotted Ringlet                        Plate 74

**Range.** Europe.

*E. manto manto* Denis and Schiffermüller 1775 TL: Vienna.
**Distribution.** Alpes-Maritimes (very local); NE Isère to Haute-Savoie; Vosges Mts. C Alps to Julian Alps. Tatra Mts.; Carpathian Mts. Bosnia-Herzegovina: Vlasic Pl.; Vranica Pl.; Jahorina Pl. 1200-2500m.
**Variation.** Many forms have been described in recognition of very marked individual, local and regional variation in size and development of pd and ocellular markings. Above 1800m in C Alps including Dolomites, f. *pyrrhula* Frey: very small; dark; all markings greatly reduced, sometimes absent. In Voges Mts., *vogesiaca* Christ: male larger; ups pd bands duller red, well developed; upf subapical black points vestigial or absent; unh pd band of more uniform width: female similar, but with unh markings variable in colour, pale yellow to bright orange-yellow, less often white (f. *bubastis* Meissner – a recurrent form in some localities in Switzerland).
**Flight-period.** Univoltine. Early July/early September.
**Habitat.** Damp, grassy, flowery meadows; woodland clearings; at high altitudes, slopes and pastures with grasses of moderate length.
**Life-history.** LHP *Festuca rubra*. Early-stage development occupies two seasonal cycles: in captivity, proportion of ova reportedly hibernate in first winter.

*E. manto constans* Eiffinger 1908 TL: Hautes-Pyrénées.
**Distribution.** Spain: Picos de Europa. Above 1500m. Pyrenees (France and Spain): Pto. de Somport to Col du Tourmalet, Pto. de Beñasque and Pic Carlit. Massif Central (Plomb du Cantal; Mont Dore). 900-2300m.
**Description.** Male ups and uns very dark, almost black; usual uns markings absent or vestigial: female paler; unh markings often vestigial.
**Flight-period and Habitat.** As for *E. m. manto*.

**Note.** *E. serotina* Descimon and de Lesse 1953 described from Hautes-Pyrénées is believed to be a hybrid of *E. manto constans* and *E. epiphron fauveaui*. Only males have been recorded, flying in September on grassy slopes near Cauterets at about 1000m. The insect appears to be extremely rare. It resembles the local form of *E. epiphron* except that:- upf ocelli in s4 and s5 are white-pupilled; uph pd ocelli ringed red, sometimes white-pupilled; unf pd band well defined; unh dark brown with paler pd band; red-ringed pd ocelli small, lacking white pupils.

## *Erebia claudina* White Speck Ringlet          Plate 74

**Range.** E Alps of Austria.

*E. claudina* Borkhausen 1789 TL: Austria.
syn: *arete* Fabricus 1787 (Invalid homonym)
**Distribution.** Austria: Hohe Tauern (Mallnitz); Salzburg Alps (Weissbriachtal). Niedere Tauern; Seetal Alps (Zirbitz-kogel); Sau Alp. 1800-2300m.
**Description.** Uph with 2 to 5 white pd points – usually 5 on unh.
**Flight-period.** Univoltine. July/early August. In some local-ities, scarce or absent in alternate years.
**Habitat.** Grassy slopes of somewhat variable character; usually above treeline.
**Life-history.** LHP uncertain: reputedly *Deschampsia cespitosa*. Relative abundance in alternate years suggests that two seasonal cycles are required for early-stage development.

## *Erebia flavofasciata* Yellow-banded Ringlet          Plate 74

**Range.** S Switzerland, N Italy.

*E. flavofasciata* Heyne 1895 TL: Campolungo Pass, Tessin.
**Distribution.** N Italy: Val Formazza; Val di Dévero; Val Antigorio; Monte Castello; Val di Tóggia; Pso. di San Giácomo. S Switzerland: Tessin (Naret Pass; Sassello Pass; Campo di Torba; Campolungo Pass); Grisons (Val Calanca; San Bernardino Pass; Julierpass; Schafberg; Tscherva Glacier; Berninapass). Very local, usually common. 1800-2600m.
**Variation.** In Engadine, f. *thiemei* Bartel: ups pd reddish spots smaller, often fewer; unh yellow pd band slightly narrower, rarely broken into ocellular rings.
**Flight-period.** Univoltine. Late June/mid August.
**Habitat.** Exposed, grass-covered or grassy and rocky slopes: grasses are usually of moderate length.
**Life-history.** LHP *Festuca ovina*. Larval development occupies two seasonal cycles.

## *Erebia epiphron* Mountain Ringlet          Plate 75

**Range.** Mountains of Europe, excluding C and S Spain, Fennoscandia, C and S Greece and Mediterranean islands.

Subject to considerable individual, local (ecological/altitudinal), regional as well as inter-seasonal variation in wing-markings, colour and, to a lesser degree, size. Considerable overlap in the variance of characters of geographically well-separated forms, coupled with confusion regarding descriptive accuracy (possibly due to non-rigorous sampling procedure), attaches some doubt to the taxonomic relevance of several named forms. Collectively, the following taxa probably embrace the full range of variation in wing-characters.

*E. epiphron epiphron* Knoch 1783 TL: Brocken, Harz Mts., W Germany.
**Distribution.** Believed to be extinct: formerly known only from Harz Mts.
**Description.** Characterised by well-developed markings and large size. Male upf pd rust-coloured band broad, usually complete, sometimes broken into discrete spots, enclosing black ocelli in s2-5; uph similar pd band enclosing black ocelli in s2-4; unh red-ringed ocelli distinctive: female markings better developed; unh reddish pd spots often confluent, forming a distinct band; ups and unh black ocelli sometimes enclosing minute white points.

*E. epiphron mackeri* Fuchs 1914 TL: Vosges Mts.
syn: *vogesiaca* Goltz 1914 (invalid homonym).
**Distribution.** France: Vosges Mts. 900-1100m.
**Description.** Resembles nominate form: smaller; upf rust-red pd bands narrower, usually broken into spots, variable; unh red-ringed ocelli reduced.
**Flight-period.** Univoltine. Mid June/mid August according to season.
**Habitat.** Sheltered gullies or hollows on open grass-covered slopes containing an abundance of grass species of moderate length: on granite rocks.
**Life-history.** LHP *Nardus stricta.* Captive larvae accept *Festuca ovina; F. rubra.*

*E. epiphron mnemon* Haworth 1812 TL: Scotland
syn: *scotica* Cooke 1943
**Distribution.** NW England: Cumbrian Mts. Scotland: Grampian Mts.; Ben Nevis; Ben Vain; Ben Lomond; Newtonmore. 350-1100m – more generally 500-800m. France: Massif Central: Cevennes (Aigoual massif); Auvergne (Monts du Cantal; Puy-de-Dôme). 900-1600m. Old records for Ireland have not been confirmed.
**Description and Variation.** Resembles *mackeri*: smaller; gc darker; upf reddish pd bands usually more extensively broken into elongate, somewhat recti-linear spots; ups and uns ocelli variable in size and number, usually very small, sometimes absent; unh rarely with pd area distinctly paler. All wing-characters very variable. Variants (f. *cebennica* Leraut 1980 and f. *mixta* de Lesse 1951) described from Massif Central, appear to fall within range of variation of *mnemon.*
**Flight-period.** Univoltine. Mid June/early August.
**Habitat.** Damp, grassy, often marshy slopes or gullies.
**Life-history.** LHP, in Britain, *Nardus stricta.* Captive larvae accept *Poa annua; Festuca ovina; Deschampsia flexuosa; D. cespitosa.*
**Note.** Discovered in 1809 by T. S. Stothard near Ambleside, Cumbrian Mts., NW England: subsequently, type-locality erroneously given as 'Scotland'.

*E. epiphron aetheria* Esper 1805 TL: not stated [(?)Austria].
**Distribution.** C European Alps: Basses-Alpes and Hautes-Alpes to Bavarian Alps, Dolomites and Austrian Alps. Mountains of Slovenia, W Croatia, Bosnia-

Herzegovina and SW Serbia. 1200-2700m.

**Description.** Resembles *mnemon*: all markings averagely poorly developed, variable; male upf red spot and ocellus in s3 often reduced: female upf pd ocelli sometimes with minute white pupils: both sexes, unh pd area paler – a feature better developed in habitats shared with *E. christi*.

**Variation.** At high altitudes in C Alps (prevalent in Engadine, W Austria and Dolomites above 1800-2000m), f. *nelamus* Boisduval 1828: small: male ups gc darker; all markings greatly reduced; upf reddish pd bands often obscure, enclosing two small subapical ocelli, often vestigial or absent; unh lacking ocelli. In Maritime Alps, Apuane Alps and C Apennines, *cydamus* Frühstorfer 1910: larger; resembles *mnemon* but markings variable.

**Flight-period.** Univoltine. Late June/July according to altitude and locality.

**Habitat.** Grass-covered slopes, usually with an abundance of grass species of moderate length: on calcareous or non-calcareous substrates.

**Life-history.** LHPs include *Nardus stricta*. At higher altitudes larval development occupies two seasonal cycles.

*E. epiphron fauveaui* de Lesse 1947 TL: E Pyrenees

**Distribution.** Spain and France: E Pyrenees (Andorra; Pic Carlit; Cambras d'Aze; Mt. Canigou). 1000-2300m.

**Description.** Resembles *mackeri*: larger; fw more pointed; upf pd band and elongate, blind ocelli usually well developed.

**Variation.** Transitional to f. *pyrenaica* west of Andorra but variable: forms resembling *aetheria* are said to become increasingly common towards Luchon: at high altitudes in C Pyrenees, specimens sometimes indistinguishable from f. *nelamus*.

**Flight-period.** Univoltine. Early June/July according to altitude and locality.

*E. epiphron pyrenaica* Herrich-Schäffer 1851 TL: Pic du Vignemale [W Pyrenees].

**Distribution.** Cantabrian Mts.; S. de la Demanda; S. de Cebollera; W Pyrenees (Basses-Pyrénées; Hautes-Pyrénées to Andorra). Above 1300m.

**Description and Variation.** Distinction from *mackeri* and *fauveaui* difficult: markings averagely reduced but variable – individual specimens often indistinguishable from the aforementioned forms. In Asturian Mts., *valdeonica* Hospital 1948: upf pd bands well developed, ocelli small, sometimes absent; uph pd reddish spots and ocelli variable, sometimes absent. Present placement of recently discovered populations of S. de Cebollera and S. de la Demanda is provisional: available material inadequate for full evaluation of racial characters.

*E. epiphron silesiana* Meyer-Dür 1852 TL: Mt. Altvater [=Mt. Praded].

**Distribution.** Czech Republic: Silesian Mts.

**Description.** Resembles nominate form: size similar; all markings averagely reduced, especially unh pd reddish spots, very obscure or absent in male, not confluent in female.

*E. epiphron transsylvanica* Rebel 1908 TL: W Transylvanian Mts.

**Distribution.** N Slovakia and S Poland: Tatra Mts. Romania: Carpathian Mts.

**Description.** Resembles *silesiana*: upf pd well developed, broad, often extending below v1; ocelli small, variable in number, usually present in s4 and s5; uph red pd markings and enclosed ocelli usually well developed; unh pd ocelli ringed red.

*E. epiphron retyezatensis* Warren 1931 TL: Retezat Mts.
**Distribution.** SW Romania: Retezat Mts. (Reported occurrence in Bosnia-Herzegovina, Montenegro and Republic of Macedonia appears to be ill-founded).
**Description and Variation.** Resembles *transsylvanica*: upf yellow-orange pd band broader near subapex (s4-6), sometimes with ray-like projections towards cell.

*E. epiphron roosi* Arnscheid and Sterba 1978 TL: Mt. Pelister.
**Distribution.** Republic of Macedonia (Sar Pl.; Jakupica Pl.; Pelister massif); NW Greece (Varnous Mts.: extremely local). 1500-2600m. Distributional relationship with *E. e. aetheria* in SW Balkans unclear.
**Description and Variation.** Male upf rust-red pd spots in s4-s5(6) contiguous and broader than those in s1b and s2, spot in s3 often vestigial, sometimes absent; pd ocelli in s4 and s5 constant; ocellus in s3 usually absent; unh pd red-ringed ocelli variable in size and number, usually vestigial, often absent; unh ocelli usually absent; pd area sometimes slightly paler. Male genitalia distinctive. On Sar Pl. above 2300m, small dark forms resembling f. *nelamus* are not uncommon.
**Flight-period.** Univoltine. Late June/mid August according to season and altitude.
**Habitat.** Grass-covered slopes, sometimes in very exposed situations: often associated with taller grass species and prostrate Juniper (*Juniperus communis nana*).

## *Erebia orientalis* Bulgarian Ringlet                     Plate 75

**Range.** Bulgaria.

*E. orientalis* Elwes 1900 TL: Rila Mts., Bulgaria.
**Distribution.** Bulgaria: Stara Pl. (Mt. Botev); Rila Mts. (Mt. Maljovica; Mt. Manchu; Kóstenets; Mt. Tcherni); Pirin Mts. (Mt. Vihren; Kameniti Dupki; Mt. Kamenica). Not recorded from Rhodopi Mts. 1800-2600m.
**Description and Variation.** Fw narrow, pointed; male upf reddish pd spots slightly larger in s4 and s5, enclosing black points; uph and unh orange-red, black-pupilled pd spots almost circular, clearly defined: female ups and uns gc greyish-brown; yellow-orange pd bands and enclosed white-pupilled ocelli well developed; upf discal and basal areas suffused reddish-brown. In Pirin Mts., *infernalis* Varga: closely similar to nominate form.
**Flight-period.** Univoltine. Generally late June/mid July: records span early June/early August.
**Habitat.** Grassy areas near treeline.
**Life-history.** Hibernation stage unconfirmed.

## *Erebia christi* Rätzer's Ringlet                          Plate 75

**Range.** SW Switzerland.

*E. christi* Rätzer 1890 TL: Laggintal, Simplon.
**Distribution.** SW Switzerland: south of Simplonpass: very local and uncommon: Rossbodental; Eggental; Laggintal; Zwischbergental. 1300-2100m.

NW Italy: Piedmont (Véglia Alp 1700m).
**Description.** Upf blind ocelli in s3-s6 co-linear (cf. *E. epiphron aetheria*).
**Flight-period.** Univoltine. Late June/early August.
**Habitat.** Steep, grassy, rocky slopes often with scattered trees and low bushes.
**Life-history.** LHP *Festuca ovina*. Larval development occupies two seasonal cycles. (Said be commoner in alternate years).
**Conservation.** In decline in some localities.

## *Erebia pharte* Blind Ringlet                    Plate 76

**Range.** C European Alps, Tatra Mts.

*E. pharte* Hübner 1804 TL: Alps of Switzerland.
**Distribution.** Central European Alps of France (N Alpes-Maritimes to Haute-Savoie: also Vosges Mts.), Switzerland, NW and NE Italy (Cottian Alps), SE Germany, Austria and W Slovenia (Julian Alps). S Poland and Slovakia: Tatra Mts. (?) Romania: Carpathian Mts. 1000-2500m, generally above 1400m.
**Description.** Ups and uns orange-red pd markings always without ocelli or black points; upf and unf pd bands sharply defined – characteristically rectilinear.
**Variation.** From W Tirol, eastwards, f. *eupompa* Frühstorfer: larger; pd bands brighter; upf pd band sometimes with ray-like, proximal extensions from s5 and s6. Above 1800m throughout range, f. *phartina* Staudinger: smaller; pd markings greatly reduced, rarely entirely absent. Occurs as an aberrant form below 1800m.
**Flight-period.** Univoltine. Early July/late August.
**Habitat.** Dry or damp alpine meadows; open grassy, flowery places in woodland at lower altitudes.
**Life-history.** LHPs *Carex ferruginea*; *C. flacca*; *Festuca ovina*; *F. quadriflora*; *F. rubra*; *Nardus stricta*. Larval development occupies two seasonal cycles.

## *Erebia melampus* Lesser Mountain Ringlet                    Plate 76

**Range.** C European Alps.

*E. melampus* Fuessli 1775 TL: Switzerland.
**Distribution.** Most of C European Alps from Maritime Alps to S Bavaria, E Austria and Dolomites. Widespread, generally common. 800-2400m.
**Description and Variation.** Upf pd reddish/orange spots irregular, usually with small black points in s4 and s5, sometimes also in s2 and s3; uph usually with 4 pd spots, with or without black points, spot in s4 largest; uns pattern similar. (cf. *E. sudetica*).
**Flight-period.** Univoltine. Early July/mid September according to altitude.
**Habitat.** Damp or dry alpine meadows; grass-covered slopes; woodland clearings.
**Life-history.** LHPs *Anthoxanthum odoratum*; *Festuca ovina*; *Poa nemoralis*. In captive rearing from ovum, life-cycle is completed without diapause in extended photo-period of S England.

## *Erebia sudetica* Sudeten Ringlet                    Plate 76

**Range.** Europe.

*E. sudetica sudetica* Staudinger 1861 TL: Silesian Mts.
**Distribution.** Czech Republic: Mt. Praded [=Mt. Altvater].
Poland: Silesian Mts. Slovakia and Poland: Tatra Mts. Roma-
nia: Carpathian Mts., including Retezat Mts. and Radna Mts.
**Description and Variation.** Ups and uns reddish, black-
pupilled pd spots in a very regular series, forming continuous
bands broken only by veins. (cf. *E. melampus*).
**Flight-period.** Univoltine. July/August.

*E. sudetica liorana* de Lesse 1947 TL: Cantal, C France.
**Distribution.** France: Monts du Cantal (Puy Mary; Le Lioran; Plomb du Cantal):
E Isère; C Savoie. Switzerland: Bernese Alps (Grindelwald): very local. 1200-2000m.
**Description and Variation.** Resembles nominate form, but pd markings reduced:
uph pd black-pupilled, reddish spots slightly smaller, usually restricted to s2-5.
**Flight-period.** Univoltine. Late June/mid August according to altitude.
**Habitat.** Damp, herb-rich meadows with long grasses, sheltered by woodland.
**Life-history.** LHP *Anthoxanthum odoratum*.

## *Erebia aethiops* Scotch Argus                    Plate 76

**Range.** C and E Europe, N Turkey, Transcaucasus, Urals,
Altai, W Siberia.

*E. aethiops* Esper 1777 TL: S Germany.
**Distribution.** Scotland. NW England: very local. France:
Massif Central; Cévennes; central E regions (sporadic in
Allier, Cher, Nièvre, E Provençe and Lorraine). Belgium to
Latvia (very local), Switzerland, Balkans and N Greece
(Rhodopi Mts.). N Italy: Apuane Alps; Ligurian Alps through
Cottian Alps and main Alpine chain. Absent from N Germany
and Fennoscandia. 0-2000m, generally 300-1500m.
**Description.** Both sexes: upf reddish pd band usually constricted in s3. Male unh
gc dark reddish-brown; basal area slightly paler, somewhat yellowish-brown; pd
band silvery-grey, well defined, enclosing small white spots, sometimes narrowly
ringed black, in s2-4: female unh gc brownish or yellowish-brown; basal and pd
areas variable; pd band yellowish-buff in combination with basal area of similar but
darker tone, or, pd band silvery-grey or violet-grey in combination with basal area
of similar but darker tone; other markings as for male but better developed.
**Variation.** Regionally/locally variable in size and development of pd markings.
Often larger in southern range. In S Scotland, f. *caledonia* Verity: smaller; wings
narrower; upf pd band narrower, often broken in s3, lacking ocellus in s3; unh
markings often less distinct. On Monte Baldo, upf red pd band often reduced
to narrow rings enclosing greatly reduced subapical ocelli; uph pd band and
ocelli similarly reduced.
**Flight-period.** Univoltine. Late July/mid September.
**Habitat.** Sparsely wooded heathland; moorland; grassy marshland; open grassy,
flowery woodland clearings and margins. On acidic and calcareous soils.

218          BUTTERFLIES OF EUROPE

**Life-history.** LHPs *Molinia caerulea*; *Sesleria caerulea*; *Carex sempervirens*; *Bromus erectus*; *Brachypodium pinnatum*; *Calamagrostis epigejos*; *Dactylis glomerata*; *Festuca ovina*; *Luzula nivea*; *Poa trivialis*; *Anthoxanthum odoratum*; *Briza media*.

## *Erebia triaria* de Prunner's Ringlet                    Plate 78

**Range.** Europe.

*E. triaria* de Prunner 1798 TL: Exilles, Piedmont.
**Distribution.** N Portugal: Serra de Gerez. Spain: S. Madrona; Montes de Toledo; S. de Gredos; S. Guadarrama; Montes Universales; S. de la Demanda; S. de Cebollera; Cantabrian Mts.; W Pyrenees (Ordessa: very local). Andorra. France: Pyrenees; Alpes-Maritimes to Vaucluse, Isère and Savoie. Italy: Ligurian Alps through Cottian Alps to Trentino-Alto Adige. S and E Switzerland. S Austria. W Slovenia (Julian Alps). S Bosnia-Herzegovina. S Serbia. Albania. 400-2500m.
**Description and Variation.** Upf ocellus in s6 (nearly always present) almost co-linear with ocelli in s4 and s5; unh very dark, obscure irroration giving a slightly roughened appearance (cf. *E. meolans*). Upf pd band variable in colour and shape; usually enclosing 5 ocelli, but those in s3 and s6 sometimes reduced to black points, rarely absent. In Spain, *hispanica* Gumppenberg: regionally variable: smaller; ups pd bands averagely paler, tending to yellow-orange; upf pd band broader near apex – more tapered towards v2 relative to nominate form; unf pd reddish, darker than upf pd band: female ups gc paler brown.
**Flight-period.** Univoltine. Mid April/mid July according to altitude and season.
**Habitat.** Bushy and grassy woodland clearings in rocky places: in Spain, often small clearings in light pinewoods on limestone.
**Life-history.** LHPs *Festuca ovina*; *Poa pratensis*; *P. alpina*; *Stipa pennata*.

## *Erebia embla* Lapland Ringlet                    Plate 77

**Range.** NE Europe, NW Russia, Urals, Siberia, N and E Altai, Transbaikal, Yakutia, Mongolia, Kamchatka, Sakhalin, N Korea.

*E. embla* Thunberg 1791 TL: Västerbotton, Sweden.
**Distribution.** S and N Norway: Hedmark; Finnmark. Sweden: Dalarne to Torne Lappmark. Finland. NE Latvia: very local: last recorded in 1985. 100-400m.
**Flight-period.** Univoltine. Mid June/July according to season.
**Habitat.** Marshes with areas of permanent water, tussock grasses, sedge and willow, often in open pine or birch woodland.
**Life-history.** LHPs: (?) *Carex* sp.; (?) *Deschampsia* sp. Hibernation stage unconfirmed.

## *Erebia disa* Arctic Ringlet                    Plate 77

**Range.** Circumpolar. Arctic Europe, Kola, Yamal and Chukot Peninsulas, Polar and Subpolar Urals, N and W Siberia, Transbaikal, Mongolia, Yakutia, Magdan, Arctic N America.

*E. disa* Thunberg 1791 TL: Lappland.

**Distribution.** Fennoscandia from 65°N to Finnmark. 300-500m.
**Flight-period.** Univoltine. Early June/late July according to season and latitude.
**Habitat.** Bogs or marshes with drier, grassy areas or heaths, usually associated with scrub or small trees and small areas of permanent water.
**Life-history.** Larval development occupies two seasonal cycles.

## *Erebia medusa* Woodland Ringlet — Plate 77

**Range.** Europe, N Turkey, Transcaucasus, S Siberia, Mongolia, N China.

*E. medusa* Denis and Schiffermüller 1775 TL: Vienna.
**Distribution.** C and E France (Cher and Allier to Ardennes and Savoie) through S Belgium (Ardennes), N Italy (including Ligurian Alps) to N Germany (S of Hannover) N Poland, S Balkans, N Greece (S to Mt. Olympus and C Pindos Mts.) and European Turkey: also reported from Alpes-de-Haute-Provençe. Widespread and locally common in SE range, sporadic elsewhere. 300-2300m.
**Description.** Uns of antennal club-tip buff (cf. *E. oeme*).
**Variation.** Geographical and altitudinal clines are evident in regard to size and wing-markings. In SE Europe, *psodea* Hübner [syn: *euphrasia* Frühstorfer; *botevi* Slaby]: larger; ups and uns yellow-orange pd spots brighter, larger, often confluent, especially in female; ocelli larger: intermediate forms occur in NW Balkans. Above about 1800m in E Central Alps, f. *hippomedusa* Ochsenheimer: small; all markings greatly reduced: transitional to nominate form at intermediate altitudes.
**Flight-period.** Univoltine. Early May/early August according to locality and altitude.
**Habitat.** Diverse. Damp, humid, grassy, flowery clearings in deciduous, coniferous or mixed woodland, often with an abundance of ferns; open grassy, flowery, woodland margins in dry or damp conditions; grassy slopes or gullies above treeline. On calcareous or non-calcareous soils.
**Life-history.** LHPs include *Festuca ovina*; *F. rubra*; *Bromus erectus*; *Milium effusum*. At higher altitudes, larval development occupies two seasonal cycles. In captive rearing from ovum, life-cycle completed without diapause in photoperiod of S England.

## *Erebia polaris* Arctic Woodland Ringlet — Plate 77

**Range.** Arctic Norway and Finland, Urals, N Siberia, Yakutia.

*E. polaris* Staudinger 1871 TL: Lappland.
**Distribution.** Arctic Norway and Finland: mainly coastal districts from 69°N to Arctic Sea. 0-400m: generally below 200m.
**Description.** Resembles *E. medusa*: ocelli smaller; unh with pale pd band, often obscure, sometimes absent.

**Flight-period.** Univoltine. Late June/late July according to season.

**Habitat.** Open, damp meadows; coastal river valleys; grassy clearings in light birch scrub.

**Life-history.** Captive larvae accept *Festuca ovina*. In captive rearing from ovum, life-cycle completed without diapause in photo-period of S England. Hibernation stage uncon-firmed.

**Note.** Regarded as a form/ssp. of *E. medusa* by some authors.

## *Erebia alberganus* Almond-eyed Ringlet          Plate 78

**Range.** N Spain (Cantabrian Mts.), Central European Alps, Peninsular Italy, Bulgaria.

*E. alberganus alberganus* de Prunner 1798 TL: Piedmont. syn: *ceto* Hübner 1804.

**Distribution.** Spain: Cantabrian Mts. Main Alpine chain from Alpes-Maritimes through Isère, Cottian Alps, S and SE Switzerland (Pennine Alps, S Bernese Alps, Lepontine Alps, Upper and Lower Engadine) to Dolomites and Hohe Tauern. Peninsular Italy: E Ligurian Alps; Abruzzi. Republic of Macedonia: Korab Pl. 900-2200m.

**Variation.** At high altitudes in E Central Alps, f. *caradjae* Caflisch: small; markings greatly reduced but lanceolate character of pd spots retained (cf. *E. medusa* f. *hippomedusa*). In W Alps, often large with well-developed markings (f. *tyrsus* Fruhstorfer). Intermediate forms are locally common.

**Flight-period.** Univoltine. Mid June/late August.

**Habitat.** Warm, flowery meadows often sheltered by woodland; grassy slopes, often south-facing.

**Life-history.** LHPs *Festuca ovina*; *Anthoxanthum odoratum*.

*E. alberganus phorcys* Freyer 1836 TL: Bulgaria.

**Distribution.** Bulgaria: Stara Pl. 1000-2000m.

**Description.** Resembles *E. a. alberganus*. All markings prominent; unh yellow pd lanceolate spots extended proximally; ocelli ringed orange.

**Flight-period.** Univoltine. July.

**Habitat.** Grassy slopes, often west-facing.

## *Erebia pluto* Sooty Ringlet          Plate 78

**Range.** Central European Alps, Peninsular Italy (C Apen-nines). A variable species, displaying a complex array of local, geographical and transitional forms. Populations whose wing-characters are sensibly constant over a substantial part of the range are described below.

*E. pluto pluto* de Prunner 1798 TL: Val Varodisiana, Piedmont.

**Distribution.** France and NW Italy: Alpes-Maritimes, through Basses and Hautes Alpes, Cottian Alps to Graian Alps. 1900-3000m.

**Description.** Male ups gc uniform silky jet black; upf pd area with trace of dark brownish suffusion, otherwise unmarked: female ups gc variable, sometimes dark grey-yellow brown (khaki), generally with pale brownish pd spots, sometimes fused into a band on fw.

**Variation.** In C Apennines (Gran Sasso), *belzebub* Costa: resembles nominate form: smallest race of the species: fw narrower; female unf copper-coloured pd area brighter.

**Flight-period.** Univoltine. Late June/late August according to altitude.

**Habitat.** Steep limestone screes; moraines.

**Behaviour.** Activity of both sexes confined largely to rocky terrain which is often devoid of vegetation. Males sometimes drink from damp soil-patches. Adults may rest on rocks for prolonged periods with open wings in cool, overcast conditions.

*E. pluto* f. *alecto* Hübner 1804 TL: Lermoos [Austria].

**Distribution.** W Tirol to Kitzbühl Alps, Hohe Tauern, Ortler Alps, Dolomites, Carnic and Julian Alps. Subspecific characters best represented and reputedly most stable in Allgäuer, Lechtaler, Karwendel and Öetztaler Alps. 1900-2700m.

**Description.** Male ups gc uniform silky dark brown or black; white-pupilled ocelli in s4 and s5 upf and s2-4 uph; unf pd area suffused reddish (cf. nominate form and f. *nicholli* (below). Female uph ocelli variable.

**Variation.** In Ortler Alps, f. *velocissima* Frühstorfer: all markings generally better developed: in both sexes, ups pd band broad though usually indistinct; subapical ocelli usually conspicuous, but variable, sometimes absent: transitional to f. *oreas* (below) in E Switzerland. In Julian Alps, male unf red pd band more distinct (f. *triglavensis* Schawerda). In Dolomites, f. *dolomitana* Schawerda: extremely variable, locally transitional to nominate form or f. *nicholli* (below).

**Flight-period, Habitat and Behaviour.** As for nominate form.

*E. pluto* f. *nicholli* Oberthür 1896 TL: Campiglio, Brenta Alps.

**Distribution.** NE Italy: Brenta Alps; Monte Baldo. Above 2000m.

**Description and Variation.** Male ups and uns gc silky dark brown or black; upf white-pupilled ocelli in s2-5, of equal size in s4 and s5, smaller but of equal size in s2 and s3 and displaced slightly distad; uph ocelli in s2-4 of equal size: ups ocellular pattern repeated on uns: female ups gc dark brown; ocelli enclosed by narrow, obscure, reddish pd bands; unf discal area reddish-brown; unh brown, veins conspicuously darker. On Monte Baldo, *burmanni* Wolfsberger: markings slightly better developed and less variable.

**Flight-period and Habitat.** As for nominate form.

*E. pluto* f. *oreas* Warren 1933 TL: Chamonix, Savoie.

syn: *glacialis* Esper 1804 (invalid homonym).

**Distribution.** France: Haute Savoie. S and E Switzerland and N Italy: Pennine Alps through Lepontine Alps to E Engadine; Bernese Oberland to Glarner Alps and Alpstein. Austria: S and E Öetztaler Alps. 1800-3000m.

**Description.** Male ups gc dark silky brown; upf with dark reddish pd band, variable, sometimes vestigial; uph sometimes with obscure reddish pd marks; unf reddish pd band with sharp proximal border, discal and basal areas suffused darker red.

**Variation.** In E Engadine, transitional to f. *velocissima*. In Bernese Oberland, f. *anteborus* Frühstorfer: transitional to nominate form but variable.

**Flight-period, Habitat and Behaviour.** As for nominate form.

**Life-history.** LHPs *Festuca quadriflora*; *F. alpina*; *Poa minor*. Ova usually laid on rocks or dead, woody plant stems, sometimes at an appreciable distance from nearest LHPs. Larvae may be found in grassy areas adjacent to screes. Larval development occupies two seasonal cycles.

## *Erebia gorge* Silky Ringlet                                    Plate 79

**Range.** S Europe.

In central Alps, complexity of variation and distribution parallels closely that of *E. pluto* with which it shares many habitats. The development of pd bands and ocelli follows roughly the same geographical pattern – the least marked forms occurring in the Apeninnes and SW Alps, whilst maximum development is achieved in SE Switzerland and associated Italian massifs. The least stable populations of both species seem to occur in the Dolomites. The main forms, described below, often show transitional character where distributions overlap. Each form is liable to appear in almost any population as an occasional variant. Some colonies appear to be unstable, producing a wide variety of forms in roughly equal proportions.

*E. gorge gorge* Hübner 1804 TL: Switzerland and Tyrol.
**Distribution.** Alps of Savoie through Alps of S and C Switzerland and N Italy (except Ober Engadine, Bernina and Ortler Alps) to Bavarian and Austrian Alps: Dolomites; Julian Alps; Velebit Pl; Dinaric Alps; Rudoka Pl.; Pirin Mts.; Rila Mts.; Carpathian Mts.; Apunseni Mts.; Tatra Mts. 1800-3000m.
**Description.** Male upf sex-brand conspicuous; reddish pd band with distinct silky appearance; subapical twin ocelli white-pupilled, additional ocelli small when present; unh variegated dark grey/greyish-brown and light grey. Both sexes: hw outer margin irregular, usually with conspicuous 'bump' at v4 – a useful diagnostic character.
**Variation.** Many populations of E Europe (Karawanken Alps, S Bosnia-Herzegovina, S Serbia and Carpathian Mts.) differ little from nominate form or appear transitional to f. *erynis* Esper (below): within this complex, upf pd band often extends to cell in s4 and s5 (*karwendeli* Zusanek; *hercegovinensis* Rebel; *vagana* Lorkovic; *rudkowskyi* Bang-Haas; *fredericikoenigi* Varga). At south-eastern limit of European range (Bulgaria), *pirinica* Buresch: larger, otherwise indistinguishable from nominate form.
**Flight-period.** Univoltine. Late June/late August according to altitude.
**Habitat.** Limestone screes; moraines.
**Life-history.** LHPs *Poa minor*; *P. alpina*; *Sesleria varia*; *Festuca alpina*. Larval development occupies two seasonal cycles.

*E. gorge* f. *ramondi* Oberthür 1909 TL: Gavarnie, Hautes-Pyrénées.
**Distribution.** Spain: Cantabrian Mts.; Spain and France: Pyrenees: Ordessa and Pic du Midi d'Ossau to Pic du Midi de Bigorre and Mont Canigou. Above 1800m.
**Description.** Resembles nominate form, but has 4 or 5 ocelli uph and unh. Specimens with additional ocellus in s6 upf resembles f. *triopes* Speyer (below). In Cantabrian Mts., often large (f. *gigantea* Oberthür).
**Flight-period and Habitat.** As for nominate form.

*E. gorge* f. *triopes* Speyer 1865 TL: Bernina Pass.
**Distribution.** Ober Engadine; Bernina Alps; Ortler Alps; Adamello Alps; Mte. Baldo. 1600-3000m. Reported as an occasional variant in Tatra Mts.
**Description.** Resembles f. *ramondi*: all ocelli better developed: upf ocelli in s4-6 of equal size, contiguous and co-linear; ocelli in s2 and s3 smaller.
**Flight-period and Habitat.** As for nominate form.

*E. gorge* f. *erynis* Esper 1805 TL: Chamonix, Haute-Savoie.
**Distribution.** SE France and NW Italy: Basses and Hautes-Alpes to Savoie, Graian and Pennine Alps. Above 1900m. From Alpes-Maritimes to Savoie, Pennine and W Bernese Alps, an increasing proportion of f. *erynis* in each population is replaced by forms resembling f. *gorge*, the distinctive characters of which also develop progressively within same geographical transition.
**Description.** Resembles f. *gorge*, but lacking ocelli.
**Variation.** In Apuane Alps and C Apennines (Monti Sibillini; Abruzzi), f. *carboncina* Verity: smaller; gc darker; pd bands narrower; ocelli very small, often absent.
**Flight-period and Habitat.** As for nominate form.

*E. gorge albanica* Rebel 1917 TL: Gropa Strelit, Albania.
**Distribution.** S Albania: Tomor Mts. (?)S Serbia: Strelizt (SE Montenegro).
**Description.** Male upf pd band narrow, short, somewhat diffuse; small white-pupilled ocelli only in s4 and s5, similar on unf; uph uniform black, unmarked; unh unicolorous dark brown with obscure, greyish antemarginal band.

## *Erebia aethiopella* False Mnestra Ringlet                 Plate 79

**Range.** France, Italy.

*E. aethiopella* Hoffmannsegg 1806 TL: Piedmont [NW Italy]. syn: *gorgophone* Bellier 1863.
**Distribution.** Alps of SE France and NW Italy: Maritimes Alps to Hautes-Alpes and Cottian Alps: very local. 1800-2400m.
**Description.** Male upf sex-brand conspicuous, extending from s1a-s4; pd band, extending to cell-end, usually with small white-pupilled ocelli in s4 and s5; uph pd band lacking ocelli (cf. *E. mnestra*).
**Flight-period.** Univoltine. Mid July/late August.
**Habitat.** Open, grassy slopes and valleys.
**Life-history.** LHP *Festuca paniculata*: oviposition and post-hibernation larval feeding observed: local occurrence of butterfly and LHP appear highly correlated.

## *Erebia rhodopensis* Nicholl's Ringlet                 Plate 79

**Range.** SE Europe.

*E. rhodopensis* Nicholl 1900 TL: Rila Mts., Bulgaria.
**Distribution.** Republic of Macedonia: Sar Pl. Bulgaria: Stara Pl.; Rila Mts.; Pirin Mts.; Rhodopi Mts. Greece: Grammos Mt. Very local. 1800-2600m.
**Description and Variation.** Resembles *E. aethiopella*: upf and unf white-pupilled subapical ocelli better developed; uph and unh pd ocelli with small white pupils. On Sar Pl., f. *sharsta* Higgins: unh brighter, gc greyish with white irroration.

**Flight-period.** Univoltine. July/August.
**Habitat.** Open grassy slopes, almost devoid of shrubs or trees.
**Life-history.** LHP unknown: captive larvae have been reared on *Poa* sp. Hibernation stage unconfirmed.

### *Erebia mnestra* Mnestra's Ringlet                    Plate 79

**Range.** Central European Alps.

*E. mnestra* Hübner 1804 TL: Swiss Alps.
**Distribution.** Alps of France (Isère; Hautes-Alpes; Savoie; Haute-Savoie), Italy (very local in Cottian Alps; Ortler Mts.; Adamello Mts.), S and SE Switerland (Valais to Engadine), Germany (Allgäuer Alps) and Austria (Oetztal Alps; Salzburg Alps; Karwendal Mts.). (?)High Tatra Mts. Generally very local, often scarce. 1500-2600m.
**Description.** Male upf sex-brand inconspicuous; pd band extending to cell-end in s4 and s5; subapical ocelli absent or sometimes represented by two, small black points; uph pd broken by veins, usually restricted to s3-5, lacking ocelli; upf brown marginal border well defined, discal and basal areas uniformly reddish, unmarked; unh uniformly brown, rarely with obscure pale pd band. (cf. *E. aethiopella*).
**Flight-period.** Univoltine. Early July/mid August.
**Habitat.** Steep slopes, dominated by grasses, including taller and coarser species.
**Life-history.** LHPs *Festuca*; *Sesleria varia*. In some localities, larval development occupies two seasonal cycles.

### *Erebia gorgone* Gavarnie Ringlet                    Plate 80

**Range.** Pyrenees.

*E. gorgone* Boisduval 1833 TL: Pyrenees.
**Distribution.** High Pyrenees. Spain: Balneario de Panticosa; Port de Beñasque; Port de la Picada; Tuc de Cabriols; Pic de l'Homme; Pto. de la Bonaigua. Andorra: Port d'Envalira (2450m). France: Col d'Aubisque; Cauterets; Cirque de Gavarnie; Col du Tourmalet. 1500-2450m.
**Description.** Male ups gc dark brown; pd bands dark red, broken by dark veins; upf sex-brand in s1a-5 conspicuous: female unh pale veins conspicuous. (cf. *E. gorge* and *E. pronoe*).
**Flight-period.** Univoltine. Mid July/late August.
**Habitat.** Grassy places amongst rocks or small areas of scree; steep slopes, dominated by grasses including some taller species.

### *Erebia epistygne* Spring Ringlet                    Plate 80

**Range.** Spain, France.

*E. epistygne* Hübner 1824 TL: not stated [Provençe]
**Distribution.** Spain: Montes Universales (La Losilla; Calomarde; Moscardon; Frias de Albarracin; Griegos; Bronchales); Serrania de Cuenca (Castillia); S. de Javalambre; S. de Calderesos (Cubillejo de la Sierra; La Yunta); S. de

Guadalajara (Cueva de la Hoz; Aguilar de Anguita; Guijo); Montseny Mts. 1000-1550m. Reports from S. de Moncayo (2300m: reported flight-period July) and C Pyrenees require confirmation. France: SW Cevennes; Provençe (widespread but local). 450-1500m.

**Variation.** In Spain, f. *viriathus* Sheldon: unh slightly greyer; marked individual/local variation of wing-characters overlaps that of nominate form.

**Flight-period.** Univoltine. Late March/late May according to season.

**Habitat.** Grassy and rocky clearings in open woodland. Limestone habitats of Montes Universales distinctive: dry, often flattish clearings, strewn with small rocks, in sparse pinewoods, with short grasses and sparse, low-growing shrubs.

**Life-history.** LHP *Festuca ovina*. In captivity, life-cycle from ovum is completed without diapause in extended photo-period of S England. Hibernation stage unconfirmed.

The following six species comprise a closely related group for which external characters are often poorly differentiated and sometimes insufficient for reliable field identification. As far as is known, no two species of the group occupy the same habitats, and is instances of geographical overlap in distribution, altitudinal separation is usually clearly apparent. Distinctive characters in male genitalia allow ready separation. For *E. cassioides*, *E. hispania* and *E. ottomana*, at least, pupal colouring and shape are appreciably different for males and females: a difference in larval coloration is less obvious and generally more variable, but female larvae are noticeably greener.

## *Erebia tyndarus* Swiss Brassy Ringlet                    Plate 80

**Range.** Central European Alps.

*E. tyndarus* Esper 1781 TL: Scheidegg, Switzerland.
**Distribution.** Pennine Alps (Col Ferret) and Berner Alps through Engadine, Ortler Alps, Allgäuer Alps to Brenner. 1200-2700m. Widespread and common. Reported occurrence in Hautes-Alpes (Col d'Izoard) requires confirmation.
**Description and Variation.** Male ups dark brown; upf with strong, brassy or greenish reflections, most apparent in fresh specimens; upf apex slightly rounded; subapical fulvous-red patch extending to cell in s4 and s5, usually enclosing twin, white-pupilled ocelli; uph sometimes with small, fulvous-red pd marks, lacking ocelli; unh grey gc and brown striae variable.

**Flight-period.** Univoltine. Generally early July/late August in prolonged emergence, sometimes extending to early October according to season and locality.

**Habitat.** Open, grassy clearings in pinewoods at lowest altitudes; grassy, stony and rocky areas above treeline.

**Life-history.** LHPs include *Nardus stricta*; *Festuca ovina*.

## *Erebia cassioides* Common Brassy Ringlet          Plate 80

**Range.** N Spain, southern C Europe, S Balkans.

*E. cassioides* Hohenwarth 1793 TL: Heilegenblut, Austria.
**Distribution.** Spain: Cantabrian Mts.; Pyrenees. France:
Pyrenees; Massif Central (Mont Dore; Mont Aigoual). Alps
of France (Alpes-Maritimes to Isère and Haute-Savoie), NW
Italy and W Switzerland (W Pennine Alps; Bernese Oberland
to Faulhorn and Grindelwald). Peninsular and NE Italy:
Apuane Alps; C Apennines; Monte Pollino; Dolomites. Aus-
tria: Hohe Tauern; Niedere Tauern. Romania: Retezat Mts.
Albania. Republic of Macedonia: Sar Pl.; Osogovske Pl.; Placenska Pl. Bulgaria:
Stara Pl.; Rila Mts.; Pirin Mts. 1600-2600m. Not reported from Greece.
**Description.** Resembles *E. tyndarus*: male upf outer margin less convex; subapical fulvous-red patch usually not extending to cell or v3; twin, white-pupilled
ocelli generally larger, contiguous; uph reddish pd marks and ocelli better
developed. In Pyrenees, Massif Central and peninsular Italy, *arvernensis* Oberthür:
resembles nominate form closely: upf twin subapical ocelli larger, white pupils
conspicuous, especially in female, additional one or two ocelli or black points
sometimes present in s2-4: female unh gc usually decidedly yellowish.
**Variation.** Whilst many forms have been described, minor regional differences
in size, gc and development of pd markings are largely obscured by individual
and local variation.
**Flight-period.** Univoltine. Late June/early September according to locality.
**Habitat.** Grass-covered slopes; grassy places amongst rocks or screes.
**Life-history.** LHPs include *Festuca ovina*. Differences in coloration are
sufficient for sexual differentiation in larval and pupal stages.

## *Erebia hispania* Spanish Brassy Ringlet          Plate 81

**Range.** Spain (Pyrenees and Sierra Nevada), France (Pyrenees), Andorra.

*E. hispania* Butler 1868 TL: Spain [Sierra Nevada].
**Distribution.** Spain: Sierra Nevada 1800-2900m. Spain and
France: W and C Pyrenees (Pto. de Portalet to Col du
Tormalet and Pto. de Viella); E Pyrenees (Andorra to Mont
Canigou). 1650-2300m
**Description and Variation.** Ups gc medium brown; all
markings generally well developed, especially upf yellow-
orange subapical patch and enclosed twin, white-pupilled ocelli (cf. *E. cassioides*).
In Pyrenees, f. *rondoui* Oberthür: smaller; fw outer margin less rounded; ups
markings better developed, especially in E Pyrenees (f. *goya* Frühstorfer).
**Flight-period.** Univoltine. In Sierra Nevada, mid June/late August according
to season and altitude: in Pyrenees, early July/mid August.
**Habitat.** Open, grassy and rocky slopes: on calcareous and non-calcareous
soils.
**Life-history.** LHPs include *Festuca ovina*. Differences in coloration are sufficient for sexual differentiation in larval and pupal stages.

## *Erebia nivalis* De Lesse's Brassy Ringlet                Plate 81

**Range.** E Central European Alps.

*E. nivalis* Lorkovic and de Lesse 1954 TL: Gross Glockner.
**Distribution.** Switzerland: very restricted: Faulhorn;
Grindelwald. 2250-2600m. NE Italy: Atesine Alps (Val di Vizze
2300-2450m). Austria: E of Öetztal: Brenner Pass; Stubaier
Alps; Zillertaler Alps; Hohe Tauern; Niedere Tauern. 2100-2500m.
**Description.** Male fw outer margin convex; upf subapical
fulvous-red patch extending to cell in s4 and s5 and v3, en-
closing small, twin, white-pupilled ocelli not contiguous; uph
pd markings small or absent; unh gc lustrous bluish-grey.
**Flight-period.** Univoltine. Early July/late August.
**Habitat.** Grassy places, often small areas amongst limestone outcrops.
**Life-history.** LHP *Festuca quadriflora*. Larval development occupies two seasonal cycles.
**Note.** Geographically and/or altitudinally separated from *E. tyndarus* and *E.
cassioides*.

## *Erebia calcaria* Lorkovic's Brassy Ringlet                Plate 81

**Range.** European Alps.

*E. calcaria* Lorkovic 1953 TL: Julian Alps.
**Distribution.** NE Italy: Piave di Cardore (Monte Cavallo;
Mte. Santo): not reported from nearby Carnic Alps. W Slovenia:
Karwanken Alps.; Julian Alps (Triglav). Above 1450m.
**Description.** Resembles *E. tyndarus*: male ups darker brown;
upf subapical white-pupilled ocelli usually very small; unh
gc lighter, silvery-grey.
**Flight-period.** Univoltine. Mid July/late August.
**Habitat.** Grassy, rocky slopes.
**Life-history.** LHPs include *Festuca ovina*. Hibernation stage unconfirmed.

## *Erebia ottomana* Ottoman Brassy Ringlet                Plate 81

**Range.** France (Massif Central), NE Italy, S Balkans, N and
C Greece, N Turkey.

*E. ottomana* Herrich-Schäffer 1851 TL: not stated.
**Distribution.** France: Massif Central. NE Italy: Monte Baldo.
S Croatia: Velebit Mts. S Bosnia-Herzegovina. S Serbia. Albania.
Republic of Macedonia. Bulgaria. N and C Greece. Widespread,
locally abundant. 850-2450m, more generally 1400-2000m.
**Description and Variation.** Ups pd markings usually well
developed. All wing-characters, including fw-shape, subject
to marked individual and local variation. Basis for regional differentiation of
Balkan and Greek populations (referrable to *bulgarica* Drenowsky [=*bureschi*
Warren], *drenowskyi* Varga, *durmitorensis* Warren, *balcanica* Rebel or nominate
subspecies) is obscure; reputed regional differences appear to fall within the
range attributable to individual, local and seasonal variation. In Massif Central,

*tardenota* Praviel: small; male ups gc dark brown; upf ocelli small: both sexes, unh markings usually well developed. On Monte Baldo, *benacensis* Dannehl: male ups gc very dark brown; upf reddish pd markings reduced to thin ocellular rings enclosing very small subapical ocelli; uph pd reddish spots vestigial: both sexes, unh markings strongly developed: in overall character, a distinctive race.
**Flight-period.** Univoltine. Mid July/August according to altitude and season.
**Habitat.** Exposed, grass-covered slopes or plains at higher altitudes; below the treeline, small, damp grassy clearings in beech, coniferous or mixed forests.
**Life-history.** LHPs include *Festuca ovina*. In extended photo-period of N Europe, captively reared larvae mature and pupate without entering diapause. Striking differences in larval colouring and pupal coloration/shape are sufficient for sexual differentiation.

## *Erebia pronoe* Water Ringlet                                    Plate 82

**Range.** Europe.

*E. pronoe* Esper 1780 TL: Styria.
**Distribution.** Pyrenees (Spain and France): Pto. de Arlas to Valle d'Arán and Andorra. E France: N Isère; N Savoie; Haute-Savoie; Jura; Doubs. Switerland: Jura Mts; Bernese Oberland and Glarner Alps to Albula Alps; more local in Valais and Tessin. Italy: Cottian Alps; Orobic Alps to Dolomites. Bavarian Alps (absent from Allgäuer Alps). Widespread in Austrian Alps to Julian Alps. Local in Dinaric Alps.
Republic of Macedonia: Sar Pl.; Vraca Pl.; Plackovica Pl. Bulgaria: Stara Pl.; Rila Mts. Slovakia and Poland: Tatra Mts. Romania: Carpathian Mts. 900-2800m.
**Description and Variation.** Male unh silvery-grey pd band with dark violet or purple reflections, contrasting with broad, brownish discal band; wing-base colour as for pd band but variable, sometimes obscure: female unh paler, bands more contrastive. In C Pyrenees, *glottis* Frühstorfer: ups reddish pd bands reduced; subapical ocelli well defined; male unh markings obscure. In Switzerland, *vergy* Ochsenheimer: upf reddish pd bands and ocelli much reduced, sometimes absent; unh markings less contrastive: in Balkans, *fruhstorferi* Warren: closely similar. In C Alps, transitional to nominate form in many areas.
**Flight-period.** Univoltine. Late June/late September according to altitude.
**Habitat.** Damp, grassy slopes or woodland clearings, often associated with small streams.
**Life-history.** LHPs *Festuca ovina*; *F. quadriflora*.

## *Erebia melas* Black Ringlet                                    Plate 82

**Range.** SE Europe.

*E. melas* Herbst 1796 TL: Perzenieska, Romanian Banat.
**Distribution.** Widespread on mountains of SW Slovenia (Mt. Nanos); W Croatia (including Velebit Planina); Bosnia-Herzegovina; SW Serbia (Montenegro); N Albania. E Serbia (Rtanj Pl.). Romania: E Apuseni Mts. (Runc Gorge 500-700m); SW Carpathian Mts. (Cerna Valley 200-1400m); Retezat Mts. (1700-2200m); Haghimas Mts. (1500-1900m); central E Transylvanian Mts. (1000-1300m). Republic of Macedonia: Sar Pl.; Jablanica Pl.; Placenska

Pl.; Kozuf Pl. Bulgaria: Stara Pl.; Rila Mts.; Pirin Mts. Greece: Mt. Phalakron; Mt. Olympus; Timfi Mts.; Mt. Timfristos; Mt. Parnassos. 900-2800m: usually above 1500m.

**Description.** Male ups velvety-black or blackish-brown; upf with twin subapical white-pupilled black ocelli, often with ocellus in s2; uph usually with pd ocelli in s2-4; unf as upf; unh with obscure dark grey variegation and obscure pale antemarginal band: female slightly browner; upf and unf orange-red pd band enclosing subapical ocelli and ocellus in s2, usually constricted in s3; all ocelli larger; unh gc brownish, irrorated grey.

**Variation.** In Apuseni Mts., *runcensis* König 1965: both sexes, all markings better developed: female upf bright orange-red pd bands wider, extending to s1b; ocelli larger; uph large pd ocelli in s1b-4, enclosed by orange-red band; unf pd bands extending into discal area; costa, apex and outer margin light grey; unh irrorated light grey; darker discal area bordered by irregular dark line; pd ocelli large; antemarginal band paler. In Haghimas Mts. (E Carpathian Mts.), *carpathicola* Popescu-Gorj and Alexinschi 1959: wing-characters inter-mediate of *melas* and *runcensis*. In SW Slovenia and Velebit Pl., *leonhardi* Frühstorfer 1918: slightly smaller, but variable: male resembles nominate form but unh almost uniform black: female dark greyish-brown; ocelli reduced; upf reddish pd bands obscure or absent; unh brown, variegated darker brown. In S Balkans and Greece, *schawerdae* Frühstorfer 1918: male resembles *leonhardi* closely, uph ocelli reduced: female brownish, variable, sometimes pale greyish-brown; ocelli smaller; fw reddish pd bands very obscure, more usually absent: some specimens in some populations of Greece and Bulgaria are indistinguish-able from *leonhardi*: morphological and distributional relationship of *leonhardi* and *schawerdae* unclear. Other named forms appear to be synonymous with, or relate to minor variation of above forms.

**Flight-period.** Univoltine. Mid July/mid September according to altitude.

**Habitat.** Rocky slopes with sparse grass; grass-covered slopes.

**Life-history.** LHP unknown: on Mt. Timfristos 1900m, hibernated larvae have been recorded feeding on a heavily perfumed grass. Captive larvae accept *Festuca ovina*.

**Note.** Lower altitudinal range in Romania, relative to W and S Balkans and Greece, may reflect adaptive compensation for significant climatic transition between the two regions: Romania is characterised by averagely lower temperatures and severe winters (possibly of ecological relevance to larval/pupal development).

## *Erebia lefebvrei* Lefèbvre's Ringlet　　　　　　　Plate 82

**Range.** Pyrenees (Spain and France), Cantabrian Mts. (N Spain).

*E. lefebvrei* Boisduval 1828 TL: Pyrenees.

**Distribution.** Spain: Picos de Europa; S. de la Demanda; E Pyrenees (Pto. de Beñasque; Puigmal; Pico de Finestrelles). France: C Pyrenees (Pic d'Anie to Pic du Midi de Bigorre and Col de Portillon): E Pyrenees (Carlit massif; Canigou massif). 1700-2700m.

**Description.** Male ups and uns gc jet black; upf reddish pd band diffuse, variable, sometimes absent; upf and uph with 3 to 5 submarginal, white-pupilled black ocelli; uns markings similar: female gc paler; all markings better developed.

**Variation.** Subject to considerable individual and local variation. In E Pyrenees, *pyrenaea* Oberthür: for most specimens, all markings reduced in both sexes: male upf reddish pd bands generally absent, vestigial in female; male uph usually without ocelli but variable. In Picos de Europa, *astur* Oberthür: resembles *pyrenaea*; markings averagely further reduced, but sufficiently variable to render individual specimens of the two populations inseparable.

**Flight-period.** Univoltine. Generally late June/late August according to altitude, locality and (?)season.

**Habitat.** Steep, limestone screes, bordered by grassy areas; rocky slopes.

## *Erebia scipio* Larche Ringlet                                Plate 83

**Range.** SE France, NW Italy.

*E. scipio* Boisduval 1832 TL: Basses Alpes.
**Distribution.** SE France: Alpes-Maritimes; Alpes-de-Haute-Provençe; Vaucluse; Drôme; Hautes-Alpes; Savoie. NW Italy: Maritime Alps. Very local. 1400-2500m.
**Flight-period.** Univoltine. Late July/late August.
**Habitat.** Steep, rocky slopes with sparse grass; screes; moraines. On limestone.
**Life-history.** LHP *Helictotrichon sedenense* – a specialized grass whose geographical and local distribution appears as restricted as that of the butterfly. Most other members of the genus have similar ecological preferences; *H. setaceum*, for example, is endemic to SW Alps and mountains of Provençe, and occurs in at least some habitats of *E. scipio* – not recorded as a LHP.

## *Erebia stirius* Styrian Ringlet                                Plate 83

**Range.** SE European Alps (NE Italy, SE Austria, W Slovenia, NW Croatia).

*E. stirius* Godart 1824 TL: Klagenfurt, Carinthia.
syn: *nerine* Freyer 1831.
**Distribution.** From Monte Baldo through Brenta Alps, Dolomites, Karawanken Alps, Julian Alps to Kapela and Velebit Mts. 700-1800m.
**Description and Variation.** Resembles *E. styx*: unf brown marginal border slightly tapered towards s1b, without projection in s1b (distinction from *E. styx*); male unh more variegated, giving a slightly roughened appearance. At high altitudes in Dolomites, f. *morula* Speyer: smaller; all markings reduced: in some localities, transitional to nominate form.
**Flight-period.** Univoltine. Late July/early September, according to altitude.
**Habitat.** Rocky and grassy slopes usually on limestone.
**Life-history.** LHP *Sesleria caerulea*.

## *Erebia styx* Stygian Ringlet                Plate 83

**Range.** SE Switzerland, N Italy, SE Germany, Austria, W Slovenia.

*E. styx* Freyer 1834 TL: not stated.
syn: *reichlini* Herrich-Schäffer 1860.
**Distribution.** Italy: Monte Generoso to Dolomites. Local in SE Switzerland: Tessin (Monte Generoso). Germany: Allgäuer Alps. Austria: Karwendel Mts. and Zillertal Alps to W Slovenia: Julian Alps (Trentadal; Mojstrovka Pass). 600-2200m. (Records for Vosges Mts. appear to have arisen from misidentification).

**Description and Variation.** Resembles *E. stirius*: unf brown marginal border of averagely uniform width with short, proximal cuspidal projection in s1b (a useful diagnostic character); male unh less variegated, appearing smoother. In Bergamasker Alps; Monte Generoso, *triglites* Frühstorfer: all markings better developed; upf pd band and subapical ocelli larger; unh ocelli sometimes absent. In Julian Alps, *trentae* Lorkovic: resembles *triglites* but markings further developed; ocelli large, pupils brilliant white: female uns gc variable.
**Flight-period.** Univoltine. Early July/early September according to locality.
**Habitat.** Warm, dry, rocky, often precipitous limestone slopes, usually with scattered bushes and trees.
**Life-history.** LHP *Sesleria varia*. Larval development occupies two seasonal cycles in some localities at higher altitude.

## *Erebia montana* Marbled Ringlet                Plate 84

**Range.** C European Alps, Apennines.

*E. montana* de Prunner 1798 TL: Piedmont.
syn: *homole* Frühstorfer 1918.
**Distribution.** From Maritime Alps (France and Italy) through main Alpine chain to Allgäuer Alps, Öetztal Alps (Brenner Pass) and Dolomites. Generally widespread and common. Also Apuane Alps and C Apennines. 1100-2500m.
**Description and Variation.** Resembles *E. styx*: unf brown marginal border internally undulate, well defined. In E Alps, *goante* Esper: ups markings generally better developed; male unh gc darker but variable. In Apuane Alps (Mont Tambura), *vandellii* Casini: larger; unh darker.
**Flight-period.** Univoltine. Mid July/mid September according to altitude.
**Habitat.** Diverse. Grassy, flowery alpine and subalpine meadows; woodland clearings; rocky and grassy slopes; in dry or damp situations. Usually on limestone.
**Life-history.** LHPs *Nardus stricta*; *Festuca alpina*; *F. ovina*.

## *Erebia zapateri* Zapater's Ringlet                Plate 84

**Range.** E Spain (Montes Universales).

*E. zapateri* Oberthür 1875 TL: Sierra de Albarracin.
**Distribution.** E Spain: Guadalajara (S. de Albarracin); Cuenca (Tragacete;

Valdemeca; Ciudad Encantada; Valdecabras); Teruel
(Albarracin; La Losilla; Colomarde; Moscardon; Griegos;
Orihuela del Tremedel; Noguera; Bronchales; S. de
Javalambre). 1050-1650m.

**Description.** Male ups gc dark brown; upf bright yellow-
orange pd band wide; uph reddish pd markings small or
absent (cf. *E. neoridas*).

**Flight-period.** Univoltine. Late July/early September: first
females emerge 10-12 days after first males (cf. *E. neoridas*).

**Habitat.** Open, grassy, sparsely bushy, pinewood clearings; very small, bushy
openings with long grasses in pine and oak woodland; stony ground with short
grasses in sparse pinewoods. On calcareous rocks, usually limestone.

**Life-history.** LHP: hibernated larvae have been recorded on three species of
Poaceae within a single colony. Posterior segment of larva, blunt – almost without 'tails'.

## *Erebia neoridas* Autumn Ringlet                    Plate 84

**Range.** NE Spain, S France, NW and C Italy.

*E. neoridas* Boisduval 1828 TL: Grenoble.

**Distribution.** Spain: Huesca (Valle d'Arazas); Lérida (S. di
Cadi); Barcelona (S. del Montseny); Gerona (S. Gallabara).
Andorra. France: C and E Pyrenees: Gavarnie; Col du
Tourmalet; Pic Carlit; Mt. Canigou. Massif Central; Alpes-
Maritimes to Vaclause, Isère and Haute-Savoie. Italy: Maritime
Alps to Susa Valley; Apuane Alps; C Apennines. 500-1600m.

**Description.** Resembles *E. zapateri*: upf pd band dull,
reddish-brown, slightly narrower near subapex, more tapered, extending to
v1; twin, subapical ocelli better developed, white-pupilled ocellus in s2; uph pd
orange-red spots often confluent, with ocelli in s2-4.

**Variation.** Individual and local variation marked. On Monte Sibillini, *sibyllina*
Verity: very small; ups pd bands mahogany-red, ocelli well developed; unh
brightly marked.

**Flight-period.** Univoltine. Early August/early October: first females appear
about two weeks after first males (cf. *E. zapateri*).

**Habitat.** Grassy, bushy places; open woodland.

**Life-history.** LHPs *Digitaria sanguinalis*; *Poa annua*; *P. pratense*; *Festuca ovina*.

## *Erebia oeme* Bright-eyed Ringlet                    Plate 85

**Range.** Europe.

*E. oeme* Hübner 1804 TL: Tirol.

**Distribution.** Pyrenees: Spain (Pto. de Beñasque; Valle
d'Arán): France (Col d'Aubisque to Mt. Canigou): Andorra.
France: Massif Central (colonies dispersed); Isère; Ain;
Savoie; Haute-Savoie; Jura. Switzerland: S Jura; Bernese Alps
to St. Gallen and Engadine. NW Italy: Ortler Alps; Dolomites.
SE Germany (Bavarian Alps) through Austrian Alps to W
Slovenia (Julian Alps), Croatia (Velebit Mts.), S Balkans and

N Greece (Rhodopi Mts.). Reported from N Carpathian Mts. (Branyiszko, Slovakia). 900-2600m: more often 1500-2000m.

**Description and Variation.** Uns of antennal club-tip black (cf. *E. medusa*). Ups and unh reddish-orange markings and ocelli well defined, but variable, giving rise to several named local and regional forms. In Switzerland, *lugens* Staudinger: pd spots and ocelli smaller: transitional to nominate form in some areas of Allgäuer Alps and N Tirol. In E Austria, Balkans and Greece, *spodia* Staudinger: larger; all markings better developed: female unh pd yellowish spots often confluent, ocelli and ocellular white pupils large: the especially well-marked forms *pacula* Frühstorfer and *vetulonia* Frühstorfer represent the limit of development in wing-characters, but appear to have no racial significance.

**Flight-period.** Univoltine. Mid June/mid August according to altitude.

**Habitat.** Damp meadows, hillside bogs, stream margins etc., usually with an abundance of long grasses; in damp, bushy, woodland clearings at lower altitudes.

**Life-history.** LHPs include *Poa alpina*; *P. pratensis*; *P. nemoralis*; *Festuca rubra*; *Carex flacca*; *C. sempervirens*; *Briza media*; *Molinia caerulea*. At high altitudes, larval development occupies two seasonal cycles.

## *Erebia meolans* Piedmont Ringlet                    Plate 85

**Range.** Europe.

*E. meolans* de Prunner 1798 TL: Piedmont.
syn: *calaritas* Frühstorfer 1918.

**Distribution.** N and C Spain: S. de Bejar; S. de Gredos; S. de Guadarrama; S. de la Demanda; Cantabrian Mts.; Pyrenees. Andorra. France: Pyrenees; Massif Central; Alpes-Maritimes to Jura and Vosges. NW, C and S Switzerland. Italy: W Ligurian Alps to Cottian Alps, Pennine Alps, Tessin and Ortler Alps: Apuane Alps; C Apennines. Germany: south  of Thuringer Wald. Austria: W Tirol; Hochschwab Mts. Records for Carpathian Mts. require confirmation. Absent from Dolomites. 600-2300m: generally below 1500m.

**Description.** Upf small ocellus in s6 (when present) displaced distad, often conspicuously so relative to ocelli in s4 and s5; unh very dark, smooth in appearance. (Cf. *E. triaria*).

**Variation.** Size and wing-markings markedly variable. In C Spain, *bejarensis* Chapman: larger; brighter; all markings well developed, upf with ocelli in s2-s6: progressively transitional to nominate form towards Cantabrian Mts. and Pyrenees. In Vosges Mts., Switzerland and E Alps, *stygne* Ochsenheimer: all markings averagely reduced but with marked local variation: in f. *valesiaca* Elwes, ups red pd markings vestigial or absent, sometimes reduced to narrow rings enclosing subapical twin ocelli on fw: prevalent in some localities in Pennine Alps.

**Flight-period.** Univoltine. Late May/mid August according to locality.

**Habitat.** Grassy, flowery woodland clearings

**Life-history.** LHPs include *Agrostis capillaris*; *Deschampia flexuosa*; *Nardus stricta*; *Festuca ovina*.

## *Erebia palarica* Chapman's Ringlet                Plate 85

**Range.** NW Spain.

*E. palarica* Chapman 1905 TL: Pajares [Asturian Mts.].
**Distribution.** NW Spain: Cantabrian Mts. (provinces of Leon; Oviedo;
Palencia; Santander). 1050-1650m.
**Description.** Resembles *E. meolans*, but larger – the largest European member of the genus; unh with slightly rough-ened appearance.
**Flight-period.** Univoltine. Late May/late July according to season and altitude.
**Habitat.** Small, grassy, clearings amongst Broom ((?) *Cytisus*) or Mediterranean Heath (*Erica arborea*), in valleys and on slopes. On non-calcareous soils.
**Life-history.** Hibernation stage unconfirmed.
**Behaviour.** Females are secretive, spending much time amongst grasses growing within the cover of Broom or Heath.

## *Erebia pandrose* Dewy Ringlet                Plate 86

**Range.** Arctic and Alpine zones of Europe, Kola and Kanin Peninsulas, Polar Urals, Altai, Sajan, Mongolia.

*E. pandrose* Borkhausen 1788 TL: Styria.
syn: *lappona* Thunberg 1791.
**Distribution.** Spain: E Pyrenees (S. dels Canals). Andorra (El Serrat 2200m). France: E Pyrenees (Col de l'Artigue; Col de Puymorens to Canigou massif); Alpes-Maritimes to Haute-Savoie. Widespread and common throughout C European Alps. Italy: C Apennines: Monti della Laga. W Slovenia: Julian Alps. Romania: Carpathian Mts. Bosnia-Herzegovina: Vranica Pl.; Prenj Pl. S Serbia: Montenegro: Sinjajevina Pl. Republic of Macedonia: Sar Pl.; Jakupica Pl. 1600-3100m. Bulgaria: Rila Mts.; (?)Rhodopi Mts.; 2400-2900m. Fennoscandia (Norway, W Sweden and N Finland): 900-1200m in south: 500-1200m in N Sweden: near sea-level on Arctic coast.
**Description.** (See *E. sthennyo*).
**Variation.** Upf reddish pd markings often reduced, more rarely absent; ocelli in s4 and s5 sometimes absent or reduced to minute points; unh gc pale silvery-grey to dark grey or greyish-brown; mediobasal, discal and submarginal lines prominent or absent. Several sspp. have been described to account for minor, regional variation.
**Flight-period.** Univoltine. Early June/mid August according to locality and altitude: emerges about mid July in Lappland according to season.
**Habitat.** Slopes, open valleys with short grasses and rocky outcrops; damp or boggy, sloping areas with low bushes.
**Life-history.** LHPs *Festuca*; *Poa*; *Sesleria*. Larval development occupies two seasonal cycles.

## *Erebia sthennyo* False Dewy Ringlet                    Plate 86

**Range.** Pyrenees (Spain, France).

*E. sthennyo* Graslin 1850 TL: Bagnères de Bigorre, Pyrenees.
**Distribution.** Spain: C Pyrenees (Pto. de Portalet; Monte Perdido; Pto. de Beñasque). France: Pic du Midi d'Ossau to Pic du Midi de Bigorre and Luchon; Port de Salau to Andorra. Recorded just east of Andorra. Above 1800m.
**Description.** Resembles *E. pandrose*, but differs in the following respects: upf ocelli closer to outer margin; dark discal line and cellular striae absent or vestigial; unf basal and discal dark striae absent; male unh pale, almost uniform grey, unmarked: female unh greyish-brown, markings vestigial or absent. Differences in male genitalia small but constant.
**Flight-period.** Univoltine. Late June/early August.
**Habitat.** Grass-covered slopes with rocky outcrops.
**Note.** Occurs in close proximity to *E. pandrose* in some districts but not known to occupy same habitats.

## *Proterebia afra* Dalmatian Ringlet                    Plate 86

**Range.** Croatia (Dalmatia), NW Greece, Turkey, Crimea, Volga region, S Urals, NW and E Kazakhstan.

*P. afra dalmata* Godart 1824 TL: Sibenik, Dalmatia.
syn: *phegea* Borkhausen 1788
**Distribution.** Croatia: Dalmatian coastal districts (Zadar to Sibenik); island of Korcula. 150-500m. NW Greece: environs of Lake Vegoritis; Askion Mts.; Vourinos Mts. 550-1250m.
**Description and Variation.** Hw with precostal vein – cf. genus *Erebia*. Both sexes: ups and uns gc, size and number of ocelli and extent and colour of upf pale suffusion variable. In Greece, *pyramus* de Louker and Dils: wing-characters and male genitalia indistinguishable from *P. afra dalmata*.
**Flight-period.** Univoltine. End April/late May.
**Habitat.** Dry, grassy, sparsely bushy limestone slopes, often gentle and undulating, strewn with small rocks. Habitats distinctive and often characterised by scattered Juniper bushes as the dominant shrub.
**Life-history.** LHP *Fesctuca ovina*. The non-adhesive ova are sometimes ejected in small numbers into grass-tufts during hovering flight: a female may also use her recurved abdomen to guide two or three ova into the inverted conical base of a tuft of LHP whilst clinging to its outer stems. In extended photo-period of S England, development from ovum proceeds to completion (November/January) without diapause. Small differences in colouring of mature larvae allow separation of sexes: female larvae are slightly darker with greener tones. Hibernating stage in nature unknown. Pupa very dark, somewhat angular in shape – unlike that of genus *Erebia*.
**Behaviour.** Females often visit flowers of *Globularia* and yellow Asteraceae.

## *Maniola jurtina* Meadow Brown                    Plate 87

**Range.** Canary Islands, NW Africa, Europe, Turkey, N Iraq, N Iran to NW Kazakhstan, S and C Urals, W Siberia.

*M. jurtina* Linnaeus 1758 TL: Europe and Africa (Sweden Verity 1953).

**Distribution.** Widespread and common. Canary Islands: La Palma; Hierro; Gomera; N Tenerife; N Gran Canaria. NW Africa (0-2500m). Most of Europe south of 63°N, including Balearic Islands, Corsica, Sardinia, Capri, Malta, Corfu, Levkas, Kithera, Crete, most W Aegean islands and E Aegean islands of Limnos and Psara. 0-1600m.

**Variation.** In Canary Islands, NW Africa, Iberian Peninsula and SW France, *hispulla* Esper: larger; male resembles nominate form; unh size and number of ocelli variable: female ups yellow-orange areas extended; all uns markings bold, highly contrastive; dark basal area bordered by conspicuous yellow suffusion. Transitional to nominate form in S France, S Italy and S Greece. In Orkney Islands, NW Scotland, including Hebrides, Isle of Man, Ireland and Scilly Isles, *splendida* White: larger; male ups gc dark brown; upf orange-fulvous pd area often enclosing subapical ocellus and extending to s2, sometimes projecting to cell-end in s4 and s5: female upf yellow-orange pd band extending into discal area; uph pd area usually suffused orange. Ovum with 11-21 longitudinal ribs, regionally variable.

**Flight-period.** Univoltine. Late May/September with prolonged aestivation in southernmost range. In Scotland and Scandinavia, mid June/mid July according to season. In most of Greece, emergence date coincides with that of S England – first week of June. In S Portugal (Algarve), mid April/September. Canary islands, late March/late September according to altitude.

**Habitat.** Diverse. Grassy, bushy, often flowery places with an abundance of taller grasses; cultivated ground; woodland clearings or margins; heaths. On calcareous or acidic soils in dry or damp conditions.

**Life-history.** LHPs include *Poa pratensis*; *Lolium pratensis*; *Festuca rubra*; *F. arundinacea*; *Agrostis stolonifera*; *A. canina*; *Bromus erectus*; *Brachypodium pinnatum*; *Holcus lanatus*; *Avenula pubescens*; *Alopecurus pratensis*; *Anthoxanthum odoratum*. Pupal gc colour extremely variable – pale green to dark reddish-purple.

**Behaviour.** In S Europe, adults retire to shade and relative cool of bushes in hottest part of the day.

## *Maniola megala*                              Not illustrated

**Range.** Greece (Aegean island of Lesbos), SW and S central Turkey.

*M. megala* Oberthür 1909 TL: Akbes, Province of Hatay.

**Distribution.** In Europe, known only from E Aegean island of Lesbos.

**Description.** The following is based upon Turkish populations. Resembles *M. jurtina* in E Mediterranean region: appreciably larger; hw outer margin averagely more undulate: male unh pd ocelli larger, more numerous: female ups gc darker brown; all uns markings darker but sharply defined and highly contrastive. Ovum with 19-21 longitudinal ribs.

**Flight-period.** Data for Greece limited: univoltine in Turkey, early May/September, aestivating in summer.

**Note.** Habitat similar to that of *M. telmessia* with which it is known to occur.

## *Maniola chia* — Not illustrated

**Range.** Greece (Aegean Islands of Chios and Inousses).

*M. chia* Thomson 1987 TL: Chios,
**Distribution.** In Europe, known only from eastern Aegean islands of Chios and Inousses: widespread and common. 50–500m.
**Description.** Individual specimens superficially indistinguishable from *M. jurtina* found in eastern Mediterranean region, but genitalia and biochemical differences distinct. Ovum has 13–14 longitudinal ribs. (No other *Maniola* species is known from Chios or Inousses).
**Flight-period.** Univoltine. Late May/late September, aestivating in summer.
**Habitat.** Grassy, rocky and bushy places; cultivated ground.

## *Maniola nurag* Sardinian Meadow Brown — Plate 86

**Range.** Sardinia.

*M. nurag* Ghiliani 1852 TL: Mt. Gennargentu, Sardinia.
**Distribution.** Sardinia. Above 500m.
**Description.** Resembles *M. jurtina hispulla*. Both sexes: smaller, ups yellow-orange areas more extensive, especially in female. Male upf sex-brand conspicuous: female markings better developed, more sharply defined.
**Flight-period.** Univoltine. Late May/early August: females appear to aestivate.
**Habitat.** Grassy, flowery places amongst bushes and rocks.

## *Maniola telmessia* — Plate 87

**Range.** Greece (Aegean islands), Turkey, Jordan, Israel, Lebanon, Iraq, SW Iran.

*M. telmessia* Zeller 1847 TL: Marmaris, Province of Mugla (Olivier 1993).
**Distribution.** In Europe, known only from E Aegean islands: Lesbos; Samos; Ikaria; Fourni; Patmos; Leros; Telendos; Kalimnos; Pserimos; Kos; Tilos; Simi; Kassos; Rhodes; Karpathos; Kastellorizo. 0–1000m. An early record for the island of Angistri, close to Peloponnesian coast, has been discredited.
**Description and Variation.** Resembles *M. jurtina*. Male upf pd yellow-orange band, often enclosing subapical ocellus, extending to v2 and projecting to cell-end or slightly beyond in s4 and s5. On Karpathos, male upf and female ups yellow-orange areas more extensive. (*M. jurtina* is absent from range of *M. telmessia* in E Aegean islands). Ovum has 14–16 longitudinal ribs.
**Flight-period.** Univoltine. Late May/late September, aestivating in summer.
**Habitat.** Grassy, rocky and bushy places; cultivated ground.

## *Maniola halicarnassus* — Not illustrated

**Range.** SW Turkey, Greece (Aegean Island of Nissiros).

*M. halicarnassus* Thomson 1990 TL: Bodrum, Province of Mugla [SW Turkey].
**Distribution.** In Europe, known only from southern Aegean island of Nissiros. 50–100m.
**Description.** The following is based upon Turkish populations: resembles *M.*

*jurtina* but male upf sex-brand large, black, conspicuous, broad at inner margin, tapering towards cell – distinctly triangular in shape: female superficially indistinguishable from *M. telmessisa*. Both sexes averagely larger than *M. telmessisa*. Male genitalia distinguishable from those of *M. megala*, *M. chia* and *M. jurtina*. Ovum has 18 longitudinal ribs.

**Flight-period and Habitat.** In Bodrum Peninsula, SW Turkey: univoltine, late May/early September, with prolonged aestivation: occurs in bushy, flowery places in company with *M. telmessisa* with which it is suspected of hybridizing.
**Note.** Uniquely for genus *Maniola*, number of larval instars variable – five or six (cf. *M. telmessia*, five; *M. jurtina*, six).

## *Hyponephele maroccana* Moroccan Meadow Brown   Plate 88

**Range.** Morocco.

*H. maroccana maroccana* Blachier 1908 TL: High Atlas, Morocco.
**Distribution.** Morocco: High Atlas (Toubkal massif; Dj. Aourach). 1700-2800m.
**Description.** Male upf orange pd patch often extending into basal area; apical ocellus large, white-pupilled; smaller ocellus usually in s2; sex-brand narrow, smoothly curved; unh greyish-brown.
**Flight-period.** Univoltine. June/August: females may emerge up to 14 days later than males.
**Habitat.** Rocky places with sparse vegetation.
**Life-history.** Hibernation stage unconfirmed.
**Behaviour.** Has been observed 'hilltopping' on summit of Adra-n-Guinnous (2788m).

*H. maroccana nivellei* Oberthür 1920 TL: Dj. Hebri, Tizi-n-Taghzeft, Middle Atlas.
**Distribution.** Morocco: Middle Atlas (Tizi-n-Taghzeft; Col du Zad; Dj. Hebri); Rif Mts. (Dj. Lakraa; Dj. Tidiquin). 1800-2200m.
**Description.** Resembles nominate form: smaller; male upf orange pd area more restricted; apical ocellus small; ocellus in s2 vestigial or absent; unh gc paler greyish-brown: female ups ocelli averagely reduced.
**Flight-period, Habitat and Life-history.** As for nominate form.

## *Hyponephele lycaon* Dusky Meadow Brown          Plate 88

**Range.** Europe, Turkey, Israel, Lebanon to C Asia (Yenisey Valley) and Kyrgyzstan.

*H. lycaon* Kühn 1774 TL: Berlin.
**Distribution.** N Portugal, Spain (except SW), S France (except coastal areas) through N Italy, S Switzerland and Austria to S Finland, Balkans and Greece. Absent from NW Europe, Scandinavia, S peninsular Italy, European Turkey and Mediterranean islands except N Sicily. Widespread and locally common in SW and SE Europe: regionally sporadic,

local and often scarce in C and NE districts. 0-2100m.
**Description.** Male upf sex-brand narrow, disrupted by v2 and v3 (cf. *H. lupina*).
**Variation.** Unh gc variable; generally greyish or greyish-brown, often whitish in limestone habitats.
**Flight-period.** Univoltine. June/August.
**Habitat.** Diverse. Bushy, grassy places, usually amongst rocks.
**Life-history.** LHPs include *Festuca ovina*; *F. rubra*; *Bromus erectus*; *Stipa pennata*: two or more species may be used in a given habitat.
**Behaviour.** In hot conditions, adults often seek shade of bushes, overhanging rocks or tree roots on earthen banks.

## *Hyponephele lupina* Oriental Meadow Brown          Plate 88

**Range.** NW Africa, S Europe, Turkey, Israel, Jordan, Lebanon, Iraq, N Iran to Tian Shan and Altai.

*H. lupina* Costa 1836 TL: Otranto [SE Italy].
**Distribution.** Morocco and Algeria: locally common. 500-2400m. N Portugal: Serra da Estrêla. S, C and NE Spain. France: very local: Aude to Hautes-Alpes and Alpes-Maritimes. Italy: N and C Apennines; Salentina Peninsula; Calabria (Aspromonte); N Sicily. Croatia: Dalmatian coast; Island of Krk. Hungary: Deliblat; Flamenda. SE Romania: Danube delta. S Serbia. Republic of Macedonia. S Bulgaria. Greece, including Lesbos, Chios, Kos, Rhodes and Crete. European Turkey. 0-2000m.
**Description.** Male ups yellowish-brown with golden reflections; upf sex-brand broad, not broken by veins (cf. *H. lycaon*); hw undulate.
**Variation.** Regionally/locally variable in size, male ups gc, length and width of sex-brand. In N Africa, Iberian Peninsula and SE France, *mauritanica* Oberthür: male ups dark greyish-brown, golden reflections inconspicuous: female ups slightly paler than nominate form. In Sicily, Balkans and Greece, *rhamnusia* Freyer: resembles nominate form: larger; male ups paler, more yellowish-brown in discal and pd areas; sex-brand conspicuous: female resembles nominate form closely.
**Flight-period.** Univoltine. Mid May/mid August according to locality: females aestivate mid summer.
**Habitat.** Hot, dry, grassy and bushy places.

## *Aphantopus hyperantus* Ringlet          Plate 88

**Range.** Europe, N Caucasus, S and C Urals, S and W Siberia, Mongolia, Amur, NE China, Korea.

*A. hyperantus* Linnaeus 1758 TL: Europe (Sweden Verity 1953).
**Distribution.** From N Spain (Cantabrian Mts. to E Pyrenees) through much of Europe, including Ireland, England, Wales and S Scotland, to 65°N in Fennoscandia, Balkans and N Greece (Macedonia; Thessaly: very local). 0-1600m. Absent from peninsular Italy and Mediterranean islands.
**Description and Variation.** Unh without pd and ante-marginal metallic line; yellow-ringed ocelli in s5 and s6 displaced basad; s4 without ocellus (cf. *C. oedippus*). In N Britain: smaller; ups and uns gc tending

to greyish yellow-brown; ocelli often small; unh ocelli sometimes replaced by small white dots (f. *arete* Müller – sporadic in S England and C Europe): in SE Europe: large; all markings bold; uns gc brighter, with brassy golden reflections.
**Flight-period.** Univoltine. Mid June/late August.
**Habitat.** Grassy, bushy places; woodland clearings; in damp or dry situations.
**Life-history.** LHPs include, *Brachypodium sylvaticum*; *B. pinnatum*; *Phleum pratense*; *Dactylis glomerata*; *Festuca rubra*; *Bromus erectus*; *B. hordeaceus*; *Cynosurus cristatus*; *Poa pratensis*; *P. nemoralis*; *Carex hirta*; *C. strigosa*; *C.* (?)*sylvatica*; *C. brizoides*; *C. panicea*; *Agrostis capillaris*; *Milium effusum*; *Elymus repens*; *Holcus mollis*; *H. lanatus*; *Deschampsia cespitosa*; *Molinia caerulea*; *Arrhenatherum elatius*; *Calamagrostis epigejos*. Two or more species/genera are often used in a single habitat. Non-adhesive ova are ejected during slow, low-level flight. Larvae feed on grass-plants well-shaded by vegetation, especially bramble.

## *Pyronia tithonus* Gatekeeper                                    Plate 89

**Range.** Morocco, Spain to S Britain, Balkans, Greece and W Turkey.

*P. tithonus* Linnaeus 1771 TL: Germany.
**Distribution.** Morocco: Rif Mts.; Ketama 1500m: very local. From Iberian peninsula through most of Europe, including S Ireland and England, to N Germany, C Poland, Balkans, Greece and European Turkey. Absent from S Italy and Mediterranean islands except S Corsica and Sardinia. Generally and often abundant but distribution significantly disjunctive in many regions of C Europe. 0-1700m.
**Variation.** In S Europe, especially hot localities, unh gc often yellowish-buff (*decolorata* Frühstorfer).
**Flight-period.** Univoltine. Early July/early September according to locality.
**Habitat.** Grassy, flowery, bushy, often in damp/humid places, usually associated with deciduous or pine woodland.
**Life-history.** LHPs include, *Phleum pratense*; *Poa annua*; *P. nemoralis*; *P. trivialis*; *P. pratensis*; *Elymus repens*; *Agrostis capillaris*; *A. canina*; *Festuca ovina*; *F. rubra*; *F. pratensis*; *Lolium perenne*; *Dactylis glomerata*; *Milium effusum*. Non-adhesive ova sometimes deposited in grass-tufts or amongst other low-growing, bushy plants, but mostly ejected during low flight into grass-rich herbage. Larvae feed on well-shaded plants, often at margins of bramble patches or other dense shrubbery.

## *Pyronia cecilia* Southern Gatekeeper                           Plate 89

**Range.** Morocco, Algeria, Tunisia, Libya, Spain, S France, Italy, SW Balkans, W Greece, NW Turkey.

*P. cecilia* Vallantin 1894 TL: Morocco.
syn: *ida* Esper 1785 (invalid homonym)
**Distribution.** Morocco. Algeria. Tunisia. 0-2200m. Portugal. Spain: S of Cantabrian Mts. and W Pyrenees; Balearic Islands. France: E Pyrenees to Ardèche and Alpes-Maritimes; Corsica. Records from S Switzerland require confirmation. Italy: very few, isolated colonies in northern districts, wide-

spread S of Modena; Sardinia; Elba; Giglio; Sicily. Balkans: W coastal districts.
(?) Albania. W and S Greece, including Corfu and Levkas: very local. European Turkey. 0-1200m.
**Description.** Male upf androconial patch segmented.
**Variation.** In western range: unh brightly marbled pale grey and white. In
eastern range: duller grey with brownish tones.
**Flight-period.** Univoltine. Early June/mid August, according to locality.
**Habitat.** Hot, dry, sparsely grassy, rocky scrubland.
**Life-history.** LHP(s) uncertain: reported use of *Deschampsia cespitosa* requires
confirmation; distribution and ecology of *D. cespitosa* and recognized ssp. –
inhabitants of wet/damp grassland – appear to correlate poorly with that of the
butterfly. Captive larvae accept *Festuca ovina, Poa nemoralis, Brachypodium
sylvaticum, Dactylis glomerata and Agrostis capillaris.*

## *Pyronia bathsheba* Spanish Gatekeeper                Plate 89

**Range.** Morocco, Algeria, W Tunisia, SW Europe.

*P. bathsheba* Fabricus 1793 TL: Morocco ('Barbaris')
syn: *pasiphae* Esper 1781 (invalid homonym)
**Distribution.** Widespread, locally common. Morocco.
Algeria. W Tunisia. 700-1700m. Portugal. Spain: south of
Cantabrian Mts.; absent from NW. France: Pyrénées-
Orientales to Ardèche and Var. 300-1700m.
**Variation.** In Europe, *pardilloi* Sagarra: generally larger; unh
pale pd band wider; ocelli better developed. Intermediate
forms occur throughout Spain.
**Flight-period.** Univoltine. Late April/July, according to locality.
**Habitat.** Grassy, bushy places; often in light woodland.
**Life-history.** LHP *Brachypodium sylvaticum.*

## *Pyronia janiroides* False Meadow Brown                Plate 89

**Range.** C Algeria, W Tunisia.

*P. janiroides* Herrich-Schäffer 1851 TL: 'Spain' [in error for
Algeria]
**Distribution.** Widespread, locally common. NE Algeria. W
Tunisia. 500-1500m.
**Description.** Male upf orange pd band proximally bordered
by androconial patch; uph orange pd band wide; unh with
2-4 yellow pd ocelli in s2-s5, ocellus in s2 often with small,
dark pupil. Both sexes, upf and unf subapical twin ocelli with
white pupils (cf. *M. jurtina*).
**Flight-period.** Univoltine. July/early September.
**Habitat.** Dry, grassy, stony places amongst scrub.
**Life-history.** LHP *Poa annua.* Hibernation stage unconfirmed.

242   BUTTERFLIES OF EUROPE

## *Coenonympha tullia* Large Heath                    Plate 90

**Range.** N Europe, temperate Asia, N America.
Variation within and between colonies, even in small regions,
may be quite marked: wing-characters most affected are:-
ups gc, pale yellowish to ochreous-yellow or brownish; ups
and unh ocelli, prominent, vestigial or absent; unh basal and
discal coloration, light or darkish brown, less often greyish;
unh whitish pd areas, extensive to vestigial. The following
forms represent the overall range of variation. Flight-periods
and habitats are similar for each form. LHPs given for *C.*
*t. tullia* are widely used by other forms/sspp. In northern range, larval development
reputedly occupies two seasonal cycles. Apart from direct interference, habitats
are very sensitive to drainage/water extraction in adjoining areas: despite official
protection afforded this butterfly, as recently as 1995/96, a colony in N Belgium
(one of two known sites in this country) was reputedly eradicated by drainage
of nearby land – designated as a human recreational facility.

*C. tullia tullia* Müller 1764 TL: Fridrichsdal, Denmark.
syn: *philoxenus* Esper 1780
**Distribution.** Small colonies generally widely dispersed in Ireland, Wales, NE
England, SE Scotland and N Germany: widespread in Fennoscandia (including
Baltic Islands) to 70°N. 0-500m.
**Variation.** Transitional to *tiphon* Rottemburg (below) in some localities.
**Flight-period.** Univoltine. Mid June/early August according to locality.
**Habitat.** Peat bogs; raised bogs; blanket bogs; damp heaths bordering wetlands.
Most habitats contain scattered trees (birch and pine), low shrubs (willow and
bilberry) and are usually identifiable by the presence of cotton grass (*Eriophorum*
sp.). Absent from alkaline or fertile soils.
**Life-history.** LHPs include *Rhynochospora alba*; *Eriophorum vaginatum*; *E.*
*angustifolia*; *Carex rostrata*.

*C. tullia rothliebii* Herrich-Schäffer 1851 TL: not stated.
**Distribution.** NW England: very local. N Belgium: a single colony known
near Antwerp – possibly now extinct. A single colony is known from NE England
(Yorkshire), within the range of nominate form. Very sporadic in Germany,
perhaps elsewhere in C and E Europe.

*C. tullia tiphon* Rottemburg 1775 TL: Halle, W Germany.
**Distribution.** E and NE France: Savoie to Nièvre and Haut-Rhin; very
restricted in Aisne and Ardennes. S Belgium: a single colony known in Ardennes.
NW Switzerland: N of Rhône Valley to Jura Mts. Bavaria and N Austria to
Baltic states and N Balkans: widespread and local. Below 1200m. Absent from
Italy and S Austria.
**Variation.** Transitional to *tullia* in some localities: specimens resembling *scotica*
(below) occur as variants in Jura Mts.

*C. tullia scotica* Staudinger 1901 TL: Scotland.
**Distribution.** Scotland, including Hebrides and Orkney islands, north of a
line from Glasgow to Aberdeen: transition to *tullia* in SE Scotland sharply
delineated. Closely related forms occur in C Sweden. 0-800m.

**Variation.** Ups gc very pale yellow in some localties; ocelli often vestigial or absent. Seasonally variable.

*C. tullia demophile* Freyer 1844 TL: Lappland.
**Distribution.** N Fennoscandia. C Norway above 200m. 0-500m.
**Description.** Upf light yellowish-brown, with darker shading towards outer margin, uph uniformly darker; unh ocelli small, but usually present. Transitional to *tiphon* in S Finland and Baltic countries.

*C. tullia lorkovici* Sirajic and Cornalutti 1976.
**Distribution.** Bosnia-Herzegovina: district of Jaice.
**Description.** Resembles *rothliebii*: averagely much larger – male fw length 18-23mm, female 18-25mm.

## *Coenonympha rhodopensis* Eastern Large Heath     Plate 90

**Range.** C Italy, S Balkans, N Greece.

*C. rhodopensis* Elwes 1900 TL: Rila Mts., Bulgaria.
syn: *occupata* Rebel 1903; *italica* Verity 1913.
**Distribution.** Italy: C Apennines (Monti Sibillini; Monte Terminillo; Abruzzi); Monte Baldo. W Croatia: Velebit Mts. Bosnia-Herzegovina: Vranica Pl; Jahorina Pl. S Serbia: Mokra Pl.; Hajia Pl. Republic of Macedonia: on all higher mountains. (?) Albania. Romania: Retezat Mts. Bulgaria: Stara Pl.; Osogovo Mts.; Vitosha Mts.; Slavyanka Mts.; Pirin Mts.; Rila Mts.; Rhodopi Mts. N Greece: Varnous Mts.; Voras Mts.; Mt. Orvilous; Vrontous Mts.; Mt. Phalakron; Rhodopi Mts. 1400-2200m.
**Description and Variation.** In both sexes, unf pale, anterior pd stripe absent (cf. *C. tullia*). Unh white mark in s3-5 always present; pd ocelli in s2, s3 and s6 present, sometimes small. In Italy and some mountains in Bulgaria and Greece, f. *italica* Verity: unh ocelli of equal size, in complete series.
**Flight-period.** Univoltine. Mid June/late July.
**Habitat.** Open, windswept, grassy plains or slopes above treeline; sometimes damp forest clearings, e.g., Rhodope Mts. (Greece) and Vitosha Mts. (Bulgaria).
**Life-history.** In captivity, larvae pupate 'upside down' – with terminal posterior segment firmly attached to a stone or other rigid surface.

## *Coenonympha pamphilus* Small Heath     Plate 90

**Range.** N Africa, Europe, Turkey, Middle East, eastwards (40-60°N) to W Mongolia.

*C. pamphilus* Linnaeus 1758 TL: Sweden.
**Distribution.** NW Africa. 0-2700m. Throughout Europe including British Isles and most Mediterranean islands to 69°N in Fennoscandia. 0-1950m. Absent from Canary Islands, Azores, Madeira, Orkney Islands, Shetland Islands and Crete: not reported from SE Aegean Islands.
**Variation.** Unh gc variable, grey to brownish; unh pd ocelli sometimes vestigial or absent. In some localities in S Europe, especially in summer broods, ups dark borders slightly wider (f. *marginata* Rühl). In NW Africa and SW Europe, f. *lyllus* Esper: ups submarginal dark borders wider;

unf with diffuse black submarginal stripe in s1-5 and oblique reddish-brown pd bar in s2-6; unh basal and discal areas light sandy-brown, sometimes with well-defined, darker distal border; pd area pale creamy-buff; ocelli vestigial, often absent. All markings subject to appreciable variation: intermediate forms occur in Italy, S Balkans and Greece. In Sicily, *sicula* Zeller: resembles *C. thyrsis* Freyer (below).

**Flight-period.** Polyvoltine: number of broods and emergence of first brood greatly dependent on altitude and locality: February/November.

**Habitat.** Grassy places of very diverse character.

**Life-history.** LHPs include *Festuca ovina*; *F. rubra*; *Poa annua*; *Anthoxanthum odoratum*; *Cynosurus cristatus*; *Dactylis glomerata*; *Nardus stricta*. Ova sometimes laid on plant-stems other than those of LHP. A proportion of larvae from early broods hibernate, in addition to those of final brood. Larvae polymorphic: greenish or reddish-brown.

## *Coenonympha thyrsis* Cretan Small Heath          Plate 90

**Range.** Crete.

*C. thyrsis* Freyer 1845 TL: Crete.
**Distribution.** Crete: widespread, locally common. 0-1800m.
**Variation.** At higher altitudes: smaller; ups black marginal borders narrower; uns markings less prominent.
**Flight-period.** (?)Univoltine. Generally early May/early July according to altitude: recorded also in late July, August and early October (see Life-history).
**Habitat.** Grassy areas of diverse character, but reportedly showing preference for relatively damp areas, compared to those frequented by *C. pamphilus* on Greek mainland.

**Life-history.** Larval polymorphism similar to that of *C. pamphilus*. In extended photo-period of S England, larval development of summer progeny is completed rapidly without diapause, suggesting partial/complete bivoltinism or possibly polyvoltinism in nature. Hibernation stage unconfirmed.

**Note.** Apart from wing-morphology and voltinism, genitalia and antennae differ significantly from those of *C. pamphilus*.

## *Coenonympha corinna* Corsican Heath          Plate 90

**Range.** Corsica, Sardinia.

*C. corinna* Hübner 1804 TL: Sardinia.
**Distribution.** Corsica. Island of Capraia (NE of Corsica). Sardinia: widespread, locally common. 0-2000m: generally below 1200m.
**Description and Variation.** Unh pale pd band irregular; ocelli vestigial or absent except in s3 and s6, when present, ocelli in s2-4 co-linear. In second and (?)subsequent broods: ups dark marginal borders wider, that of upf sometimes with internal cuspidal projection along v3. On Island of Capraia, f. *trettaui* Gross: transitional to *C. elbana* (below).
**Flight-period.** Polyvoltine. Mid May/August.
**Habitat.** Grassy, bushy and rocky places; open woodland; margins of cultivation.

## *Coenonympha elbana* Elban Heath — Plate 90

**Range.** W Italy (Elba, Giglo and nearby mainland).

*C. elbana* Staudinger 1901 TL: Elba.

**Distribution.** W Italy: Islands of Elba, Giglio and Giannutri; coastal area of Tuscany (Mte. Calvi; Mte. Massoncello; Mte. Ballone; Mte. della Uccellina; Mte. Argentario; Grosseto). 0-800m.

**Description.** Unf dark antemarginal and submarginal lines prominent; unh pale pd band and proximal dark border almost linear in s2-s4; ocelli usually in complete series (cf. *C. corinna*).

**Flight-period.** Polyvoltine. Early May/September.

**Habitat.** Grassy, bushy places.

**Note.** Specific status not established: perhaps better regarded as form/ssp. of *C. corinna*.

## *Coenonympha dorus* Dusky Heath — Plate 91

**Range.** NW Africa, SW Europe to C Italy.

*C. dorus dorus* Esper 1782 TL: Toulouse, France.

**Distribution.** Portugal. Spain. France: Pyrénées-Orientales to Lozère, Haute-Alpes and Alpes-Maritimes; (?)Lot. Italy: very local: Maritime Alps; N and C Apennines. 100-1700m.

**Description.** Uph pd ocelli in s1c-4 in a proximally convex curved line – characteristic of nominate form and derivatives (cf. *C. vaucheri*).

**Variation.** Ups coloration and uns markings subject to considerable regional, local and individual variation. In NW Spain and N Portugal, *bieli* Staudinger: male ups darker, smokey-brown, ocelli vestigial; uns markings less contrastive, ocelli small: similar forms occur in E Spain and in some localities in S France. In C Italy, *aquilonia* Higgins: resembles *C. dorus*: male upf pd band, narrow, yellow-fulvous; unh pd ocelli small but series complete.

**Flight-period.** Univoltine. Early June/mid August.

**Habitat.** Dry, grassy and bushy places, often in woodland clearings; hot, dry rocky slopes and gullies, usually amongst scrub.

**Life-history.** LHPs *Agrostis canina*; *A. alba*; *Festuca ovina*.

*C. dorus fettigii* Oberthür 1874 TL: Province of Oran [Telaghre] Algeria.

**Distribution.** Morocco: Middle Atlas; High Atlas; Rif Mts. Algeria. Tunisia. 800-2200m.

**Description.** Male upf yellow-fulvous pd band sometimes extending into discal area; upf ocelli small or absent; unh discal area pale yellowish-grey, distal margin poorly defined except at anterior, paler pd area; ocelli very small, usually absent in s1, s4 and s5.

**Variation.** Subject to marked individual and regional/altitudinal variation with some wing-characters more stable in some populations: distributional and ecological relationship of named forms/ssp. unclear. In C and E Algeria and W Tunisia (800-1600m), *nicholasi* Rothschild: male ups orange pd area more extensive; unh gc paler; anterior pale pd area averagely larger: female marginal brown borders narrower. InW Morocco (800-2200m), *inframaculata* Oberthür: resembles *fettigii* closely: variable, especially in Rif Mts.

**Flight-period.** Univoltine. Mid June/late August according to locality and altitude.

**Note.** Accorded specific rank by some authors (see *C. dorus austauti* (below)).

*C. dorus austauti* Oberthür 1881 TL: Nemours, Algeria.

**Distribution.** NE Morocco: local: Beni-Snassen.W Algeria: Sounai; Nedroma; Maghnia; Lalla Marina; Zough-el-Beghal; Masser Mines. 600-900m.

**Description.** Resembles nominate form. Upf apical ocellus dark, large, blind, clearly ringed orange; uph series of blind pd ocelli usually complete; unh white-pupilled, orange ringed ocelli well developed; silver-grey antemarginal line conspicuous; proximal, central margin of pale discal band linear; antemarginal area of s1c-3 yellowish-buff. Similar forms occur in S Spain.

**Flight-period.** Univoltine. Mid June/early August.

**Habitat.** Dry, rocky places with sparse vegetation.

**Note.** Often accorded specific rank: in absence of biological data, extensive range of superficial variation of above taxa precludes definitive evaluation.

## *Coenonympha vaucheri* Vaucher's Heath                    Plate 91

**Range.** Morocco.

*C. vaucheri vaucheri* Blachier 1905 TL: High Atlas, Morocco.

**Distribution.** Morocco: High Atlas (Imilchil; Tizi-n-Test; Oukaïmeden;Tizi-n-Talremt; Amizmiz;Tizi-n-Melloul;Tizi-n-Tieta). 1800m to at least 3000m – a male was recorded at the summit of Dj.Toubkal (4167m) in June 1994.

**Description.** Male ups gc orange, sometimes largely obscured by dark fuscous suffusion; upf subapical ocellus, large, dark, blind, usually ovoid bridging s4 and s5 – distinctive; uph series of blind pd ocelli in s1c-4 almost linear (cf. *C. dorus*), occasional, smaller ocellus in s5 displaced basad; uns markings sharply defined; unf gc dusky-orange, contrasting with yellowish pd area; subapical ocellus with twin, silver-white pupils; unh dark, brownish basal area enclosing distinctive pale mark in cell; dark submarginal band enclosing small, white-pupilled ocelli in s1c-6; pale pd band distal edge irregular, with ray-like projections tending to penetrate submarginal band, especially along v4: female similar: larger; ups gc paler, generally lacking dark suffusion; markings better defined.

**Flight-period.** Univoltine. Late May/August or September according to season.

**Habitat.** Grassy slopes; more often, dry, rocky slopes with sparse vegetation.

**Life-history.** Hibernation stage unconfirmed.

*C. vaucheri annoceuri* Wyatt 1952 TL: Annoceur, Middle Atlas.

**Distribution.** Morocco: Middle Atlas (Tizi-Tarhzeft;Tizi-n-Taghzeft; Col du Zad;Tizi-bou-Zabel; Annoceur). 1800-2300m.

**Description.** Resembles nominate form. Usually smaller; ups brighter, lacking dark suffusion; ocelli smaller.

**Flight-period.** Univoltine. Late May/early August, according to season.

**Habitat and Life-history.** As for nominate form.

*C. vaucheri rifensis* Weiss 1979 TL: Dj. Lakraa, Rif Mts.

**Distribution.** Morocco:W Rif Mts. 1900-2200m.

**Description.** Resembles *annoceuri*. Small; ups and uns paler; upf subapical ocellus averagely smaller; unh submarginal band paler, contrasting poorly with pale pd band.
**Flight-period.** Univoltine. Late June/early August.
**Habitat and Life-history.** As for nominate form.

*C. vaucheri beraberensis* Lay and Rose 1979 TL: Tizi-n' Ouguerd-Zegzaoune, Morocco.
**Distribution.** Morocco: High Atlas (Tizi-n' Ouguerd-Zegzaoune; Dj. Aourach; Imlil; Lake Tislit). 2150-3000m.
**Description.** Resembles nominate form. Larger; ups pd areas sharply defined, paler somewhat yellowish; marginal dark borders heavy; upf and unf subapical ocellus larger, prominent; unf pale yellow pd and orange basal areas well-delineated, contrastive; unh markings indistinguishable from those of nominate form.
**Flight-period.** Univoltine. Mid June/July.
**Habitat.** Hot valleys and rocky slopes.
**Life-history.** Hibernation stage unconfirmed.
**Note.** Taxonomic relationship of above forms not clearly understood: overall *known* variation in most wing-characters very marked (cf. *C. dorus*).

## *Coenonympha arcania* Pearly Heath          Plate 91

**Range.** W Europe, Turkey, Transcaucasus, S Russia, S and C Urals.

*C. arcania* Linnaeus 1761 TL: Sweden.
syn: *amyntas* Poda 1761.
**Distribution.** From N and C Spain through most of Europe (except Britain) to Norway (Oslo Fjord), S Sweden (S of Uppland, including Öland and Gotland), Balkans, N and C Greece and European Turkey. 50-1800m.
**Description and Variation.** Unh irregular, creamy-white pd band and ocelli conspicuous, ocellus in s6 proximal to pd band (cf. *C. darwiniana*). In E Spain, *chlorinda* de Sagarra: uph inner margin fulvous-orange, sometimes extending to anal angle, variable.
**Flight-period.** Univoltine. Mid May/mid August in a prolonged emergence.
**Habitat.** Grassy, flowery, bushy places; damp or dry woodland clearings.
**Life-history.** LHPs *Poa pratensis*; *Melica ciliata*; *Holcus lanatus*.

## *Coenonympha darwiniana* Darwin's Heath          Plate 91

**Range.** Alps of France, S Switzerland and Italy .

*C. darwiniana* Staudinger 1871 TL: Switzerland (Valais).
**Distribution.** France: very local: Alpes-Maritimes; Alpes-de-Haute-Provençe. S Switzerland: restricted to southern alpine slopes (Valais to Graubunden). Italy: Venosta to Dolomites. 800-2100m.
**Description.** Unh ocelli ringed yellow, ocellus in s6 contained within white pd band (cf. *C. arcania*).
**Flight-period.** Univoltine. Early June/August.
**Habitat.** Flowery, grassy places.

248     BUTTERFLIES OF EUROPE

## *Coenonympha gardetta* Alpine Heath     Plate 91

**Range.** France, Italy, S Switzerland, Germany and Austria.

*C gardetta* de Prunner 1798 TL: Val Varaita, Alpes-Maritimes. syn: *satyrion* Esper 1804; *philea* Hübner 1800 (invalid homonym); *neoclides* Hübner 1805.
**Distribution.** France: NE Massif Central; Alpes-Maritimes; Basses Alpes. Italy: Cottian Alps to Dolomites. S Switzerland: Valais to Engadine. Germany: Bavarian Alps. Austria: Tirol; Karawanken Mts. Reported from mountains of Bosnia-Herzegovenia, SW Serbia (Kopaonik Pl.) and Albania. 800-2900m: rarely below 1500m.
**Description and Variation.** Ups extensively or entirely greyish; unh ocelli not ringed yellow, usually enclosed in white pd band (cf. *C. darwiniana*). At lower altitudes, f. *macrophthamica* Stauder: upf basal area often with fulvous-orange flush; upf with small apical ocellus; unh ocelli larger.
**Flight-period.** Univoltine. Late June/mid September according to altitude.
**Habitat.** Exposed alpine meadows at higher altitude; grassy slopes with sparse bushes and trees at lower levels.

## *Coenonympha arcanioides* Moroccan Pearly Heath   Plate 92

**Range.** Morocco, N Algeria, N Tunisia.

*C. arcanioides* Pierret 1837 TL: Oran, Algeria.
**Distribution.** Morocco. N Algeria. N Tunisia. Local but widespread from coastal hills to northern slopes of Middle Atlas. 0-1800m.
**Description.** Upf gc fulvous; dark fuscous outer marginal border and apex enclosing small, subapical blind ocellus; uph dark fuscous with submarginal orange line in anal angle; unf discal area dusky orange, sharply divided from paler pd band; subapex, inner and outer margins greyish; subapical yellow-ringed, white-pupilled ocellus large, conspicuous; unh gc dark brown; irregular white pd band prominent; small, white-pupilled pd ocelli usually present in s1c-5; fw and hw with metallic antemarginal line: female similar: larger; ups paler.
**Flight-period.** Polyvoltine. April/September.
**Habitat and Behaviour.** Dry, rocky, grassy places amongst scrub, often in gullies near oleander bushes and broom ((?)*Genista* sp.) amongst which adults often secrete themselves when disturbed.
**Life-history.** Hibernation stage unconfirmed.

## *Coenonympha leander* Russian Heath     Plate 92

**Range.** S Balkans, N Greece, Turkey, NW Iran, Transcaucasus, S Urals.

*C. leander* Esper 1784 TL: Russia, Volga.
**Distribution.** Locally common. Romania: S Carpathian Mts. Republic of Macedonia. Bulgaria. N Greece: Varnous Mts.; Vernon Mts.; Askion Mts.; N Pindos Mts.; E Thrace. 350-1900m.
**Variation.** In Pindos Mts. (Tzoumérka Mts. to Grammos Mt. 1000-1900m),

*orientalis* Rebel: resembles nominate form except unh white ocellular rings confluent, extending proximally to form prominent pd band; variable, some individuals transitional to nominate form.
**Flight-period.** Univoltine. Generally mid May/early August according to altitude and locality: in NE Greece, mid April/May.
**Habitat.** Warm, grassy, flowery, bushy woodland margins/clearings.
**Life-history.** Captive larvae accept *Festuca ovina*; *Brachypodium sylvaticum*.

## *Coenonympha glycerion* Chestnut Heath                    Plate 92

**Range.** Europe, Russia, N Kazakhstan, Mongolia.

*C. glycerion glycerion* Borkhausen 1788 TL: not stated.
syn: *iphis* Denis and Schiffermüller 1775 (invalid homonym)
**Distribution.** France: E Pyrenees; Massif Central; Provençe to Ardennes. Italy: W Ligurian Alps to Cottian Alps; Venosta; C Apennines. Switzerland to S Finland, Balkans and N Greece (Rhodopi Mts.). 250-2100m, generally below 1800m.
**Description.** Unh white discal marks in s1c and s4 distinctive; pd white-pupilled ocelli uneven in size, variable; orange antemarginal line in anal angle.
**Variation.** Unh markings, size and number of ocelli subject to marked regional variation: unh ocelli sometimes absent (f. *bertolis* Prunner), especially at higher altitudes.
**Flight-period.** Univoltine. Early June/late August according to locality.
**Habitat.** Grassy, bushy places; woodland clearings: in damp or dry conditions.
**Life-history.** LHPs *Brachypodium sylvaticum*; *Cynosurus cristatus*; *Briza media*; *Melica ciliata*; *Bromus erectus*; *B. hordeaceus*.

*C. glycerion iphioides* Staudinger 1870 TL: Castile, Spain.
**Distribution.** Spain: Cantabrian Mts. and Pyrenees to Montes Universales. 600-1600m. Not reported from Portugal.
**Description.** Resembles *C. glycerion*: larger; upf apical ocellus absent; unh pd series of ocelli complete. Transitional to nominate form at higher altitudes in Pyrenees and Montes Universales (f. *pearsoni* Romei). Darker, somewhat greyish forms occur on damp acidic soils.
**Flight-period.** Univoltine. Late May/August.
**Habitat.** As for nominate form.
**Note.** Considered specifically distinct by some authors.

## *Coenonympha hero* Scarce Heath                    Plate 92

**Range.** NE France, S Scandinavia, C Europe, S and C Urals, Tobol River, W Siberia, Mongolia, Amur, Korea, Japan.

*C. hero* Linnaeus 1761 TL: S Sweden.
**Distribution.** Colonies generally very small, few in number and widely dispersed. France: Allier; Nièvre; Saône-et-Loire; Ain; Jura; Haut Rhin; Bas Rhin; Seine-et-Marne; Meuse; Moselle. NW, NE and C Switzerland. S and E Germany. N

Austria. Poland to S Fennoscandia (Denmark, only on
Sjælland) and Baltic states. 50-700m.
**Description.** Ups very dark brown; uph ocelli prominent;
unh ocellus in s6 not displaced basad; pd ocelli with irregular
proximal pale band; antemarginal silver-grey and orange lines
conspicuous (cf. *C. oedippus*).
**Flight-period.** Univoltine. Mid May/early July according
to season and locality.
**Habitat.** Damp or wet meadows dominated by grasses,
usually on infertile, peat-based soils; less often drier, grassy woodland clearings
or herb-rich, flowery meadows.
**Life-history.** LHPs *Leymus arenarius* [=*Elymus arenarius*]; *Hordeum marinum*;
*Hordelymus europaeus*.
**Conservation.** One of the more seriously threatened of the European species:
in rapid decline in many regions. Despite well-publicized European legislation
to protect endangered European butterfly species, the essential, concomitant
need to afford *equivalent* protection to habitats appears to have been largely or
entirely ignored. In the case of *C. hero*, conversion of habitats to conifer or
poplar plantations continues.

## *Coenonympha oedippus* False Ringlet                    Plate 92

**Range.** Europe, W Russia, Urals, S and W Siberia, N Kazakhstan, Mongolia, China, Japan.

*C. oedippus* Fabricus 1787 TL: S Russia.
**Distribution.** Very sporadic, usually extremely local:
Pyrénées-Atlantiques to Charante-Maritime and Charante;
Sarthe; Seine-et-Marne; Savoie; Isère. Switzerland: Rhine
Valley; Tessin. Italy: Varese; Treviso; Friuli-Venezia Giulia.
Slovenia. Austria. Poland. Hungary. (?)Albania. No recent
records from Germany or Bulgaria. Extinct in Belgium.
Records for N Spain require confirmation. 150-500m.
**Description and Variation.** Unh ocellus in s6 displaced basad (cf. *C. hero*);
ocellus in s5 (often very small) not displaced basad (cf. *A. hyperanthus*). Unh
pale band proximal to pd ocelli variable, often absent. In some localities in
Austria and Hungary, *hungarica* Rebel: ups and uns ocelli reduced, locally
variable, rarely absent on female uph.
**Flight-period.** Univoltine. Early June/early August.
**Habitat.** Wet meadows and peripheral areas of damp, grassy, open scrubland,
invariably associated with rivers or lakes.
**Life-history.** LHPs *Poa palustris*; *P. pratensis*; *P. annua*.
**Conservation.** A seriously threatened species – circumstances pertaining to
*C. hero* apply equally to *C. oedippus*.

## *Pararge aegeria* Speckled Wood                         Plate 93

**Range.** N Africa, Europe, Turkey, Israel, Syria, Transcaucasus, S and C Urals.

*P. aegeria aegeria* Linnaeus 1758 TL: S Europe and Algeria.
syn: *vulgaris* Zeller 1847.

**Distribution.** Widespread and common. NW Africa: north-ern coast to southern slopes of High Atlas. 0-2500m. Iberian Peninsula. Balearic Islands. SW and S France. S Switzer-land. Italy. Corsica. Sardinia. Sicily. Aegean Islands of Crete, Lesbos, Samos, Kos and Karpathos. Not reported from Rhodes. First noted on Madeira in 1976, now widespread. 0-1500m.

**Description.** In both sexes: gc orange; fw outer margin concave below subapex; (cf. *P. xiphioides* and *P. xiphia*).

**Variation.** From NW France to Maritime Alps, eastwards into C France, tran-sitional to *tircis* (below): intermediate forms also occur in SW Britain (Scilly Isles and Channel Islands), S Greece (Peloponnesos) and Samos. In exceptionally hot summers, specimens with gc corresponding to nominate form have been reported from C England. In NW Africa, unh gc pale buff to dark, reddish-brown.

**Flight-period.** Bivoltine or trivoltine, late February/early October according to locality and altitude.

**Habitat.** Deciduous, coniferous and mixed woodland. In hot localities of S Europe, often associated with treelined rivers or small streams.

**Behaviour.** Prefers shady areas with dappled sunlight, where males often bask on sunlit leaves or woodland floor. Males are very territorial.

**Life-history.** LHPs include *Brachypodium sylvaticum*; *B. pinnatum*; *Holcus lanatus*; *Cynodon dactylon*; *Agrostis gigantea*; *Dactylis glomerata*; *Elymus repens* [= *Triticum repens*; *Agropyron repens*; *Elytrigia repens*]. Madeira, *B. sylvaticum*. Hibernates as a larva or pupa.

*P. aegeria tircis* Butler 1867 TL: France.
syn: *egerides* Staudinger 1871.

**Distribution.** British Isles, C and E France, N and C Switzerland to 64°N in Fennoscandia (including Baltic Islands), Balkans and Greece, Corfu, Thassos, Lesbos and European Turkey. 0-1750m.

**Description.** Resembles nominate form: in both sexes, gc yellow or creamy-white.

**Variation.** In southern range, gc of late broods tends towards that of nominate form.

**Flight-period.** Bivoltine. Late March/mid June and late June/early October.

**Habitat and Life-history.** As for nominate form.

**Note.** Circumstances relating to variation in gc suggest strong ecological influence (temperature/humidity). Although phenotype of populations of Thassos and Lesbos (NE Aegean Islands) has not been reported, these islands fall within geographical range of *tircis* (widespread in N Turkey; recorded from Gelibolu Peninsula and some coastal sites in NW Turkey: replaced by nominate form in S Turkey).

## *Pararge xiphiopides* Canary Speckled Wood                   Plate 93

**Range.** Canary Islands.

*P. xiphioides* Staudinger 1871 TL: Canary Islands.
**Distribution.** Canary Islands: Gomera; La Palma; Tenerife; Gran Canaria. 200-2000m.
**Description.** Fw outer margin linear: unh with white band extending from costa to cell (cf. *P. xiphia*).

**Flight-period.** Polyvoltine. Recorded throughout the year.

**Habitat.** Laurel and Chestnut forests; less often in Pine or other woodland.

**Life-history.** LHPs: Tenerife, *Brachypodium sylvaticum*; *Carex divulsa*; *Agrostis tenuous*; *Luzula forsteri*; *Oryzopsis miliacea*; *Dactylis glomerata*: La Palma, *Brachypodium sylvaticum*; *B. pinnatum*. Hibernation stage unconfirmed.

## *Pararge xiphia* Madeiran Speckled Wood — Plate 93

**Range.** Madeira.

*P. xiphia* Fabricius 1775 TL: Madeira

**Distribution.** Madeira. 0-1000m.

**Description.** Fw outer margin slightly convex: unh with small white mark on costa (cf. *P. xiphioides*).

**Flight-period.** Polyvoltine. Recorded in all months with no apparent discontinuity but with reduced abundance June/August.

**Habitat.** Laurel and chestnut forests.

**Life-history.** LHPs *Brachypodium sylvaticum*; *Holcus lanatus*; *Agrostis gigantea*. Hibernation stage unconfirmed.

## *Lasiommata megera* Wall Brown — Plate 94

**Range.** N Africa, Europe, Turkey, Israel, Lebanon, Syria, Iraq, Iran, Transcaucasus, Turkmenistan.

*L. megera* Linnaeus 1767 TL: Austria and Denmark.

**Distribution.** Widespread and common. N Africa. 0-3000m. Most of Europe, from Ireland, S Scotland, S Scandinavia (including Baltic Islands), S Lithuania, S Latvia (possibly extinct) to Iberian peninsula, S Greece, European Turkey and most Mediterranean islands. Absent from N Denmark, Estonia and Finland. 0-2300m.

**Description.** Upf with two, transverse cellular bars (cf. *L. maera*).

**Variation.** Both sexes, unh gc brownish in N Europe, greyish in S Europe. On Corsica, Sardinia, Capraia, Montecristo and Balearic Islands, *paramegaera* Hübner: resembles nominate form, but smaller; upf dark pd lines in s1b and s2 thinner or vestigial; uph irregular pd band absent. Transitional forms occur with nominate form in Balearic Islands and Sicily.

**Flight-period.** Bivoltine or trivoltine. Early April/October according to locality and altitude.

**Habitat.** Diverse. Grassy, rocky slopes/gullies; flowery meadows; woodland clearings associated with open stony ground, paths etc.

**Life-history.** LHPs include *Dactylis glomerata*; *Agrostis tenuis*; *A. gigantea*; *A. capillaris*; *Deschampsia flexuosa*; *Holcus lanatus*; *Festuca ovina*; *Brachypodium sylvaticum*; *B. pinnatum*.

**Behaviour.** Males are very alert and easily disturbed from paths, stones, rock faces or walls on which they often bask. Shelter provided by overhanging rocks are favoured roosting sites. Commonly found 'hilltopping': recorded near summit of Dj. Toubkal, High Atlas (4160m).

**Note.** Population of Sardinia and (?)Corsica accorded specific status (*L. tigellius* Bonelli 1826) by some authors.

## *Lasiommata maera* Large Wall Brown                    Plate 94

**Range.** N Africa and Europe to W Siberia and Tian Shan.

*L. maera maera* Linnaeus 1758 TL: Sweden (Verity 1953).
syn: *monotonia* Schilde 1885; *hiera* Fabricus 1777.
**Distribution.** Morocco. Middle Atlas; Rif Mts. Algeria:
Djurdjura massif. Records for Tunisia require confirmation.
800-2500m. From Iberian Peninsula (except SW), Sicily,
Greece and European Turkey (including many Ionian and
Aegean Islands) through most of Europe to 68°N in Fenno-
scandia (including Öland). Absent from Britain, N Belgium,
Holland, NW Germany, Denmark, N Finland, Balearic Islands, Corsica, Sardinia
and Crete. 0-2000m.

**Description and Variation.** Upf with one transverse cellular bar (cf. *L. megera*);
uph without transverse discal line (cf. *L. petropolitana*); unh gc variable, light
grey to greyish-brown. In Fennoscandia, f. *borealis* Fuchs: smaller; ups dark
suffusion more extensive, but upf subapical yellow/orange patch retained. In
Iberian Peninsula and Mediterranean region, f. *adrasta* Illiger: female upf orange-
fulvous pd area extended towards base: second brood smaller; ups orange
markings more extensive.

**Flight-period.** Univoltine in north, mid June/late August; bivoltine in south,
late April/June and June/late September. Reported trivoltinism in NW Africa
requires confirmation.

**Habitat.** Dry, grassy, rocky or stony places, including steep slopes and screes.

**Life-history.** LHPs include *Glyceria fluitans*; *Deschampsia flexuosa*; *Calamagrostis epigejos*; *C. arundinacea*; *C. varia*; *Nardus stricta*; *Hordeum marinum*; *Agrostis
capillaris*; *Luzula luzuloides*; *Holcus mollis*; *Festuca rubra*; *F. ovina*.

**Behaviour.** Recorded 'hilltopping' in Atlas Mts., and at 2900m in Sierra Nevada.

*L. maera meadewaldoi* Rothschild 1917 TL: Tizi Gourzá, Morocco.
syn: *alluaudi* Oberthür 1922.
**Distribution.** Morocco: High Atlas; known only from Toubkal massif (Tizi
Gourzá; Oukaïmeden; Tizi-n-Test). 2100-3700m, more generally 2200-3200m.

**Description.** Resembles nominate form: larger (male fw 27-30mm; female fw
up to 32mm); male ups gc rusty-brown; unf gc dull yellow-orange with greyish
tone; unh gc greyish-brown: female ups gc dull fulvous-orange; unf fulvous-
orange; unh gc grey-brown: in both sexes, ups and uns ocellular white pupils
prominent.

**Flight-period.** Voltinism uncertain: possibly univoltine. Generally mid June/
August; records span late May/early September.

**Habitat.** Rocky slopes; cliffs; barren mountain ridges; steep grassy slopes –
more usually, females frequent the latter habitat.

**Note.** Regarded as specifically distinct by some authors. Known circumstances
of occurrence suggest possible ecological influence on size, wing-markings and
voltinism. Univoltinism, relating to cooler conditions prevalent at higher altitude,
implies an extended period available for larval development, resulting in larger
imagines relative to bivoltine forms at lower altitude. Adaptive alteration in wing-
colour/pattern is also not unexpected: within the European range of the species,
a correlation of phenotype and voltinism with climatic conditions is apparent.

## *Lasiommata petropolitana* Northern Wall Brown Plate 94

**Range.** Pyrenees, eastwards on most larger mountain massifs to Fennoscandia, N Turkey, N Siberia and Amur.

*L. petropolitana* Fabricius 1787 TL: Petrograd.
syn: *hiera* auct.
**Distribution.** Generally local. Higher mountain ranges of S Europe from Pyrenees, through Central Alps to Carpathian Mts., Balkans and N Greece. 500-2250m. Also, Norway, Sweden (including Gotland), Finland, Latvia and Estonia. 100-1200m. Absent from (?) Spain, Andorra, Massif Central, Denmark, Peninsular Italy, S Greece and Mediterranean islands.
**Description.** Uph with irregular, transverse discal line (cf. *L. maera*).
**Flight-period.** Univoltine. Late April/early August according to altitude. Possibly a partial second brood at low altitudes in southern range.
**Habitat.** Grassy, stony, sandy or rocky banks and gullies in woodland clearings or margins.
**Life-history.** LHPs include *Calamagrostis epigejos*; *Festuca ovina*; *Dactylis glomerata*. Hibernates as a larva or pupa.
**Behaviour.** Adults often rest on bare ground or fallen tree-trunks. Shelter provided by overhanging rock-ledges or exposed tree-roots on earthen banks are favoured roosting/resting sites.

## *Lopinga achine* Woodland Brown Plate 95

**Range.** C Europe, Russia and NC Asia to Amur, Yssuri and Japan.

*L. achine* Scopoli 1763 TL: Carniola.
syn: *deianira* Linnaeus 1764.
**Distribution.** (?)N Spain: province of Vizcaya. France (C Pyrenees), through Switzerland (Jura; Valais; Tessin), N Italy (N of Po Valley to Julian Alps), Germany to SE Sweden (Östergötland; Gotland), Baltic states (including Dagö and Ösel), S Finland, N and E Balkans, (?)S Romania and (?)NE Bulgaria (first and last record 1902). Absent from Britain, Belgium, Holland, NW Germany and Denmark. 200-1500m. Generally very sporadic and local: reputedly in decline in France, Switzerland and N Italy.
**Variation.** Uns pale band, proximal to pd spots, variable in width and colour.
**Flight-period.** Univoltine. Early June/late July.
**Habitat.** Grassy, bushy, often small clearings, in deciduous woodland; bushy margins of coniferous forests/plantations: in damp or dry conditions on calcareous and non-calcareous soils.
**Life-history.** LHPs *Brachypodium sylvaticum*; *B. pinnatum*.

## *Ypthima asterope* African Ringlet Plate 95

**Range.** Greece (Aegean Islands), Turkey, Middle East to India, Africa.

*Y. asterope* Klug 1832 TL: Syria and SW Saudi Arabia.
**Distribution.** Greece: known only from E Aegean Islands of Samos, Rhodes,

Simi and Kastellorizo. 0-250m.
**Flight-period.** Polyvoltine. Early April/late October.
**Habitat.** Hot, stony, grassy places; dry stream-beds.
**Life-history.** Captive larvae accept *Poa annua*.

## *Kirinia roxelana* Lattice Brown                   Plate 95

**Range.** SE Europe, Turkey, Cyprus, Israel, Lebanon, Syria,
N Iraq, W Iran.

*K. roxelana* Cramer 1777 TL: Istanbul.
**Distribution.** Widespread but local. SW Croatia (Dalmatian
coast). S Bosnia-Herzegovina. Serbia. S Romania. Albania.
Republic of Macedonia. Bulgaria. Greece, including Corfu,
Levkas and most E Aegean islands. European Turkey. Not
reported from Crete. 0-1750m.
**Flight-period.** Univoltine. Late April/September, according
to locality. Fertilized females, along with a small number of males, appear to
aestivate in hottest/driest summer months.
**Habitat.** Generally hot, dry bushy places, often in light, pine woodland: less
often in cooler, damper conditions at higher altitudes.
**Life-history.** Ova are laid in bark crevices on well-shaded bushes or trees.
Unfed larvae sometimes enter brief diapause: feeding appears to be initiated by
moisture and reduced temperature. Larvae, unusual and distinctive: long in
proportion to width; pale green with paler, longitudinal stripes mimicking the
veins and glossy reflections of grass-blades; posterior segment slender, with
long 'tails'; head with two, lateral, slender, forward-projecting processes –
resembling 'horns'. The small larva rests vertically in the fold of a wide grass-
blade with the tips of its 'tails' and 'horns' splayed side-ways, coincident with
leaf-edges: thus positioned, the larva closely resembles a small, green spider
and is well camouflaged.
**Behaviour.** Both sexes appear to spend much time in the interior, often deep
shade of bushes, thickets or small trees: adults quickly retreat to such cover
when disturbed. Males sometimes roost amongst rocks in exposed places,
females more usually in bushes. In hot, calm conditions, both sexes sometimes
gather at dusk in appreciable numbers on stony beds of dry watercourses, from
which they are easily disturbed during early hours of darkness.

## *Kirinia climene* Lesser Lattice Brown             Plate 95

**Range.** SE Europe, Turkey, Ukraine, Caucasus, N Iran.

*K. climene* Esper 1783 TL: not stated.
**Distribution.** Very local and sporadic. (?)E Serbia. (?)SW
Romania. (?)NE Albania. Republic of Macedonia: near
Skopje, Gostivar, Lake Ochrid and Lake Prespa. NW Bul-
garia: reported from Sliven (SE Stara Pl.) in 1896; presently
known only from Vratsa (Gorna Kremena). NW Greece: N
Pindos Mts.; Limni Mikri Préspa. 700-1600m. Records for
district of Drama, N Greece require confirmation.
**Variation.** Uph orange pd band variable, sometimes absent: female unh gc

usually yellowish, less often greyish.

**Flight-period.** Univoltine. Mid June/late July.

**Habitat.** Grassy, bushy clearings in damp or dry mature deciduous or mixed woodland.

**Life-history.** Larva closely resembles that of *K. roxelana*. Larvae feed on a robust, wide-stemmed grass. Larger larvae rest on stems opposite to a developing inflorescence: thus situated, a larva appears as an extension of the stem-node, rendering detection difficult.

**Behaviour.** Adults often visit the forest canopy, where they roost on tree-trunks or underside of thicker tree-branches.

257

# Hesperiidae Latreille 1809

This ancient and cosmopolitan family is readily distinguished from all other butterflies by several structural characters. The head of the adult insect is large, having similar proportions to the thorax, which itself is robust. The eyes are large and the distinctive antennae widely separated. Wing-veins are unbranched throughout their length. Males of the genera *Pyrgus*, *Muschampia* and *Carcharodus* have a costal fold on the fore-wing containing androconia. All species have a characteristic flight, some flying very fast and close to the ground. Some are known or suspected migrants. Larvae are usually cylindrical but in some genera tend to be bulbous in the posterior segments. The head is large. In some genera, a 'collar' immediately behind the head may be marked with conspicuous white or yellow spots. In all European species for which the life-history is known, larvae live, feed and pupate in the security of shelters formed from leaves held in place by silk. Modification to the design of these structures may occur during larval development, a sequence of events well-illustrated by the genus *Pyrgus*, whose staple host-plants are species of *Potentilla* – plants with palmate, that is, three or five-lobed leaves. Newly-hatched larvae feed singly on the concealed surfaces of overlapping leaves, drawn loosely together by a few strands of silk. Increasingly elaborate and secure constructions are employed in later instars. Half-grown larvae roll up individual leaves to form a tightly closed tubular tent, whereas larvae in their final instar adopt an entirely logical engineering strategy in which the outer edges of the three central lobes of a palmate leaf are drawn together, whilst the excess length of the central lobe is pulled down so as to form the lid of an irregular tetrahedron – a box. These structures are remarkably strong and difficult to tease open: situated on the more robust stems of the host-plant or concealed at its base amongst leaf litter; they also serve as hibernacula or pupation sites.

## *Pyrgus malvae* Grizzled Skipper — Plate 97

**Range.** Europe, NW Turkey, Tian Shan, Mongolia, N China, Korea.

*P. malvae malvae* Linnaeus 1758 TL: Aland Island, Finland.
**Distribution.** From W France, Wales, S England, N and C Switzerland and N and E Austria to 65°N in Fennoscandia (including Baltic Islands), S Greece (including Lesbos) and European Turkey. Absent from Iberian peninsula, SW and S France and Italy – replaced by *P. malvae malvoides* (below). 0-1900m.
**Variation.** Aberrations with greatly extended and sometimes confluent white markings upf are not uncommon, especially in Greece.
**Flight-period.** Univoltine (May/early July) or bivoltine (April/early June and late July/August) according to locality and altitude. Univoltine in N Europe, also in Greece and perhaps elsewhere in SE Europe.
**Habitat.** Diverse. Grassy, flowery places.
**Life-history.** LHPs *Potentilla recta*; *P. sterilis*; *P. tabernaemontani*; *P. pedata*; *P. palustris*; *P. erecta*; *P. anglica*; *P. argentea*; *Fragaria vesca*; *Agrimonia eupatoria*; *Rubus*

*fruticosus*. Hibernates as a pupa. In captivity, diapause may extend over two seasonal cycles.

*P. malvae malvoides* Elwes and Edwards 1897 TL: Biarritz.
**Distribution.** Spain. Portugal. W and S France (Charante-Maritime through Massif Central to Haute-Savoie). SE Switzerland (S Engadine). SW Austria (S of Innsbruck). Italy, including Istria and Sicily. Absent from Balearic Islands, Corsica and Sardinia. 0-1800m. Exact distributional relationship with nominate form uncertain.
**Description and Variation.** Wing-markings as for nominate form: male genitalia distinct. Interbreeds freely with nominate form in areas of distributional overlap, producing hybrids of intermediate character in male genitalia. In C Spain, ups white markings often reduced in second brood.
**Flight-period.** Generally bivoltine, April/June and late July/August: univoltine at high altitudes, June/July.
**Habitat.** As for nominate form.
**Life-history.** LHP: S Spain, *Potentilla pensylvanica*. Hibernates as a pupa.

## *Prygus melotis*                          Not illustrated

**Range.** Turkey, Israel, Lebanon, Jordan, Syria, (?)N Iraq, Transcaucasus.

*P. melotis* Duponchel 1834. TL: Lebanon.
**Distribution.** According to *Guide des Papillons d'Europe* (Higgins and Riley, translated and adapted by Bourgoin 1988), this species occurs on the Kykladian island of Melos [= Milo or Milos]. Equivalent information is not given in any original, English edition of this field guide. Staudinger (1870), Seitz (1906) and de Jong (1972) refer to the presence of the species on Melos. Warren (1926) also mentions 'the island of Milo' in quoting Greece amongst... 'the only reliable records I can find for Europe'. Of the five, poorly labelled, Greek specimens extant in the collection of the Natural History Museum, London, none of the data-labels refer specifically to this island or give locality data more precise than 'Greece': a large and remotely located label referring to 'Is of Milo' is pinned in the case carrying these and many other specimens including those of other *Pyrgus* species. The most recent of the five specimens is a male taken by Elwes in 1962; the only reference to site of capture are the letters 'GR'. A search for *P. melotis* on Melos by Mr J. G. Coutsis of Athens in May 1985 proved negative.
**Description.** Unh extensive white, somewhat striated suffusion is very striking, rendering this species quite unlike any other European member of the genus.

## *Pyrgus alveus* Large Grizzled Skipper                Plate 97

**Range.** N Africa, Spain, Europe, Turkey, Transcaucasus, S and W Siberia, Urals, Transbaikal, Mongolia, N China.

*P. alveus alveus* Hübner 1803 TL: Germany.
**Distribution.** From W and C France (Massif Central; Jura Mts.; Vosges Mts.: very local and sporadic in other regions) through S Belgium to 60°N in Norway, Sweden (including Öland and Gotland), Baltic states and Finland, Balkans and Greece (local but widespread in northern and central mountains:

very local and scarce above 1400m on Mt. Chelmos). Absent from Britain, NW France, Holland, N Germany and Denmark. 800-2000m.

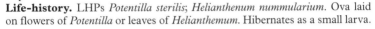

**Variation.** On Mt. Chelmos: large; both sexes, ups with striking whitish/yellowish suffusion (super-scaling).
**Flight-period.** Univoltine. Late June/mid August according to locality and altitude.
**Habitat.** Dry or damp grassy, flowery places: meadows; woodland clearings; sheltered gullies/hollows on subalpine slopes.
**Life-history.** LHPs *Potentilla sterilis*; *Helianthenum nummularium*. Ova laid on flowers of *Potentilla* or leaves of *Helianthemum*. Hibernates as a small larva.

*P. alveus centralhispaniae* Verity 1925 TL: Montes Universales, Spain.
**Distribution.** N Portugal and Spain: most mountainous areas including Sierra Nevada and S Pyrenees: widespread, often very local. S France: Pyrénées-Orientales sporadically through Cevennes, Massive Central to Côte-d'Or (S of Dijon); Haute-Savoie to Provençe. Italy: Maritime Alps to Dolomites; C Apeninnes. 900-1800m. Exact distributional relationship with nominate form uncertain. Absent from Mediterranean islands: records for Sicily require confirmation.
**Variation.** Populations of Cantabrian Mts. (*accretus* Verity), S Spain (Sierra Nevada; S. de Segura; S. de la Sagra) and Apeninnes (*centralitaliae* Verity) differ in small characters in male genitalia.
**Flight-period.** Univoltine. Early June/mid August.
**Habitat.** As for nominate form.
**Life-history.** LHPs *Potentilla* spp.; *Helianthemum nummularium*.

*P. alveus scandinavicus* Strand 1903 TL: Dovre, Norway.
syn: *ballotae* Oberthür 1910.
**Distribution.** Local in Norway and Sweden to 63°N. Absent from Denmark and Finland. 100-1100m.
**Description.** Resembles nominate form: smaller; ups white markings slightly larger, clearly defined; male genitalia distinctive. Considered specifically distinct by some authors.
**Flight-period.** Univoltine. Late June/August according to season.
**Habitat.** At higher altitudes, barren stony ground with damp, grassy hollows or small, sheltered streams: at lower levels, dry soils with sparse grass.
**Life-history.** LHPs *Potentilla* sp.; *Agrimonia eupatoria*; (?)*Polygala vulgare*. Hibernates as an ovum.

*P. alveus numidus* Oberthür 1910 TL: Lambessa, Algeria.
**Distribution.** Morocco and Algeria: Middle Atlas; High Atlas. 1500-2800m.
**Flight-period.** Univoltine. Late May/late June.
**Habitat.** Grassy, flowery slopes.
**Life-history.** LHP *Helianthemum croceum*.

## *Pyrgus armoricanus* Oberthür's Grizzled Skipper — Plate 97

**Range.** N Africa, Europe, Turkey, Transcaucasus, NW Asia, S Urals.

*P. armoricanus* Oberthür 1910 TL: Rennes, France.
**Distribution.** Morocco and Algeria: Middle Atlas. 1500-1800m. Iberian

peninsula, Sardinia, Corsica, Sicily, through France (except NW and NE) to Denmark (restricted to Sjælland and Bornholm), S Sweden (restricted to S Skåne), Balkans, Greece (including Kithira and Crete) and European Turkey. 50-1700m.

**Description.** Ups light coloration and bright yellowish unh characteristic and distinctive (cf. *P. alveus*).

**Variation.** In NW Africa, *maroccanus* Picard: larger; all markings better developed. In S Greece, Kithira, Crete and European Turkey, *persicus* Reverdin: distinguished by small difference in male genitalia.

**Flight-period.** Generally bivoltine (May/June and July/late August): univoltine in northern range (late June/July). Has been reported from C Pyrenees late April: in Sardinia, most abundant in October.

**Habitat.** Grassy, rocky gullies/slopes, often hot, dry bushy places with an abundance of flowers.

**Life-history.** LHPs *Potentilla tabernaemontani*; *P. reptans*; *P. arenaria*; *Fragaria vesca*; *Helianthemum nummularium*. Ova laid on flowers of *Potentilla* or leaves of *Helianthemum*.

**Behaviour.** Attracted to flowers of *Thymus* and *Achillea*.

## *Pyrgus foulquieri* Foulquier's Grizzled Skipper          Plate 97

**Range.** NE Spain, S France, C Italy.

*P. foulquieri* Oberthür 1910 TL: Larche, Basses Alpes.
syn: *bellieri* Oberthür 1910.

**Distribution.** Spain: Catalonia: very local. S France: Massif Central; Aveyron to Bouches-du-Rhône, Var, Alpes-Maritimes, Isère and Savoie. Italy: Maritime Alps to Cottian Alps; Apennines (Mte. Sibillini; Abruzzi; Mte. Aurunci): very local. 500-1800m.

**Description.** Resembles *P. alveus centralhispaniae*: uph pale markings better developed; pd spots larger; unh gc yellowish-brown.

**Variation.** In C Italy, *picenus* Verity: smaller; ups paler; unh yellowish, slightly mottled yellowish-brown.

**Flight-period.** Univoltine. Mid July/August.

**Habitat.** Grassy flowery places.

**Life-history.** LHP *Potentilla* sp.

## *Pyrgus warrensis* Warren's Skipper          Plate 97

**Range.** E Central European Alps.

*P. warrensis* Verity 1928 TL: Grisons, Switzerland.
syn: *alticola* Evans nec Rebel

**Distribution.** Widespread but very local in E Switzerland (Albulapass; Julier Pass; Bernina Pass). Italy: Ortler Alps (Pso. dello Stelvio); Dolomites (Pso. Falzarego; Pso. di Sella; Pso. di Pardoi) and Austria (Brenner Pass; Hohe Tauern). 1800-2600m.

**Description.** Resembles *P. a. alveus*: smaller; markings less prominent.

**Flight-period.** Univoltine. July/August.
**Habitat.** Sheltered hollows, gullies and slopes with short turf and *Thymus*.

## *Pyrgus serratulae* Olive Skipper                    Plate 98

**Range.** Spain, C Europe to Balkans and Greece, Turkey, Caucasus, S and C Siberia, Mongolia, Transbaikal.

*P. serratulae* Rambur 1839 TL: Spain.
**Distribution.** Spain: Sierra Nevada; S. de Segura; Cantabrian Mts.; S. de la Demanda; S. de Guadarrama; Serrania de Cuenca; Montes Universales; Pyrenees. C France through C Germany to S Lithuania, Latvia (very local and rare last reported in 1988), northern and peninsular Italy (C Apeninnes), Balkans, S Greece and European Turkey. Absent
from Portugal, NW and NE France, Belgium, Holland and NW Germany. 50-2400m.
**Description.** Both sexes: uns gc and markings distinctive and characteristic.
**Variation.** In SE Europe, f. *major* Staudinger: consistently larger. Large forms occur sporadically in hot, low-lying localities elsewhere in S Europe.
**Flight-period.** Univoltine. Generally mid May/July: emergence prolonged at higher altitudes: reported from C Pyrenees late April.
**Habitat.** Open grassy, flowery places; damp woodland clearings; hot, dry scrubland at low altitudes.
**Life-history.** LHPs *Potentilla recta*; *P. pedata*; *P. tabernaemontani*; *P. hirta*; *P. nevadensis*; *P. reptans*.

## *Pyrgus carlinae* Carline Skipper                    Plate 98

**Range.** Portugal, Spain, S and C France, W and C Switzerland, S Germany, Austria, E Turkey, Armenia.

*P. carlinae carlinae* Rambur 1839 TL: Dalecarlia [in error].
**Distribution.** SE France and NW Italy (Maritime Alps to Savoie). SW Switzerland: Valais to Tessin (Campolungo Pass appears to be the most easterly location). A single record for Austria requires confirmation. Generally 1350-1900m: confirmed at 2900m on Col de Torrent and 950-1050m in various sites in France and Switzerland: records below this range require confirmation.
**Flight-period.** Univoltine. Late July/August.
**Habitat.** Open, flowery meadows; grassy, woodland clearings.
**Life-history.** LHPs *Potentilla verna*; *P. reptans*; *P. hirta*; *P. tabernaemontani*.

*P. carlinae cirsii* Rambur 1839 TL: Fontainebleau, France.
syn: *fritillum* Denis and Schiffermüller 1775
**Distribution.** Portugal and Spain: widespread and common. 800-1600m. S and C France. Switzerland: Vaud; Valais; Jura Mts. Very sporadic and local in S Germany, Austria and W Hungary. 300-1300m. Distributional relationship with nominate form uncertain. Records for NW Italy require confirmation.
**Description.** Resembles nominate form: ups white markings better developed:

male genitalia distinct. Hybridizes with nominate form in areas of distributional overlap. Regarded as specifically distinct by some authors.

**Variation.** Unh gc locally/regionally variable, yellow-brown to reddish-brown.

**Flight-period and Habitat.** As for nominate form.

**Life-history.** LHPs *Potentilla reptans*; *P. erecta*; *P. verna*; *P. sterilis*; *P. cinerea* (Montes Universales).

## *Pyrgus onopordi* Rosy Grizzled Skipper          Plate 98

**Range.** Morocco, Algeria, SW Europe.

*P. onopordi* Rambur 1839 TL: Granada, Spain.

**Distribution.** Morocco and Algeria: Middle Atlas; High Atlas; Rif Mts. 0-2800m. Portugal and Spain: widespread. S France (Pyrénées-Orientales to about 46°N in Rhône Valley). Italy: generally widespread, sporadic in NE. 0-2000m.

**Description.** Both sexes: unh large white anvil-shaped spots in s4 and s5 distinctive and characteristic.

**Flight-period.** Bivoltine or trivoltine. April/early October.

**Habitat.** Flowery meadows, sheltered streams and gullies in open grassland.

**Life-history.** LHP: S Spain (Sierra Nevada), *Malva neglecta*. Ova laid on upperside of leaves. Captive larvae accept *Malope malachoides*.

## *Pyrgus cinarae* Sandy Grizzled Skipper          Plate 98

**Range.** Central E Spain, S Balkans, Greece, Turkey, S Urals.

*P. cinarae cinarae* Rambur 1839 TL: Sarepta.

**Distribution.** Albania. Republic of Macedonia. Bulgaria. N Greece. European Turkey. Sporadic and local. 750-1600m.

**Flight-period.** Univoltine. Mid June/early August.

**Habitat.** Open, grassy, flowery places: also, dry, rocky terrain on calcareous and non-calcareous soils. Often occurs with *P. sidae*, *P. serratulae* and, in drier biotopes, *S. phlomides*.

**Life-history.** LHP: Greece, *Potentilla recta*. Ova laid on flower-buds.

*P. cinarae clorinda* Warren 1927 TL: Cuenca, C Spain.

**Distribution.** C Spain: province of Cuenca (Montes Universales); very local. 900-1200m. Confirmed records include: Uña; Tragacete; Valdecabras; Huelamo; Ciudad Encantada. A tentative record from S. de Albarracin, pertaining to material collected by Querci in 1925, has not been confirmed.

**Description.** Both sexes: ups and uns gc more yellowish, especially male unh.

**Flight-period.** Univoltine. Mid July/early September.

**Habitat.** Flowery, grassy, bushy pinewood clearings.

## *Pyrgus sidae* Yellow-banded Skipper          Plate 98

**Range.** W Spain, SE France, C Italy, Balkans, Turkey, Iran, Transcaucasus, NW Asia, S Urals, NW Kazakhstan, W Tian Shan.

*P. sidae sidae* Esper 1784 TL: Volga, S Russia.

**Distribution.** S Bosnia-Herzegovina. S Serbia. S Romania. Bulgaria. Albania. N Greece. European Turkey. 50-1750m, generally above 600m.

**Flight-period.** Univoltine. Generally mid May/late June; NE Greece, near sea-level, early April/May.
**Habitat.** Grassy, flowery banks/meadows, rocky gullies and slopes: most habitats contain an abundance of flowers, which often include *Vicia* and *Achillea* – much favoured nectar-sources.
**Life-history.** LHP: Greece, *Potentilla recta*. Ova laid amongst flower-stamens. As an inhabitant of disturbed ground (areas of cultivation, roadsides, wasteland etc.), the ecological requirements of *Abutilon theophrasti* [=*A. avicennae*] (Malvaceae), widely quoted as a LHP, do not appear compatible with those of the butterfly.

*P. sidae occiduus* Verity 1925 TL: Tuscany.
**Distribution.** W Spain: restricted to S. de Gredos. 700-1300m. SE France: Hérault; Bouches-du-Rhône; Var; Alpes-de-Haute-Provençe; Alpes-Maritimes. Italy: NW coastal district; Módena to Golfo di Gaeta; Belluno; Istria; 100-1400m.
**Description.** Resembles nominate form: smaller; ups spotting less prominent; unh yellow discal band generally paler. Specimens of intermediate character are not uncommon.
**Flight-period.** Univoltine. Mid June/early July.
**Habitat.** Flowery grassland and scrub.

## *Pyrgus carthami* Safflower Skipper                    Plate 98

**Range.** SW and C Europe, Balkans, N Greece, Turkey, Urals, S Russia, C Asia, Koptedagh.

*P. carthami* Hübner 1813 TL: Bavaria.
syn: *fritillarius* auct. nec Poda 1761.
**Distribution.** NE Portugal, Spain and peninsular Italy (C Apeninnes and Calabria) to S Lithuania, Balkans, N Greece (known only from Mt. Phalakron and Menikion Mts.) and European Turkey. Absent from W central Spain, Britain, N and W France, Belgium, Holland, N Germany and Mediterranean islands. Old records for Latvia appear to relate to misidentification. 600-1800m.
**Description.** Male uph white, elongate submarginal markings usually prominent; unh white markings narrowly bordered pale grey, distinctive and characteristic.
**Variation.** In S Spain, f. *nevadensis* Oberthür: ups white markings better developed; unh markings more sharply defined.
**Flight-period.** Univoltine. Late June/September in prolonged emergence.
**Habitat.** Sheltered gullies/hollows on open, grassy slopes; flowery meadows: often amongst rocks, bushes or in open woodland.
**Life-history.** LHPs *Potentilla cinerea* (N Greece and Montes Universales); *P. arenaria*; *P. heterophylla*; *P. hirta*; *P. tabernaemontani*. Ova laid singly on upperside of leaf. Hibernates as a small larva.

## *Pyrgus andromedae* Alpine Grizzled Skipper                Plate 99

**Range.** Europe.

*P. andromedae* Wallengren 1853 TL: Dovre, Norway.
**Distribution.** Spain and France; Pyrenees. Alps of France,
Italy, Switzerland, Germany and Austria. Slovenia: Julian
Alps. Norway: Finnmark; Troms; Nordland; Nord-
Trøndelag. Sweden:Torne Lappmark. 25-1000m. S Bosnia-
Herzegovina. SW Serbia (Montenegro) and Republic of
Macedonia: restricted to Sar Pl. 1200-3000m.
**Description.** Unh prominent white spot and white streak in
s1c gives a striking impression of an exclamation mark – useful diagnostic feature.
**Flight-period.** Univoltine. Scandinavia, mid June/July: C and SE Europe,
generally July, records span mid May/late August.
**Habitat.** Sheltered, grassy places in open moorland, heaths and alpine grassland.
**Life-history.** LHPs: Scandinavia, *Potentilla thuringiaca*; *Alchemilla glomerulans*;
*Malva* sp.

## *Pyrgus cacaliae* Dusky Grizzled Skipper                Plate 99

**Range.** C and SE Europe.

*P. cacaliae* Rambur 1839 TL: 'Alps'.
**Distribution.** Alps of France, Italy, Switzerland, Germany
and Austria. Bulgaria: Rila Mts. Romania: Bucegi Mts. 1800-
2800m. Records for Pyrenees, including Andorra (1978) require
confirmation.
**Description.** Ups white markings small in both sexes; uns
markings indistinct, giving overall 'washed-out' appearance;
unh gc extends to v1b; lacking basal spot in s2. (Cf. *P.
andromedae*).
**Flight-period.** Univoltine. June/August.
**Habitat.** Sheltered hollows/gullies in open alpine grassland, often near low
bushes or scrub.
**Life-history.** LHPs *Potentilla* sp; *Sibbaldia* sp.

## *Pyrgus centaureae* Northern Grizzled Skipper                Plate 99

**Range.** N Fennoscandia, Arctic Russia, Altai Mts., Tchuja
Mts., S and E Siberia, Mongolia, Transbaikal, Arctic N
America southwards to Rocky Mts. and Appalachian Mts.

*P. centaureae* Rambur 1839 TL: Lappland.
**Distribution.** Norway, Sweden and Finland: 60°N-North
Cape: widespread but generally absent from coastal regions.
0-950m.
**Description.** Unh white veins prominent and distinctive.
**Flight-period.** Univoltine. Mid June/July according to
season.
**Habitat and Life-history.** Marshes, bogs and damp heath containing an
abundance of LHP, *Rubus chamaemorus*.

## *Spialia sertorius* Red Underwing Skipper          Plate 99

**Range.** N Africa, S Europe. W Asia to Altai Mts., Tibet and Amur.

*S. sertorius sertorius* Hoffmannsegg 1804 TL: Germany.
syn: *hibiscae* Hemming 1936
**Distribution.** Portugal. Spain. France. S Belgium and NW Germany to W Czech Republic, Austria and Italy. Widespread and common. Reports from Corsica and Hungary require confirmation. 0-1650m.
**Description.** First brood: uns gc creamy-yellow: second brood, uns gc reddish.
**Flight-period.** Bivoltine. April/June and Mid July/August.
**Habitat.** Diverse. Hot, dry, flowery scrubland at sea-level: at higher altitudes, grassy slopes; flowery meadows; woodland clearings; bushy places.
**Life-history.** LHPs: principally *Sanguisorba minor*: also (?)*Potentilla verna*; (?)*Rubus ideaus*. Oviposition, early-stage development/morphology appears to parallel that of *S. orbifer* (below).

*S. sertorius therapne* Rambur 1832 TL: Corsica.
**Distribution.** Corsica and Sardinia. 0-1500m.
**Description and Variation.** Resembles nominate form: smaller; upf cell-mark roughly square; unh gc reddish-brown, marginal markings reduced. Forms transitional to nominate form have been reported from Corsica.
**Flight-period.** Bivoltine. Late April/mid June and August/early September.
**Habitat.** Grassy, flowery places, often amongst low bushes and rocks.

*S. sertorius ali* Oberthür 1881 TL: Provinces of Oran and Constantine, Algeria.
**Distribution.** Morocco: Anti-Atlas; High Atlas; Middle Atlas; Rif Mts. Algeria. Tunisia. 500-2500m.
**Description.** Ups gc colour paler, markings bolder, especially white discoidal spot; unh reddish-brown with darker striae; white discoidal spot conspicuous, white marginal spots elongate, veins pale brown.
**Flight-period.** Bivoltine (April/June and August/early September) or trivoltine (late February/October) according to locality and altitude.
**Habitat.** Rocky, flowery slopes and gullies; dry water courses.
**Life-history.** LHP *Sanguisorba magnolii*.

## *Spialia orbifer* Orbed Red-underwing Skipper          Plate 99

**Range.** Sicily, E Europe, Balkans, Middle East, Afghanistan, S Russia, S Urals, Tian Shan.

*S. orbifer* Hübner 1823 TL: Hungary.
**Distribution.** Sicily. (?)E Czech Republic. Slovakia. S Poland. (?)SE Austria. Hungary. Balkans. Greece, including Corfu, Levkas, Kefalonia, Zakynthos, Kithera, Skopelos, Skyros, Limnos, Lesbos, Chios, Ikaria, Samos, Kos, Simi and Rhodes. European Turkey. Not reported from the Kykladian archipeligo, Crete or Karpathos. 0-2000m. Distributional relationship with *S. sertorius* unclear.

**Variation.** Both sexes: first brood, uns gc creamy-yellow; second brood, uns reddish or rust-brown.
**Flight-period.** Bivoltine. Mid April/June and Mid July/August: in Greece, emergence of first brood variable (mid April/late May) according to locality, altitude and season.
**Habitat.** As for *S. sertorius*.
**Life-history.** LHP *Sanguisorba minor*. Ova laid singly amongst flower-buds. Initially, the small larva feeds entirely within the globular, compound flower: when too large to remain concealed, larva transfers to a leaf where it lives in a loose shelter gathered together with silk. In captivity, mature larvae of the first brood occasionally enter diapause, hibernating amongst dead leaves at base of LHP. Rolled-up stem-leaves serve as pupation sites.

## *Spialia phlomidis* Persian Skipper — Plate 99

**Range.** S Balkans, Greece, Turkey, N Israel, Lebanon, Syria, N Iran, S Russia, Transcaucasus.

*S. phlomidis* Herrich-Schäffer 1845 TL: Turkey.
**Distribution.** (?)S Croatia. SW Serbia. Albania. Republic of Macedonia. Bulgaria. Greece. Sporadic and usually very uncommon. 650-1650m, generally below 1000m.
**Flight-period.** Univoltine. Late May/June.
**Habitat.** Hot, dry, often rocky places; dry grassland with sparse, low-growing scrub. Usually on calcareous soils.
**Life-history.** LHP not recorded for Europe: Lebanon, *Convolulus libanotica*: Greece, circumstantial evidence indicates *Convolulus* sp.

## *Spialia doris* Aden Skipper — Plate 99

**Range.** Morocco, Egypt, Arabia, Somalia, India.

*S. doris daphne* Evans 1949 TL: Ziz Valley, High Atlas, Morocco.
**Distribution.** Morocco: widespread but local: Anti-Atlas (Tizi-n-Bachkoum; El Drââ Valley; Tizi-n-Tinififft); High Atlas (Ziz Valley; Er Rachidia). 400-1750m.
**Flight-period.** Bivoltine. Late March/May and late August/September.
**Habitat.** Very hot, dry gullies with very sparse vegetation.
**Life-history.** LHPs *Convolulus lanatus*; *C. captmedusae*; *C. trabutianus*. (Sinai peninsula, *Ipomoea stolonifera* (also Convolulaceae)).
**Behaviour.** Flight very fast and low.

## *Muschampia tessellum* Tessellated Skipper — Plate 100

**Range.** SE Europe, Turkey, Middle East to S Siberia, Mongolia and N China.

*M. tessellum* Hübner 1803 TL: S Russia.
**Distribution.** Republic of Macedonia. Bulgaria. NW Greece: Vernon Mts.; Kerkeni Mts.; Askion Mts; Mt. Cholomon; Mt. Olympus. 800-1100m. Also, SE Aegean island of Simi 0-100m. European Turkey.

**Variation.** Upf rarely with additional pair of obscure, elongate white spots in s1b (cf. *M. cribrellum*); unh gc yellowish, sometimes pale, delicate green.
**Flight-period.** Univoltine. Mid May/mid August in prolonged emergence: average peak emergence early June.
**Habitat and Behaviour.** Open, grassy, sunny places with an abundance of flowers, especially *Vicia*, *Achillea* and *Thymus*, upon which both sexes are fond of resting and feeding.
**Life-history.** LHP: NW Greece, *Phlomis samia*. Larva feeds within shelter of a small fold, secured by silk, near the edge and upper stem of a basal leaf. Hibernates as an immature larva. Prior to feeding, larger, post-hibernated larvae sever the leaf-stem vein sustaining that part of the leaf upon which they subsequently feed: possibly, this practice serves to counter the plant's chemical defences. (LHP in S Ural Mts., *Phlomis* (?) *tuberosa*: not confirmed as an European LHP although often quoted as such: apparently absent from *M. tessellum* habitats in N Greece).

## *Muschampia cribrellum* Spinose Skipper                    Plate 100

**Range.** Balkans, Caucasus, S Siberia, S Urals, Kazakhstan, Altai, Mongolia, Amur, N and W China.

*M. cribrellum* Eversmann 1841 TL: S Russia.
**Distribution.** E Hungary. Romania: Cluj; Hunedoara. Republic of Macedonia: district of Skopje. 800-850m.
**Description.** Resembles *M. tessellum*: smaller; ups and uns white markings more conspicuous; upf with two pairs of elongate white spots in s1b.
**Flight-period.** Univoltine. Mid May/mid June.
**Habitat.** Dry, flowery grassland with scattered bushes.
**Life-history.** LHP(s) uncertain: reportedly *Potentilla* sp. (cf. *M. tessellum* and other members of the genus).

## *Muschampia proto* Sage Skipper                    Plate 100

**Range.** NW Africa, Portugal, Spain, S Europe, Turkey.

*M. proto* Ochsenheimer 1808 TL: Portugal.
**Distribution.** Morocco: Middle Atlas. Algeria. 1200-1700m. Portugal. Spain. S France. Italy: Monte Gargano; Calabria; N Sicily. (?) Albania. Republic of Macedonia. Greece, including Kithira, Karpathos and Simi. 0-1600m.
**Variation.** Uns gc seasonally variable, especially in female: greenish in spring emergence; brownish, orange or pinkish mid/late summer. In N Africa and occasionally in S Spain, f. *fulvosatura* Verity: large; markings well developed. Common features in male genitalia of *M. proto* from southern Aegean island of Simi and *M. mohammed* from N Africa have been reported.
**Flight-period.** Univoltine. April/October, emergence prolonged.
**Habitat.** Flowery places, often amongst mixed scrub on dry, rocky slopes or dry grassland: habitats often dominated by LHP.

**Life-history.** LHPs: NW Africa, *Phlomis crinita*; *P. bovei*: Europe, *P. fruticosa*; *P. lychnitis*; *P. herba-venti*. Larva feeds, hibernates and pupates within a shelter formed usually from a single leaf.

## *Muschampia mohammed* Barbary Skipper                 Plate 100

**Range.** Morocco, Algeria, (?) Tunisia.

*M. mohammed* Oberthür 1887 TL: Lambessa, Algeria.

**Distribution.** Morocco: Middle Atlas: very local (Azrou; Ifrane; Oulmès). Algeria: (Teniet-el-Haad; Sebdou; Tlemcen; Lambessa; Aures Mts.; Djurdjura Massif). 1500-1800m. A recent tentative record from Tunisia requires confirmation.

**Description and Variation.** Resembles *M. proto*. Hw outer margin distinctly undulate; veins brownish; unh discal spot, large, pale, nacreous: unh gc dark brown in first brood, reddish-brown in second brood.

**Flight-period.** Bivoltine or trivoltine. March/October according to locality and altitude.

**Habitat.** Rocky, flowery places.

**Life-history.** LHPs *Phlomis crinita*; *P. bovei*.

## *Muschampia leuzeae* Algerian Grizzled Skipper          Plate 100

**Range.** Algeria.

*M. leuzeae* Oberthür 1881 TL: Mascara, Algeria.

**Distribution.** Algeria: Blida; Chrea; Col de Ben-Chicao; Tenient-el-Had; Djurdjura Massif: local and uncommon. 1200-2000m.

**Description.** Resembles *M. proto*. Ups gc dark grey; upf discoidal spot very large; unh pattern reticulate.

**Flight-period.** Univoltine. Mid May/July.

**Habitat.** Dry, flowery grassland.

**Life-history.** LHP *Phlomis*.

## *Carcharodus alceae* Mallow Skipper                      Plate 101

**Range.** S and C Europe, Turkey, Yemen, S and C Urals, W Kazakhstan, Turkestan, N Pakistan, N India, Altai, Tian Shan.

*C. alceae* Esper 1780 TL: Germany.

**Distribution.** In Europe, widespread and common south of 50°N including most Mediterranean islands. 0-2000m. Not confirmed in NW Africa. Presence in coastal district of SW Iberian peninsula from Lisbon to Cádiz not confirmed – apparently replaced entirely by *C. tripolinus* (below): distributional detail of the two species unknown in this region; only *C. alceae* has been confirmed in Málaga and Granada.

**Description.** Male unf without hair-tuft. Indistinguishable from *C. tripolinus* by external characters: male genitalia distinct.

**Flight-period.** Polyvoltine. Early April/October in three or more broods.

**Habitat.** Diverse. Usually open flowery places, often with long grasses and light scrub, but well adapted to hot, dry, rocky terrain.
**Life-history.** LHP principally *Malva sylvestris*: a common and widespread plant, adaptable to a wide range of conditions and remarkably resistant to grazing and trampling. Less commonly used LHPs include *M. neglecta*; *M. moschata*; *M. pusilla*; *Alcea rosea* [=*Althaea rosea*]. (Unexpected use of *Chrozophora hierosolymitana* (Euphorbiaceae) has been reported from E Palearctic range). Mature larva hibernates at base of LHP in a loose but strong structure formed from dead leaves held together by silk. Second brood larvae from Mediterranean region, captively reared below ambient temperature, often enter and remain in diapause until following spring.
**Behaviour.** Under certain conditions which appear to relate to a reduction of light and/or temperature, males have the curious habit of lowering their wings below the plane of the thorax whilst recurving their abdomens in the opposite direction: captive specimens kept in darkness have been noted to retain this posture for several hours. This practice is exhibited by other members of the genus.

## *Carcharodus tripolinus* False Mallow Skipper  Not illustrated

**Range.** Morocco, Algeria, Tunisia, Libya, SW Portugal, SW Spain.

*C. tripolinus* Verity 1925. TL: Garian plateau, Libya.
**Distribution.** Morocco. Algeria. Tunisia. Widespread from Sahara Desert to northern coast. 0-2500m. S Portugal and S Spain: confirmed in coastal districts from Lisbon (Estoril) to Cádiz. Exact distributional relationship with *C. alceae* unknown.
**Description.** Unf without hair-tuft. Inseparable from *C. alceae* on basis of wing-characters: male genitalia distinct.
**Flight-period.** Polyvoltine. March/September.
**Habitat.** Hot, dry flowery and grassy places, rocky gullies and slopes.
**Life-history.** LHP *Malva sylvestris*.
**Conservation.** Intense human activity on southern coast of Iberian peninsula poses a serious threat to habitat.

## *Carcharodus lavatherae* Marbled Skipper          Plate 101

**Range.** N Africa, Europe to 47°N, Turkey, Transcaucaus, S Urals.

*C. lavatherae lavatherae* Esper 1783 TL: S France.
**Distribution.** Morocco and Algeria: Middle Atlas: local and uncommon. Spain through S France (including Massif Central) S Switzerland, Italy (except northern central plains) to NE Balkans and N Greece. 200-1600m. N Greece appears to be limit of SE European range, where it occurs in isolated colonies interspersed with *C. lavatherae tauricus* (below).

**Description.** Male unf without hair-tuft. Both sexes: ups greenish or yellowish-brown with darker marbling; upf inner margin often conspicuously reddish-

brown or dull orange; unh whitish, usually tinged creamy-yellow; markings vague.
**Flight-period.** Univoltine. Mid May/late July. Reports of a second brood require confirmation.
**Habitat.** Hot, rocky gullies or dry grassy banks with sparse scrub: usually on limestone.
**Life-history.** LHPs *Stachys recta*; *S. germanica*; *S. arvensis*. Ova laid on calyx. Small larvae feed between overlapping leaves loosely drawn together with silk.
**Behaviour.** In very hot conditions, males may gather in large numbers to take moisture from damp soil: in intermittent sunshine, feeding insects appear to regulate their temperature by careful adjustment in wing-separation.

*C. lavatherae tauricus* Reverdin 1915 TL: Taurus Mts.
**Distribution.** Bosnia-Herzegovina. (?)S Serbia. (?)Albania. Republic of Macedonia. Romania. Bulgaria. NW Greece. European Turkey (Gelibolu). 500-1100m. Replaces nominate form in Turkey and elsewhere in eastern range.
**Description.** Resembles nominate form: ups greenish/olive gc replaced with greyish or greyish-brown; uns gc chalky-white. In N Greece, nominate form and *tauricus* exist in small populations having no apparent ecological separation. Whilst male genitalia of the two forms are identical in shape, the uncus, tegumen and brachia of *tauricus* are consistently more robust – features readily apparent to the naked-eye.
**Flight-period.** Univoltine. Mid June/July.
**Habitat.** Grassy, flowery places with scrub and scattered trees.
**Life-history.** LHP: NW Greece, *Stachys plumosa*. Ova laid singly on calyx. Larger larvae feed in loosely rolled-up leaves. Mature larva dark grey, almost black, with extensive yellow mottling and fine, pale, long hairs. Small larvae hibernate in the shelter of dead leaves near base of host-plant. Pupates in final feeding station.

## *Carcharodus boeticus* Southern Marbled Skipper    Plate 101

**Range.** Iberian peninsula, S France, W Switzerland, NW and C peninsular Italy.

*C. boeticus* Rambur 1839 TL: Andalusia.
syn: *marrubii* Rambur 1840.
**Distribution.** N Portugal. Spain, south of Pyrenees. France: E Pyrenees; Cevennes; Provençe. SW Switzerland; Valais. Italy: Piedmont; Appenines; Sicily. Progressively more dispersed in eastern range. 500-1600m.
**Description.** Male unf with hair-tuft. Both sexes: unh white markings arranged in a distinctive reticulate pattern.
**Variation.** Ups gc becomes progressively paler in later broods, culminating in a light sandy-brown in late summer: colour of hair-tuft follows same trend and becomes smaller.
**Flight-period.** Voltinism dependent on locality: univoltine in Switzerland (July), trivoltine in S Spain (May, June/July and August/September).
**Habitat.** Hot, dry gullies, rocky slopes with sparse vegetation and scrub.
**Life-history.** LHP (?)*Marrubium vulgare*. Hibernates as a small larva.

## *Carcharodus stauderi*                    Plate 101

**Range.** N Africa, eastwards to Turkey, N Iran and Afghanistan.

*C. stauderi* Reverdin 1913 TL: El Kantara, Algeria.
**Distribution.** Morocco. Algeria. Tunisia. Widespread. 700-2400m. Greece: known only from E Aegean islands of Kos, Simi and Rhodes: near sea-level.
**Description and Variation.** Male unf with hair-tuft. Resembles *C. boeticus* closely: all markings extremely variable: male genitalia distinct.
**Flight-period.** Polyvoltine. NW Africa, records span March/October: Aegean Islands, May/June.
**Habitat.** Hot, dry, rocky, flowery places.
**Life-history.** LHP: Morocco, *Marrubium vulgare*. Elsewhere in range, *Ballota hirsuta* (Hoggar Mts., S Algeria); *Phlomis floccusa* (Egypt); *Phlomis aurea* (Sinai peninsula).

## *Carcharodus flocciferus* Tufted Marbled Skipper       Plate 102

**Range.** Morocco, Spain, S and SE Europe, E Turkey, Transcaucasus, S Siberia, S Urals, Kazakhstan, Altai.

*C. flocciferus* Zeller 1847 TL: Sicily.
syn: *alchymillae* Hemming 1936
**Distribution.** Morocco: W Rif Mts.: very local and rare. 1500-2000m. Spain: sporadic, very local and generally uncommon: Cantabrian Mts.; S. de Gredos; S. de Guadarrama; S. de Segura; Montes Universales; S. de la Demanda; Pyrenees: records for Sierra Nevada require confirmation. S France: Massive Central. Central European Alps. Peninsular Italy and Sicily. S Poland. N Hungary. Slovenia: Julian Alps. Widespread but sporadic and local in C and S Balkans. Bosnia-Herzegovina: Vranica Pl.; Prenj Pl. SW Serbia: Orjen Pl.; Sinjajevita Pl. (?)Albania. Republic of Macedonia: Sar Pl.; Bistra Pl.; Placenska Pl.; Mt. Pelister. Romania: Carpathian Mts.. SW Bulgaria: Rila Mts.; Pirin Mts. Greece: Grammos Mt.; Pindos Mts.; Askion Mts.; Vourinos Mts.; Voras Mts.; Mt. Orvilos; Mt. Phalakron; Rhodope Mts.; Mt. Chelmos. Reports for Sardinia require confirmation. 1000-2000m.
**Description.** Resembles *C. orientalis*: often larger; male unf dark hair-tuft prominent; ups gc darker grey; unh gc darker, often with bluish or violet tones in fresh specimens; whitish stripe and discoidal spot prominent.
**Flight-period.** Bivoltine in W and C Europe: late May/June and late July/August: apparently univoltine in Greece, early July/mid August.
**Habitat.** Grassy, flowery slopes or meadows, rocky gullies, sometimes in woodland clearings: often in damp places. Shows a marked preference for relatively cooler/damper conditions prevalent in upper-half of altitudinal range. Although usually separated by altitude and/or habitat-character from *C. orientalis* (below), which generally occurs in hotter and drier conditions below 1500m, the two species occur together very occasionally at about 1000m in Greece.
**Life-history.** LHPs *Stachys recta*; *S alpina*; *S. officinalis*; *S. germanica*; *S. palustris*;

*S. sylvatica*; *S. scardica*. In last two instars, larva feeds in a fully enclosed tent fashioned from leaves at crown of LHP. Hibernates as a small larva near base of LHP. Larva and pupa closely similar to that of *C. orientalis*. Pupates in final feeding station.

**Behaviour.** Both sexes fond of resting on tops of tall flower-stems, especially those of LHP (cf. *C. orientalis*).

## *Carcharodus orientalis* Oriental Marbled Skipper    Plate 102

**Range.** SE Europe, Turkey, Moravia, N Iran, S Urals.

*C. orientalis* Reverdin 1913 TL: S Greece.

**Distribution.** N Hungary. S Croatia: Dalmatian coast. S Serbia. (?)Albania. Republic of Macedonia. Bulgaria: Stara Pl. Greece, including Corfu, Kithera, Kea, Skyros, Limnos, Lesbos, Samos, Kos and Kalimnos. European Turkey. 25-1650m.

**Description and Variation.** Uns gc pale with obscure white markings (cf. *C. flocciferus*): male unf with prominent dark hair-tuft. Subject to marked individual variation in size and ups coloration.

**Flight-period.** Bivoltine or trivoltine (April/August) according to locality and altitude.

**Habitat.** Hot, dry, rocky, flowery slopes, gullies or grassland: often amongst sparse scrub or bushes. (See *C. flocciferus*).

**Life-history.** LHP: S Greece, *Stachys* sp. Half-grown, post-hibernated larva feeds in rolled-up leaves.

**Behaviour.** Males often sit on stones or soil in hot conditions (cf. *C. flocciferus*).

## *Erynnis tages* Dingy Skipper                         Plate 102

**Range.** Europe to 62°N, eastwards to Amur.

*E. tages* Linnaeus 1758 TL: Europe.

**Distribution.** Generally widespread and common from S Europe (including European Turkey) to Ireland, S Scotland, S Scandinavia (including Sjælland, Öland and Gotland) and (?)Estonia (including Dagö and Ösel). Possibly extinct in Latvia: very rare and local in Holland, N Belgium and Lithuania. In decline in Ireland and Britain. Absent from S Portugal, Gibraltar, SW Spain (Huelva) and Mediterranean islands except Corfu. A record for Kykladian island of Tinos requires confirmation. 50-2000m.

**Variation.** Male upf with costal fold (cf. *E. marloyi*). Ups gc variable, pale brown (f. *brunnea* Tutt) to dark brown with dark, greyish-blue overtones (f. *clarus* Caradja). Ups markings variable, obscure to prominent. In W Ireland, *baynesi* Huggins: ups light brown; markings prominent. Darker forms appear to associate with cooler conditions at higher altitudes, e.g. Switzerland above 1500m.

**Flight-period.** Voltinism dependent on locality, altitude and season: usually univoltine in N and C Europe, late April/mid June: at least partially bivoltine in S Europe, early April/early June and late June/late August. A partial second brood may occur in N Europe in favourable seasons. From Mediterranean region, captively reared larvae from first brood often enter and remain in diapause until following spring.

**Habitat.** Diverse. Damp or dry grassy, flowery places.

**Life-history.** LHPs principally *Lotus corniculatus*; *L. uliginosus*; *Hippocrepis comosa*. Conspicuous orange ova laid singly on upper surface of leaves. Larvae feed in an open but strong cage-like structure formed from leaves and silk. Full-grown larva hibernates amongst leaves of LHP bound together with silk. Pupates within hibernaculum in early spring.

**Behaviour.** See *E. marloyi* (below).

## *Erynnis marloyi* Inky Skipper                        Plate 102

**Range.** S Balkans, Turkey, Lebanon, Syria, N Iraq, N Iran, Transcaucasus.

*E. marloyi* Boisduval 1834 TL: Peloponnesos, S Greece.
**Distribution.** Albania. Republic of Macedonia. NW, C and S Greece, including Corfu, Lesbos, Chios and Samos. European Turkey. 600-2000m.
**Description.** Male upf without costal fold (cf. *E. tages*).
**Flight-period.** Univoltine. Mid May/late June.
**Habitat.** Dry gullies; rocky slopes: on calcareous rocks, usually limestone.

**Behaviour.** Females are fond of feeding on flowers of *Thymus*. 'Hilltopping', sometimes involving 20 or more male specimens, is a common occurrence. Especially wary and readily disturbed. Flash-assisted photographs taken in bright sunlight often record no trace of the butterfly, it having been startled by the flash or the noise of the camera-shutter mechanism and taken flight during the very short period of exposure. The exceptionally keen reflexes thus indicated may be related to the insect's common practice of sitting on white stones in the hot sun, for, in such positions, these almost black butterflies are very conspicuous and a clear target for the predatory and ubiquitous lizard. As it would appear that *E. marloyi*, like the lizard, benefits from the absorption of solar radiation in maintaining its activity, its dark colour is advantageous, possibly even necessary to ensure its survival. Similar responses have also been recorded for its similarly coloured cogener, *E. tages*.

## *Heteropterus morpheus* Large Chequered Skipper      Plate 102

**Range.** N Spain, much of C Europe, Italy, Denmark, Sweden, Lithuania, Balkans, SE Bulgaria, NW Turkey, C Asia, Amur, Korea.

*H. morpheus* Pallas 1771 TL: Samara, S Russia.
syn: *steropes* Denis and Schiffermüller 1775.
**Distribution.** N Spain: Oviedo to San Sebastion. France: Pyrénées-Atlantiques through Nièvre (W and N of Massif Central) to Brittany and Somme (W of Somme Valley). Channel Islands: Jersey ((?)introduced). Very local in S Belgium, N Holland and NW Germany. Italy: Lazio; Piedmont through Dolomites to Trieste. Denmark: restricted to Lolland and Falster. Sweden:

restricted to S Skåne. NE Germany to C and E Latvia (very local in C and S
Lithuania), through E Czech Republic, E Austria to N Balkans, SE Bulgaria
(Primorsko) and European Turkey. 0-1000m.

**Flight-period.** Univoltine. Late June/July.

**Habitat.** Woodland clearings with tall grasses: usually in damp places; commonly associated with marshy heaths.

**Life-history.** LHPs *Calamagrostis canescens*; *Brachypodium sylvaticum*; *Molinia
caerulea*; *Phragmites australis*. Ova laid on stems. Larva feeds in a tube formed
from a grass blade. Half-grown larva hibernates within its feeding station. The
green pupa suspends itself within a loose structure formed from grass stems
bound with silk.

## *Carterocephalus palaemon* Chequered Skipper    Plate 103

**Range.** C, N and E Europe, C and N Asia to Japan. N America.

*C. palaemon* Pallas 1771 TL: Russia.

**Distribution.** From N Pyrenees through C France, N Italy
(common in Dolomites) to Arctic Circle, Balkans and N Greece
(Rhodopi Mts.). Locally common in W Scotland. Extinct in
England. Absent from Iberian peninsula except Val d'Aran
(E Pyrenees), W and S France, Peninsular Italy, N Belgium,
N Holland, Denmark, S Sweden, Albania, Republic of Mac-
edonia and SE Bulgaria. 200-1600m.

**Description.** Uns of antennal club-base dark in male, yellow in female.

**Flight-period.** Univoltine. Mid May/June at lower altitudes, July at 1600m.

**Habitat and Behaviour.** Grassy, woodland clearings: often in damp places:
on calcareous or acidic soils. Both sexes attracted to nectar of *Ajuga repans*; *A.
pyramidalis*; *A. genevensis* (bugle) and *Endymion non-scriptus* (bluebell).

**Life-history.** LHPs *Molinia caerulea*; *M. c. arundinacea*; *Calamagrostis epigejos*;
*Brachypodium sylvaticum*; *B. pinnatum*; *Bromus ramosus*; *Dactylis glomerata*;
*Alopecurus pratensis*; *Phleum pratense*. Ova laid singly on grass-blades. Larva
feeds in a tube formed from a grass-blade by drawing together and securing
edges with silk. Mature larva pale green, but assumes an adaptive straw or buff
colour during hibernation amongst dead grass-blades bound together with silk.
Pupates within hibernaculum in early spring.

## *Carterocephalus silvicolus* Northern Chequered Skipper Plate 103

**Range.** NE Germany, N Poland, Baltic states, Fennoscandia
to Siberia, Amur, Japan.

*C. silvicolus* Meigen 1829 TL: Brunswick, Germany.
syn: *sylvius* Knoch 1781 (invalid homonym).

**Distribution.** NE Germany: Helmstedt through Lüchow
to Schwerin See. N Poland. Baltic countries: widespread and
common. Denmark: restricted to Lolland. Norway: very sporadic from Telemark and Akerhaus through Nord-Trøndelag
to Troms (69°N). Sweden: Skåne, Småland and Gotland;
Närke, Söderland, Uppland and Dalarne to Arctic Circle. Finland: widespread
and common. 0-(?)200m.

**Flight-period.** Univoltine. Late May/late June according to locality and season.
**Habitat.** Damp, sunny, sheltered, flowery woodland clearings.
**Life-history.** LHPs *Bromus ramosus*; *Brachypodium sylvaticum*; (?)*Milium effusum*; *Cynosurus cristatus*.

## *Thymelicus acteon* Lulworth Skipper          Plate 103

**Range.** Canary Islands, NW Africa, Europe to 54°N, Turkey, Cyprus, Israel, Jordan, Lebanon, Iraq, Iran.

*T. acteon acteon* Rottemburg 1775 TL: Lansberg-an-der-Warthe, Germany.
**Distribution.** Morocco. Algeria. Tunisia. 0-1800m. Common and widespread in most of Europe to about 54°N. In Britain, restricted to the Dorset coast, S England. Recorded from Sicily, Elba, Corfu, Evia, Naxos, Syra, Tinos, Aegina, Andros, Paros, Crete, Thassos, Samos and Rhodes. Absent from Balearic Islands, Corsica, Sardinia, N Belgium, Holland, N Germany, NE Poland and Baltic countries. 0-1600m.
**Variation.** In NW Africa, f. *oranus* Evans: ups darker, tending to greenish or greyish-brown. Similarly-coloured races occur in Spain, Elba, Crete and other E Mediterranean islands.
**Flight-period.** Univoltine. Mid May/early August in prolonged emergence.
**Habitat.** Grassy and flowery places, usually amongst scrub: often hot, dry situations. In S England, restricted to coastal chalk grassland.
**Life-history.** LHPs *Brachypodium pinnatum*; *B. sylvaticum*; *Elymus repens*; *Calamagrostis epigejos*. Usually, several ova laid in a row on underside of a stem-leaf. Hibernates as a newly-hatched larva within a cocoon on grass-blade.

*T. acteon christi* Rebel 1894 TL: Canary Islands.
**Distribution.** Canary Islands: Hierro (Pic del Risco 300m); La Palma; Gomera; Tenerife; Gran Canaria. 100-1000m.
**Description.** Ups gc brownish; upf yellow-orange markings well defined.
**Flight-period.** Voltinism uncertain: February/late September in two or three broods.
**Habitat.** Flowery, grassy places in margins of laurel forests.

## *Thymelicus hamza* Moroccan Small Skipper          Plate 103

**Range.** Morocco, Algeria, Tunisia, Libya.

*T. hamza* Oberthür 1876 TL: Oran, Algeria.
**Distribution.** Widespread but local. Morocco. Algeria. Tunisia. 500-2400m.
**Description.** Resembles *T. acteon* closely: upf rarely with traces of orange pd markings; unh greyish, with orange wedge-shaped marking extending from outer margin to wing-base at v2.
**Flight-period.** Univoltine. May/late June.
**Habitat.** Flowery grassland; rocky gullies and slopes.

## *Thymelicus lineola* Essex Skipper                    Plate 103

**Range.** N Africa, Europe, C Asia, Tian Shan, Amur. Introduced to N America.

*T. lineola* Ochsenheimer 1808 TL: Germany.

**Distribution.** Morocco. Algeria. Throughout Europe, including S England, S Fennoscandia (including Baltic Islands), Baltic countries, European Turkey, Sicily and Corsica. Absent from Sardinia. 0–2200m.

**Description.** Resembles *T. sylvestris*: generally smaller: ups narrow, black outer marginal borders more prominent; black veins usually prominent, highlighted by finely tapered, black suffusion expanding towards outer margins: male upf sex-brand short, broken at v2: uns of antennal tip black or dark brown (cf. *T. sylvestris*).

**Variation.** In N Africa, f. *semicolon* Staudinger: ups black marginal borders wider, black veins prominent.

**Flight-period.** Univoltine. May/August in prolonged emergence.

**Habitat.** Flowery places containing long grasses: woodland clearings; bushy places; open fields. *T. sylvestris* almost always shares same habitats.

**Life-history.** LHPs *Phleum pratense*; *Holcus mollis*; *Calamagrostis epigejos*; *Dactylis glomerata*; *Agrostis capillaris*; *Brachypodium pinnatum*; *B. sylvaticum*; *Arrhenatherum elatius*; *Triticum aestivum*; *Alopecurus pratensis*; *Carex acutiformis*; *Lolium perenne*; *Phalaris arundinacea*; *Anthoxanthum odoratum*; *Elymus repens* [=*Agropyron repens*; *Triticum repens*; *Elytrigia repens*]. Ova laid between base of stem-leaf and stem. Hibernates as a fully-formed larva within ovum-case.

**Note.** In S England, consolidation and extension of range in recent decades may be due, partly or largely, to new and highly integrated habitat provided by the verges of new road systems. Has spread rapidly in N America since its accidental introduction to Ontario in about 1910, and in other sites subsequently. An economic pest on *Phleum* spp., the transportation of which, as hay-bales, appears mainly responsible for the rapidity of expansion.

## *Thymelicus sylvestris* Small Skipper                    Plate 103

**Range.** NW Africa, Europe, Turkey, Middle East, Iran, Caucasus, S Urals.

*T. sylvestris* Poda 1761 TL: Graz, Austria.
syn: *flavus* Brünnich 1763; *thaumas* Hufnagel 1766

**Distribution.** Widespread and very common. Morocco. Algeria. 0–2600m. From Spain, Sicily, European Turkey and Greece (including Corfu, Kithera, Limnos, Lesbos, Chios, Samos, Kalimnos, Kos and Simi) to Wales, England, Denmark (including Fyen) and Baltic states. Absent from Balearic Islands, Corsica, Sardinia and Crete. 0–1900m.

**Description.** Resembles *T. lineola*: generally larger: ups black veins usually less conspicuous: upf male sex-brand extends to v3: uns of antennal tip fulvous (cf. *T. lineola*).

**Variation.** Rarely, upf male sex-brand greatly reduced or absent. In S Europe, f. *syriacus* Tutt: large; ups gc brighter.

**Flight-period.** Univoltine. May/July.
**Habitat.** Diverse. Flowery clearings in woodland or scrub containing tall grasses.
**Life-history.** LHPs *Holcus lanatus*; *H. mollis*; *Phleum pratense*; *Brachypodium sylvaticum*. Ova laid in small groups. Ovum much rounder than that of *T. lineola*. Hibernates as a newly-hatched larva within a cocoon attached to a grass-blade.
**Behaviour.** Ovipositing females are usually very fastidious and may take 10-15 minutes inspecting LHP stems before laying.

## *Thymelicus hyrax* Levantine Skipper                 Plate 103

**Range.** Greece, Turkey, Iran, Syria, Lebanon, Israel.

*T. hyrax* Lederer 1861 TL: Antakya.
**Distribution.** Greece: S Parnassos massif; Askion Mts.; 600-800m: E Aegean islands of Samos, Chios, Lesbos and Rhodes. 0-250m.
**Description.** Resembles *T. sylvestris*: uns hw more greenish.
**Flight-period.** Late April/late June.
**Habitat.** Hot, dry, rocky places.
**Behaviour.** On Mt. Parnassos, both sexes are greatly attracted to the flowers of a small, bushy *Thymus* sp.

## *Hesperia comma* Silver-spotted Skipper               Plate 104

**Range.** NW Africa, Europe, Turkey, temperate Asia to Amur. NW America.

*H. comma* Linnaeus 1758 TL: Sweden.
syn: *sylvestris* auct. nec Poda
**Distribution.** Morocco. Algeria. Widespread and common. 1500-2800m. Throughout Europe except low-lying regions of southern Iberian peninsula and much of central Scandinavia (including Baltic Islands). Largely absent from S Italy. Absent from Mediterranean islands except N Sicily. 0-2300m.
**Variation.** In Lappland and at higher altitudes elsewhere, f. *catena* Staudinger: smaller; ups darker fulvous, tending to brown; uns gc darker green. In N Africa, f. *benuncus* Oberthür: ups brighter; unh pd silver/whitish spots often confluent, basal spots also fused; unh veins paler, sometimes white.
**Flight-period.** Univoltine. Late June/mid September according to locality.
**Habitat.** Open, flowery places with short grass containing an abundance of *Festuca ovina*. On calcareous and non-calcareous soils.
**Life-history.** LHP principally *Festuca ovina*: rarely, *Lolium perenne*. Natural use of *Lotus corniculatus* and *Ornithopus perpusillus* requires confirmation: captive larvae accept *L. corniculatus* and *Coronilla varia* spontaneously. Ova laid singly, usually one per grass tuft. Hibernates as an ovum or unfed larva in N and C Europe but as a mature larva amongst roots of LHP in Mediterranean region. (In Alaska, two seasonal cycles are required for development, hibernating as an ovum in first winter and as a larva or pupa in second winter). In N and C Europe, mature larva are green, greyish-green or olive-brown: dusky-pink specimens have been recorded in S Spain, S France, NW Italy and NW Greece.

## *Ochlodes venatus* Large Skipper                           Plate 104

**Range.** Europe, Turkey, temperate Asia to China and Japan.

*O. venatus faunus* Turati 1905 TL: Italy and S France.
syn: *sylvanus* Esper 1777 (invalid homonym).
**Distribution.** Widespread and common in most of Europe
to 64°N. Absent from N Africa, Ireland and Mediterranean
islands except Sicily and Corfu. 0-1800m: above 1000m in
S Spain.
**Variation.** At high altitudes and in colder, northern localities,
f. *alpinus* Hoffmann: smaller; darker.
**Flight-period.** Generally univoltine, June/August: (?)bivoltine in Spain, re-
corded in May, June, July and August.
**Habitat.** Sunny, grassy, woodland margins/clearings: most often with some
deciduous trees, bushes and shrubs, especially *Rubus fruticosus* (bramble). Most
habitats are humid and often contain an abundance of ferns, especially bracken
(*Pteris aquilina*).
**Life-history.** LHPs *Dactylis glomerata*; *Molinia caerulea*; *M. c. arundinacea*;
*Brachypodium pinnatum*; *B. sylvaticum*; *Poa pratensis*; *Festuca arundinacea*;
*Calamagrostis epigejos*; *Luzula pilosa*; *Holcus lanatus*; *Elymus repens*; *Juncus effusum*;
*Agrostis capillaris*; *Phleum pratense*; (?)*Bromus erectus*. Ova laid on underside of
grass-blade. Larvae feed inside a tube formed by drawing together edges of a
grass-blade. Hibernates as a large larva.
**Behaviour.** Both sexes attracted to bramble blossom and often rest or bask on
the leaves of this shrub.

## *Gegenes nostrodamus* Mediterranean Skipper                Plate 104

**Range.** Mediterranean coastal region, Turkey, Middle East,
Arabia, Iraq, Iran, Afghanistan, Pakistan, NW India.

*G. nostrodamus* Fabricius 1794 TL: 'Barbaria' (Algeria).
**Distribution.** Very local and sporadic in predominantly
Mediterranean coastal regions. Morocco: northern coast near
sea-level; Taroudannt 250m; High Atlas (Tizi-n-Test 1880m;
Tizi-n-Bachkoum 1400-1600m). Algeria. Tunisia. Spain:
scattered colonies from southern coast to Soria and Zaragoza.
Mallorca. Corsica. Sardinia. Elba. W Italy. NW Sicily. W
Croatia: Dalmatian coast. SW Serbia: Zelenika. Albania. Republic of Macedonia:
Ohrid; Crna Valley; Vardar Valley (Gevgelija). Greece: coastal districts 0-250m;
NW Pindos Mts. 400-1200m; Crete 0-100m. Occurs with *G. pumilio* in some
localities on Crete.
**Description.** Unh cilia-like hairs on costa long and dense (cf. *G. pumilio*).
**Flight-period.** Bivoltine or trivoltine (late April/October) according to locality:
in province of Soria, bivoltine (May/June and late July/August). Usually very
scarce in first brood.
**Habitat.** Hot, dry gullies; stony/sandy flood-plains of rivers, usually amongst
sparse vegetation.
**Life-history.** LHP not recorded for Europe: in Sinai peninsula, ova and larvae
have been recorded on *Aeluropus* and *Panicum* spp. (Poaceae).

**Behaviour.** Flight very fast and low. Males often sit on stones or soil in full sun: extremely wary but returns quickly to original resting site when disturbed. Females perch on tall grass or flower-stems in early morning: much less in evidence at other times of day.

## *Gegenes pumilio* Pigmy Skipper                  Plate 104

**Range.** Mediterranean coastal region, eastwards to Iran and Himalayas. Sporadically throughout Africa.

*G. pumilio* Hoffmannsegg 1804 TL: Naples.
syn: *pygmaeus* Cyrilli 1787 (invalid homonym); *aetna* Boisduval 1840; *lefebvrei* Rambur 1842.
**Distribution.** Generally very local in predominantly Mediterranean coastal regions. Algeria. Tunisia: Aïn Draham. S Spain. Mallorca. SE France: Var; Alpes-Maritimes. Corsica. Sardinia. Elba. W Italy. Sicily. Malta. S Croatia: Heretva Valley 0-4m. SW Serbia. Albania. Greece: mainly coastal districts (0-400m), also inland at moderate to high altitude (Pindos Mts. 500-1000m; Mt. Tymphristos 1200-1800m); Corfu (Mt. Pantokrator, 910m); Spetsai; Paros; Crete; Samos; Kos; Rhodes; Kastellórizo. Not reported from E Italy, NE Greece or European Turkey. 0-1800m. Occurs with *G. nostrodamus* in some localities on Crete.
**Description.** Unh cilia-like hairs on costa short and sparse (cf. *G. nostrodamus*).
**Variation.** Chromosome number in W Mediterranean region (CN=24) differs substantially from that of E Mediterranean (Turkey and Lebanon) and SW Saudi Arabia (CN=41): cytological data are very limited and do not include Italy, Balkans or Greece. Whilst two species of insect may be implicated, this observation is possibly an example of polyploidy, that is, duplication/multiplication of a chromosome set in which all superfluous sets are inactive: if so, the number of active sets – the only ones in genetic control – may be equal in different populations. (It is assumed that inexact multiplicity of CN in present example is due to experimental error: a small range of inter-population variance in chromosome number is probably tolerable (cf. *Lysandra coridon*)).
**Flight-period.** Bivoltine or trivoltine according to locality: records span mid April/late October. Generally very scarce in first brood.
**Habitat and Behaviour.** As for *G. nostrodamus*.
**Life-history.** LHP(s) (?)unknown in Europe. In S Africa, *Ehrhartia erecta* (Poaceae): although sometimes quoted for Europe/NW Africa, this plant genus is not known from either region. Captive larvae have been reared on *Cynodon dactylon* and *Hyparrhenia hirta* (Poaceae): both species, plus *Imperata cylindrica* [=*Saccharum cylindricum*] have been quoted as LHPs but their natural use is apparently unconfirmed.

## *Borbo borbonica* Zeller's Skipper                  Plate 104

**Range.** SW Spain. Gibraltar. Throughout Africa, including coastal districts of NW Morocco, Algeria, Libya and islands of Madagascar, Mauritius and Reunion. Egypt, Israel, Lebanon, Syria.

*B. borbonica zelleri* Lederer 1855 TL: Syria.
**Distribution.** Very local in coastal districts. Morocco: Rabat; Kenitra; Larache;

Tangier. Algeria: Algiers. SW Spain: Algeciras. Gibraltar. Not reported from Tunisia. 0-50m.

**Description.** Upf pd spots hyaline; spot in s1b yellow; unf brown; unh yellowish-brown; palpi buff: female similar; larger; unh with 3 small, well-defined, pale pd spots. (cf. *Gegenes nostrodamus* and *G. pumilio*).

**Flight-period.** Voltinism uncertain. Records span June/November: most observations relate to August/October.

**Habitat.** Hot, dry, rocky, coastal gullies and sandy hills with sparse vegetation.

**Life-history.** LHPs: N Africa *Leersia hexandra*; *Sorghum alepense* (Poaceae).

**Behaviour.** Reputedly an occasional migrant.

## *Pelopidas thrax* Millet Skipper                          Plate 104

**Range.** Greece (Aegean islands), W and SW Turkey, Israel, Lebanon, Syria, Iraq, Arabia, Africa, Kashmir, Far East.

*P. thrax* Hübner 1821 TL: Java.

**Distribution.** Greece: known only from Samos and Rhodes. 0-75m. Possibly over-looked on other Aegean islands in proximity to Turkish coast.

**Description.** Male upf narrow, white sex-brand distinctive. In both sexes, fw hyaline spots distinctive (cf. *Gegenes nostrodamus* and *G. pumilio*).

**Flight-period.** Voltinism uncertain: Greek records relate to June. Reportedly bivoltine in Turkey, May/July and late September/mid October.

**Habitat.** Hot, dry, grassy places in low-lying coastal districts.

**Life-history.** LHP unknown in Europe: in N Africa, *Panicum miliaceum*. In Lebanon, an occasional pest on cereal crops.

**Behaviour.** Flight low and powerful. Reportedly a migrant.

# Checklist

Papilionidae

*Papilio machaon* Swallowtail ❏
*Papilio saharae* Desert Swallowtail ❏
*Papilio hospiton* Corsican Swallowtail ❏
*Papilio alexanor* Southern Swallowtail ❏
*Iphiclides podalirius* Scarce Swallowtail ❏
*Zerynthia polyxena* Southern Festoon ❏
*Zerynthia rumina* Spanish Festoon ❏
*Zerynthia cerisy* Eastern Festoon ❏
*Archon apollinus* False Apollo ❏
*Parnassius apollo* Apollo ❏
*Parnassius phoebus* Small Apollo ❏
*Parnassius mnemosyne* Clouded Apollo ❏

Pieridae

*Aporia crataegi* Black-veined White ❏
*Pieris brassicae* Large White ❏
*Pieris cheiranthi* Canary Islands' Large White ❏
*Artogeia rapae* Small White ❏
*Artogeia mannii* Southern Small White ❏
*Artogeia ergane* Mountain Small White ❏
*Artogeia napi* Green-veined White ❏
*Artogeia balcana* Balkan Green-veined White ❏
*Artogeia bryoniae* Mountain Green-veined White ❏
*Artogeia krueperi* Krueper's Small White ❏
*Pontia edusa* Eastern Bath White ❏
*Pontia daplidice* Bath White ❏
*Pontia chloridice* Small Bath White ❏
*Pontia callidice* Peak White ❏
*Euchloe crameri* Western Dappled White ❏
*Euchloe simplonia* Mountain Dappled White ❏
*Euchloe ausonia* Eastern Dappled White ❏
*Euchloe insularis* Corsican Dappled White ❏
*Euchloe tagis* Portuguese Dappled White ❏
*Euchloe falloui* Scarce Green-striped White ❏
*Euchloe belemia* Green-striped White ❏
*Elphinstonia charlonia* Greenish Black-tip ❏

*Elphinstonia penia* Eastern Greenish Black-tip ❏

*Anthocharis cardamines* Orange Tip ❏

*Anthocharis belia* Moroccan Orange Tip ❏

*Anthocharis damone* Eastern Orange Tip ❏

*Anthocharis gruneri* Gruner's Orange Tip ❏

*Zegris eupheme* Sooty Orange Tip ❏

*Colotis evagore* Desert Orange Tip ❏

*Catopsilia florella* African Migrant ❏

*Colias phicomone* Mountain Clouded Yellow ❏

*Colias nastes* Pale Arctic Clouded Yellow ❏

*Colias palaeno* Moorland Clouded Yellow ❏

*Colias chrysotheme* Lesser Clouded Yellow ❏

*Colias aurorina* Greek Clouded Yellow ❏

*Colias myrmidone* Danube Clouded Yellow ❏

*Colias hecla* Northern Clouded Yellow ❏

*Colias hyale* Pale Clouded Yellow ❏

*Colias crocea* Clouded Yellow ❏

*Colias caucasica* Balkan Clouded Yellow ❏

*Colias alfacariensis* Berger's Clouded Yellow ❏

*Colias erate* Eastern Pale Clouded Yellow ❏

*Gonepteryx rhamni* Brimstone ❏

*Gonepteryx cleopatra* Cleopatra ❏

*Gonepteryx farinosa* Powdered Brimstone ❏

*Leptidea sinapis* Wood White ❏

*Leptidea reali* Réal's Wood White ❏

*Leptidea duponcheli* Eastern Wood White ❏

*Leptidea morsei* Fenton's Wood White ❏

Lycaenidae

*Cigaritis zohra* Donzel's Silver-line ❏

*Cigaritis siphax* Common Silver-line ❏

*Cigaritis allardi* Allard's Silver-line ❏

*Apharitis myrmecophilia* Desert Leopard ❏

*Thecla betulae* Brown Hairstreak ❏

*Quercusia quercus* Purple Hairstreak ❏

*Laeosopis roboris* Spanish Purple Hairstreak ❏

*Satyrium acaciae* Sloe Hairstreak ❏

*Satyrium ilicis* Ilex Hairstreak ❏

*Satyrium esculi* False Ilex Hairstreak ❏

*Satyrium spini* Blue-spot Hairstreak ❑
*Satyrium w-album* White-letter Hairstreak ❑
*Satyrium pruni* Black Hairstreak ❑
*Satyrium ledereri* Orange-banded Hairstreak ❑
*Callophrys rubi* Green Hairstreak ❑
*Callophrys avis* Chapman's Green Hairstreak ❑
*Tomares ballus* Provence Hairstreak ❑
*Tomares nogelii* Nogel's Hairstreak ❑
*Tomares mauretanicus* Moroccan Hairstreak ❑
*Lycaena helle* Violet Copper ❑
*Lycaena phlaeas* Small Copper ❑
*Lycaena dispar* Large Copper ❑
*Lycaena vigaureae* Scarce Copper ❑
*Lycaena ottomana* Grecian Copper ❑
*Lycaena tityrus* Sooty Copper ❑
*Lycaena alciphron* Purple-shot Copper ❑
*Lycaena thersamon* Lesser Fiery Copper ❑
*Lycaena thetis* Fiery Copper ❑
*Lycaena phoebus* Moroccan Copper ❑
*Lycaena hippothoe* Purple-edged Copper ❑
*Lycaena candens* Balkan Copper ❑
*Lampides boeticus* Long-tailed Blue ❑
*Cacyreus marshalli* Geranium Bronze ❑
*Leptotes pirithous* Lang's Short-tailed Blue ❑
*Cyclyrius webbianus* Canary Blue ❑
*Tarucus theophrastus* Common Tiger Blue ❑
*Tarucus rosaceus* Mediterranean Blue ❑
*Tarucus balkanicus* Little Tiger Blue ❑
*Azanus ubaldus* Desert Babul Blue ❑
*Azanus jesous* African Babul Blue ❑
*Zizeeria knysna* African Grass Blue ❑
*Everes argiades* Short-tailed Blue ❑
*Everes decoloratus* Eastern Short-tailed Blue ❑
*Everes alcetas* Provençal Short-tailed Blue ❑
*Cupido minimus* Little Blue ❑
*Cupido carswelli* Carswell's Little Blue ❑
*Cupido osiris* Osiris Blue ❑
*Cupido lorquinii* Lorquin's Blue ❑
*Celastrina argiolus* Holly Blue ❑

*Glaucopsyche alexis* Green-underside Blue ❏

*Glaucopsyche melanops* Black-eyed Blue ❏

*Turanana endymion* Odd-spot Blue ❏

*Maculinea alcon* Alcon Blue ❏

*Maculinea rebeli* Mountain Alcon Blue ❏

*Maculinea arion* Large Blue ❏

*Maculinea telejus* Scarce Large Blue ❏

*Maculinea nausithous* Dusky Large Blue ❏

*Iolana iolas* Iolas Blue ❏

*Pseudophilotes baton* Baton Blue ❏

*Pseudophilotes panoptes* Panoptes Blue ❏

*Pseudophilotes vicrama* ❏

*Pseudophilotes abencerragus* False Baton Blue ❏

*Pseudophilotes barbagiae* Sardinian Blue ❏

*Pseudophilotes bavius* Bavius Blue ❏

*Scolitantides orion* Chequered Blue ❏

*Chilades trochylus* Grass Jewel ❏

*Maurus vogelii* Vogel's Blue ❏

*Plebejus martini* Martin's Blue ❏

*Plebejus allardi* Allard's Blue ❏

*Plebejus pylaon* Zephyr Blue ❏

*Plebejus argus* Silver-studded Blue ❏

*Plebejus loewii* Loew's Blue ❏

*Plebejus idas* Idas Blue ❏

*Plebejus argyrognomon* Reverdin's Blue ❏

*Vacciniina optilete* Cranberry Blue ❏

*Kretania psylorita* Cretan Argus ❏

*Kretania eurypilus* Eastern Brown Argus ❏

*Eumedonia eumedon* Geranium Argus ❏

*Aricia agestis* Brown Argus ❏

*Aricia artaxerxes* Mountain Argus ❏

*Aricia morronensis* Spanish Argus ❏

*Ultraaricia anteros* Blue Argus ❏

*Pseudaricia nicias* Silvery Argus ❏

*Albulina orbitulus* Alpine Blue ❏

*Agriades glandon* Glandon Blue ❏

*Agriades pyrenaicus* Gavarnie Blue ❏

*Cyaniris semiargus* Mazarine Blue ❏

*Agrodiaetus iphigenia* Chelmos Blue ❏

*Agrodiaetus damon* Damon Blue ❏

*Agrodiaetus dolus* Furry Blue ❏

*Agrodiaetus ainsae* Forster's Furry Blue ❏

*Agrodiaetus escheri* Escher's Blue ❏

*Agrodiaetus amanda* Amanda's Blue ❏

*Agrodiaetus thersites* Chapman's Blue ❏

*Agrodiaetus admetus* Anomalous Blue ❏

*Agrodiaetus fabressei* Oberthür's Anomalous Blue ❏

*Agrodiaetus agenjoi* Agenjo's Anomalous Blue ❏

*Agrodiaetus humedasae* Piedmont Anomalous Blue ❏

*Agrodiaetus violetae* Andalusian Anomalous Blue ❏

*Agrodiaetus aroanensis* Grecian Anomalous Blue ❏

*Agrodiaetus ripartii* Ripart's Anomalous Blue ❏

*Agrodiaetus nephohiptamenos*
        Higgins' Anomalous Blue ❏

*Agrodiaetus galloi* Gallo's Anomalous Blue ❏

*Neolysandra coelestina* Pontic Blue ❏

*Plebicula dorylas* Turquoise Blue ❏

*Plebicula golgus* Nevada Blue ❏

*Plebicula nivescens* Mother-of-pearl Blue ❏

*Plebicula atlantica* Atlas Blue ❏

*Meleageria daphnis* Meleager's Blue ❏

*Lysandra coridon* Chalk-hill Blue ❏

*Lysandra philippi* Macedonian Chalk-hill Blue ❏

*Lysandra hispana* Provençe Chalk-hill Blue ❏

*Lysandra albicans* Spanish Chalk-hill Blue ❏

*Lysandra bellargus* Adonis Blue ❏

*Lysandra punctifera* Spotted Adonis Blue ❏

*Polyommatus icarus* Common Blue ❏

*Polyommatus andronicus* Phalakron Blue ❏

*Polyommatus eroides* False Eros Blue ❏

*Polyommatus eros* Eros Blue ❏

*Polyommatus menelaos* Taygetos Blue ❏

Riodinidae

*Hamearis lucina* Duke of Burgundy Fritillary ❏

Libytheidae

*Libythea celtis* Nettle-tree Butterfly ❏

Danaidae

*Danaus plexippus* Milkweed or Monarch                    ❑
*Danaus chrysippus* Plain Tiger                           ❑

Nymphalidae

*Charaxes jasius* Two-tailed Pasha                        ❑
*Apatura iris* Purple Emperor                             ❑
*Apatura ilia* Lesser Purple Emperor                     ❑
*Apatura metis* Freyer's Purple Emperor                  ❑
*Thaleropis ionia*                                        ❑
*Limenitis populi* Poplar Admiral                        ❑
*Limenitis reducta* Southern White Admiral              ❑
*Limenitis camilla* White Admiral                       ❑
*Hypolimnas misippus* False Plain Tiger                 ❑
*Neptis sappho* Common Glider                           ❑
*Neptis rivularis* Hungarian Glider                     ❑
*Nymphalis antiopa* Camberwell Beauty                   ❑
*Nymphalis polychloros* Large Tortoiseshell             ❑
*Nymphalis xanthomelas* Yellow-legged Tortoiseshell     ❑
*Nymphalis vau-album* False Comma                       ❑
*Inachis io* Peacock Butterfly                           ❑
*Vanessa atalanta* Red Admiral                           ❑
*Vanessa indica* Indian Red Admiral                     ❑
*Vanessa cardui* Painted Lady                            ❑
*Vanessa virginiensis* American Painted Lady            ❑
*Aglais urticae* Small Tortoiseshell                    ❑
*Polygonum c-album* Comma Butterfly                     ❑
*Polygonum egea* Southern Comma                         ❑
*Araschnia levana* Map Butterfly                        ❑
*Argynnis pandora* Cardinal                             ❑
*Argynnis paphia* Silver-washed Fritillary             ❑
*Argynnis laodice* Pallas's Fritillary                 ❑
*Argynnis aglaja* Dark Green Fritillary                ❑
*Argynnis adippe* High Brown Fritillary                ❑
*Argynnis niobe* Niobe Fritillary                       ❑
*Argynnis elisa* Corsican Fritillary                   ❑
*Issoria lathonia* Queen of Spain Fritillary           ❑
*Brenthis hecate* Twin-spot Fritillary                 ❑

*Brenthis daphne* Marbled Fritillary ❑

*Brenthis ino* Lesser Marbled Fritillary ❑

*Boloria pales* Shepherd's Fritillary ❑

*Boloria napaea* Mountain Fritillary ❑

*Boloria aquilonaris* Cranberry Fritillary ❑

*Boloria graeca* Balkan Fritillary ❑

*Proclossiana eunomia* Bog Fritillary ❑

*Clossiana euphrosyne* Pearl-bordered Fritillary ❑

*Clossiana titania* Titania's Fritillary ❑

*Clossiana selene* Small Pearl-bordered Fritillary ❑

*Clossiana chariclea* Arctic Fritillary ❑

*Clossiana freija* Frejya's Fritillary ❑

*Clossiana dia* Weaver's Fritillary ❑

*Clossiana polaris* Polar Fritillary ❑

*Clossiana thore* Thor's Fritillary ❑

*Clossiana frigga* Frigga's Fritillary ❑

*Clossiana improba* Dusky-winged Fritillary ❑

*Melitaea cinxia* Glanville Fritillary ❑

*Melitaea arduinna* Freyer's Fritillary ❑

*Melitaea phoebe* Knapweed Fritillary ❑

*Melitaea aetherie* Aetherie Fritillary ❑

*Melitaea didyma* Spotted Fritillary ❑

*Melitaea deserticola* Desert Fritillary ❑

*Melitaea trivia* Lesser Spotted Fritillary ❑

*Melitaea diamina* False Heath Fritillary ❑

*Mellicta athalia* Heath Fritillary ❑

*Mellicta deione* Provençal Fritillary ❑

*Mellicta varia* Grisons Fritillary ❑

*Mellicta parthenoides* Meadow Fritillary ❑

*Mellicta aurelia* Nickerl's Fritillary ❑

*Mellicta britomartis* Assmann's Fritillary ❑

*Mellicta asteria* Little Fritillary ❑

*Hypodryas maturna* Scarce Fritillary ❑

*Hypodryas intermedia* Asian Fritillary ❑

*Hypodryas cynthia* Cynthia's Fritillary ❑

*Hypodryas iduna* Lappland Fritillary ❑

*Euphydryas aurinia* Marsh Fritillary ❑

*Euphydryas desfontainii* Spanish Fritillary ❑

Satyridae

*Melanargia galathea* Marbled White ❏
*Melanargia lachesis* Iberian Marbled White ❏
*Melanargia russiae* Esper's Marbled White ❏
*Melanargia larissa* Balkan Marbled White ❏
*Melanargia occitancia* Western Marbled White ❏
*Melanargia arge* Italian Marbled White ❏
*Melanargia ines* Spanish Marbled White ❏
*Hipparchia fagi* Woodland Grayling ❏
*Hipparchia alcyone* Rock Grayling ❏
*Hipparchia syriaca* Eastern Rock Grayling ❏
*Hipparchia ellena* Algerian Grayling ❏
*Hipparchia neomiris* Corsican Grayling ❏
*Hipparchia volgensis* Delattin's Grayling ❏
*Hipparchia semele* Grayling ❏
*Hipparchia cretica* Cretan Grayling ❏
*Hipparchia christenseni* ❏
*Hipparchia aristaeus* Southern Grayling ❏
*Hipparchia azorina* Azores Grayling ❏
*Hipparchia caldeirense* Oehmig's Grayling ❏
*Hipparchia miguelensis* Le Cerf's Grayling ❏
*Hipparchia mersina* ❏
*Hipparchia pellucida* ❏
*Neohipparchia statilinus* Tree Grayling ❏
*Neohipparchia fatua* Freyer's Grayling ❏
*Neohipparchia hansii* Austaut's Grayling ❏
*Neohipparchia powelli* Powell's Grayling ❏
*Peudotergumia fidia* Striped Grayling ❏
*Pseudotergumia wyssii* Canary Grayling ❏
*Chazara briseis* The Hermit ❏
*Chazara prieuri* Southern Hermit ❏
*Pseudochazara atlantis* Moroccan Grayling ❏
*Pseudochazara graeca* Grecian Grayling ❏
*Pseudochazara hippolyte* Nevada Grayling ❏
*Pseudochazara geyeri* Grey Asian Grayling ❏
*Pseudochazara mamurra* Brown's Grayling ❏
*Pseudochazara orestes* Dils' Grayling ❏
*Pseudochazara mniszechii* Dark Grayling ❏
*Pseudochazara cingovskii* Macedonian Grayling ❏

*Pseudochazara anthelea* White-banded Grayling ❑
*Oeneis norna* Norse Grayling ❑
*Oeneis bore* Arctic Grayling ❑
*Oeneis glacialis* Alpine Grayling ❑
*Oeneis jutta* Baltic Grayling ❑
*Satyrus actaea* Black Satyr ❑
*Satyrus ferula* Great Sooty Satyr ❑
*Minois dryas* Dryad ❑
*Berberia abdelkader* Giant Grayling ❑
*Berberia lambessanus* ❑
*Kanetisa circe* Great Banded Grayling ❑
*Arethusana arethusa* False Grayling ❑
*Erebia ligea* Arran Brown ❑
*Erebia euryale* Large Ringlet ❑
*Erebia eriphyle* Eriphyle Ringlet ❑
*Erebia manto* Yellow-spotted Ringlet ❑
*Erebia claudina* White Speck Ringlet ❑
*Erebia flavofasciata* Yellow-banded Ringlet ❑
*Erebia epiphron* Mountain Ringlet ❑
*Erebia orientalis* Bulgarian Ringlet ❑
*Erebia christi* Rätzer's Ringlet ❑
*Erebia pharte* Blind Ringlet ❑
*Erebia melampus* Lesser Mountain Ringlet ❑
*Erebia sudetica* Sudeten Ringlet ❑
*Erebia aethiops* Scotch Argus ❑
*Erebia triaria* de Prunner's Ringlet ❑
*Erebia embla* Lapland Ringlet ❑
*Erebia disa* Arctic Ringlet ❑
*Erebia medusa* Woodland Ringlet ❑
*Erebia polaris* Arctic Woodland Ringlet ❑
*Erebia alberganus* Almond-eyed Ringlet ❑
*Erebia pluto* Sooty Ringlet ❑
*Erebia gorge* Silky Ringlet ❑
*Erebia aethiopella* False Mnestra Ringlet ❑
*Erebia rhodopensis* Nicholl's Ringlet ❑
*Erebia mnestra* Mnestra's Ringlet ❑
*Erebia gorgone* Gavarnie Ringlet ❑
*Erebia epistygne* Spring Ringlet ❑
*Erebia tyndarus* Swiss Brassy Ringlet ❑

*Erebia cassioides* Common Brassy Ringlet ❏
*Erebia hispania* Spanish Brassy Ringlet ❏
*Erebia nivalis* De Lesse's Brassy Ringlet ❏
*Erebia calcaria* Lorkovic's Brassy Ringlet ❏
*Erebia ottomana* Ottoman Brassy Ringlet ❏
*Erebia pronoe* Water Ringlet ❏
*Erebia melas* Black Ringlet ❏
*Erebia lefebvrei* Lefèbvre's Ringlet ❏
*Erebia scipio* Larche Ringlet ❏
*Erebia stirius* Styrian Ringlet ❏
*Erebia styx* Stygian Ringlet ❏
*Erebia montana* Marbled Ringlet ❏
*Erebia zapateri* Zapater's Ringlet ❏
*Erebia neoridas* Autumn Ringlet ❏
*Erebia oeme* Bright-eyed Ringlet ❏
*Erebia meolans* Piedmont Ringlet ❏
*Erebia palarica* Chapman's Ringlet ❏
*Erebia pandrose* Dewy Ringlet ❏
*Erebia sthennyo* False Dewy Ringlet ❏
*Proterebia afra* Dalmatian Ringlet ❏
*Maniola jurtina* Meadow Brown ❏
*Maniola megala* ❏
*Maniola chia* ❏
*Maniola nurag* Sardinian Meadow Brown ❏
*Maniola telmessia* ❏
*Maniola halicarnassus* ❏
*Hyponephele maroccana* Moroccan Meadow Brown ❏
*Hyponephele lycaon* Dusky Meadow Brown ❏
*Hyponephele lupina* Oriental Meadow Brown ❏
*Aphantopus hyperantus* Ringlet ❏
*Pyronia tithonus* Gatekeeper ❏
*Pyronia cecilia* Southern Gatekeeper ❏
*Pyronia bathsheba* Spanish Gatekeeper ❏
*Pyronia janiroides* False Meadow Brown ❏
*Coenonympha tullia* Large Heath ❏
*Coenonympha rhodopensis* Eastern Large Heath ❏
*Coenonympha pamphilus* Small Heath ❏
*Coenonymphia thyrsis* Cretan Small Heath ❏
*Coenonympha corinna* Corsican Heath ❏

*Coenonympha elbana* Elban Heath ❑
*Coenonympha dorus* Dusky Heath ❑
*Coenonympha vaucheri* Vaucher's Heath ❑
*Coenonympha arcania* Pearly Heath ❑
*Coenonympha darwiniana* Darwin's Heath ❑
*Coenonympha gardetta* Alpine Heath ❑
*Coenonympha arcanioides* Moroccan Pearly Heath ❑
*Coenonympha leander* Russian Heath ❑
*Coenonympha glycerion* Chestnut Heath ❑
*Coenonympha hero* Scarce Heath ❑
*Coenonympha oedippus* False Ringlet ❑
*Pararge aegeria* Speckled Wood ❑
*Pararge xiphioides* Canary Speckled Wood ❑
*Pararge xiphia* Madeiran Speckled Wood ❑
*Lasiommata megera* Wall Brown ❑
*Lasiommata maera* Large Wall Brown ❑
*Lasiommata petropolitana* Northern Wall Brown ❑
*Lopinga achine* Woodland Brown ❑
*Ypthima asterope* African Ringlet ❑
*Kirinia roxelana* Lattice Brown ❑
*Kirinia climene* Lesser Lattice Brown ❑

Hesperiidae

*Pyrgus malvae* Grizzled Skipper ❑
*Prygus melotis* ❑
*Pyrgus alveus* Large Grizzled Skipper ❑
*Pyrgus armoricanus* Oberthür's Grizzled Skipper ❑
*Pyrgus foulquieri* Foulquier's Grizzled Skipper ❑
*Pyrgus warrensis* Warren's Skipper ❑
*Pyrgus serratulae* Olive Skipper ❑
*Pyrgus carlinae* Carline Skipper ❑
*Pyrgus onopordi* Rosy Grizzled Skipper ❑
*Pyrgus cinarae* Sandy Grizzled Skipper ❑
*Pyrgus sidae* Yellow-banded Skipper ❑
*Pyrgus carthami* Safflower Skipper ❑
*Pyrgus andromedae* Alpine Grizzled Skipper ❑
*Pyrgus cacaliae* Dusky Grizzled Skipper ❑
*Pyrgus centaureae* Northern Grizzled Skipper ❑
*Spialia sertorius* Red Underwing Skipper ❑

*Spialia orbifer* Orbed Red-underwing Skipper ❑

*Spialia phlomidis* Persian Skipper ❑

*Spialia doris* Aden Skipper ❑

*Muschampia tessellum* Tessellated Skipper ❑

*Muschampia cribellum* Spinose Skipper ❑

*Muschampia proto* Sage Skipper ❑

*Muschampia mohammed* Barbary Skipper ❑

*Muschampia leuzeae* Algerian Grizzled Skipper ❑

*Carcharodus alceae* Mallow Skipper ❑

*Carcharodus tripolinus* False Mallow Skipper ❑

*Carcharodus lavatherae* Marbled Skipper ❑

*Carcharodus boeticus* Southern Marbled Skipper ❑

*Carcharodus stauderi* ❑

*Carcharodus flocciferus* Tufted Marbled Skipper ❑

*Carcharodus orientalis* Oriental Marbled Skipper ❑

*Erynnis tages* Dingy Skipper ❑

*Erynnis marloyi* Inky Skipper ❑

*Heteropterus morpheus* Large Chequered Skipper ❑

*Carterocephalus palaemon* Chequered Skipper ❑

*Carterocephalus silvicolus*

Northern Chequered Skipper ❑

*Thymelicus acteon* Lulworth Skipper ❑

*Thymelicus hamza* Moroccan Small Skipper ❑

*Thymelicus lineola* Essex Skipper ❑

*Thymelicus sylvestris* Small Skipper ❑

*Thymelicus hyrax* Levantine Skipper ❑

*Hesperia comma* Silver-spotted Skipper ❑

*Ochlodes venatus* Large Skipper ❑

*Gegenes nostrodamus* Mediterranean Skipper ❑

*Gegenes pumilio* Pigmy Skipper ❑

*Borbo borbonica* Zeller's Skipper ❑

*Pelopidas thrax* Millet Skipper ❑

# Glossary

**Abdomen.** The part of the body behind the thorax.

**Aberration.** An abnormal individual form of usually rare occurrence arising from an environmentally induced or genetic cause.

**Aestivation.** A state of torpor (diapause) in summer heat or drought.

**Allopatric.** Two or more forms having essentially separate areas of distribution.

**Anal angle.** Small apical area enclosed by inner and outer margins of the hind-wing.

**Anal fold.** A fold in the hind-wing inner margin.

**Androconia (sing. Androconium).** In male butterflies, specialized wing-scales (often called scent-scales) possessing gland cells containing special chemicals for attracting females.

**Antennae (sing. Antenna).** Paired, jointed sensory organs – clubbed in the case of butterflies – arising from the head of an insect.

**Anterior.** Towards the head in reference to axis of head thorax and abdomen. Applicable to adult, larvae or pupa. (Cf. posterior).

**Apex.** The point of coincidence of the costal and outer margins.

**Apical area.** Of fore-wing, area just inside and contiguous with apex. (Cf. subapex).

**Auct. (*auctorum*).** Indicating the use of a name for a purpose other than that intended by the original author.

**Basad.** Towards the wing-base.

**Basal.** Of the wing-base.

**Bivoltine.** Having two annual broods.

**Caterpillar.** *See* larva.

**Calcareous.** Referring to rocks/soils having an alkaline (basic) reaction.

**Cell.** In reference to wings, the generally closed area defined by the subcostal, medial and discoidal veins in the basal and discal areas of the fore-wings and hind-wings: due to the absence of one or more elements of the discoidal vein, the cell on the hind-wing is sometimes open. (See also discocellular).

**Cephalic.** Of the head.

**Chevron.** A wedge-shaped mark.

**Chitin.** A tough, sometimes brittle material from which the hard parts of an insect are formed, e.g. exoskeleton.

**Chromosome.** Within the nucleus of each living cell, small bodies carrying the genes.

**Chrysalis.** *See* pupa.

**Cline.** A progressive, usually continuous change in one or more characters over a geographical or altitudinal range. *Euchloe tagis* is an example of a geographical cline; good examples of altitudinal clines are provided by some *Erebia* spp. for which populations at highest altitudes tend to be smaller and have reduced wing-markings. The term is also applicable to equivalent change in relative proportions of individuals having two or more distinctive forms, e.g., ratio of 'brown' to 'blue' females in populations of some lycaenid butterflies. A combination of clinal types is apparent for some species, e.g. *Erebia gorge*. Although many clines correlate with climatic variables, often temperature and humidity, causal/functional relationships are not necessarily implied.

**Club.** The thickened, terminal part of the antenna.

**Code.** See International Commission on Zoological Nomenclature.

**Colony.** A small, locally isolated population.

**Compositae.** Disused plant family name for Asteraceae.

**Conspecific.** Belonging to the same species.

**Costa.** The front (leading) edge of fore-wing or hind-wing.

**Costal fold.** A narrow, thin membrane folded back on the upper surface of forewing costa containing androconia.

**Cremaster.** Tiny hooks at the abdominal tip of a pupa giving support by attatchment to a silk pad spun by the larva prior to pupation.

**Cruciferae.** Disused plant family name for Brassicaceae.

**Cryptic.** Colouring and/or pattern adopted for the purpose of protection from predators or concealment from prey.

**Cuspidal.** Two segments of curved lines meeting and terminating at a sharp point.

**Cytology.** The study of cells.

**Dentate.** Tooth-like. Often applied to small cuspidal projections on outer margin of wings.

**Desiccation.** In plants, excessive loss of water from plant tissues caused by high temperature and/or drought. Usually a reversible condition but relevant to the nutritional quality of plant used as a larval host-plant.

**Diapause (noun or verb).** Suspension of activity or development in any metamorphic stage. (See also aestivation and hibernation).

**Dimorphism.** The occurrence of two distinct forms within the same population: hence, sexual dimorphism, seasonal dimorphism, etc.

**Discal.** The central portion of wing from costa to inner margin: hence, discal band, discal markings etc.

**Discocellular.** Of the veins associated with the cell.

**Discoidal.** Of the area associated with the cell: hence discoidal spot.

**Dispersion.** Of adult butterfly behaviour, extension of local range. (*See also* migration).

**Distad.** In the direction away from the body.

**Distal.** The point furthest away from the centre of the body.

**DNA.** Abbreviation for deoxyribonucleic acid, a complex molecule from which the chromosome, and the genes it carries, is made.

**Dorsal.** Of the back – upper surface of the body (cf. ventral).

**Dorsal Nectary Organ.** In the larvae of many species of the Lycaenidae, a gland located in the dorsal region of the 7th segment producing a sweet secretion attractive to ants. Often called the 'honey-gland'.

**Dorsum.** The back.

**Ecdysis.** The process of shedding the larval skin or pupal case.

**Ecology.** The study of the relationships of animals and plants with each other and their environment.

**Elongate.** Of extended or lengthened form – stretched.

**Endemic.** Restricted to a well-defined region – found nowhere else: hence, endemic species, form, etc.

**Exuvium.** The cast skin of a larva.

**Falcate.** Hook-shaped.

**Faculative.** A beneficial, but non-essential association: e.g., that between the larval (or pupal) stages of many lycaenid butterflies and ants. (See also obligate).

**Family.** A basic unit of taxonomic classification, usually comprising an assemblage of genera considered to be closely related on account of certain shared characters.

**Fauna.** Collectively, the animals of a region.

**Flora.** Collectively, the plants of a region.

**Form.** Any taxonomic unit subordinate to subspecific classification applicable to ecological, seasonal or sexually dimorphic/polymorphic forms.

**Frons.** The area between the eyes on the front the head ('face'), often bearing a hair-like tuft.

**Fuscous.** Smokey greyish-brown.

**Genitalia.** Located in the terminal abdominal segments, the male or female sexual organs, by which means the spermatophore of the male is transferred to the female during copulation.

**Genotype.** The total genetic characters of an organism.

**Genus.** A basic unit of taxonomic classification, usually comprising a number of species considered to be more closely related to each other than to other species of other genera.

**Girdle.** A silken thread supporting the midsection of a pupa.

**Gramineae.** A disused plant family name for Poaceae (the grasses).

**Gynandromorph.** An individual having both male and female characters. Various degrees of gynandromorphism are possible: in bilateral gynandromorphism, sexual characters/components of left and right-hand sides of an adult insect are sharply delineated by the vertical axial plane of the head, thorax and abdomen. Gynandromorphs are infertile.

**Hair-tuft.** A grouping of hair-like androconia.

**Hibernaculum.** For butterflies, a protective structure within which hibernation occurs, fashioned by a larva (or, collectively and co-operatively by larvae) for its own use or that of its pupa.

**Hibernation.** The dormant stage in which an animal passes the winter. (See also diapause).

**Homonym.** A name given (inadvertently) to two different species within the same genus. According to international code (International Commission on Zoological Nomeclature), the first published name must be adopted upon recognition of oversight.

**Honey-gland.** *See* Dorsal Nectary Organ.

**Hyaline.** Translucent, glass-like membranes: part of the wing-structure of some butterflies.

**Hybrid.** The progeny of two species arising from cross-fertilization: hence, hybridization. Adult hybrids are infertile: characteristically, the early-stages arising from cross-fertilization have poor viability.

**I.C.Z.N.** *See* International Commission on Zoological Nomenclature.

**Imago.** The adult or 'perfect' insect.

**Infrasubspecific.** Any taxonomic unit subordinate to subspecific classification.

**Inner margin.** Of the wings, the margin closest to the body.

**Instar.** A stage of larval development between skin changes.

**Internal (syn: proximal).** The point closest to the body.

**International Commission on Zoological Nomenclature.** The body responsible for the International Code of rules governing the application of the scientific names of animals.

**Invalid name.** A scientific name inconsistent with rules of the International Code governing the application of such names.

**Irrorate.** Covered with minute, coloured dots - 'dusted' or minutely speckled.

**Jullien Organ.** Distinctive, dark, stiff rods (or batons) present in the male genitalia of certain butterflies.

**Lapsus calami.** An author's error, for example, inaccuracy in the description of a type locality or the mis-spelling of a name.

**Larva (pl. larvae).** The second (growth) stage in the development of an insect.

**Leguminosae.** Disused plant family name for Fabaceae.

**Lunule.** A crescent-shaped mark.

**Macular.** Spotted.

**Marginal.** Of fore-wing or hind-wing, the wing area contiguous with the outer margin.

**Mediobasal.** Central transverse line of basal area.

**Mediodiscal.** Central transverse line of wing – bisecting the discal area.

**Melanism.** Increased development of black pigment.

**Metamorphosis.** Transformation of one structure into another: in butterflies, the transitions of larva to pupa, and pupa to adult.

**Migrant.** Of butterflies, survival strategy depending partly or wholly on dispersion and establishment of temporary breeding colonies over an extensive geographical area. (See Dispersion).

**Mimic (n. or v.).** A species (animal or plant) bearing a close resemblance, in part or whole, to another, used as a model: to adopt, in part or whole, the superficial characters of another species.

**Mimicry.** The close, superficial resemblance of one organism (animal or plant) to another of a different species, adopted for the purpose of gaining advantage through deception, e.g. to evade a predator or to conceal from prey.

**Monophagous.** Restricted to a single larval host-plant.

**Morphology.** The study of structure and form: in butterflies, in any developmental stage, includes visible external characters, such as wing-markings in the adult stage.

**Nacreous.** Resembling mother-of-pearl.

**Nominate form.** Having characters corresponding to type specimen upon which species description is based – the typical form, often referred to (more correctly according to the present Code) as the nominotypical form.

**Nominotypical form.** *See* nominate form.

**Nom. nud. (*nomen nudum*).** A proposed scientific name unaccompanied by formal description and therefore unacceptable according to the rules of the International Code.

**Obligate.** Of association, necessary - unavoidable. Applicable to that of the larval stage (or part of) of some lycaenid butterflies and ants.

**Ocellus (pl. ocelli).** An 'eye-spot': a rounded spot (often black), usually with a central white pupil or pale spot, often enclosed by a pale or coloured annulus. When the pupil is absent, the spot is said to be 'blind'.

**Oligophagous.** Restricted to a single genus of larval host-plants.

**Osmeterium.** An eversible (erectile), fleshy organ held within the first thoracic segment of the larva of certain butterflies.

**Oviposit.** To lay eggs.

**Ovipositor.** Located in the tip of the female abdomen, a specialized structure through which eggs are extruded during egg-laying.

**Ovum (pl. ova).** Egg.

**Palearctic.** Of the biogeographical region comprising Europe (including Canary Islands, Azores and Madeira) and the extra-tropical areas of Africa and Asia.

**Palp (pl. Palpi).** In adult butterfly, one of pair of sensory organs located on the front of the head.

**Phenotype.** Pertaining to the appearance of an organism arising from the inter-action of its genetic character with that of its environment.

**Photoperiod.** Day-length, period between dawn and dusk.

**Polygenetic.** A wing-character or other feature controlled by a contribution from several genes.

**Polymorphism.** The occurrence of two or more forms of a single species within the same population.

**Polyphagous.** Having a range of larval host-plants belonging to more than one plant genus.

**Polyploidy.** Within a cell, the multiplication of chromosome sets in which superfluous sets are inactive (non-functional).

**Polyvoltine.** Having two or more annual broods (number of which may be unknown or unspecified).

**Population.** Individuals of a species living together or in sufficiently close proximity to sustain, over time, a high probability of maintaining uniform (within limits of normal variation) genetic character.

**Postdiscal.** Of the wings, the area between the discal and submarginal areas.

**Posterior.** Towards the abdominal extremity relative to axis of head, thorax and abdomen.

**Proboscis.** The feeding tube of the adult butterfly.

**Proximal (syn: internal).** The point closest to the body.

**Pupa (pl. pupae).** The third developmental stage of an insect in which the final transformation to the adult insect occurs.

**Race.** A distinctive population of a species approximating to, but generally considered subordinate to a subspecies.

**Range.** The total (unless otherwise specified or implied) geographic area within which a species or subspecies occurs: distribution need not be continuous.

**Reticulate.** A network pattern.

**Sagittate.** Arrow-shaped.

**Scandinavia.** Geographical region of Europe comprising Denmark, Norway and Sweden.

**Sex-brand.** A grouping of androconia – often in conspicuous patches.

**Space.** Of the wings, an area of wing membrane between two veins.

**Species (pl. species).** A basic unit of formal taxonomic classification referring to a group of individuals of an organism capable of interbreeding and producing healthy, fertile offspring. Such groups are incapable of cross-breeding with other groups to produce healthy, fully fertile offspring.

**Spermatophore.** The sperm sac transferred to the female during copulation.

**Sphragis.** A hard structure formed on the ventral surface of the terminal abdominal segments of a fertilized (female) butterfly to prevent further copulation.

**Stria (pl. striae).** A narrow line or streak.

**Subapex.** Of the fore-wing, the area inside the apex: hence subapical area.

**Subgenus.** A sub-unit of taxonomic classification pertaining to a closely related group of species within a genus.

**Submarginal.** Of fore-wing or hind-wing, the wing area between that just inside the outer margin and the post-discal area. (Closest to the outer margin is the marginal (or sometimes antimarginal) area).

**Subspecies.** A population occupying a distinct geographical region, separate from other populations of the same species, and having constant and clearly different characters. Such populations have the potential to interbreed (e.g., in captivity) and, therefore, cannot overlap.

**Symbiosis.** Living together – a close and often obligatory association of two species: e.g. the associations of ants and lycaenid larvae.

**Sympatric.** Two or more species occurring in the same habitat or otherwise in sufficiently close proximity to sustain a high probability of inter-breeding, if biologically possible.

**Synonym.** Different (scientific) names given to the same taxon: only the first published name is valid.

**Systematics.** The study of the diversity of biological organisms and the description of their relationships.

**Taxon (pl. taxa).** Any defined biological unit (species, subspecies or form etc.) or group of units (genus, family, subfamily, tribe, etc). Although taxa are almost always given scientific names, a taxon may be properly defined solely according to its site of origin.

**Taxonomy.** The classification of animals and plants.

**Thorax (a. thoracic).** The middle section of an insect's body: in the adult butterfly, the clearly separate portion, bearing the wings and legs, between the head and the abdomen. The thorax itself consists of three segments, more clearly apparent in the larva – prothorax (front), mesothorax (middle) and metathorax (last).

**Toponym.** Name designating type locality. (Taxonomic names often derive from type locality).

**Tornus.** Junction of inner and outer margins, on fore-wing or hind-wing.

**Trivoltine.** Having three annual broods.

**Tundra.** Grassy, treeless, Polar regions with permanently frozen subsoil (permafrost). In lower latitudes, tundra-like zones, conforming closely to arctic climatic conditions, occur at high altitudes.

**Type locality.** The geographical site of capture of the type specimen.

**Type specimen.** The single specimen accepted as the basis of the description of a taxon.

**Umbelliferae.** Disused plant family name for Apiaceae.

**Undulate.** Wavy, scalloped.

**Univoltine.** Having one annual brood (generation).

**Valid name.** According to the rules of the International Code, an acceptable scientific name.

**Variety.** A poorly defined sub-unit of taxonomic classification below the rank of subspecies – in definable terms, inseparable from a form.

**Vein.** In an insect's wing, the semi-rigid tubes supporting the wing membrane.

**Venation.** The arrangement of veins in an insect's wing.

**Ventral.** Below the central plane of the body: hence ventral surface of the wings. (Cf. Dorsal).

**Voltinism.** Number of annual broods (generations): hence, univoltine, bivoltine, trivoltine, polyvoltine.

# Bibliography

The following includes source publications and botanical reference works, amongst which will be found many useful bibliographies.

Abadjiev S. 1992. *Butterflies of Bulgaria. Part 1. Papilionidae and Pieridae.* - Veren Publishers, Sofia.
Abadjiev S. 1993. *Butterflies of Bulgaria. Part 2. Nymphalidae: Libytheinae and Satyrinae.* - S. Abadjiev, Sofia.
Abadjiev S. 1995. *Butterflies of Bulgaria. Part 3. Nymphalidae: Apaturinae and Nymphalinae.* - S. Abadjiev, Sofia.
Agosti, D. and Collingwood, C. A. 1987. A provisional list of the Balkan ants (Hym., Formicidae) and a key to the worker caste. 1. Synonymic list. - Mitt. schwiz. ent. Ges., 60:51-62.
Agosti, D. and Collingwood, C. A. 1987. A provisional list of the Balkan ants (Hym., Formicidae) and a key to the worker caste. 1. Synonymic list. - Mitt. schwiz. ent. Ges., 60:51-62.
Baldock, D. W. and Bretherton, R. F. 1981. Butterflies in Corfu (Kerkyra) in late August, 1980, with a provisional list of all species known from it: (Parts 1 and 2). - *Proc. Trans. Br. ent. nat. Hist. soc.*, 14:8-10, 101-107.
Bateman, G. (Ed.) 1986. *The Oxford Encylopedia of Trees of the World.* - Peeridge Books, London.
Baynes, E. S. A. 1964. *A revised catalogue of Irish Macrolepidoptera.* - Hampton.
Benyamini, D. 1984. The butterflies of the Sinai Peninsula (Lep.: Rhopalocera). - *Nota lepid.*, 7(4):309-321.
Benyamini, D. 1990. [*A field guide to the butterflies of Israel including butterflies of Mt. Hermon and Sinai*]. - Keter Publishing House Ltd., Jerusalem. [In Hebrew].
Bernardi, G. 1961. Biogéographie et spéciation des Lépidoptères Rhopalocères des îles mediterranéennes. - *Colloques int. Cent. natn. Rech. scient.*, 94:181-215.
Bernardi, G. 1971. *C. r. somm. Séanc. Soc. Biogéogr.*, des Lépidoptères des îles égéennes. - *C. r. somm. Séanc. Soc. Biogéogr.*, 1971:21-32
Bink, F. A. 1992. Ecologische Atlas van de Dagvlinders van Noordwest-Europa. [In Dutch].
Bretherton, R. F., De Worms, C. G. M. and Johnson, G. 1963. Butterflies of Corsica. - *Entomologist's Rec. J.Var.*, 75:93-104.
Bretherton, R. F. 1966. A distribution list of the butterflies (Rhopalocera) of western and southern Europe. - *Trans. Soc. Br. Ent.*, 17:1-94.
Buszko, J. and Maslowski. 1993. *Atlas motyli Polski:Vol. 1. Motyle dzienne (Rhopalocera).* [In Polish].
Carlstrom, A. 1987. *A Survey of the Flora and Phytogeography of Rodhos, Simi, Tilos and the Marmaris Peninsula (SE Greece, SW Turkey).* - Department of Systematic Botany, University of Lund, Lund.
Chneour, A. 1954. Macrolepidoptera de Tunisie I, II, Rhopalocera, Gryocera. - *Bull. Soc. Sci. nat. Tunis.*, 7:207-239.
Chneour, A. 1963. Vingt-six ans de travail d'un lépidoptèriste en Tunisie. - *Alexanor*, 3:104-110.
Coutsis, J. G. 1969. List of Grecian Butterflies. - *Entomologist* 102:264-268.
Coutsis, J. G. 1978. List of Grecian Butterflies: additions and corrections. - *Entomologist's Rec. J.Var.*, 90:300-301.
Coutsis, J. G. 1984. Description of the Female Genitalia of *Hipparchia fagi* Scopoli, *Hipparchia semele* Linnaeus (Satyridae) and their Related Taxa. - *J. Res. Lepid.* 22(1983)(3):161-203.

Dacie, J.V., Dacie, M.K.V., Grammaticos, P. and Coutsis, J.G. 1982. Butterflies in northern Greece: July-August 1980. - *Entomologist's Rec. J.Var.* 94:18-20.

Davies, P. H. *et al* (Eds.) 1965-75. *Flora of Turkey and the eastern Aegean islands,Vols. 1-5.* - Edinburgh.

De Lesse, H. 1970. Les nombres de chromosomes à l'appui d'une systématic du groupe de *Lysandra coridon* (Lycaenidae). - *Alexanor*, 6(5):203-224.

De Lesse, H. 1970. Formules chromosomiques de quelques Rhopalocères paléarctiques (Lep.). - *Bull. Soc. ent. Fr.*, 75(7-8):214-216.

De Lesse, H. 1972. Variations géographiques des nombres chromosomiques chez les Lycaenidaede. - *C. r. somm. Séanc. Soc. Biogéogr.*, 48:32-38.

Ebert, G. (Ed.) 1993. *Die Schmetterlinge Baden-Württembergs.*Vols. 1 and 2. - Eugen Ulmer, Stuttgart.

Fernandez-Rubio, F. 1991. *Guia de Mariposas Diurnas de la Peninsula Ibérica, Baleares, Canarias, Azores y Madeira.*

Fiedler, K. 1991. Systematic, evolutionary, and ecological implications of myrmecophily within the Lycaenidae (Insecta: Lepidoptera: Papilionoidea). - *Bonn. zool. Monogr.*, 31:1-156.

Fiedler, K. 1991. European and North West African Lycaenidae (Lepidoptera) and their associations with ants. - *J. Res. Lepid.* 28(1989)(4):239-257.

Ford, E. B. 1957. *Butterflies.* - Collins, London.

Ford E. B. 1975. *Ecological Genetics.* - Chapman and Hall, London.

Forster, W. and Wohlfahrt, T. A. 1976/77. *Die Schmetterlinge Mitteleuropas. Vol 2. Tagfalter. (2 Auflage).* - Franckh'sche Verlagshandlung, Stuttgart.

Geiger, W. (Ed.) 1987. *Les papillons de jour et leurs biotopes.* - Ligue Suisse pour la Protection de la Nature, Bâle. [In German or French].

Gomez-Bustillo, M. R. and Fernandez-Rubio, F. 1974. *Mariposas de la Peninsula Ibérica: Ropalóceros.Vols. 1 and 2.* - Ministerio de Agricultur, Madrid.

Gonseth, Y. 1987. Atlas de Distribution des Papillons Diurnes de Suisse (Lep.; Rhopalocera). - *Doc. faun. Helv.*, 5:1-242 [In French or German].

Gozmany, L. 1968. Nappili lepkek - Diurna. - *Fauna Hungariae*, 91:1-204.

Gross, F.J. 1978. Beitrag zur Systematik von *Pseudochazara*-Arten. - *Atalanta (Würzburg)*, 9:41-103.

Hackray, J. and Sarlet, L. G. 1969-74. Catalogue des Macrolépidoptères de Belgique. - *Lambillionea* (supplement), 67(1969) *et seq.*

Hartig, F. and Amsel, H. G. 1952. Lepidoptera Sardinica. - *Fragm. ent.*, 1(1951):1-159.

Heath, J. (Ed.) 1970. *Provisional atlas of the Insects of the British Isles. 1. Lepidoptera Rhopalocera: Butterflies.* - Biological Records Centre, Huntingdon.

Heath, J. (Ed.) 1976. *The moths and butterflies of Great Britain and Ireland.* Vol. 1. - Blackwell Scientific Publications and Curwen, Oxford and London.

Heath, J. 1981. Threatened Rhopalocera (butterflies) in Europe. - *Nature Environ. Ser.*, 23:1-157.

Henriksen, H. J. and Kreutzer, Ib. 1982. *The Butterflies of Scandinavia in Nature.* - Skandinavisk Bogforlag, Odense. [In English or Danish].

Hesselbarth, G., Van Oorschot, H. and Wagener, S. 1995. *Die Tagfalter der Türkei. Vols. 1-3.* Berger-Juling Electronic Publishing, Bonn.

Higgins, L. G. 1941. An illustrated Catalogue of the Palearctic *Melitaea*. - *Trans. R. Ent. Soc. Lond.*, 91(7):175-365.

Higgins, L. G. 1950. A descriptive Catalogue of the Palaearctic *Euphydryas* (Lepidoptera: Rhopalocera). - *Trans. R. Ent. Soc. Lond.*, 101(12):435-499.

Higgins, L. G. 1955. A descriptive Catalogue of the genus *Mellicta* Billberg (Lepidoptera: Nymphalidae) and its species, with supplementary notes on the genera

*Mellitaea* and *Euphydryas*. - *Trans. R. Ent. Soc. Lond.*, 106(1):1-131.

Higgins, L. G. 1975. *The Classification of European Butterflies*. - Collins, London.

Higgins, L. G. and Riley, N. D. 1984. *A Field Guide to the Butterflies of Britain and Europe*. - Collins, London.

Høegh-Guldberg, O. and Jarvis, F. V. L. 1969. Central and north European *Ariciae* (Lep.). Relationships, heredity, evolution. - *Natura jutl.*, 15:1-106.

Howarth, T. G. 1973. *South's British Butterflies*. - Warne and Co. Ltd., London.

Hruby, K. 1964. Prodomus Lepidopter Slovenska. - *Vydav. Slov. Akad. Vied*, Bratislava.

Ivinskis, P. 1993. *Checklist of Lithuanian Lepidoptera*. - Vilnius.

Izenbek, B. A. 1980. The Butterflies of the Lithuanian SSR. - *Nota lepid.*, 3(3-4):126-135.

Jong, R. de, 1972. Systematics and geographic history of the genus *Pyrgus* in the Palaearctic region. - *Tijdschr. Ent.*, 115:1-121.

Jong, R. de, 1974. Notes on the genus *Carcharodus* (Lepidoptera, Hesperiidae). - *Zool. Mededelingen*, 48(1):1-9.

Jong, R. de, 1978. Monograph of the genus *Spialia* Swinhoe. - *Tijdschr. Ent.*, 11:23-146.

Kaisila, J. 1962. Immigration und Expansion of der Lepidopteren in Finnland in den Jahren 1869-1960. - *Acta ent. fenn.*, 18:1-452.

Koch, M. 1984. *Wir bestimmen Schmetterlinge*. - Neumann, Leipzig.

Kremsky, J. 1925. Przyczynek do fauny motyli Podlasia [Macrolepidoptera of Poland. - *Polskie Pismo ent.*, 4:35-62. [In Polish].

Krzywicki, M. 1981. Anmerkungen zur Tagfalterfauna Bulgariens. - *Nota lepid.* 4(1-2):29-46.

Kudrna, O. 1985/86/90. *Butterflies of Europe*: Vols. 1, 2 and 8. AULA-Verlag, Wiesbaden.

Kudrna, O. 1977. *A Revision of the Genus Hipparchia Fabricus*. E.W. Classey Ltd., Faringdon.

Larsen, T. B. 1983. Insects of Saudi Arabia: Lepidoptera; Rhopalocera (A mongraph of the butterflies of the Arabian Peninsula). - *Fauna of Saudi Arabia*, 5:333-478.

Larsen, T. B. 1984. *Butterflies of Saudi Arabia and its neighbours*. - Stacey International, London.

Le Cerf, F. 1972. *Atlas des Lépidoptères de France. 1. Rhopalocè*res. - Paris.

Leestmans , R. 1965/66/68. Étude biogéographique sur les Lépidoptères diurnes de la Corse. - *Alexanor* 5:17-24, 89-96, 113-120, 179-189, 194-194, 281-288, 297-304, 345-352.

Lempke, B. J. 1937/53/54/56/57. Catalogus der nederlandse Macrolepidoptera. - *Tijdschr. Ent.*, 79:238-315; 96:239-305; 97:301-345; 98(1955):283-355; 100:155-216.

Lukhtanov, V. and Lukhtanov, A. 1994. *Die Tagfalter Nordestasiens*. - Eitschberger, Marktleuthen.

Manley, W. B. L. and Allcard, H. G. 1970. *A Field Guide to the Butterflies and Burnets of Spain*. - E. W. Classey Ltd., Hampton.

Mariani, M. 1939. Fauna Lepidopterorum Siciliae. - *Memorie Soc. ent. ital.*, 17(1938):129-187.

Markgraf, F. 1931. *Pflanzen aus Albanien*. - Wien.

Niculescu, E. V. 1961. Lepidoptera. Fam. Papilionidae (Fluturi). - *Fauna Repub. pop. rom.*, 11(5):1-103. [In Romanian].

Niculescu, E. V. 1963. Lepidoptera. Fam. Pieridae (Fluturi). - *Fauna Repub. pop. rom.*, 11(6):1-202. [In Romanian].

Niculescu, E. V. 1965. Lepidoptera. Fam. Nymphalidae (Fluturi). - *Fauna Repub. pop. rom.*, 11(7):1-361. [In Romanian].

Nordstrom, F. 1955. De Fennoskandiska dagfjärilarnas utbredning. - *Acta Univ. Lund (N.F.)* 66(1):1-176.

Nordstrom, F. and Wahlgreen, E. 1935-41. *Svenska fjärilar.* - Nordisk Famijeboks Förlags, Stockholm.

Oberthur, C. 1915. Faune des Lépidoptères de la Barbarie. - *Étud. Lép. comp.*, 10:7-459.

Oberthur, C. 1922. Les Lépidoptères du Maroc. - *Étud. Lép. comp.*, 19(1):1-403; 19(2):71-90, 165-195.

Oehmig, S. 1977. Die Tagfalter Madeiras. - *Ent. Z. Frankf.a.M.*, 87:169-176, 189-199.

Oehmig, S. 1983. *Hipparchia azorina* (Strecker, 1899) (Satyridae) Biology, Ecology and Distribution on the Azores Islands. - *J. Res. Lepid.*, 20(1981)(3):136-160.

Olivier, A. 1993. *Butterflies of the Greek island of Ródos.* - Vlaamse Vereniging Voor Entomologie, Antwerp.

Pittaway, A. R. 1985. Fauna of Saudi Arabia. Lepidoptera: Rhopalocera of Western Saudi Arabia. - *Fauna of Saudi Arabia*, 7:172-197.

Popescu-Gorj, A. 1964. *Catalogue de la collection de Lépidoptères "Prof.A. Ostrogovich" du Museum d'Histoire Naturelle "Grigore Antipa" Bucarest.* - Museum d'Histoire Naturelle "Grigore Antipa", Bucarest.

Rebel, H. 1903. Studien über die Lepidopterenfauna der Balkanländer. 1. Bulgarien und Ostrumelien. - *Annln. naturh. Mus.Wien.* 18:123-347.

Rebel, H. 1904. Studien über die Lepidopterenfauna der Balkanländer. 2. Bosien und Herzegowina. - *Annln. naturh. Mus.Wien*, 19:97-377.

Rebel, H. 1913. Studien über die Lepidopterenfauna der Balkanländer. 3. Sammelergebenisse aus Montenegro, Albanien, Mazedonien und Thrazien. - *Annln. naturh. Mus.Wien*, 27:281-334.

Rebel, H. 1926. Lepidopteran von den Balearen. - *Dt. ent. Z. Iris*, 40:135-146.

Rebel, H. 1934. Lepidopteran von den Balearen und Pityusen. - *Dt. ent. Z. Iris*, 48:122-138.

Rebel, H. and Zerny, H. 1931. Die Lepidopterenfauna Albaniens. - *Denkschr.Akad. Wiss.Wien*, 103:37-161.

Romaniszyn, J. and Schille, F. 1930. Fauna motyli Polski. 1. - *Pr. monogr. Kom. fizjogr.*, 6(1929):1-555. [In Polish].

Schaider P. and Jaksic, P. 1988. *Die Tagfalter von jugoslawisch Mazedonien.* - Schaider, Munchen.

Scott, J. A. 1986. *The Butterflies of North America.* - Stanford University Press, Stanford, California.

Sichel, G. 1963. Elenco dei Ropaloceri della Sicilia nord-orientale nella collezione dell'I.N.E. - *Fragm. ent.*, 4:49-61.

Stoyanov, N. and Kitanov B. 1966. *Plants of the high mountains of Bulgaria.* - Sofia.

Strid, A. 1986. *Mountain Flora of Greece.* Vol 1. - Cambridge University Press (Cambridge, London, New York, New Rochelle, Melbourne, Sydney).

Stubbs, A. E. 1982. Conservation and the future for the field entomologist. - *Proc. Trans. Br. ent. nat. Hist. soc.*, 15:55-66.

Tax, M. H. 1990. *Atlas van de Nederlandse dagvlinders.*

Tennent, J. 1996. *The Butterflies of Morocco, Algeria and Tunisia.* - Gem Publishing Company, Wallingford.

Thurner, J. 1964. Die Lepiddopterenfauna Jugoslawisch Mazedoniens. 1. Rhopalocera, Gryocera und Noctuidae. - *Posebno Izd. prirod. Muz. Skopje*, 1:1-158.

Thomas, J. A. and Lewington, R. 1991. *The Butterflies of Britain and Ireland.* - Dorling-Kindersley, London.

Thomson, E. 1967. *Die Grosschmetterlinge Estlands.* - Rauschenbusch Verlag, Stollhamm.

Thomson, G. 1980. *The Butterflies of Scotland.* - Croom Helm, London.

Times Books. 1994. *The Times Atlas of the World - Comprehensive Edition.* - HarperCollins, London.

Tolman, T. W. *The Butterflies of Greece.* [In preparation].

Tronicek, E. 1949. Contribution to the Knowledge of the Lepidopterological fauna of Crete. - *Acta ent. Mus. natn. Pragae*, 26:1-15.

Tutin, T. G., *et al* (eds.) 1964-80. *Flora Europaea. Vols. 1-5.* - Cambridge University Press, England.

Valletta, A. 1972. *The butterflies of the Maltese Islands.* - Valletta, Malta.

Varga, Z. 1975. Geographische Isolation und subspeziation bei den Hochgebirgs-Lepidopteren der Balkanhablinsel. - *Acta ent. jugosl.*, 11:5-39.

Verity, R. Revision of the athalia group of the genus *Melitaea* Fabricius, 1807 (Lepidoptera, Nymphalidae). - *Trans. R. Ent. Soc. Lond.*, 89(14):591-706.

Verity, R. 1940-1953. *Le Farfalle Diurne d'Italia.* Vols. 1-5. - Florence.

Viidalepp, J. 1966. [Baltic butterflies and their distribution (Rhopalocera and Gyrocera)]. - *Ucen. Zap. tartu. gos. Univ.*, 180:3-39. [In Russian, English summary].

Viidalepp J. 1979. [Additions to the fauna of the butterflies of Tuva]. - *Ucen. Zap. tartu. gos. Univ.*, 483:15-16. [In Russian, English summary].

Vikhodtsevskii, N. 1958. [New and rare butterflies in the fauna of Bulgaria]. - *Izv. zool. Inst. Sof.*, 7:358-365 [In Bulgaria, French summary].

Warren, B. C. S. 1926. Monograph of the Tribe Hesperiidi (European species) with revised classification of the subfamily Hesperiinae (Palaearctic species) based on the Genital Armature of the Males. - *Trans. Ent. Soc. Lond.*, 74(1):1-170.

Warren, B. C. S. 1936. Monograph of the Genus *Erebia.* - British Museum [Natural History], London.

Weidemann, H. J. 1986/88. *Naturführer - Tagfalter. Vols 1 and 2.* - Neumann-Neudamm, Melsungen. [In German].

Wiemers, M. 1995. The butterflies of the Canary Islands: A survey on their distribution, biology and ecology. - *Linn. belg.*, 15(2):63-84; 15(3):87-118.

Willemse, L. 1975. Distribution records of Rhopalocera in the Greek mainland and Crete. - *Ent. Ber., Amst.*, 35:141-149.

Willemse, L. 1980. Some interesting faunistical data of Rhopalocera in Greece. - *Ent. Ber., Amst.*, 40:156-158.

Willemse, L. 1981. More about the distribution of Rhopalocera in Greece. - *Ent. Ber., Amst.*, 41:41-47.

Willien, P. 1990. Contribution lépidoptérique française à la Cartographie des Invertébrés Européens (C.I.E.). Le genre *Erebia* (Lépidoptères: Nymphalidae: Satyrinae). - *Alexanor*, 16(5):259-290.

Zerkowitz, A. 1946. The Lepidoptera of Portugal. - *J. New York ent. Soc.*, 54:51-87, 115-165, 211-261.

# Index of English Names

The numbers in Roman type refer to the text pages, those in bold refer to the colour plate in the centre of the book on which that species is illustrated.

310

# Index of Scientific Names